Professional
BizTalk® Server 2006

Professional
BizTalk® Server 2006

Darren Jefford
Kevin B. Smith
Ewan Fairweather

1807
WILEY
2007

Wiley Publishing, Inc.

Professional BizTalk® Server 2006

Published by
Wiley Publishing, Inc.
10475 Crosspoint Boulevard
Indianapolis, IN 46256
www.wiley.com

Copyright © 2007 by Wiley Publishing, Inc., Indianapolis, Indiana

Published simultaneously in Canada

ISBN: 978-0-470-04642-5

Manufactured in the United States of America

10 9 8 7 6 5 4 3

Library of Congress Cataloging-in-Publication Data:
Jefford, Darren, 1978-
  Professional BizTalk server 2006 / Darren Jefford, Kevin B. Smith, Ewan Fairweather.
    p. cm.
  Includes index.
  ISBN 978-0-470-04642-5 (paper/website)
  1. Microsoft BizTalk server. 2. Client/server computing. I. Smith, Kevin B., 1967- II. Fairweather, Ewan, 1983- III. Title.
  QA76.9.C55J445 2007
  005.2'768--dc22
                        2007009237

For general information on our other products and services please contact our Customer Care Department within the United States at (800) 762-2974, outside the United States at (317) 572-3993 or fax (317) 572-4002.

Trademarks: Wiley, the Wiley logo, Wrox, the Wrox logo, Programmer to Programmer, and related trade dress are trademarks or registered trademarks of John Wiley & Sons, Inc. and/or its affiliates, in the United States and other countries, and may not be used without written permission. BizTalk is a registered trademark of Microsoft Corporation in the United States and/or other countries. All other trademarks are the property of their respective owners. Wiley Publishing, Inc., is not associated with any product or vendor mentioned in this book.

Wiley also publishes its books in a variety of electronic formats. Some content that appears in print may not be available in electronic books.

About the Authors

Darren Jefford

Darren Jefford (`http://blogs.msdn.com/darrenj`) has worked for Microsoft UK for more than five years. He is a principal consultant within the Application Development Consulting (ADC) team, where he works with a variety of customers and partners to architect, develop, and test solutions built on the Microsoft platform, leveraging the entire breadth of Microsoft development technologies.

Recent customer work has led Darren to focus on BizTalk Server and Visual Studio Team System, alongside the core .NET platform. As a result, Darren recently coauthored *Professional Visual Studio Team System 2005* (Wrox).

Darren has previously worked as a consultant and as a software engineer for a number of software houses in the UK, developing market-trading platforms and financial software using a wide range of Microsoft technologies, including C++, COM, and SQL Server.

Darren cut his developer's teeth on the Sinclair Spectrum and BBC Micro and then upgraded to an 8086, which hooked him on the PC platform. He subsequently learned C++, which led to a junior software development role at the tender age of 15.

Darren is married to Julieann, with whom he has two fantastic young children, Lucy and Toby, who take up most of his time. Between his family and Microsoft, there isn't much time left, but whenever possible he takes time out to tinker with digital photography, play the guitar, and follow Formula 1.

Darren is the author of Chapters 1, 2, 3, 5, 6, 7, 9, 12, 13, and 14.

> I'd like to dedicate this book to my fantastic wife Julieann for making this project even remotely possible. Her patience, encouragement, understanding, and unwavering support through the long, lonely evenings and single-parent Sundays were key and helped make the book what it is.
>
> Thanks also to Lucy and Toby, who had to do without Daddy for many weekends. You both mean the world to me! This year will be full of undistracted and dedicated weekends and as many princess dresses and Spiderman outfits as you need! Sincere thanks also to Ann and Michael for taking my family in most Sundays while I focused on the book!
>
> Thanks also to my parents for everything. Without you, none of this would have been possible.

My five-year-old daughter Lucy was very excited that her Daddy was writing a book and spent a lot of time composing a story that she wanted to put inside her "daddy's book." So here it is!

The Rainbow Wish

by Lucy Anna Jefford

Once upon a time there was a little princess called Anna and she was a very good girl. One day she helped her friend called Poppy who had fallen down. A fairy saw this good deed and granted her a wish. It was a Rainbow wish, she could wish for any color in the rainbow. Princess Anna said to the fairy that she wanted everything that belonged to her to turn pink. When she went to her bedroom, she was very sad because she couldn't find anything because everything was the same color: PINK!

The End

For my Daddy x x x x x x x x x

Kevin Smith

Kevin Smith (http://www.kevinsmith.co.uk) worked for Microsoft for more than eight years. He held roles in the .NET and BizTalk Server product groups and Microsoft Consulting Services. Kevin shipped three versions of BizTalk Server (2000, 2002, and 2004) and holds six U.S. design pattern awards for his software designs that shipped in the product. For the 2004 release of BizTalk Server, Kevin was a technical lead software design engineer in the Core Engine team and was responsible for the design and implementation of the Messaging Engine.

After shipping the 2004 release of BizTalk, Kevin joined Microsoft Consulting Services to help enterprise customers to design and develop mission-critical applications built on the Microsoft platform. Many of these applications were built using BizTalk Server. During that period he worked on mission-critical BizTalk applications that are deployed worldwide, focusing mostly in the financial services space.

Kevin now works for a leading European investment bank as a senior architect. In his current role, he is responsible for designing and developing strategic parts of the bank's trading platform.

Before working for Microsoft, Kevin worked for IBM as a lead software developer, designing and developing scalable systems using C++ and COM. Prior to working for IBM, he worked for AT&T.

Kevin is married to Gail, and they have an amazing daughter, Natasha, who takes up most of his time outside of work. Kevin's hobbies include mountain biking, windsurfing, and photography.

Kevin is the author of Chapters 4, 8, and 10.

To Gail: For all your love and support. The last few years have made us both stronger. I cherish you, our family, and the time we spend together.

To Natasha: You have filled my life with love and joy. I am so blessed to have you in my life; words really cannot express what you mean to me.

To Mum and Dad: Without your support and encouragement, none of this would have been possible.

To Gareth, Antony, and Nigel: For always being there for me; you guys are the best brothers anyone could wish for.

My daughter Natasha is very proud of her dad writing a book and wanted to add her own story.

The Little Diplodocus and the Little Allosaurus

by Natasha Jade Smith

Once upon a time there was a little long-necked dinosaur that lived in the grass. The little baby dinosaur was a diplodocus. She played with her baby allosaurus friend. The allosaurus didn't want to eat her because she was too cute. He didn't want to eat any herbivores like other allosauruses ate. He only wanted to eat plants — he was a herbivore allosaurus. The other allosauruses said, "Don't play with your food." And then the baby allosaurus said, "This isn't my food." Then the mother allosaurus got angry and roared at the baby allosaurus. The little baby allosaurus and the little baby diplodocus got scared. And then they ran away to play and they stayed friends.

The End

Ewan Fairweather

Ewan Fairweather (http://blogs.msdn.com/ewanf) has worked for Microsoft UK for three years. He works for the Premier Field Engineering team. In this role, he works with enterprise customers, helping them to maintain and optimize their BizTalk applications. This involves providing both proactive and reactive onsite assistance within the UK and the rest of Europe. Ewan has also worked in a dedicated capacity on some of the world's largest BizTalk deployments, predominantly within financial services.

Prior to joining Microsoft, Ewan worked as a Cisco Certified Academy Instructor (CCAI) for a regional training organization, delivering advanced routing and networking courses.

Ewan holds a first-class honors bachelor of science degree in Computing with Management from the University of Leeds. Outside of work, Ewan's hobbies include reading and regularly going to the gym.

Ewan is the author of Chapter 11.

To Samantha: Thank you for supporting me through this and for reminding me that I could do it.

To Mum and Dad: Thanks you for always being there to guide me to make the right decisions.

To Shona and Kieran: You are the best brother and sister I could ask for. I'm very proud of you both.

Credits

Acquisitions Editor
Katie Mohr

Development Editor
John Sleeva

Production Editor
Debra Banninger

Copy Editor
Foxxe Editorial Services

Editorial Manager
Mary Beth Wakefield

Production Manager
Tim Tate

Vice President and Executive Group Publisher
Richard Swadley

Vice President and Executive Publisher
Joseph B. Wikert

Compositor
Maureen Forys, Happenstance Type-O-Rama

Proofreader
James Brook, Word One

Indexer
Robert Swanson

Anniversary Logo Design
Richard Pacifico

Acknowledgments

This book would not have been complete without the awesome contributions by my two coauthors. Kevin Smith who authored three chapters and technically reviewed much of the book, keeping me on my toes! Special thanks to Ewan Fairweather, for stepping in to write the Administration chapter at late notice when I realized I couldn't do the topic justice with my background. Kevin and Ewan brought unique viewpoints and have helped produce a book that I'm immensely proud of.

A very big thank you to the various technical reviewers who waded through the chapters in various forms, providing highly valuable feedback and highlighting things that we'd overlooked. Without you, this book would not be as complete or accurate. Yossi Dahan and Jon Fancey went way beyond the call of duty and reviewed every chapter. Thanks, also, to the following for their valuable input on various chapters: Doug Girard, Kris Horrocks, James Musson, Thomas Canter, Richard Seroter, Mick Badran, John Plummer, Paul Thorpe, and anybody I've inadvertently missed.

Thanks also go out to Microsoft and the fantastic Application Development Consulting team with whom I have worked with over the last five years. Without the fantastic Microsoft learning environment and the dynamics of our team, I can't imagine ever being capable of writing a technical book. Here's to the ADC team, Ken Watson, and Steve Leaback!

Of course, I have to thank Wiley — specifically Katie Mohr and John Sleeva, who had to put up with my ever-moving deadlines and performed fantastic edits.

Thanks also go out to David Stewart, our librarian at the Microsoft UK library. We had many chats about the trials and tribulations of writing a book, and he advised on many aspects, which I found invaluable throughout.

Last, but not least, sincere thanks to Dave Thomas, Keith Everitt, Totem Systems, and Simon Dutton, all of whom helped me get to where I am today!

In closing, this book has been incredibly hard work for all involved. Looking back over the content now, it's been well worth it and I hope you find it useful.

— **Darren Jefford**

Writing a book like this is no easy feat. I'm sure there will be those who love it and those who won't. BizTalk is a very large and complex product. No single person has a really deep understanding across *all* the product's feature areas. The product is quite simply too big. Speaking as someone who spent more than six years in one way or the other working on BizTalk, I know all too well how true that is!

During the writing of this book, we drew on the expertise of many individuals around the world. I'd like to especially thank each and every one of those individuals — for their help not only during the writing of this book but also leading up to that time. Much of the content is a culmination of many years of product group and real-world experience — the blood, sweat, and tears of many, many people!

First and foremost, I'd like to thank the BizTalk Server Product Group in Redmond. You guys are *rock stars*! You have always been laser-focused on the customer; that is a testament to the product today. From a

Acknowledgments

personal perspective, I feel truly honored to have worked with so many talented individuals for so long, and to have been part of what is quite simply an amazing team. There are so many people in the product group that have helped and contributed in some way. I'd like to thank you all for your help over the years, and for making my time in Redmond such an amazing experience — one that I will always look back on with great fondness. I'd like to especially thank Bill Lo, Joe Sharp, Derek LaSalle, Balasubramanian Sriram, and Jean-Emile Elien for your support, encouragement, and the opportunities that you gave to me during my time in the .NET and BizTalk Server product groups to design and build some amazing technology which has literally changed the landscape of the industry.

During the writing of this book, I hounded a bunch of my friends and colleagues, all of whom are authorities for their feature areas. As always, you guys found the time to help out and to provide the deep technical answers I was looking for. I'd like to especially thank the following for putting up with my questions during the writing of this book: Tolga Yildirim, Kartik Paramasivam, John Taylor, Anil Balakrishnan, Lee Graber, Jayu Katti, Paul Ringseth, Sanjib Saha, Kevin Lam, Raied Malhas, Yossi Levanoni, Jurgen Willis, John Rummell, Andy Wu, and Patric McElroy.

I'd like to give a special thank you to Jon Fancey for his tireless efforts reviewing all my chapters and indeed much of the rest of the content. He had some great ideas and feedback about additional things to cover, which, of course, meant even more work!

Much of the content in this book is drawn from the experience gained while working on real-world projects with which I was either directly or indirectly involved through Microsoft Consulting Services. I'd like to give a special thank you to Maurice Magnier and Andy Nichol for believing in me, for your support, and for giving me the opportunity to work on some of the biggest and scariest projects that the industry had to throw at us. Hmm, should I really be thanking you gents? I guess I must be a bit of a maniac! I had an amazing time and learned a great deal from those projects. Also, off the back of some of those projects, we managed to drive a lot of great ideas and requirements back into the product group to help make BizTalk a better product.

Last, thanks to Darren for persuading me to do this book, despite turning you down three or four times on the grounds that it was too much work. You kept at me. Dude, I was right! But now that its over, I'm glad we wrote it (although I tell you, there were times…).

— **Kevin Smith**

First, I'd like to say a big thank you to Darren and Kevin for giving me the fantastic opportunity to contribute to this book. You gave me clear guidelines on what it was you wanted me to cover and both of you were always there when I needed assistance. It truly has been a privilege to work with you.

A number of people have gone above and beyond to assist me in the writing of this book. I'd like to thank Lee Graber from the BizTalk Server Product Group for answering my many questions about the internals of the MessageBox. To Yossi Dahan and Jim Allen, thank you for both stepping in at short notice to review the content I'd written and for providing very valuable feedback. I'd also like to thank Christian Bolton for providing advice and guidance on SQL Server.

The support of the PFE team at Microsoft has been invaluable. Andy Gitsham and Kevin Wooldridge have always believed in me and have consistently pushed me forward to achieve greater things. I'd like to thank Neil Armstrong for unwavering support and Ben Kennedy for providing invaluable advice.

Finally, I'd like to thank Phil McLear for giving me the opportunity to get where I am today.

— **Ewan Fairweather**

Foreword

Mission-critical enterprise integration applications are among the most challenging, valuable, and rewarding applications to build and deliver. Since you've picked up and are thumbing through a book on BizTalk Server, I'm guessing you know this as well, probably from firsthand experience. Looking back, I've spent the better part of the last 15 years building both applications, as well as platform and server products in this space. For the last six years I've had the privilege of being part of the BizTalk Server development team — first as a group program manager and later as a product unit manager for the core BizTalk Server team. During this time I've seen many fads and trends come and go, and while some of them brought useful advances that helped address key issues, there is still no substitute for the kind of real-world, best-practices type of advice that the authors have included in this book.

The focus in recent years on Service Oriented Architectures (SOAs), and Web services are really the culmination of the types of systems and the architectural and operational constraints that integration developers have been working to address for a long time. Today, BizTalk Server has more customers than any other product in the BPM, SOI space — a great testament to the value we've delivered to enterprise customers, as well as the skills and talents of the many thousands of BizTalk application developers around the world. Our philosophy of maintaining an open dialog with our customers and delivering innovations within a well-integrated server product is as important today as it was for the initial release of BizTalk Server back in 2000. As customers continue to tell us that standards-based messaging and loosely coupled services are critical to their plans for enterprise applications, WS-* and common workflow technologies are becoming even more important additions to the enterprise developer's toolbox. BizTalk Server 2006 R2 continues to deliver on these customer demands with additional integration to the Windows Communication Foundation, Windows Workflow Foundation, and Windows SharePoint Server services and technologies. BizTalk Server 2006 R2 will also deliver a key set of technologies, such as full-function, native EDI processing and RFID extensions that integrate an independent device driver layer into the higher-order BizTalk functions.

Of course, our work is not yet done. As part of the Connected Systems Division, the BizTalk product team will continue to deliver key platform innovations and premium server products that meet the needs of Microsoft's most demanding enterprise customers. As a BizTalk "old-timer," it is truly gratifying to see this increase in investment as well as the continued focus on delivering these key innovations as part of a well-integrated connected application platform stack.

In the meantime, this book will provide an invaluable resource for professional developers and architects. Darren and Kevin have many years' worth of real-world, hands-on experience helping customers architect, develop, and deploy solutions using both BizTalk Server as well as other parts of the Microsoft technology stack. I've known Kevin Smith since I first joined Microsoft and the BizTalk Server product team in mid-2001. We worked together throughout the BizTalk Server 2004 product cycle, when Kevin led the development of key parts of the core BizTalk Server Messaging Engine. Darren has a strong background as a C++ developer and brings more than 10 years of experience developing mission critical, server-based systems, from real-time stock-trading platforms to Internet banking applications. Darren has worked with BizTalk Server since 2002, although most of his experience is with the 2004 and 2006 releases. As members of Microsoft Consulting Services, both Kevin and Darren have designed and successfully delivered some of the biggest, most challenging BizTalk Server applications for some of Microsoft's most strategic enterprise customers. It is rare to find such a strong combination of both "insider" knowledge of the internal workings of BizTalk Server, combined with the invaluable experience that comes from building and delivering these types of solutions for customers. Together, Kevin and Darren are uniquely positioned to understand and share which approaches and processes work as well as those which don't.

Reading through the draft copy, I was impressed by the amount of detail and applied knowledge they've captured. This book will prove an indispensible resource for the solution architects and developers already familiar with BizTalk Server and BizTalk solutions who want to drill more deeply into the key areas of the product. It is a very valuable set of material that could have only been written by insiders with deep experience both developing the product as well as many years architecting and delivering solutions for our most demanding enterprise customers.

Finally, a foreword to a book on BizTalk Server wouldn't be complete without a "shout out" to the members of the extended BizTalk family that I've had the pleasure and privilege of working with over the past six years. This group of amazingly talented and passionate individuals includes both those in the core product group and the many, many developers, solution architects, and IT professionals around the world who have used BizTalk Server to deliver the most amazing, innovative, and valuable solutions to their clients, customers, and employers. Simply put, it would not have been possible without you.

— **Patric McElroy**, Product Unit Manager, BizTalk Server

Contents

Acknowledgments ix

Foreword xi

Introduction xxi

Chapter 1: Technology Primer 1

XML Schema 1

XML Namespaces 2

XPath 3

   The local-name Function 5

   The count Function 5

Serializable Classes 7

   Generating Serializable Classes from Schema 8

   Serializable Classes and Performance 11

   BizTalk Development and Serializable Classes 12

Summary 12

Chapter 2: BizTalk Architecture 15

Why BizTalk? 15

   Phase 1 15

   Phase 2 17

   Phase 3 18

Architecture Overview 20

Messages 21

Adapters 21

Pipelines 22

Subscriptions 23

MessageBox 25

Orchestrations 31

Enterprise Single Sign-On 32

Business Activity Monitoring 33

Rules Engine 34

Hosts 34

Summary 36

Contents

Chapter 3: Adapters   37

Overview   37
Architecture   38
Communication Semantics   39
Ports   39
Filtering   42
Dynamic Send Ports   44
Enlistment   45
Hosting   46
Configuration Settings   47
Retry Semantics   47
Service Windows   49
Tracking   50
Context Properties   53
Batching   54
In-Order Delivery   54
Writing a Custom Adapter   55
In-Box Adapters   56
File   57
MSMQT   64
MSMQ   66
Windows SharePoint Services   68
SQL   71
SOAP   72
HTTP   80
SMTP   81
POP3   82
EDI   82
MQSeries   83
FTP   84
WCF   85
WSE   86
Line of Business (LOB) Adapter Pack   87
Summary   87

Chapter 4: Pipelines   89

Architecture and Concepts   89
Understanding IBaseMessage   90
Pipeline Architecture   93
Pipelines and Transactions   97

Pipeline Stages   **98**
    Receive Pipeline Stages   100
    Handling Pipeline Failures   104
    Send Pipeline Stages   106
Pipeline Configuration   **107**
    Default Pipelines   108
    BizTalk Framework (BTF 2)   109
Developing a Custom Pipeline Component   **113**
    The Core Tenets   114
Creating a Pipeline Component   **117**
    The Pipeline Component Wizard   117
    Pipeline Interfaces and Attributes   118
    Compression Stream Implementation   121
    Decompression Stream Implementation   124
    Assemblers and Disassemblers   126
    BizTalk Stream Implementations   126
    Testing a Pipeline/Pipeline Components   130
Summary   **131**

Chapter 5: Orchestrations   **133**

The Orchestration Execution Environment   **133**
    Implementation   134
    Activation   141
    Subscriptions   143
    Persistence Points   144
    Dehydration   149
    Versioning   150
    Logical Ports   153
Orchestration Development   **160**
    Designing the Process   160
    Messaging   178
    Coding   197
    Transactions   208
    Transformations   211
    Debugging   217
    BPEL4WS   219
Summary   **220**

Chapter 6: Business Activity Monitoring   **221**

Overview   **221**

Contents

BAM Fundamentals   **222**
    Conceptual Overview   224
    Database Structure   229
Tracking Profile Editor   **238**
    Using the TPE   238
    To TPE or Not to TPE?   250
BAM API   **251**
    Creating Activities   251
    Updating Data Items   251
    Continuation   252
    References   254
    Activity References   255
    Custom References   256
    Generating Typed APIs   257
    Event Streams   258
    Custom Interceptor   261
Applied BAM   **262**
    Deploying the Database Infrastructure   279
    Writing Activity Data   280
    Using Activity Data   288
    SQL Server Reporting Services   289
    BAM Portal   299
Summary   **308**

Chapter 7: Business Rules Engine   311

BRE Basics   **311**
    Rule Expressions   311
    Rete Analysis Network   312
    Evaluating Rules   316
    Forward Chaining   321
Business Rule Composer   **324**
    Creating Policies   324
    Creating Rules   326
    Predicates   327
    BRE Functions   327
    Fact Sources   328
    Vocabularies   334
Hosting   **344**
Testing   **344**
    Test Policy   344
    The PolicyTester Class   345

Contents

Invoking Rules   **347**
  .NET Helper Class   348
  Call Rules Shape   349
  Problems   352
Short-Term/Long-Term Facts   **353**
  Long-Term Fact Retriever Example   354
Tracking Interceptor   **357**
  DebugTrackingInterceptor   357
  Custom Interceptors   358
  Sample Custom Interceptor   359
Rule Store   **361**
Updating and Caching Rules   **361**
Custom Rules Editor   **362**
Deploying Rules   **364**
  Programmatically Deploying Rules   365
Summary   **366**

Chapter 8: Testing   **367**

Overview   **367**
The Build Process   **370**
Unit Testing   **371**
Functional Testing   **373**
  BizUnit   375
  Code Coverage   383
Integration Testing   **386**
Performance Testing and Tuning   **387**
  Load Profile   387
  Performance Testing Tools – Load Generation   389
  Identifying Performance Bottlenecks   391
  Code Profiling   396
  Automating Performance Testing   401
Stress Testing   **406**
  Mixing It Up   407
  Overload Testing   407
User Acceptance Testing   **408**
Disaster Recovery Testing   **409**
  Testing, Documenting, and Fine-Tuning Procedures   410
  Ensuring Zero Data Loss upon Failover   410
Production Support Testing   **411**
  Deploying New Solution Artifacts   412
  Handling Suspended Messages and Orchestrations   412
  Archiving BAM Data   413
Summary   **413**

Contents

Chapter 9: Performance and Scalability   415

Laying the Foundations   **416**
   Hardware   416
   Software   421
   Checklist   428
Monitoring   **428**
   Strategy   429
   BizTalk   439
   SQL Server   450
   Dependent Systems   453
Common Symptoms   **455**
   Orchestration Completed/Sec Drops Off Suddenly   455
   High Memory Usage   458
   Web Service Problems (SOAP Adapter)   459
   Low Throughput (Not Achieving the msg/Sec)   461
   Heavy BAM Usage   462
   Spool Increasing Steadily   462
Summary   **463**

Chapter 10: Low Latency   465

What Is Low Latency?   **465**
The BizTalk Processing Model   **466**
Measuring Latency   **469**
Tuning BizTalk for Low Latency   **472**
   Host Throttling   474
   MessageBox Sizing   475
   Disk Subsystem   476
   Other Things That Affect Latency   477
   Mixing Low-Latency and High-Throughput Scenarios   477
Orchestration Inline Sends   **479**
   What You Lose with Inline Sends   480
   Executing Pipelines from Orchestration   481
   Inline Orchestration Send Port   483
   Adding Resilience   487
   Initializing Correlation Sets   488
   Inline Web Service Calls   489
Summary   **493**

Chapter 11: Administration   495

What to Manage   **496**

Contents

The Administration Toolkit   **496**
   BizTalk Server Administration Console   497
   Health and Activity Tracking (HAT)   498
   BTSTask and BTSDeploy   498
   WMI   499
   BizTalk Explorer   499
Regular Administration Tasks   **500**
   Application Deployment   500
   Managing Hosts   513
   Clustering Hosts   515
Troubleshooting BizTalk   **516**
   Checking the Health of Your BizTalk System   516
Essential ESSO Maintenance   **523**
   The Master Secret Server   523
   Backing Up the Master Secret Key   524
   Moving the Master Secret Server   524
   Clustering Options for the Master Secret Server   525
Tools to Assist You   **526**
   BizTalk Best Practices Analyzer (BPA)   526
   Hidden Tools with BizTalk 2006   528
Troubleshooting DTC Problems   **534**
   Checking Firewall Configuration   535
   Verifying NetBIOS Resolution   535
   Checking MSDTC Security Options   535
   Checking Windows XP SP2 Registry Settings   537
   Checking DTC Connectivity   538
Preventive Administration Tasks   **538**
   Microsoft Baseline Security Analyzer   538
   UK SDC BizTalk 2006 Documenter   539
   MPSReports   540
SQL Server — From a BizTalk Perspective   **541**
   SQL Server Agent Jobs   544
   Backing Up the BizTalk Databases — The Supported Method 546
   Log Shipping   551
   DTA Purging and Archiving   554
   Checking the Performance of Your BizTalk Database Server 560
   Database Separation   562
BizTalk Monitoring   **563**
   Microsoft Operations Manager   563
   BizTalk Management Packs   565
   MOM Operator Console   571
Summary   **573**

Contents

Chapter 12: End-to-End Scenarios   **575**

  The Scenarios   **576**
  The Business Process Management Scenario   **576**
    Highlights   577
    Installation   582
  The Service-Oriented Scenario   **582**
    Highlights   584
    Installation   588
  The Business-to-Business Scenario   **588**
    Highlights   588
    Installation   590
  Summary   **590**

Chapter 13: BizTalk Best Practices   **591**

  Processing Large Messages   **591**
  Looping/Storing Messages   **593**
  Storing Configuration Data   **593**
  Subscribing to Failure Messages   **597**
  No Suspended Messages/Orchestrations   **598**
  Loosely Coupling   **599**
  Process Manager Pattern   **602**
  Instrumenting Your Solution   **602**
  First In, First Out   **604**
  Summary   **604**

Chapter 14: Windows Workflow Foundation and BizTalk   **605**

  Introducing Windows Workflow Foundation   **605**
    Workflows   606
    Activities   607
    Hosting   608
    Runtime Services   609
    Workflow Designer   613
    Rules Engine   613
  BizTalk Server and Windows Workflow   **615**
    Positioning   615
    BizTalk Version "Next" (vNext)   616
    BAM Interceptor for Windows Workflow   616
    BizTalk, WF, and SharePoint   623
  Summary   **624**

  Index   **627**

Introduction

BizTalk Server has seen tremendous growth since the groundbreaking 2004 release. Customers and partners alike have implemented many mission-critical and highly complex solutions based on the BizTalk platform, bringing Microsoft technology to the heart of organizations (which was largely unheard of before).

The BizTalk Server platform is incredibly powerful and arguably complex; much of this is not necessarily because of the product but because of the problem spaces that it typically occupies. I've yet to come across a straightforward set of requirements for a BizTalk solution. It is used as the central backbone of huge organizations, the integrator between disparate and complex applications, and the platform for entire financial trading platforms, and the list goes on.

Such scenarios are incredibly complex; they demand high and sustained message rates, can tolerate no downtime or data loss, and are often central to an organization's operation. If the solution were to fail, an organization could lose significant amounts of money or incur regulatory penalties.

I like to borrow a well-known tag line to describe BizTalk in situations such as this, "with great power, comes great responsibility." BizTalk Server is incredibly powerful and can be applied to solve many scenarios. To do so, however, you have to architect, develop, test, and administer such a solution responsibly.

Any compromises in these stages can lead to any number of problems: the solution might not scale, it might fail when deployed, and, in extreme cases, might lead to loss of data. None of these are due to the product, but instead, how you make use of it. For example, if you use an unreliable transport method such as HTTP, you can expect, under certain conditions, data to be lost (an unreliable network, for instance). This isn't due to BizTalk but to the nature of certain transports.

I have assisted a variety of organizations with all aspects of solution development (not just BizTalk but the entire Microsoft development stack), from the initial architecture discussions, to development, and through to performance and scalability testing.

From this work with a variety of technologies, I've been in an enviable position of assisting many customers create completely different types of applications, from stock-trading platforms to central payment processing hubs. I've observed firsthand the challenges that come up regardless of technology and, more importantly, how they can be avoided.

The compelling drive for me to create this book resulted from two main factors. First, after working with these customers I had a clear view of what worked, what didn't, and the things to highlight early on to avoid problems later in the development life cycle of a BizTalk solution.

The next compelling drive was that such real-world, best-practice advice was tied up inside a small number of people's heads. This clearly doesn't scale to help the broader base of BizTalk customers, and it's often frustrating (to both sides) to be called on site to see the same issues crop up again and again.

These problems, in my experience, are not the fault of the product or the customer per se but instead represent the learning curve required for enterprise software development. It's a hard problem space, and tiny mistakes or oversights have big consequences.

This book is positioned to help address this. It's a fusion of how the product works under the covers and cutting-edge best practices designed to enable you to make best use of the product within your solution.

The decision to write a book was a tortuous one. I loved the idea of writing a book, but I was given a number of reality checks by colleagues with regard to the effort required — something that (with a young family) I wasn't sure I could commit to, and I decided to shelve the project.

The final straw, however, came in late in 2005. While onsite with a customer, I was asked the following question: "Why does it take Darren Jefford or Kevin Smith to come in to help us understand these problems and highlight the types of things we should be aware of? This type of information isn't in the documentation…."

I went home and inked the deal with Wiley, and sometime later this book was born. In answer to that original question: *Laurie, you asked for it and here it is!*

— Darren Jefford

Who This Book Is For

The main content of this book is intended to be a valuable resource for architects, developers, testers, and administrators involved in the development of a BizTalk Server 2004 or 2006 solution.

This book is not meant as a gentle introduction to BizTalk Server. It drills deeply into the technical details of the product. (Chapter 2 acts as an introduction to the overall architecture to ensure that everyone starts from the same base understanding.)

Experienced .NET developers familiar with XML, schemas, XPath, and serializable classes can proceed straight to Chapter 2. Chapter 1 acts to ensure that developers are aware of some key concepts that can be invaluable when developing and debugging a solution. In my experience, these concepts are not as well understood as you might imagine. If you are a developer, you should read the entire book from end to end. This will enable you to fully appreciate the features and best practices you should be considering at every stage.

Architects should read the entire book, if possible. If this isn't possible, Chapters 2, 4, 5, 6, 10, 12, and 13 should be considered mandatory reading to enable you to make best use of the BizTalk product.

Testers responsible for designing and implementing tests for BizTalk Server solutions should read Chapter 2 to understand the overall architecture, along with Chapters 8 and 9 to understand how to approach testing.

Administrators tasked with deploying and maintaining a BizTalk Server solution will find content aimed specifically at this role in Chapter 11, although it's useful for all roles to have an appreciation of how to administer a BizTalk Server solution. Chapters 2, 6, 8, 9, and 13 also contain valuable information that will enable administrators to participate in the entire development life cycle to ensure that the resulting solution is easy to manage and maintain.

What This Book Covers

Professional BizTalk Server 2006 focuses on the BizTalk Server 2006 release. The 2006 release, however, is built on and adds new features to the 2004 foundation, meaning that almost everything covered in this book is applicable to projects utilizing BizTalk Server 2004. Any differences are highlighted throughout the book. Key features of the yet-to-be released BizTalk Server 2006 R2 are also covered throughout the book.

The book begins by covering some underlying technology concepts and introducing the overall BizTalk architecture. It then covers the main technology areas in detail: adapters, pipelines, orchestration, and so on.

The latter part of the book then covers techniques and approaches such as testing, low latency, best practices, and administration, before finishing up with positioning BizTalk Server and Windows Workflow.

How This Book Is Structured

This book is broadly structured to represent the different areas of BizTalk Server along with approaches and techniques that apply to BizTalk Server development.

Broadly speaking, Chapter 2 covers all the key architectural components of BizTalk Server and introduces the key terms you will see throughout the book. From this point, you can read the chapters in any order, although reading them in order may help your understanding if you're not familiar with BizTalk.

❑   **Chapter 1: Technology Primer** — This chapter primes the reader on some key technologies that each developer should have a basic understanding of to aid with development and debugging. This chapter covers XML schemas, namespaces, XPath, and serializable classes.

❑   **Chapter 2: BizTalk Architecture** — This chapter is the only chapter that really deals with explaining the basic BizTalk principles. It positions the value that BizTalk brings to solutions and compares using BizTalk to writing a custom solution without BizTalk. It then runs through all the key architectural pieces of BizTalk and explains what they do and how they work.

❑   **Chapter 3: Adapters** — This chapter covers key adapter concepts — such as ports, tracking, hosting, and context properties — and then drills into each adapter supplied with BizTalk to explain what the adapter does, which context properties it promotes, and, where appropriate and relevant, provides a walk-through to show how to use the adapter.

The chapter also details the new R2 adapters at a high level, and in time for publication we'll add downloadable content to demonstrate how to write an adapter using the new WCF Adapter framework shipped with BizTalk Server 2006 R2 (not available at the time of writing).

❑ **Chapter 4: Pipelines** — This chapter covers the core principles of pipelines and details how they work. The chapter then highlights how pipeline components should be developed and provides an example.

The chapter also covers the Messaging Engine architecture and how it works. Understanding this is *key* to being able to exploit the architecture to the fullest.

❑ **Chapter 5: Orchestrations** — This chapter introduces BizTalk orchestrations and the environment within which they execute. It discusses key areas such as persistence points and logical ports before covering how orchestrations can be developed and which features are available.

❑ **Chapter 6: Business Activity Monitoring** — This chapter introduces the Business Activity Monitoring (BAM) technology and details how BAM can be used to instrument your BizTalk solution and your entire enterprise. The chapter then shows how a fictional scenario can be instrumented and how you can make use of the information collected by BAM.

❑ **Chapter 7: Business Rules Engine** — This chapter discusses the key principles that underpin the Rules Engine and then covers all the concepts to enable effective use of the Rules Engine within your solution.

❑ **Chapter 8: Testing** — This chapter starts by describing the types of testing you must apply to your BizTalk solution, including unit testing, functional testing, integration testing, and performance testing.

The chapter goes on to discuss how BizUnit can be used to automate testing, how you can perform code coverage of your BizTalk solution, how LoadGen can be used to generate load, and how you can profile your solution using the Visual Studio profiler.

❑ **Chapter 9: Performance and Scalability** — This chapter covers all the things you must have in place before beginning any performance testing. Forgetting these often leads to bad performance results.

The chapter then explains how to monitor BizTalk, SQL, and IIS, explaining all the relevant performance counters and what they actually mean. It also provides a complete reference on what BizTalk throttling is and how it works, including an explanation of all the various throttling states.

The final section of the chapter discusses a number of common symptoms of problems. These are problems that customers run into regularly and include high CPU usage and sudden processing drop-off. The chapter explains the common reasons for these problems and things to check to identify the underlying problem.

❑ **Chapter 10: Low Latency** — This chapter covers what low latency means to BizTalk solutions and how you can measure it. It then drills into a variety of techniques that you can employ to reduce latency for your solution.

❑ **Chapter 11: Administration** — This chapter describes everything required to administer BizTalk effectively. It's a great resource for administrators as well as developers. The chapter covers the key administration tools and tasks that you need to undertake, and highlights areas that are often overlooked, such as SSO maintenance, suspended instances, subscriptions, and the like.

The chapter also covers in great detail how the SQL Server used by BizTalk needs to be looked after, including backups, log shipping, and how you can monitor the performance of the SQL Server. The chapter also covers MOM and how it can be used in conjunction with the BizTalk Management Pack to greatly simplify management.

❑ **Chapter 12: End-to-End Scenarios** — This chapter highlights all the End-to-End scenarios that were shipped as part of BizTalk 2006. These are often overlooked but provide full working solutions of real-world customer scenarios that have been fully tested and demonstrate best practices.

Each scenario is supplied with complete source code and provides implementations that you can use within your own solution. We cover each scenario and highlight key deliverables in each scenario such as the code required to use the SSO store for configuration data and an adapter to enable messages to be sent for manual repair.

❑ **Chapter 13: BizTalk Best Practices** — This chapter discusses a number of best practices and techniques that have been used in a range of projects, including handling large messages, storing configuration data, subscribing to failure messages, and instrumenting your solution.

❑ **Chapter 14: Windows Workflow and BizTalk** — This chapter positions the key concepts of Windows Workflow and discusses how it compares with BizTalk Server. It then demonstrates how the BAM Interceptor for Windows Workflow works and explains how BizTalk, WF, and SharePoint can be used together to enable compelling solutions.

What You Need to Use This Book

To formalize your understanding of the concepts in this book and to make use of features discussed throughout, you will need access to the following software:

❑ Windows XP, Windows Server 2003

❑ BizTalk Server 2006

❑ Visual Studio 2005

❑ SQL Server 2005

If you have an MSDN license, you can obtain all the software through your media or MSDN Subscriber Downloads.

The complete source code for the samples is available for downloading at www.wrox.com.

Conventions

To help you get the most from the text and keep track of what's happening, we've used a number of conventions throughout the book.

> **Boxes like this one hold important, not-to-be forgotten information that is directly relevant to the surrounding text.**

Tips, hints, tricks, and asides to the current discussion are offset and placed in italics like this.

As for styles in the text:

- ❑ We *highlight* new terms and important words when we introduce them.
- ❑ We show keyboard strokes like this: Ctrl+A.
- ❑ We show filenames, URLs, and code within the text like this: `persistence.properties`.
- ❑ We present code in two different ways:

```
In code examples we highlight new and important code with a gray background.
The gray highlighting is not used for code that's less important in the present
context, or has been shown before.
```

Source Code

As you work through the examples in this book, you may choose either to type in all the code manually or to use the source code files that accompany the book. All the source code used in this book is available for downloading at `www.wrox.com`. Once at the site, simply locate the book's title (either by using the Search box or by using one of the title lists) and click the Download Code link on the book's detail page to obtain all the source code for the book.

Because many books have similar titles, you may find it easiest to search by ISBN; this book's ISBN is 978-0-470-04642-5.

Once you download the code, just decompress it with your favorite compression tool. Alternatively, you can go to the main Wrox code download page at `www.wrox.com/dynamic/books/download.aspx` to see the code available for this book and all other Wrox books.

Errata

We make every effort to ensure that there are no errors in the text or in the code. However, no one is perfect, and mistakes do occur. If you find an error in one of our books, such as a spelling mistake or faulty piece of code, we would be very grateful for your feedback. By sending in errata you may save another reader hours of frustration and at the same time you will be helping us provide even higher quality information.

To find the errata page for this book, go to www.wrox.com and locate the title using the Search box or one of the title lists. Then, on the book details page, click the Book Errata link. On this page, you can view all errata that has been submitted for this book and posted by Wrox editors. A complete book list including links to each book's errata is also available at www.wrox.com/misc-pages/booklist.shtml.

If you don't spot "your" error on the Book Errata page, go to www.wrox.com/contact/techsupport.shtml and complete the form there to send us the error you have found. We'll check the information and, if appropriate, post a message to the book's errata page and fix the problem in subsequent editions of the book.

p2p.wrox.com

For author and peer discussion, join the P2P forums at p2p.wrox.com. The forums are a Web-based system for you to post messages relating to Wrox books and related technologies and interact with other readers and technology users. The forums offer a subscription feature to e-mail you topics of interest of your choosing when new posts are made to the forums. Wrox authors, editors, other industry experts, and your fellow readers are present on these forums.

At http://p2p.wrox.com, you will find a number of different forums that will help you not only as you read this book but also as you develop your own applications. To join the forums, just follow these steps:

1. Go to p2p.wrox.com and click the Register link.
2. Read the terms of use and click Agree.
3. Complete the required information to join as well as any optional information you wish to provide, and click Submit.
4. You will receive an e-mail with information describing how to verify your account and complete the joining process.

You can read messages in the forums without joining P2P, but in order to post your own messages, you must join.

Once you join, you can post new messages and respond to messages other users post. You can read messages at any time on the Web. If you would like to have new messages from a particular forum e-mailed to you, click the Subscribe to this Forum icon by the forum name in the forum listing.

For more information about how to use the Wrox P2P, be sure to read the P2P FAQs for answers to questions about how the forum software works as well as many common questions specific to P2P and Wrox books. To read the FAQs, click the FAQ link on any P2P page.

1

Technology Primer

Microsoft .NET software development relies on a wide range of technologies and "tricks of the trade." Some of these you might not be familiar with and others you may already use on a day-to-day basis. We'll cover a number of areas of particular relevance and value to BizTalk Server development projects to ensure we're all on the same page as we progress through the book.

Specifically, this chapter introduces the following concepts that apply to software development in general rather than to BizTalk in particular. In my experience, understanding these concepts is key to development and debugging.

- ❏ XML Schema
- ❏ XML namespaces
- ❏ XPath
- ❏ Serializable classes

This chapter is meant simply to be an introduction to these topics and does not cover them in depth or discuss all of their aspects; there are many books and online resources that will cover them in depth. If, however, you are familiar with these topics then feel free to move on to the next chapter.

XML Schema

XML Schema is a World Wide Web Consortium (W3C) standard for defining the structure and content of Extensible Markup Language (XML) documents. In short, this means that you can define how an XML document should look and what types any data in it should conform to; it is a form of data contract, if you like. BizTalk is driven by messages, which, in most cases, are based on an XML schema that must be deployed to BizTalk.

The following is an example of a simple schema used to describe a person:

```
<xs:schema xmlns:xs="http://www.w3.org/2001/XMLSchema">
  <xs:element name="Person">
    <xs:complexType>
      <xs:sequence>
        <xs:element name="Name" type="xs:string"/>
        <xs:element name="Age" type="xs:int"/>
      </xs:sequence>
    </xs:complexType>
  </xs:element>
</xs:schema>
```

This schema defines an element called `Person` that contains a complex type, which, in its simplest form, is a collection of subelements (like a class in object-oriented programming). Two further elements with differing data types have been defined within this complex type.

The following is the XML document that conforms to this schema:

```
<Person>
  <Name>Lucy</Name>
  <Age>5</Age>
</Person>
```

Defining the schema in this way enables you to enforce how you expect data to be encoded or represented. This schema can be given to any consumers of your application to ensure that they respect this contract and it enables them to communicate with you easily.

You can also use the schema to validate any incoming XML documents, which can eliminate the need for extensive data checking inside your application and improve the overall reliability of your solution.

> BizTalk Server 2000 and 2002 used an earlier "schema" standard called Document Type Definition (DTD). DTD has subsequently been superseded by XML Schema, hence the native support for schemas in BizTalk Server 2004 and 2006.
>
> If you have DTD files that you wish to leverage, you can migrate them to XML Schema by using the Add Generated Items feature, which is accessible by right-clicking your BizTalk project in the Visual Studio Solution Explorer.

XML Namespaces

Namespaces in XML documents are conceptually the same as namespaces in .NET. Any types you define are "enclosed" within the context of the specified namespace. This ensures against name clashes and allows content from multiple sources to be stored within the same document but still be isolated, as required.

Namespaces are used within XML documents and, therefore, BizTalk messages. Namespaces can often be the cause for problems when integrating different systems, when a message doesn't use the correct namespace and, therefore, doesn't comply with the appropriate schema.

The following XML document specifies that the `Person` element and its contents are within the `"http://www.wiley.com"` namespace. (This is called a *default namespace*.)

```
<Person xmlns="http://www.wiley.com/person">
  <Name>Lucy</Name>
  <Age>5</Age>
</Person>
```

The following XML document shows how you can explicitly set the namespaces, in contrast to the default namespace example shown before. The `Person` element is contained within the `"http://www.wiley.com/person"` namespace, and the `Address` element is defined within the `"http://www.wiley.com/address"` namespace.

Instead of having to prefix the nodes with the full namespace name, you can use aliases. In this instance, we've used `ps` and `ad`, which allows easier reading and, of course, a smaller payload on the wire, as less text will need to be transmitted.

```
<ps:Person xmlns:ps:="http://www.wiley.com/person"
xmlns:ad:="http://www.wiley.com/address">
  <ps:Name>Lucy</ps:Name>
  <ps:Age>5</ps:Age>
  <ad:Address>
      <ad:Town>Chippenham</ad:Town>
  </ad:Address>
</ps:Person>
```

As you can see, namespace names are typically specified as URLs, which can be confusing because people tend to assume that they must point to something on the Internet. They don't have to but often do. A namespace name can be any form of URL.

This holds true for .NET namespaces as well. Microsoft, for example, tends to prefix its code in the `Microsoft` or `System` namespaces.

XPath

XPath is a navigation language for finding information held in an XML document. Navigation is described using "expressions," which in their basic form are analogous to the paths you use to navigate the filesystem on Windows.

XPath is used by BizTalk messaging and orchestrations to retrieve interesting pieces of data from a message, which can then be used to route the message or perform a conditional business process. As with namespaces, a little understanding of XPath can go a long way toward helping you diagnose problems during development.

An XPath expression returns a node or collection of nodes called a *node set* and in some cases the result of a function — a integer representing a count for example. The XPath expression `/ps:Person/ps:Name` will return the Name node of the following XML document.

```
<ps:Person  xmlns:ps="http://www.wiley.com/person"
xmlns:ad:="http://www.wiley.com/address">
  <ps:Name>Toby</ps:Name>
  <ps:Age>3</ps:Age>
  <ad:Address>
  <ad:Town>Chippenham</ad:Town>
  </ad:Address>
</ps:Person>
```

As you may have noticed, the namespace prefixes have been used in the XPath expression. Because XPath is "namespace aware," if namespaces are omitted, it will be unable to find the node. Omitting the namespaces in this way will cause XPath to use only the default namespace. So if `/Person/Name` were to be used, it would not exist outside of the correct namespace.

The .NET code to retrieve the Name element from the preceding document is shown below. Note that the namespace alias used in the XPath query is different from the alias used in the XML document above.

Aliases are not part of the document structure; they just refer to the namespace name. Under the covers, the namespace alias is expanded to the full namespace. In the following code, you can see that you have to register a namespace prefix so that it will point at the namespace name. This alias can be anything, as long as it points to the underlying namespace definition.

> **Developers are often confused by namespace aliases. When faced with XML documents that BizTalk has received or generated, you might find that the namespace aliases differ from a sample XML document you are working against and assume they are wrong, when in fact they are actually the same.**
>
> **I have seen issues with Web services deployed on other platforms, where the developers have assumed that the namespace alias will be a fixed name and subsequently the webservice fails to work when a perfectly valid XML document is transmitted that uses different alias names. This is incorrect behavior on the service end and should be corrected wherever possible**

This alias is then used in the XPath expression to retrieve the Name element. The following code uses the .NET `XPathDocument` and `XPathNavigator` classes, which are part of the `System.Xml` namespace and provide the ability to use XPath expressions efficiently against XML documents:

```
XPathDocument doc = new XPathDocument("person.xml");
XPathNavigator nav = doc.CreateNavigator();

XmlNamespaceManager nsmgr = new XmlNamespaceManager(nav.NameTable);
nsmgr.AddNamespace("p", "http://www.wiley.com/person");

foreach ( XPathNavigator node in nav.Select("/p:Person/p:Name",nsmgr))
{
  Console.WriteLine(node.Value);
}
```

The XPath language is comprehensive and offers a variety of mechanisms with which to retrieve data. We won't cover them all here, but we will pull out a couple of useful techniques for BizTalk Server development.

> **You may have noticed the use of** XPathDocument **and** XPathNavigator **in these examples rather than** XmlDocument, **which is often used. The** XPathDocument **uses a read-only, in-memory tree that is optimized for XPath expressions and the Extensible Style Language Transformation (XSLT) language.**

The local-name Function

As you've probably already noticed, BizTalk uses XPath in a number of areas — pipeline component configuration and property promotions are two examples. In both of these areas, BizTalk builds the XPath statement for you but uses an XPath function called local-name.

As the name implies, the local-name function returns the name of the XML element in the local context. Therefore, if an XML element has a namespace prefix, it's considered to be within that namespace. Using local-name removes the namespace prefix and returns the raw element name, thus eliminating the need to jump through the hoops you had to when using the XmlNamespaceManager previously.

The following code returns exactly the same information as the previous code sample and is far simpler as a result of using the local-name function. You should also bear in mind that use of the local-name function incurs slightly more overhead because it has to perform extra processing.

```
XPathDocument doc = new XPathDocument("person.xml");
XPathNavigator nav = doc.CreateNavigator();

foreach (XPathNavigator node in nav.Select("/*[local-name()='Person']/*
[local-name()='Name']"))
{
  Console.WriteLine(node.Value);
}
```

About 90 percent of all the XPath "problems" I've ever seen have been rooted in namespace problems. A quick way to see if you're hitting such problems is to try using local-name in your XPath expressions. Although I wouldn't recommend it by default for everything, as it may cause problems in a project where there could be conflicting types. Namespaces are there for a reason!

The count Function

The count XPath function, as the name implies, enables you to count the number of elements matching an XPath expression, which is useful if you want to calculate the number of line items in an order, for example.

The following XML document and code counts the number of Person elements present in the XML document.

```
<People xmlns="http://www.wiley.com/people">
```

```
  <Person>
    <Name>Lucy</Name>
    <Age>5</Age>
  </Person>
  <Person>
    <Toby>
    <Age>3</Age>
  </Person>
</People>

XPathDocument doc = new XPathDocument("person.xml");
XPathNavigator nav = doc.CreateNavigator();

int count = Convert.ToInt32(nav.Evaluate("count(/*[local-name()='People']/
*[local-name()='Person'])"));
```

This technique is handy for times when you need to calculate the number of items in an XML document and then initiate a Loop shape in a BizTalk orchestration.

A number of other XPath functions are supported. Table 1-1 lists the functions supported at the time of this writing for reference. Check the MSDN documentation for the latest list.

Table 1-1: XPath Functions

Node-Set	String	Boolean	Number	Microsoft Extensions
count	concat	boolean	ceiling	ms:type-is
id	contains	false	floor	ms:type-local-name
last	normalize-space	long	number	ms:type-namespace-uri
local-name	starts-with	not	round	ms:schema-info-available
name	string	true	sum	ms:string-compare
namespace-uri	string-length			ms:utc
position	substring			ms:namespace-uri
	substring-after			ms:local-name
	substring-before			ms:number
	translate			ms:format-date
				ms:format-time

Serializable Classes

Serializable classes are one of the more powerful features of the .NET Framework and, sadly, one of the most overlooked, largely because there is no native IDE support to generate them and, therefore, their existence is not obvious to developers.

Despite this, you do end up using them whenever you return a class type from an ASP.NET Web service method. Under the covers a serializable class is generated for you to handle the class being transmitted across the wire in a Simple Object Access Protocol (SOAP) envelope.

By their very definition, serializable classes are classes that can have their "content" dehydrated for later use. The .NET implementation allows serializable classes to be dehydrated to any form of `Stream`.

Many API's in the .NET Framework use the concept of streams, which represent an abstract view of data by presenting it in a contiguous sequence of bytes that you can read or write. Thus, they isolate you from any underlying data store, such as a file, serial port, or network connection. This is useful because it enables you to write to and read from a variety of "stores" using the same application programming interface (API).

The following code uses a `StreamReader` to write to a `Memory` and `File` stream demonstrating the ability to use a generic "writer" against different stores.

```
using (MemoryStream ms = new MemoryStream())
{
    StreamWriter writer = new StreamWriter(ms);
    writer.WriteLine("Hello World!");
}

using (FileStream fs = new FileStream("output.txt", FileMode.Create))
{
    StreamWriter writer = new StreamWriter(fs);
    writer.WriteLine("Hello World");
}
```

If you want to serialize a .NET class to a stream, you need to decorate the class with a `[Serializable]` attribute, which tells the .NET runtime that your class is allowed to be serialized.

The following code demonstrates how to serialize a class to a file:

```
[Serializable]
  public class Person
  {
      public string    Name;
      public string    Town;
      public int       Age;
  }

  class Program
  {
      static void Main(string[] args)
      {
          using (FileStream fs = new FileStream("output.txt",FileMode.Create))
```

```
        {
            Person p = new Person();
            p.Name = "Lucy";
            p.Age = 5;
            p.Town = "Chippenham";

            XmlSerializer xs = new XmlSerializer(typeof(Person));
            xs.Serialize(fs,p);
        }
    }
}
```

The resulting `output.txt` file contains the following XML document that contains all the data of the `Person` class:

```
<?xml version="1.0"?>
<Person xmlns:xsi="http://www.w3.org/2001/XMLschema-instance"
xmlns:xsd="http://www.w3.org/2001/XMLSchema">
  <Name>Lucy</Name>
  <Town>Chippenham</Town>
  <Age>5</Age>
</Person>
```

As you can see, all the component parts of the class have been written out automatically by the `XmlSerializer` — a process often called *dehydration*. To rehydrate the class, use the same technique, but use the `Deserialize` method, instead.

```
using (FileStream fs = new FileStream("output.txt",FileMode.Open))
{
  XmlSerializer xs = new XmlSerializer(typeof(Person));
  Person p = xs.Deserialize(fs) as Person;
}
```

The resulting XML document can be customized in myriad ways. You can specify what namespaces elements are members of, whether variables are dehydrated as attributes or elements, or even to just omit certain elements from dehydration.

So, you've seen how to serialize classes and data into a variety of stores, but how does this technique help with BizTalk Server development?

Generating Serializable Classes from Schema

Consider the following schema, which represents the evolved XML `Person` type that we've used previously:

```
<xs:schema xmlns:xs="http://www.w3.org/2001/XMLschema">
  <xs:element name="Person">
    <xs:complexType>
      <xs:sequence>
        <xs:element name="Name" type="xs:string"/>
        <xs:element name="Age" type="xs:int"/>
        <xs:element name="Address">
```

```
        <xs:complexType>
          <xs:sequence>
            <xs:element name="Town" type="xs:string"/>
          </xs:sequence>
        </xs:complexType>
      </xs:element>
    </xs:sequence>
  </xs:complexType>
</xs:element>
</xs:schema>
```

You need to be able to generate an XML document that conforms to this schema. As mentioned previously, you can create a `Person` class and decorate it with the appropriate serialization attributes. However, this requires you to manually transcribe all the schema "settings" into a serializable class, when in fact all you really want to do is have a class generated from the provided schema that will generate an XML document conforming to the schema automatically.

This is where `XSD.EXE` comes in. Visual Studio 2005 and the previous .NET versions ship with a command-line tool called `XSD.EXE` that can generate serializable classes from a schema definition, and vice versa. Using `XSD.EXE /C` to pass the schema name as a parameter results in a serializable class definition, as follows:

```
[System.CodeDom.Compiler.GeneratedCodeAttribute("xsd", "2.0.50727.42")]
[System.SerializableAttribute()]
[System.Diagnostics.DebuggerStepThroughAttribute()]
[System.ComponentModel.DesignerCategoryAttribute("code")]
[System.Xml.Serialization.XmlTypeAttribute(AnonymousType=true)]
[System.Xml.Serialization.XmlRootAttribute(Namespace="", IsNullable=false)]
public partial class Person {

    private string nameField;

    private int ageField;

    private PersonAddress addressField;

    /// <remarks/>
    [System.Xml.Serialization.XmlElementAttribute(Form=System.Xml.schema
.XmlschemaForm.Unqualified)]
    public string Name {
        get {
            return this.nameField;
        }
        set {
            this.nameField = value;
        }
    }

    /// <remarks/>
    [System.Xml.Serialization.XmlElementAttribute(Form=System.Xml.schema
.XmlschemaForm.Unqualified)]
    public int Age {
        get {
```

```
                return this.ageField;
        }
        set {
            this.ageField = value;
        }
    }

    /// <remarks/>
    [System.Xml.Serialization.XmlElementAttribute(Form=System.Xml.schema
.XmlschemaForm.Unqualified)]
    public PersonAddress Address {
        get {
            return this.addressField;
        }
        set {
            this.addressField = value;
        }
    }
}

/// <remarks/>
[System.CodeDom.Compiler.GeneratedCodeAttribute("xsd", "2.0.50727.42")]
[System.SerializableAttribute()]
[System.Diagnostics.DebuggerStepThroughAttribute()]
[System.ComponentModel.DesignerCategoryAttribute("code")]
[System.Xml.Serialization.XmlTypeAttribute(AnonymousType=true)]
public partial class PersonAddress {

    private string townField;

    /// <remarks/>
    [System.Xml.Serialization.XmlElementAttribute(Form=System.Xml.schema
.XmlschemaForm.Unqualified)]
    public string Town {
        get {
            return this.townField;
        }
        set {
            this.townField = value;
        }
    }
}
```

As you can see, there are a number of extra attributes present on the class definition, which are there to control the XML serialization to ensure that the XML document conforms to the schema definition and that some property "setters" and "getters" have been provided. This strong-typing approach removes any problems associated with handling XML documents manually.

Serializing this class across the wire will result in an XML document that strictly adheres to the XML schema. You haven't had to write any XmlDocument code to manually build an XML document and ensure it conforms to the schema — it's all been done for you! This is a very powerful technique.

Using the XmlSerializer to construct XML documents that conform to a given XSD schema is one approach that works well for some scenarios. Other common approaches include loading a "template" XML document and replacing tokens with the required data, or using the XmlWriter class to build the instance document.

The XmlSerializer approach has the advantage that a valid XML document will be automatically constructed for you thus removing the need to write such code along with compile-time checks to ensure that, for example, you are using the correct data-types for XML elements.

Other approaches typically require details of the schema such as the structure to be encoded within a template XML document or within code that creates a valid document, if the schema is changed you will need to ensure that these are changed. However, a thorough set of validation tests as detailed in Chapter 8 could identify such problems automatically.

There are other aspects that you should consider when selecting an approach, such as the required performance, rate of schema change, and ease of programming model and size and complexity of the XML documents that you are creating.

You can now use the `XmlSerializer`, as shown before, to serialize this class. The following is an example of using this generated class:

```
Person p = new Person();
p.Name = "Lucy";
p.Age = 5;
p.Address = new PersonAddress();
p.Address.Town = "Chippenham";

using ( MemoryStream ms = new MemoryStream() )
{
    XmlSerializer xs = new XmlSerializer( typeof(Person) );
    xs.Serialize(ms, p);
}
```

Serializable Classes and Performance

When you first use the `XmlSerializer` in your application against a given type, a dynamic class is created and compiled on the fly to represent the serialized class. This has an obvious performance overhead, but it will be cached for subsequent requests.

This cache is maintained per the common language runtime (CLR) `AppDomain`, which is fine for applications such as BizTalk, as there is by default one `AppDomain` per BizTalk host. This means that any orchestrations and .NET code will be run within the same `AppDomain` for all subsequent requests. For other applications, where the `AppDomain` is torn down each time, this may be an issue.

The .NET Framework 2.0 release introduced a new tool, `sgen.exe`. `sgen.exe`, which enables you to pregenerate a serialization assembly and deploy this to your server to avoid the first-time compilation hit (which I would recommend that you measure to gauge the impact).

Serializing a .NET class does have an obvious CPU penalty, so bear in mind the size of your class and the frequency with which you serialize classes. It should be noted that for large complex schemas the programming model provided by serializable classes can be complex and may therefore not be appropriate. Another consideration is around message size, as we will discuss later in detail in Chapter 4. BizTalk processes messages in a forward-only streaming fashion, for large messages this approach will cause the entire message to be loaded into memory, which is not desirable.

BizTalk Development and Serializable Classes

Typically, all messages passing into and out of BizTalk are based on an underlying XML schema.

A typical BizTalk solution has systems on either side of BizTalk: systems that provide data into BizTalk and systems that BizTalk queries or updates during message processing. These systems, therefore, have to use the same message formats, along with any custom .NET components written by you and used by your BizTalk solution.

By leveraging serializable classes, you can leverage these same schemas everywhere to produce strongly typed classes that enable developers to easily work the messages and not have to fiddle with XML documents and schemas. Adopting such an approach enables the seamless interchange of data between all the key parts of your solution and removes the usually painful process of integrating the components of your solution.

Within BizTalk orchestrations you often need to pass a BizTalk message into C# class libraries for processing. If you declare the interface to use serializable classes generated from the XML schema underlying the BizTalk message, you can pass this message directly into your class library and have a strong-typed representation of your class. Thus, you eliminate any need to use XPath to retrieve data or to use the XmlDocument API.

You can also use these schemas in "schema-aware" products such as Microsoft InfoPath to produce a rich interactive form with little or no development effort, to allow users to fill in data and submit it to a back-end processing system, such as BizTalk, via a Web service.

InfoPath will validate all data inputted against the underlying XML schema, thus providing a data validation layer driven by the XML schema. This validation, of course, will then occur at all points in your solution where the schema is used.

Summary

This chapter has covered four technologies and approaches that are key to effective BizTalk Server development and debugging. Although this chapter is simply an introduction, it should give you the bare minimum information required to understand what's going on under the covers and why certain technologies behave the way they do.

XML schemas are at the center of BizTalk development. They define how messages flowing into and out of BizTalk should be represented and what they must include.

Namespaces are used as part of XML documents to protect against elements with the same name causing conflicts and also to convey ownership. However, they often cause problems during development because developers fail to indicate which namespace an element belongs to (for example, when querying for elements using XPath).

XPath enables you to interrogate an XML document and retrieve information to use during processing. This technique is invaluable; when combined with an XPathDocument, it provides a fast, streaming approach to retrieving data from your XML document without, for example, loading the entire document into memory.

Serializible classes are a key concept to understand, as they can greatly simplify the complexity of your solution and enable any applications using your BizTalk solution or being called by BizTalk to leverage the same schemas and classes. They also eliminate the need to write any custom code to handle and validate messages.

The following chapter discusses the BizTalk architecture at a high level to formalize its concepts and explain the value BizTalk brings to your solution.

BizTalk Architecture

In this chapter we'll cover the architecture of BizTalk Server, which we will refer back to as the book progresses. The chapter is meant to set the scene for the rest of the book and not to explore every nook and cranny of the architecture, which would take a book in itself.

We cover each main functional area of BizTalk later in the book, but instead of explaining the basics we discuss how that functionality works and how it should be used within your project.

Why BizTalk?

Before we start discussing how BizTalk is architected, let's take a step back and think about how you would implement your own solution without BizTalk. This is an approach I use often with my customers, to counter scenarios where developers just want to *write code*. Sure, you can write the code, but the devil is in the details.

It's also important to remember that BizTalk is not a universal panacea for all software problems and must be used in the right place. You should not be using it for all your applications — *just where it makes sense*. I always try to get customers to consider what value they are seeking from BizTalk in each use case. If they struggle with the answer, perhaps BizTalk is not the best solution.

We'll use a fictional scenario to illustrate some of the reasoning behind why BizTalk is architected the way it is.

Phase 1

A new software project is designed by your organization. You need to take travel itinerary bookings that arrive at this new system as individual files on the Windows filesystem (a directory). These files must be collected and the contents transformed from the third-party data structures to your internal format.

Once this has been done, you need to interface to flight, hotel, and rental car booking Web services hosted by third-party suppliers.

Custom Development

You start with a Windows service that can be executed unattended on a server. This Windows service, once started, can use the `FileSystemWatcher` class provided in the .NET framework to monitor a directory for the arrival of files.

The `FileSystemWatcher` class handles all the directory monitoring and raises events when a file arrives. The service can then use the .NET `ThreadPool` class to process multiple files at once. Each of these processing threads can then read the contents of the file into memory and remove it from the disk to avoid reprocessing.

The contents of the file (which are in XML format) need to be transformed into a generic XML document based on a standard schema. To do this, you need to create an XSL transform that will transform the source XML document to the destination XML document. This XSLT transform must be created manually, using the standard XML editor built into Visual Studio 2005.

Once you have created a transform, you can use the `XslTransform` class to perform the transformation between the two formats. To easily access the contents of the message, you should use a serializable class to create a strongly typed class for the message.

The next step is to call the three booking Web services with the relevant parts of the XML document (for example, the contents of the *Flights* part of the message will need to be passed to the Web service).

You can add three Web references to the project and then invoke each one in turn. You will need to manually transpose the data from the source message into the format required by the Web service. Typically, you can do this by manually assigning the data from one class instance to another.

You can then successfully invoke the three Web services.

BizTalk Development

You start by adding the predefined XML schemas used to define the file format to a BizTalk project, and then create a new BizTalk orchestration.

This BizTalk orchestration has a receive shape linked to a logical one-way port to instruct BizTalk to *deliver* the message to the orchestration. You then add a Web reference to each of the three booking Web services.

The next step is to construct the messages required to invoke the Web services based on the source data retrieved from the file. Three Transform shapes are used on the orchestration and a graphical map is created for each booking Web service, using the file message provided to the orchestration. The graphical transformation is simple and just requires connections to be drawn between the source and destination XML documents.

You would then deploy the solution to BizTalk, which will create the Web service send ports automatically and you then need to create a new receive location using the File adapter to retrieve the files from the hard drive.

Phase 1 Summary

As you can already see, the BizTalk solution doesn't require a line of custom code — it just requires configuration and deployment to meet the Phase 1 requirements. The custom solution, on the other hand, requires a fair amount of code to solve the problem.

The development effort for the custom solution is not that great, so there isn't a clear winner in the development stakes. However, a significant amount of testing is required, especially around the error handling of the network communications and other failure conditions — none of which is required for the BizTalk solution, as this is handled by the *platform*. Handling "unhappy" scenarios like this typically requires significant amounts of development effort and architectural thought up front.

Phase 2

After the solution delivered by Phase 1 has been deployed for a while, its importance to the business function increases. Therefore, the solution needs to be scaled to support the future load and to be resilient to failure from itself or from the booking Web services it's dependent on.

Custom Development

As a custom developer, you would have to take the design back to the drawing board to accommodate these new requirements. The design of Phase 1 means that the message retrieved from the directory is held in memory during processing and the invocation of the booking Web services.

Consider adding hardware failure to this scenario. The message is held in memory, so in the event of a power failure the message would be lost; the filesystem is nontransactional, so a lightweight transaction cannot be used, either.

A transactional store must be used while the message is being processed so that in event of failure it will remain within a durable store for later processing rather than being lost. A SQL Server database is the straightforward option in this case, requiring at least that a database table be designed to hold "in-progress" messages pending successful processing, at which point they can be removed.

This database will need to be well designed to cater to the high level of insert and delete operations. It must also undergo stress testing and index tuning to prevent it from becoming a bottleneck, which it quickly will become if not designed appropriately.

The Windows service will need to be modified to have a "pending" processing thread that wakes up at scheduled intervals to check if there are any messages that have been held in the database table for a long time pending processing. It will then need to reprocess them, as they will likely have experienced a failure.

A further resilience scenario involves not the service implementation but the dependant Web services. If, for example, the flight booking Web service is unavailable and you've exhausted the retry pattern, you want to *suspend* processing until the Web service is available.

For example, if the flight booking Web service is down for a few hours, you may end up with hundreds of messages awaiting processing in-memory. This is clearly not sustainable or resilient, so the Windows service would need to further leverage the database covered above to store the pending messages.

Another problem with the Phase 1 design is race conditions. With the introduction of the new scaling requirements, multiple machines running the Windows service could easily end up processing the same file twice without some form of locking (i.e., the FileSystemWatcher can raise events to multiple machines at the same time). Using an exclusive lock when opening the file will mitigate this, however.

The FileSystemWatcher also suffers from problems related to understanding when a file has finished writing. Typically, the FileSystemWatcher will report multiple events for the same file and before writing has finished, as it relies on filesystem events. When you try to access said file, you can experience a locking problem because writing is still occurring. You then need to queue the file and attempt processing later.

You can then deploy the Windows service on multiple machines all configured to *watch* the same directory to process files. With this design, a machine can fail, but another machine will seamlessly carry on processing, and any in-memory files will be safe in the database table.

BizTalk Development

To address this scenario, an extra BizTalk server would be joined to the BizTalk Server group, providing instant resilience in case of failure of the original BizTalk server, and this extra server will use the same BizTalk MessageBox hosted on a SQL server.

The SQL server hosting the BizTalk MessageBox would then need to be clustered in an active-passive configuration, using the standard clustering support built into the Windows platform, and leverage a shared-disk array.

The shared BizTalk MessageBox architecture enables seamless load-balancing between multiple servers and provides instant extra scalability without any custom code.

When the dependent booking Web services are unavailable, the BizTalk adapter will automatically retry per the configured retry-interval and, once this has been exhausted, suspend the message for Administrator intervention to resume using standard BizTalk administration tools.

Phase 2 Summary

You can clearly see in this case that these new requirements, which apply to virtually all systems (Phase 1 wasn't particularly real-world but provides a useful comparison, nonetheless), have required the custom developer to take the entire solution back to the drawing board for a complete rearchitecting involving extensive amounts of custom development, which needs to be tested and supported.

The BizTalk solution hasn't required writing any code for Phase 2 (or Phase 1), and we've just leveraged the in-built resilience and scalability by adding an additional server, which can be done on the fly to an existing solution. BizTalk is the clear winner in this solution. The development cost is significantly less, and the support costs, which, in my experience, are responsible for more than the development costs, are incredibly reduced, due to Microsoft's support for the BizTalk platform and its components.

Phase 3

Phase 2 of the solution has been in production for some time and is becoming increasingly important to both the company responsible for the solution and the providers of the booking services. Due to growth within the industry, message loads are expected to grow extensively within a short space of time.

In light of this importance, a contract is drawn up to define the service level agreements (SLAs) in place. Also, following a processing dispute, new requirements have been introduced to track messages to identify processing problems and SLA violations.

Custom Development

The custom developer needs to introduce message tracking to the Phase 2 solution. This tracking system will need to store details of the message, including the message body contents, before it's transformed, as well as after to provide a record of what the message contained before and after transformation, to ensure that the transformation hasn't altered the core payload of the message.

Leveraging the database introduced in Phase 2 would be the straightforward option and would require at its simplest another table to hold message bodies, using a data type capable of storing message bodies (such as image or text). As with Phase 2, such a table will be subject to great load, so it will need to be heavily tested and tuned to ensure that it doesn't become a bottleneck during processing.

To implement SLA monitoring, precise timing will need to be implemented at all key stages of processing (e.g., when the payment arrives, when the payment transformation starts and ends). You'll also need to record timestamps on either side of each booking Web service call in order to calculate the call's duration and identify times when the supplier of the booking service violates the agreed-upon SLA. A tracking portal must then be implemented to provide first-line support and developers with easy access to the tracking data recorded during processing.

Extensive performance tuning and benchmarking will be required to achieve the best performance with the custom solution. Also, depending on the performance characteristics, some form of load throttling must be implemented across the entire solution to prevent the overloading of the processing system or the dependent solutions. All these activities require extensive development expertise from experienced developers.

BizTalk Development

The BizTalk solution has basic Message Tracking on by default, and Message Body tracking must be turned on at the receive location level to record the incoming message and at the orchestration level to record the transformed message.

Business Activity Monitoring (BAM) can be used to record to fulfil the SLA requirement. The business milestones to track are defined in an Excel spreadsheet using the BAM add-in. The database infrastructure required to store this information in a performant and scalable way is created automatically by the BAM administration tool, requires no development or coding, and is fully supported by Microsoft.

The BizTalk developer then simply uses the Tracking Profile Editor (TPE) to annotate the orchestration at the points at which BAM will record the milestones. This can be instantly deployed to a live system to start tracking.

The built-in BAM portal will provide an easy interface to the BAM data recorded — again without any coding.

The BizTalk Messaging Engine has extensive throttling controls built in to allow fine-grained control over message processing and to protect the engine from being overloaded. All this is configurable on the fly, using the BizTalk administration tool.

Phase 3 Summary

From Phase 2 to Phase 3, you can clearly see that the custom solution has again undergone significant changes to accommodate the new requirements. At the same time, the BizTalk solution has remained custom-code-free throughout, remains fully supported, and really demonstrates the value of BizTalk. It also provides a real-world example of why BizTalk is architected the way it is.

> *It's worth stressing that although this contrived and admittedly simplified scenario has required no code, it's rare that a typical solution doesn't contain custom code. Writing custom code is not a weakness or something to avoid per se. Minimizing plumbing code, however, is incredibly valuable, as it's very hard to get right, especially when subjected to high load, and is often the cause of performance and scalability problems.*

Architecture Overview

Figure 2-1, which we'll reference as we progress through this chapter, depicts the BizTalk architecture.

The receive ports on the left side consist of adapters, the End Point Manager (EPM), and receive pipelines, and are responsible for bringing messages into BizTalk from a source system and storing them in the BizTalk MessageBox.

Orchestrations in the center are an optional feature of BizTalk in that you can choose to leverage orchestrations to process messages, as required. Messages that are processed by orchestrations are retrieved from the BizTalk MessageBox, and any messages sent from an orchestration are stored in the BizTalk MessageBox.

The send ports on the right side consist of adapters, the End Point Manager (EPM), and send pipelines, and are responsible for collecting outbound messages from the BizTalk MessageBox and transmitting them to the destination system.

The following sections walk you through all the key components, to deepen your understanding of how all the architectural pieces work together.

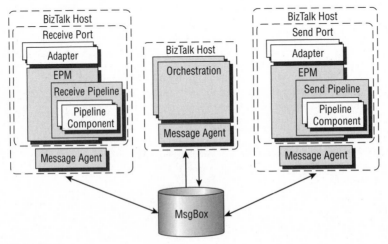

Figure 2-1

Messages

Messages are the lifeblood of every BizTalk solution. Any data, regardless of type, is represented as a message within BizTalk. Typically, messages are represented as XML documents, although you can also handle messages represented in binary format. Doing so, however, will limit the features you can use. For example, you cannot use the BizTalk Mapper or Rules Engine on binary-formatted messages.

A BizTalk message has at least one underlying part, which is typically the body of the message. If you want to hold multiple pieces of data within one message, you can create a multipart message.

BizTalk also offers the ability to track message bodies, which can then be viewed using the Health and Activity Tracking (HAT) tool. HAT is not enabled by default, as it introduces significant overhead and should be used only if absolutely necessary.

See Chapter 6 for more information on an alternative approach. BizTalk messages are covered in more detail in Chapters 4 and 5.

Adapters

Adapters provide connectivity for BizTalk to and from the outside world. The rest of the BizTalk engine is thus isolated from whatever requirements or communication semantics a remote system may impose.

In most cases, adapters work with a transport and have no underlying knowledge of the data that will be sent or received. They receive a byte stream from the wire and feed the BizTalk engine. Adapters are for the most part data agnostic — that is, that they are not concerned with whether they are receiving XML, flat file, or binary data.

In the receive case, the adapter is responsible for listening or polling for data and wrapping that data in a BizTalk message. In the case of listening, it may listen on a endpoint (or URL) for incoming data and will communicate with the remote system in whichever way is required (authentication, transactions, handshaking, etc.). In the polling scenario, the behavior will typically involve periodically checking an endpoint for new data that needs to be received into BizTalk.

In the send case, the adapter is responsible for receiving messages from the BizTalk MessageBox and transmitting them to the remote system, using their associated transport or protocol.

The SQL adapter retrieves an XML message from the BizTalk MessageBox and ultimately creates rows in a remote SQL Server database, all based on the contents of the XML message. The adapter is responsible for transferring the message from BizTalk to the remote system without the rest of the BizTalk engine requiring any endpoint specifics — true isolation.

Once an adapter has received the message, it's then responsible for passing that message to the BizTalk Messaging Engine for processing. The Messaging Engine will process the message in a pipeline after receiving a message and before sending a message.

See Chapter 3 for a more detailed discussion of adapters.

Pipelines

Pipelines provide the ability to perform data processing and validation operations on incoming and outgoing messages. Incoming messages use receive pipelines, and outgoing messages use send pipelines. The canonical use of pipelines is to normalize inbound data into XML and denormalize outbound data from XML into whatever the desired format may be, although this is by no means mandatory. A common misconception is that BizTalk is always required to normalize data into XML format; this is not true.

BizTalk provides four pipelines in-box that are suitable for most scenarios.

The following pipelines are available on the receive side:

❑ `XmlReceive` — The `XmlReceive` pipeline contains the XML Disassembler pipeline component.

❑ `PassThruReceive` — The `PassThruReceive` pipeline contains no pipeline components.

And the following pipelines are available on the send side:

❑ `XmlTransmit` — The `XmlTransmit` pipeline contains the XML Assembler component.

❑ `PassThruTransmit` — The `PassThruTransmit` pipeline contains no pipeline components.

As described in Tables 2-1 and 2-2, pipeline execution is split into multiple processing stages, each of which is designed to perform a specific type of processing. Note that each stage can optionally contain pipeline components, as required. Pipelines are covered in more detail in Chapter 4.

Messages flow through these pipeline stages and pipeline processing, like all processing in BizTalk, is stream based. BizTalk uses this to avoid having to load the entire message into memory, since loading large messages into memory could bring down the BizTalk process by causing an out-of-memory condition.

Table 2-1: Receive Pipeline Stages

Stage	Description
Decode	In the Decode stage any processing required to enable the message to be processed by subsequent stages is performed. Common examples are decryption or decompression, which must be performed before, say, disassembly or validation.
Disassemble	Depending on the component, the Disassemble stage will be responsible for identifying the type of message, conversion to XML, as required, or splitting up a message into separate, discrete messages.
Validate	The Validate stage is responsible for performing message validation. This is typically used to validate an XML message against an XML schema.
Resolve Party	The Resolve Party stage is used to identify the sender of the message, typically using an X509 Certificate or the Windows user, which is supplied by the adapter.

Table 2-2: Send Pipeline Stages

Stage	Description
Pre-Assemble	In the Pre-Assemble stage any processing required to enable the message to be processed by subsequent stages is performed. This stage is often used to make any last-minute changes to an XML, message before it's converted to a flat file by the Assemble stage.
Assemble	The Assemble stage is the opposite of the Disassemble stage in that it is responsible for converting the message from XML, typically to a different format such as a flat file. It's also possible to assemble multiple messages into one output message.
Encode	The Encode stage is used to perform any final changes to a message. Typically, these include encoding, encryption, or compression.

When a pipeline component is invoked, it may read the message data from the message stream and perform what normalization or translation is required. So in the case of the Flat File Disassembler pipeline component, it will be responsible for reading the flat-file contents from the stream and applying the flat-file schema parsing and transformation to create an XML message.

Out of this Flat File Disassembler pipeline component, a new stream will be returned, but it will contain the new XML document instead of the flat-file format. This will then be passed on through the pipeline to the next pipeline component.

Typical uses of pipeline components are flat-file assembly/disassembly, batching/debatching of messages, validating messages against XML schemas, validating digital signatures, encryption/decryption, and so on.

A number of pipeline components are included in the box with BizTalk, and new ones can be written easily. Custom pipeline component development is fairly common and is required far more often than custom adapters.

For a more detailed discussion of pipelines and instructions for how to construct a pipeline component, see Chapter 4.

Subscriptions

Once a message has been processed by the adapter and associated pipeline, it needs to be routed to an interested party. A BizTalk orchestration or send port can register its interest in a specific message via subscriptions.

A subscription is made up of a number of conditions to ensure that a subscriber gets the message it requires. When a message is processed, metadata is derived from the message content, the transport adapter, and the BizTalk port that the message was received over and is written to the *context* of the message. These context properties are evaluated against the subscriptions in order to determine how to route the message.

In a typical `XMLReceive` pipeline, the XML Disassembler component will populate the `MessageType` context property, among others. This property, in the case of an XML message, contains the namespace and root node of the associated schema, thereby uniquely identifying a message type.

BizTalk orchestrations and send ports can then subscribe to all messages of a certain schema type or use any combination of context properties, such as the name of the receive port that received the message, the name of the customer sending the message, and the like.

These subscriptions are held within the Subscription table of the BizTalkMsgBoxDb SQL database and are evaluated when a message is published to the MessageBox by the BizTalk Message Agent, which is run as part of the BizTalk host.

Figure 2-2 shows the subscription query feature of the BizTalk Server 2006 Administration Console, which displays all the subscriptions currently registered with BizTalk. This is useful for understanding which messages are being *waited for* and for determining their ultimate destination (an orchestration or send port).

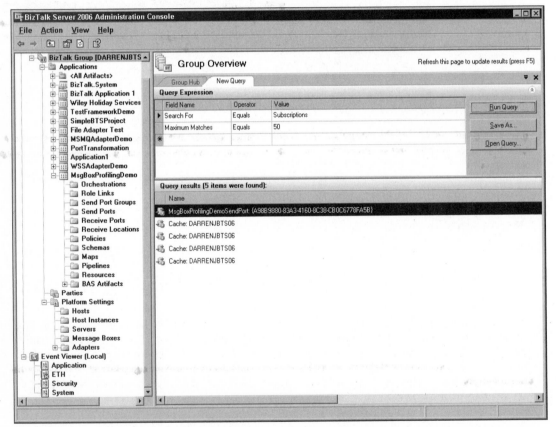

Figure 2-2

Double-clicking a subscription enables you to understand the precise details of a subscription. Figure 2-3, for example, shows a send port subscription that is subscribing to all messages that originate through a receive port called MsgBoxProfilingDemoRecvPort.

Subscriptions are covered in more detail in Chapters 3, 5, and 11.

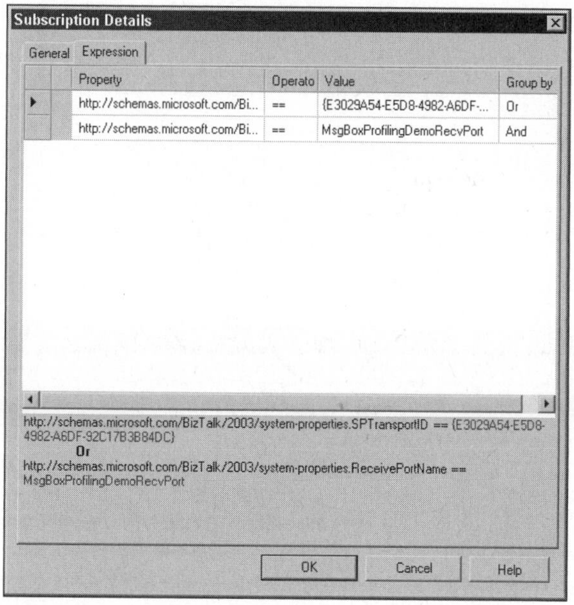

Figure 2-3

MessageBox

Once the message has passed from the adapter and through the pipeline, the BizTalk Message Agent, which runs as part of a BizTalk host instance, is responsible for evaluating who has subscribed to this message and committing it into the BizTalk MessageBox. Figure 2-4 shows all the engine concepts we've shown so far, in context. We cover BizTalk hosts later in this chapter.

The BizTalk MessageBox is implemented as a SQL Server database and is shared between all BizTalk servers in a BizTalk group. Multiple MessageBoxes can be utilized in very specific high-load or latency-critical scenarios. However, due to the requirements of using a distributed transaction across multiple MessageBoxes, and the necessity to disable message publication on the master MessageBox, you typically need to scale from one to three MessageBoxes to achieve scalability. (This should be tested in a performance and scalability lab.)

The MessageBox is the heart of any BizTalk solution in that without it nothing would work. All inbound and outbound messages, along with orchestration execution, dehydration, rehydration, and message tracking, rely on the BizTalk MessageBox.

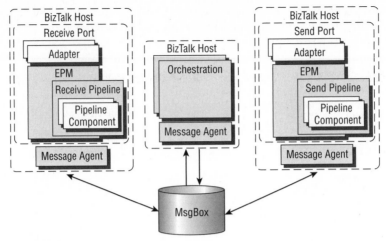

Figure 2-4

As you'll see when we discuss the MessageBox further, it's a publish/subscribe design. Messages are published to the BizTalk MessageBox; if there is more than one subscriber to a given message, both subscribers will receive a copy of the message.

In the case of BizTalk receiving a message, the Message Agent will receive a message once it has passed through an adapter and associated pipeline. The Message Agent must first write the promoted properties from the Message Context into the `BizTalkMsgBoxDb` database by using the `bts_InsertProperty` stored procedure, which ultimately places the properties into the `MessageProps` SQL table (all of which happens in a single roundtrip to the MessageBox database).

The promoted properties available will vary depending on the adapter and pipeline combination. The most common promoted property is `MessageType`, which provides the message type that is then used for orchestration subscriptions, for example.

The Message Agent then calls the `bts_FindSubscriptions` stored procedure held in the BizTalk MessageBox to establish which subscriptions, if any, match this message. This stored procedure queries the Subscription and Predicate SQL tables and joins them with the properties inserted for the batch of messages in the previous step to identify potential subscribers.

There is a series of Predicate SQL tables — `EqualsPredicates`, `ExistsPredicates`, `GreaterThanPredicates`, `GreaterThanOrEqualPredicates`, `GreaterThanPredicates`, `LessThanOrEqualPredicates`, LessThanPredicates, and NotEqualPredicates — which match all of the possible subscription expression combinations. For example, the following subscription will be placed in the `EqualsPredicates` table because it uses the = predicate.

```
ReceivePortName = "MsgBoxProfilingDemoRecvPort"
```

Depending on the subscription, any number of the preceding SQL tables will be used to represent a subscription.

Figure 2-5 shows the contents of the EqualsPredicates table when a send port is configured to subscribe to all messages processed by a receive port called `MsgBoxProfilingDemoRecvPort`. This is the same subscription that was shown in Figure 2-3.

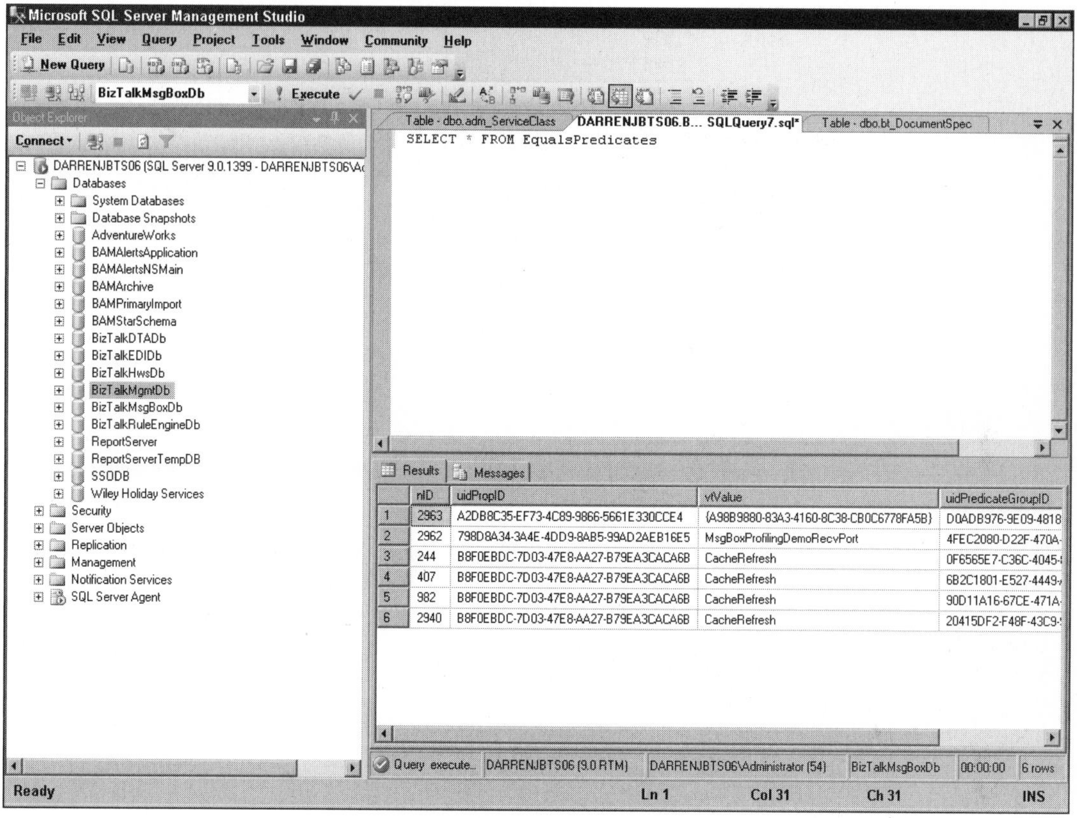

Figure 2-5

The Message Agent then calls the `bts_InsertMessage` stored procedure to insert the BizTalk message into the `Spool` SQL table, along with basic metadata about the message, such as the number of parts. As part of this stored procedure's execution, it internally calls the `int_InsertPart` stored procedure, which places the raw body of the message into the `Parts` table.

As part of this stored procedure, the `int_EvaluateSubscriptions` stored procedure, which, among other validation steps, inserts a reference to the message into the relevant Host Queue SQL table, follows the naming convention `<HostName>Q`. For example, the default BizTalkServerApplication host will be called `BizTalkServerApplicationQ`. This is useful when analyzing what work is currently waiting to be processed by which host in your system. See the "Hosts" section later in this chapter for more details.

In the case of a multipart message, the BizTalk Message Agent then calls the `bts_InsertMessage` stored procedure again for each additional part of the message, which, in turn, is placed in the `Parts` table.

Figure 2-6 illustrates a SQL Server profiler trace captured through the SQL Management Studio tool. This trace shows the stored procedures being invoked when a message is received by BizTalk. The trace statements highlighted with a bookmark on the left side show the interactions we've just discussed.

EventClass	TextData
SQL:BatchStarting	select collationname(0x0904D00000)
SQL:BatchCompleted	select collationname(0x0904D00000)
RPC:Completed	exec bt_GetDocSpecInfoByID @id=N'{CA7B4DE5-1F37-473C-967F-C21C7BE49990}'
Audit Logout	
RPC:Completed	exec [dbo].[bts_InsertProperty] @uidBatchID=N'{649B5162-3338-414F-A061-AF63EC2D6D17}',@nOrderID=0,@uidMessage
RPC:Completed	exec [dbo].[bts_InsertProperty] @uidBatchID=N'{649B5162-3338-414F-A061-AF63EC2D6D17}',@nOrderID=0,@uidMessage
RPC:Completed	exec [dbo].[bts_InsertProperty] @uidBatchID=N'{649B5162-3338-414F-A061-AF63EC2D6D17}',@nOrderID=0,@uidMessage
RPC:Completed	exec [dbo].[bts_InsertProperty] @uidBatchID=N'{649B5162-3338-414F-A061-AF63EC2D6D17}',@nOrderID=0,@uidMessage
RPC:Completed	exec [dbo].[bts_InsertProperty] @uidBatchID=N'{649B5162-3338-414F-A061-AF63EC2D6D17}',@nOrderID=0,@uidMessage
RPC:Completed	exec [dbo].[bts_FindSubscriptions] @uidBatchID=N'{649B5162-3338-414F-A061-AF63EC2D6D17}'
RPC:Completed	declare @p17 int set @p17=1 exec [dbo].[bts_InsertMessage] @uidMessageID=N'{5F72C398-3788-4D97-9994-824089(
RPC:Completed	declare @p17 int set @p17=0 exec [dbo].[bts_InsertMessage] @uidMessageID=N'{5F72C398-3788-4D97-9994-824089(
RPC:Completed	exec [dbo].[bts_InsertTrackingData] @uidServiceID=N'{D87BC2D5-80AE-4CD5-B66B-CCA77437D311}',@uidInstanceID=N'
SQL:BatchStarting	IF @@TRANCOUNT > 0 COMMIT TRAN
RPC:Completed	declare @p4 bigint set @p4=25630 exec TDDS_GetTrackingData @DestinationID=1,@PartitionID=2,@LastReadSeqNum
SQL:BatchCompleted	IF @@TRANCOUNT > 0 COMMIT TRAN
RPC:Completed	declare @p4 bigint set @p4=25489 exec TDDS_GetTrackingData @DestinationID=1,@PartitionID=0,@LastReadSeqNum

Figure 2-6

The details of the SQL Server profiler trace are shown below. You can clearly see the `InsertProperty` stored procedure being called for each promoted property. The `uidPropertyID` value references context properties that have been registered with BizTalk and are held in the `bt_DocumentSpec` table held within the BizTalkMgmtDb (BizTalk Management Database).

```
exec [dbo].[bts_InsertProperty]
@uidBatchID=N'{649B5162-3338-414F-A061-AF63EC2D6D17}',
@nOrderID=0,
@uidMessageID=N'{5F72C398-3788-4D97-9994-82408966C8EF}',
@uidPropertyID=N'{70715D47-142A-41B4-8FDC-9E3DBA78BD13}',
@vtValue=N'c:\msgdrop\*.xml'
Go

exec [dbo].[bts_InsertProperty]
@uidBatchID=N'{649B5162-3338-414F-A061-AF63EC2D6D17}',
@nOrderID=0,@uidMessageID=N'{5F72C398-3788-4D97-9994-82408966C8EF}',
@uidPropertyID=N'{133445B0-B87A-482E-9A98-0A82CFED3896}',
@vtValue=N'{9438DC3B-16AE-466C-B53F-9F723D195FB4}'
Go

exec [dbo].[bts_InsertProperty]
@uidBatchID=N'{649B5162-3338-414F-A061-AF63EC2D6D17}',
@nOrderID=0,@uidMessageID=N'{5F72C398-3788-4D97-9994-82408966C8EF}',
@uidPropertyID=N'{798D8A34-3A4E-4DD9-8AB5-99AD2AEB16E5}',
@vtValue=N'MsgBoxProfilingDemoRecvPort'
Go

exec [dbo].[bts_InsertProperty]
@uidBatchID=N'{649B5162-3338-414F-A061-AF63EC2D6D17}',
@nOrderID=0,@uidMessageID=N'{5F72C398-3788-4D97-9994-82408966C8EF}',
@uidPropertyID=N'{7D0D2D40-4906-4AB0-9578-D4593F7848D7}',
@vtValue=N'FILE'
```

```
Go

exec [dbo].[bts_InsertProperty]
@uidBatchID=N'{649B5162-3338-414F-A061-AF63EC2D6D17}',
@nOrderID=0,@uidMessageID=N'{5F72C398-3788-4D97-9994-82408966C8EF}',
@uidPropertyID=N'{F4E068C3-48AE-49EC-8CCA-FB3B542348B2}',
@vtValue=N'http://MsgBoxProfilingDemo.Schema1#Root'
Go

exec [dbo].[bts_FindSubscriptions]
@uidBatchID=N'{649B5162-3338-414F-A061-AF63EC2D6D17}'
go

exec [dbo].[bts_InsertMessage]
@uidMessageID=N'{5F72C398-3788-4D97-9994-82408966C8EF}',
@uidBatchID=N'{649B5162-3338-414F-A061-AF63EC2D6D17}',
@uidSubscriptionID=N'{A98B9880-83A3-4160-8C38-CB0C6778FA5B}',
@uidPredicateGroupID=N'{E924947A-FE38-45A1-A37A-0789715D996B}',
@uidInstanceID=NULL,
@fMessageRoutedTwice=1,
@nRefCount=1,@nNumParts=0,@OriginatorSID=NULL,@OriginatorPID=NULL,
@dtExpiration=''1899-12-30 00:00:00:000'',

@fTrackMessage=0,@nvcMessageType=NULL,@uidPartID=NULL,@nvcPartName=NULL,
@nPartSize=0,@fSuccess=@p17output,@imgPart=NULL,@imgPropBag=NULL,
@fPartExistsInDB=0,@imgContext=NUL

exec [dbo].[bts_InsertMessage]
@uidMessageID=N'{5F72C398-3788-4D97-9994-82408966C8EF}',
@uidBatchID=N'{649B5162-3338-414F-A061-AF63EC2D6D17}',
@uidSubscriptionID=NULL,@uidPredicateGroupID=NULL,@uidInstanceID=NULL,
@fMessageRoutedTwice=0,@nRefCount=0,@nNumParts=1,@OriginatorSID=NULL,
@OriginatorPID=N's-1-5-7',@dtExpiration=''1899-12-30
00:00:00:000'',
@fTrackMessage=0,@nvcMessageType=N'http://MsgBoxProfilingDemo.Schema1#Root',
@uidPartID=N'{9C30EE5F-0B4B-484D-AF16-D8B8C84F822B}',
@nvcPartName=N'body',@nPartSize=119,@fSuccess=@p17output,
@imgPart=<removed for brevity>
```

So, in the case of the `InsertProperty` call (highlighted in bold above), you will see a GUID being passed as the `uidPropertyID` parameter that identifies the property being populated. The underlying property name is actually `ReceivePortName`. The following is the SQL query to resolve this from the GUID:

```
SELECT * FROM bt_DocumentSpec WHERE id LIKE '798D8A34-3A4E-4DD9-8AB5-99AD2AEB16E5%'

Returns:

http://schemas.microsoft.com/BizTalk/2003/system-properties#ReceivePortName
```

As you can see in the SQL Profiler trace above, the first call to `bts_InsertMessage` passes a `SubscriptionID` in the `uidSubscriptionID` parameter, the value of which was returned from the `bts_FindSubscriptions` stored procedure as a subscriber to this message.

The value passed is {A98B9880-83A3-4160-8C38-CB0C6778FA5B}, which matches the send port subscription, as you can see in Figure 2-7.

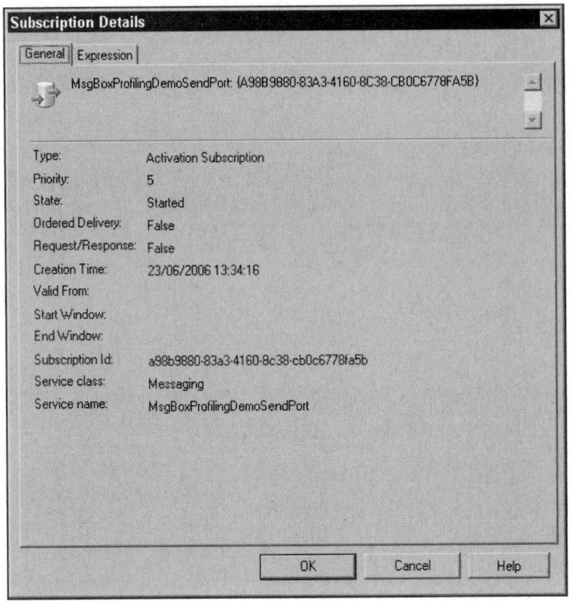

Figure 2-7

Once all this is complete, the promoted properties inserted in the first step of this process are then removed because the message routing has been completed.

Subscription processing is complex and has been covered for reference purposes to help you during debugging. In short, you just need to remember that once a message arrives at the Message Agent, subscribers are evaluated, the message is inserted, and references are then added into the host instance queue, ready for processing by the subscriber hosted by the host instance.

Each host instance polls the database at a regular interval to look for new work in the queue. Multiple threads (called *dequeue threads* internally) are used by the host instance, and multiple machines may run a given host instance for resilience and scalability.

The `bts_DequeueMessages_<HostInstanceName>` stored procedure is then used by these dequeue threads to retrieve messages for processing. Each call to `bts_DequeueMessages` will retrieve as many messages as possible for processing up to a configurable limit.

The default for the batch size is set to 20 and is configurable on a service-class-wide setting, which we discuss more in Chapter 9. You can also configure how aggressively the host instance calls the `bts_DequeueMessages` stored procedure, which in low-latency scenarios can improve the latency (although at the expense of your SQL server).

The architecture of BizTalk and its use of the MessageBox means that messages may be routed based on their content — typically referred to as content-based routing (CBR). CBR is an extremely powerful concept and one that is very easy to configure in BizTalk. You configure a receive location and one or more send ports, which subscribe to properties of the incoming messages. They are then sent to a remote system or endpoint using whatever transport is required.

CBR is a perfectly valid use of BizTalk and, when combined with custom pipeline components, can be all that is required to provide your solution. Most scenarios, however, use orchestrations, enabling BizTalk to be utilized to implement complex business processes.

Orchestrations

BizTalk orchestrations enable you to implement a business process using a visual design tool called the *Orchestration Designer*. The Orchestration Designer enables you to express your business process using a combination of *shapes*, which are provided via a Toolbox and dragged onto the design surface.

Figure 2-8 shows the Orchestration Designer, with the available shapes on the left side in the Toolbox.

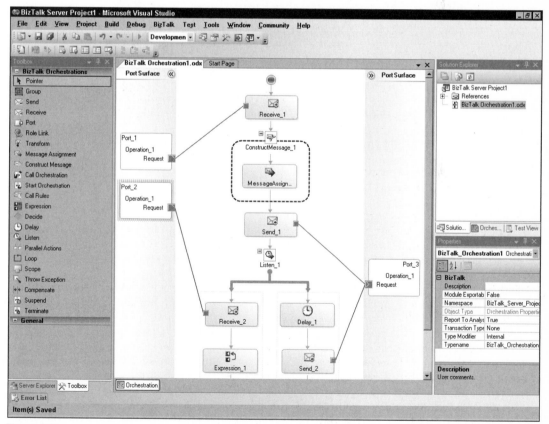

Figure 2-8

The design surface is hosted in Visual Studio and is very developer-centric. There is also a Visio add-in that allows business processes to be expressed using simplified concepts. The resulting Visio diagram can be imported into the main Orchestration Designer to be implemented fully.

Once created, the orchestration is compiled into .NET code and, ultimately, into a .NET assembly; it also leverages the .NET side-by-side (SxS) functionality, which allows multiple versions of an orchestration to be deployed at any time.

An orchestration can be created either by a message that it subscribes to or by being invoked by another orchestration. In the case of an orchestration subscribing to a message, the orchestration must have a Receive shape at the top.

The developer then creates a BizTalk message using Visual Studio and the Orchestration View pane, and specifies the schema for the message being requested. The Receive shape is then configured to use this message. The next step is to create a port on the orchestration design surface and link this to the Receive shape.

This process effectively describes the subscription required for the orchestration and enables messages to be routed to the orchestration.

The orchestration engine is responsible for creating orchestrations when messages arrive. During orchestration execution, you commonly reach *wait* points. These wait points are typically Receive shapes (i.e., the orchestration must wait for an undefined period for a message to arrive or a Delay shape, which causes the orchestration to sleep for a defined period).

Maintaining these orchestrations in-memory during these periods would cause excessive system resources to be used, which for many scenarios may lead to an out-of-memory condition or resource starvation — for example, running out of threads within a thread pool. To counter this, the orchestration engine can elect to *dehydrate* an orchestration. This involves serializing the state of the orchestration to the MessageBox, thereby removing it from memory. The engine will automatically rehydrate it when the message being waited on arrives or the delay period expires.

The processing of orchestrations is stateless; all of the orchestration's state is held within the orchestration instance. This means that an instance of an orchestration does not have any affinity for a specific machine. An orchestration, therefore, may be dehydrated on one machine and rehydrated on another machine at a later time.

We cover all the orchestration concepts in Chapter 5, including some of the more complex business processes that can be implemented.

Enterprise Single Sign-On

Enterprise Single Sign-On (SSO) is an integral part of a BizTalk solution and provides a resilient and secure store for information. By default BizTalk uses SSO to provide secure and centralized storage of adapter configuration and any usernames and passwords required for access to remote systems (which adapters can then retrieve).

Using the SSO provides a secure store for this configuration data. Because it's held centrally, the configuration data can be changed once and all the BizTalk Servers will retrieve this configuration data on startup.

Chapters 11 and 12 discuss SSO in more detail.

Business Activity Monitoring

Business Activity Monitoring (BAM) is an extremely valuable and powerful feature of BizTalk. It was introduced in the 2004 release and was extended further in BizTalk Server 2006.

When BizTalk is used to solve business problems, the processing within those solutions is often a black box, making it very difficult for business users and technical support personnel to get a view into what is happening. This is true of not only BizTalk solutions but many IT projects that involve the processing of business data and logic. Providing visibility into this processing is critical to these users. Typically, they need to understand where backlogs of processing occur and get a view as to why. They also need to understand the numbers and types of business transactions being processed.

Understanding where a given request or message is at any point in time may be problematic. You have the various BizTalk administration tools, but they paint the picture in a very technical way; they talk about orchestrations and messages, which are opaque terms to anyone other than the developers, and they don't really convey exactly what stage of processing they are currently in.

This is where Business Activity Monitoring comes in. BAM enables any messaging or business process to be fully instrumented in terms that any data consumer can understand. The first step requires a *wish list* of data to be collected. This is described in terms of business milestones, which are represented as timestamps, and business data, which can be represented as string, int, or float data types.

Once a wish list has been created, you need to provide storage for this instrumentation data. SQL Server provides an ideal location for this, given its transactional behavior and ability to handle high loads.

The BAM administration tool provisions all the database infrastructure required to store this instrumentation data in a performant manner. Huge amounts of instrumentation data can be collected with low impact on the overall system performance. Those of you who have implemented tracing for high-load systems will appreciate that this is not a trivial problem to solve.

Once the wish list and database infrastructure are created, you need to get the data into this infrastructure. In most cases the Tracking Profile Editor (TPE) provides a graphical drag-and-drop way to tell the BizTalk engine to collect timestamps and message data and match these to the wish list. This process creates a tracking profile. All this can be done retrospectively to an existing system, as required.

The tracking profile can then be deployed at runtime for data collection and modified over time without causing any downtime to the system.

Once data is stored in your database infrastructure, you need to make it available to the interested parties. BizTalk Server 2006 introduced the BAM portal (covered later in the book), which provides a generic Web interface into the data collected by BAM. Because the data is stored in a SQL database, you can, of course, create your own portal using tools such as SQL Reporting Services or integrate the data into an existing tool or application using SQL queries if your requirements are not met by the BAM portal.

Measures and dimensions (explained in Chapter 6) can also be defined at the wish list creation stage. These are then used to provision an Online Analytical Processing (OLAP) cube, which the BAM infrastructure will automatically populate, and to provide a data warehouse, which can be interrogated using any business intelligence tool or Excel with PivotTables.

Chapter 6 covers this subject in far more detail, but it's also worth noting here that you can leverage the BAM components on servers other than BizTalk, effectively providing an end-to-end and enterprise-wide instrumentation technology.

Rules Engine

In any BizTalk solution, there is an element of conditional logic. Many of these solutions effectively implement a form of business logic in a programming language such as C#.

When this business logic is subject to change or when the owners of such business rules want to have control to make changes on their own terms, the Rules Engine can be a very powerful technology, as it enables the business logic to be abstracted from the code.

BizTalk Server 2004 introduced the Business Rules Engine (BRE), which introduced no major changes for the 2006 release. The BRE is a standard forward-inferencing rules engine that implements the Rete algorithm. (We cover what this really means in Chapter 7.)

Nontechnical business users can define rules using the Business Rule Composer. Within this graphical user interface (GUI) tool they can define policies — a concept used to group multiple rules together. These rules will each rely on any combination of data source; valid data sources are XML documents, SQL Server database tables/rows, or .NET classes.

Data sources present a problem for business users, because they won't know where data they rely on to evaluate a rule exists and how to get hold of it. Imagine, for example, a user writing an XPath statement! To avoid this, the BRE uses what are known as *vocabularies*, which enable developers to map business-friendly names onto the underlying data. Business users can simply drag the logical data item onto their rule without knowing where or how that data is stored.

Policies are versioned and can be deployed into your BizTalk Server environment without causing any downtime. Policies are stored in the Rules Engine SQL Server database. BizTalk Server maintains a cache of the policies in memory to avoid database roundtrips, thus improving performance.

Rules execution can be tracked, providing clear traceability as to why certain rules were used in given scenarios and the results of policy execution.

Hosts

A BizTalk *host* is a logical representation of a runtime process. Each host may contain a combination of Receive or Send adapters (and their associated receive and send ports) or orchestrations.

Once you have defined a BizTalk host, you can then create instances of it. When creating an instance, you specify the name of a physical server for the host instance to execute on along with a *service account* for the host to run under. Hosts can be either in-process or isolated. An in-process host instance executes as a Windows service. The BizTalk tools automatically create this service when a new host is created. Isolated host instances execute in a non-BizTalk process, such as an ASP.NET worker process.

A host can have multiple instances, and this enables you to run a BizTalk host on more than one server. Furthermore, each BizTalk Server can run any combination of hosts.

Running a host on multiple boxes is important for distributing load around your BizTalk Server group. A common problem with performance testing occurs when a solution is deployed with all the adapters and orchestrations in the default `BizTalkServerApplication` host, due to the conflicting resource requirements of the different types of processing.

Because large parts of the BizTalk engine are written in .NET, which itself leverages the built-in CLR thread pool, if you run the SOAP adapter and your orchestrations in the same host, they will fight over limited resources, such as threads. When running multiple orchestrations, each using a thread pool thread, it's easy to *starve* the SOAP adapter of threads to process outbound messages. This results in the SOAP adapter raising errors and then retrying the message later. For the most part, this is due to the fact that the Orchestration Engine uses the .NET `ThreadPool` very aggressively.

The default rule of thumb to avoid this, and a general best practice, is to use a separate host for receive, orchestration, and send operations. You can run each host on each BizTalk server, which should be the basic starting point for most solutions, of course. A performance test will determine the optimum host and host instance combination for your solution.

By default, BizTalk has two default hosts: `BizTalkServerApplication` and `BizTalkServer-IsolatedHost`. The `BizTalkServerApplication` host is the default host for any adapters or orchestrations that you create and for outbound SOAP messages generated by BizTalk, whereas the `BizTalkServerIsolatedHost` is used for messages received via the SOAP adapter.

There are several good reasons for this split. In-bound SOAP messages are handled by Internet Information Server (IIS), not the BizTalk Server engine, unlike other adapters. Also, you can think of messages being received from IIS as being far less trusted than those from other adapters; in many cases they will be received over an untrusted network, such as the Internet. Many adapters, such as the SOAP adapter, need to be hosted by processes other than the BizTalk NT Service. The isolated host model enables this and effectively means that an adapter may be hosted outside of BizTalk. For these scenarios, the adapter actually loads the BizTalk Messaging Engine and, subsequently, the Message Agent into its process address space. This ensures that the same out-of-process communication is required regardless of whether the adapter is hosted by BizTalk or as an isolated adapter.

This split allows you to run an isolated host under a different service account with bare minimum permissions to the BizTalk MessageBox, delivering a great security solution. Of course, you can configure each BizTalk host instance with a different service account, enabling the same approach to be used throughout your deployment.

It's also worth mentioning the tracking host, which is responsible for moving all message-tracking data from the BizTalk MessageBox into the Tracking database and, as we'll discuss in Chapter 6, any BAM data from the BizTalk MessageBox into the BAMPrimaryImport SQL database.

Any host can perform tracking operations; by default, the standard BizTalkServerAppplication host is configured to be the tracking host. Of course, you can configure a dedicated host to perform tracking as required.

Summary

In this chapter, we have highlighted, with the use of a fictional integration scenario, how complex it can be to create a solution without BizTalk and, conversely, how the same solution can more easily be created using BizTalk. Although this scenario was contrived, it highlights the things you should consider when architecting your solution and deciding whether to use BizTalk.

The chapter then walked you through the key architectural pieces of BizTalk to explain how everything fits together, setting the scene for the rest of the book. The next chapter covers BizTalk adapters, detailing the fundamental concepts and the various adapters available in the box.

3

Adapters

Adapters are the communication interface for BizTalk to and from the outside world. They perform whatever communication semantics or protocols that the remote system requires, thus hiding any complexity that is required when interfacing with remote systems, particularly legacy ones.

Adapters are commonly referred to as *bit shovelers* because of the way they move the binary bits from the outside world into BizTalk and from BizTalk back out to the outside world, effectively feeding the BizTalk engine with work — like a fireman feeding coal into the engine of a steam train.

No conversion or translation of messages is performed by adapters; they purely bring the bits into BizTalk so that pipelines can then optionally perform any data translation, such as converting a flat file to an XML document.

This chapter begins with an overview of the adapter architecture along with features offered to adapters, and then the remainder of the chapter discusses each of the mainstream adapters.

Overview

BizTalk Server 2006 comes with a number of adapters in the box, and a number of third parties provide adapters at extra cost for just about every system, new and old, regardless of platform.

The 2006 release includes extra adapters that were purchased by Microsoft from iWay, as these were the most commonly requested and used by BizTalk customers; this should mean that most systems you need to interface with have adapters in the box with BizTalk.

Adapters are really extensions of the BizTalk engine. Custom adapters can be written but need to be designed and developed with care since they are multithreaded server-side components. Microsoft intentionally designed a low-level programming API for adapters, allowing custom adapters to take advantage of the full set of functionality that out-of-the-box adapters enjoy. In short, custom adapters are treated as first-class citizens by the BizTalk engine.

This does, however, have implications. Custom adapter code needs to be written in a robust and resilient manner, which makes the task of developing custom adapters relatively significant. A poorly written adapter may starve BizTalk, introduce a performance bottleneck, or consume valuable (and not free) resources such as memory.

A common solution to interfacing with systems where an adapter isn't available or economically viable is to wrap (expose) the remote system via a Web service and call this via the SOAP adapter. This, of course, has a higher overhead than a native and richer adapter approach but is a useful technique to bear in mind.

Architecture

A common misconception is that orchestrations wishing to receive messages from an adapter are directly coupled. In fact, messages flow from an adapter through a pipeline into the BizTalk MessageBox and are then subsequently dispatched to an orchestration.

As Figure 3-1 depicts, all external messages flow into BizTalk through adapters, which then hand them off to the End Point Manager (EPM), which executes a receive pipeline before being committed to the appropriate host queue in the SQL Server MessageBox by the BizTalk Message Agent.

As we covered in the last chapter, BizTalk hosts are responsible for *hosting* adapters and/or orchestrations. The best-practice starting configuration is shown in Figure 3-1, which has a host for receive, orchestration, and send.

The Message Agent for the appropriate host will poll its host queue in the MessageBox, and when messages are available, it will handle orchestration instantiation or send port invocation.

If an orchestration sends messages, there is again no direct coupling between the orchestration and send ports; instead, the messages are published to the MessageBox, where the MessageBox subscriptions are evaluated. The messages are then sent via the appropriately configured send port and appropriate adapters.

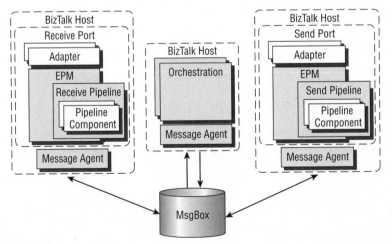

Figure 3-1

Communication Semantics

BizTalk adapters can support one-way or two-way message exchange patterns when sending or receiving data. Depending on the transport, an adapter can support both of these. In-bound two-way message exchanges are referred to as *request-response*, whereas outbound two-way message exchanges are referred to as *solicit-response*.

The File adapter, for example, is a one-way adapter because there is no return path involved. The SOAP adapter typically implements a request-response method, where there is always a response to match a request. The SOAP adapter can be configured to use a one-way message exchange pattern, which will, in turn, cause the SOAP adapter to not expect a response to be returned. This is due to the underlying SOAP transport supporting both approaches.

Ports

Ports are physical communication endpoints used by BizTalk to send or receive messages. When you create a port, you must select the appropriate communication type, which, in the case of receive ports, defines how an external system must communicate to BizTalk and, in the case of send ports, defines how BizTalk must communicate to an external system.

> If you are using BizTalk orchestrations, each logical port defined within the orchestration is mapped to the physical port using binding. In content-based routing scenarios, however, there is no need to perform this mapping because there is no concept of logical ports.

Receive Ports

Receive ports can be configured with one or more receive locations, each of which maps to an endpoint (URL) for a specific adapter. This enables one receive port to be exposed by many different physical endpoints in order to receive messages. This technique is often overlooked because it's assumed that receive ports have a one-to-one mapping with a BizTalk adapter; however, there is instead another level that enables multiple adapters to be utilized.

Consider a scenario where you have created a BizTalk orchestration that wants to receive a travel itinerary. You define an orchestration with a logical receive port, and at deployment time you bind this logical receive port to a physical receive port. This physical receive port can then define two receive locations, one that uses the FTP adapter and another that uses the File adapter.

This would enable travel itinerary messages to be received by either adapter and routed directly to the orchestration, without it having any knowledge of multiple endpoints being defined, completely decoupling the orchestration from the physical transport medium. Further, each receive location has a pipeline associated with it, so the format of the data received on each endpoint may be different and normalized into a common format in the receive pipeline. For example, one receive location may receive data in XML conforming to schema A, while the other may receive its data in flat-file format. Both could be normalized to a common XML format conforming to schema B before being fed to the orchestration that is responsible for processing the messages.

Figure 3-2 illustrates a receive port with two receive locations associated with it, each of which uses a different adapter.

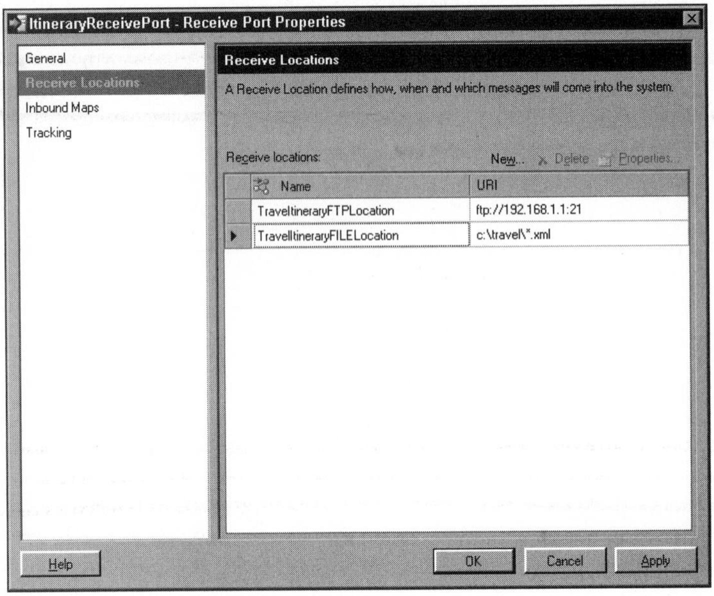

Figure 3-2

Send Ports

Send ports, unlike receive ports, are a one-to-one mapping in that you define one send port and map it directly to one BizTalk adapter. Of course, multiple send ports can use the same adapter type. This send port, in the case of BizTalk orchestration, is then mapped to a logical send port in a BizTalk orchestration via binding. The exception to this is dynamic send ports, which we'll discuss shortly.

In some scenarios, you may want to send a message via a choice of send ports; perhaps you have a multicast scenario where one message needs to be transmitted to multiple endpoints, or you have multiple endpoints but want to select the specific send point to use at runtime by evaluating a piece of data.

This is where send port groups come in. As the name implies, a *send port group* can contain one or more send ports. In the case of BizTalk orchestrations, this send port group can be mapped directly to a logical send port via binding. Any messages then sent to this send port group will result in a copy of the message being sent via each send port that is configured to be part of the send port group.

Figure 3-3 shows the Send Port Group Properties dialog box. As you can see, two send ports have been selected to be part of this send port group.

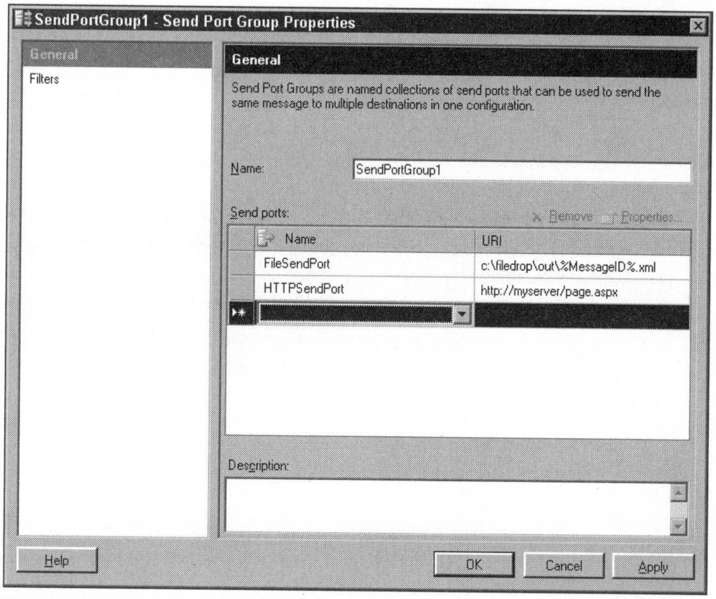

Figure 3-3

If instead of broadcasting messages to all the send ports, you want to select a particular send port within a send port group based on data held in the message, you can apply filters to each send port based on message data that has been promoted using property promotions. The filtering feature is covered later in this chapter.

Property promotions are covered in more depth in Chapter 5. They are the process by which BizTalk can extract key pieces of a message for use within message routing — a customer type, for example. It's worth noting that if you have multiple send ports configured to subscribe to the same message and/or using the same filters you should insure that you make use of send port groups which perform significantly better than individual send ports.

The advice from the product team is that eight or more identical send ports should make use of send port groups to avoid MessageBox and CPU overhead. However, you should insure that you test both combinations for your scenario to understand the impact.

Mapping

Each receive or send port can apply a BizTalk map transformation (which is essentially an XSL to a message). In the case of receive ports, the transformation occurs after the BizTalk adapter has received the message and after the pipeline has been executed. In the case of the send port, the transformation is performed before the send pipeline has been executed.

This is a particularly useful technique to convert a message from a native external format to your internal representation. Imagine receiving travel itineraries from a number of third-party travel agents, each of which represents them in a different XML schema.

In situations where you cannot impose a standard schema on users of your solution, you could create a BizTalk Map for each travel agent, which converts their XML schema into your native format. You can then configure each transformation at the port level, using the BizTalk Administration Console.

In the case of a receive port, you can configure one or more maps via the Inbound Maps section of the Receive Port properties dialog box. Figure 3-4 shows two maps configured on a receive port. The appropriate map will be selected at runtime based upon the type of message received. (Send ports can be configured to use maps via the Outbound Maps section of the Send Port properties dialog box.)

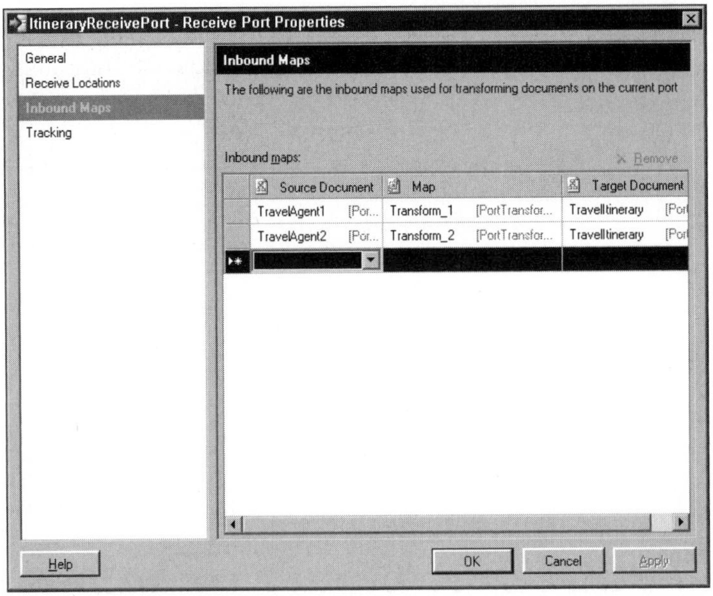

Figure 3-4

This way, your solution orchestrations and components have to deal with only one schema instead of many, greatly simplifying the development and maintenance of your solution because it enables the message engine to dynamically choose the appropriate map based on the message type. Note that you must use the XmlReceive pipeline that populates the BTS.MessageType context property used by this mapping step.

Filtering

We touched on filtering when we covered send port groups. Filters enable you to dynamically determine which send port will be used to process a message or which Orchestration will process a message. Filters use message context properties, which can be based on message data, among other things.

As we cover in more detail in Chapter 5, you can make various elements of your BizTalk message available to the runtime using property promotions. BizTalk pipelines can then extract this data from the body of the message and make it available in the message context.

A filter can leverage context properties that you have promoted manually, or use any of the built-in context properties that are populated by the adapters, pipeline components, or the engine. Filters are sometimes used to enable selection of the appropriate send port within a group based on message data, but most often when you are configuring standard, content-based routing.

Figure 3-5 shows a send port filter configured to subscribe to messages that arrive through a receive port called *FileReceive*. With this configured, any messages arriving through that receive port would be collected by the send port and sent onwards. Send port filters can be configured on a send port through the BizTalk Administration Console.

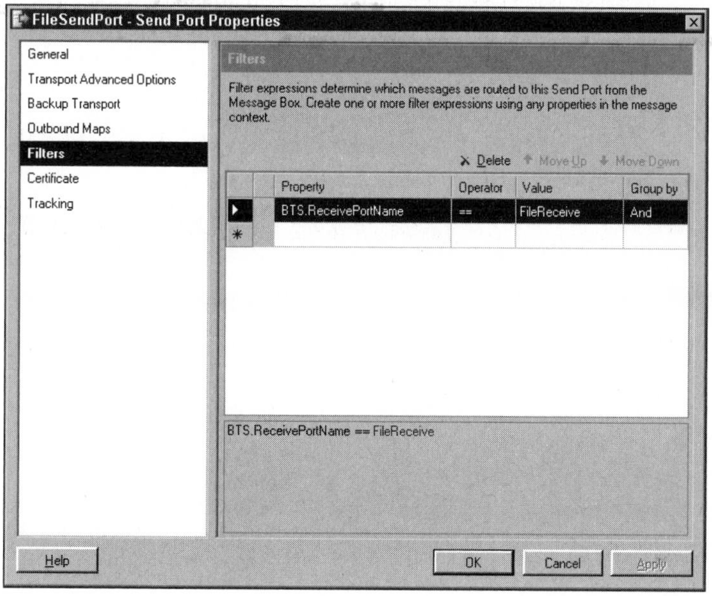

Figure 3-5

You can also apply filters to Receive shapes on BizTalk orchestrations. This can enable two orchestrations to process the same type of messages but process them differently based on data held within the message. You have probably already guessed that subscriptions and filters are how BizTalk exposes its publish/subscribe infrastructure.

Imagine a Travel Itinerary processing orchestration. If you're a premium member, perhaps your itinerary has its processing fast-tracked, whereas if you're a standard member, it's processed in the usual way. Using filtering on the Receive shape of each orchestration would allow you to solve this requirement by executing different orchestrations and, therefore, business processes.

Note, however, that if you ever need to change the filter applied to a Receive shape, you must recompile and redeploy the orchestrations — it cannot be changed on the fly or stored within configuration files.

Dynamic Send Ports

We've covered send ports and how they are created and configured at deployment time. In some instances, however, you may want to control the adapter used dynamically at runtime rather than at deployment time or modify configuration settings such as endpoint address at runtime.

Dynamic send ports exist for exactly this scenario. They enable you to select the adapter used and control any transport configuration, such as the endpoint URI, from within a BizTalk orchestration.

You can create a dynamic port by dragging a port onto the orchestration surface as usual but during configuration select Dynamic as the Port Binding. Dynamic is available only when creating a send port and can be used on both one-way and request-response ports. Figure 3-6 shows the configuration dialog box that is accessed when creating a logical receive port on an orchestration.

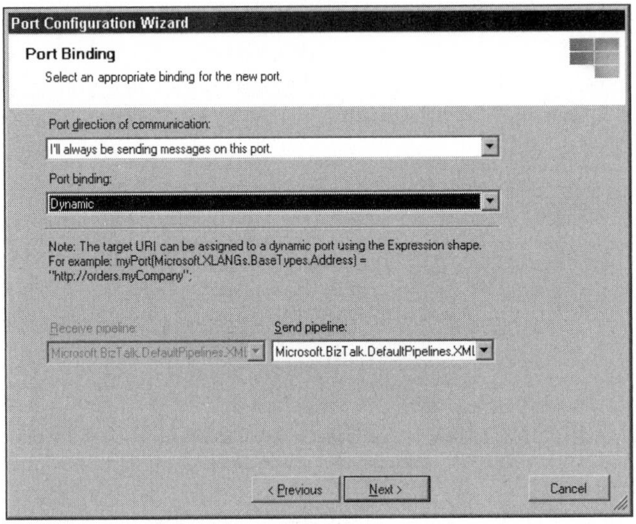

Figure 3-6

At this creation stage you must also select the send pipeline to be used when the dynamic port is invoked from BizTalk orchestration. At runtime, the engine uses the prefix of the endpoint URL (the engine uses the system context property "OutboundTransportLocation" for this) to determine which adapter to use. For example, the following URL will cause the HTTP adapter to be used:

```
http://www.wiley.com/ProfessionalBizTalk2006
```

The following example will cause the File adapter to be used (the engine selects the appropriate adapter by using a mapping database table: BizTalkMgmtDb.adm_AdapterAlias; each adapter may register one or more prefixes/aliases at setup time):

```
FILE://\\PODrop\Outbound
```

Enlistment

The process of enlistment creates the underlying subscriptions required for a send port or orchestration in the BizTalk MessageBox. These subscriptions will then be evaluated when a message arrives in the MessageBox to establish what BizTalk should do with the message.

If no subscriptions match the incoming message, the message will be suspended; hence, it's important to always ensure that your subscriptions are in place for live systems. With BizTalk Server 2006, however, these messages can be resumed — unlike in BizTalk Server 2004, which had no automatic resuming ability for this scenario.

It's important to remember that you can have a send port or orchestration enlisted but not started. That way, messages will be queued in the MessageBox until the send port or orchestration is restarted. This is useful when you want to receive messages but not process them until later in the day or if there is some form of system problem that you wish to fix before processing. (Versioning, which is covered in Chapter 5, uses this technique.) Not having them enlisted will cause the messages to be suspended.

You can enlist a send port by right-clicking on a send port within the BizTalk Administration Console and selecting Enlist (see Figure 3-7). We cover orchestration enlistment in Chapter 5.

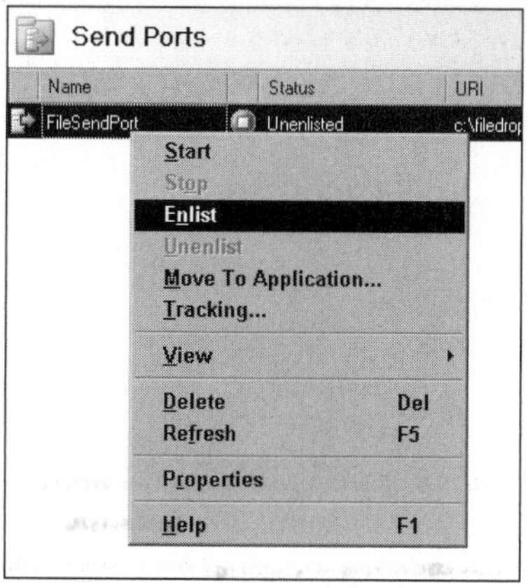

Figure 3-7

You can see all active subscriptions (and therefore enlistments) in the BizTalk Server 2006 Administration Console by clicking on the BizTalk Group. Then click the New Query tab and select Subscriptions from the Value drop-down list, as shown in Figure 3-8.

Note that this view shows both send port and orchestration subscriptions along with internal cache subscriptions which are used by the BizTalk engine and should be ignored.

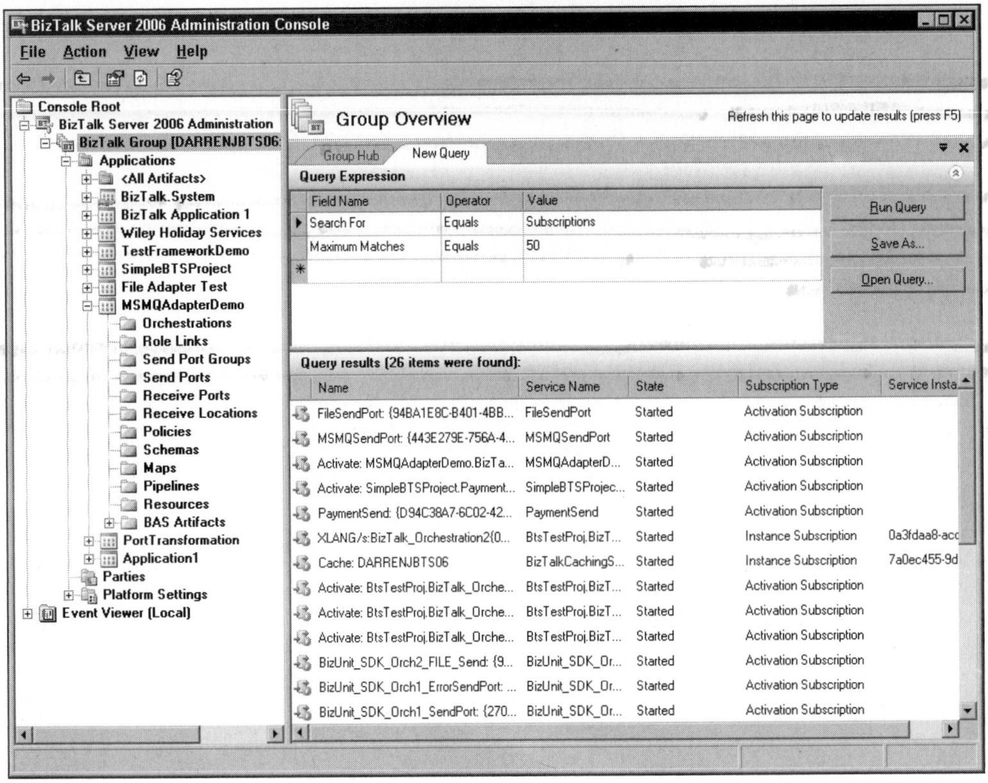

Figure 3-8

Hosting

When you create a receive or send port, you need to have it hosted (loaded in memory) by BizTalk in order for it to successfully send and receive messages. Hosting, as we discussed in the previous chapter, is the technique that BizTalk uses to "load" adapters, pipelines, and orchestrations.

During the binding phase of deployment, you can choose which BizTalk host to use for each receive, send port and Orchestration. Once configured, the host will make your receive and send ports available for operation.

Each BizTalk host can run on any combination of servers to provide high availability and the ability to leverage multiple machines for processing in-bound messages. You can think of a host as merely a definition; you must then define one or more host instances that are created on a BizTalk Server.

These host instances are represented as Windows services on each configured BizTalk Server and can be created through the BizTalk Administration Console.

All adapters, with the exception of the FTP adapter, can be safely run on multiple machines without running the risk of duplicating in-bound messages.

> The FTP protocol has no locking semantics, so the BizTalk FTP adapter is not able to prevent another FTP adapter running on another BizTalk Server from processing the same file.
>
> Therefore, the FTP adapter must be hosted only on one BizTalk Server. This is clearly a problem for high availability, in that you risk not being able to process in-bound files if the BizTalk Server hosting the FTP adapter is not available for any reason.
>
> Chapter 11 covers the workaround for this scenario.

Using hosts can allow you to isolate in-bound message processing to one or more servers and free the remaining BizTalk Servers in your BizTalk group to focus on processing the messages instead of being *distracted* by processing in-bound messages and using up valuable CPU cycles. We cover such a technique in Chapter 5.

Configuration Settings

All the configuration settings for adapters are stored in the Single Sign-On (SSO) database. There are two reasons for this. First, they are stored in one central place so that they don't have to be duplicated across multiple servers, leading to configuration mismatches, and it makes provisioning of new servers straightforward.

The other reason is security. Adapter configurations that include usernames and passwords need to be secured. The SSO functionality provides a heavily secured store from which to do this.

It's a popular misconception among developers that they don't need the SSO functionality, as they *don't use it*. In fact, it's required to allow BizTalk to operate and should, therefore, be configured to enable high availability. This is covered in Chapter 11.

Many BizTalk solutions end up with additional configuration information required to be stored somewhere, which typically is in the BizTalk XML configuration file (`btsntsvc.exe.config`). However, ensuring the file is kept up-to-date on all servers becomes a management nightmare. Developers can make use of SSO in the same way as the adapters to store custom configuration (see Chapter 13).

Retry Semantics

One of the most overlooked advantages of using a BizTalk adapter over a custom communications solution is catering for the "unhappy" scenarios that occur when sending messages. These occur when the destination system is down or is rejecting the message for any reason.

This unplanned downtime of the remote system could persist for a long period time, during which you must keep the message destined for the remote system in a secure location, and then retry transmitting the message at varying intervals.

Given that the message might be in this retry state for a long period of time, it should be held in a transactable store to ensure it's not lost — if a BizTalk Server is restarted, for example. BizTalk provides this capability via the BizTalk MessageBox.

Eventually, after the message has exhausted the configured retry pattern, it will be suspended pending administrator intervention. An administrator, through the BizTalk Administration Console, can resume or terminate the messages. Resuming enables the message processing to be attempted and is useful for scenarios when, say, an orchestration hasn't been enlisted. This process is covered in Chapter 11.

This default behavior of the message being suspended when the retry pattern is exhausted can be overridden by subscribing to failure messages, which we cover in Chapter 13.

In most failure scenarios of remote endpoints you shouldn't "flood" the remote system with retries that are destined for failure; instead, you should pause transmitting messages until the endpoint is repaired. BizTalk can still generate outbound messages, but they will be held in the MessageBox until the send port is restarted.

BizTalk will automatically disable a send port after a series of errors within a certain period of time, thus preventing the "flood" situation in which you continually send messages to a failed endpoint. BizTalk will then just hold the messages in the MessageBox until the send port is reactivated. Disabling a send port in this way leaves the send port enlisted and, therefore, the subscription remains enabling messages to queue up in the MessageBox.

As I'm sure you can appreciate, such retry logic is very hard to implement by hand. BizTalk provides all these semantics in the BizTalk runtime, which each adapter leverages. All configuration of these settings can be done via the BizTalk Administration Console and can be changed dynamically at runtime.

Figure 3-9 shows the default retry settings for a BizTalk send port. You can access these settings by right-clicking a send port in the BizTalk Administration Console, choosing Properties and then the Transport Advanced Options. The default settings will cause each message to be retried three times, with a 5-minute delay between each attempt, which you can alter in line with your requirements.

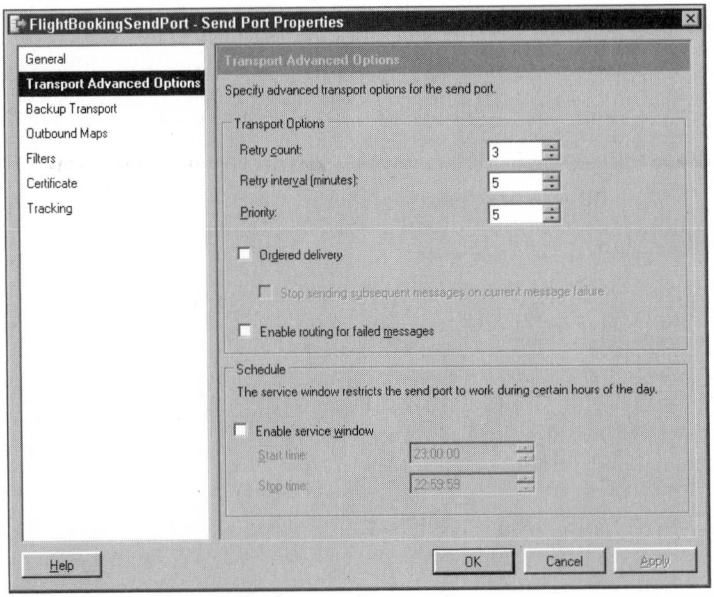

Figure 3-9

In some scenarios, you might implement a secondary transport to use in case the primary transport fails. BizTalk provides this functionality via the Backup Transport setting. Backup Transport is configured completely independently of the primary transport and can utilize a completely different adapter and retry interval.

If the backup transport also fails and exceeds the retry interval, the message will be suspended in the same way as if no backup transport had been configured.

Figure 3-10 shows the Backup Transport configuration dialog box, which you can access from the Send Port Properties. The figure demonstrates a different transport being utilized and a different retry interval of 60 minutes between each retry.

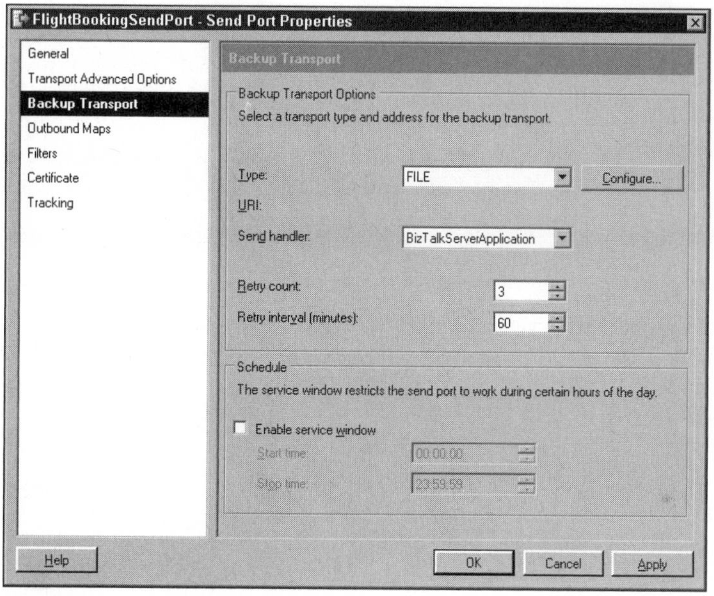

Figure 3-10

Service Windows

All receive locations and send ports enable you to specify a service window, which restricts the time period in which the receive location or send port operates.

This is useful for when a dependent system is not operational between, say, 23:00 and 00:00, so configuring a service window on a send port in this way would stop the send port within the configured time period but still build messages up in the MessageBox ready for the send port to be started again once the service window became active.

Figure 3-11 shows a service window configured on a send port. Service windows are configured through the BizTalk Administration Console through the Receive or Send Port properties.

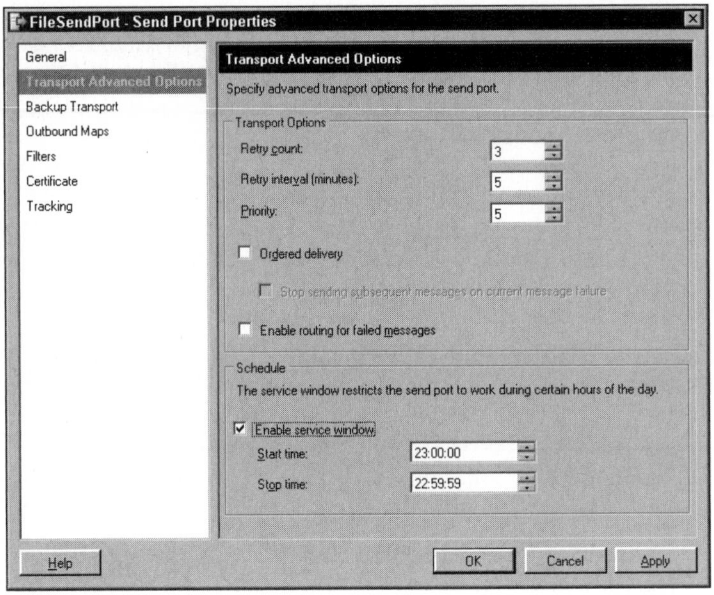

Figure 3-11

Tracking

You can configure each receive and send port to track detailed information about the message passing through. By default, tracking is turned off because it introduces a significant performance impact. You should only enable tracking only when absolutely necessary.

If you have specific tracking requirements or want to gain further information to assist with debugging, tracking can be a very valuable technique. Remember, however, if you turn it on for diagnostic purposes, be sure to turn it off.

Figure 3-12 shows the Tracking section of the Receive Port Properties dialog, where you can select tracking for message bodies and message properties. Tracking can be enabled on both receive ports and send ports through the BizTalk Administration Console.

Tracking can occur before the port processes the message or after. If you select "before port processing," the message will be tracked in the form it came off the wire or from the BizTalk MessageBox, whereas if you select "after port processing," any port processing will occur before tracking.

Tracking message properties requires less overhead than tracking message bodies and will just store any promoted properties and make them available via the Health and Activity Tracking tool (HAT).

Tracking message bodies enables you to later save them to disk using the HAT tool. To do this, enable message body tracking on your receive or send port and push at least one message through BizTalk to enable a message to be tracked.

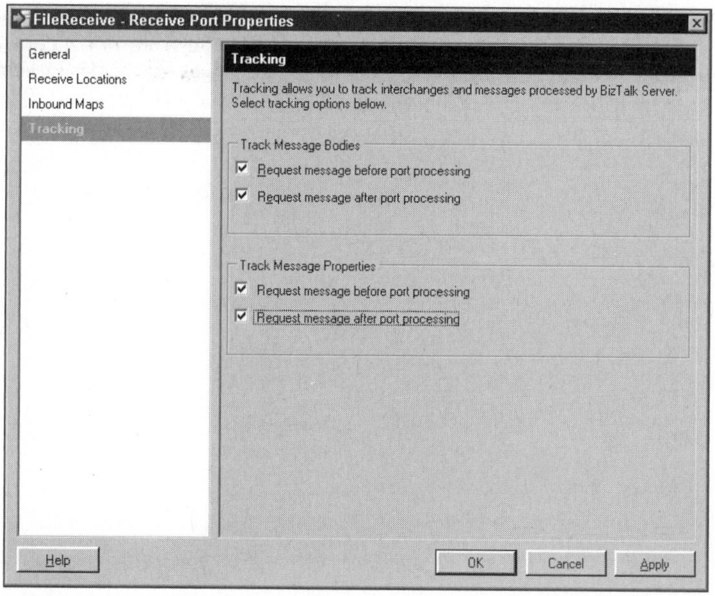

Figure 3-12

Open the HAT tool, click Find Message, and select the schema of the message you passed through the configured receive or send port. Click Run Query, select the message you want to view the message body of, and then choose Save All Tracked Messages, as shown in Figure 3-13.

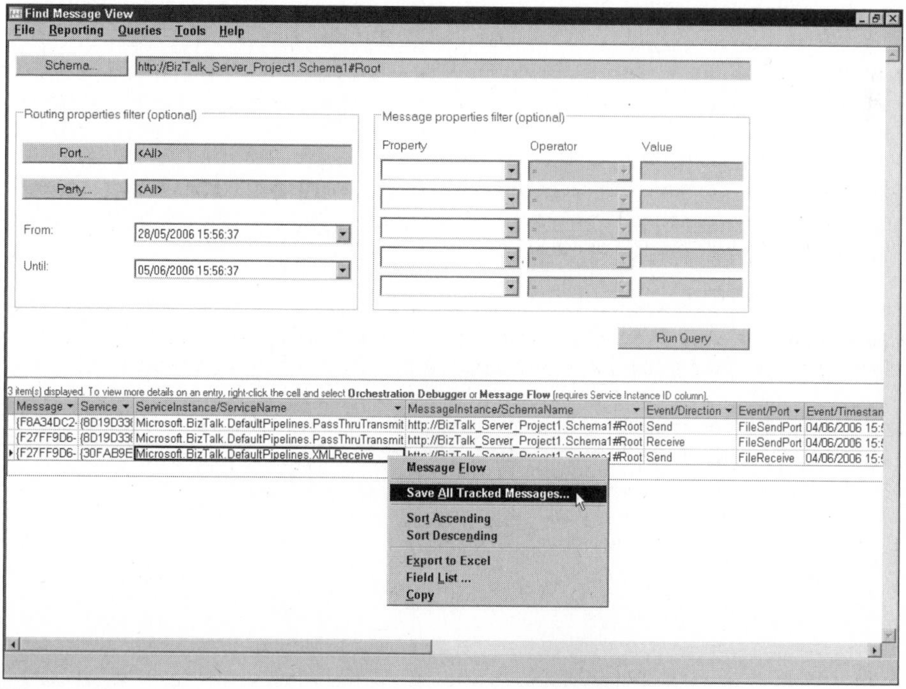

Figure 3-13

Choose a directory for the message body to be extracted to and you will see that two files are created for each tracked message saved: one with an XML extension and another with an OUT extension. The XML file contains all the context properties associated with the message, and the OUT file contains the message body. This file doesn't have an XML extension because it isn't always XML (it depends on the input message format).

The following sample context properties file clearly shows all the properties promoted by the adapter and pipeline:

```
<MessageInfo>
  <ContextInfo PropertiesCount="22">
    <Property Name="FileCreationTime" Namespace="http://schemas.microsoft.com/
BizTalk/2003/file-properties" Value="6/4/2006 3:10:11 PM"/>
    <Property Name="ReceivedFileName" Namespace="http://schemas.microsoft.com/
BizTalk/2003/file-properties" Value="c:\drop\msg.xml"/>
    <ArrayProperty Name="PartNames" Namespace="http://schemas.microsoft.com/
BizTalk/2003/messageagent-properties">
        <ArrayElement1 Value="body"/>
    </ArrayProperty>
    <Property Name="ActivityIdentity" Namespace="http://schemas.microsoft.com/
BizTalk/2003/messagetracking-properties" Value="{6C766D9F-B678-4CF9-B49A-
79EA0C9A3110}"/>
    <Property Name="PartyName" Namespace="http://schemas.microsoft.com/
BizTalk/2003/messagetracking-properties" Value=""/>
    <Property Name="PortName" Namespace="http://schemas.microsoft.com/
BizTalk/2003/messagetracking-properties" Value="FileReceive"/>
    <Property Name="InboundTransportLocation" Namespace="http://schemas.microsoft
.com/BizTalk/2003/system-properties" Value="c:\drop\*.xml"/>
    <Property Name="InterchangeID" Namespace="http://schemas.microsoft.com/
BizTalk/2003/system-properties"        Value="{649F182E-16D0-4155-8C6A-
5494FF0C7D69}"/>
    <Property Name="ReceiveInstanceID" Namespace="http://schemas.microsoft.com/
BizTalk/2003/system-properties" Value="{746FCF2F-CC87-422D-9C27-
4779BB6193D9}"/><Property Name="ReceiveLocationName" Namespace="http://schemas
.microsoft.com/BizTalk/2003/system-properties" Value="FileReceiveLocation"/>
    <Property Name="ReceivePortID" Namespace="http://schemas.microsoft.com/
BizTalk/2003/system-properties"        Value="{B2EAC49D-0E39-4BAE-AA22-
C35634F9ADA0}"/>
    <Property Name="ReceivePortName" Namespace="http://schemas.microsoft.com/
BizTalk/2003/system-properties" Value="FileReceive"/>
  </ContextInfo>
...
  <PartInfo PartsCount="1">
    <MessagePart ID="{A7C1E7BD-4AC2-40F5-98EE-562D717C3875}" Name="body"
FileName="C:\dump\{d796bd1d-adf1-47ea-b65f-b44b209e0638}_{A7C1E7BD-4AC2-40F5-98EE-
562D717C3875}_body.out" Charset="UTF-8" ContentType="text/xml"/>
  </PartInfo>
</MessageInfo>
```

The message body file contents are shown below, again for reference. You can see the raw body of the message, which, as you would expect, is kept separate from the context properties:

```
<ns0:Root xmlns:ns0="http://BizTalk_Server_Project1.Schema1">
  <Data1>Hello</Data1>
  <Data2>World</Data2>
</ns0:Root>
```

Message bodies should be available for tracking within a minute of the message being processed by BizTalk. If you receive errors from HAT when attempting to save the message, ensure that the SQL Server Agent is running on the SQL server that processes tracked messages. If this isn't running, you won't be able to access message bodies until the `TrackedMessages_Copy_BizTalkMsgBoxDb` job is executed.

If a message is suspended for whatever reason, it is possible to locate it within the BizTalk Administration Console and save the message contents to disk by right-clicking on the message instance.

> If you have a requirement for message body tracking along with high-throughput requirements, you should consider using Business Activity Monitoring (BAM) to store message bodies. We discuss this in Chapter 6.
>
> Another common requirement is to store message bodies for incoming messages for a short period. This can be done through message tracking, but an alternative, and often easier, approach is to create an additional send port configured to use the File adapter. This send port is then configured to subscribe to all incoming messages using a filter and will then store every incoming message in a file location.

If you are planning to use message body tracking within your solution, refer to Chapter 11, which covers how to configure purging and archiving to prevent against problems within your live environment as the tracking data builds up.

Context Properties

Context properties are used extensively by BizTalk adapters. On the receive side, the adapter will populate them to provide contextual metadata describing how a message has been processed. On the send side, context properties will be used by the adapter to control how it transmits a particular message. In fact, on the send side, the adapter's configuration is delivered to it as message context properties.

An example of a context property is the filename of a file that BizTalk has retrieved from a filesystem using the File adapter. The File adapter writes the filename into the context during processing; this can then be accessed via pipeline components and BizTalk orchestrations.

As briefly discussed before, context properties are also used for dynamic ports. They enable you to control adapter settings, such as the Web service address, on the fly without having to reconfigure a send port.

We cover the context properties that each adapter exposes later in this chapter.

Batching

Batching is an optimization within the engine, enabling a receive location to process multiple units of work as part of the same batch, thereby reducing the number of BizTalk MessageBox roundtrips required and enabling asynchronous processing for messages. This can increase the throughput and scaling of your solution.

Most receive locations use batching by default, where appropriate. For example, the SOAP adapter has no notion of batching, because messages are pushed into BizTalk rather than pulled.

In the case of the File adapter, the "Number of messages in a batch" is set to 20 by default and can be configured through the BizTalk Administration Console when creating or modifying a receive port. This means that the File adapter will start by creating a batch by collecting all the files available in the configured directory. This batch will then be submitted to the BizTalk MessageBox by the adapter when there are no further files available or when the configured batch size is exceeded.

So, if 19 files are present, they will all be collected within one batch and submitted. If 25 messages are present, 20 will be collected and submitted, followed by the remaining 5 in another batch. There is also a "Maximum batch size (in bytes)" setting that can restrict the size of the batch in terms of bytes rather than files.

The default settings are suitable for most scenarios. However, if you are processing very large files, you may not want the File adapter to collect twenty 30MB files at a time. The reason for this is that BizTalk will process each batch of messages sequentially on a single thread, meaning that there will be no scalability, since all 30 large files will be processed by one thread.

For this scenario, using a batch size of one will mean that each batch (or in this case, message) is processed on a single thread, leading to much better scalability. Alternatively, the batch size could be controlled by using the maximum batch size (in bytes). This would be a better solution because it will dynamically adjust the number of messages in a batch according to their size.

In-Order Delivery

By its very design, BizTalk publishes messages to the BizTalk MessageBox in batches. These messages are published in the order that the engine received them from an adapter. BizTalk maintains order within an adapter's batch but not across batches, so an adapter requiring messages to be published in order needs to ensure that it publishes a single batch of messages at a time.

Once messages are published to the MessageBox, order needs to be maintained throughout the next hop to and from the MessageBox, whether it is to an orchestration or to a send port. Marking an orchestration receive port as requiring in-order delivery will ensure that messages are delivered to the orchestration in the order that they were published to the MessageBox. In-order delivery can be achieved at the send-port level by marking the send port as "Ordered delivery" in the Transport Advanced Options for the port. This will ensure that messages are delivered to the send port in the order that they were published to the send port.

Not all receive-side adapters can support ordered delivery. It may only be supported if the transport protocol has a notion of order that the receive adapter may use. For example, in-order delivery using the File adapter does not typically make sense, because the naming and the sorting of the files plays a large role in the ordering, making it very nondeterministic and tightly coupled between the sender and the receiver. The HTTP protocol also makes ordered delivery challenging because Web servers are, by their nature, designed to be highly scalable. Imposing order at this level would cripple the performance. To achieve in-order semantics over HTTP, the client would need to send a single request and wait to see that it had been successfully processed before sending the next message in the ordered sequence.

However, transports such as MSMQ, when used in a transactional manner, do respect in-order delivery for both receiving and sending, although there are caveats even for them. Only a single BizTalk host can be used to read messages from a given queue if order is to be maintained. This is because two or more BizTalk servers reading from the same queue would effectively publish interleaved batches of messages, which would break the ordering. BizTalk does not provide any mechanism to synchronize receive adapters between hosts. Typically, this would mean clustering the BizTalk receive host where the MSMQ receive adapter is hosted to provide a highly available solution while ensuring only one server is processing the queue. So BizTalk can be used to process messages in order, but there are some caveats!

Orchestration convoys are key to enabling in-order delivery and are discussed in Chapter 5.

Writing a Custom Adapter

In my experience, most BizTalk solutions can be delivered without writing any custom adapters by relying on the built-in adapters. These, with the additions provided by BizTalk Server 2006, cater to most integration scenarios.

Writing a custom BizTalk adapter is a nontrivial exercise and should not be taken lightly. Adapters must "feed" the BizTalk engine as fast as possible to ensure that the BizTalk platform can perform at its best. Therefore, adapters need to make heavy use of threading and asynchronous programming.

The bottom line is that, if you are to write an adapter, you must ensure that you allocate this task to a developer who is experienced in writing server-side code. In addition, it is critical that you allocate adequate time for testing the adapter.

The adapter API exposed by BizTalk was largely designed for the adapter vendor community and is fairly low level. Custom adapters are treated as first-class citizens by BizTalk. Thus, the level of functionality exposed to them enables fine-grained control over the processing semantics of the engine. The BizTalk SDK ships with a BaseAdapter sample that a number of Microsoft adapters are based on and should be the starting point for any adapters that you choose to write. In fact, the BaseAdapter was derived from a library that the BizTalk products adapters use internally.

BizTalk Server 2006 R2 will introduce the .NET 3.0 Adapter Framework, which enables adapters to be created not only for BizTalk but also for any .NET-enabled application, such as Microsoft Office or your own application. This extends the concept of adapters broadly across the Microsoft platform and will make development of non-BizTalk solutions that require information from disparate back-end systems easier to develop.

Remember, not all solutions are a good fit for BizTalk, so using a BizTalk adapter within your own custom solution is entirely reasonable.

The .NET 3.0 Adapter Framework is built on Windows Communication Foundation (WCF) and thus enables usage across the Microsoft platform, SharePoint, Office, etc. Construction of an adapter using the framework is far simpler than using the native BizTalk Adapter Framework. If you're about to start writing an adapter, it may be worth considering BizTalk Server 2006 R2.

At the time of this writing, the Adapter Framework was not formalized enough to write a section detailing how to construct an adapter. However, around the time of publication, a guide will be published on the Wiley site, for downloading, which will itself be included in later printing of this book.

A number of adapters built using the Adapter Framework will be made available with the R2 release. We cover these later in the chapter.

In-Box Adapters

This section walks you through the main BizTalk adapters that come in the box, to cover what they offer, detail how they work under the covers, and provide a working example for the adapters that are most frequently used and that can cause problems for developers.

There are, of course, additional adapters over and above those that are covered in this chapter that were provided for the first time in BizTalk Server 2006. These are used for what's commonly termed as line-of-business (LOB) integration and are typically used less often than the adapters covered in his chapter. These new adapters are:

- ❏ JD Edwards EnterpriseOne
- ❏ JD Edwards OneWorld XE
- ❏ ODBC Adapter for Oracle Database
- ❏ PeopleSoft
- ❏ SAP
- ❏ Siebel eBusiness Applications
- ❏ TIBO Enterprise Message Service
- ❏ TIBCO Rendezvous

In addition, BizTalk Server 2006 also now includes Microsoft Host Integration Server 2006 (HIS), which provides BizTalk Adapters for Host System 2006 that leverage technologies supplied as part of HIS 2006.

BizTalk Adapters for Host System 2006 includes a number of additional adapters that you use within your solutions. See the HIS documentation for full details on the adapters and their limitations. For reference, they are:

- ❏ The Microsoft BizTalk Adapter for Host Application provides access to IBM Mainframes (CICS and IMS) or midrange iSeries (AS/400) server programs.
- ❏ The Microsoft BizTalk Adapter for DB2 provides access to IBM Mainframe DB2 for Z/OS, IBM midrange DB2/400, and IBM DB2 Universal Database of open platforms (AIX, Linux, Solaris, and Windows).

❑ Microsoft BizTalk Adapter for Host Files provides access to IBM mainframe zSeries VSAM datasets and IBM midrange iSeries AS/400 physical files.

❑ Microsoft BizTalk Adapter for WebSphere MQ provides direct messaging with remote MQSeries queue managers deployed on non-Windows platforms.

This WebSphere MQ adapter is in contrast to the built-in BizTalk 2006 MQSeries adapter, which requires that WebSphere MQ Server for Windows be installed in between BizTalk and a remote queue manager when the remote queue manager is deployed on a non-Windows platform, this adapter can communicate directly to MQSeries queues as it uses the MQSeries client.

File

The File adapter is arguably one of the most frequently used adapters that BizTalk provides. As the name implies, it can monitor a filesystem directory for files matching a configured extension to arrive.

The File adapter works in two modes. After detecting a new file, the File adapter places a lock on it to ensure that another thread or machine doesn't try to process the file at the same time. It maintains the lock until the file has passed through the pipeline and has been successfully written to the MessageBox. Alternatively, it can be configured to rename the file to prevent another process from picking up the file while it is being processed.

If the MessageBox persistence of the message is successful, the file is deleted from the filesystem. Conversely, if an error occurs during adapter or pipeline processing, the file is returned to the filesystem and will be processed again. In the case where it was renamed, it will be renamed to its original name.

Context Properties Promoted

The File adapter exposes a number of context properties during processing, which are shown below for reference. Refer to the BizTalk documentation for detailed information on each one.

AllowCacheOnWrite (Boolean)	CopyMode (int)	FileCreationTime (DateTime)
Password (string)	ReceivedFileName (string)	Username (string)
UseTempFileOnWrite (Boolean)		

As with all adapters, the context properties populated by the File adapter can be used in later routing or processing. The File adapter makes two context properties available for in-bound messages.

FileCreationTime and ReceivedFileName are populated by the File adapter and hold the creation timestamp of the file along with the filename of the file held on the filesystem. You can access these properties within an orchestration by using the message context, which you can do through the Expression Editor within a Message Assignment or Expression shape. An example of this is shown in Figure 3-14. Note that the additional properties in the figure are for use only with dynamic ports and will not be populated automatically.

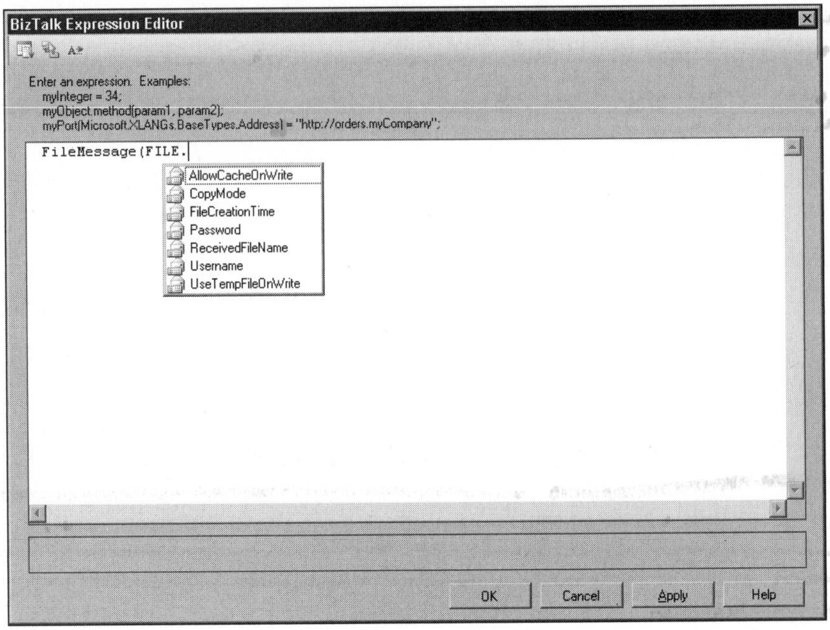

Figure 3-14

The `AllowCacheOnWrite` property indicates whether you want to allow the operating system to use filesystem caching. Be careful here because enabling this can lead to data loss in some edge cases — for example, consider the scenario whereby BizTalk has written the file to disk via the adapter and continues under that premise but the operating system hasn't physically written the file yet.

The `CopyMode` property defines how the File adapter should handle writing the file. There are three possible settings for this property:

❑ A setting of 0 will cause the File adapter to append to an existing file or create a new one, if it doesn't exist.

❑ A setting of 1 will create a new file and an error will occur if the file already exists. The standard retry logic will then apply. This is the default setting for `CopyMode`.

❑ A setting of 2 will overwrite an existing file or create a new a one, if it doesn't already exist. Care should obviously be taken with this setting, because a misconfiguration could lead to data loss.

The `Username` and `Password` properties are used to provide alternative credentials when writing to a network share. By default, the username and password of the BizTalk host hosting the File adapter will be used — that is, integrated authentication is used by default, which is the most secure mode of operation since user credentials do not need to be stored.

The `UseTempFileOnWrite` property indicates that the File adapter should first write the file contents to a temporary file and then rename the file to the actual filename when writing has finished. This is useful when you have another application monitoring the directory for files that isn't intelligent enough to identify when writing has finished.

File Adapter Walk-through

This section describes how to configure a simple content-based routing scenario using the File adapter.

The Receive Port

The first step is to create a new receive port. To do so, open the BizTalk Server 2006 Administration Console.

A default BizTalk application should be available, within which you can create a receive port. You can, however, create a new application by right-clicking Applications and choosing New Application.

Expand your chosen application, right-click the Receive Ports folder, and then choose New ⇨ One-way Receive Port. The Receive Port Properties dialog opens, as shown in Figure 3-15.

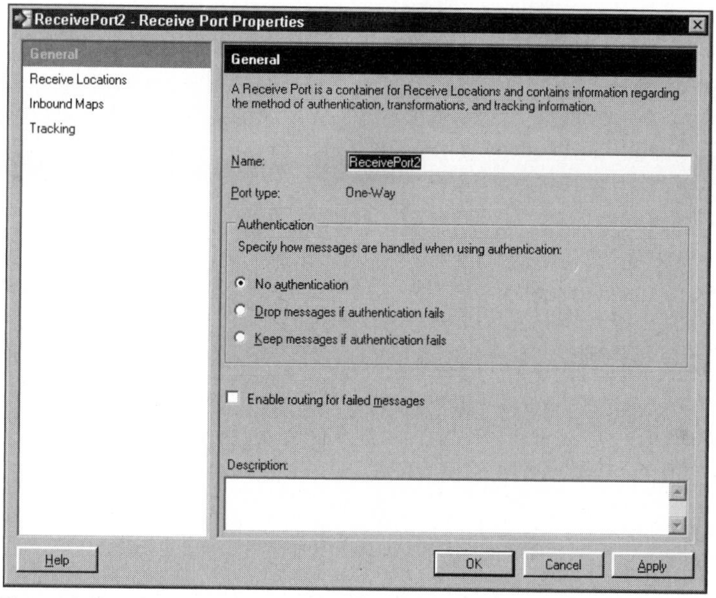

Figure 3-15

Provide a name for your receive port and select Receive Locations on the left-hand side to create a receive location that will read files from a directory. Click New. The Receive Location Properties dialog box appears, as shown in Figure 3-16.

Provide a name for the receive location. Now you need to select the adapter to use for this receive port by clicking the Type drop-down list and selecting the File adapter. Then click Configure. The File adapter-specific configuration dialog box appears, as shown in Figure 3-17.

The File Mask shown in the dialog box enables you to specify the files that the receive port will collect. By default, this is configured to *.xml, but this can be configured to any file mask that you require. Click Browse to select a folder where files will be placed for processing.

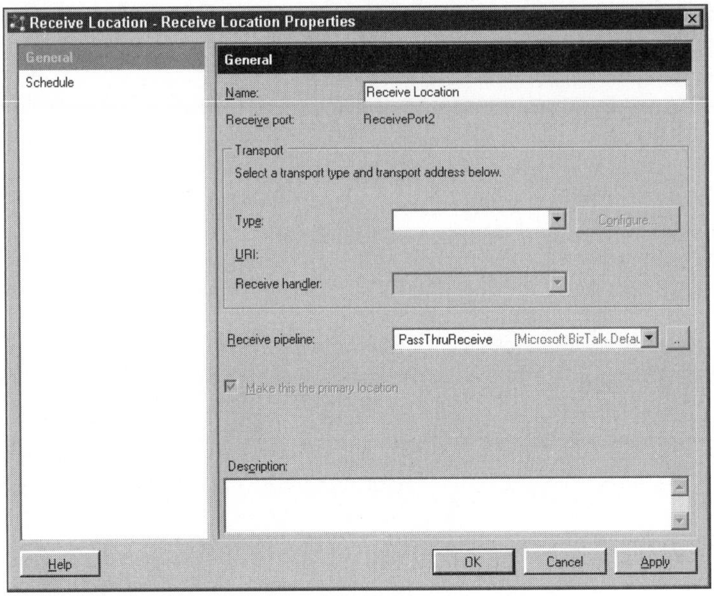

Figure 3-16

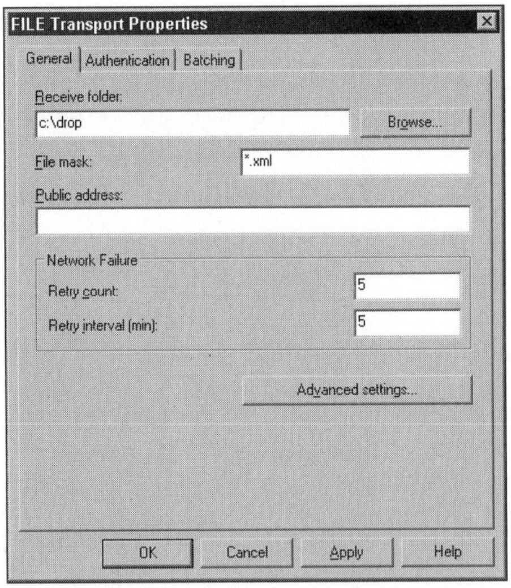

Figure 3-17

Click OK to complete the Adapter Configuration section and you are returned to the Receive Location dialog box. You now have the option of selecting a receive handler. Receive handlers in this context are BizTalk hosts that are available to "host" the File adapter.

This demo uses the standard `BizTalkServerApplication` host. In a real-world scenario, however, you would typically create a receive-specific host to allow you to host the receive adapters on specific boxes to balance load.

You can also configure the pipeline used by the receive location at this stage. Because you are not doing anything specific with the messages, you can set this to the default PassThruReceive pipeline, which will perform no pipeline processing. Click OK to complete the creation of the receive port.

To start this receive port, click Receive Locations, right-click the newly created receive location, and then choose Enable. BizTalk will now retrieve messages from the directory specified and place them in the BizTalk MessageBox.

The Send Port

Once the message has been published into the MessageBox by the receive port, you need to do something with it. For the purposes of this simple demo, you will create a send port to subscribe to messages from the receive port and send them out to another directory on the filesystem.

Start by creating a new send port by right-clicking the Send Ports folder under our application in the BizTalk Server Administration Console and choosing New ⇨ Static One-way Send Port.

The Send Port Properties dialog box appears, as shown in Figure 3-18. Enter a name for the send port, select the File Adapter from the Type drop-down list, and select Configure to provide the configuration settings for the File adapter.

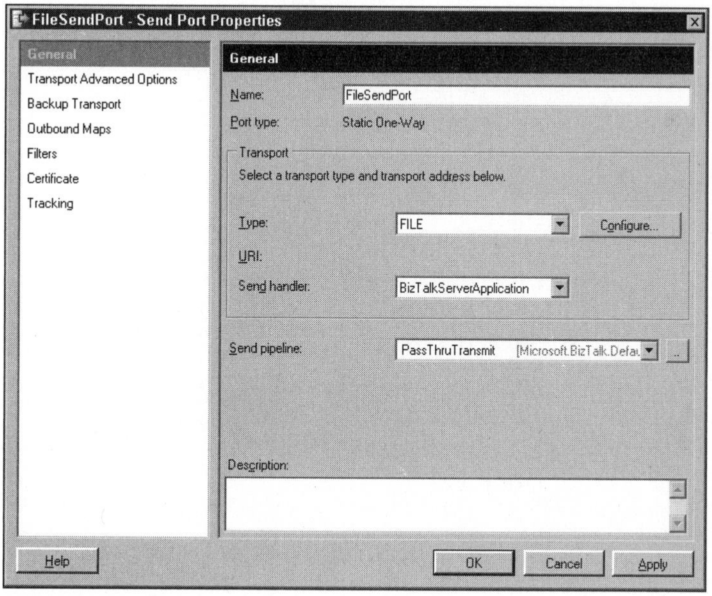

Figure 3-18

Provide a directory name for messages to be written to, as shown in Figure 3-19. Note the File name property defaults to %MessageID%.xml, which will cause the new file to use the BizTalk Internal MessageID (a GUID) as the filename. A number of other expansion macros are available for configuring here, including %datetime%, %sourcefilename%, and %time%.

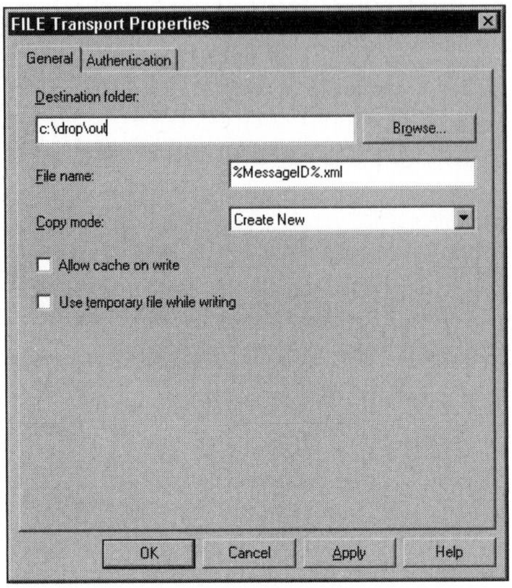

Figure 3-19

Select OK to complete the send port configuration, leaving the defaults for the send handler and send pipeline.

To enable content-based routing, you need to configure which messages this send port is going to sub-scribe to and send to the filesystem directory. Do this by configuring a filter that will filter on all mes-sages received by the receive port configured in the first step.

Click the Filters section on the left-hand side of Send Port Properties, as shown in Figure 3-20, and select the BTS.ReceivePortName context property from the Properties drop-down list. Next, type the name of the receive port that you created in the first step. Note that this is the name of the receive port, not the receive location. Click OK to complete the send port configuration.

To enable the send port, right-click the send port and choose Start. The Start process will first enlist the send port, which establishes a subscription in the MessageBox for all messages received via the receive port configured in the first step and then enables the send port.

Now you can drop a file with an .XML extension (this is the default wildcard mapping on a File adapter) into the directory used by the receive location, and it will be collected by BizTalk, processed, and then transmitted to the send port location.

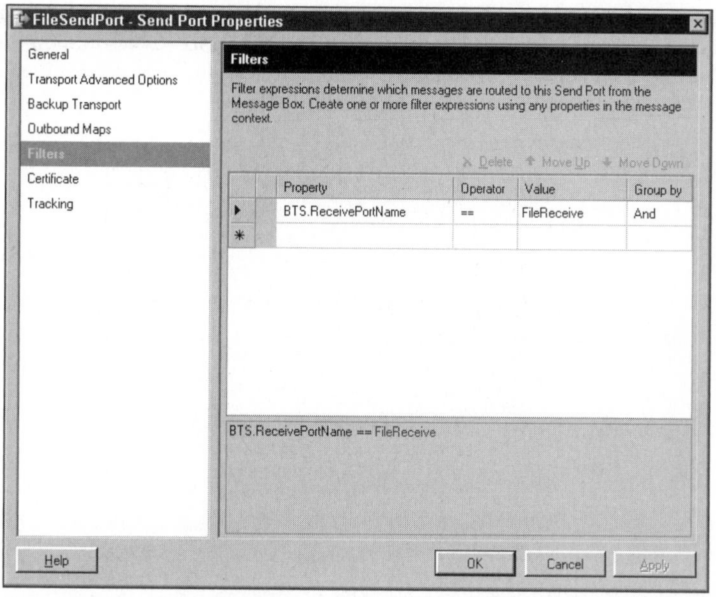

Figure 3-20

Security

A typical problem encountered when configuring the File adapter is the service account used by the BizTalk host not having read and write permissions to the configured directory. If you have problems with your receive or send port that uses the File adapter, check the Event Viewer for a series of events that indicate you don't have the correct permissions. Figure 3-21 shows an example of a receive port not having read and write permission to a directory.

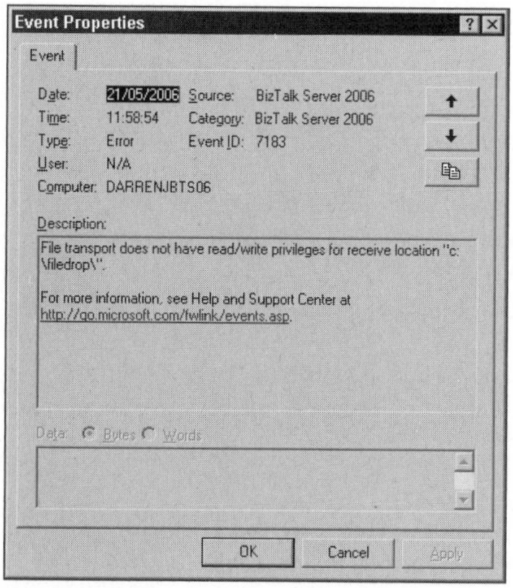

Figure 3-21

BizTalk will shut down the receive or send port after a series of errors. If, for example, a send port using the File adapter doesn't have the correct permissions, after three failed attempts it will shut down the send port. Therefore, if messages are not being picked up or sent as required, be sure to check that the ports are actually active. Figure 3-22 shows the Event Viewer message you will see if the port has been shut down due to this.

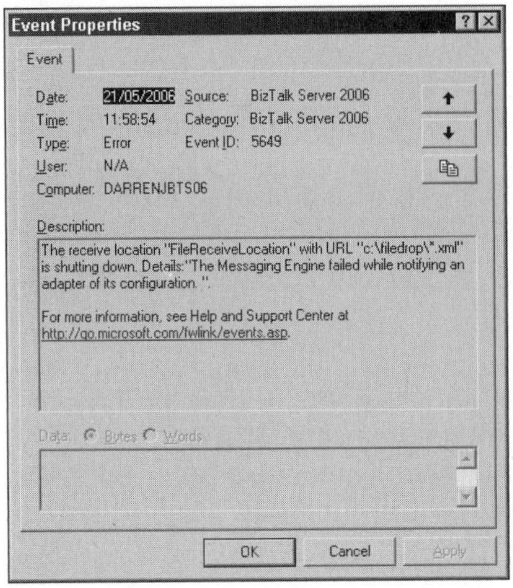

Figure 3-22

MSMQT

The MSMQT adapter, introduced with BizTalk Server 2004, sparked a fair amount of confusion among developers regarding its relationship with MSMQ.

The reasoning behind MSMQT was to address performance concerns caused by the so-called *double-hop* introduced by using MSMQ along with the ability to send messages larger than 4MB.

Figure 3-23 shows the communication required to transmit a message from a MSMQ client to a BizTalk Server.

As you can see, the message first is transmitted to the server hosting MSMQ, and the message is stored in the MSMQ Message Store, which is implemented on the filesystem. BizTalk using the MSMQ adapter then has to retrieve the message from the MSMQ queue and place it into the MessageBox.

There are two main concerns with this approach. First, the message when held in the MSMQ queue is held on the filesystem. For an enterprise-class deployment, the queue would need to be made resilient, which will typically mean clustering the servers and mounting the queue on a either RAID or SAN storage. This is in addition to the effort required to make BizTalk resilient.

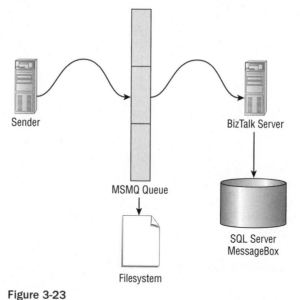

Figure 3-23

The second concern is that the message has had to perform a double-hop — the first to the MSMQ queue, often held on a separate server, and the second to the BizTalk MessageBox via the BizTalk MSMQ adapter hosted on a BizTalk Server. This has an obvious performance impact that may cause a throughput issue for your scenario.

MSMQT removes both concerns by exposing an MSMQ *listener* via the MSMQT adapter that is hosted by BizTalk Server. This listener *listens* on the MSMQ TCP/IP port and fully implements the MSMQ communication specification. There is no intermediate filesystem queue with MSMQT; once the message has been received, it's written to the MessageBox and an acknowledgment is returned. In other words, the MSMQ stack is hosted in BizTalk, and it uses the BizTalk MessageBox for its queue storage requirements.

The BizTalk MessageBox database is a secure transactional store and is typically made resilient by using either RAID or SAN disk systems and SQL Server active/passive cluster. This, therefore, resolves the resilience problem introduced by MSMQ.

Avoiding this extra hop does improve performance, but MSMQT was also implemented to provide in-order delivery. This is fine *if* you want in-order delivery, of course, which in many circumstances is not required. To implement in-order delivery, the MSMQT adapter has only one operating system thread per queue to process incoming messages, which under load becomes a bottleneck.

The utilization of one thread is done by design, because to implement in-order delivery, you must process messages sequentially. Using multiple concurrent threads would break the in-order semantics.

In my experience, the performance bottleneck of this one-thread processing greatly outweighs the performance gains of not having the double-hop approach.

In short, if you don't need in-order delivery, use the MSMQC adapter and deal with the resilience issue as appropriate for your requirements. If you do need in-order delivery, consider both the MSMQ and

MSMQT adapters. The MSMQT adapter should perform slightly faster in this scenario compared to the MSMQ adapter, as it avoids a further hop. The performance for an MSMQT scenario can be improved by *spraying* messages over multiple queues instead of using a single queue to receive messages. This effectively increases the level of concurrency and will improve the performance.

It's also worth noting that the MSMQC adapter, which is covered in the next section, also enables large-message support through the use of chunking. In light of this and the points made above, you should not consider using the MSMQT adapter in any solution unless you need the in-order delivery semantics — but ensure that you have a real need for this approach. Another point to consider is that the MSMQT adapter will stream large messages into memory, making it a better choice if you have to process very large messages, as the memory profile is kept low.

> **The MSMQT adapter is not installed by default. To install the adapter, open the BizTalk Server 2006 Administration Console, expand the Platform Settings Node, right-click Adapters, choose New Adapter, and select MSMQT from the drop-down list.**

Context Properties Promoted

The MSMQT adapter exposes a number of context properties during processing, which are shown below for reference. Refer to the BizTalk Documentation for detailed information on each one.

Acknowledge (uint)	AdminQueue (string)	AppSpecific (uint)
ArrivedTime (DateTime)	Authenticated (Boolean)	AuthLevel (Boolean)
Class (short)	CorrelationId (string)	Extension (string)
HashAlg (uint)	InboundResponseQueue (string)	IsAuthenticated (Boolean)
IsFirstInTransaction (Boolean)	IsLastInTransaction (Boolean)	IsSecurityEnabled (Boolean)
IsXactMsg (Boolean)	Label (string)	MsgID (int)
Priority (int)	ResponseQueue (string)	SenderID (string)
SentTime (DateTime)	Signature (string)	SourceMachineGuid (string)
TimeToReachQueue (uint)	TransactionId (int)	Version (string)

MSMQ

The MSMQ adapter was introduced after the launch of BizTalk Server 2004 as an add-on (named MSMQC — C for "classic") and is shipped in the box with BizTalk Server 2006.

The MSMQ adapter polls the configured MSMQ queue for new messages. This polling interval is set to ½ second and is not configurable. Once messages are available, they are retrieved from the MSMQ queue. Messages can be retrieved from the queue in the scope of a transaction, if the queue is configured as transactional. This ensures that the message is not removed from the queue until the message has been safely committed to the BizTalk MessageBox.

In-order delivery can be configured on a queue-by-queue basis, unlike MSMQT, which always assumes in-order delivery. Not using in-order delivery will result in a significant increase to messaging through-put, as multiple threads can be utilized to read messages from the MSMQ queue. It is, however, important to remember that if you want to receive messages from an MSMQ queue in order, only a single BizTalk host can be active at a given time. This is different from other adapters that may be made resilient by ensuring that two or more receive hosts are configured for a given adapter. To make MSMQ resilient for in-order delivery, you will need to cluster two receive hosts for the MSMQ adapter.

As covered in the previous section, the MSMQ adapter can also handle messages larger than 4MB through the use of chunking. You must, however, use MQRTLarge.dll instead of the standard MSMQ API to transmit large messages. MQRTLarge, however, presents the same API as normal MSMQ.

The MSMQT adapter uses streaming throughout because it's effectively a new code base. Be aware that the MSMQ adapter, in contrast, is built against MQRTLarge, which uses the same approaches as MSMQ. Therefore, it will load the entire message into memory throughout processing. So, if you're processing seriously large messages, you need to be aware of this limitation and may need to consider using the MSMQT adapter.

Context Properties Promoted

The MSMQ adapter exposes a number of context properties during processing, which are shown below for reference. Refer to the BizTalk Documentation for detailed information on each one.

Acknowledge (uint)	AdminQueue (string)	AppSpecific (uint)
ArrivedTime (DateTime)	Authenticated (Boolean)	AuthLevel (Boolean)
Class (short)	CorrelationId (string)	Extension (string)
HashAlg (uint)	InboundResponseQueue (string)	IsAuthenticated (Boolean)
IsFirstInTransaction (Boolean)	IsLastInTransaction (Boolean)	IsSecurityEnabled (Boolean)
IsXactMsg (Boolean)	Label (string)	MsgID (int)
Priority (int)	ResponseQueue (string)	SenderID (string)
SentTime (DateTime)	Signature (string)	SourceMachineGuid (string)
TimeToReachQueue (uint)	TransactionId (int)	Version (string)

Many of these are not populated in every scenario; for example, any transaction-related properties, such as `IsFirstInTransaction`, will not be present if transactional queues are not used.

For example, a typical nontransactional MSMQ message causes the MSMQ adapter to populate the following properties.

Acknowledgement	AppSpecific	ArrivedTime
Authenticated	BodyType	CorrelationId
Id	InboundTransportLocation	LabelValue
MessageType	Priority	ResponseQueue
SentTime		

Windows SharePoint Services

The Windows SharePoint Services (WSS) adapter was introduced with BizTalk Server 2006. There was, however, an unsupported adapter available for download for BizTalk Server 2004.

The WSS adapter can poll a configured WSS document library for new documents to arrive and can also transmit documents to a configured WSS document library.

Context Properties Promoted

The WSS adapter exposes a number of context properties during processing, which are shown below for reference. Refer to the BizTalk documentation for detailed information on each one.

ConfigAdapterWSPort (int)	ConfigCustomTemplatesDocLib (string)	ConfigCustomTemplatesNamespaceCol (string)
ConfigNamespaceAliases (string)	ConfigOfficeIntegration (string)	ConfigOverwrite (string)
ConfigPropertiesXml (string)	ConfigTemplatesDocLib (string)	ConfigTemplatesNamespaceCol (string)
ConfigTimeout (int)	Filename (string)	InArchivedMsgUrl (string)
InCreated (DateTime)	InCreatedBy (string)	InEditUrl (string)
InFileSize (int)	InItemId (int)	InLastModified (DateTime)
InLastModifedBy (string)	InListName (string)	InListUrl (string)
InOfficeIntegration (string)	InPropertiesXml (string)	InTitle (string)
IsIconUrl (string)	TransmittedFileLocation (string)	Url (string)

A typical BizTalk message received from a SharePoint document library, for example, causes the WSS adapter to populate the following properties, which are a subset of the total number available.

Filename (string)	InCreated (DateTime)	InCreatedBy (string)
InEditUrl (string)	InFileSize (int)	InIconUrl (string)
InItemId (int)	InLastModified (DateTime)	InLastModifiedby (string)
InListName (string)	InListUrl (string)	InOfficeIntegration (string)
InPropertiesXml (string)	InTitle (string)	Url (string)

WSS Adapter Walk-through

This section walks you through the configuration of the WSS adapter to demonstrate sending a BizTalk message to a Windows SharePoint Services document library. We'll skip the creation of the receive port, as we covered this earlier in the chapter (refer to the "File Adapter Walk-through" section).

After creating the receive port, you need to create a new send port. From the BizTalk Server 2006 Administration Console, navigate to your application, right-click Send Ports, and then choose New ➪ Static One-way Send Port.

Type a name for your send port, select the Windows SharePoint Services Adapter from the Type drop-down list, and then click Configure to display the Windows SharePoint Services Transport Properties dialog box, as shown in Figure 3-24.

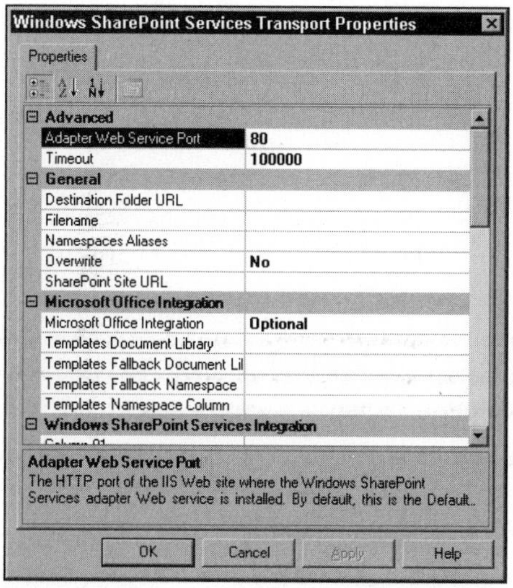

Figure 3-24

69

There are a number of configuration settings, but you need to apply only two for the purposes of this demo. The first setting is the SharePoint Site URL, which is the URL to the SharePoint site containing the document library where you'd like BizTalk to place the message. An example of the syntax is `http://darrenjbts06/sites/WSSDemo/`.

The final setting you need to apply is the Destination Folder URL. Unlike the name of the property, this is the name of the document library under the previously configured SharePoint site. An example of this syntax is `Shared Documents`. Figure 3-25 shows the configured settings.

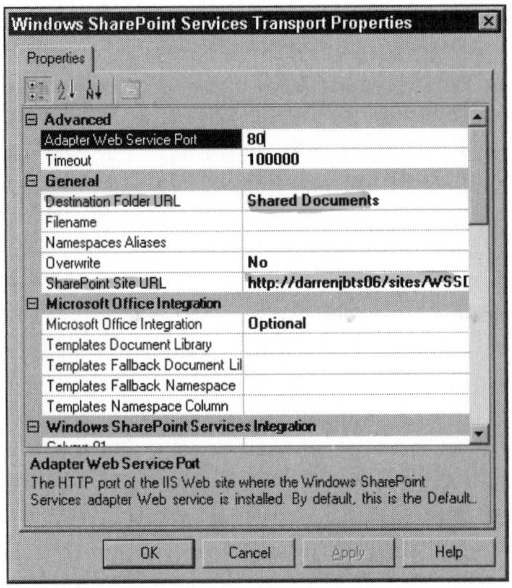

Figure 3-25

You then need to configure a filter on this send port to subscribe to messages received via receive port that you've configured separately. On the Send Port configuration dialog box, choose Filters and supply the following filter condition, customized to your receive port name:

```
BTS.ReceivePortName == WSSDemoReceivePort
```

Start the receive and send port and drop a file in the receive location. You will see it appear on the configured SharePoint document library, as shown in Figure 3-26.

> The BizTalk host running the WSS adapter will use the host service account when communicating to the Windows SharePoint Services server. This, by default, will not have access to communicate to the SharePoint Server.
>
> To grant access to the Host Service Account, you must add the Host Service Account to the SharePoint Enabled Hosts Windows Group on the SharePoint Server and then restart the BizTalk host.
>
> You must then grant at least Contributor access to this Service Account on the WSS site.

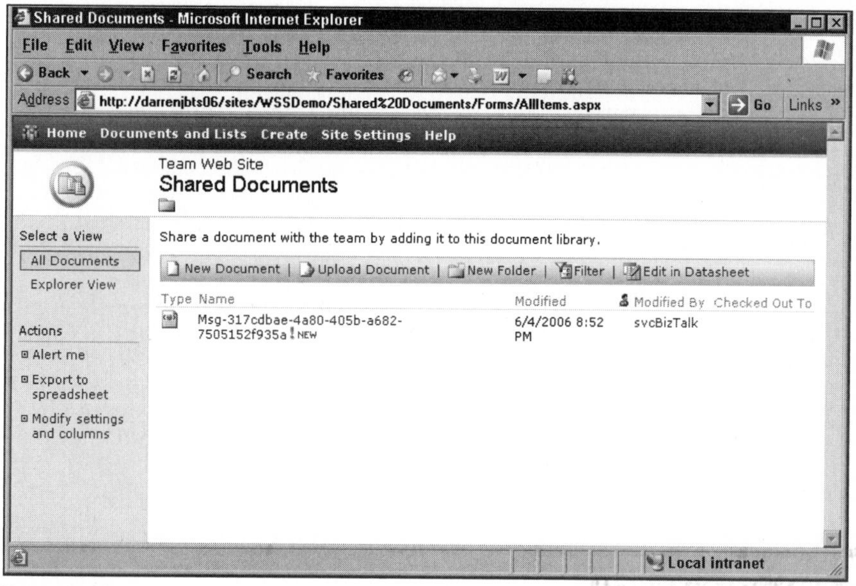

Figure 3-26

SQL

The SQL adapter enables BizTalk to poll a SQL Server database via a SQL query or stored procedure to retrieve rows as one or more XML messages. Conversely, the SQL adapter can be used to insert, update, or delete rows in SQL Server tables using the SQL updategrams or by invoking predefined stored procedures.

It's worth bearing in mind that because the SQL adapter is a pull adapter, you must engineer a form of read flag on your records to ensure that rows are not read again when the adapter polls for data again. The query that's used to retrieve records must be designed to check this read flag on each adapter poll.

The SQL adapter depends on the SQLXML functionality exposed by SQL Server and does not communicate via the native SQL Server TDS (Tabular Data Stream). Therefore, any SQL queries or stored procedures must return data in XML using the FOR XML constructs, not standard rowsets.

The SQL adapter relies on special XML schemas to be created at design time using Visual Studio's Add Generated Items Wizard, which you can access by right-clicking on a BizTalk project in the Solution Explorer and choosing Add Generated Items.

This wizard guides you through the creation of these schemas, which is achieved by supplying the query or stored procedure to invoke. The wizard then takes a sample result set and builds a schema based on it.

The BizTalk documentation has complete step-by-step instructions on how to generate schemas and configure the SQL adapter.

Context Properties Promoted

The SQL adapter exposes a number of context properties during processing, which are shown below for reference. Refer to the BizTalk documentation for detailed information on each one.

connectionString (string)	documentRootElementName (string)	documentTargetNamespace (string)
outputRootElementName (string) — used for send ports only	pollingInterval (int)	pollingUnitOfMeasure (string)
pollWhileDataFound (Boolean)	sqlCommand (string)	

SOAP

The SOAP adapter enables BizTalk to send and receive messages via Web services that utilize the SOAP protocol and the HTTP transport.

BizTalk doesn't have the capability to natively expose HTTP ports to the outside world; instead, it exposes Web service endpoints via ASP.NET Web services hosted in IIS. The SOAP adapter, like the HTTP adapter, is an isolated adapter, meaning that the adapter hosts the BizTalk Messaging Engine rather than the Messaging Engine hosting the adapter.

For Web services to be invoked, BizTalk leverages the underlying .NET Web services stack to communicate with remote Web services and, therefore, is subject to the usual configuration.

> **Because the SOAP adapter leverages the underlying .NET Framework stack, it will by default be limited to two concurrent outbound calls to each Web server. After two concurrent calls, further requests will be queued, waiting for one of the two calls to complete.**
>
> **This is not a bug but instead is in line with the HTTP 1.1 standard. The HTTP 1.1 specification specifies that a "single-user client SHOULD NOT maintain more than 2 connections with any server or proxy." This is to ensure that a user cannot overload a remote Web server. All the various Microsoft HTTP stacks respect this restriction.**
>
> **See Chapter 9 for more details and how to change this setting.**

Web services typically use the request-response pattern; therefore, the SOAP adapter supports request-response semantics, although you can also configure it to use one-way messaging.

One-way messaging is often not used because of delivery guarantees. The HTTP specification specifies that as soon as the bits are successfully read by the destination system, an HTTP 200 response code will be returned.

The HTTP 200 response code is defined as "The request was successfully received, understood, and accepted," at which point the client assumes that the message has been successfully processed. However, there are no guarantees on the server end; the message may fail during processing or be lost during a power outage. The implications of this in the context of BizTalk are that the message will not have been persisted to the MessageBox when the 200 response code is returned to the sending client. This can provide a window of opportunity for data loss in a failure scenario.

If you can handle messages potentially not being delivered successfully or have an "out-of-band" NACK mechanism, you can consider one-way messaging.

> When deploying a BizTalk Server solution that exposes Web services, many organizations raise concerns around placing BizTalk and SQL Server machines in their Demilitarized Zone (DMZ). The standard policies of many companies prohibit anything other than Web servers.
>
> There are a number of solutions to this. If placing BizTalk and SQL Server in the DMZ is not an option, you might consider using Microsoft ISA Server as a reverse proxy to forward the Web service requests from the DMZ to your corporate domain.

Context Properties Promoted

The SOAP adapter exposes a number of context properties during processing, which are shown below for reference. Refer to the BizTalk documentation for detailed information on each one.

AssemblyName (string)	AffiliateApplicationName (string)	AuthenticationScheme (string)
ClientCertificate (string)	ClientConnectionTimeout (int)	MethodName (string)
Password (string)	ProxyAddress (string)	ProxyPassword (string)
ProxyPort (int)	ProxyUserName (string)	UnknownHeaders (string)
UserDefined (string)	UseHandlerSetting (Boolean)	Username (string)
UseProxy (Boolean)	UseSoap12 (Boolean)	UseSSO (Boolean)

SOAP Adapter Walk-through

This walk-through demonstrates how to invoke a Web service via orchestration. The SOAP adapter is straightforward to use, but there are a few tricks of the trade along the way to make things easier.

In the interests of clarity, we'll skip the creation of the receive port, as we covered this earlier in the chapter. For the purposes of a sample, you should create a receive port that uses the File adapter to retrieve messages from the filesystem, making testing easier.

You can now create an orchestration that subscribes to this incoming message. Ensure that the message being received has a good range of data, which you can then pass on to the Web service.

For the purposes of this walk-through, you will receive a Travel Itinerary message and then call a Flight Booking Web service, passing the Flights held within the Travel Itinerary message.

Start with your BizTalk orchestration. Within Visual Studio, right-click your project in the Solution Explorer and choose Add New Web Reference, as you would do in a normal Visual Studio project. Browse to your Web service, and then click OK to create the Web reference.

Visual Studio then creates the Web reference and automatically creates an orchestration port type for this Web service, which you can view via the Orchestration View pane in Visual Studio. It also creates a schema for the Web service request and response messages, which it retrieves from the Web service WSDL document.

Figure 3-27 shows the resulting files, which you can see under the Web References node.

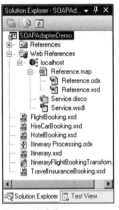

Figure 3-27

The next step is to create a logical port on our orchestration that maps to the port type created by the Add Reference step. To do this, you need to use the Port Configuration Wizard.

This wizard is started by dragging a Port shape from the Toolbox onto the orchestration design surface, or by right-clicking the Port sections at either side of the orchestration and choosing New Configured Port.

Within the first wizard step, type a sensible port name to identify the port and click Next to display the Port Type dialog box. Instead of creating a new port, you want to select the port type that's already been created as a result of the Add Web Reference step. Click the Use an existing Port Type radio button and select the Port Type under the Web Port Types node, as shown in Figure 3-28.

Click Next to display the Port Binding dialog box, which, as you can see in Figure 3-29, is already configured to the Web service endpoint referenced when you added the Web Reference to the project. This setting is then carried forward into the send port configuration when you deploy. Click Next to complete the wizard.

Figure 3-30 shows the resulting orchestration port in the Orchestration Designer when you complete the port creation step.

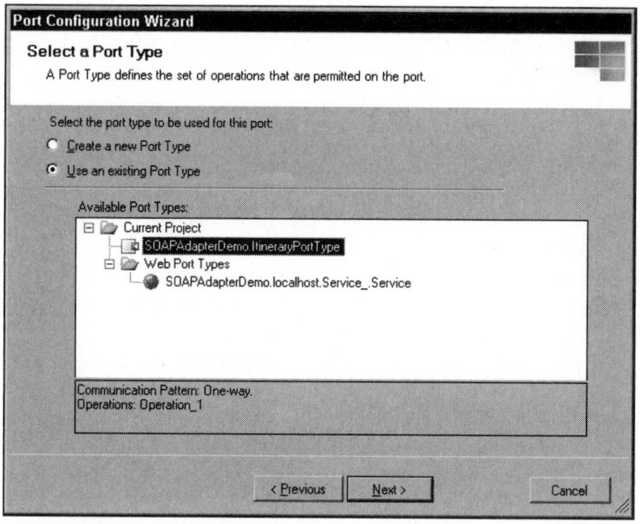

Figure 3-28

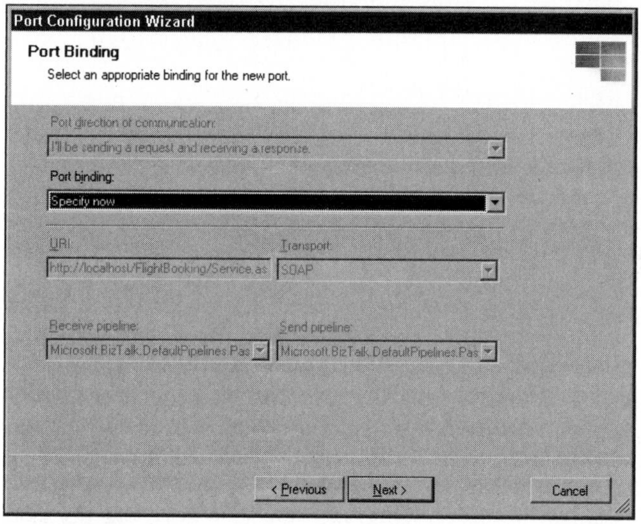

Figure 3-29

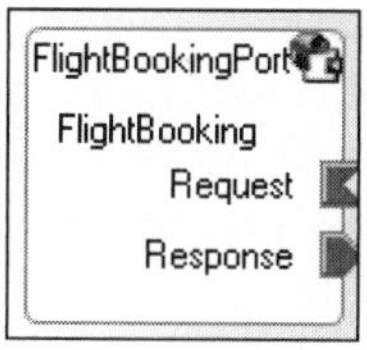

Figure 3-30

Now that you have your orchestration port, you need to create two BizTalk messages that map to each of the Web service Request and Response schemas. This enables you to create the message data required for calling the Web service and to receive the response data to process.

To do this, create two new BizTalk messages through the Orchestration View pane within Visual Studio by right-clicking Messages and choosing New Message. Then map each to the appropriate Request or Response schema listed under the Web Message Types section of the Message definition, as shown in Figure 3-31. Unfortunately, the drop-down list that you can see in the figure is not resizable, which can make identification of the schemas harder than it should be.

For the purposes of this walk-through, you will call the Request message `FlightBookingRequestMessage` and the Response message `FlightBookingResponseMessage`.

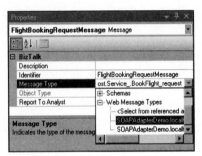

Figure 3-31

You now have two BizTalk messages that point at the underlying Web service schemas. However, you have to populate the request message with the appropriate content; the second response message will be populated when the response is received from the remote Web service.

There are a number of ways to achieve this. We'll start with the straightforward approach and detail alternative options that might be useful for your scenarios.

Transform

The first approach uses the BizTalk Mapper to transform data from any number of input BizTalk messages into the output message, which, in this case, is the Web service request message.

We'll focus on this common approach in the walk-through but outline other options you can use in conjunction or instead.

Drag a new Transform shape onto your BizTalk orchestration. The Orchestration Designer will also create a Construct Message shape around the Transform shape. Select the Construct Message shape and select the Web service request message that you need to "construct" via the Messages Constructed property, which you can find in the Properties pane when the shape is selected.

To create the transformation, double-click the Transform shape. You will be presented with the Transform Configuration dialog box. Within this dialog, select the Source and Destination Messages. In this scenario, the Source message will be the message received in the BizTalk orchestration, and the Destination message will be the Web service request message that you are constructing.

Click OK and the BizTalk Mapper is displayed. The exact mapping and functoid configuration will depend on your scenario, but our simplistic scenario mapping is shown in Figure 3-32 — a clear one-to-one mapping, which will not always be the case.

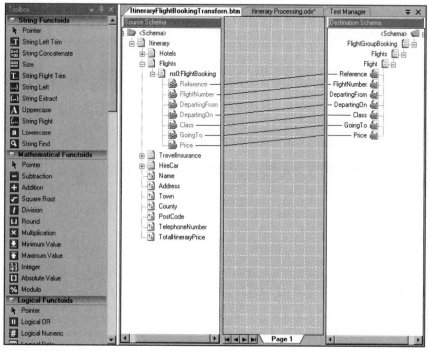

Figure 3-32

After the map has been created, simply create Send and Receive shapes and map them to the appropriate port connection, as shown in Figure 3-33, and your Web service invocation via a BizTalk orchestration is complete.

Manual Message Construction

If you don't have all the required data to construct a Web service request message, using a Transform shape on its own is not enough.

As you have seen already, the Add Web Reference operation creates a schema for your underlying Web service request message. Using the technique we covered in Chapter 1, you can construct a serializable class that will be serialized into an XML document that conforms to this schema.

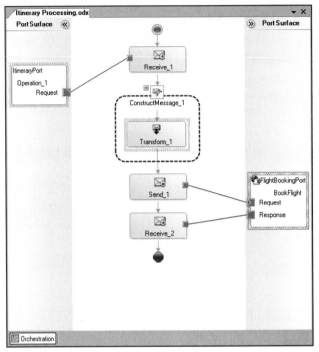

Figure 3-33

This class can then be populated by hand using a .NET class library, returned back to BizTalk, and cast into a BizTalk message seamlessly.

> To avoid type clashes between the underlying BizTalk representation of the schema (which is also represented as a class), ensure that your XSD-generated serializable class is located within a different .NET namespace.

This approach gives you complete control over message construction and is often the simplest way to construct Web service messages that cannot be created directly within a BizTalk orchestration.

So, taking the previous scenario, you now need to populate the Web service request message with the appropriate contents. Start by generating a serializable class from the Web Reference schema.

Take a copy of the `reference.xsd` file located under the Web References node of Solution Explorer and use `XSD.exe` to generate a serializable class. Supply a namespace via the `/namespace` command-line parameter.

Next, create a .NET class library project that contains the generated serializable class created by `XSD.exe`, and then create a static method (for ease of use from BizTalk orchestration) that has a return type of this serializable class.

Within this method, construct the message, as you require, an example of which follows:

```
        static public MessageConstructionHelper.FlightGroupBooking
GetFlightGroupBookingMessage()
        {
            MessageConstructionHelper.FlightGroupBooking booking = new
FlightGroupBooking();
        booking.Flights = new ArrayOfArrayOfFlightGroupFlightFlightFlight[1];

        booking.Flights[0] = new ArrayOfArrayOfFlightGroupFlightFlightFlight();
        booking.Flights[0].DepartingFrom = "London";
        booking.Flights[0].DepartingOn = System.DateTime.Now;
        booking.Flights[0].GoingTo = "Seattle";
        booking.Flights[0].FlightNumber = "DJ01";
        booking.Flights[0].Price = 1000;
        booking.Flights[0].Class = "Business";
        booking.Flights[0].Reference = System.Guid.NewGuid().ToString();


        return booking;
        }
```

Within the BizTalk Project, right-click the project in Solution Explorer, choose Add Reference, and select the previously created class library from the Projects tab.

You now have an assembly that creates a message of the correct type. Next, you need to call this from the BizTalk orchestration.

Drag a Message Assignment shape from the orchestration Toolbox, which will, in turn, also create a Construct Message shape around the Message Assignment shape. Select the Construct Message shape, and select the Web Service request message that you need to "construct" via the Messages Constructed property, which will be visible via the Properties pane when the shape is selected.

Double-click the Message Assignment shape and the BizTalk Expression Editor appears, from within which you need to call the .NET component and assign the return variable to the BizTalk message.

This is done in exactly the same way as in normal .NET programming; an example follows. Note that Web service messages are multipart messages, so there are two elements to the message (FlightBooking-RequestMessage.FlightGroupBooking, rather than just FlightBookingRequestMessage, which you would use in other scenarios).

```
FlightBookingRequestMessage.FlightGroupBooking =
MessageConstructionHelper.HelperClass.GetFlightGroupBookingMessage();
```

Finally, simply create Send and Receive shapes and map them to the appropriate port connection, and your Web service invocation is complete.

Distinguished Properties

There are also some scenarios in which you need to use a combination of approaches. Perhaps you construct the message using a BizTalk transform but then need to add an extra property later in your

BizTalk orchestration (perhaps held within an orchestration variable that isn't available to the BizTalk Mapper).

In such a case, you can choose to promote elements manually on the Web service schema created by the Add Web Reference step, and then set them using an Expression shape. To do so, open the schema held under the Web References node of Solution Explorer and perform a distinguished promotion in the usual way.

We cover distinguished promotions in Chapter 5. Simply put, they are a mechanism by which parts of your message schema can be made easily available for retrieval or storage within a BizTalk orchestration, preventing orchestration developers from having to use XPath expressions.

Note that this approach modifies an autogenerated schema that will be overwritten if you refresh the Web reference at a later point.

You can, of course, use the built-in XPath function to change message properties without promotion, if you prefer, although this can lead to brittleness or coding errors. This approach is covered in the Chapter 5.

HTTP

The HTTP adapter enables BizTalk to receive messages via an HTTP post to a configured IIS virtual directory and, conversely, to send messages via HTTP to a remote Web server.

Like the SOAP adapter, BizTalk itself doesn't have the capability to natively expose HTTP ports to the outside world but instead exposes HTTP endpoints via an ISAPI extension hosted in IIS. The ISAPI extension hosts the BizTalk Messaging Engine, which in turn "posts" messages into the BizTalk MessageBox.

For HTTP endpoints to be invoked on the send side, BizTalk leverages the underlying .NET framework HTTP stack and with the usual configuration.

> You can use SSL to secure messages sent by a send port that uses the HTTP adapter by prefixing a URI with `https://` instead of the usual `http://`.
>
> Receive ports require additional configuration within IIS. See the IIS documentation for more information.

Context Properties Promoted

The HTTP adapter exposes a number of context properties during processing, which are shown below for reference. Refer to the BizTalk documentation for detailed information on each one.

AffiliateApplicationName (string)	AuthenticationScheme (string)	Certificate (string)
ContentType (string)	EnableChunkedEncoding (Boolean)	InboundHttpHeaders (string)
MaxRedirects (int)	Password (string)	ProxyName (string)
ProxyPassword (string)	ProxyPort (int)	ProxyUserName (string)
RequestTimeout (int)	SubmissionHandle (string)	UseHandlerProxySettings (Boolean)
UseProxy (Boolean)	UserHttpHeaders (Boolean)	Username (string)
UseSSO (Boolean)		

SMTP

The SMTP adapter is a send-only adapter, allowing BizTalk to send e-mail messages to any SMTP-compliant mail server, including Microsoft Exchange Server.

The SMTP adapter is a one-way adapter; the underlying SMTP protocol doesn't support a synchronous sending mechanism. However, you can supply a valid e-mail address as the From address and request a delivery receipt, which will be sent to the configured From address. You will then have to process these delivery receipts yourself; the adapter will not handle these for you.

Authentication is done either by using standard authentication or by using Windows-based security with the process identity configured for the BizTalk host hosting the SMTP adapter.

Context Properties Promoted

The SMTP adapter exposes a number of context properties during processing, which are shown below for reference. Refer to the BizTalk documentation for detailed information on each one.

Attachments	CC (string)	DeliveryReceipt (Boolean)
EmailBodyFile (string)	EmailBodyFileCharset (string)	EmailBodyText (string)
EmailBodyTextCharset (string)	From (string)	MessagePartsAttachments (int)
Password (string)	ReadReceipt (Boolean)	ReplyBy (DateTime)
SMTPAuthenticate (int)	SMTPHost (string)	Subject (string)
Username (string)		

POP3

The POP3 adapter is a receive-only adapter, allowing BizTalk to receive messages by polling a mailbox on any POP3-compliant mail server, including Microsoft Exchange Server.

By default, the POP3 adapter uses MIME decoding for any messages retrieved from a POP3 adapter, but it can be configured for plain text, MIME-encrypted, MIME-encoded and signed, and MIME-encrypted and signed.

Authentication is performed using standard Basic Authentication, Digest, or Secure Password Authentication (SPA), which uses the process identity of the BizTalk host hosting the POP3 adapter.

Context Properties Promoted

The POP3 adapter exposes a number of context properties during processing, which are shown below for reference. Refer to the BizTalk documentation for detailed information on each one.

CC (string)	Date (string)	DispositionNotificationTo (string)
From (string)	Headers (string)	ReplyTo (string)
Subject (string)	To (string)	

EDI

The EDI adapter is a cut-down version of the full-featured, third-party Covast EDI adapter, which you can purchase from Covast (www.covast.com).

The in-box EDI adapter supports many of the common EDI standards, including X12 and EDIFACT. BizTalk Server 2006 R2, however, will provide fully featured EDI support through a complete EDI solution, offering support for EDITFACT, X12, and the secure communication protocol EDIINT AS2, along with features such as the ability to construct new EDI schemas and debatching.

Context Properties Promoted

The EDI adapter exposes a number of context properties during processing, which are shown below for reference. Refer to the BizTalk documentation for detailed information on each one.

EDIFACT_D93A (string)	EDIFACT_D95A (string)	EDIFACT_D95B (string)
EDIFACT_D97B (string)	EDIFACT_D98A (string)	EDIFACT_D98B (string)
Msgsrv_msrvcd (string) — send only	prtnr3_compsep (string) — send only	prtnr3_decsep (string) — send only

prtnr3_elmsep (string) — send only	prtnr3_errlevel (string) — send only	prtnr3_ona_01 (string) — send only
prtnr3_oun3_01 (string) — send only	prtnr3_relchar (string) — send only	prtnr3_segterm (string) — send only
prtnr3_tagsep (string) — send only	prtnr3_techack (string) — receive only	prtnr3_techack (string) — send only
prtnr3_wrapyn (string) — send only	qfenda_accalldoc (string)	qfenda_deffmtver_edifact (string) — send only
qfenda_deffmtver_x12 (string) — send only	Uri (string)	X12_2040 (string)
X12_3010 (string)	X12_3060 (string)	X12_4010 (string)

MQSeries

The MQSeries adapter enables BizTalk to send and receive messages to an IBM MQSeries queue. MQSeries offers reliable messaging semantics in the same way as MSMQ and is widely used for interop scenarios between BizTalk and legacy systems.

The MQSeries adapter is unable to communicate natively to an MQSeries queue hosted on a non-Windows platform. The adapter is architected in two parts. First, a BizTalk MQSeries adapter is hosted in BizTalk in the usual manner. This adapter communicates to the other half of the adapter, a COM+ application (the MQ Agent) that is deployed on the Windows server where MQSeries is deployed.

The reasoning for this is that at the time the MQSeries adapter was developed, remote transactional messaging was not possible with MQSeries. Therefore, the MQ Agent is used to ensure that transactional semantics using COM+ distributed transactions. The design gives very high performance, largely because the adapter moves batches of messages over the wire in atomic transactions, which is very efficient.

There is now, however, another MQSeries adapter (Microsoft BizTalk Adapter for WebSphere MQ) that is shipped as part of Microsoft Host Integration Server 2006 (included with BizTalk). It provides direct messaging with remote MQSeries queue managers deployed on non-Windows platforms, thus removing the need to deploy an intermediate installation of MQSeries on Windows. This adapter is not designed to replace the in-box adapter and differs from it by using the MQ Extended Client, which supports distributed transactions. Because this adapter is client based, it will not perform as well as the in-box adapter in high-throughput scenarios. You should test both adapters within your environment before making a decision.

The BizTalk documentation fully covers all the deployment scenarios and options when considering a MQSeries adapter deployment.

Context Properties Promoted

The MQSeries adapter exposes a number of context properties during processing, which are shown below for reference. Refer to the BizTalk documentation for detailed information on each one.

MQMD_AccountingToken (string)	MQMD_ApplIdentityData (string)	MQMD_ApplOriginData (string)
MQMD_BackoutCount (uint)	MQMD_CodedCharSetId (uint)	MQMD_CorrelId (string)
MQMD_Encoding (uint)	MQMD_Expiry (uint)	MQMD_Feedback (uint)
MQMD_Format (string)	MQMD_GroupID (string)	MQMD_MsgFlags (uint)
MQMD_MsgId (string)	MQMD_MsgSeqNumber (uint)	MQMD_MsgType (uint)
MQMD_Offset (uint)	MQMD_OriginalLength (uint)	MQMD_Persistence (uint)
MQMD_Priority (uint)	MQMD_PutApplName (string)	MQMD_PutApplType (uint)
MQMD_PutDate (string)	MQMD_PutTime (string)	MQMD_ReplyToQ (string)
MQMD_ReplyToQMgr (string)	MQMD_Report (uint)	MQMD_UserIdentifier (string)
MQXQH_RemoteQMgrName (string) — send only	MQXQH_RemoteQName (string) — send only	

FTP

The FTP adapter enables BizTalk to send and receive messages to and from an FTP (File Transfer Protocol) server.

The FTP protocol is often used when moving files between organizations or to and from a legacy system, such as a mainframe. The FTP protocol doesn't have any file-locking support. This means you cannot have a host running the FTP adapter active on more than one BizTalk server. By doing so, you could run the risk of files being processed multiple times because there is no way for the FTP adapter to indicate to another BizTalk server that the file is currently being processed. Running the FTP adapter host on one machine is not a major problem, apart from in a failure scenario in which the BizTalk server responsible for retrieving FTP files stops and files are no longer retrieved. See Chapter 11 for details on how you can mitigate this risk.

In all other adapter scenarios, you can run the adapter on multiple servers to give you high availability. In the case of the FTP adapter, you can install the FTP host on multiple machines but only start them in a failure condition, which could be automated using Microsoft Operations Manager, for example.

As you'll see in the context properties section below, you can specify FTP commands that can be executed before and after a file is put on the remote FTP server. These can be specified dynamically within an orchestration or configured on a send port through the BizTalk Administration Console.

The available FTP commands that you can use with these settings can be found within the FTP specification, at `http://www.w3.org/Protocols/rfc959/4_FileTransfer.html`.

A common use for these commands is to change the directory following an upload or to upload a file with a given filename and to then rename it once the upload has finished. This prevents processing of the file before the file has been completely written. This is done through the use of the RNFT and RNTO commands.

Context Properties Promoted

The FTP adapter exposes a number of context properties during processing, which are shown below for reference. Refer to the BizTalk documentation for detailed information on each one.

AfterPut (string)	BeforePut (string)	Password (string)
ReceivedFileName (string)	RepresentationType (string)	SSOAffiliateApplication (string)
UserName (string)		

WCF

BizTalk Server 2006 R2 will provide a Windows Communication Foundation (WCF) adapter to enable native invocation of Web services that can optionally make use of the WS:* Specifications supported by WCF, such as WS:Security. At the time of this writing the WCF adapter will only be available with the R2 release and will not be back-ported to the 2006 release. A number of BizTalk engine changes were required within R2 to support the WCF approach so the adapter cannot be simply installed on a 2006 server.

Often the remote services consumed by the WCF adapter will be native WCF services, but they can be services exposed from a third-party platform that make use of the WS:* specifications.

As things evolve, the WCF adapter is likely to be the primary adapter used for Web service communication, replacing the SOAP adapter.

R2, as you would expect, will also provide a wizard to enable orchestrations or schemas to be published as WCF services, as well as a wizard to enable service references to be added to an orchestration in the same way as Web service references.

The following adapters directly map the WCF bindings shipped as part of WCF (the "Custom" adapters enable you to utilize any custom binding):

❑ **WCF-WSHttp adapter** — The WCF-WSHttp adapter, likely the most commonly used adapter, provides support for the implemented WS:* specifications. The specifications used are WS:Security for message protection and integrity, and WS:Transaction, which enables transactions around the BizTalk MessageBox and any external applications that support WS:Transaction.

All communication is performed using HTTP or HTTPS, if transport-level security is required.

❑ **WCF-BasicHttp adapter** — The WCF-BasicHttp adapter is the adapter you should consider when you must invoke ASP.NET Web services (ASMX) or other Web services that conform to the WS:Basic Profile 1.1 and don't make use of the WS:* specifications.

❑ **WCF-NetTcp adapter** — The WCF-NetTcp adapter provides exactly the same features as the WCF-WSHttp adapter, but instead of using HTTP as the communication method, it uses TCP sockets along with a binary encoding.

This is the preferred choice for communication between BizTalk and WCF-based services because it offers significant performance improvements over HTTP (upwards of 150% improvement in some cases), especially if you have a large payload. Due to the proprietary nature of the binary encoding, it's not possible to use this method for interoperability scenarios.

❑ **WCF-NetMsmq adapter** — The WCF-NetMsmq adapter provides all the features and benefits of MSMQ, such as reliable, in-order delivery via WCF. The NetMsmq binding itself utilizes MSMQ under the covers but enables you to leverage MSMQ using the familiar WCF approach.

❑ **WCF-NetNamedPipe adapter** — The WCF-NetNamedPipe adapter enables cross-process communication within the boundaries of a machine. This enables scenarios in which you have discrete services that your solution must consume, but instead of taking the performance hit of a network roundtrip, you can still respect service isolation and only pay the performance penalty of cross-process communication.

❑ **WCF-Custom adapter** — The WCF-Custom adapter enables you specify a custom WCF binding and behavior for use with a receive or send port. This is ideal for scenarios in which you have a requirement to utilize a proprietary transport of encoding type.

❑ **WCF-CustomIsolated adapter** — The WCF-CustomIsolated adapter offers the same customization capabilities as the WCF-Custom adapter but is designed for use within IIS where a receive location, for example, is hosted in a process other than BizTalk. This is directly analogous to the isolated adapters in BizTalk 2004 and 2006 today.

WSE

A Web Services Enhancements (WSE) adapter is available for download that can be used with BizTalk Server 2006. However, this supports only WSE 2.0, which is not wire compatible with WCF services.

As you may know, WSE was a tactical delivery of technology to enable early adopters to make use of the new WS:* specifications prior to the release of WCF (formerly known as Indigo). In light of WCF now being broadly available through the .NET Framework 3.0 release, the WSE adapter should no longer be considered.

BizTalk Server 2006 R2 ships with a WCF adapter. Prior to R2, you could invoke WCF services via the SOAP adapter, which, of course, prevents you from being able to utilize the WS:* specifications. WCF can, however, be used in line from a BizTalk orchestration with BizTalk 2006 if you cannot make use of R2 but you will have to handle adapter provided semantics such as retries manually. See Chapter 10 for more information on how you can mitigate this.

Line of Business (LOB) Adapter Pack

As we introduced earlier in the chapter, BizTalk 2006 R2 introduces the .NET 3.0 Adapter framework to simplify adapter construction and to enable adapters to be used across the Microsoft platform, not just BizTalk.

A number of key adapters that enable application integration to third-party products were identified to be rewritten using this new adapter framework. This will enable .NET- and WCF-enabled applications to benefit from the seamless integration without BizTalk having to be involved, unless it adds value and makes sense, of course.

Thus, the LOB adapter pack was created and is available as part of BizTalk Server 2006 R2, or it can be purchased separately for use within your own application or in conjunction with, say, Microsoft Office.

The following adapters are available as part of the LOB Adapter Framework and can be utilized through BizTalk Server 2006 R2 by using the WCF adapter or by using WCF directly within your own application:

❑ Microsoft BizTalk .NET Adapter for Oracle

❑ Microsoft BizTalk .NET Adapter for SAP

❑ Microsoft BizTalk .NET Adapter for Siebel

❑ Microsoft BizTalk .NET Adapter for TIBO Rendezvous

Summary

This chapter covered the core adapter concepts that are key to understand in order to design and develop effective BizTalk solutions. It covered the disconnected nature of BizTalk, explaining that adapters do not communicate directly to orchestrations and instead communicate via the BizTalk MessageBox.

It introduced the concepts of ports along with key but often overlooked abilities, such as being able to configure ports on the fly using dynamic ports and to perform mapping at the port level as messages are received or sent instead of having to involve a BizTalk orchestration.

It then walked through a number of the key adapters, detailing what features they offer to you as a BizTalk developer, and covering the range of context properties that each adapter makes available, which can be key to know when developing a solution. It also provided step-by-step instructions for a few key adapters.

Chapter 4 will cover the next step in the journey that a message takes through the BizTalk architecture: pipelines. Pipelines are invoked following adapter processing for in-bound messages and are invoked before an adapter for outbound messages.

Pipelines

BizTalk Server is a message-based system; it is both data agnostic and transport agnostic, meaning that it can connect to a wide range of different transport protocols and systems and process a wide variety of different data formats. When receiving data from systems, you typically need to do something with the data that you receive. Often, you will need to parse that data and convert it into a common format that is easier to work with. Similarly, when you communicate with a system, you will need to format the data that you pass to that system into the format that the receiving system is expecting. The lion's share of this parsing and formatting of data in BizTalk is performed in pipelines.

Pipelines are the conduits through which messages pass, and as messages pass through, the data that they represent can be changed — metadata may be extracted from the message data and inserted into the message context, or, conversely, message context data may be inserted into the message content. In this chapter, we are going to cover an overview of the pipeline architecture and then cover how to write a custom pipeline component that respects the core pipeline principles.

Architecture and Concepts

As mentioned in the introductory paragraph, BizTalk is both transport and data agnostic. The BizTalk architecture is designed so that the processing responsibilities within the Messaging Engine are clearly demarcated. This simplifies the process of designing integration solutions and provides greater flexibility. Consider the following distinction between adapters and pipelines:

❑ **Adapters** are the components that deal with the transportation of data; they are responsible for moving data from the *wire* into the BizTalk engine. One way to think of them is as *bitshovelers* — that is, they move bits from the wire into BizTalk, and vice versa, without caring too much about the format those bits represent.

The SOAP adapter is an exception to this, since it serializes and deserializes the SOAP packet at the adapter.

❑ Pipelines, on the other hand, are concerned with the processing of the data. They are responsible for recognizing the format of the data, converting the data from one format to another, validating that the format is correct, and performing security checks for some scenarios. Pipelines are not concerned what mode of transport that data was received or sent over.

This demarcation of responsibilities provides a great deal of flexibility. For example, if you were to write a TCP-IP adapter and followed the design principles, you could use it to send data that was formatted as XML, flat file, EDI, and so on. That adapter code would not have to be changed to support different data formats.

Every BizTalk pipeline will be either a send or receive pipeline. As messages enter BizTalk they are executed through a receive pipeline, and as they leave they will be executed through a send pipeline. The request-response message exchange pattern causes a receive pipeline to be executed for the request message and a send pipeline to be executed for the response message. Similarly, for the solicit-response message exchange pattern, a send pipeline will be executed for the solicit message and a receive pipeline will be executed to process the response message.

For the 2006 release of BizTalk, the engine team enhanced the Pipeline Manager, which is responsible for executing pipelines. The enhancements mean that pipelines can now be executed from orchestrations as well as from messaging ports. This opens up a whole raft of scenarios that previously required a lot of custom code to achieve. The pipeline concepts covered in this chapter are for the most part applicable regardless of whether the pipeline is being executed in the traditional way or from an orchestration.

Understanding IBaseMessage

BizTalk processes messages internally. Messages flow through the BizTalk engine and are processed in different ways by different parts of the engine. The engine is extensible at various points during processing, and each of these extensibility points in turn processes messages in some manner. So before you really dig into pipelines it's important to understand in a little more detail what a message is. When programming against BizTalk, whether you are writing adapters, pipeline components, or orchestrations, you will be dealing with a BizTalk message. For adapter and pipeline components, this means programming against the IBaseMessage interface; for orchestrations, you program against the abstract class XLANGMessage. Conceptually, both are very similar, and for all intents and purposes, the XLANGMessage maps down to IBaseMessage. In this chapter, we refer specifically to IBaseMessage, since this is the interface that pipeline components will be dealing with.

> Internally, the BizTalk engine uses the IBTMessage interface, which extends IBaseMessage; this interface supports the additional functionality required by the Message Agent and other parts of the engine.

IBaseMessage makes no assumptions about the underlying data format that it is representing; in fact, the data associated with the message is simply a reference to a Stream. This is necessary in order to deal with any message format, even binary messages. Figure 4-1 illustrates the class diagram for IBaseMessage.

> For the remainder of this discussion I'll refer to IBaseMessage simply as a message.

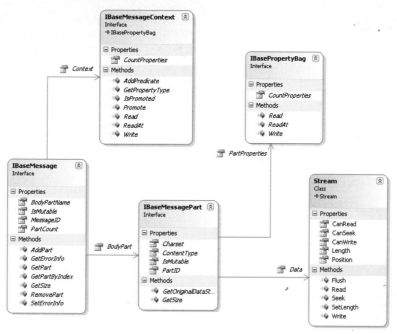

Figure 4-1

Understanding Message Parts

Every message has zero or more message parts. Each message part implements the `IBaseMessagePart` interface. Each part may have a `Stream` associated with it, and this `Stream` contains the data for the part. Although the message may have many parts associated with it, one of these parts is special — it is the *body* part. The body part is the message part that has the *wire-level* data associated with it, typically, the data that adapters receive or send will be held in the message body part. In other words, the body part typically contains the payload that is sent or received over the wire. (One thing to consider here is that the `Stream` associated with a message part will usually be processed in a forward-only streaming model; we'll discuss this in a lot more detail shortly.)

You may be wondering why BizTalk supports the notion of multipart messages, but the answer is simple. This enables the use of Multipurpose Internet Mail Extensions (MIME) encoding and other protocols that enable messages to contain attachments. With the use of a multipart message, the body data can be separated from the attachments. This means that the body can be processed independently of the attachments, which are simply flowed with the message. These attachments may be ignored while processing the body part of the message, which simplifies processing. So, prior to transmitting the message, the body part and attachments can be encoded into a single stream of data, which will of course be held in the message body part. The SOAP adapter is an exception to this. When using the SOAP adapter each parameter maps on to an individual part.

Additionally, a message may have no parts associated with it; in fact, BizTalk internally uses control messages that for some scenarios have no parts, such as delivery notifications. For example, a BizTalk *ACK* has no message parts. The engine flows control messages between different subservices to control the behavior, and some of these messages have no body, but only a message context that is used to notify different subsystems of various events.

Keep in mind that messages are immutable once they have been written to the MessageBox. Each message part has its own part context of type IBasePropertyBag, and the purpose for this is to hold state associated with the individual part; the data's content-type and charset are, for example, held on the part context.

Understanding Message Contexts

This brings us to IBaseMessageContext. The message context derives from IBasePropertyBag, and it is responsible for holding properties that are associated with the message. The properties may be derived from the message data, meaning that as the message is processed, various key values of the data may be extracted and placed in the message context, thereby simplifying the consumption of that data at a later stage. For example, a purchase order number embedded in a message may be extracted and written to the context. Downstream components do not need to parse the message again, instead they may simply read the message context property. Properties associated with the receive port/location over which the message was received may be placed in the context, enabling messages to be differentiated according to their source URL and the properties of the port which they were received on.

The context may also be used to flow state between different processing elements within the engine. This is useful because the engine is stateless; allowing state to be associated with the message simplifies the processing of that message.

But the context is not only about flowing metadata and state for the message; it is also a fundamental part of the subscription evaluation process that is used to route messages. Message context properties can be written or promoted, and when a context property is promoted, it may be used in the routing of messages. The MessageBox considers only properties that are promoted when evaluating subscriptions.

Message properties have a namespace associated with them; this is to prevent collisions if two properties are defined with the same name by different applications. Many of the properties that BizTalk defines and uses internally live in the http://schemas.microsoft.com/BizTalk/2003/system-properties namespace. Since the context is a property bag, each item in the context requires a key to put and get the value for that property. To prevent collisions, the key for each property is defined in the format namespace#name; for example, the name of the system property to identify the receive port on which a message was received is:

```
http://schemas.microsoft.com/BizTalk/2003/system-properties#ReceivePortName
```

This means that a custom property that I define for my application, AckRequired, does not clash with or interfere with any other properties of the same name, for example, BizTalk's system property called AckRequired. This is important because if custom code were to overwrite key BizTalk system properties, this would interfere with the processing of messages and lead to undefined behavior, similarly, this also prevents different applications from interfering with each other.

The correct way to read, write, and promote properties is shown as follows. First, a reference to the following assemblies needs to be added to your project. You can find these assemblies in the following directory: %PROGRAMFILES%\Microsoft BizTalk Server 2006\.

```
Microsoft.XLANGs.BaseTypes.dll
Microsoft.BizTalk.GlobalPropertySchemas.dll
```

The reference for the XLANG assembly is for PropertyBase, which is defined in the Microsoft .XLANGs.BaseTypes namespace, while the other reference is the assembly where all of the BizTalk context properties are defined; this includes the system namespace and the properties for all of the adapters. You can explore which properties are packaged in this assembly using *ILDasm*, as shown in Figure 4-2.

Figure 4-2

Note that you need to declare a static property of the appropriate type; this provides a level of type safety when specifying the name and namespace of the context property that you are using. The following code illustrates the reading, writing, and promoting of the AckRequired property from the BizTalk system namespace.

```
using Microsoft.XLANGs.BaseTypes;

// Declare property: ackRequired
private static PropertyBase ackRequired = new BTS.AckRequired();

...

// Read context property
bool ackReqValue = (bool)inmsg.Context.Read(ackRequired.Name.Name,
  ackRequired.Name.Namespace);

// Write context property
inmsg.Context.Write(ackRequired.Name.Name, ackRequired.Name.Namespace, true);

// Promote context property
inmsg.Context.Promote(ackRequired.Name.Name, ackRequired.Name.Namespace, true);
```

Pipeline Architecture

To really understand pipelines, it's important to understand the architecture of pipelines and how they work under the hood. Figure 4-3 illustrates the BizTalk stack from the adapter to the MessageBox. The diagram illustrates how the engine *pulls* the stream of data through the pipeline and adapter; the arrows indicate who is doing the pulling of the data. As you read through this section you may find it helpful to refer back to this diagram. The numbers on the diagram represent the order in which the stream is read once the pipeline has been "wired up." The following processing takes place at that time:

- ❏ When a message is delivered out of the pipeline the stream is largely unread. There are exceptions to this that I will discuss later, but to simplify matters at this stage lets assume that the first read is performed by the Messaging Engine.

- ❏ This stream read triggers a stream read on the previous message stream, which in turn triggers a stream read on the previous. This propagates back to the "wire" stream, (read number 7), the adapter will read data from the "wire" and return it on the stream read, this will be returned back up the chain to the Messaging Engine which initially issued the stream read.

- ❏ The Messaging Engine will write the data that it has read to the MessageBox via the Message Agent at the point when it is appropriate.

In the following sections in this chapter I will discuss this process in much more detail.

In order to maintain a flat memory model while processing messages of arbitrary sizes and under high load, the engine processes all messages in a forward-only streaming manner with message data flowing through the engine. This is the case from the moment the message enters into BizTalk all the way through the product. The way that BizTalk processes message data is analogous to water flowing through a pipe, as opposed to loading all the water into a really large bucket and passing that along. The forward-only streaming model means that message streams may only be read; they can't be seeked back to the beginning. Forward-only streams hold only a small part of the stream data in an in-memory buffer, as opposed to a memory stream in which all the stream data is held in memory.

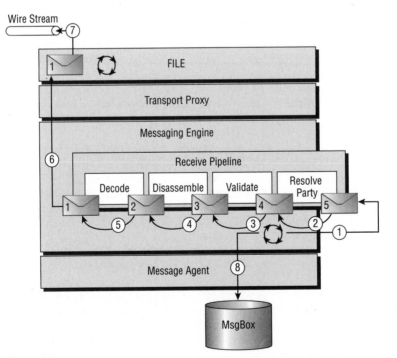

Figure 4-3

Message Processing

The data flow starts at the adapter, which connects to the *wire* (for the purpose of this discussion, the wire is an abstract concept and is dependent on the transport protocol; an example would be an HTTP connection for messages received using the HTTP receive adapter). Typically, the adapter does not read all the wire data before creating the message and submitting it; instead, when it receives new data, it creates a BizTalk message and attaches the wire stream to the message. At that point, it submits the message into BizTalk. There are, of course, transport-specific optimizations, whereby a specified amount of data is loaded into the message stream — for example, for an HTTP ISAPI extension IIS delivers the first 48KB of data; the remainder of the data is fetched asynchronously. For this scenario, since IIS delivers the first 48KB of data up front, all this data is loaded into the message stream; the rest of the data will be loaded on demand. You'll see how the rest of the data is "pulled" from the wire shortly.

The Messaging Engine accepts the new message (typically, a number of messages would be submitted in one batch by the adapter for performance reasons) and performs some pre-pipeline processing on it. The pipeline is then executed, passing in the message that was submitted by the adapter; remember, at this point the wire stream still has not been pulled (i.e. the stream has not been read). When receiving or sending messages, the pipeline is executed by the Messaging Engine. This means that for a receive port it will be executed in the receive host and for the send port in a send host. As mentioned earlier, it can be executed in an orchestration host, which is discussed in more detail in Chapter 10. When the pipeline is executed, the components at each stage of the pipeline are executed; you will drill into pipeline stages and their responsibilities later in the chapter in the section on pipeline stages.

Each pipeline component processes the message. Remember, the processing model is stream based, so each pipeline component does not read the data stream yet, at least not in its entirety, since that would break the streaming model and run the risk of hitting an out-of-memory exception. (There are exceptions to this that I'll discuss later in the chapter.) Basically, each pipeline component that changes the data clones the input message passed to it. The new message is the return parameter (disassemblers and assemblers work a little differently; we'll get to them later in the chapter). The stream on the output message, however, needs to be wired up to the stream on the input message so that, when `Stream.Read` is called on the output stream, it in turn calls `Stream.Read` on the input stream, processes the data that it reads from it, and then returns the processed data. All the methods on the output stream need to be wired up in this manner, as appropriate. We'll look at this in more detail shortly.

At this point, the pipeline has been executed in the sense that the APIs on all of the pipeline components have been called. In fact, all that has really happened is that the pipeline has been wired up and is ready to execute. Typically, a message is produced from the pipeline. In fact, for a receive pipeline, a single input message could result in zero or more messages to be extracted; zero in the case that the pipeline was a consuming pipeline, and multiple in the case that the input message was disassembled into multiple messages. A *consuming pipeline*, as the name implies, is a pipeline that consumes a message but does not emit a message. Later, I will discuss how BizTalk implements reliable messaging for BizTalk Framework (BTF), which will illustrate an example of a consuming pipeline.

The Messaging Engine then begins its work, which in turn drives the execution of the pipeline by reading the streams of the message returned from the pipeline execution. The engine processes each message returned from the pipeline. It iterates through each message part and fetches its stream. It then reads the stream, which in turn triggers a read on every stream back to the network stream that the adapter created. This reading of the stream drives the various pipeline components — for example, as the stream that the flat file disassembler created and wired up is read, the flat-file disassembler does its work of converting the flat file into XML data.

Large Message Processing

The Messaging Engine monitors the amount of data that was read and currently in memory. Once the amount of data exceeds the `Large message threshold` configured, the engine starts flushing the data to the MessageBox in chunks of the `Large message fragment size`. These values are configured at the BizTalk group level. Figure 4-4 illustrates the dialog box and the default values.

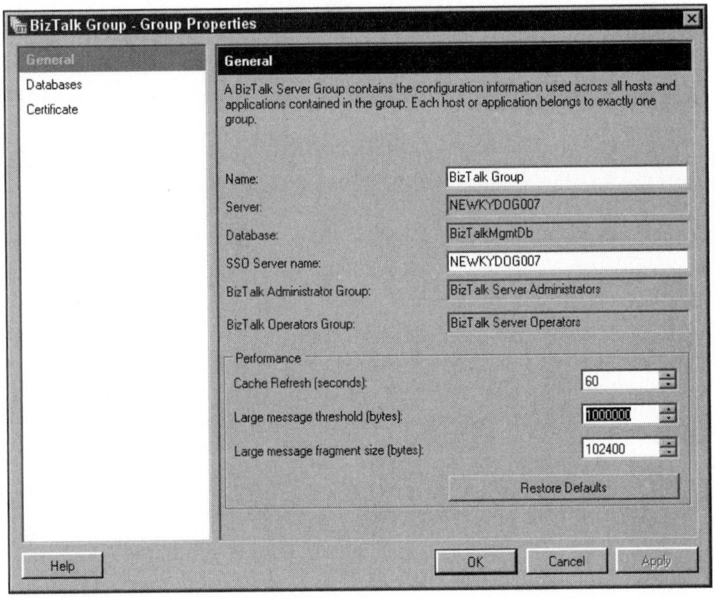

Figure 4-4

The optimum values for this configuration are dependent on the physical environment where BizTalk is operating. Tests have historically shown that sending data in 100KB chunks gives the optimum performance (though this can of course vary from scenario to scenario). The `Large message fragment size` represents the size of the chunks of data that flow between BizTalk and SQL Server. A message can be made up of many fragments that are persisted individually by the engine; when the messages are dequeued, the Message Agent and MessageBox stitch these fragments together to rebuild the message.

This, of course, also happens in a streaming manner. In theory, there is no limit to the size that a message may be; in practice, however, the .NET XML stack means that limit is around 4GB. Also, additional work is performed prior to committing the data to the MessageBox; for example, if an inbound map has been configured, this will be executed prior to the flush.

Pipeline execution on the send side is very similar to the receive side, in terms of its stream- based processing. The main difference is that it is the adapter that is pulling on the stream, rather than the Messaging Engine. Essentially, the stream of data is pulled from the MessageBox by the adapter. As mentioned, receive pipelines may produce zero or more output messages for a given input message; this is called *disassembly*. Send pipelines have complementary functionality called *assembly*, where one or more messages can be fed into a send pipeline to produce a single message as output. This functionality has always been present in BizTalk assembler components, though the 2006 release makes it usable; I discuss this in more detail when I discuss the Assemble pipeline stage.

Pipelines and Transactions

Next, it's important to understand the scope of transactions and where they may be used in relation to pipeline components. Only receive pipelines support transactions. There are two variations:

- ❑ A pipeline component in the receive pipeline can enlist in the adapter's transaction (assuming that the adapter uses transactions), which is also used when publishing to the MessageBox.

- ❑ If the adapter does not support transactions, then the transaction will be between the pipeline component and the MessageBox.

For both cases, this will be a distributed transaction. Distributed transactions are used only for these scenarios and scenarios where BizTalk is deployed with multiple MessageBoxes in a single BizTalk group. This means that when you are using a transacted adapter and a pipeline component that supports transactions, the messages are received, processed in the pipeline components, and published to the MessageBox — all in one atomic transaction. This is illustrated in Figure 4-5, which has a pipeline component (Txn Comp) that atomically adds an identifier from the message into a duplicate database table; this unit of work is performed atomically with the dequeueing of the message from the MSMQ queue and the publication of the message to the MessageBox. In this scenario, it ensures that the duplicate entry is made only if the message is published successfully to the database.

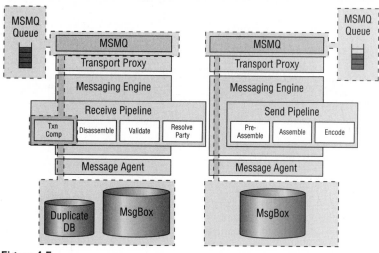

Figure 4-5

You should note that for a pipeline component to enlist in the transaction it needs to fetch the transaction from the pipeline context by calling IPipelineContextEx.GetTransaction. A common mistake is to assume that a ServicedComponent will automatically be enlisted in the transaction; it will not. Instead, it creates a separate unrelated transaction. In the scenario where a transacted adapter is used, the call to IPipelineContextEx.GetTransaction simply passes to the pipeline component the transaction reference that was passed to the engine by the adapter. In the scenario where the adapter does not support transactions or is not using transactions, the same call causes the engine to create a new DTC transaction and pass this to the pipeline component. In both scenarios, the engine also uses this same transaction when performing the publication of the message to the MessageBox.

Send pipelines do not support transactions; a pipeline component in the send pipeline can use transactions if your scenario requires it, but be aware that BizTalk will not use this transaction in any way. There is no way to hook the transaction on the send side using a pipeline component.

Pipeline Stages

As mentioned previously, pipelines are broken down into a number of stages. These stages are executed sequentially, although there are some complications, which I cover when I discuss the disassembler in more detail. Broadly speaking, pipeline stages are a logical grouping for similar types of processing. Each stage can have 0 or up to 255 pipeline components configured in it, with the exception of the assembler stage, which can have 0 components or 1 component in it. A pipeline with no components in any stages represents a *pass-through* pipeline, which, as the name implies, performs no processing on the message. Pass-through pipelines are often used for binary messages because they simply allow the message to flow through. Each stage is assigned an `execution mode`, which determines how the components within that stage are executed. There are three execution modes: *all*, *first recognized*, and *all recognized*.

❑ Most of the stages in both the send and receive pipelines are assigned the *all* execution mode with the exception of the Disassemble stage. The *all* execution mode does, of course, cause every pipeline component in that stage to be executed. They are executed in the order that they are specified in the stage. This means that, effectively, each stage is like a mini-pipeline in itself; the implications of this will be a little clearer when I discuss disassembly in more detail.

❑ Next is the *first recognized* mode. This execution mode is a little more interesting. Stages marked with this execution mode iterate through the components until they find a match, at which point the component is executed, leaving the remaining components unexecuted. The only stage that uses this mode by default is the Disassemble stage in the receive pipeline, as you'll see shortly. This mode may also be used in the discovery of the format of the message. Any stage can use the *first recognized* mode, though the components in that stage should implement the `IProbeMessage` interface. If they don't they are treated in the same way as the *all* execution mode. I discuss this discovery mechanism more when I drill a little deeper into the Disassemble stage, but essentially the `IProbeMessage` interface enables pipeline components to choose whether they want to process a message.

❑ The final execution mode is *all recognized*. This mode is not currently used in any stages out of the box. It works in the same manner as *first recognized*, except that it will execute all the components that recognize the format of the data.

Pipeline templates use a *policy file* to define the characteristics of each pipeline stage; these include the minimum and maximum number of components in a given stage, the execution mode of the stage, and the name of the stage. These policies files are installed in the directory `%PROGRAMFILES%\Microsoft BizTalk Server 2006\Developer Tools\Pipeline Policy Files`. The policy files may be cloned or changed to provide a limited level of constraint enforcement on the types of pipelines that may be developed. You should be aware that the order or type of the stages cannot be changed, although stages can be removed completely.

In the following example policy file, I've copied the standard policy file used out of the box for all BizTalk receive pipelines — `BTSReceivePolicy.xml` — and modified the names of some of the stages and the number of components they allow. My policy file has been tailored to my scenario, which receives compressed messages; it needs to perform the following processing on messages received: decompression, disassemble, validate, and, finally, cross-field validation. It allows only one component to be used in all stages, except for the Disassemble stage, which may have up to 255 components. In addition, I have renamed the stages to encourage the deployment of particular types of components. For example, the Decode stage has been renamed as the Uncompress stage, since this scenario always receives compressed data over the wire.

```xml
<?xml version="1.0" encoding="utf-8"?>
<Document xmlns:xsd="http://www.w3.org/2001/XMLSchema"
    xmlns:xsi="http://www.w3.org/2001/XMLSchema-instance" CategoryId =
    "F66B9F5E-43FF-4f5f-BA46-885348AE1B4E" FriendlyName = "SwiftReceive">
  <Stages>
    <Stage _locAttrData="Name" _locID="1" Name = "Uncompress" minOccurs = "1"
      maxOccurs = "1" stageId = "9d0e4103-4cce-4536-83fa-4a5040674ad6"
      execMethod = "All">
    </Stage>
    <Stage _locAttrData="Name" _locID="2" Name = "Disassemble" minOccurs = "1"
      maxOccurs = "-1" stageId = "9d0e4105-4cce-4536-83fa-4a5040674ad6"
      execMethod = "FirstMatch">
    </Stage>
    <Stage _locAttrData="Name" _locID="4" Name = "Validate" minOccurs = "1"
      maxOccurs = "1" stageId = "9d0e410e-4cce-4536-83fa-4a5040674ad6"
      execMethod = "All">
    </Stage>
    <Stage _locAttrData="Name" _locID="3" Name = "CrossFieldCheck"
      minOccurs = "1" maxOccurs = "1"
      stageId = "9d0e410d-4cce-4536-83fa-4a5040674ad6" execMethod = "All">
    </Stage>
  </Stages>
</Document>
```

To use the policy file, you need to create a new pipeline template. These live in the directory %PROGRAM-FILES%\Microsoft BizTalk Server 2006\Developer Tools\BizTalkProjectItems. The following is my new pipeline template. Notice that it references the name of my new pipeline policy file.

```xml
<?xml version="1.0" encoding="utf-16"?>
<Document xmlns:xsd="http://www.w3.org/2001/XMLSchema"
xmlns:xsi="http://www.w3.org/2001/XMLSchema-instance"
PolicyFilePath="SwiftBTSReceivePolicy.xml" MajorVersion="1" MinorVersion="0">
  <Stages>
  </Stages>
</Document>
```

Once the pipeline template has been deployed, you will be able to create a new pipeline using the new pipeline template by selecting Add ➪ New Item from a BizTalk project. Figure 4-6 illustrates the new pipeline that uses two custom pipeline components, the Decompressor and CrossFieldCheck pipeline components. The policy file specifies that exactly one component is required in the Uncompress, Validate, and CrossFieldCheck stages; failure to comply with the policy results in a compilation error. The Uncompress stage is the renamed Decode stage, and the CrossFieldCheck stage is the renamed ResolveParty stage.

Unfortunately, there is no way to define a new type of stage, although renaming stages in this way can help to provide a graphical prompt for the type of pipeline component that should be configured in the stage.

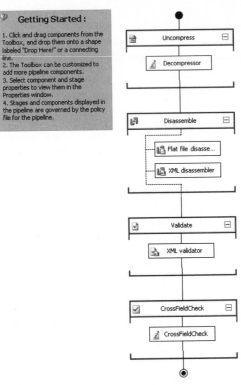

Figure 4-6

Receive Pipeline Stages

The receive pipeline has four stages:

❑   Decode

❑   Disassemble

❑   Validate

❑   ResolveParty

The canonical example of the processing that the receive pipeline performs is to take the wire-formatted message and convert it into a valid XML document. It is a common misconception that the resulting document must be an XML document, though BizTalk is, of course, geared toward normalizing inbound documents to XML, and the mapping that may be configured at the port level requires the data to be in XML format. As you have seen previously, the policy file enforces number of components that are deployed to each of these stages; by default, all stages may be empty.

Decode

The type of processing that is typically configured in the Decode stage is to prepare the message for the Disassemble stage. This may mean decoding and decrypting of messages. Typical examples of this include MIME and SMIME. MIME supports the notion of attachments, and as you have seen previously, `IBaseMessage` supports multiple parts. The MIME/SMIME component takes advantage of this when decoding messages, as it may create a message with a body part and a number of attachments (additional message parts). The Decode stage can be used for any type of processing that is required to prepare the message for the Disassemble stage. As you saw previously, it could be used to uncompress the input message. It is also common to deploy message-tracking components to this stage to collect and publish data and statistics pertaining to the wire message received. Chapter 6 will discuss this in more detail.

Disassemble

The Disassemble stage is typically concerned with two types of processing:

- ❑ The recognition and conversion of the input message to XML
- ❑ The disassembling of message interchanges into many individual messages

First and foremost, it is responsible for the recognition and conversion of the input message to XML. As mentioned earlier, BizTalk does not require that conversion be to XML, although all of the disassemblers out of the box do output messages in XML format. For many scenarios, the input message may be formatted as an XML message, in which case it will be processed by the `XmlDisassembler`. For this scenario, the disassembler is responsible for recognizing the message type and promoting to the message context the properties that have been specified in the schema for that message type. The message context property `MessageType` in the system namespace is promoted to the message context by the disassembler when it recognizes the message. The recognition of the message essentially means that the disassembler determines which XSD schema the message conforms to.

The schema may be decorated with a number of schema properties that are of interest. This happens when properties are marked as requiring promotion in BizTalk XSD Editor. The values for these properties are extracted from the message content and promoted to the message context, and as such they may be used for document routing. The disassembler performs this by first fetching the XSD schema for the message. This schema is annotated by the BizTalk tools to indicate what properties need to be promoted. The annotations contain the name of the context properties, the namespace, and the XPath expression that may be used to query the value. The SDK sample `ArbitraryXPathPropertyHandler` demonstrates how this may be achieved.

One thing to note here is that there is a cost associated with promoting properties. Since they all need to be evaluated downstream for every message publication, the number of properties that are promoted should be limited to those that really need to be promoted. That said, the assembler has the opposite concept of moving message context properties into the message content, referred to as *demotion* of properties. For property demotion to work in the assembler component, the properties need to be promoted; this is sometimes at odds with reducing the number of properties that are promoted, though when dealing with messages formatted as flat file it is an extremely powerful mechanism to set the fields of the message content. For scenarios where the values are not required for message routing, but are instead only required to be read by orchestrations, it makes more sense to use distinguished fields, this avoids the unnecessary performance hit.

The second type of processing, the Disassemble stage, is is responsible for the disassembling of message interchanges into many individual messages. A message interchange is a single message that is a batch of many individual messages. Often, these individual messages are wrapped by a header and trailer. The term *interchange* originates from Electronic Data Interchange (EDIFACT), which is a type of flat-file format. Each of these individual messages is treated independently once it leaves the disassembler component and flows through BizTalk.

Previously, I mentioned that the stages after the Disassemble stage are, effectively, like subpipelines; hopefully, now this comment starts to become clear. For every message that is output from the disassembler, the rest of the pipeline is executed prior to fetching the next message from the disassembler. The disassembler interfaces expose a `GetNext` method signature, which is used to drive the fetching of messages in this manner. The input message is fed into the disassembler, and then `GetNext` is called to fetch the first output message. The engine keeps calling `GetNext` until the disassembler returns `null` to indicate that there are no more messages, at which point the input message has been completely processed. For every message that is returned from a `GetNext` call, the rest of the pipeline is executed, which in effect means that the Validate and ResolveParty stages are subpipelines of the Disassemble stage.

As mentioned previously, the Disassemble stage may contain many disassemblers by default, and the first that recognizes the message executes. To achieve this, the pipeline component inspects the message and determines the format of the message; this is called *message probing*. The probing capabilities of the Disassemble stage enable different message formats to be received over the same URL. The pipeline can dynamically identify the format and schema of the message that is being processed. In order for a disassembler to take advantage of probing, it needs to implement the `IProbeMessage` interface, which has a single method, `Probe`, that returns `true` if the disassembler decides that it wants to process the message. The `Probe` method typically reads a small portion of the message data stream in order to make a choice as to whether or not it is capable of processing the message.

When Large Interchanges Are Too Large

As discussed earlier in the chapter, the Messaging Engine monitors the amount of memory being used when processing a batch of messages submitted by an adapter and periodically writes that data to the MessageBox in order to keep the memory usage flat. This is not only true when processing an individual message that is large but also when disassembling messages.

Although the size of the individual messages may be small, disassembling a large number of them can nevertheless cause an out-of-memory scenario. For example, suppose that the engine was processing a large interchange containing 100,000 messages. As the engine pulls messages from the Pipeline Manager, it reads the stream for each message. For each message pulled from the pipeline, the engine keeps track of the amount of memory that the message uses. When that amount of memory exceeds the `Large message threshold` configured, the engine starts publishing those messages pulled from the pipeline to the MessageBox in *subbatches*. The number of messages published to the MessageBox in a subbatch is determined when their associated data exceeds the `Large message fragment size`.

These subbatches are published using a DTC transaction. This transaction is not committed until the entire batch of messages that was submitted by the adapter has been processed. This means that a DTC transaction is held open while processing this large interchange to ensure that the entire batch of messages is published to the MessageBox atomically. Publishing the subbatches of messages to the MessageBox helps to relieve memory pressure as it builds.

For most scenarios, this process is not a problem; however, when the size of an interchange exceeds a given threshold, the number of locks held open in SQL Server will exceed the maximum number of locks available (the limit in 64-bit SQL Server is higher). At this point, the transaction is aborted, and the message is either suspended or returned to the adapter to determine what to do with it. These locks are held open for the duration of the DTC transaction, so for very large interchanges this may be tens of minutes.

The maximum number of messages in an interchange that can be disassembled is on the order of 400,000. However, remember that the Messaging Engine is processing pipelines on its threadpool, which means that, at any given time, the number of pipelines being executed could be as many as the number of threads in the threadpool. While there will typically only be one or two threads per CPU actually executing, all of the threads in the threadpool typically have been scheduled and context switched out, so usually a pipeline is executing for every thread in the threadpool. This dramatically reduces the size of interchanges that can be handled concurrently because the number of SQL locks now needs to be shared among a lot more large interchanges. The BizTalk Performance Characteristics white paper gives the following formula for calculating the number of messages in an interchange that can be handled before running out of locks in SQL Server. You should note that this formula is only a rough guide — the 200,000 is half of the maximum number of messages in a single interchange to give some contingency:

```
Maximum number of messages per interchange <= 200,000 / (Number of CPUs * BatchSize
    * MessagingThreadPoolSize)
```

As a rule of thumb, if you need to disassemble very large interchanges that are larger than 5000 messages, arguably the best approach is to presplit them before they enter into BizTalk, unless you can guarantee that only a single large message interchange is to be processed at a given time. Of course, every scenario is different, so the bottom line is that if you have a scenario where you are handling large interchanges, you need to test it. Be aware that this does not mean running a single message through. You need to test burst loading in order to ensure that the threadpool is loaded. If you take the presplitting approach, you could later assemble the messages before sending them outbound, if required. There are two approaches that I have either used myself or seen used, both of which may be used to successfully split very large message interchanges before they enter into BizTalk. The first involves the development of a custom adapter to perform the split; the adapter submits the individual messages into BizTalk. The second approach uses SQL Server Integration Services to split the interchange and subsequently save the individual messages in a staging table in SQL Server, the BizTalk SQL adapter may then used to receive the messages from the staging area in SQL Server.

Recoverable Interchanges

When a disassembler component processes an interchange of messages, the output messages are disassembled from the input message one at a time in a streaming manner. The implications of this are that a badly formatted message buried in the middle of an interchange can present problems when processing the messages that follow, due to the stream-based processing. All of the messages within an interchange are logically related; therefore, they all need to be persisted to the MessageBox together.

BizTalk Server 2004 took the approach of suspending the entire interchange in the scenario where it contained a single bad message; in that scenario no messages would be published. While this approach worked for many messages, it's clearly not a one-size-fits-all solution. BizTalk Server 2006 introduces the concept of a *recoverable interchange*. A recoverable interchange effectively means that the engine will try to publish the good messages in an interchange and suspend the messages that are bad. This happens in an atomic operation, so logically all of the messages are guaranteed to be in the MessageBox; the good messages are published, while the bad ones are suspended. This approach is more suited to scenarios where it is more appropriate to process as many of the messages as possible, where you need to continue processing in the event of failures. The recoverable interchange option is configured on the disassembler (by setting the RecoverableInterchangeProcessing property on the disassembler), and it is supported on a case-by-case basis, since the disassembler needs to be able to move to a position in the stream where it can find the next message to process.

Validate

The Validate stage is responsible for ensuring that the messages that are produced upstream of it are valid. Typically, this means ensuring that a given message is validated against a collection of XSD schemas. As previously mentioned, every message extracted by the Disassemble stage results in the Validate stage being executed. BizTalk ships with an XML Validator that performs this task.

> *Schema validation is not always sufficient to ensure that a message is valid. For example, SWIFT messages require cross-field validation, whereby the population of one field requires other fields to be populated in a specific manner. The BizTalk A4Swift accelerator achieves this by using a custom pipeline component that executes BRE rules over the XML message to perform the cross-field validation.*

ResolveParty

The ResolveParty stage is used to determine the party that BizTalk received the message from. Pipeline components in this stage achieve this by mapping the sender's certificate or the sender's security identifier (SID) to the corresponding BizTalk party. The component writes the party ID to message context property `SourcePartyID`. If the party cannot be resolved, the `SourcePartyID` is set to be anonymous, that is, `"s-1-5-7"`. Downstream, the engine sets the message context property `OriginatorPID` to equal the `SourcePartyID` if the host has been configured as Authentication Trusted.

The Party Resolution pipeline component reads the message context properties `WindowsUser` and `SignatureCertificate`. Typically, the `WindowsUser` message context property is populated by the adapter. For example, if the message was received using the HTTP receive adapter, IIS authenticates the sending user, and the adapter writes the value of the sending user to this message context property. The `SignatureCertificate` property is typically populated with the thumbprint of the client authentication certificate by either an adapter or the MIME/SMIME decoder pipeline component.

Handling Pipeline Failures

A receive pipeline failure means that the message is not published to the MessageBox; instead, it is typically either given back to the adapter that submitted it or suspended in the MessageBox. The choice as to which action happens is up to the adapter. The reason for this is the forward-only streaming model that is used. If execution of the receive pipeline fails, the Messaging Engine attempts to suspend the message that was submitted to it by the adapter. However, before it can suspend the message, it needs to seek the stream back to the beginning; otherwise, there could be data loss, since the part of the stream that has already been consumed may be lost. So the engine calls the `Stream.CanSeek` property. If the property indicates that the stream can be "seeked," the engine then attempts to seek it to the beginning. If this is successful, then the engine suspends the message. If on the other hand it cannot be "seeked," the message is given back to the adapter, which determines what it wishes to do with the message.

Of course, for some adapters the fact that the stream has been consumed means that it is forced to return the error to the client. For example, when HTTP receives data greater than 48KB, this data is not kept in memory and so cannot be "seeked." In other scenarios, it may be possible for the adapter to suspend that message by seeking the stream back to the beginning; for example the FILE adapter can typically seek the stream back to the beginning, since the data is on disk. The approach means that the adapter can control whether messages that fail in the pipeline may be suspended, by wrapping the data stream and controlling the return value of the `Stream.CanSeek` property.

> *One thing to bear in mind here is that allowing messages to be suspended is typically not a good thing; usually, it requires manual intervention to resolve those messages. If there are thousands of them, this can be a very labor-intensive process.*

BizTalk Server 2006 adds a new mechanism for handling failures in the receive or send port. It is enabled when you configure `Enable routing for failed messages` at the receive or send port level. Figure 4-7 illustrates the receive port configuration.

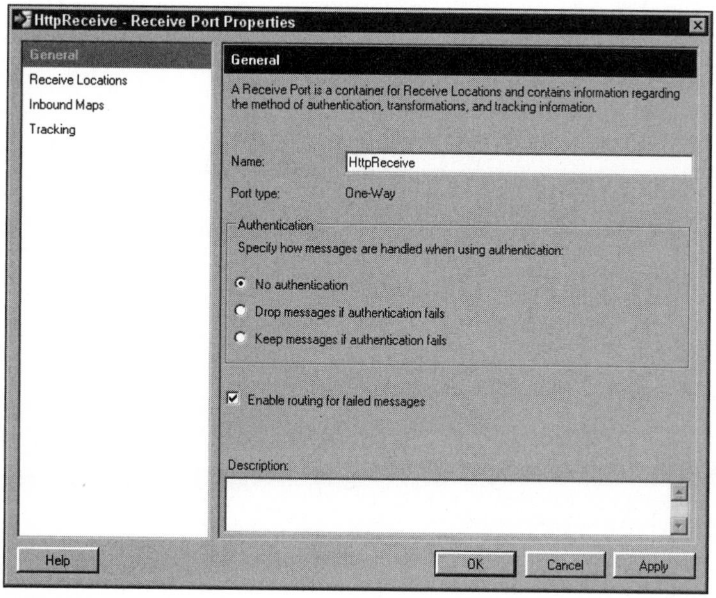

Figure 4-7

When this option is configured and a message fails during receive processing, the engine demotes all of the existing message context properties and promotes a number of `ErrorReport` message context properties that may be used to route the message to either a send port or an orchestration. This is very powerful, since it enables you to move to a more automated approach when dealing with messages that fail processing. For example, the failed messages could be "enqueued" to an error queue that the sending application reads, thereby pushing the responsibility of the error processing back to the client. Alternatively, you could route these messages to an orchestration that has some logic designed to repair the messages automatically. The `ErrorReport` properties contain a number of properties related to the error, such as the `ErrorType` (which always contains the value `FailedMessage`), `FailureCode`, and `FailureCategory`.

The `ErrorReport` properties also contain a number of useful properties that are copied from the failed message, for example, `ReceivePortName` and `InboundTransportLocation`. These properties may be used to route the message to the correct error handling service. For example, configuring a filter expression on an orchestration receive port as follows would enable the failed messages to be routed to it:

```
(ErrorReport.ErrorType == "FailedMessage") && (ErrorReport.ReceivePortName == "HttpReceive")
```

You should note that the orchestration message type needs to be `System.Xml.XmlDocument`, since at the point of failure it is likely that the message type has not been established. This enables documents of any type to be routed to the repair orchestration.

Send Pipeline Stages

The send pipeline has three stages: Pre-Assemble, Assemble, and Encode. The canonical example of the processing that the send pipeline performs is to take the XML message that has been processed by BizTalk and to format the message so that it is ready to be sent over the wire. You can think of it along the lines of performing the reverse of the actions that the receive pipeline performed.

Pre-Assemble

The Pre-Assemble stage is the first stage in the send pipeline. The stage is designed to enable custom processing of the message prior to its being processed by the Assemble stage. This is often useful when sending non-XML messages, since it's the last point in the pipeline where the message can be easily manipulated. It is far easier to query and modify XML data than data that is formatted in flat-file format, for example.

Assemble

The Assemble stage is essentially the opposite of the Disassemble stage in the receive pipeline. The Assemble stage is responsible for two types of functionality:

❑ Formatting the message to be sent over the wire

❑ Assembling the messages

First, it is responsible for formatting (sometimes referred to as *serializing*) the message to the format that will be sent over the wire. Typically, at the point when the Assemble stage is executed, the message is in XML format; this stage is responsible for formatting the message as flat file, or possibly adding an envelope to an XML message. If you recall, the Disassemble stage promotes message properties from the message content to the message context. These properties can be used for routing the message. Similarly, the Assemble stage includes the concept of demoting message context properties; this involves moving values from the message context and setting them in the message content.

The second type of processing that is performed in the Assemble stage is what this stage's name implies: the assembling of messages. Of course, this is the opposite of the disassembling process that takes place in the receive pipeline. Here, many individual messages are assembled into a single message interchange. The interchange could also be wrapped with a header and trailer.

There are, however, some caveats around this. Typically, the assembling of messages into interchanges in this manner requires a degree of business logic in order to determine which messages should be fed into the pipeline in order to be assembled together. Business logic of this nature belongs in orchestrations where a high level of control may be expressed over the messages that need to be assembled. In BizTalk Server 2004 the only way to assemble messages into a single interchange was to write some code in your orchestration to parse and assemble the messages yourself, and there is no way in either BizTalk 2004 or 2006 to perform message assembly in the send port. As mentioned previously, in BizTalk 2006 the Pipeline Manager can be hosted by an orchestration. The pipeline APIs are packaged in the `Microsoft.XLANGs.Pipeline.dll` assembly and may be driven from orchestrations. Chapter 10 discusses the execution of pipelines from orchestrations in more detail. Assembly of message interchanges can be achieved in orchestrations by developing your orchestration to build a collection of messages that logically make sense to assemble into a single message interchange. This collection of messages can then be passed into the pipeline and assembled. The SDK has a sample that demonstrates how message interchanges can be assembled by executing the send pipeline from an orchestration: `%PROGRAMFILES%\Microsoft BizTalk Server 2006\SDK\Samples\ Pipelines\Aggregator`.

Encode

The Encode stage is the last stage to be executed before the message is sent over the wire. Typically, it is used to encode, encrypt, and sign the message. This may be used for scenarios that require messages to be securely transmitted to external partners, ensuring that the message may not be "sniffed" or tampered with on route. BizTalk provides the MIME/SMIME pipeline component for this purpose. The BizTalk architecture is designed to be flexible to meet myriad scenarios — for example, if you are using a transport that natively supports the transmission of messages in a secure format, there would be no need to encrypt the message in the pipeline. However, decoupling the encryption of the message from the transport of the message means that you can use the encryption provided by the pipeline component over any transport. This is, of course, very powerful.

The Encode stage may also be used for other types of processing that make sense before message transmission. For example, compressing the message prior to transmission is a common technique used to increase message throughput. Effectively, this means trading CPU cycles for network bandwidth, and usually provides increased message throughput; in fact, the BizTalk engine does this itself when communicating with the MessageBox database. All message data is sent compressed over the wire to and from the database. The nature of XML means that a high compression ratio is usually achieved; this can be as high as 10:1 for larger documents. This not only provides better throughput but also means that the storage requirements are lower.

Pipeline Configuration

Pipelines may be configured in two ways:

- ❑   By type
- ❑   By instance

Most people are very familiar with configuring them by type. For this, the components in the pipeline are configured in Visual Studio at development time. After you have configured the pipeline, you deploy it, and that configuration is then *baked* into the deployed pipeline and will be used at runtime. This configuration is delivered to the engine at runtime from the database; it is persisted in the database during the deployment process when it is extracted from the compiled pipeline assembly. This works well and is the usual way that people tend to configure pipelines. The problem with this approach is that if you need different configuration for two ports using the same pipeline, you must create two pipelines, configure them, and deploy them. Clearly, this approach has limitations, and it means that you'll end up creating and deploying far more pipelines.

BizTalk 2004 introduced the notion of pipeline instance configuration. For this, the pipeline is still configured at development time, but an instance of that pipeline that is used in a specific send port or receive location may have its own independent configuration. This configuration is delivered to the pipeline at execution time and overwrites the type level configuration. This feature was rarely used in BizTalk 2004 because of the overhead associated with setting it up. First, you had to manually create the XML configuration file in the format that the pipeline was expecting (the tools support to create that configuration was of course the trusty Notepad!). Then you had to write some code to call the object model to set the configuration on the pipeline instance. It's hardly surprising that it was rarely used. The BizTalk team did not have the bandwidth to ship a user interface for this feature in the BizTalk 2004 release due to a raft of higher-priority features.

BizTalk 2006 has now added that user interface, and consequently instance-based pipeline configuration is now very simple. In general, I would encourage you to use this instead of creating lots of different pipeline types that are essentially identical apart from their configuration. All pipelines can be configured in this manner. Figure 4-8 shows the user interface used to configure the pipeline for a send port. Clicking on the ellipsis button (...) to the right of the send pipeline brings up the configuration dialog for that pipeline instance. Note that every component in that pipeline that takes configuration can be configured in this single dialog box. Your life is made easier by having a single place to enter all your configuration.

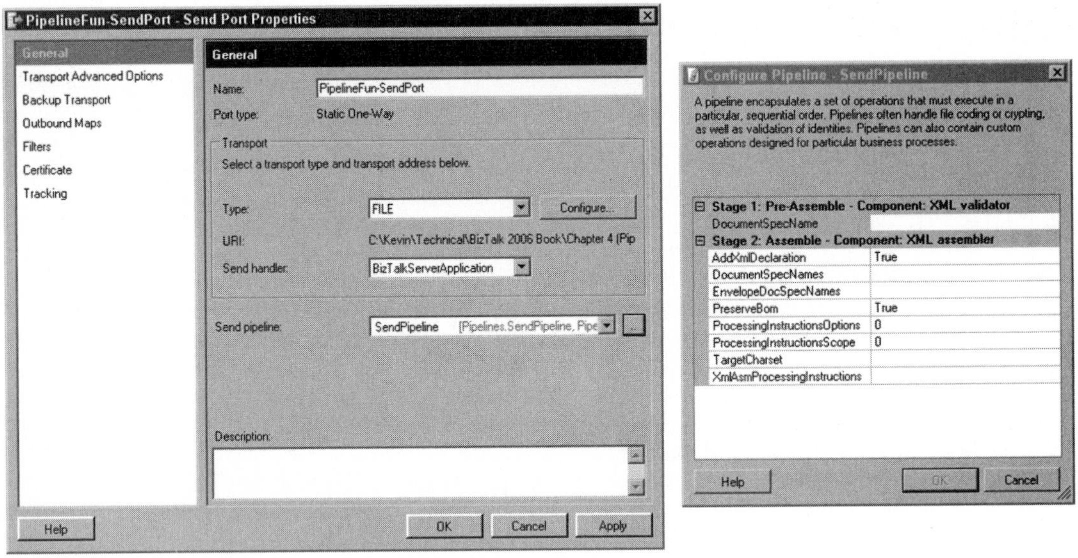

Figure 4-8

Default Pipelines

BizTalk ships with a number of default pipelines. These pipelines are created during the installation of BizTalk and can be used to expedite the development of a solution. Now that you understand instance-based pipeline configuration, it should be obvious that for many scenarios you will not need to create new pipelines but instead can use the existing default pipelines with your own instance-based configuration.

The first of these is the pass-through pipeline. There is one of these for receiving (PassThruReceive) and one for sending (PassThruTransmit). The send pass-through pipeline is essentially an empty pipeline; it contains no pipeline components and performs no processing of the message. Pass-through pipelines have a variety of uses. On the receive side, they can be used to bring in binary data to BizTalk. For example, for scenarios where binary files need to be moved, a pass-through pipeline can be used on both the receive and the send sides. The send pass-through pipeline is used frequently for scenarios where no outbound processing is required. For example, consider the scenario in which the message has been formatted in an orchestration ready to be transmitted. Executing a send pipeline with an XML assembler may add no additional value. But you would incur a performance overhead for the pleasure, typically in the order of a double-digit percentage over using a pass-through pipeline! The moral here is to minimize the pipeline components that are configured in your pipelines if you are trying to squeeze the maximum performance out of a system.

In addition, there are two additional default pipelines: XMLReceive and XMLTransmit. As the names imply, these are for processing XML messages on the receive and send sides, respectively. The XMLReceive pipeline has an empty Decode stage, the XML disassembler in the Disassemble stage, an empty Validate stage, and the party resolution component in the ResolveParty stage. The XMLTransmit pipeline has only the XML assembler in the Assemble stage, with the Pre-Assemble and Encode stages empty.

BizTalk Framework (BTF 2)

The BizTalk Framework (BTF 2) was introduced in BizTalk Server 2000. For the remainder of this discussion, this will simply be referred to as BTF.

> *BTF 1 was developed prior to BizTalk Server 2000 shipping. Only limited support surfaced in BizTalk 2000. BTF 2 was a significant enhancement to BTF 1.*

BTF was developed primarily to provide transport-agnostic reliable messaging. Interestingly, this has only recently been superseded by the reliable messaging in .NET 3.0 — WCF. The WCF implementation, of course, needs to be bound to a durable reliable messaging transport, such as MSMQ. In addition, BTF also provided SOAP with Attachments, which, as the name implies, enabled the transmission of multiple documents within a single SOAP envelope. This has since been superseded with the W3C standard Message Transmission Optimization Mechanism (MTOM). So BTF is essentially a specification for a number of SOAP headers, and BizTalk provides support out of the box for generating and handling these SOAP headers.

> **.NET 3.0 WCF implements WS-ReliableMessaging. However, it should be noted that at the time of this writing, the WCF service will send an acknowledgment back to the sender as soon as it receives a message; that is, WCF does not give the application the opportunity to persist the message before sending the acknowledgment to the client. The implications of this are that there are opportunities to lose messages should the receiver process die after the acknowledgment has been sent but before it persists the message that it received. So WCF at present enables reliable messaging at the wire level. At the time of writing this, Microsoft plans to address this issue in a future version of .NET. For durable messaging, a binding to MSMQ would be required.**

Although BTF was essentially a tactical solution to provide transport-agnostic reliable messaging, it is still supported in BizTalk today. In the future, the preferred mechanism to enable reliable messaging using Web services will be WCF.

Taking a closer look at how it works under the covers will help to give you ideas about how to design and solve similar problems, using pipeline components. Specifically, I will illustrate how reliable messaging is achieved using BTF. I won't cover how to configure BTF — the documentation is very adequate in that area.

BTF uses two pipeline components to facilitate reliable messaging: the BTF disassembler and the BTF assembler. To understand how BTF works, let's take a look at two scenarios.

Receiving BTF Reliable Messages

The first is for the receipt of a BTF reliable message from a trading partner. Figure 4-9 illustrates this.

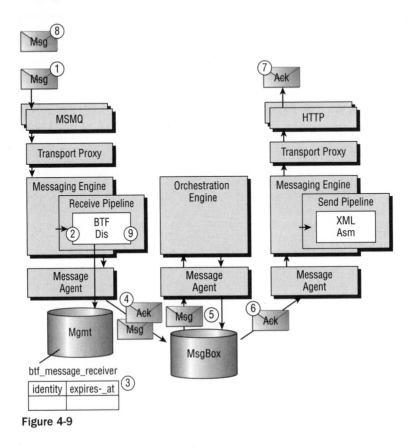

Figure 4-9

On the receive side, a reliable messaging solution needs to ensure idempotency — that is to say, that a given message will be accepted only once; all subsequent messages that represent the same instance will be discarded. The protocol typically means that every time a message is received, a receipt or acknowledgment for that message should be returned to the sender. Always returning the acknowledgment covers the scenario in which a previous acknowledgment was lost. So a reliable messaging implementation should make no assumptions around the delivery of a message or the subsequent acknowledgment for that message.

The following sequence of events takes place when receiving a BTF reliable message:

1. The scenario starts with a new BTF reliable message being received. It can be received via any transport adapter. This message will have been sent from another system that implements the BTF protocol. That other system does not need to be BizTalk and does not necessarily need to be running on the Microsoft platform.

2. Next, the message is processed by the BTF disassembler. The disassembler is based on the XML disassembler but has some additional functionality. First, it extracts the identity of the message. This is a property defined in one of the BTF headers in the SOAP envelope. The envelope will be extracted and all the BTF properties will be written to the message context.

3. The disassembler will then try to insert the new identity into the `BizTalkMgmtDB.btf_message_receiver` database table. If a row for that identity already exists, the BTF disassembler will catch the exception and thus recognize this as a message that has already been received. This is how BTF achieves idempotency. Because the disassembler uses the transaction from the pipeline context, BizTalk can guarantee that the message is received only once. If the message has already been received once, it will not be published; instead, the pipeline will consume the message.

4. The disassembler will always produce an acknowledgment, regardless of whether it is publishing a new message or simply acknowledging a message that has already been received. This is to cater to the scenario in which the receipt was lost and never made its way back to the sender. Both the message received (assuming that it's the first time it was received) and the acknowledgment to the message are published to the MessageBox. The acknowledgment will be routed using dynamic routing by extracting the "reply to" address from the message received and using it as its destination address.

5. For this scenario, the actual message will be processed by an orchestration. The message that is delivered to the orchestration will be the message that was in the body of the SOAP envelope.

6. The acknowledgment is delivered to the Messaging Engine to send to its destination.

7. The acknowledgment is transmitted using the appropriate transport, as defined in the BTF message that was received.

8. The next step in the scenario illustrates the receipt of the same message again. As you will see shortly, BTF will keep sending a message until it either expires or an acknowledgment for the message is received.

9. The BTF disassembler will again try to insert the identity of the message into the database, but this time it will fail. The message will be eaten by the disassembler, although an acknowledgment will still be generated by the disassembler and subsequently sent back to the sender.

This scenario showed that by using a transactional receive pipeline component, you can design a solution to give idempotency. The key point to remember here is that the pipeline component in the receive pipeline must fetch the DTC transaction from the pipeline context. The component needs to enlist in the transaction when inserting the record into the database. I have worked with many customers who needed to implement an idempotent solution. The BTF design pattern is a good choice because it is transport agnostic and the adapter does not need to support transactions.

Sending BTF Reliable Messages

The next scenario to discuss is the sending of a BTF reliable message. The sender of a reliable message also needs to be able to receive an acknowledgment for the messages that it sends, and needs to keep sending the message until it either expires or an acknowledgment for it is received. Figure 4-10 illustrates the scenario.

1. The scenario starts with the message being delivered to the BTF send port.

2. The BTF assembler processes the message.

3. The BTF assembler checks the `BizTalkMgmtDB.btf_message_sender` database table to see if the message that it is sending has already been acknowledged. If the message hasn't, it wraps the message in a SOAP envelope and adds the BTF headers to that envelope. The assembler will then return the message so that it can be processed. If the message has already been sent or the message has expired, the assembler will return `null`, meaning that it will consume the message. Because the assembler is simply reading the database, the lack of transactional support in the send pipeline does not matter.

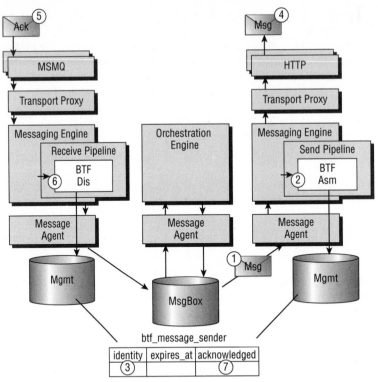

Figure 4-10

4. The message is then sent using the configured transport, assuming that an acknowledgment was not previously received for it.

5. Step 5 assumes that some time has passed and an acknowledgment has been received for the reliable message that was previously sent. The receiver of the message knew where to send the acknowledgment because the sender put a reply to URL in the appropriate SOAP header.

6. The BTF disassembler then processes the acknowledgment. It updates the `BizTalkMgmtDB.btf_ message_sender` database table to indicate that an acknowledgment for the message was received. The disassembler will consume this acknowledgment; there is no need to publish it, because it is purely a protocol communication message and of no business value.

The more observant of you will have figured out that a piece of the puzzle is missing. In order for the reliable protocol to work correctly, the sender must keep sending the message until an acknowledgment has been received. This is at odds with the usual protocol that the Messaging Engine uses, whereby once a message has been successfully sent by an adapter, the engine will delete the message from the application queue. Clearly, if the message has been deleted from the application queue, it cannot be resent. So, to support this scenario, the engine uses the system message context property `BTS.IsReliable` to determine when a reliable message is being sent. If it detects that a reliable message has been successfully sent, instead of deleting the message it will treat it as a regular retry. It uses the retry interval that has been set on the message context to determine when the message will be redelivered to the send port. This is the final piece of the puzzle. By ensuring that the message is resent even if transmission is successful, the sender will keep sending the message until either an acknowledgment is received or the message has expired.

Developing a Custom Pipeline Component

For some scenarios, it's necessary to create your own pipeline components. Sometimes this may mean creating your own component from scratch or creating a wrapper around an existing pipeline component to provide some additional functionality. For example, the BizTalk Swift accelerator has its own disassembler and assembler. Under the covers, these components invoke the BizTalk flat-file disassembler and assembler, layering some additional functionality on top. The disassembler, for example, catches all exceptions and promotes message context properties to enable failed messages to be routed so that they can go to a portal and be repaired. This ability to route failed messages is now provided by the engine in the BizTalk 2006 release, as mentioned earlier in the chapter.

> *This is a very interesting design, and I would encourage you to take a look. The portal allows the badly formatted message to be opened in InfoPath forms, repaired, and then resubmitted to BizTalk to continue its processing.*

If you need to develop a custom pipeline component, the first question to ask yourself should be, "Do my requirements extend any existing pipeline components?" If they do, it's worth considering extending an existing component before jumping in to develop a new component from scratch. There are many advantages to extending the existing components, including reduced time to develop your scenario. In addition, you will be leveraging code that is heavily tested by Microsoft and hence will be of a high quality from both a performance and reliability perspective.

Pipeline components are executed on the server side. There are implications surrounding this that you should be aware of if you are new to server-side development. Chapter 10 discusses some of the considerations about this from a testing perspective. Essentially, server-side code is less forgiving than client-side code; it cannot leak *any* memory, and exception handling should be designed in a way to make the code robust and resilient. Server-side components are typically executed in an asynchronous, multi-threaded environment that introduces a whole raft of associated challenges and is generally much harsher. For example, if you write a pipeline component that opens a database connection (you should do this in a pipeline component only if you really need to), make sure that you proactively close/release that connection as early as you can. You should never rely on the garbage collector to release resources, since for some scenarios it may not be able to keep up; doing so may result in what appear to be memory leaks in the BizTalk process.

That said, the BizTalk pipeline component model does a very good job of keeping the programming model relatively simple, but it is wise to keep in mind the environment where your pipeline component will be executing. Pipeline components are executed on a single thread. While the engine is multi-threaded, pipelines are not shared across threads. At any one time the engine is executing multiple pipelines all on different threads. This simplifies the programming model for pipeline components. However, on the downside (as I discussed earlier), the processing model is stream based, which has implications for the implementation. The programming model is such that the pipeline APIs are executed to *wire* up the pipeline and the messages being processed in it; the stream is then read by the engine, which executes the pipeline component. Of course, if you are not performing streaming processing, you don't need to worry about this; however, you will need to worry about hitting an out-of-memory condition, which will most likely pull the BizTalk Server process down. This stream-based programming model does add a degree of complexity to the pipeline component.

Later in this section, I will cover how to develop a pipeline component. I will walk through the development of a pipeline component that can be used to compress and decompress messages as they exit and enter into BizTalk. As mentioned earlier, trading CPU cycles to compress message data in order to save network bandwidth is a technique that can often be used to increase throughput, though compression cannot be used for all scenarios.

The Core Tenets

When writing pipeline components, it's important to consider the following guidelines:

❑ **Release resources as early as possible** — With .NET, you should try to acquire resources as late as possible and release them as early as possible in order to get the most out of the .NET garbage collector (GC). If you are opening database connections in your pipeline components, make sure that you open them as late as possible and close them as early as possible. Make sure that you always release resources in all failure scenarios. Use the .NET using statement if it is appropriate. For unmanaged resources that need to live for the duration of the pipeline component — perhaps you are accessing a native stream — you should add them to the resource tracker that your pipeline component may fetch from the pipeline context. For these resources your pipeline component does not have any opportunity to release them, because they may only be released once the pipeline has executed. Your pipeline component has no way of understanding when that time is. The engine ensures that all native resources that are added to the resource tracker are released at the appropriate time, which is after the pipeline has been completely executed, regardless of whether it was successful or failed.

❑ **Don't create threads in your pipeline component** — As mentioned previously, the programming model for pipeline components is single-threaded; although multiple threads will each process an individual pipeline, pipelines are not shared across threads. All processing should be performed on the thread that the components' APIs are called on. To date, I've not come across a scenario where it makes sense to create a thread in a pipeline component in order to perform some work. The Messaging Engine is designed and tuned to manage the threadpool that your pipeline component executes on. Under the covers, the engine's threadpool uses an *I/O completion port*, which is a Windows kernel object that ensures that threads are used in an optimal manner. Completion ports achieve this by using a *first in, first out* queue for threads. This helps to ensure that threads run hot, which reduces the number of context switches that occur. This threadpool is not exposed for pipeline components to use; it is intended only for the engine to use. Components that require threads (for example, adapters) should typically use the .NET threadpool. That said, you won't get better performance by creating your own threads in a pipeline component and will most likely have a negative impact on the performance of the engine as a whole.

❑ **Process messages in a streaming manner** — We've discussed this quite a bit already, and soon I'll illustrate a concrete example of how this should be done. In short, you should not load the entire message into memory unless you can guarantee that it will always be small. If you are processing XML documents, you should consider using the .NET XMLReader class, which provides forward-only, read-only, noncached parsing for XML. The XMLReader class uses a similar model to Simple API for XML (SAX) parsers, except that XMLReader uses a pull model, whereas SAX uses a push model, meaning that with SAX you have no control over the reading on the XML because it raises events that you have to respond to. The pull model that the XMLReader uses means that you invoke it; this makes it easier to hook it into the streaming pipeline processing model that BizTalk uses. Essentially, every message read on the message stream would invoke the XMLReader to parse the next section of the document. BizTalk makes extensive use of the XMLReader; for example, the XMLDisassembler uses it. Similarly, for producing or serializing XML the XMLWriter should be used for the same reasons. It may be used for producing forward-only, write-only, noncached XML, which is in line with the BizTalk streaming model.

Many people tend to use the .NET XmlDocument when processing messages in pipeline components. BizTalk 2000 and 2002 used the native version of the DOM in the engine, and as a consequence, the product suffered from a number of issues associated with the processing of large documents. The XmlDocument loads the entire XML document into memory to enable random access to the XML, including the ability to change values of elements and attributes as well as restructure the XML. For small messages this may seem to be fine, and many projects start with a limited scope in which the use of the DOM is acceptable; however, often either the scope increases to include large message processing or the components of that project are shared with another project. Before you know it, you are debugging memory issues. In general, you should try to avoid using the DOM for those reasons. It is also worth noting that the DOM adds a large memory footprint to the message size, which can be in the order of 10X. BizTalk's ability to process large messages using a flat memory model is only as good as the weakest of the components in the processing chain.

❑ **Instrument your code** — BizTalk, like most Microsoft products, uses software-tracing technology internally to instrument the source code. BizTalk actually uses kernel-mode software tracing which provides excellent flexibility. The tracing can be enabled or disabled at runtime, it can be switched on or off at an individual subsystem level, and the verbosity of the trace can be adjusted at runtime. For example, it supports information-, warning-, and error-level trace information. If you have ever raised a BizTalk issue with Microsoft Product Support Services (PSS), during the diagnosis they may have given you instructions to enable software tracing while reproducing your scenario. Software tracing, when done well, is incredibly powerful and saves hours of painful debugging; when done poorly, it's next to useless. To give you an idea of what I would expect from good tracing, consider software tracing in the BizTalk engine code. In previous versions, the tracing was less satisfactory, so at the beginning of the development cycle of BizTalk Server 2004, the development team made the call that we would try to do a great job of tracing. The driving force behind this was to reduce the overhead associated with troubleshooting customer problems. When I was developing the Messaging Engine, every method entry and exit was traced, including various parameters passed that were of interest, for example, message IDs and interchange IDs. Each method would trace any information that was "interesting," for example the branch that a key if/else condition took. A single message in an end-to-end scenario, passing through all pipeline components and orchestrations, would generate around 1MB of formatted data using the highest level of trace. During the development cycle, we troubleshot and fixed a very large percentage of the bugs without ever attaching a debugger. The trace information gave us all the information that we needed to pinpoint the problem. As the team moved through the development process and bugs were found that could not be identified due to insufficient trace, typically as part of fixing the bug, the trace statements were beefed up for next time.

Good software tracing should enable you to follow the flow of execution through your code, and it should identify all of the key decisions that the code made. A common mistake made when tracing server-side code is that no transaction reference is traced. This means that you, effectively, end up with a whole bunch of trace statements and no way of identifying the particular flow of execution through the stack for your problem scenario. This transaction reference differs from scenario to scenario, and it should be something that makes sense for your scenario. If you can't enable your software tracing and get a detailed picture of what your code is doing, then it's probably not good enough. Also, you should take care not to swing too far in the other direction. Only trace those parts of the code that are important and relevant when troubleshooting.

❑ **Minimize the message context promotions** — Every message context property that is promoted needs to be evaluated by the MessageBox. This does not come for free. In general, the cost of promoted properties is relatively flat until the number of properties exceeds 10. After that point, the performance is impacted more. You should only promote properties if you either want them to be used for message routing or want them to be demoted in the send pipeline, that is, you want to move the value of the context property from the context to the message content. If you simply need to set context properties in your pipeline components in order to flow metadata with the message, you should use `IBaseMessageContext.Write` instead of `IBaseMessageContext.Promote`. Alternatively, if you need to access the data in an orchestration, you could write them as distinguished fields; the ArbitraryXPathPropertyHandler sample in the SDK illustrates how to do this.

❑ **Get your transaction from the pipeline context** — As mentioned earlier in the chapter, only the receive pipeline supports transactions. If you need to use transactions in a pipeline component in the receive pipeline because you want the component's work to be atomically committed with the publication of the message, you must get the transaction from the pipeline context. The following example illustrates the correct way to do this:

1. First, the transaction is fetched form the `IPipelineContextEx` interface, which means that you need to cast the `IPipelineContext` interface.

2. You can then get the transaction and cast it to an `ITransaction`.

3. You then need to enlist in the connection in the DTC transaction that you fetched from the pipeline context:

```
public IBaseMessage Execute(IPipelineContext pc, IBaseMessage inmsg) {
    IPipelineContextEx pcx = pc as IPipelineContextEx;

    if (null != pcx) {
        ITransaction txn = (ITransaction)pcx.GetTransaction();

        if(null != txn) {
            using (SqlConnection conn = new SqlConnection(_ConnectionString)) {
                conn.EnlistDistributedTransaction(txn);

                // Do txn work...
            }
        }
    }

    return inmsg;
}
```

At this point, your pipeline component is set up and ready to do its work against the enlisted resource manager.

Creating a Pipeline Component

In this section, I walk you through the creation of a pipeline component. I've chosen a scenario that will help you understand how to implement a streaming pipeline component. There are several pipeline component samples in the BizTalk SDK, and I encourage you to look at those, also. The pipeline component that I have chosen is a compression/decompression component; it will not have any stage affinity — in other words, it can be deployed to any pipeline stage. That said, typically, I would expect it to be used as the first component of a receive pipeline and the last component in a send pipeline, configured to decompress in the receive pipeline and compress in the send pipeline.

The Pipeline Component Wizard

When you create a new pipeline component, there are a number of options available to you: you could write it completely from scratch, you could take one of the SDK samples and modify it to meet your requirements, or you could simply use Martijn Hoogendoorn's Pipeline Component Wizard, which can save you heaps of time.

> *The Pipeline Component Wizard can be downloaded from the following GotDotNet workspace:*
> `http://www.codeplex.com/btsplcw/`.

The Wizard creates all of the boilerplate code that you would normally need to create, and leaves you simply to implement the interesting bits such as how your component will process messages. Once the wizard has been installed, the new Visual Studio template "BizTalk Server Pipeline Component Project" for BizTalk projects will be available, as shown in Figure 4-11. The wizard is self-explanatory, so there is little value in walking through each screen; instead, I want to focus on the implementation of the pipeline component.

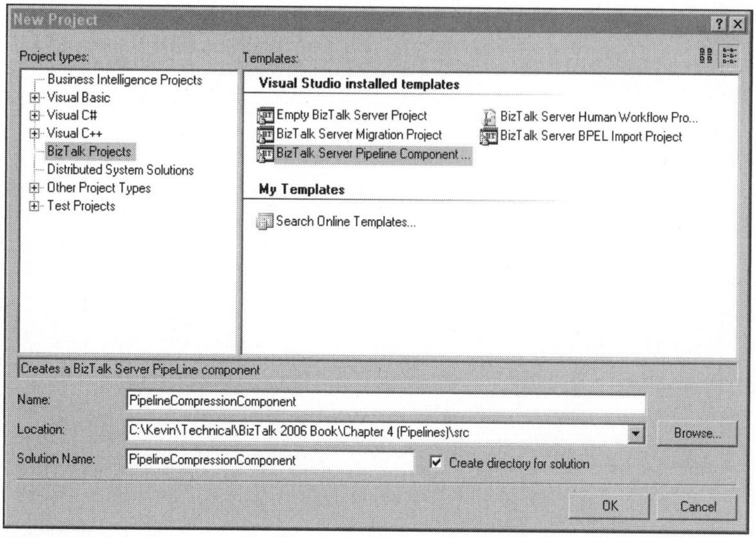

Figure 4-11

Pipeline Interfaces and Attributes

Using the wizard I created a new pipeline component called `PipelineCompressionComponent`. Start off by looking at this class, the attributes it has defined for it, and what interfaces it implements.

```
[ComponentCategory(CategoryTypes.CATID_PipelineComponent)]
[System.Runtime.InteropServices.Guid("d05a2d3d-fa83-4ee8-ac3b-2945ff9e0b8d")]
[ComponentCategory(CategoryTypes.CATID_Any)]
public class PipelineCompressionComponent :
Microsoft.BizTalk.Component.Interop.IComponent, IBaseComponent,
IPersistPropertyBag, IComponentUI
{
  ...
}
```

The first attribute, `CategoryTypes.CATID_PipelineComponent`, is used by the tools. At design time, the tools will enumerate all classes in all assemblies in the `%PROGRAMFILES%\Microsoft BizTalk Server 2006\Pipeline Components` directory. If any of those classes implement this category type, the designer recognizes them as a pipeline component. The next interesting attribute is `CategoryTypes.CATID_Any`. This category type defines what stage the pipeline component may be deployed to, and as the name implies, this component is stage agile, meaning that it may be deployed in any stage. A pipeline component may only be dragged into a stage that is appropriate for its category type. The class implements four interfaces. I want to skip `IComponent` for now (I come back to it shortly) and first discuss `IBaseComponent`. This is really just boilerplate code; the interface is used by the design surface to get the name, version, and description of the pipeline component so that it can be displayed.

```
public interface IBaseComponent
{
  string Name { get; }
  string Version { get; }
  string Description { get; }
}
```

IPersistPropertyBag

The next interface, `IPersistPropertyBag`, is an ActiveX interface designed for the persistent storage of properties, and this is exactly what BizTalk uses it for.

```
public interface IPersistPropertyBag
{
  void GetClassID(out System.Guid classID);
  void InitNew();
  void Load(IPropertyBag propertyBag, int errorLog);
  void Save(IPropertyBag propertyBag, bool clearDirty, bool saveAllProperties);
}
public interface IPropertyBag
{
  void Read(string propName, out object ptrVar, int errorLog);
  void Write(string propName, ref object ptrVar);
}
```

The two methods of interest on this interface are `Save` and `Load`. Pipeline components are created by BizTalk not only at runtime but also at design time. When a BizTalk project uses a pipeline component it is loaded by Visual Studio, the BizTalk design time creates the pipeline component and calls its `IPersistPropertyBag.Load` method, passing the component an `IPropertyBag` that contains the configuration for the component. The pipeline component uses the property bag to set its member variables accordingly. The following code snippet shows the code for my pipeline component, which has two properties. An enumeration (`CompressionMode`) indicates whether it's doing compression or decompression, and another (`CompressionType`) indicates the type of compression to use (GZip or Deflate). The Pipeline Manager also invokes the `Load` method at runtime; it calls this after creating the component in order to initialize it with its configuration prior to being executed.

```
public virtual void Load(IPropertyBag pb, int errlog)
{
  object val = null;
  val = this.ReadPropertyBag(pb, "Compress");
  if ((val != null))
  {
    this.Compress = ((CompressionMode)(val));
  }

  val = this.ReadPropertyBag(pb, "Algorithm");
  if ((val != null))
  {
    this.Algorithm = (CompressionType)val;
  }
}
```

The design time calls the `IPersistPropertyBag.Save` method, passing the pipeline component a property bag. The pipeline component is responsible for writing its configuration into the property bag, which the designer then persists. Both of these methods are used to pass configuration between the component and the designer as the configuration in the designer is changed by the user.

```
public virtual void Save(IPropertyBag pb, bool fClearDirty,
  bool fSaveAllProperties)
{
  this.WritePropertyBag(pb, "Compress", Convert.ToInt32(Compress));
  this.WritePropertyBag(pb, "Algorithm", Convert.ToInt32(Algorithm));
}
```

The BizTalk Pipeline Designer uses reflection to discover the public properties that a pipeline component has, and these properties are displayed in the Pipeline Designer's properties.

IComponentUI

The next interface, `IComponentUI`, has one method, `Validate`, and a property, `Icon`. The `Validate` method is called prior to design time, persisting the configuration in the BizTalk management and SSO databases; this gives the pipeline component an opportunity to validate the configuration that has been set on it. Any errors may be returned as an `IEnumerator`; these errors appear as compile-time errors in Visual Studio. The `Icon` property, not surprisingly, is used to define what icon is used by the designer when displaying the component in the Toolbox.

```
public interface IComponentUI
```

```
{
  IntPtr Icon { get; }
  IEnumerator Validate(object projectSystem);
}
```

IComponent

The last interface that my pipeline component implements is IComponent. It has a single method: Execute.

```
public interface IComponent
{
  IBaseMessage Execute(IPipelineContext pContext, IBaseMessage pInMsg);
}
```

This method is called by the Pipeline Manager at runtime. The following code shows the implementation for the compression/decompression pipeline component. The method takes the input message and returns the output message. As you can see, the code is very straightforward — the method gets the data stream for the body part of the input message, wraps it with either a CompressionStream or DecompressionStream stream, and then replaces the original stream on the message with the new wrapped stream. The original message is returned with a new stream attached to it. One thing to watch out for is how you get the stream from the message part. IBaseMessagePart.Data should typically not be used; this property *may* clone the stream and return the cloned version of the stream. (The stream is not always cloned; the behavior is dependent on the adapter and pipeline components upstream of the pipeline component.) The implication of this is that to clone the stream it needs to be read in its entirety, which breaks the streaming model. This is a common mistake; you should always use the IBaseMessagePart.GetOriginalDataStream method to fetch the orginal stream. Because this pipeline component is marked to be stage agile, and it also supports both compression and decompression, it is flexible in how it can be used.

```
public IBaseMessage Execute(IPipelineContext pc, IBaseMessage inmsg)
{
  Stream oldStream = inmsg.BodyPart.GetOriginalDataStream();
  Stream newStream;

  if (CompressionMode.Compress == _Compress)
  {
    newStream = new CompressionStream(oldStream, _Algorithm);
  }
  else
  {
    newStream = new DecompressionStream(oldStream, _Algorithm);
  }

  inmsg.BodyPart.Data = newStream;

  return inmsg;
}
```

As with many pipeline components, the clever bits for this one are actually in the stream implementation and not the pipeline component as such.

Compression Stream Implementation

The compressor pipeline component needs to compress data in a streaming fashion. To facilitate this, .NET 2.0 ships with two new classes that can be used for compressing and decompressing streams: GZipStream and DeflateStream, to support the GZip and Deflate algorithms, respectively. The constructor for both of these classes takes a stream; when using the classes for compression, this is the stream that the compressed data is written to when Stream.Write is called on the GZipStream or DeflateStream class.

For my pipeline component, I need a stream that wraps the BizTalk message data stream and processes it in a streaming manner to either compress or decompress the data. This stream wrapper must be able to keep a flat memory model regardless of whether it is compressing 3KB or 3GB. The programming model that the GZipStream and DeflateStream class use means that the compressed data must be written to a stream. You could read the uncompressed data in its entirety and write it into a virtual stream; this would keep a flat memory model, since the virtual stream spills over to disk. (Don't worry if you are unfamiliar with the virtual stream concept. I will cover it later in the chapter.) But this would not really be in the spirit of the pipeline design and would cause the data for every Stream.Read to be copied to disk for large messages; messages whose size is less than the large message threshold would be loaded entirely into memory. The virtual stream should really be your last resort when you need your large streams to be seekable and should not be used as an easy way out. So instead, I've implemented my own stream. Figure 4-12 illustrates the design for this compression stream.

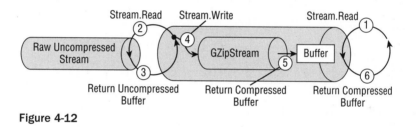

Figure 4-12

You'll take a look at the code shortly, but here's how the compression stream works:

1. A consumer of the CompressionStream calls Stream.Read.

2. The CompressionStream in turn calls Stream.Read on the underlying uncompressed stream, which it has a reference to.

3. The underlying uncompressed stream returns the buffer of uncompressed data.

4. The CompressionStream calls Stream.Write on the GZipStream in order to compress the data.

5. The CompressionStream was created, passing in a reference to itself to the GZipStream. This means that when the Write method is called on the GZipStream stream, the Write method is called on the CompressionStream. The CompressionStream implementation of Write copies the buffer containing the compressed data to its own internal buffer.

6. The CompressionStream's internal buffer is copied to the buffer passed on its Read and then returned.

This implementation means that the CompressionStream has control over how much data it holds in memory, which it does using a buffer. Data flowing through this stream is streamed and not bulk loaded.

This approach is more in line with how the BizTalk pipeline components that ship out of the box are implemented. In addition, the CompressionStream can provide some other capabilities, such as the ability to use either the GZip or the Deflate algorithm. The following code illustrates the implementation for the CompressionStream class.

The constructor takes the input stream and an enumeration to tell it which compression algorithm to use; this will ultimately be configured through the pipeline component. For the purposes of this walk-through, assume that you use the GZipStream. You should note that when you create GZipStream, you pass in this as the target stream. It will be clear why you do this shortly. This is a forward-only stream, so properties such as CanSeek, Length, and Position always return false.

```
namespace BizTalk.PipelineComponents.Compression
{

    public enum CompressionType { GZip = 0, Deflate = 1 }

    public class CompressionStream : Stream {
        private const int tempBuffSz = 4096;
        private List<byte> compressedBuffer = new List<byte>();
        private byte[] tempBuff = new byte[tempBuffSz];
        private bool streamClosed = false;
        private Stream rawStream;
        private Stream compressedStream;

        public CompressionStream(Stream s, CompressionType compressionType) {
            this.rawStream = s;
            if (compressionType == CompressionType.GZip) {
                this.compressedStream = new GZipStream(this,
                    CompressionMode.Compress, true);
            }
            else if (compressionType == CompressionType.Deflate) {
                this.compressedStream = new DeflateStream(this,
                    CompressionMode.Compress, true);
            }
            else {
                throw new ArgumentException("Invalid compression type");
            }
        }

        public override bool CanRead { get { return true; } }

        public override bool CanSeek { get { return false; } }

        public override bool CanWrite { get { return true; } }

        public override void Flush() { this.compressedStream.Flush();}

        public override long Length {
            get { throw new NotSupportedException("Length"); }
        }

        public override long Position {
            get {
                throw new NotSupportedException("Position");
```

```
        }
        set {
            throw new NotSupportedException("Position");
        }
    }

    public override int Read(byte[] buffer, int offset, int count) {
        ArgumentValidation.CheckForNullReference(buffer, "buffer");

        int rawRead = 0;
        int bytesReturned = 0;

        if (this.compressedBuffer.Count == 0 && !this.streamClosed) {
            if(this.tempBuff.Length < count) {
                this.tempBuff = new byte[count];
            }

            rawRead = this.rawStream.Read(this.tempBuff, 0,
                this.tempBuff.Length);

            if (rawRead > 0) {
                this.compressedStream.Write(this.tempBuff, 0, rawRead);
            }
            if (0 == rawRead || this.compressedBuffer.Count == 0) {
                this.compressedStream.Close();
                this.streamClosed = true;
            }
        }

        if (this.compressedBuffer.Count > 0) {
            bytesReturned = (count < this.compressedBuffer.Count) ? count :
                this.compressedBuffer.Count;

            this.compressedBuffer.CopyTo(0, buffer, offset, bytesReturned);
            this.compressedBuffer.RemoveRange(0, bytesReturned);
        }

        return bytesReturned;
    }

    public override long Seek(long offset, SeekOrigin origin) {
        throw new NotSupportedException("Seek");
    }

    public override void SetLength(long value) {
        throw new NotSupportedException("SetLength");
    }

    public override void Write(byte[] buffer, int offset, int count) {
        ArgumentValidation.CheckForNullReference(buffer, "buffer");

        byte[] buff = new byte[count];
        Buffer.BlockCopy(buffer, offset, buff, 0, count);
        this.compressedBuffer.AddRange(buff);
    }
```

```
override public void Close(){
    if (this.rawStream != null) {
        this.rawStream.Close();
        this.rawStream = null;
    }

    if (this.compressedStream != null) {
        this.compressedStream.Close();
        this.compressedStream = null;
    }
  }
 }
}
```

The first interesting method is Read. In this example, Read is called from the next upstream pipeline component and ultimately driven by the engine. You first check that you were passed a non-null buffer, since if you get a null reference exception, you want to know why. Next, Read is called on the underlying stream that you are compressing to get a buffer of data to compress. If you get back some data, you pass it to the Write method on the GZipStream. This causes it to compress the data. Now, remember you passed this as the target stream; what happens next is that the GZipStream invokes the Write method on the CompressionStream class, passing in the data that it has compressed.

The Write method creates a byte[] buffer to hold the compressed data that was passed into it. It copies the data passed into the method to the new buffer. This buffer is then added to a generic byte list, which is a member variable of the class. The generic byte list is an internal buffer that is used to decouple the client of the CompressionStream class from the underlying compression stream. At this point, the call to Write returns to the Read implementation. The amount of data that the client requested is then copied from the generic byte list to the buffer that the caller passed in. The amount of data that was written is then returned. The last call to Read will cause Close to be called on the GZipStream, which causes a last write to be called, as GZipStream writes the remainder of the compressed data.

Decompression Stream Implementation

The DecompressionStream is a lot simpler. You still need to implement your own stream, but for the most part, the Stream methods simply pass through to the GZipStream. The stream containing the compressed data is passed into the constructor, which is, in turn, passed to the constructor of the GZipStream. A Read on the DecompressionStream, in turn, causes a Read on the GZipStream, which, under the covers, calls Read on the stream containing the compressed data. The constructor also enables selection of which compression method, or in this case decompression algorithm, to use. As before, the stream is a forward-only stream, which is reflected in properties such as CanSeek. Figure 4-13 illustrates the wiring-up of the streams.

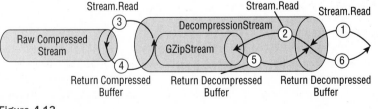

Figure 4-13

The following code shows the implementation for the DecompressionStream. As you can see, the class is very simple.

```
namespace BizTalk.PipelineComponents.Compression
{
    public class DecompressionStream : Stream
    {
        Stream decompressionStream;

        public DecompressionStream(Stream s) {
            decompressionStream = new GZipStream(
                s, CompressionMode.Decompress, true); }

        public DecompressionStream(Stream s, CompressionType compressionType) {
            if (compressionType == CompressionType.GZip) {
                decompressionStream = new GZipStream(
                    s, CompressionMode.Decompress, true); }
            else if (compressionType == CompressionType.Deflate) {
                decompressionStream = new DeflateStream(
                    s, CompressionMode.Decompress, true); }
        }

        public override void Flush() { throw new NotSupportedException("Flush"); }

        public override long Seek(long offset, SeekOrigin origin) {
            throw new NotSupportedException("Flush"); }

        public override void SetLength(long value) {
            throw new NotSupportedException("Flush"); }

        public override int Read(byte[] buffer, int offset, int count) {
            return decompressionStream.Read(buffer, offset, count);
        }

        public override void Write(byte[] buffer, int offset, int count) {
            throw new NotImplementedException();}

        public override bool CanRead { get { return true; } }
        public override bool CanSeek { get { return false; } }
        public override bool CanWrite { get { return false; } }

        public override long Length {
            get { throw new NotSupportedException("Length"); } }

        public override long Position {
            get { throw new NotSupportedException("Position"); }
            set { throw new NotSupportedException("Position"); } }
    }
```

This section has illustrated how to create a custom pipeline component and how it should be written in order to process messages in a forward-only streaming fashion that will be good citizens in the BizTalk runtime. Hopefully, this has demystified the process and illustrated that it is actually reasonably straightforward to write custom pipeline components that will be able to handle messages regardless of their size.

Assemblers and Disassemblers

The two main interfaces that I have not discussed so far are IDisassemblerComponent and IAssemblerComponent, and both of these interfaces are slightly more complicated in that they support multiple messages moving into or out of the component, respectively.

If you recall, the execution mode of the Disassemble pipeline stage is by default set to FirstMatch. This, of course, implies that disassemblers typically implement the IProbeMessage interface so that they are given the opportunity to determine whether they recognize the message. I will discuss the MarkableForwardOnlyEventingReadStream shortly, which will give you some insight into how you implement Probe when using forward-only streaming.

IDisassemblerComponent implements two methods, as can be seen in the following code. The Pipeline Manager first calls the Disassemble method, passing the pipeline context and the message to disassemble. Next, the GetNext method is called, which should return a message if there is one to return. Otherwise, a return value of null signifies that all of the messages have been disassembled from the input message. Each time the engine calls the GetNext method it reads the stream for all message parts, as has been described previously. When Stream.Read returns zero bytes the engine will again call GetNext to fetch the next message. This cycle repeats until GetNext returns null.

```
public interface IDisassemblerComponent
{
  void Disassemble(IPipelineContext pContext, IBaseMessage pInMsg);
  IBaseMessage GetNext(IPipelineContext pContext);
}
```

Assemblers should implement the IAssemblerComponent interface, which is essentially the reverse of the IDisassemblerComponent interface. At runtime, the engine first calls the AddDocument method. This is called one or more times, adding messages that need to be assembled. Once all of the messages have been added, the engine then calls the Assemble method, which returns the new message. By now, it should be pretty clear what happens next — the engine then enumerates all of the message parts and reads the streams for all of those. This, in turn, drives the assembly of the messages. If you recall, the streaming process on the send side is driven by the adapter. So it is the adapter that will be reading the stream and ultimately driving the assembly of the messages.

```
public interface IAssemblerComponent
{
  void AddDocument(IPipelineContext pContext, IBaseMessage pInMsg);
  IBaseMessage Assemble(IPipelineContext pContext);
}
```

BizTalk Stream Implementations

The use of streams in pipeline components is clearly very important; having seen an example stream implementation, you will no doubt find it interesting to learn about some of the stream implementations that you may be able to reuse.

When you are writing pipeline components for BizTalk, there are often scenarios when a component needs to know when its stream is read or to be informed before the first or after the last read is invoked on it. For example, the BizTalk party resolution pipeline component needs to read the SignatureCertificate from the message context; however, this property will be written to the message context in a nondeterministic manner; an upstream pipeline component may need to completely consume the message data before it can write this message context property. In this scenario, the party resolution waits for the last stream read event to take place. Once that event has fired, it is guaranteed that the property will have been written if it exists.

To facilitate this and many other scenarios, under the hood BizTalk implements and uses a number of wrapper streams. These streams are packaged in the `Microsoft.BizTalk.Streaming.dll` assembly. I'm not going to discuss all of the streams implemented in this assembly, but there are two or three that are particularly interesting and worth discussing, since they'll give you ideas about how you can solve similar problems.

EventingReadStream

The first stream is the `EventingReadStream` abstract class. This enables you to receive events, as in the preceding party resolution scenario. The following code illustrates how the input stream can be wrapped using the `CForwardOnlyEventingReadStream` class. The events are triggered as appropriate when the stream is read.

```
using Microsoft.BizTalk.Streaming;

public IBaseMessage Execute(IPipelineContext pc, IBaseMessage inmsg)
{
  Stream data = inmsg.BodyPart.GetOriginalDataStream();
  CForwardOnlyEventingReadStream fes = new CForwardOnlyEventingReadStream(data);
  fes.AfterLastReadEvent += new AfterLastReadEventHandler(OnLastRead);
  fes.BeforeFirstReadEvent += new BeforeFirstReadEventHandler(OnFirstRead);
  fes.ReadEvent += new ReadEventHandler(OnRead);

  inmsg.BodyPart.Data = fes;

  return inmsg;
}

private static void OnFirstRead(object src, EventArgs args)
{
  // Handle event...
}

private static void OnRead(object src, EventArgs args)
{
  ReadEventArgs rea = args as ReadEventArgs;
  // Handle event...
}

private static void OnLastRead(object src, EventArgs args)
{
  // Handle event...
}
```

MarkableForwardOnlyEventingReadStream

The MarkableForwardOnlyEventingReadStream is a useful stream if you are writing *probing* components, that is, components that implement the IProbeMessage interface. In order to support probing in a forward-only manner, you need the ability to read the beginning of the message data stream and then set the position of the stream back to the beginning so that you can parse the data for real. Multiple components must have the ability to probe the message, so this means reading the beginning of the message multiple times. MarkableForwardOnlyEventingReadStream enables this scenario. The following code snippet illustrates the calling of this stream. First, the stream is used to wrap the raw message stream. Next, the position that the stream is currently in, is *marked*. The following example reads the first 64 bytes of the message. This is enough of the message to determine whether the component recognizes the data. After the stream has been read, the position of the stream is reset to the position where it was previously marked.

```
MarkableForwardOnlyEventingReadStream mes = new
  MarkableForwardOnlyEventingReadStream(rawStream);

byte[] buffer = new byte[1024];

mes.MarkPosition();
int read = mes.Read(buffer, 0, 64);
WriteDataToConsole(buffer, 0, read);

Console.WriteLine("### MarkableForwardOnlyEventingReadStream.ResetPosition ###");
mes.ResetPosition();
WriteStreamToConsole(mes);
```

The output from the preceding code is illustrated in the following block. As you can see, the first 64 bytes are written, and then once the position of the stream has been reset, the entire stream is written, including the 64 bytes that were previously written. The MarkableForwardOnlyEventingReadStream stream achieves this by copying the data read from the wrapped stream while the stream is marked to a buffer. When the stream position is reset, the data stored in the buffer will be read until the buffer is emptied, at which point the wrapped stream is read and its data returned.

```
<ns0:CBRInputRecord xmlns:ns0="http://CBR.CBRInputSchema">
  <I
### MarkableForwardOnlyEventingReadStream.ResetPosition ###
<ns0:CBRInputRecord xmlns:ns0="http://CBR.CBRInputSchema">
  <Identity>
    <UserID>UserID_0</UserID>
    <LastName>LastName_0</LastName>
    <FirstName>FirstName_0</FirstName>
    <Initial>Initial_0</Initial>
  </Identity>
</ns0:CBRInputRecord>
```

The IProbeMessage interface is very simple and has a single method. The following code illustrates an implementation of Probe using the MarkableForwardOnlyEventingReadStream. The buffer of data read from the stream is passed to a helper method, CanRecognizeData, that parses that fragment of data to determine whether it understands the data. The position of the stream is reset before the method returns.

```
public bool Probe(IPipelineContext pContext, IBaseMessage pInMsg)
{
  MarkableForwardOnlyEventingReadStream mes = null;

  mes =
  new MarkableForwardOnlyEventingReadStream(
    pInMsg.BodyPart.GetOriginalDataStream());
  mes.MarkPosition();

  byte[] buffer = new byte[64];
  int read = mes.Read(buffer, 0, 64);
  mes.ResetPosition();

  return CanRecognizeData(buffer, 0, read);
}
```

Virtual Stream — When You Can't Use Forward-Only Streaming

There are scenarios where you can't adopt a forward-only streaming model. For example, decoding an SMIME-encoded message typically means that the entire message must be read in order to decode it. If the message is only 100KB, this is probably not a problem, but what about if the message is 100MB? You wouldn't want to load all of that data into your process address space, because of the risk of pulling the process down. There are many such scenarios, and they are not always restricted to pipeline processing. For example, when executing XSL transforms over large messages, by default the entire message needs to be loaded into memory. BizTalk 2004 used the XslTransform class to transform messages; under the hood this loads the message into an XPathDocument, which holds the message in memory. This clearly has implications for mapping large messages.

Another scenario when forward-only streaming cannot be used is when processing the response message for a solicit-response HTTP adapter. The processing of this message could fail in the receive pipeline.

Failure while processing the response of a large message that is processed in a forward-only streaming manner presents challenges. First, since it is a response, there is no way to inform the Web server that an error has occurred due to the way the HTTP protocol works. This means that the response needs to be suspended by BizTalk to avoid a data-loss scenario; however, since the message was processed using forward-only streaming, much of the data may have already been consumed. And since the stream is not seekable, there is no way to get this data back. What is needed is a mechanism to read the entire stream from the adapter, using a flat memory model, and to provide the ability to seek the stream in the event of a failure scenario.

For these scenarios BizTalk has the concept of a *virtual stream*, also sometimes referred to as a *scalable stream*. The concept is relatively simple — the stream is treated as a MemoryStream until the amount of data that has been written into it exceeds a given threshold; the threshold is configurable, but typically 1MB is a reasonable value. When the amount of data in the stream exceeds the threshold, the virtual stream spills the data over to a temporary disk file. Since the storage for the stream is on the disk, the stream is seekable; it also means that the data is not held in memory. Instead, each `Stream.Write` causes the data to be written to the file stream. The virtual stream concept is quite simple yet extremely useful for a number of scenarios.

There is, of course, a a small performance hit once the stream changes to persistence mode. The virtual stream is packaged in the `Microsoft.BizTalk.Streaming.dll` assembly. The type is `Microsoft.BizTalk.Streaming.VirtualStream`, and you can use the `VirtualStream` in your pipeline components and adapters if your streams need to be seekable. Alternatively, there is also a virtual stream implemented in the SDK: `%PROGRAMFILES%\Microsoft BizTalk Server 2006\SDK\Samples\Pipelines\ArbitraryXPathPropertyHandler\VirtualStream.cs`.

> *Unfortunately, at the time of writing, the virtual stream implementation in the SDK has a couple of bugs in the* `SetLength` *and* `Write` *methods. For these methods the last statements,* `wrappedStream.SetLength(length)` *and* `wrappedStream.Write(buffer, offset, count)`, *respectively, should both be in* `else` *blocks corresponding to their previous* `if` *blocks.*

You may be interested to know that the 2006 release of BizTalk introduces the `ScalableXPathDocument` class, which is used to get around the need to load the entire document into memory when executing an XSL transformation. This class also uses the virtual stream concept though in a slightly more complex form. The `ScalableXPathDocument` implements the `IXPathNavigable` interface. The `IXPathNavigable.CreateNavigator` method, however, returns a `ScalableXPathNavigator` class, which derives from the standard .NET `XPathNavigator` class. This class implements the virtual stream concept to enable BizTalk to execute XSL transforms over large messages by buffering the data to disk.

Testing a Pipeline/Pipeline Components

Chapter 8 covers testing in detail. That said, sometimes the development cycle for pipeline components and schemas can be quite iterative; deploying and testing these changes can take longer than is desirable when rapidly iterating on the code. In other scenarios, you may need more agility around the process of testing your pipelines, pipeline components, schemas, and input messages. In fact, ideally, you may want to have unit tests for these artifacts that the development team can execute prior to checking source code into the source repository, without the need to deploy the BizTalk solution. In those scenarios, the BizTalk SDK ships with a very useful command-line utility, `Pipeline.exe`, that may be used to test pipelines outside of BizTalk (you should note that this is only a simulator).

> *The utility is located at* `%PROGRAMFILES%\Microsoft BizTalk Server 2006\SDK\Utilities\PipelineTools\Pipeline.exe`.

`Pipeline.exe` can be used to execute the uncompiled pipeline file (.BTP) or the compiled .NET assembly. The utility can also be used to show the output message(s) from the pipeline as well as the message context properties for the message(s) that are produced by the pipeline. From this, you can also see if the properties are promoted. Figure 4-14 illustrates the utility.

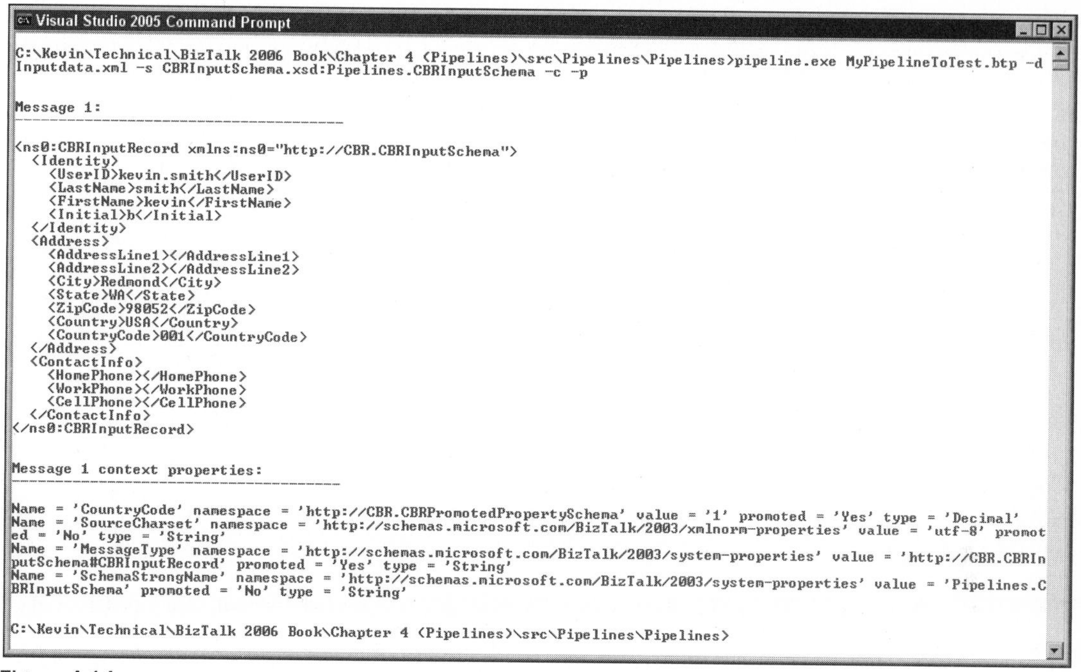

Figure 4-14

Summary

This chapter has given you some insight into the role that pipelines play in BizTalk, how they may be customized, and how BizTalk processes data under the hood. Understanding the processing model that BizTalk uses will help you to exploit the architecture to its fullest. It will also help you to avoid some of the pitfalls that are present, such as those that occur when you are disassembling very large message interchanges. Pipelines provide a powerful and extensible programming model that may be exploited to support myriad scenarios. They use stream-based processing, which is fundamental to the BizTalk architecture. From adapters to the Messaging Engine to the MessageBox to the Orchestration Engine, understanding the stream-based processing model will help you to develop more robust and scalable components for BizTalk.

5

Orchestrations

As you've already seen in Chapter 3, using BizTalk Server to implement content-based routing solutions is relatively straightforward. Routing messages based on the content within those messages is often the first step toward solving a business problem, but often a business process will need to be followed to determine how messages will be processed.

BizTalk orchestration enables you to graphically design business processes using a sequence diagram metaphor instead of the conventional approach of writing extensive amounts of source code. This sequence metaphor means that a business process may graphically illustrate a business process, thereby providing a representation of the business process that is easier to understand than code.

The business process is expressed graphically through BizTalk orchestration as a number of shapes, each performing specific operations such as send, receive, executing business rules, branching, looping, sequential processing, and correlation. Coding a business process in this abstracted way greatly removes the amount of plumbing code required to implement a business process. In short, you can concentrate on solving the business problem rather than on technical implementation.

The Orchestration Execution Environment

This section covers the environment that underpins BizTalk orchestration and details the many features that are required to enable business processes to be expressed and executed within BizTalk.

We'll start with covering how BizTalk orchestrations are implemented under the covers and detail how they are activated and versioned. We'll also cover persistence points, which you must understand to create BizTalk orchestrations that perform and scale well.

After covering these fundamentals, we'll cover orchestration development in more detail.

Implementation

In this section, we'll detail how BizTalk orchestrations are actually implemented under the covers. Although this is completely transparent to a solution developer, it's often important to understand how things work under the covers to enable effective debugging.

Although not essential, it is useful to understand how orchestrations are compiled and subsequently executed at runtime. When designing your BizTalk orchestration using the Orchestration Designer, each orchestration will have an associated ODX file. This file represents the shapes in the orchestration and their associated configuration, including any code that has been written in expression shapes. The collection of these defines the orchestration.

The ODX file contains both XML and a language that, on first sight, looks like C# but is in fact a private BizTalk language called X#. Interestingly, both the XML and X# represent the orchestration and either can be generated from the other.

You might be wondering why the ODX file contains two definitions of the orchestration in two separate formats, XML and X#. You can think of this in terms of the runtime and design-time requirements of the orchestration. The XML representation is used by the Orchestration Designer. Being XML, it is easy for the designer and other tools to parse and update as the user creates and modifies the orchestration.

After the orchestration has been designed, it needs to be executed at runtime. The toolset enables you to compile it into a .NET assembly and deploy it. The X# representation is used during this compilation process. It is this .NET assembly that represents the orchestration, and this assembly that is executed at runtime.

> Prior to BizTalk Server 2004, orchestrations were interpreted at runtime instead of being compiled, as they are today. In many scenarios, this resulted in less than ideal performance, leading many customers requiring high performance not to utilize BizTalk orchestrations.
>
> This move to compiled orchestrations in BizTalk Server 2004, and subsequently 2006, provided significant performance improvements for orchestrations when compared with BizTalk 2000 and 2002-based orchestrations.

Let's take a look at the XML representation first. The following XML shows a fragment of an orchestration designed using the Orchestration Designer and depicts the XML to represent the orchestration shown in Figure 5-1.

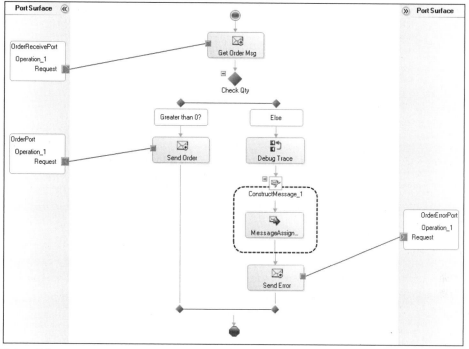

Figure 5-1

As you can see, a `Decision` element is used to represent the Decision shape. Each branch within the Decision shape is represented as a `DecisionBranch` and so on. The key elements of the XML fragment are highlighted in bold.

```
<om:Element Type="Receive" OID="AAD1B9C7-3572-343D-A7D8-99D10E80BD22"
ParentLink="ServiceBody_Statement" LowerBound="1.1" HigherBound="100.1">
  <om:Property Name="Activate" Value="True" />
  <om:Property Name="MessageName" Value="OrderMessage" />
  <om:Property Name="PortName" Value="OrderReceivePort" />
  <om:Property Name="OperationName" Value="Operation_1" />
  <om:Property Name="OperationMessageName" Value="Request" />
  <om:Property Name="Name" Value="Receive_1" />
  <om:Property Name="Signal" Value="True" />
</om:Element>
<om:Element Type="Decision" OID="76D618E4-5B99-34B0-8E58-EA1D5062C3F1"
ParentLink="ServiceBody_Statement" LowerBound="1.1" HigherBound="100.1">
  <om:Property Name="Name" Value="Decision_1" />
  <om:Property Name="Signal" Value="False" />
  <om:Element Type="DecisionBranch" OID="A516D08D-CB0D-35A3-BE43-F73038727F98"
ParentLink="ReallyComplexStatement_Branch" LowerBound="1.1" HigherBound="100.1">
    <om:Property Name="Expression" Value="OrderMessage.Qty&gt;0" />
    <om:Property Name="IsGhostBranch" Value="True" />
    <om:Property Name="Name" Value="Rule_1" />
    <om:Property Name="Signal" Value="True" />
```

```
      <om:Element Type="Send" OID="ECE0FB0D-33B5-3F91-94DF-BBCE04C0F95E"
ParentLink="ComplexStatement_Statement" LowerBound="1.1" HigherBound="100.1">
        <om:Property Name="MessageName" Value="OrderMessage" />
        <om:Property Name="PortName" Value="OrderPort" />
        <om:Property Name="OperationName" Value="Operation_1" />
        <om:Property Name="OperationMessageName" Value="Request" />
        <om:Property Name="Name" Value="Send_1" />
        <om:Property Name="Signal" Value="True" />
      </om:Element>
    </om:Element>
    <om:Element Type="DecisionBranch" OID="F3E5B92C-83EC-3913-950D-1A6706D4E05B"
ParentLink="ReallyComplexStatement_Branch" LowerBound="1.1" HigherBound="100.1">
      <om:Property Name="IsGhostBranch" Value="True" />
      <om:Property Name="Name" Value="Else" />
      <om:Property Name="Signal" Value="False" />
      <om:Element Type="VariableAssignment" OID="4063EC12-AD39-3D44-A95C-37F977B83165"
ParentLink="ComplexStatement_Statement" LowerBound="1.1" HigherBound="100.1">
        <om:Property Name="Expression" Value="System.Diagnostics.Trace.WriteLine
(&quot;An error occurred&quot;);&#xD;&#xA;" />
        <om:Property Name="Name" Value="Expression_1" />
        <om:Property Name="Signal" Value="True" />
      </om:Element>
      <om:Element Type="Construct" OID="4C1DB720-CC04-346A-937F-6ED43E8268A8"
ParentLink="ComplexStatement_Statement" LowerBound="1.1" HigherBound="100.1">
        <om:Property Name="Name" Value="ConstructMessage_1" />
        <om:Property Name="Signal" Value="True" />
        <om:Element Type="MessageRef" OID="D520A860-D487-3740-9D49-034382403D55"
ParentLink="Construct_MessageRef" LowerBound="1.1" HigherBound="100.1">
    <om:Property Name="Ref" Value="ErrorMessage" />
    <om:Property Name="Signal" Value="False" />
        </om:Element>
        <om:Element Type="MessageAssignment" OID="F7983B77-7A01-3DEE-98AB-C0E0496C0CE6"
ParentLink="ComplexStatement_Statement" LowerBound="1.1" HigherBound="100.1">
    <om:Property Name="Expression" Value="ErrorMessage =
OrchestrationHelper.MessageConstruction.ConstructErrorMessage(&quot;Quantity is
invalid&quot;, OrderMessage.OrderReference);&#xD;&#xA;" />
    <om:Property Name="Name" Value="MessageAssignment_1" />
    <om:Property Name="Signal" Value="True" />
        </om:Element>
      </om:Element>
      <om:Element Type="Send" OID="8920BC21-1960-3FC8-93E1-C11981954EEB"
ParentLink="ComplexStatement_Statement" LowerBound="1.1" HigherBound="100.1">
        <om:Property Name="MessageName" Value="ErrorMessage" />
        <om:Property Name="PortName" Value="OrderErrorPort" />
        <om:Property Name="OperationName" Value="Operation_1" />
        <om:Property Name="OperationMessageName" Value="Request" />
        <om:Property Name="Name" Value="Send_2" />
        <om:Property Name="Signal" Value="True" />
      </om:Element>
    </om:Element>
  </om:Element>
</om:Element>
```

As mentioned, the X# looks and feels like C# but is missing some common features, such as looping constructs (`for`, `while`). This quickly becomes apparent when using the Expression shape in a BizTalk solution.

This might seem limiting but in fact encourages you to define such looping constructs using orchestration shapes from the Toolbox in the Orchestration Designer. This is intended to enable the higher-level abstraction of business processes. Code that requires more complex logic may be written in a .NET assembly and invoked from an Expression shape. Trying to express very complex logic in an orchestration is typically not appropriate and usually leads to a very large and verbose orchestration, making it hard to read, understand, and maintain.

The following code snippet shows the X# code for the orchestration shown in Figure 5-1. This X# is syntactically identical to the XML definition of the orchestration; both fully represent the orchestration. In fact, during the development process of BizTalk 2004, the Orchestration Engine development and test teams wrote orchestrations for many test scenarios in raw X# before the Orchestration Designer was ready and fit for use. That said, you should, of course, understand that Microsoft does not support the development of orchestrations by writing raw X#, though you can have some fun with it!

```
[Microsoft.XLANGs.BaseTypes.BPELExportable(false)]
module SampleOrcProject
{
  internal porttype OrderPortType
  {
    oneway Operation_1
    {
      Order
    };
  };
  internal porttype OrderReceivePortType
  {
    oneway Operation_1
    {
      Order
    };
  };
  internal porttype OrderErrorPortType
  {
    oneway Operation_1
    {
      Error
    };
  };
  [Microsoft.XLANGs.BaseTypes.BPELExportable(false)]
  internal service BizTalk_Orchestration1
  {
    [Microsoft.XLANGs.BaseTypes.LogicalBinding()]
    port uses OrderPortType OrderPort;
    [Microsoft.XLANGs.BaseTypes.LogicalBinding()]
    port implements OrderReceivePortType OrderReceivePort;
    [Microsoft.XLANGs.BaseTypes.LogicalBinding()]
    port uses OrderErrorPortType OrderErrorPort;
    message Order OrderMessage;
    message Error ErrorMessage;
    body ()
    {
      [Microsoft.XLANGs.BaseTypes.DesignerPosition(
        "875d4b97-bb55-4154-950d-162276c7cd86")]
```

```
activate receive (OrderReceivePort.Operation_1, OrderMessage);
[Microsoft.XLANGs.BaseTypes.DesignerPosition(
  "73926b3c-b0e2-4b95-979f-d886db03a338")]
if (OrderMessage.Qty > 0)
{
  [Microsoft.XLANGs.BaseTypes.DesignerPosition(
    "763ddbbf-a364-4f19-8506-9e9bf3c78db1")]
  send (OrderPort.Operation_1, OrderMessage);
}
else
{
  [Microsoft.XLANGs.BaseTypes.DesignerPosition(
    "33e54d68-8571-4e29-bccd-f329bf998780")]
  System.Diagnostics.Trace.WriteLine("An error occurred");
  [Microsoft.XLANGs.BaseTypes.DesignerPosition(
    "a85d7e9f-4bed-4f4d-b50d-d32e2072190e")]
  construct ErrorMessage
  {
    [Microsoft.XLANGs.BaseTypes.DesignerPosition(
      "68f337cc-10ed-484f-b72c-773dc7445fe2")]
    ErrorMessage =
      OrchestrationHelper.MessageConstruction.ConstructErrorMessage(
      "Quantity is invalid",OrderMessage.OrderReference);
  }
  [Microsoft.XLANGs.BaseTypes.DesignerPosition(
    "707ef593-4c48-429c-bba7-014ea8c87397")]
  send (OrderErrorPort.Operation_1, ErrorMessage);
  }
 }
}
}
```

The preceding X# can, in fact, be used to generate the XML for the ODX. This can be done by executing the following command, which will generate DemoOrch.ODX by using the token parser in the XSharp compiler tool:

```
XSharpP -dump -tokenparse demoOrch.xs /outd:. /outf: DemoOrch
```

Similarly, you can delete the X# code from the bottom on an ODX. The Orchestration Designer will generate the X# from the XML in the ODX when you save and compile the ODX.

As mentioned, the X# code is used during the compilation process to ultimately generate an MSIL assembly that is deployed and executed at runtime. The BizTalk X# compiler, XSharpP.exe, translates the X# into C# code. This C# is then compiled down to MSIL using the .NET C# compiler, and it is this assembly that is executed at runtime. In fact, all BizTalk artifacts are embedded into C# code, which is then compiled into .NET assemblies and subsequently deployed (the assembly being the unit of deployment offering versioning and security).

The C# code can be viewed as effectively scripting the XLANG runtime engine to take advantage of the services that it exposes. These services enable the rich programming semantics that orchestrations enable, such as persistence and correlation. The XLANG engine, in turn, scripts the Message Agent APIs that are responsible for managing the persistence of service instances (i.e., orchestrations) in a transitionally consistent manner.

In BizTalk 2004, the C# code was deleted automatically after compilation. The following Registry key allowed the user to keep the generated C# source files:

```
HKCU\Software\Microsoft\VisualStudio\7.1\BizTalkProject\GenerateCSFiles=1
(GenerateCSFiles is a DWORD)
```

In BizTalk 2006, the following Registry key can be used to generate the C# source for the release builds:

```
HKCU\Software\Microsoft\VisualStudio\8.0\BizTalkProject\GenerateCSFiles=1
(GenerateCSFiles is a DWORD)
```

Setting the `Generate Debugging Information = True` property by right-clicking on the project in Visual Studio and selecting Properties ➪ Configuration Properties ➪ Build will ensure that the C# files are created for debug builds in BizTalk 2006. These C# files will be saved to the same directory as their associated ODX files and are named `<YourOrchestrationName>.odx.cs`.

The generated C# code contains a number of classes, which are derived from the following classes: `ServiceContext`, `ExceptionHandlingContext`, `AtomicTransactionContext`, or `LongRunningTransactionContext`.

Each of these corresponds to a scope or the entire service instance. (BizTalk refers to orchestration types as *services* and instances of orchestrations as *service instances*; you will notice that the tools refer to orchestrations as service instances.) At the service level, there is a `ServiceContext` and then a context to describe the transactional nature of the service (either `ExceptionHandlingContext`, `AtomicTransactionContext`, or `LongRunningTransactionContext`).

The code in the body of a service or scope is called a *segment*. Each segment is a function in the C# code. `Segment0` will be defined for the `ServiceContext`, and `segment1` for the actual code of the body of the service. In addition, there will be a segment for each block of a Parallel shape and for each compensation or exception handler.

A segment is a switch statement that creates a state machine. Special return values are returned when the segment is blocked at a Receive or Timer shape. This enables the segment to be rescheduled to execute where it left off when a message gets delivered to the service.

The following code snippet illustrates part of `segment1` that represents the main scope for the service.

```
public Microsoft.XLANGs.Core.StopConditions segment1(Microsoft.XLANGs.Core.StopConditions
stopOn)
{
  Microsoft.XLANGs.Core.Envelope __msgEnv__ = null;
  bool __condition__;
  Microsoft.XLANGs.Core.Segment __seg__ = _segments[1];
  Microsoft.XLANGs.Core.Context __ctx__ = (Microsoft.XLANGs.Core.Context)_stateMgrs[1];
  __BizTalk_Orchestration1_root_0 __ctx0__ = (__BizTalk_Orchestration1_root_0)_stateMgrs[0];
  __BizTalk_Orchestration1_1 __ctx1__ = (__BizTalk_Orchestration1_1)_stateMgrs[1];

  switch (__seg__.Progress)
  {
  case 0:
    __ctx__.PrologueCompleted = true;
```

```
      if ( !PostProgressInc( __seg__, __ctx__, 1 ) )
        return Microsoft.XLANGs.Core.StopConditions.Paused;
      goto case 1;
   case 1:
      if ( !PreProgressInc( __seg__, __ctx__, 2 ) )
        return Microsoft.XLANGs.Core.StopConditions.Paused;
      Tracker.FireEvent(__eventLocations[0],__eventData[0],_stateMgrs[1].TrackDataStream );
      if (IsDebugged)
        return Microsoft.XLANGs.Core.StopConditions.InBreakpoint;
      goto case 2;
   case 2:
      if ( !PreProgressInc( __seg__, __ctx__, 3 ) )
        return Microsoft.XLANGs.Core.StopConditions.Paused;
      Tracker.FireEvent(__eventLocations[1],__eventData[1],_stateMgrs[1].TrackDataStream );
      if (IsDebugged)
        return Microsoft.XLANGs.Core.StopConditions.InBreakpoint;
      goto case 3;

   ...

   case 24:
      if (!__ctx1__.CleanupAndPrepareToCommit(__seg__))
        return Microsoft.XLANGs.Core.StopConditions.Blocked;
      if ( !PostProgressInc( __seg__, __ctx__, 25 ) )
        return Microsoft.XLANGs.Core.StopConditions.Paused;
      goto case 25;
   case 25:
      if ( !PreProgressInc( __seg__, __ctx__, 26 ) )
        return Microsoft.XLANGs.Core.StopConditions.Paused;
      __ctx1__.OnCommit();
      goto case 26;
   case 26:
      __seg__.SegmentDone();
      _segments[0].PredecessorDone(this);
      break;
   }
   return Microsoft.XLANGs.Core.StopConditions.Completed;
}
```

This is all very interesting to know, but can it really help you other than understanding how the product works under the hood?

In fact, the C# source files can be of great use. For example, you can debug your orchestrations by setting breakpoints in the C# code, assuming that you have your symbols set up correctly. In addition, they can be used during performance tuning. Chapter 8 discusses how the Visual Studio Profiler can be used to identify bottlenecks in your code. Having the C# source code for your orchestrations can enable you to identify where performance bottlenecks are in your orchestrations.

You can also inspect the BizTalk assemblies using `ildasm`, which is supplied as part of the .NET framework, or the fantastic .NET Reflector tool, written by Lutz Roeder (http://www.aisto.com/roeder/DotNet/). Figure 5-2 shows a BizTalk orchestration compiled into a .NET assembly using Reflector.

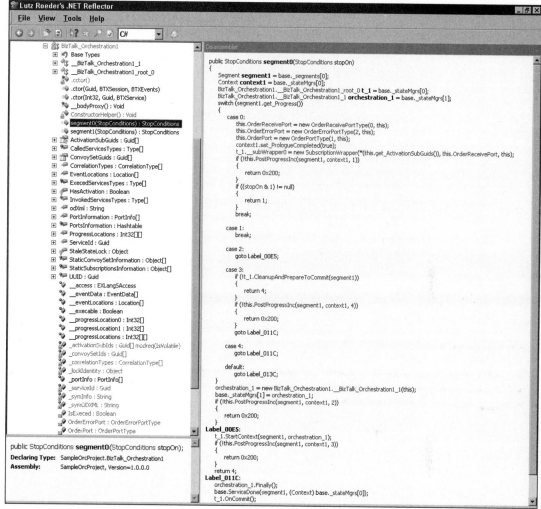

Figure 5-2

This section has covered BizTalk internal information mostly for informational purposes. It's important to appreciate how it works under the covers because it helps you understand why BizTalk behaves the way it does — as bizarre as it might seem at times!

Activation

BizTalk orchestrations can be instantiated in one of two ways:

❑ By a message arriving in the MessageBox to which an orchestration has subscribed. This is called an activating receive.

❑ Following an invocation from another orchestration.

Let's take a look at both ways.

Activating Receive

The first scenario, when an orchestration is created following a message's arrival, is the most common method and is called an *activating receive* because a message's arrival *activates* a new instance of an orchestration.

An activating receive is created by dragging a Receive shape onto an orchestration as the first shape. You cannot have an activating receive in any other position within an orchestration, because that cannot be used to *activate* the orchestration. You would be trying to start the orchestration when it had already been started.

> There are two exceptions to this rule. The Listen and Parallel shapes can appear at the top of an orchestration and can contain two or more activating receives.
>
> These exceptions are detailed further in "The Parallel Shape" and "The Listen Shape" sections of this chapter.

On the Receive shape, you must select the BizTalk message that it will populate with the inbound message. This step, therefore, implies to the BizTalk engine which type of message you wish to subscribe to and process within the orchestration. The final step is to then set the `Activate` property of the Receive shape to `true`, which indicates an activating receive.

With all of this information, the BizTalk Engine knows that when a message matching the type referenced by the Receive shape arrives, it needs to create a new instance of the orchestration and hand it the message. This is called a *subscription*.

Invoked

The second scenario is when an orchestration is created from another orchestration. This is configured by dragging a Call Orchestration or Start Orchestration shape onto the orchestration design surface. The differences between these two shapes are covered in the "Flow Control Shapes" section. The other orchestration shapes are covered later in this chapter.

When configuring either of these shapes, you must select the orchestration that you want to be invoked and specify any parameters to be passed. Messages and ports are the most often used parameter types because most scenarios hand off messages to new orchestrations and, in some cases, pass ports between orchestrations to enable callback scenarios.

Invoking orchestrations in this way is typically used when refactoring orchestrations; if you have the same core business process logic duplicated in multiple places, it's easier to place it in one shared orchestration.

Another potential use for an invoked orchestration is to control on what BizTalk servers certain orchestrations run. (This only applies to orchestrations invoked using the Start Orchestration shape.) If, for example, you have an auditing orchestration that must be executed multiple times during a business process and you want to *off-load* the performance overhead of this auditing step, you can invoke the auditing orchestration but place it in a different BizTalk host and therefore on another potentially dedicated server.

This enables you to install an instance of this BizTalk host on another machine, and hand off the processing overhead and not have it interfere with the core business process execution. You must consider the hand-off overhead to ensure that utilizing such a technique isn't introducing more overhead than the actual operation; thus, such a decision would need to be taken in the scalability labs.

A good example of this would be payment processing. A payment-processing system will need to commit the payment as quickly as possible, as a customer or member of staff will be waiting for the result.

However, additional steps might be required to complete the business process. Auditing is a good example of this. Decoupling the auditing process in this way enables the main payment process to complete and thus not require the end user to wait for additional processes to complete.

Again, this approach can be used only by orchestrations invoked using the asynchronous Start Orchestration shape, not the Call Orchestration shape.

Subscriptions

As you've already learned, by creating Receive shapes and configuring them to use BizTalk messages, you are ultimately defining subscriptions to messages, which the BizTalk engine then honors.

These subscriptions are only created inside the BizTalk MessageBox when an orchestration is enlisted using the BizTalk administration tool. A key thing to remember is that stopping an orchestration using the administration tool does leave the subscription in place.

Leaving the subscription in place enables messages to arrive and to be queued inside the MessageBox. If, however, the subscription is removed by unenlisting the orchestration, then messages destined for that orchestration will be suspended — unless, of course, there is another orchestration also subscribing to the same message.

Administration of orchestrations in this way is done through the BizTalk Administration Console or, in the case of development, the BizTalk Explorer inside Visual Studio can also be used.

Subscriptions are also automatically created by BizTalk when dealing with a Send/Receive orchestration messaging patterns. This enables BizTalk to route a reply back to the requesting orchestration. Send ports, when enlisted, also create subscriptions to messages to ensure that messages destined to be transmitted by BizTalk are subscribed to and ultimately delivered to the remote endpoint.

In the case of an Activation subscription, you can control the subscription further by adding a filter expression. A *filter expression* enables you to filter orchestration messages based on message data or message context properties (perhaps those created by adapters) and is specified on a Receive shape via the `Filter` property. Message properties used in a filter expression must be promoted using property promotions, as the filtering is performed at the messaging layer. Property promotions are covered later in this chapter.

Figure 5-3 shows a filter expression being configured on a Receive shape within the Orchestration Designer in Visual Studio, and Figure 5-4 shows the resulting filtered subscription shown via the BizTalk Administration Console.

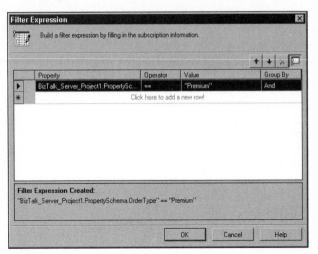

Figure 5-3

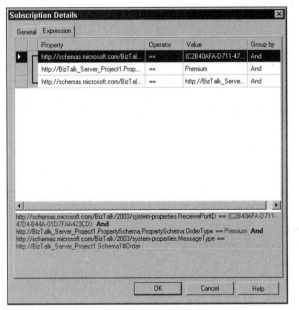

Figure 5-4

Persistence Points

BizTalk itself has been designed to be entirely stateless at the BizTalk Server layer. This architectural principle is crucial to the scalability of any solution dealing with long-running business processes and indeed for any form of reliability.

This stateless model is achieved by persisting the in-memory representation of an orchestration and any associated messages in SQL Server, which acts as a durable store. The engine does this in an intelligent manner rather than persisting the entire orchestration each time. It will persist only the parts that it needs to.

This state is *server agnostic*, meaning that it can be used by any server that has been configured for that type of orchestration.

Messages and orchestrations are always processed within the scope of a SQL transaction. So if a BizTalk Server were to suffer a power outage, for example, a message being consumed by an orchestration while in memory would not be lost. Instead, the transaction (and hence any orchestration state or messages) would be rolled back to its last good state that was persisted in the BizTalk MessageBox.

Orchestrations also persist their state at various points during execution, effectively creating a checkpoint. This checkpointing (referred to as *persistence points*) is crucial to provide resilience against failure. BizTalk leverages the standard .NET serialization techniques to implement persistence.

Consider the scenario whereby an orchestration has checkpointed during execution. If that BizTalk server were to suffer a power outage, another BizTalk server could continue the orchestration from the checkpoint rather than having to start the orchestration from the beginning, as it would have to without this checkpoint.

This is a great optimization but has overhead. The cost of serializing the orchestration out of memory into the BizTalk MessageBox will impact the CPU utilization of the BizTalk server and the SQL server, impact network bandwidth, and impact the amount of I/O for the database. Such impact is a necessary evil, and BizTalk has been tuned to reduce the impact. For example, the state is compressed before being written to the MessageBox, which effectively trades CPU cycles for network bandwidth. The XLang compiler does an excellent job of collapsing multiple persistence points into one where possible. It can do this because it has implicit knowledge of the orchestration.

Orchestration developers, however, can implement orchestrations that cause unnecessary persistence points. Causing an extra one or two persistence points per orchestration might not seem like a problem, but if your orchestration is being executed 100,000 times, that's a lot of CPU processing on both the BizTalk servers and SQL servers that could be avoided, not to mention the additional I/O for SQL Server and additional network traffic between the BizTalk and SQL Server.

When designing an orchestration, it's not clear exactly what will cause a persistence point to be created, because there are no straightforward visual cues or compiler warnings. Hence, it is easy to fall into the trap of making the solution perform less than it could.

The following things incur a persistence point during orchestration execution:

❑ **Send shape** — After the Send shape has committed the message to the BizTalk MessageBox, the orchestration will checkpoint. That way, if the orchestration later rolls back, the Send shape will not be executed again, and thus message duplication is avoided.

Consider the orchestration shown in Figure 5-5, which has three Send shapes in a row. Now that you know the orchestration will checkpoint after each Send shape, you know that you have introduced three extra persistence points per execution of the orchestration.

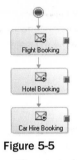

Figure 5-5

This is clearly going to be less than optimal with many of these orchestrations executing. Modifying the orchestration as shown in Figure 5-6 to wrap all the Send shapes in an atomic scope removes two of the persistence points, because the atomic scope will not "commit" the messages to the MessageBox until the atomic scope completes, thus batching the persistence points into one.

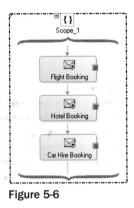

Figure 5-6

Another pattern to avoid is the use of a Parallel shape to perform two sends. Because the send operation is completely asynchronous (and therefore returns immediately to the orchestration) to the BizTalk orchestration, performing two sends does nothing other than incur further persistence points. Figure 5-7 shows such a Parallel shape being used in this way.

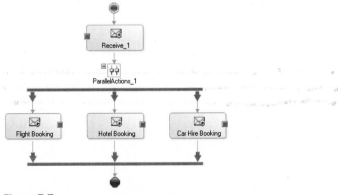

Figure 5-7

❑ **Atomic scope** — The atomic scope causes a persistence point when the atomic scope completes. This makes a lot of sense because once an atomic scope has completed it will have committed any ACID transaction(s). Therefore, in a failure condition rolling back and reexecuting the atomic scope is likely to be unacceptable.

As you'll see in the discussion of the persistence points incurred by Send shapes, this one persistence point behavior is extremely beneficial in some scenarios. Any shapes that cause a persistence point will not incur a persistence point when hosted inside an atomic scope, because the persistence points will be collapsed into one (batching). This is due to the nature of an atomic transaction. Everything within an atomic scope must complete successfully, and any failure will cause an entire atomic transaction to be rolled back.

However, I've found a number of customers utilizing atomic scopes heavily within a BizTalk solution to work around the serialization requirements of a BizTalk orchestration. Although this addresses their issues around serialization, it incurs an extra persistence point each time, thus impacting performance.

As you'll see later in this chapter, any classes or types used by your orchestration must be serializable. So if you call a .NET class library, it must be marked with the `[Serializable]` attribute. When the BizTalk orchestration then checkpoints or dehydrates, the class library can be serialized along with the orchestration.

> Your class may have no state requirements and therefore be stateless, but you must ensure that your class is still marked as serializable and that you mark properties as nonserializable using `[NonSerialized]` attributes. Another approach is to mark your methods as static.

Sometimes, developers want to make use of .NET Framework types that are not serializable. A very common example is `System.XML` types, such as `XmlNode`. Use of these types will be blocked by the orchestration compiler or at runtime because it would cause a failure when persisting the orchestration.

Developers quickly found that they could make use of these types within atomic scopes because persistence cannot happen within an atomic scope. (It's all or nothing.) Atomic scopes are there for a reason, but they were not designed for such a scenario. These types can also be used by adopting a stateless model whereby they are not held as member variables; hence, the fact that they do not support serialization is not relevant.

As already discussed, persistence has an underlying cost to performance, and introducing unnecessary persistence points in this way can seriously impact performance.

> In fact, one customer introduced their own logging implementation for BizTalk, scattering approximately 50 instrumentation points among orchestrations. The logging implementation relied on `System.Xml` types and, therefore, required each instrumentation point to be encased within an atomic scope.
>
> A simple business process applied to one message caused in excess of 200 persistence points and introduced far higher SQL disk I/O than required. Elimination of these persistence points delivered approximately an 800 percent performance improvement!

- ❑ **Start Orchestration shape** — Using a Start Orchestration shape to asynchronously launch another orchestration causes a persistence point because this is effectively just sending a message to the BizTalk MessageBox.

- ❑ **End of a long-running scope** — If you use a long-running scope and mark it as transactional (atomic or long running), the Orchestration Engine will persist the orchestration when the scope completes. Long-running scopes configured with a transaction type of none incur no persistence points.

- ❑ **End of Orchestration** — The end of an orchestration, which is indicated by the red circle, incurs a persistence point as you would expect, as the orchestration has completed. The Orchestration Engine will automatically optimize this persistence point if, for example, you have a Send shape or transactional scope as the last shape in your orchestration. It does this by batching the persistence points up into one.

This can easily be demonstrated by the two orchestration snippets shown in Figures 5-8 and 5-9. Figure 5-8 shows an orchestration that will incur one persistence point which is due to the optimized End of Orchestration and Send shapes.

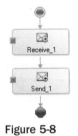

Figure 5-8

Figure 5-9 shows an orchestration that will incur two persistence points: one for the Send shape and one for the End of Orchestration. The Orchestration Engine has been unable to optimize in this scenario because it has a shape between the two shapes.

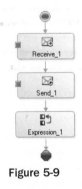

Figure 5-9

- ❑ **Receive, Delay, and Suspend shapes** — The use of Receive, Delay, or Suspend shapes does not create persistence points per se, but as covered in the next section, it will make the orchestration become a candidate for dehydration, which, if performed, effectively causes a persistence point. This is out of your control and is included here purely for reference.

Another factor to bear in mind is the size of your orchestration state. Reducing the number of variables and messages will make a big difference to your state size. In addition, scoping variables and messages using Scope shapes can mean that they can go out of scope and therefore reduce your state size.

Persistence points are key to good orchestration design, and it's imperative that you monitor the number of persistence points caused by your solution during development and, wherever possible, minimize them.

You can monitor the number of persistence points incurred by your solution through the `Persistence Points` performance counter located under the `XLANG/s Orchestrations` performance object in `PerfMon`. It's useful to monitor this counter while submitting one message to your solution, to understand the number of persistence points for each message.

Dehydration

Business processes are typically long running because they execute over extended periods of time and are always asynchronous in terms of messaging. If an orchestration sends a message using a Send shape, the process of physically sending the message is done asynchronously to the orchestration. Once the message has been published to the BizTalk MessageBox, the orchestration carries on executing until it reaches a waiting point, such as a Receive shape.

Waiting points are typically Receive and Delay shapes. In these cases, there is no reason for the orchestration to remain in memory to wait for a message to arrive or a delay period to expire. In fact, such a delay could take hours or days. At these points, the orchestration becomes a candidate for dehydration. The Orchestration Engine may dehydrate your orchestration after such a delay has exceeded the engine threshold and persist it into the BizTalk MessageBox.

You can think of dehydration as an extension of persistence. It leverages the same persistence approach to write the state of the orchestration to a durable store, but instead of leaving it in memory, it will remove the orchestration from memory pending the wait condition being satisfied (a message arriving or a delay period expiring).

When it is time to rehydrate the orchestration, the engine will load (rehydrate) the orchestration from the MessageBox and execute it on the most appropriate server. The Orchestration Engine will only dehydrate orchestrations if it deems it necessary, and it will use number of factors to determine whether dehydration is required. Memory pressure is a typical example.

If you initiate a shutdown of the BizTalk service, the Messaging Engine will wait for approximately 60 seconds to allow all messaging activity to complete. During this time, orchestrations have the ability to dehydrate cleanly, which they will in almost all cases. However, if an orchestration instance fails to dehydrate, it will be terminated.

If the shutdown is not controlled, such as during a power failure, the orchestration will continue from its last persistence point, which can mean that your orchestration shapes are executed more than once.

The BizTalk engine will make a decision on whether to dehydrate based on a number of dehydration thresholds, which can be set in the `btsntsvc.exe.config` configuration file. They are not present by default but can be added as required.

In my experience, dehydration works extremely well, and it's extremely rare that you need to modify the default dehydration settings. For systems under heavy load it may be advantageous to tune them, but this should be done carefully during a performance and scalability test to ensure that by adjusting them you are not causing extra problems.

The main settings that you can change are `MinThreshold` and `MaxThreshold`, which default to 1 second and 1800 seconds (30 minutes), respectively. The decision to dehydrate is complex. In simple terms, the engine monitors the system to ensure that private bytes and virtual bytes are not under pressure and also to see how long it took to satisfy this wait point in the orchestration last time. This way, it can make an educated decision on whether it's worth dehydrating if moments later it will be rehydrating anyway. However, if the system is under resource pressure, it's important to dehydrate more aggressively to protect the overall system. You can find highly detailed information on the dehydration calculations performed at the following URL: `http://msdn2.microsoft.com/en-us/library/aa561238.aspx`, but I provide a high level summary below for ease of understanding.

For example, if the BizTalk Server is not under memory pressure and a Receive shape has previously taken 2 minutes to complete on an orchestration instance, then this is less than the `MaxThreshold` and won't necessarily cause orchestration dehydration.

However, if the BizTalk Server is under memory pressure and a Receive shape has previously taken 2 minutes to complete, this is greater than the `MinThreshold` and will therefore cause dehydration.

A snippet showing these configuration settings, along with their default values, is shown below. See `http://msdn2.microsoft.com/en-us/library/aa559350.aspx` for further information on these settings.

```
<xlangs>
<Configuration>
  <Dehydration MaxThreshold="1800" MinThreshold="1"
    ConstantThreshold="-1">
    <VirtualMemoryThrottlingCriteria OptimalUsage="900"
      MaximalUsage="1300" IsActive="true" />
    <PrivateMemoryThrottlingCriteria OptimalUsage="50"  MaximalUsage="350"
      IsActive="true" />
    <PhysicalMemoryThrottlingCriteria OptimalUsage="50" MaximalUsage="350"
      IsActive="false" />
  </Dehydration>
</Configuration>
</xlangs>
```

Versioning

Versioning of BizTalk orchestrations is a critical feature, especially when orchestrations have implemented a business process that can be long running. A common example is when a message is sent to an external party and a response message is received after, say, an order has been completed.

Deploying a modified orchestration during such a long-running orchestration could cause any number of problems, including backward compatibility issues, and is thus not supported. Imagine a custom C# class that you serialize out to a file pending later deserialization. If you then modify this class extensively and attempt to deserialize the state back, you'll likely run into compatibility problems.

Instead, BizTalk leverages the .NET side-by-side capability by utilizing the Global Assembly Cache (GAC). The GAC enables multiple versions of .NET assemblies to be deployed side by side. Because an orchestration is compiled into a .NET assembly, it can leverage this feature. So, if you have an orchestration already deployed and have instances of this orchestration dehydrated, you can modify the orchestration, update the version number, and deploy to your BizTalk servers.

After this new version has been deployed, you will see both versions in the GAC. When one of the dehydrated orchestrations wakes up, it will continue to use the original .NET assembly version, not the new version. Any new activations of this orchestration (i.e., not orchestrations rehydrating) will use the new orchestration version deployed as part of the new assembly. This approach ultimately drains the number of orchestrations using the original version, at which point you can then undeploy the version, as required.

You should ensure that any schemas used by your BizTalk solution are housed in a separate BizTalk project and therefore deployed in a different assembly. Having your orchestrations and schemas combined in the same assembly will prevent versioning from using this approach, as you cannot have multiple versions of the same schema deployed at any one time. Thus, you are required to undeploy all orchestrations and schema assemblies and prevent any form of in-place upgrade.

Any orchestration invoked directly through the use of a Call Orchestration shape will create further hard dependencies between orchestrations and thus make versioning more complicated because you need to version and deploy each one, despite only making changes to one orchestration.

To avoid this, you should consider a loosely coupled approach between your orchestrations — either through the Start Orchestration shape or by using direct ports. You should, however, bear in mind that the Start Orchestration approach will have a higher performance overhead as it goes via the MessageBox. The direct-binding approach adds further complexity to your project, which can make understanding how everything connects together harder.

As with most things, there are trade-offs with each approach that you must consider upfront: performance or manageability? If you don't foresee having to change an orchestration regularly, you might not want to loosely couple it. If you want the best absolute performance, you should tightly couple your orchestrations, although this makes maintenance harder. Review each area of your solution early on in your development life cycle and apply the right design to suit your requirements.

To perform this upgrade, you need to complete the following steps, in order. It's advisable to script all these steps and test the upgrade step thoroughly before going live.

1. Deploy the new orchestration version to the BizTalk Server, preferably using the MSI installation method.

2. Configure the new orchestration in the same way as the previous version; ensure that the host bindings and port binding are identical. This is done using the BizTalk Administration Console.

3. Disable the activating receive port used by the orchestration to prevent any messages from being received during this maintenance window. This is to prevent duplicate processing of messages during this maintenance window.

    It's advisable to disable only the receive port that activates the orchestration and not other receive ports that the orchestration may use, because this will prevent dehydrated orchestrations from completing during the maintenance window.

4. Unenlist the original orchestration through the BizTalk Administration Console. This will remove the orchestration subscription from the MessageBox and therefore prevent new instances of this orchestration version from being created. You can easily distinguish between the new and old versions through the BizTalk Administration Console, as shown in Figure 5-10.

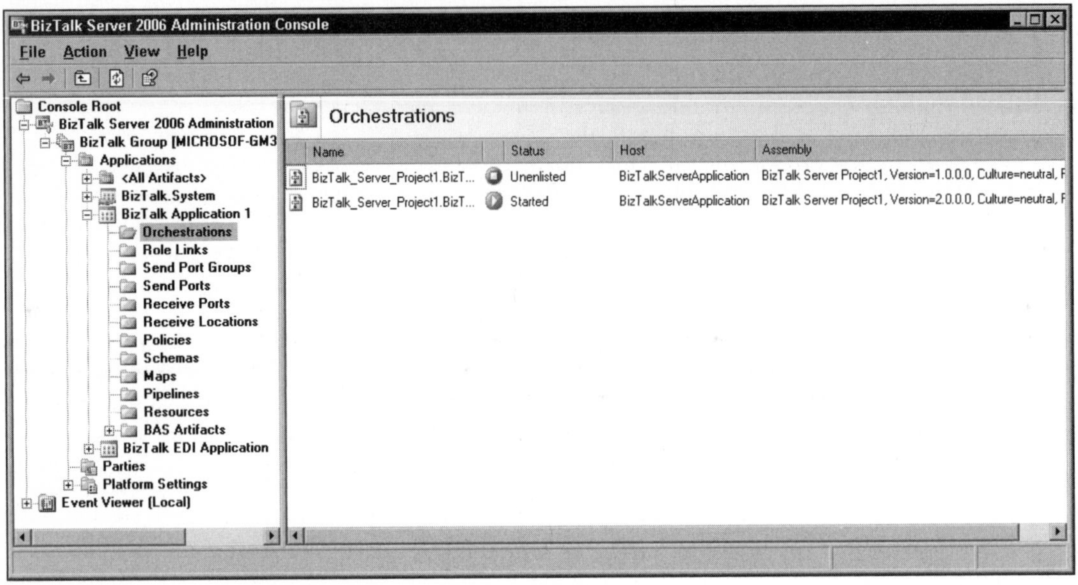

Figure 5-10

5. Enlist the new orchestration version through the BizTalk Administration Console. This creates a new subscription in the MessageBox that enables new instances of this orchestration to be created when the message it's waiting for arrives.

6. Finally, enable the receive port that you disabled in the first step. This allows messages to arrive in the BizTalk MessageBox.

For scenarios where you cannot tolerate having the Receive port shut down even momentarily (perhaps the sending system has no notion of retries), you can leave the Receive port enabled while you perform the upgrade. This approach, however, leaves the potential for incoming messages to be suspended during the process of unenlisting the old version and enlisting the new version. The gap between the two operations can leave no subscription for a given message; hence, it may be suspended.

Performing the unenlist and enlist via a script minimizes this window. Either way, you can resume any suspended messages that may occur using the BizTalk Administration Console, so ensure that this is checked following an upgrade.

> .NET publisher policy files (which enable you to manually redirect the loading of .NET assemblies to new versions) are not supported by BizTalk for versioning, because BizTalk can utilize a private cache for assemblies. This means that you may not achieve the desired result until the BizTalk service has been restarted, and you can, of course, suffer rehydration problems.

Logical Ports

This section introduces the concept of logical ports, which are used during orchestration development to express the way messages can be sent and received by an orchestration.

When creating and configuring Send and Receive shapes, you specify a BizTalk message that the shapes will use. In the case of a Receive shape, this configuration step indicates to which message types the orchestration is subscribing and is used as the basis of the orchestration subscription. These Send and Receive shapes must also be connected to a logical port to be successfully configured and to indicate how a message should arrive in the orchestration.

Logical ports define entry and exit points for messages on your orchestration and place no dependency on the physical deployment of the orchestration. Logical port design, at its simplest, defines only the communication pattern used and the message type, enabling you, at deployment, to attach whichever adapter your environment requires, giving you complete flexibility.

The only messaging decisions you need to make at the orchestration design stage is which message types you're going to use and which communication pattern each port will utilize. Valid communication patterns are One-Way, Solicit/Response, and Request/Response. This pattern decision does to some extent influence which adapter you can use at deployment as, for example, the File adapter supports only One-Way messaging, but the SOAP adapter supports all available communication patterns.

Port Creation

The choice of communication pattern is entirely dependent on the requirements imposed on your solution. If you want to send a response to a source system, a Request/Response pattern should be used. If you just want to receive messages with no direct response, a One-Way pattern is suitable.

The orchestration design surface has two port surfaces on either side, shown as vertical bars, where ports can be defined. There is no difference between the sides, but the separate port surfaces allow you to locate a port in such a way that the orchestration has minimal lines crossing across it — purely a layout feature that you should use to make your orchestration easier to read. These port surfaces are shown in Figure 5-11.

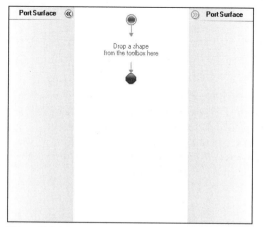

Figure 5-11

You can create ports either by dragging a Port shape from the toolbox onto the port surface or by right-clicking the port surface and choosing `New Port` or `New Configured Port`. The latter option is identical to the first but launches the Port Configuration Wizard instantly, rather than requiring you to manually launch it.

At this stage, it's prudent to give the port a sensible name, as this identifier is shown when binding the orchestration at deployment time. (Having Port_1 and Port_2 displayed doesn't help when figuring out which port is which.)

Port Type

The next step is to create or select a port type used by the port. The port type defines the communication pattern and message types that a port will use and can be shared among multiple ports, as required.

A port type can be created directly using the Orchestration View pane in Visual Studio, but it's usually done through the wizard used to create a port. Figure 5-12 shows the Port Type section of the Port Configuration Wizard.

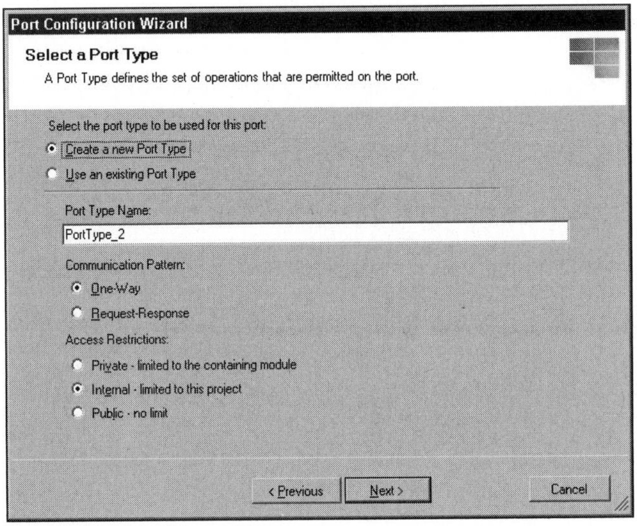

Figure 5-12

Type definitions such as port types are shared within a project. It can make sense in some instances to define these all in one empty orchestration, which keeps the type definitions defined in one central place rather than spread across your entire solution.

As you can see, this step of configuring the port type enables you to define the communication pattern utilized by this port type along with access restrictions. You can think of access restrictions in exactly the same way as you would restrict access to a .NET class in, say, C# (`public`, `private`, etc.).

❏   Private means that this port type can be used only within this orchestration.

❏   Internal means that the port type can be used across different orchestrations within the project.

❏   Public means this port type can be used by anyone.

The default of internal works for most scenarios. Public is typically used only when you need to expose an orchestration as a Web service, which, for obvious reasons, needs to be public.

The next step of the Port Configuration Wizard requires you to specify the direction of communications used by the port, either send or receive.

Port Binding

The final setting required at this stage is what port binding should be used. The default is usually set to Specify Later, which enables you to bind your logical ports to physical receive or send ports at deployment time, which is advisable in almost all cases. Another option is Specify Now, which enables you to configure the physical port at development time, which is effectively hard-coding your configuration. This is not advisable, because any configuration changes will require the orchestration to be recompiled and deployed.

The final option at this stage is direct port binding; the various options for this are shown in Figure 5-13.

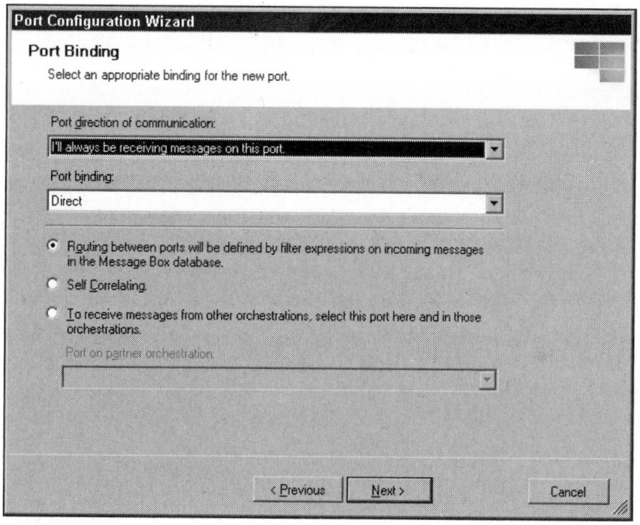

Figure 5-13

Direct port binding enables you to loosely couple orchestrations together or loosely couple orchestrations from the message source. Orchestrations with direct bound ports are not bound to physical ports at deployment time but instead rely on messages arriving from other receive ports or being created from other orchestrations at runtime.

Such an approach is particularly useful when you want to implement a publish-and-subscribe messaging architecture and want to slot in new orchestrations without modifying the rest of your architecture. This is discussed further in Chapter 13.

A common scenario that I like to use when explaining direct ports is an insurance-brokering system. One insurance quote message arrives in the MessageBox and is consumed by an orchestration that generates an internal quotation message.

This internal quotation message then needs to be sent to *n* insurance providers. Instead of manually calling *n* orchestrations to handle this, one message is sent to the MessageBox by using a direct port, and any number of insurance provider orchestrations subscribe to this message. You can add further insurance provider orchestrations at any point in the future without modifying any parts of your solution.

As you can see in Figure 5-13, there are three options for direct ports. We'll cover this briefly now as they are important to understand when developing orchestrations. This is touched on this further in Chapters 12 and 13.

Filter Expressions

Messages sent through this type of port will be published to the MessageBox, and the ultimate destination (orchestration or send port) will be decided through the evaluation of subscriptions to this message type.

This approach can be used by orchestrations wishing to process a message differently, depending on the contents of the message. This can be performed by configuring a filter on the Receive shape within the orchestration. This is covered later in this chapter in the "Property Promotions" section.

Send ports can also subscribe to these messages and apply filters, as required. This was covered in Chapter 3.

Self-Correlating Ports

Self-correlating ports enable you to implement a pattern whereby a child orchestration can call back to the parent orchestration that created it. This can obviously be performed using the Call Orchestration shape, but this is a synchronous invocation in that the parent orchestration must wait for the child to complete.

The Start Orchestration shape can be used to counter this, but this method, unlike the Call Orchestration method, doesn't provide a way for the child orchestration to return anything back to the parent orchestration because it allows only `in` parameters and explicitly doesn't allow `out` or `ref` parameters.

Self-correlating ports enable child orchestrations to communicate back to the calling orchestration. This is useful for implementing the Scatter and Gather pattern, which, as in the Insurance example above, enables you to *scatter* work out to child orchestration and then *gather* the responses back. You can find an example of this pattern that uses self-correlating ports at `http://go.microsoft.com/fwlink/?LinkId=73703`.

The following steps detail how self-correlating ports can be configured. In these steps, you are going to asynchronously invoke a child orchestration using the Start Orchestration shape and enable the child orchestration to return a message back to the parent orchestration. These steps do not cover how you will invoke the parent orchestration, which is a straightforward task for you to implement. (A File-adapter–based receive location is great for a demo.)

1. Create two orchestrations: one to act as the parent orchestration and another to act as the child orchestration, which, when invoked from the parent, will return a response.

2. In the parent orchestration, create a new logical port (for the purposes of this example, called `ChildOrchestrationResponsePort`), configured with a One-Way communication pattern set to receive messages, and choose Direct as the Port Binding and select Self Correlating.

3. In the child orchestration, right-click Orchestration Parameters in the Orchestration View pane and choose New Configured Port Parameter. Enter a name for this port, and then click Next.

4. Choose Use an existing port type to display the port types available, and then select the port type created in the previous step. Finally, click Next and choose "I will be sending messages on this port."

    A logical port will appear on the orchestration design surface. You can now wire up a Send shape to this port to return a message to the calling orchestration. Create this message in whichever way you feel appropriate.

5. Back in the parent orchestration, drag a Start Orchestration shape onto the orchestration and configure it to invoke the child orchestration. The port parameter will be shown and will automatically be mapped to the appropriate port on your orchestration.

6. The final step is to add a Receive shape to your orchestration to receive the response back from the child orchestration. Create a message that is configured to be the same type used by the child orchestration and wire it up to the self-correlating port you created initially (`ChildOrchestrationResponsePort`).

This is a powerful technique to enable communication between orchestrations that are created asynchronously and avoids the pain of creating and managing correlation sets.

Partner Ports

The last option for direct ports is partner orchestration ports. Like the previous options, these enable communication between orchestrations but offer slightly different features that may be required to implement your solution.

You may wonder why you might use partner ports over and above the Call or Start Orchestration shapes that we've already covered. Like partner ports, these enable inter-orchestration communication.

The main difference is that partner ports use a messaging paradigm rather than an invocation with parameters paradigm. This enables convoy-style and publish-subscribe–style messaging between your orchestrations, which is not possible with the invocation approach. Another difference is the ability to loosely couple orchestrations, which can enable them to be modified easily once the system is live.

Two different types of communication patterns can be implemented using partner ports: forward partner direct binding and inverse partner direct binding. As we've already seen, a port type can be shared among ports on other orchestrations, but partner ports enable a particular port instance to be shared between orchestrations, thus enabling direct communication, albeit through the BizTalk MessageBox.

Forward partner direct binding enables an orchestration to expose a port that can then be invoked by other orchestrations in order to pass messages. In the forward partner scenario, the orchestration that is being called has no explicit knowledge of the sending orchestration, but the calling orchestration does have explicit binding to the called orchestration.

This enables the calling orchestration to be modified and deployed without requiring any changes to the called orchestration.

This communication pattern is useful when you want to share an orchestration between multiple calling orchestrations. An example of this is a set of message brokers that are sending messages to a central servicing orchestration through forward direct binding. The servicing orchestration requires a number of messages to complete a business process for a given customer.

The servicing orchestration is activated by the first message for a specific customer, and subsequent messages sent by other broker orchestrations are directed to this instance.

Inverse partner direct binding, as the name implies, is the reverse of forward partner direct binding in that it enables an orchestration to expose a specific logical port instance that subscribing orchestrations can listen to and subsequently process any messages that are sent via this logical port — a publish-and-subscribe model, if you will.

In this communication pattern, the listening orchestration is explicitly bound to the sending orchestration, but the sending orchestration has no knowledge of the subscribers, which enables subscriber orchestrations to be added or modified without any changes being required to the sending orchestration. Changes to the sending orchestration, however, will require modification of listening orchestrations.

> *Chapter 12 discusses inverse partner direct binding in more detail and provides an example of how it can be used to loosely couple a long-running orchestration to improve manageability.*

The following sections detail how to configure forward and inverse partner direct binding.

Forward Partner Direct Binding

Complete these steps to configure forward partner direct binding:

1. Create two orchestrations: one to act as the parent orchestration (`ParentOrc`) and another to act as the child orchestration (`ChildOrc`) that will be invoked from the parent.

2. In the child orchestration, you need to create a port that can be used from the parent orchestration. To do this, create a new logical port (for the purposes of this example, called `ChildOrcExposedPort`) and when prompted in the wizard, create a new port type called `ChildOrcExposedPortType`.

3. Configure this port with a One-Way communication pattern and set to receive messages.

4. Choose Direct as the port binding and select "to receive messages from other orchestration." Select the port that you just created from the drop-down list (`<YourBizTalkProjectName>.ChildOrc.ChildOrcExposedPort`). This is effectively saying that you want to receive any messages sent to the `ChildOrcExposedPort`.

5. Configure a Receive shape to receive a message of the appropriate type and wire it up to the `ChildOrcExposedPort`.

6. In the parent orchestration (`ParentOrc`), create a new port with a name of your choosing. Instead of creating a new port through the Port Configuration Wizard, however, choose "use an existing port type" and select the port type created in the previous step (`<YourBizTalkProjectName>.ChildOrcExposedPortType`).

7. In the next step of the Port Configuration Wizard, choose Send as the direction of communication.

8. The final step of the wizard is to choose Direct as the port binding and select "to send messsages to other orchestrations." Select the port that you created from the drop-down list

(`<YourBizTalkProjectName>.ChildOrc.ChildOrcExposedPort`). This is effectively saying that you want any messages sent using this logical port to be sent to the `ChildOrcExposedPort` port exposed from the `ChildOrc` orchestration.

Inverse Partner Direct Binding

Complete these steps to configure inverse partner direct binding:

1. Create two orchestrations: one to act as the parent orchestration (`ParentOrc`) and another to act as the child orchestration (`ChildOrc`). Messages will be sent through a logical port created on the parent orchestration, and the child orchestration will subscribe to them. Extra subscribers can be added by following the same steps used for the child orchestration.

2. In the parent orchestration, you need to create a port that can be used from the child orchestration. To do this, create a new logical port (for the purposes of this example, called `ParentOrcExposedPort`), and when prompted in the wizard, create a new port type called `ParentOrcExposedPortType`.

3. Configure this port with a One-Way communication pattern, and set it to receive messages.

4. Choose Direct as the port binding, and select "to receive messages from other orchestration." Select the port that you just created from the drop-down list (`<YourBizTalkProjectName>.ParentOrc.ParentOrcExposedPort`). This is effectively saying that you will send messages to any subscribers to this `ParentOrcExposedPort` port, which will remain unknown to the parent orchestration.

5. Configure a Send shape to send a message of the appropriate type, and wire it up to the `ParentOrcExposedPort`. This message will then be sent to all subscribers to this send port.

6. In the child orchestration, you need to create a logical port that subscribes to all messages sent to the `ParentOrcExposedPort`. Create a new port with a name of your choosing, but instead of creating a new port type through the Port Configuration Wizard, choose "use an existing port type" and select the port type created in the previous step (`<YourBizTalkProjectName>.ParentOrcExposedPortType`).

7. In the next step of the Port Configuration Wizard, choose receive as the direction of communication.

8. The final step of the wizard is to choose Direct as the port binding and select "to receive messages from other orchestrations." Select the port that was created in the parent orchestration (`<YourBizTalkProjectName>.ChildOrc.ParentOrcExposedPort`). This is effectively saying that you want any messages sent to the `ParentOrcExposedPort` exposed by the `ParentOrc` orchestration to be sent to this orchestration.

Additional subscribing orchestrations can be added by following the steps for the child orchestration. However, you will need to configure appropriate filters on the Receive shape of each subscribing orchestration to prevent all subscribing orchestrations from receiving the same message.

This exact technique is used in conjunction with a broker orchestration within the BPM scenario covered in Chapter 12 to split a large monolithic orchestration into a number of discrete processing stage orchestrations that can be modified on the fly, thus enabling easy modification of the business process. This is an implementation of the Process Manager pattern. Inverse binding can also be used to implement the Recipient List pattern.

As you can see, logical ports are a critical part of orchestration design and enable complex messaging patterns to be used when implementing your business processes. It's important to understand the various options available to you to ensure that you pick the most effective approach for your solution.

Orchestration Development

Now that we've covered some of the orchestration fundamentals, we'll move on to discussing how you can develop BizTalk orchestrations to implement your business processes.

Designing the Process

This section describes the way in which you can design your process using BizTalk orchestration. We'll cover the messages and the various orchestration shapes available.

Visio Designer

As you'll see in the next section, the usual Orchestration Designer is a developer-focused tool and is not suitable for use by, say, business analysts looking to express a business process. BizTalk Server 2004 and 2006 delivered a Visio-based Orchestration Designer called the *Orchestration Designer for Business Analysts* (ODBA).

ODBA is available as a free designer for download from Microsoft and doesn't require any BizTalk components to be installed, and at the time of writing requires Microsoft Visio 2003 and is not compatible with Office 2007. You can download ODBA from `http://go.microsoft.com/fwlink/?LinkId=47543`.

ODBA enables a business analyst to define the basic business process using simplified Visio shapes and then export this business process to a BizTalk orchestration file (`.ODX`), which is compatible with the Visual Studio Orchestration Designer covered next.

While there is ODBA, in my experience with customers it doesn't really fill the void between developers and analysts. Customers often find it more productive to sit the analyst and developers down together to formalize the process and even design the first draft of the orchestration together using the Orchestration Designer.

That said, we'll cover the basics of the Visio Designer here for completeness. If it works for your organization, then by all means use it, even if it's just for documenting the process and you don't make use of the Export to Orchestration feature.

Walk-through

Figure 5-14 shows a fictional business process developed using ODBA. Note the reduced number of shapes available on the left-hand side Toolbox compared to the Orchestration Designer, which we will cover in the next section.

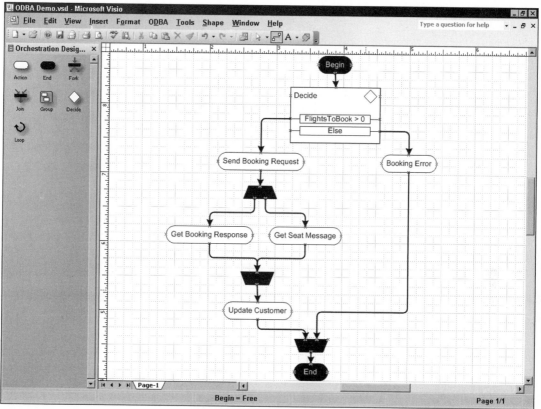

Figure 5-14

As you can see, this is a pretty effective way of enabling nondevelopers to express business processes, and Visio is already often used by organizations for exactly this reason. ODBA can go one step further, however, and export this abstract business process to the skeleton of a BizTalk orchestration.

By using the Export to BizTalk option on the ODBA menu, you can create an .ODX orchestration file. The export process will first verify that your business process doesn't invalidate any rules before creating the ODX file.

The BizTalk developer can then take this exported orchestration file and add it to the appropriate BizTalk project in Visual Studio. Figure 5-15 shows the orchestration created from the business process shown in the previous figure.

As you can see, the action shapes are translated into a group shape. This enables developers to then place however many shapes that are required to implement that process step. Unfortunately, conditions and names given to shapes do not make the translation, which can make it complicated to understand.

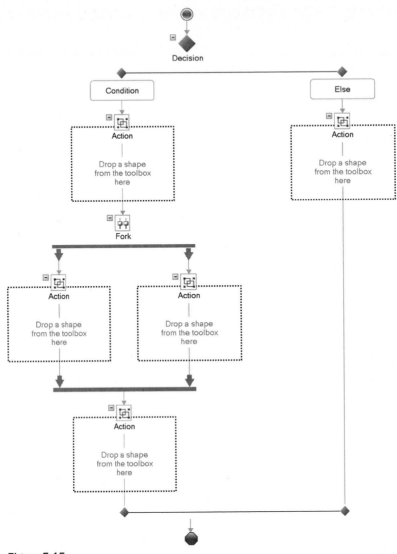

Figure 5-15

Roundtripping can also be performed; it enables you to import a BizTalk orchestration into Visio. Results can be mixed, especially with regard to layout. Previous to BizTalk Server 2006, roundtripping was often used as a workaround for the poor printing support — printing was improved in BizTalk Server 2006, however.

Figure 5-16 shows an example of an orchestration imported into Visio. I've deliberately picked a small orchestration for clarity reasons. The orchestration shown is used in Chapter 6.

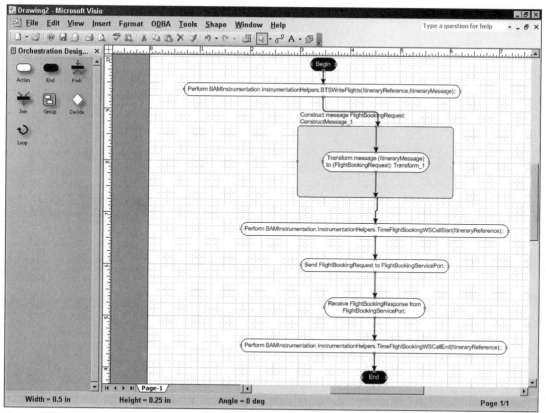

Figure 5-16

ODBA was extended in the 2006 release of BizTalk to include the ability to model BAM activities and to view BAM data alongside the Visio diagram. BAM is covered in more detail in Chapter 6, but for now you can think of a BAM activity as a SQL table that collects tracking information for your business process.

When clicking Show/Hide Business Data of Interest on the ODBA menu, you will see a Data of Interest window appear on the Vision Design surface, as shown in Figure 5-17.

Right-clicking this and choosing Edit Business Data Items enables you to add Activity Items, which will form your BAM Activity. The dialog box used to create Activity Items is shown in Figure 5-18, and the resulting Data of Interest pane is shown in Figure 5-19.

Once all the Activity Items have been defined, you can export a BAM definition file from Visio, which can be directly used to provision the BAM infrastructure, or imported into a fully featured Excel worksheet to create Activity Views and the like via the Import XML option.

We have mentioned a number of BAM concepts here that will be explained in Chapter 6.

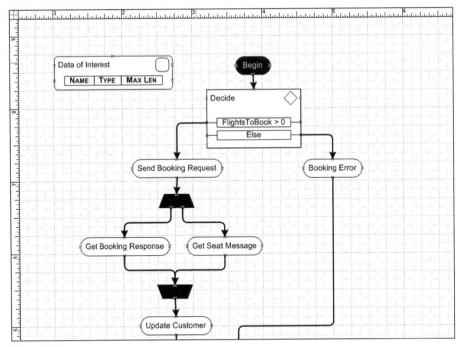

Figure 5-17

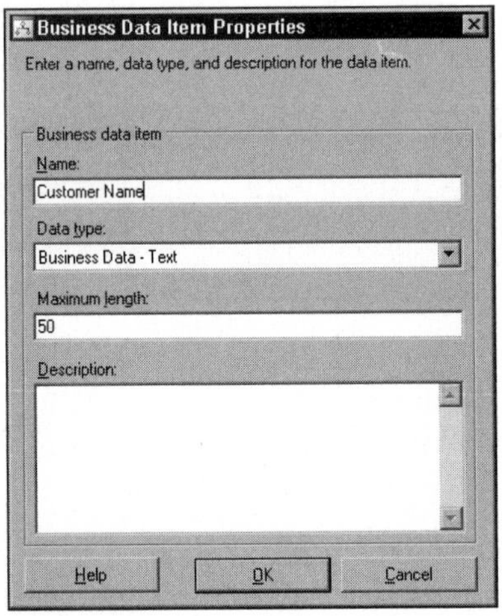

Figure 5-18

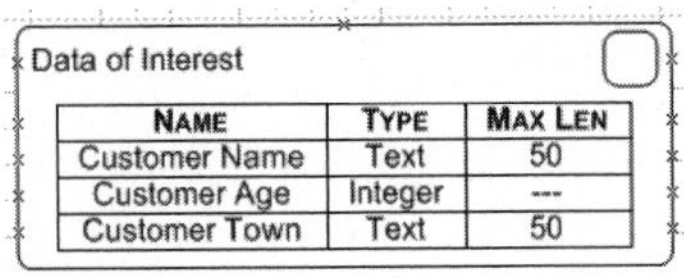

Figure 5-19

Orchestration Designer

The Orchestration Designer is hosted within Visual Studio and provides a developer-centric design tool to create BizTalk orchestrations. The Orchestration Designer makes use of the core Visual Studio features such as a toolbox for orchestration shapes, property pane for configuring orchestration shapes and ports, and so on. We will cover all these areas as we work through the remainder of this chapter.

> **The orchestration design surface is a proprietary development by the BizTalk team and doesn't leverage the rich-design surface developed for Visual Studio 2005 and used by the distributed system designers or DSL tools. This is because these technologies are new investments by Microsoft and weren't available within the BizTalk development timescales.**

BizTalk Server 2006 introduced zoom support for orchestrations, which was a much requested feature by 2004 developers when working with large orchestrations. It is advisable, however, to consider refactoring your orchestration into more manageable parts wherever possible and use the Call Orchestration shape, which offers no real performance overhead, since it is analogous to a method call in C#, unlike the Start Orchestration shape, which goes via the BizTalk MessageBox. Approach refactoring in the same way as you would functions in traditional coding.

See Chapter 13 for more advice on how best to factor and design your BizTalk orchestrations.

Messages

Messages are the building blocks of any orchestration, effectively forming the input and output mechanisms. Every message is effectively treated as a multipart message in that a message can have one or more parts to it. Even if your message has only one part, it is still capable of having multiple parts under the covers. See Chapter 4 for more information on message internals.

It's worth nothing that while most BizTalk messages are represented as XML, they are not required to be XML and can indeed hold any type, including a pure binary message. Of course, this limits the BizTalk tools that can be used. For example, you cannot use the BizTalk Mapper on binary messages.

Each message used within a BizTalk orchestration is represented as the underlying XLANGMessage type. This isn't directly exposed at the orchestration level, but you can gain access to it by casting your BizTalk message to a variable of type `Microsoft.XLANGs.BaseTypes.XLANGMessage`. You need to add an assembly reference to `Microsoft.XLANGs.BaseTypes.dll` (which you can find in `%PROGRAMFILES%\ Microsoft BizTalk Server 2006`) to gain access to the type.

The `XLANGMessage` class has a collection of `XLANGParts` represented via the `Item` property. Unless you have a multipart message, you will find the body of your message at the 0th element (`MyXLANGPart MyPart = MyXLANGMessage.Item[0];`).

Each part can either be defined by an XML schema or any .NET class that is serializable either to XML or implementing its own serialization. Messages are typically represented in XML, which can make development significantly easier because you can leverage native features such as the BizTalk Mapper. If you have no need to convert the messages to XML at any point within BizTalk, however, don't convert them for the sake of it; this introduces unnecessary processing overhead.

> Defining a Message Part type to be an `XmlDocument` **enables you to receive messages that are of any type, including binary.**

BizTalk has implemented a streaming-based model for message processing throughout to ensure that if large messages are being used they are not loaded into memory and thus incur the memory overhead. See Chapter 4 for more information on the streaming model used and Chapter 13 for information on how to approach the processing of large messages.

BizTalk versions prior to 2004 did not implement this model and had issues regarding large-message capability, which were largely resolved in 2004 and 2006 versions.

As discussed later in the chapter, BizTalk messages are immutable and cannot be changed at any point. To change any element of this message requires you to create a new message, assign the original message to it, and then perform any changes. Any message construction like this must be performed within the scope of a Construct Message shape and nowhere else.

Each BizTalk message also has a message context associated with it; this message context flows with the BizTalk message and is a dictionary of properties defined by name and a property namespace to prevent name collision. The message context is used heavily by adapters and pipeline components to provide data on how the message was processed, transport information, and so on.

As you'll see later in this chapter, the message context can be used to great effect by developers to store processing information, and it can also be used for property promotions. Again, see Chapter 4 for more information on messages and context.

Creating a BizTalk Message

An orchestration message is created using the Orchestration View pane in Visual Studio. If this isn't visible inside your IDE when you have an active BizTalk project, click View ➪ Other Windows ➪ Orchestration View.

Right-clicking the Messages node within the Orchestration View pane enables you to create a new message, which you must use to configure the underlying type via the `Message Type` property in the Properties pane. Most BizTalk messages use a schema type to represent the message, although you can select a .NET class via this property by either selecting one of the commonly used types shown in the `Message Type` property drop-down list or by browsing to a type in a referenced .NET assembly.

This class must support serialization to enable the .NET class to be serialized into an XML representation. Solution developers often start by defining a schema using the BizTalk Schema Editor and then use `xsd.exe /c` to create a serializable class that, when serialized, automatically creates an XML document that adheres to the schema. We discuss this further in the "Coding" section of this chapter. The `XmlDocument` type can be selected if you want to handle binary messages.

Once the type has been selected, the message is ready to use and you can then configure a Send or Receive shape to use this message.

Creating a Multipart BizTalk Message

As we've already covered, BizTalk messages are always capable of having multiple parts, although in most cases, including the message created in the previous section, messages only ever have one part — the body part. A message, however, can have multiple parts, which is a useful technique to segregate message data. For example, binary attachments or processing metadata could be kept in a separate part.

Multipart messages are created in a very similar manner to normal messages. First, create a BizTalk message as usual, but select Create New Multi-part Message Type from the Message Type property in the Properties window, as shown in Figure 5-20.

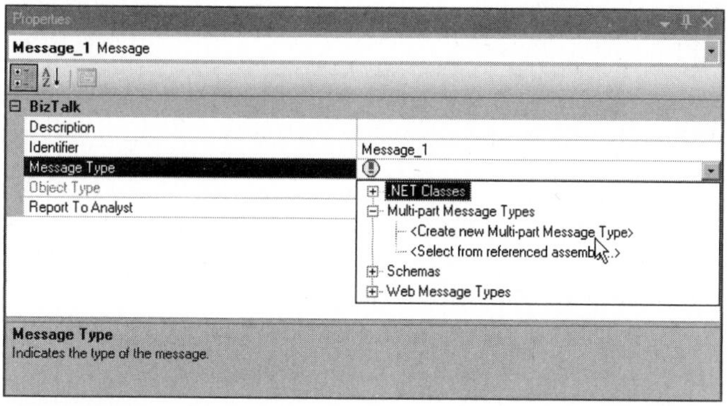

Figure 5-20

This will then create a new multipart message type in the Types section of the Orchestration View pane. From here, you can create multiple parts and configure the type of each one in the same way you did in the previous section. This is shown in Figure 5-21.

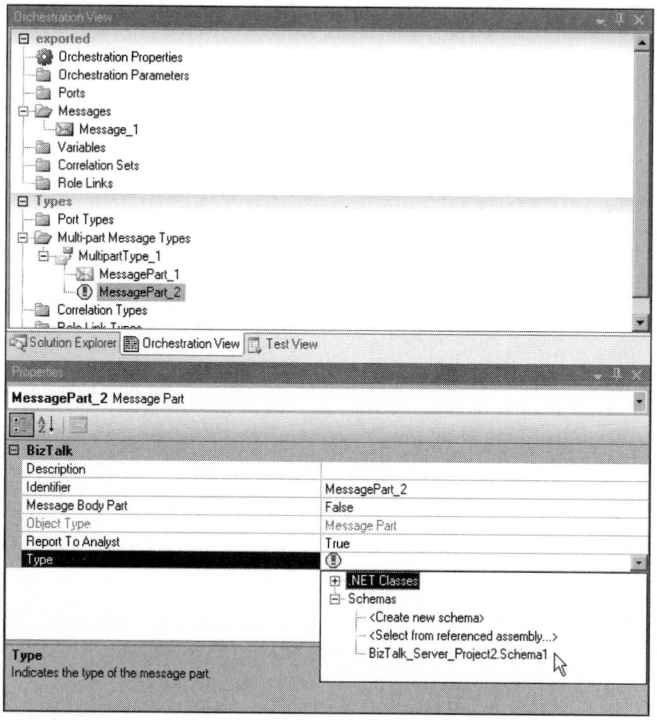

Figure 5-21

These multiple parts can then be directly accessed within the orchestration as child properties of the BizTalk message (see Figure 5-22). Additional message parts can be added dynamically from within an orchestration, as required. This is a useful technique for when you need to store a dynamic number of messages within an orchestration and can be done without creating a new message within a Construct Message shape.

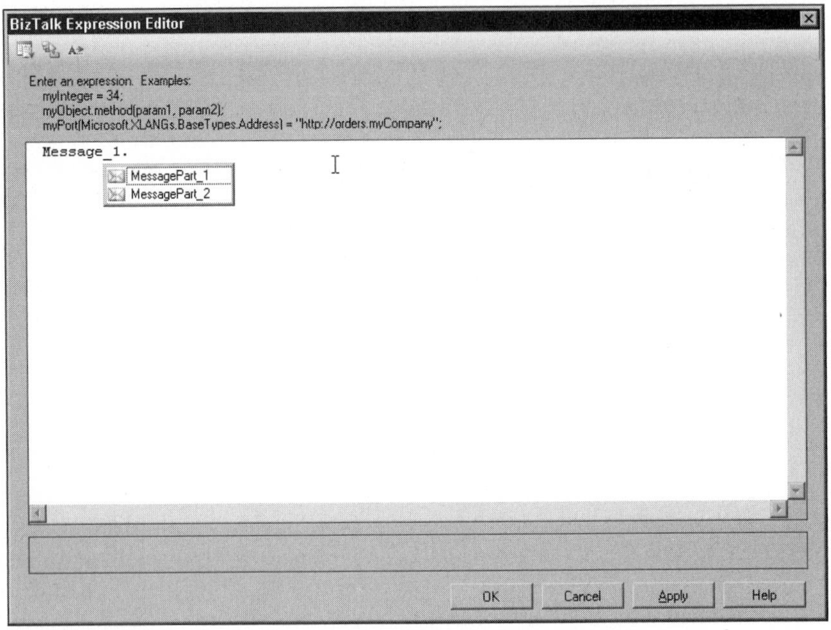

Figure 5-22

Some good examples of using multiple parts are when you need to receive a variable number of messages inside an orchestration, which will then be aggregated at a later stage; storing "out-of-band" processing metadata; or if you use the SWIFT accelerator, using multiple parts for repair messages: one to store the XML representation of the message and another part to contain the original flat-file contents, which can be used in case the repair tool needs the original message.

Parts can be dynamically added by casting your multipart message to an XLANGMessage and using the AddPart method. This can be done within an Expression shape or, preferably, a helper .NET class, which can be easily tested via a unit test.

The following is an example of a helper .NET class that simplifies how parts can be added to and retrieved from a BizTalk message. This can be called straight from a BizTalk orchestration, passing the BizTalk message in question.

```
[Serializable]
public class PartHelper
{
  public static void AddPart(XLANGMessage msg, string partName, object part)
  {
    msg.AddPart(part, partName);
```

```
        }

    public static object GetPart(XLANGMessage msg, string partName, Type t)
    {
        XLANGPart part = msg[partName];
        return part.RetrieveAs(t);
    }
}
```

From an Expression shape within a BizTalk orchestration, you can use the preceding helper class as follows: In this example we are storing some processing metadata (a string literal of "Preprocessed") inside a part called ProcessingStage, and then retrieving the part information into an orchestration string variable. As mentioned previously, you can store any serializable type as the part contents — a C# class is a classic example.

```
PartHelper.AddPart(OrderMessage, "ProcessingStage", "Preprocessed");

OrcStringVariable = (System.String)PartHelper.GetPart(msg,"ProcessingStage",
typeof(System.String));
```

The Receive Shape

The Receive shape, as the name implies, enables you to indicate to the Orchestration Engine that you wish to have a message conforming to a particular schema delivered to the orchestration. This message delivery can be further restricted from the schema type by using a filter.

The general rule is that all orchestrations must start with an activating receive, which means a Receive shape with its Activate property set to True. As touched on earlier in this chapter, there are exceptions to this rule. The Listen and Parallel shapes can be used but must contain an activating receive as the first shape in each branch. We cover this in detail in the respective sections of the chapter. Another exception is an orchestration configured with parameters to enable invocation from another orchestration.

> Failing to set the Activate property to True will generate the following compile-time error, which plagues even the hardened orchestration developer and causes great confusion to new developers because the error doesn't really give much clue as to the problem!
>
> ```
> "you must specify at least one already-initialized correlation set
> for a non-activation receive that is on a non-selfcorrelating port"
> ```
>
> Setting the Activate property to True on the Receive shape resolves this error.

Once a Receive shape has been dragged onto the orchestration surface, it must be configured as indicated by the usual exclamation mark smart tag.

The first step before configuring a Receive shape is to create a BizTalk message, as discussed in the previous step, and select it via the Message property on the Receive shape.

You can optionally configure filters on a activating receive shape to restrict the messages that will cause the orchestration to be activated. These filters can make use of any message context properties that have been promoted.

An activating receive shape could have a filter applied to not only receive order messages but also order only messages where the `Customer Type == "Premium"`. Another orchestration could have a receive filter that is interested only in messages where the `Customer Type == "Normal"`. This way, one orchestration can perhaps perform fast-track processing for your premium customers.

This technique is often combined with the use of direct ports to loosely couple orchestrations; a *processing flag* can be set on a message prior to its being posted back to the MessageBox, which indicates the next processing stage required for this message. Another orchestration can subscribe to this message but with a filter relating to this processing stage, and so on. Unlike the Call or Start Orchestration shape, there is no formal binding between these orchestrations, so new processing stage orchestrations can be introduced or existing ones modified without producing a modification of the remaining solution.

You can apply filters through the `Filter Expression` property exposed by the Receive shape. Once the filters have been compiled, you cannot modify them unless the orchestration is recompiled and redeployed.

The Send Shape

The Send shape, as you would expect, enables you to send a message. Contrary to popular belief, the actual process of sending the message to the ultimate destination is decoupled from the Send shape. The Send shape solely commits the message to the BizTalk MessageBox and then returns immediately allowing the orchestration to continue.

A Send shape is often immediately followed by a Receive shape, meaning that once the message has been committed to the MessageBox, the orchestration then becomes a dehydration candidate as it's awaiting arrival of the response message.

Send shapes can be configured to enable delivery notifications, which we discuss later in the "Messaging" section of this chapter. Delivery notifications cause the orchestration to wait at the Send shape until the message has been successfully transmitted to the destination system, rather than engaging in the usual behavior of continuing once the message has been committed to the MessageBox. The orchestration can still dehydrate while waiting for this acknowledgment, but the orchestration will not continue processing.

Delivery notifications are covered further in the "Messaging" section of this chapter.

Flow Control Shapes

There are a number of flow control shapes that can be used by orchestration developers to control the flow of the business process:

- ❑ Loop
- ❑ Delay
- ❑ Decide
- ❑ Parallel
- ❑ Listen
- ❑ Start Orchestration
- ❑ Call Orchestration

The Loop Shape

The simplest flow control shape is the Loop shape, which, when dragged onto the orchestration design surface, enables you to drag any combination of orchestration shapes within the *scope* of the Loop shape, as shown in Figure 5-23.

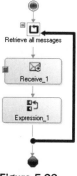

Figure 5-23

Each shape within the scope of the Loop shape will be executed repeatedly while the condition specified on the Loop shape is true.

The Delay Shape

The Delay shape allows you to put the orchestration to *sleep* for a configured period of time. The sleep period is provided by way of a .NET `TimeSpan`. The delay shape is configured by double-clicking it in the Orchestration Designer or by clicking the exclamation mark smart tag displayed on the shape.

To make an orchestration delay for 1 day, the following `TimeSpan` can be used:

```
new System.TimeSpan(1,0,0,0);
```

This time period can be stored in configuration to enable it to be modified once the solution is live. Chapter 13 discusses how you can store configuration data using the centralized SSO store.

A delay shape will not always cause the orchestration to dehydrate. If the delay period specified on the Delay shape is greater than the dehydration thresholds, then it will dehydrate; anything less, however, will not necessarily cause dehydration.

The Decide Shape

The Decide shape enables you to branch orchestration processing based on a Boolean expression, directly analogous to the `if` statement in C#. Each Decide shape includes an `else` branch and right-clicking the Decide shape enables you to add extra branches (analogous to the `else if` statement in C#) by selecting New Rule Branch.

The Decide shape is often used to evaluate contents of a BizTalk message, for example, when checking to see if the customer is a Premium Customer for whom processing is then fast tracked.

Distinguished promotions are often used for this scenario to enable easy retrieval of message data (and are discussed in the "Messaging" section of this chapter).

The Parallel Shape

In my experience, the Parallel shape provokes the most confusion. If you're approaching it from a developer's mind-set, you would likely assume the Parallel shape would enable you to process multiple branches at the same time — the business process equivalent of spinning up multiple threads.

In fact, this is not what happens. You do not get a thread per Parallel shape branch. Instead, you must use the Parallel shape from a business user's mind-set. To illustrate this, consider the orchestration shown in Figure 5-24.

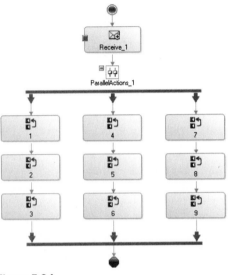

Figure 5-24

This orchestration has three parallel branches. The first branch has three Expression shapes configured to write debug trace out using the `System.Diagnostics.Debug.WriteLine()` method. The first shape will output 1, second shape 2, and so on. The second and third branches complete the same pattern but with different numbers.

If the Parallel shape were to execute multiple threads, you would expect to see interleaved numbers, but in fact you would see that each branch is executed in its entirety from left to right. This is shown in Figure 5-25. Note that the entire branch will not be executed if a shape that causes a delay (Receive or Delay) is executed. In the case of a delay, the next branch will start execution and so on.

The Parallel shape enables you to complete different stages of business process without having to wait for another part of the business process to complete. Figure 5-26 shows a simplified typical example. A Travel Itinerary message is received by the orchestration, and the flights are booked, followed by the hotel.

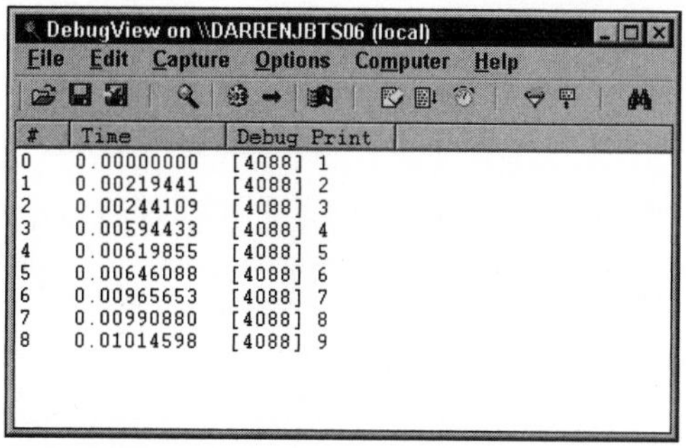

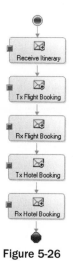

Figure 5-25

Figure 5-26

If for example, the Flight Booking response message took a few hours to process, it would leave the hotels unbooked until after the Flight Booking response had been received. In that case, you might want to perform both elements of the business process in parallel to seek a booking at the earliest opportunity.

If this orchestration was redesigned to use the Parallel shape, it not only is more understandable but also operates each business process logically in parallel, as shown in Figure 5-27.

To ensure that you understand exactly how the Parallel shape works in this case, we'll walk through the order the Parallel shape executes the orchestration shapes.

1. The Tx Flight Booking shape

2. The Rx Flight Booking shape (the shape then enters a wait condition, potentially leading to dehydration)

3. The Tx Hotel Booking shape

4. The Rx Hotel Booking shape (the shape then enters a wait condition, potentially leading to dehydration)

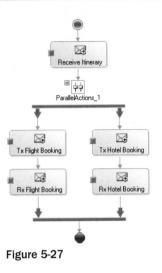

Figure 5-27

The order in which the response messages arrive will then dictate which shape is completed first — either Rx Flight Booking or Rx Hotel Booking. Continued processing of the orchestration below this Parallel shape will not continue until all branches have been completed.

> In some scenarios, you might use the same variable or message in multiple branches. To prevent a branch from modifying data in use by another branch, you must use such messages or variables within a Scope shape configured as synchronized, which prevents the modification of data shared across multiple branches.

As detailed earlier in this chapter, the Parallel shape is a special case in that it can be used as the first shape inside an orchestration. Other shapes cannot be used in this way.

This pattern is useful when you don't know which message will arrive first to start a new orchestration, but you require both messages to ultimately arrive. The usual approach of having two Receive shapes within your orchestration achieves the same ultimate goal but means that the message retrieved by the first Receive shape must be received and processed before the second. Adopting this Parallel shape approach means that the first message to arrive can be processed while waiting for the remaining message.

This is called a *parallel convoy* and is covered later in this chapter in the "Convoys" section, along with an example.

The Listen Shape

The Listen shape is arguably one of the most powerful shapes in any orchestration developer's toolbox, and is often overlooked. The Listen shape, as the name implies, allows you to *listen* for any combination of messages to arrive or delays to expire through the use of multiple branches, but, crucially, only one branch can succeed — the first one wins.

Consider the scenario shown in Figure 5-28. This Listen shape has two branches: The first branch has a Receive shape waiting for a message to arrive, and the second branch has a Delay shape waiting for a configured period before continuing.

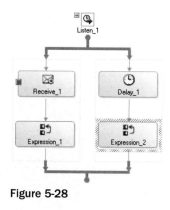

Figure 5-28

If a message arrives in this configuration, the Delay branch will be terminated and can no longer continue down that branch. Processing continues down the Receive shape branch. Conversely, if the delay period completes before a message arrives, then the Receive branch is terminated and orchestration processing continues down the Delay branch.

This send-wait-retry pattern is often used to implement a message retry style of pattern in that you send a message and expect a reply. In the case where a reply isn't received within an expected SLA, you can then resend the message or apply some other compensating action.

Figure 5-29 shows this common send-wait-retry pattern.

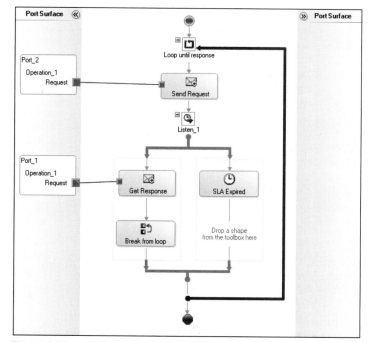

Figure 5-29

A particular interrupt pattern, which is discussed in Chapter 12, makes use of the listen shape to identify if an orchestration needs to be interrupted. This is implemented through the use of a Listen shape that has two branches: one with a Receive shape and another with a Delay shape set to wait for a delay period of 0.

This usage illustrates the left-to-right behavior of the Listen shape in that it will execute branches from left to right. If no interrupt message is present, it will instantly execute the delay branch, but the Delay branch will not instantly execute if an interrupt message is present, because it checks the leftmost branch first.

Another common use for the Listen shape is when you have the possibility of receiving two or more different types of messages but can't predict which one you'll receive in advance. You can have multiple branches in your Listen shape, both with Receive shapes configured to accept different BizTalk messages. The first message to arrive will "win," and the remaining branches will be terminated. Again, the Listen shape will be executed from left to right, so if both messages are present, the leftmost branch containing a Receive shape will execute.

As with the Parallel shape, the Listen shape is a special case in that it can be used as the first shape inside an orchestration. The preceding pattern can be used as long as each branch within the Listen shape starts with a Receive shape and is marked as an activating receive. The first message to arrive will activate the orchestration and the other branches will be terminated.

The Start Orchestration Shape

The Start Orchestration shape is used to invoke another BizTalk orchestration asynchronously, thus enabling the calling or parent orchestration to continue processing.

Breaking orchestrations up into discrete smaller orchestrations is a good approach, especially when there is a common pattern or implementation that can be used by multiple orchestrations. Follow the same approach that you would use when refactoring code.

When configuring the Start Orchestration shape, you must first specify the orchestration that should be invoked. You can do this either by double-clicking the shape or by selecting the target orchestration via the `Called Orchestration` property. You can use orchestrations within the current Visual Studio project or a referenced project.

> A word of warning, however: Invoking orchestrations in this way creates an implied dependency between the two orchestrations, which will require that the orchestrations be deployed in the right order and stopped/started together. Any modifications to one orchestration may require modification to the other and cause both to have to be redeployed.
>
> Although this is not a major problem, you need to be aware of it. An alternative approach to address this is to loosely couple your orchestrations through the use of direct ports, which is covered in the "Logical Ports" section of this chapter and in more detail in Chapter 13.

Unlike the Call Orchestration shape, the Start Orchestration shape provides an interesting design technique: The Start Orchestration shape causes a new orchestration to be created via the BizTalk MessageBox. Interestingly, this can enable you to invoke an orchestration that is held within a different BizTalk host. However, this MessageBox *hop* does introduce a performance overhead, something you should consider when choosing between the Call and Start Orchestration shapes.

You might ask why this is useful. As discussed in the "Activation" section of this chapter, there can be scenarios in which there are elements of your business process that are not critical to perform immediately, and you may want to off-load this processing to later in the business day or do it on a separate dedicated server to keep your core processing servers from being affected and to improve the latency of your processing.

I'll use the same example that I mentioned earlier in the chapter. A payment-processing system will need to commit the payment as quickly as possible because a customer or member of staff will be waiting for the result.

However, additional steps can be required to complete the business process. Auditing is a good example. Decoupling the auditing process in this way enables the main payment process to complete and thus not require the end user to wait for additional processes to complete.

Configuring the *invoked* orchestration in a separate BizTalk host will enable you to then execute this orchestration on preconfigured machines.

The Call Orchestration Shape

The Call Orchestration shape, like the Start Orchestration shape, enables you to invoke another orchestration — the difference being that this invocation is done synchronously, meaning that the calling or parent orchestration must wait for the invoked orchestration to complete before processing can continue.

Unlike the Start Orchestration shape, the orchestration (even if it's configured to use a different BizTalk host) will run within the same host as the parent orchestration, because the invocation is performed *in-memory* and introduces little to no overhead, unlike the Start Orchestration shape, which works via the BizTalk MessageBox.

Rules Engine

The BizTalk Rules Engine Call Rules shape enables you to invoke a rules policy created using the Business Rules Composer. As part of rules invocation, you can pass BizTalk messages and variables as parameters to your rules policy. It's worth noting that the Call Rules shape will always execute the most recent version of a rules policy that has been deployed. If you want to control the version executed, you can execute the policy manually (see Chapter 7).

BizTalk Server 2004 required that the Rules Engine be called within an atomic scope, which, as we've already discussed, introduces an extra persistence point that is not desirable, for performance reasons.

To address this, it was possible to invoke the Rules Engine via an Expression shape to avoid the persistence point overhead. This technique was used to great effect in a number of projects. BizTalk Server 2006, however, has lifted this requirement.

A message can actually be changed during a Rules Engine execution to, for example, set some data on the message. This does not break the immutable message rule discussed earlier but instead causes the creation of a new message.

Be aware, though, that because this new message will not contain any of the context properties present on the original message, you will need to manually set these again or ensure that you make a copy of the original message first so that you can bulk copy all the context properties after the Call Rules shape has been executed — for example: `NewMessage(*) = OriginalMessage(*);`.

We cover the Rules Engine in further detail in Chapter 7, including how to invoke the Rules Engine via an Expression shape if you're still using BizTalk Server 2004.

Messaging

Now that you've seen how you can express your process using BizTalk orchestration, we'll discuss BizTalk messaging to explain how messages can be constructed and queried, along with messaging patterns that enable complex business process requirements to be implemented.

Construction

BizTalk messages are considered to be immutable throughout all elements of the BizTalk architecture. Within an orchestration, you must clone a message to modify any message data, and this can only be done within a special orchestration shape called the *Construct Message* shape.

The Construct Message shape allows only the Message Transform and Message Assignment shapes to be dragged within its scope. The Message Transform shape allows a message to be created following execution of a BizTalk Map.

The Message Assignment shape, as the name implies, allows messages to be constructed from other messages and is primarily used to assign an existing message to another and to then perform modification. It also enables messages to be created from .NET types, `XmlDocuments`, and so on. As discussed earlier, messages are immutable, and therefore the Message Assignment shape must be used in order to construct a new message based on another, which can then be modified while in the scope of a Construct Message shape.

Context

Each BizTalk message has an associated context; this context is used to hold out-of-band metadata and is often used to make routing decisions and to make available various transport information for use later in the processing.

As you learned in Chapter 3, adapters and pipelines place a significant amount of data into the context of messages. For example, the File adapter stores the originating filename into the context and the MSMQ adapter stores the message priority.

Selected elements of context data can be marked as *promoted*, which enables the BizTalk runtime to use such properties to make routing decisions. Subscriptions, for example, can only make use of promoted properties. An example of this is that a send port can subscribe to messages with, say, an Order Value of

> 5000, meaning that the send port will retrieve any messages that have a message property called Order Value greater than 5000. This can only be performed if the Order Value property is promoted.

As you'll see later in this section, you can add extra custom context properties as required that will flow with the BizTalk message as it passes through the system.

Promoting

When developing a BizTalk solution, you're frequently in a position where you need to access pieces of data from a BizTalk message. Rarely do you need the entire message to perform a business process or routing.

As already discussed in the book, it's not advisable to have the entire message body in memory during processing, especially when dealing with large message bodies and high throughput.

Promotions enable you to take a piece of data from a message and make it easily available to the BizTalk messaging infrastructure and developers. This data can then be used for content-based routing and correlation, and by orchestration developers to branch the orchestration flow based on message data. Alternatively, you can use the xpath function from within a BizTalk orchestration, which we cover in the "Coding" section of this chapter. However, this requires the XPath expression to be encoded within the orchestration, which can be less than ideal if your schema structure changes.

The process by which properties are promoted does have performance overhead, so it's advisable to minimize the number of promotions that you have. Promote properties only if you need them. Distinguished promotions incur less of performance overhead than property promotions.

Distinguished Promotions

Distinguished promotions are simply XPath statements defined by the BizTalk developer using the BizTalk Schema Designer. A distinguished promotion can be any element of data within an XML schema, but, crucially, it must only exist once; therefore, repeating elements are not supported.

Distinguished promotions are available only within the scope of an orchestration and therefore can only be used by orchestration developers and not the BizTalk runtime.

Because these promotions are visible only within an orchestration, there is less overhead associated with using them compared to property promotions. So, unless you need to use the data for correlation or routing or within an adapter or pipeline component, you should, by default, use distinguished promotions.

To promote a property as a distinguished promotion, perform these steps:

1. Open the XML schema within Visual Studio and choose the element you wish to promote from the left tree view.

2. Right-click the element, choose Promote from the context menu, and then select Show Promotions. The Promotions dialog box will appear.

3. Ensure that the Distinguished Promotions tab is selected, and then click Add to mark that property as requiring a distinguished promotion, as shown in Figure 5-30.

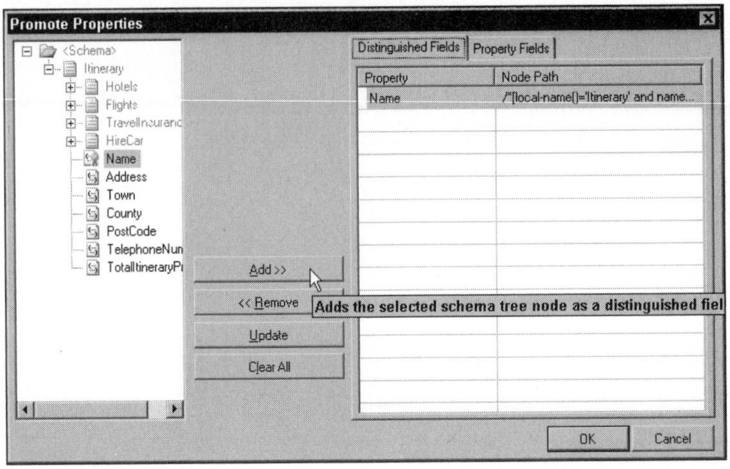

Figure 5-30

Distinguished promotions can then be accessed within a BizTalk orchestration as a property of a message, as shown in Figure 5-31, which shows the Expression Editor shape being used.

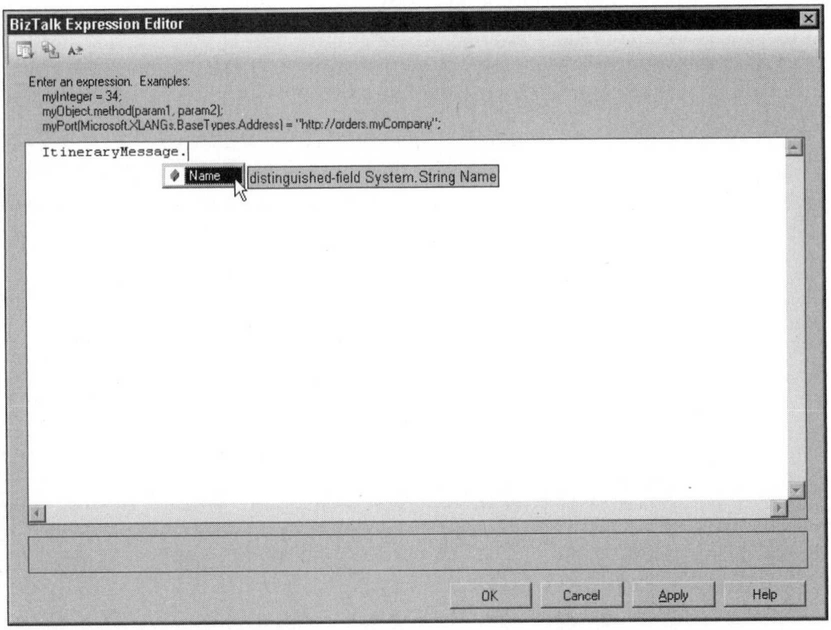

Figure 5-31

Property Promotions

Now that we've covered distinguished promotions, let's discuss property promotions and how they differ.

The key difference is that property promotions are visible at both the messaging infrastructure layer and Orchestrations. Property promotions are made available within Orchestrations by storing the promoted property in the Message context of a given message. Unlike distinguished promotions, property promotions are limited to 255 characters.

Property promotions are typically used when you wish to make elements of your message available so they can be used for content-based-routing scenarios. For example, you could promote the Customer Type element of your Order Message and have two orchestrations that subscribe to an Order Message.

One orchestration could have a receive filter applied that to a Receive shape is set to only be interested in Order messages where the `Customer Type == "Premium"`, and the other orchestration has a receive filter applied that is only interested in messages where the `Customer Type == "Normal"`. This way, one orchestration can perhaps perform fast-track processing for your premium customers.

Another scenario is that with send ports you can apply filters in the same way to select which send port to use based on data held within the message, often called *content-based routing*.

Any context properties can also be viewed at runtime using the BizTalk administration tools. When viewing a message, you can view the standard BizTalk messaging information as well as all context properties. The only exception to this is the properties that have been marked as *sensitive*.

Walk-through

How do you get data from your message into the context of a message? We'll walk through an example to build up on what we've just discussed.

1. Start by creating a list of properties that you want to be placed in the context. To do this, right-click your BizTalk solution, choose Add ➪ New Item from the context menu, and then select Property Schema under the Schema Files node, as shown in Figure 5-32.

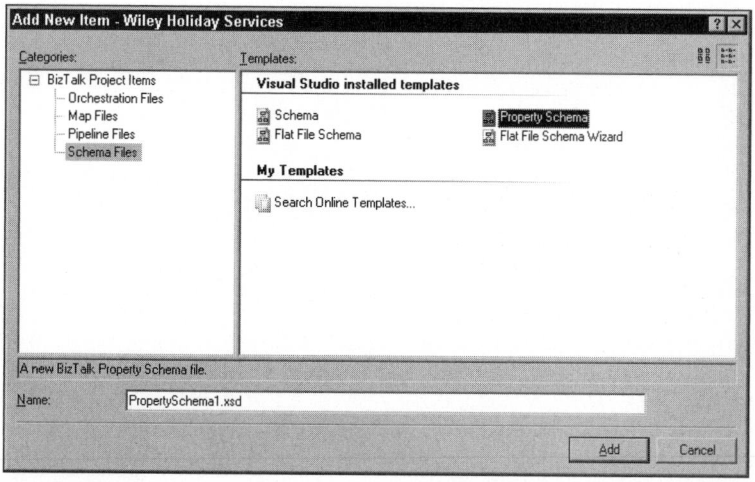

Figure 5-32

2. Modify the namespace of the property schema through the properties pane in Visual Studio. Namespaces are used to qualify and uniquely identify property promotions to the BizTalk runtime.

3. Add an element for each required property and select the appropriate schema type, which is identical to the way you build an XML schema using the BizTalk Schema Editor. This property schema step is effectively extending the context properties available to BizTalk messages. Of course, a message will not be required to use it. As covered in Chapter 3, a number of context properties are made available by BizTalk out of the box.

    Note that in the properties pane of Visual Studio, you can set the `Sensitive Information` property to `true` on property items, which will cause the property not to be tracked and therefore not to be visible to the administration tools.

Now that you've created these custom context properties, you need to populate them with data extracted from the message.

In many scenarios, you use the XML Disassembler component that's present in the standard `XmlReceive` pipeline to populate these custom context properties. You can manually promote data, which we cover later in this section. To configure this, you must select the appropriate data items from your message schema and configure a property promotion for each.

To do this, perform the following steps:

1. Open the XML schema within Visual Studio, and choose the element you want to promote from the left tree view.

2. Right-click the element, choose Promote from the context menu, and then select Show Promotions.

3. When the Promotions dialog box appears, ensure that the Property Fields Tab is selected. First, the Property Schema must be referenced to provide the list of custom context properties you have created previously.

4. Now, select the element for promotion from the left tree view and choose Add.

As you can see in Figure 5-33, the element is moved to the Property Fields List section of the dialog box, and you can then select the custom context property you wish the element to populate at runtime. Note that at this stage you can select the XPath expression shown in the Node Path column to view and edit the XPath expression.

This step adds extra annotations to the top of your XML schema, which indicates how to perform the promotions to the `XmlReceive` pipeline. These annotations are shown below for reference; they show a property promotion and a distinguished promotion.

```
<b:imports>
  <b:namespace prefix="ns4"
uri="http://Wiley_Holiday_Services.PropertySchema.PropertySchema"
     location=".\propertyschema.xsd" />
</b:imports>
<xs:annotation>
  <xs:appinfo>
    <b:properties>
```

```
    <b:property name="ns4:CustomerType" xpath="/*[local-name()='Itinerary' and
namespace-uri()='http://Wiley_Holiday_Services.Itinerary']/*[local-name()='Customer
Type' and namespace-uri()='']" />

        <b:property distinguished="true" xpath="/*[local-name()='Itinerary' and
namespace-uri()='http://Wiley_Holiday_Services.Itinerary']/*[local-name()=
'TotalItineraryPrice' and namespace-uri()='']" />
    </b:properties>
  </xs:appinfo>
</xs:annotation>
```

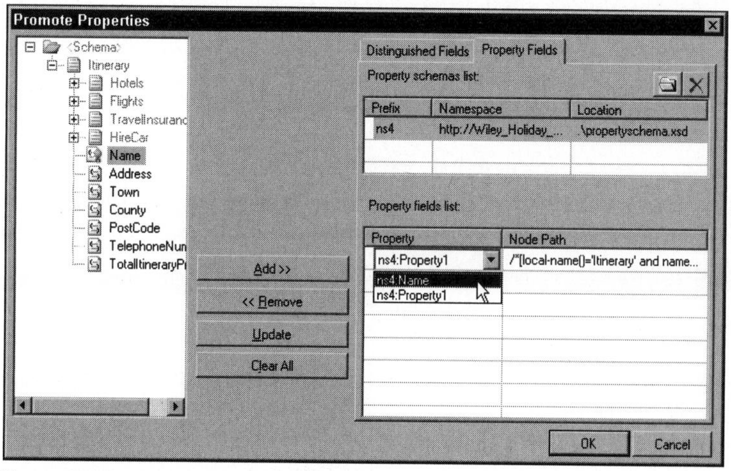

Figure 5-33

Once these steps are complete and the solution is deployed, the custom context property will be populated by the `XmlReceive` pipeline and made available to rest of the BizTalk runtime.

Orchestrations can access the Property Promotion by using the Context Property notation shown in Figure 5-34. Receive shape and Send Port filters are also common consumers of context properties when you apply content-based routing semantics.

It is possible to shortcut the previous steps by selecting Quick Promotion when right-clicking a schema element for promotion, which automatically creates a property schema and a matching element name, and configures the promotion. However, if you want to have complete control over naming, using the previous steps is advisable.

Advanced Property Promotion

The standard approach to property promotions is acceptable for most scenarios, but there are scenarios that require a manual approach. The most common of these is when you wish to populate a context property at runtime with data that is not present in the message (or even to store "out-of-band" data that you need for processing but that isn't part of the core message). Remember, however, that promotion does incur performance overhead, so ensure that you are promoting only the items that you need.

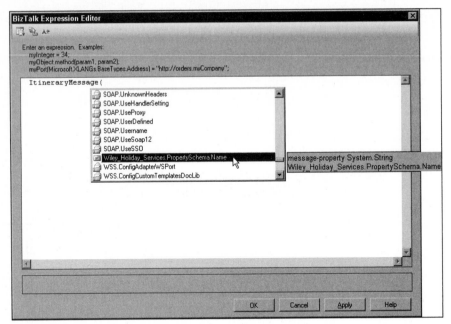

Figure 5-34

Some developers elect to *bend* their XML schema to include such processing data in the message schema. Although this works, it's not really part of the message and, in my view, "dirties" the purity of the message. Utilising a context property enables you to store bits of information metadata required during processing without changing your schema, and it's worth bearing in mind that often you don't control the schema, so modification is not an acceptable option.

To utilize a context property, you must still define a property schema in the usual way, but you need to modify a configuration setting for each property. When you create a new element in your property schema, it defaults to a Property Schema Base setting of `MessageDataPropertyBase`, which indicates to BizTalk that the property will be populated with data from the BizTalk message. In this case, the data isn't part of the message, so this setting needs to be changed to `MessageContextPropertyBase` to indicate that the data will not be sourced from the BizTalk message. Figure 5-35 shows this setting.

This custom context property can be used from anywhere within a BizTalk solution, be it pipeline component or BizTalk orchestration. Modification of a context property is treated as a message modification, so it can only be done with a Message Assignment shape within a Construct Message shape. Figure 5-36 shows a Message Assignment shape contained within the required Construct Message shape. Figure 5-37 shows the expression code required to set the context property within an orchestration.

This works really well and is a crucial technique for most BizTalk solutions, which, sadly, most BizTalk developers are not aware of. It's also important to bear in mind that if you duplicate the message later to make a modification (an example would be using the Message Assignment shape), you must remember to copy the context property values; otherwise, the new message will not have the properties present.

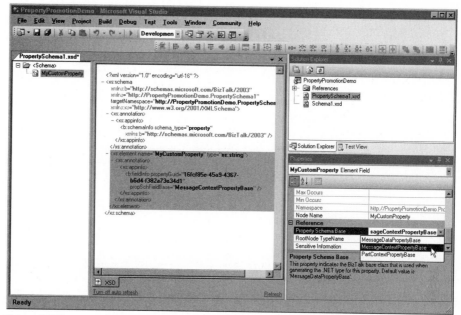

Figure 5-35

Figure 5-36

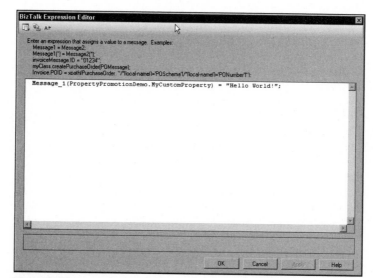

Figure 5-37

> `Message_2(*) = Message_1(*);` **can be used within a Message Assignment shape as a brute-force copy of all the context properties and can be used to ensure that you don't lose any context properties when modifying messages.**

Although this technique works fine for storing data in context properties, you will run into problems if you use this context property for content-based routing. By default, properties written in this way (`MessageContextPropertyBase`) will not be promoted; they are present in the context but are not available for routing. The only way to force the property to be promoted is to send the message using a Send shape configured to Initialize or Follow a Correlation Set that uses this context property. You can then use that property for both content-based routing and correlation.

In other scenarios, you may want to populate context properties from within a custom pipeline component, which is easily done using the `Context` property on an `XLANGMessage`, as shown below. See Chapter 4 for more information.

```
MyXLANGMessage.Context.Promote("MyCustomProperty",
"http://PropertyPromotionDemo.PropertySchema1", "Hello World");
```

Correlation

Correlation is an important concept to understand, as it's required to implement many business processes effectively. Message correlation is all about ensuring that you can route messages back to the right caller.

Imagine a scenario in which two messages of the same type are committed to the BizTalk MessageBox by two different orchestrations for transmission. The appropriate send port will collect and transmit the messages. In turn, two responses will be received and committed to the BizTalk MessageBox.

Because these two messages conform to the same underlying XML schema, BizTalk views them as the same type and needs to ensure that each orchestration waiting for a response gets the right message. If you imagine a bank statement scenario, it would be bad for me to see someone else's statement because the wrong message was routed to my orchestration! This scenario is further complicated when you consider that there will most likely be multiple instances of the orchestration, running in multiple processes, on multiple servers. The message needs to be correlated to the right instance running in the right process on the right server.

BizTalk has a concept of correlation to avoid exactly this scenario. It does this by requiring a developer to identify one or more pieces of data present in the initial message or the message context, which when combined, produce a unique identifier. Often, there is a unique identifier already present in the message which can be used as is; a common example of such a unique identifier is a GUID (globally unique identifier).

This unique identifier must be present somewhere in the return message or message context and allows BizTalk to then identify which dehydrated orchestration the message is ultimately destined for. It could be that the unique identifier is actually a pair of properties that together form a unique identifier.

Correlation is implemented as part of the messaging platform and therefore requires that any data to be used as a unique identifier for correlation to be promoted into the message-context using property promotions. (Remember that distinguished promotions are only available within orchestration.)

Developers need to worry about correlation only when dealing with non-request-response ports such as the MSMQ, MQSeries, and File adapters. Adapters that support request-response messaging internally perform the correlation for you as the BizTalk engine and adapter manage both the request and response. With separate request-response messaging, on the other hand, different adapter threads will manage them and therefore there will be no linkage between the two messages. This requires you to indicate to the BizTalk engine how to link these messages, which is where correlation comes into play.

The Mechanics of Correlation

Configuring correlation is a relatively simple affair, as you'll see in the next section, where you walk through a simple scenario. Conceptually, you start by identifying which element(s) of data you wish to use as the correlation token.

These elements must be available as context properties and therefore promoted using property promotions or manually using the appropriate API. A correlation set is then created, which references a correlation type. The correlation type is purely a list of context properties that make up this correlation type; the correlation set, however, contains these properties but with values assigned during use.

Consider a scenario in which you are sending a message and then receiving a response message that needs to be correlated. This initial sending action needs to *initialize* the correlation set. By initializing it, you are simply instructing BizTalk to extract the context property value at this stage and populating your correlation set — think of it as variable initialization.

The receiving step needs to *follow* this correlation set, instructing BizTalk to take the value(s) held in the correlation set and ensuring that any incoming messages with context properties matching these in your correlation set are routed back to this orchestration instance.

Knowing how the orchestration utilizes subscriptions, you might expect that an orchestration waiting for a correlated message would use a special subscription in the BizTalk MessageBox that would be evaluated when a message is delivered.

If you use the BizTalk Administration Console to view active subscriptions when you have an orchestration waiting for a correlated message, you will see that no subscriptions are present. Instead, active correlations are recorded in the ConvoySetInstances table held in the BizTalk MessageBox (BizTalkMsgBoxDb) database.

When the message is inserted into the MessageBox, the int_EvaluateSubscriptions stored procedure is invoked to identify subscribers. This stored procedure has a special case for convoys and handles delivery to the orchestration.

It can sometimes be useful to identify which correlations are currently active. Although this isn't possible through the BizTalk Administration Console, querying the ConvoySetInstances SQL table can help. Another alternative is to use the sample viewer created by Stephen W. Thomas, which you can download from www.biztalkgurus.com/Tools/Convoy-Subscription-Viewer.html. This tool is for BizTalk Server 2004 but works fine with the 2006 release.

A common misconception is that any data used as part of a correlation type must exist in the same *place* in all messages. In fact, messages conforming to completely different message schemas can work with correlation, as it relies on context properties that are isolated from the physical message structure. Pipeline components typically find the data and promote it into the context properties prior to correlation being performed.

Correlation Walk-through

I like to use a highly contrived but simple scenario to explain how correlation works in practice and the steps required to get it to work. The scenario has to be simple to avoid any extra complexity clouding what's going on under the covers.

So, disclaimer aside, you're going to use BizTalk to implement one of the most expensive calculators you'll come across! The calculator adds two numbers and generates an output message with the result. Each number is delivered into BizTalk via separate messages. Once the first message has been received, an orchestration is created, which then waits for a further message. You have to ensure that the second message reaches the right orchestration; otherwise, the calculation will deliver incorrect results.

This walk-through happens to use a sequential convoy. Correlation doesn't have to be used in conjunction with a convoy, but this particular walk-through necessitates a sequential convoy.

1. Create the schemas to represent our messages — in this case, an Add and Equals message. These are straightforward and are shown in Figures 5-38 and 5-39, respectively.

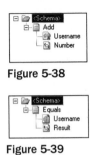

Figure 5-38

Figure 5-39

Note that both messages have a `Username` attribute to provide a unique identifier and configured to be given a property promotion, by selecting the `Username` attribute on the Add message created in the previous step and choosing Quick Promotion. Remember that any message elements used for correlation must be property promotions.

2. Create the BizTalk orchestration that will receive two Add messages, calculate the total, and return an Equals message.

    Start by creating the three messages used by the orchestration. For this demonstration, you'll use the names `LHSAddMessage` and `RHSAddMessage` when naming the BizTalk messages, which will represent the left-hand and right-hand parts of the equation (e.g., 6 + 2), and an `EqualsMessage` to hold the equation's result. The Add messages will conform to the Add Message schema, and the `EqualsMessage` will conform to the Equals schema.

3. Create a Receive shape for the first Add message (`LHSAddMessage`). Drag this onto the orchestration design surface, and set the `Activate` property to `True` and the `Message` property to `LHSMessage`. Create a logical port configured to receive messages on the orchestration, and connect this to this Receive shape.

4. You now need to receive a further Add message to complete your calculation. If you were to drag another Receive shape onto the orchestration configured to receive a message of the same type, you would run the risk of getting another user's message. The basic subscription created only distinguishes message type.

In fact, the Orchestration Designer prevents you from falling into this trap by detecting this messaging problem during compilation and indicating that you should use correlation.

5. Configure another Receive shape as you did in the previous step, but set the Message property to RHSMessage, and instead of creating a new logical port for this Receive shape, connect this shape to the same logical port used by the previous Receive shape.

    Because you are using a sequential convoy, you must select the same logical port for this scenario. It's not required for vanilla correlation scenarios.

6. To ensure that the second Receive shape receives only an Add message with the same username that the first Add message received, you need to enable correlation, which instructs the messaging infrastructure to route the message correctly.

    The first step to enabling correlation is to create a correlation set, which can be done through the Orchestration View pane in Visual Studio. Right-click Correlation Sets in this pane, choose New Correlation Set, and then provide a friendly name, such as AddMessageCorrelationSet.

7. During runtime, this correlation set will be used to hold the correlation token values. The next step is to define what correlation tokens will be used. This is done by selecting Create New Correlation Type from the Correlation Type drop-down list on the Correlation Set properties Window (see Figure 5-40).

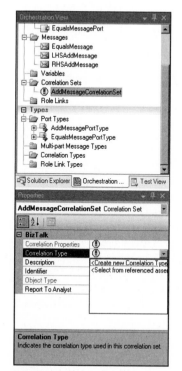

Figure 5-40

8. Once the correlation type is created, provide a friendly name, such as `AddMessage-CorrelationType`, and click the Correlation Properties button in the Correlation Type properties window to configure the properties used (see Figure 5-41).

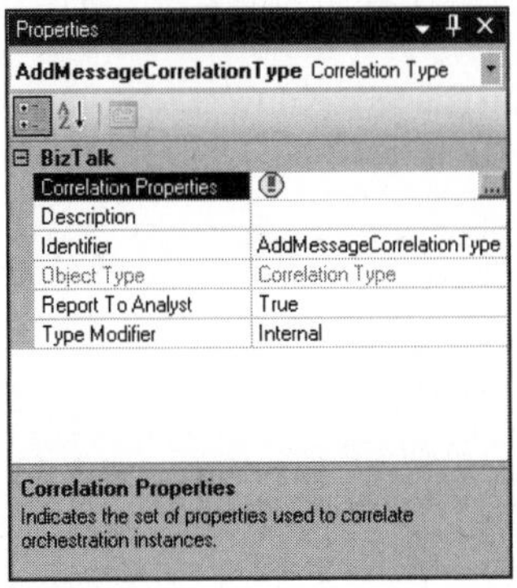

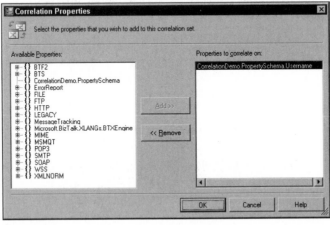

Figure 5-41

9. The Correlation Properties are the context properties that you want to use for correlation. The Correlation Properties dialog box shows all the built-in context properties that BizTalk makes available, along with any custom context properties that you've created via a property schema in your project.

10. In this scenario, you can see the `Username` property under the `CorrelationDemo` `.PropertySchema` node. Select this, and click Add to select this for correlation, as shown in Figure 5-42.

Figure 5-42

This completes configuration of the correlation set. Now, you need to use this correlation in the BizTalk orchestration. You must first initialize the correlation set with the data it will later use when correlating messages. Do this on the Receive shape by selecting the `AddMessageCorrelationSet` on the Initializing Correlation Set property, as shown in Figure 5-43.

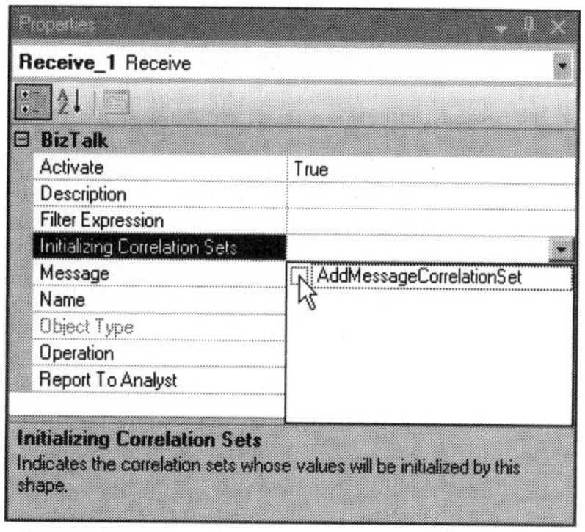

Figure 5-43

This instructs the orchestration's runtime to copy values of the properties specified in our Correlation Type into your correlation set when a message is received.

The next and final step is to configure the second Receive shape that will receive the next Add message to follow this correlation set. Therefore, when another message arrives in the MessageBox containing the same username, it will be correlated back to this orchestration instance.

To do this, select the second Receive shape and pick `AddMessageCorrelationSet` on the Following Correlation Sets property, as shown in Figure 5-44.

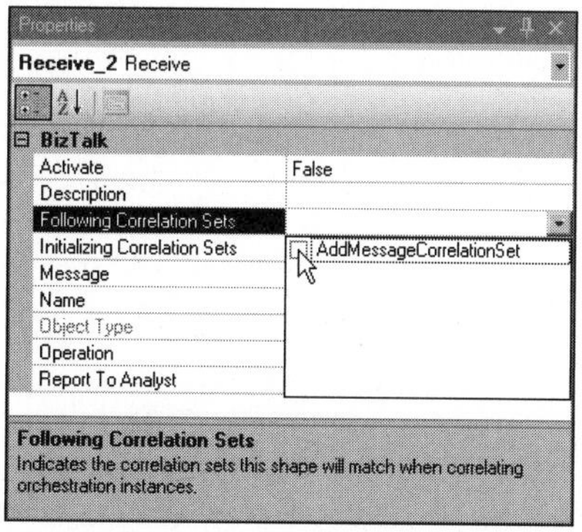

Figure 5-44

That's everything configured to enable correlation for this scenario. The remainder of the orchestration is shown for reference in Figure 5-45 but does little more than use the BizTalk Mapper to add the two numbers and then send an Equals message.

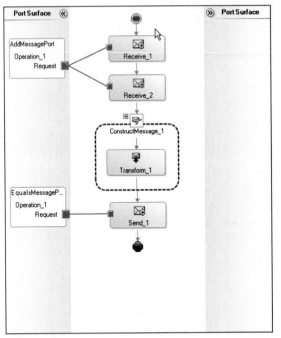

Figure 5-45

Convoys

In my experience, many orchestration developers struggle with the concept of convoys. Strictly speaking, you don't need to know anything about convoys, as they're an internal mechanism utilized by BizTalk to avoid messaging race conditions. You can think of this as BizTalk detecting a complex messaging pattern and doing the heavy lifting required to get such a pattern to work reliably.

However, I think it is important to at least have an appreciation of what a convoy is and what BizTalk will do to support your business process designed using orchestration. So why do you need convoys? BizTalk, as already discussed, is driven by a publish-and-subscribe model, which is fine for many scenarios. Some business processes, though, require subtle differences that can't be served by the traditional publish-and-subscribe scenario. You'll look at some of these now.

The Race Condition

As you've already seen, a BizTalk orchestration places an activation subscription into the BizTalk MessageBox when an orchestration is enlisted. If the orchestration also has other (nonactivation) Receive shapes for different messages, there's no subscription present for these until the Receive shape is executed.

If you consider the orchestration in Figure 5-46, you can see that there are two Receive shapes shown, which seems simple enough. The first Receive has been marked as an activating Receive, as usual.

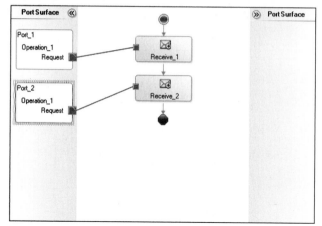

Figure 5-46

While it looks fine, this can lead to a problem. When the orchestration is enlisted, a subscription will be created for the message requested by the Receive_1 shape. What will happen if the message requested by the Receive_2 shape arrives first?

Because there's no subscription present in the MessageBox for the Receive_2 message, it will be suspended. This would be a bad thing. It's not reasonable to expect that all messages will always arrive in the right order. The system responsible for sending the first message, for example, might have a communications problem leading to the message not arriving at BizTalk until later.

In fact, the Orchestration Compiler detects this for you and doesn't let the orchestration shown above compile. This is a form of race condition; expecting a BizTalk developer to detect and resolve such a problem is a tall order and is a Messaging Engine feature, so the BizTalk engine itself resolves this for you, which is nice!

Another form of race condition scenario occurs when you require, say, three messages to complete a business process. If all three messages arrive at once, you don't want each to start their own orchestration; instead, you want to logically have the first message start an orchestration and for that to then consume the remaining two messages. For the developers among you, this is a form of thread synchronisation object — a critical section, if you like.

The Singleton Pattern

In some scenarios, you may wish to process a number of messages using one orchestration instance rather than multiple instances. This limits the parallelism you would otherwise get, so it should only be used if absolutely necessary.

While you can achieve this singleton behavior with standard correlation and a subscription, by setting a Receive filter to Batch = '1024', you need to know the batch in advance — which, of course, you won't. You need a dynamic runtime singleton orchestration that takes the value from the first message and streams in the remaining messages. This is what a convoy gives you — the synchronization object behavior where the first message is processed first, followed by the rest.

It's important to remember that singleton in this scenario can be the usual definition where you have one orchestration, but it is typically a singleton per "group" of messages, grouped per correlation set.

Convoy Types

Convoys exist to address these messaging problems, and they involve the implementation of a special case at the BizTalk MessageBox layer when subscriptions are evaluated.

During the enlistment of an orchestration, the requirement for a convoy is detected automatically. A normal subscription is placed in the MessageBox, which subscribes to the message type as usual, along with further criteria to ensure that all the context properties used as part of the correlation set exist.

Then as convoys need to be created, they are inserted into `ConvoySetInstances`. When messages arrive in the MessageBox, the subscription evaluation takes these into consideration when establishing where messages need to be routed.

Sequential Convoys

A *sequential convoy* is used to describe a messaging pattern whereby messages are received in order, one after another until some form of condition is reached — such as the last message in a batch.

There are two types of sequential convoys. The names are pretty confusing but the convoys themselves quite simple once you get your head around them.

Uniform Sequential Convoy

The first sequential convoy is the *uniform sequential convoy*. Uniform means that the convoy can only contain messages of the same type. A uniform sequential convoy can only receive messages from the same logical orchestration port. It is not possible to receive sequential convoy messages from different logical ports on an orchestration.

An example of this type of convoy is shown in Figure 5-47, and a sequential convoy was used as part of the previous correlation walk-through. The only configuration required is that, as usual, the first Receive shape be marked as an activation receive and initialize a correlation set.

Subsequent Receive shapes are required to follow the correlation set as initialized by the initial correlation set.

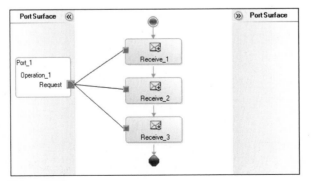

Figure 5-47

Non-Uniform Sequential Convoy

The second kind of sequential convoy is a *non-uniform sequential convoy*; non-uniform means that the convoy can, unlike a uniform sequential convoy, handle messages of different types. These messages must come from the same logical orchestration port. This convoy also imposes an order in which the messages must arrive, which is different from a uniform sequential convoy, where there are no order guarantees.

The ability to handle different message types on a logical port is counterintuitive in the Orchestration Designer and has led many developers to assume that it's not possible, whereupon they pursue a less optimal orchestration design. Extra message types can be added by creating extra operations on a logical port. This can be done by right-clicking the port and choosing New Operation.

An example of this convoy is shown in Figure 5-48. Note the logical port has three operations signifying three different message types being used as part of this convoy. Configuration is the same as for a uniform sequential convoy, apart from the port's being configured with ordered delivery.

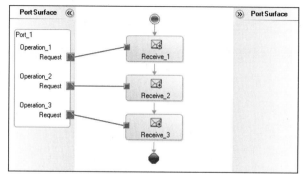

Figure 5-48

Parallel Convoys

A *parallel convoy* is used to describe a messaging pattern whereby messages can be received in any order, but they must all be received before the orchestration can continue. This enables messages to be processed as they arrive, rather than waiting for them to arrive in sequence.

A parallel convoy is implemented by using a Parallel shape with multiple branches, each containing a Receive shape. If you wish to activate an orchestration with this convoy, each Receive shape must be marked as an *activating receive*.

A correlation set has to be created as usual for these Receive shapes, and each Receive shape within the Parallel shape must be marked as initializing the correlation set.

The astute among you will have noticed that you cannot have more than one activating receive in an orchestration, and only one *thing* can initialize a correlation set. So why does BizTalk allow this pattern?

It's a special case specific to this convoy. The first branch of the Parallel shape to execute activates the orchestration and initializes the correlation set. Subsequent branches follow the correlation set, even though they are set to initialize it.

An example of a parallel convoy is shown in Figure 5-49.

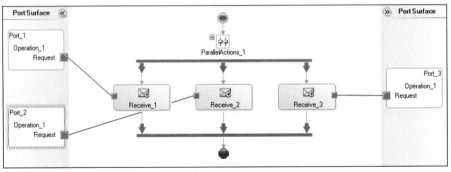

Figure 5-49

Delivery Notifications

As already covered in the "Send Shape" section of this chapter, Send shapes are completely decoupled from the actual operation of delivering the message to the destination system. Delivery notifications provide you with the ability to wait for the message to be delivered successfully to the destination system and only continue orchestration processing when an acknowledgment is returned. Alternatively, they are used to notify an orchestration that a transmission failed.

Delivery notifications can be enabled on a logical port configured with a communication direction of Send. To enable delivery notifications, select the logical send port, and via the Properties Pane select `Transmitted` as the `Delivery Notification`.

Any Send shapes connected to a delivery notification enabled logical port should be placed within a long-running scope along with an exception handler configured to catch a `DeliveryFailureException`. This exception will be thrown if the message delivery fails and will contain information to help identify why. You don't have to wrap the Send shape with a scope in this way, but it's a good practice to ensure that your orchestration doesn't throw unhandled exceptions and suspend pending a manual administrative task.

While delivery notifications seem like a good thing they actually incur a large performance hit, so they should only be considered if you absolutely need such functionality. In high-load scenarios, an alternative custom implementation may be more advisable.

Delivery notifications impact performance for a few reasons. The first is that you are reducing the throughput of your orchestrations, as they have to wait for delivery of the message along with the subsequent acknowledgment message before continuing and will likely cause further dehydration, thus increasing MessageBox load further. You can think of Delivery notification as adding a virtual Receive shape under your Send shape.

Delivery notifications work by subscribing to the Acknowledgment (ACK) and Negative Acknowledgment (NACK) messages. These are BizTalk system messages that the engine automatically publishes, as required. They are actually special messages, because the absence of a matching subscription will not cause them to be suspended; instead, they will simply be ignored.

An example of a NACK message is shown below for reference:

```
<ns0:NACK Type="NACK" xmlns:ns0="http://schema.microsoft.com/BizTalk/2003/
NACKMessage.xsd">
       <NAckID>{BD6682EE-1741-4856-8CC7-B2EE36B7874E}</NAckID>
       <ErrorCode>0xc0c01c10</ErrorCode>
       <ErrorCategory>0</ErrorCategory>
       <ErrorDescription>The FILE send adapter cannot open file
C:\Foo\DeliveryNotification\out\{505A3211-9081-4720-827B-A0DE2BD124FD}.xml for
writing. </ErrorDescription>
       </ns0:NACK>
```

If your BizTalk solution is under high load, these ACK/NACK messages go into the spool of messages awaiting processing. As the distribution of messages to subscribers is not performed in order nor are the ACK/NACK messages treated with higher priority, you run the risk of orchestrations waiting longer than expected for an acknowledgment.

Another point to consider is that send ports themselves implement error-handling and retry semantics, so it may be a long time before the adapter gives up transmitting a message and subsequently suspends it, which will cause BizTalk to publish a NACK to the MessageBox.

If you must use delivery notifications, it's strongly advised that you test the difference it makes to your solution performance to see that it's acceptable. A rule of thumb for the amount of performance difference they can make is around 30 percent.

For atomic scope scenarios where you want to utilize a transactable adapter (an adapter that supports transactions), you must use delivery notifications to ensure that the atomic scope only completes when the messages have transactionally been delivered to the destination system. Note, however, that the Atomic Scope transaction does not bridge to the destination system but instead doesn't commit until the ACK message is received from the adapter.

You can use inline sends as an alternative to delivery notifications (see Chapter 10).

Coding

Now that we've covered the messaging concepts relating to BizTalk orchestration, let's discuss how you can add custom code to your BizTalk orchestration.

Expression Shape

The Expression shape enables you to execute code from within your BizTalk orchestration. As discussed earlier in the chapter, the language used to write code looks like C# but in fact is X#.

The functionality exposed by the Expression shape is used by a number of other shapes, including Decide and Message Assignment. The Expression functionality offers full IntelliSense functionality in the same way as the Visual Studio editors.

Typical uses of the Expression shape are to call .NET class libraries and debugging calls. Because .NET orchestrations themselves become .NET assemblies, there is no interop cost between orchestrations and .NET assemblies, meaning that you shouldn't worry if you end up calling out to .NET components regularly.

Developers frequently lament that the Expression shape has a small editing window that is not resizable and offers no coloring in line with Visual Studio. I like to think these "deficiencies" are deliberate, because the Expression shape is not the place to write pages of code. Instead, it's designed for the snippets of code required to help you out during orchestration development. A .NET class library is the right place for any heavy lifting that can't be expressed using the Orchestration Designer and keeps your business process abstracted from any code.

Having custom code in an external .NET class library offers a number of other benefits. Because it can be shared with other projects and as it's separate from BizTalk, you can implement unit testing to test independently of the BizTalk runtime.

Variables

Variables can be defined at both the orchestration and scope level and can be based on any .NET class type or value types. Variables can be added via the Orchestration view under the Variables node and on a scope by selecting the scope in the Orchestration Designer and expanding it in the Orchestration View pane to show the Variables node.

From a performance perspective (and therefore minimizing the size of your state during persistence), you should not declare variables and messages globally (that is, at the orchestration level) unless absolutely required. You should instead use Scope shapes, which enable you to declare variables for a short period of time. This is the same approach you would use during coding. For example, you can declare a variable within an `if` code block that is garbage collected once the code block has been executed.

Variables can be assigned a default value via the Properties pane, which is useful for initializing, for example, Boolean values to `false` for use as a loop condition. This initialization is performed at the beginning of the orchestration if they are defined at the orchestration level, or when a scope is started if they are defined at a scope level.

It's interesting to note that variables are transactional. So, if you were to change them within an atomic scope, the changes would not be visible until after the scope had committed.

As variables are part of the orchestration state, any type used must be capable of being serialized. This doesn't apply to variables that are part of an atomic scope, as persistence cannot occur during atomic scope execution. The `XmlDocument` class is not serializable but has been "special cased" by the Orchestration Engine to allow it to be serialized. This does not occur for any other type.

Calling .NET Components

Invoking .NET assemblies from BizTalk orchestrations is a simple affair. Because orchestrations are themselves .NET assemblies, no interop or marshaling is required between orchestrations and .NET assemblies.

You must add an assembly reference to your BizTalk project the same way you would with a normal .NET project. As all BizTalk assemblies must be installed in the Global Assembly Cache (GAC), you must ensure that any assemblies referenced by BizTalk components are installed into the GAC and are present when you deploy a BizTalk solution. This can be done automatically by using the Export MSI feature of the BizTalk Administration Console and ensuring that the assemblies are selected as dependent resources.

Why the hard dependency on the GAC, you may ask? The GAC is typically positioned for use when you wish to share one instance of a .NET assembly with multiple programs and don't wish to duplicate the DLL across multiple program locations on a given machine.

Utilizing the GAC also enables you to store multiple versions of a .NET assembly at the same time. If you are not using the GAC, this is not possible, because the Windows file system does not allow multiples files sharing the same name to be present in a directory.

BizTalk has to have a good versioning story, especially with regard to long-running business processes. Ensuring that all BizTalk components are installed in the GAC enables a solid versioning approach for all BizTalk solutions.

Once an assembly reference has been added, you need to be able to invoke it from an orchestration. If the class has static methods, then any assembly methods can be accessed directly using an Expression shape (e.g., `MyNameSpace.Class.MyStaticMethod("Hello World");`).

In nonstatic cases, you must define an `Orchestration` variable assigned to the class type that you wish to use. This variable will then need to be initialized within an Expression shape before use.

Figure 5-50 shows the Orchestration Variable pane, and Figure 5-51 shows an example of calling a .NET assembly via an Expression shape.

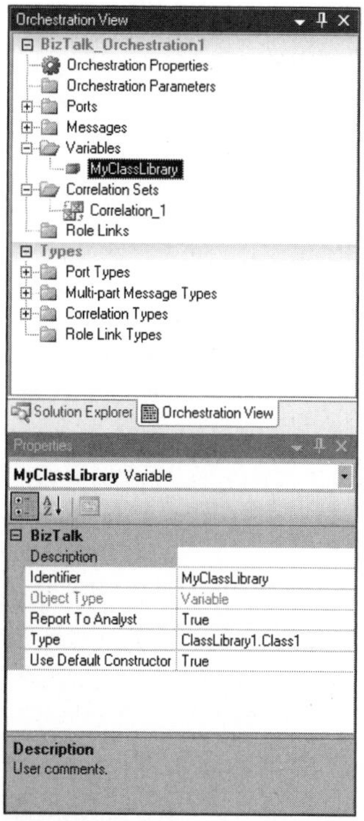

Figure 5-50

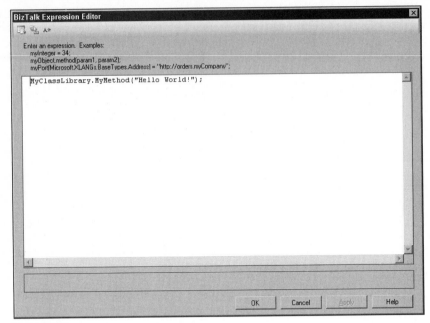

Figure 5-51

If you need to invoke a COM component, you must invoke it within an atomic
scope, as COM components are not serializable. An alternative approach is to wrap
your COM component with a .NET class that handles serializing the state manually.

Best Practice

I often see developers passing BizTalk messages into .NET components to perform processing steps,
which is absolutely the right thing. However, the common choice made by developers is to use the
XmlDocument type on the method signatures. This works absolutely fine but has a number of bad side
effects on any subsequent coding. Perhaps most problematic is how the developer retrieves message
data from this XmlDocument. The tendency is to use XPath queries or even traverse the document manually using the DOM. While this typically works well enough, it produces brittle code and often can be
hard for most developers to get right due to XPath's being namespace aware and thus requiring developers to understand namespaces and how to form sensible XPath statements.

The other major, and most important, downside to using the XmlDocument type on the method signatures is that you are driving a deep dependency on the structure of your XML messages into your entire
solution. With your .NET components coding directly to the structure, it makes the inevitable modification of the schemas as development progresses incredibly hard to handle, as you need to change many
aspects of your solution.

XPath statements and DOM traversing are effectively *loosely typed* errors, which means that inconsisten-
cies are not captured at compile time but instead at runtime, making detection harder. The same points
all apply to code that manually creates an XML document for, say, return to BizTalk. Manually constructing XML documents is tiresome, unnecessary, and above all, brittle.

These concerns lead me to strongly advise against passing messages in this untyped way but instead to pass them as strongly typed classes derived from the XML schema that ultimately is the *owner* of the structure. This way, when the schema does need to be modified, the serializable classes can be regenerated and any dependent components will recompile and raise breaking changes at compile time.

Unfortunately, you cannot directly cast a BizTalk message to a serializable class. Instead, you must pass it to a BizTalk *façade* method that accepts an XLANGMessage and then uses the RetrieveAs method to retrieve the Message-Part in a more accessible type. To access the XLANGMessage type, you need to add a reference to the Microsoft.XLang.BaseTypes assembly.

You can use the RetrieveAs XLANGPart method to retrieve the part in a variety of ways; a few common approaches are shown here:

```
// XMLDocument approach
void BTSMyDotNetMethod( XLANGMessage msg )
{
   XmlDocument doc = msg[0].RetrieveAs(typeof(XmlDocument));
}


// Stream approach
void BTSMyDotNetMethod( XLANGMessage msg )
{
   StreamReader rdr = new StreamReader(msg[0].RetrieveAs(typeof(Stream) );
}
```

These are great but don't give you the strong typing that you're after. Instead, if you generate .NET serializable classes using XSD from the schemas backing your BizTalk messages, then you can utilize these directly. We covered this concept in Chapter 1.

These serializable classes give you a strongly typed class, which, when serialized, produces an XML document that adheres to the schema — all without any XML or schema intervention from the developer. The following code shows a serializable class being populated:

```
CustomerSchemaClass Customer = new CustomerSchemaClass();
Customer.Name = "Toby Jefford";
Customer.Address = "23 Railway Cuttings";
```

The best-practice advice, therefore, is to construct methods that, as appropriate, take and return serializable classes generated by XSD.EXE. BizTalk cannot natively cast XLANGMessages to a serializable class, so you must provide a façade *helper* method to do this for you. This is also a benefit as the underlying method can then be used by other non-BizTalk solutions and when writing unit tests, whereas a method accepting an XLANGMessage makes no sense to anything other than BizTalk. Because XLANGMessage is a BizTalk-specific type, a vanilla .NET application would not have any idea what this type was.

Serializable classes can be cast directly back to BizTalk messages as return parameters without any extra work. Here's an example with an initially generated serializable class (CustomerSchemaClass) that uses xsd.exe from a customer schema.

A BizTalk Expression shape can natively call the BTSDoStuffFacade method, passing a BizTalk message, which, in turn, retrieves a serializable class from the message part.

The BTSDoStuffFacade method then calls the internal DoStuff method with the serializable class as a parameter. The internal DoStuff method then can perform its work and, for the purposes of this example, returns a new serializable class directly back to BizTalk via the BTSDoStuffFacade method to indicate how a message can be returned to an orchestration.

```
public CustomerSchemaClass BTSDoStuffFacade(XLANGMessage MyXLANGMessage)
{
  CustomerSchemaClass c =
    MyXLANGMessage[0].RetrieveAs(typeof(CustomerSchemaClass) );

  return DoStuff (c);
}

public CustomerSchemaClass DoStuff (CustomerSchemaClass c)
{
  // Your code here

  // Create a new CustomerSchemaClass to return back to an Orchestration
  CustomerSchemaClass NewCustomerClass = new CustomerSchemaClass();

  // Your code here

  return NewCustomerClass;
}
```

Making such classes static can also make it slightly easier to invoke from BizTalk, but you need to ensure the classes don't maintain any state.

> Although I recommend this approach as your de facto stance for calling .NET components, it may not be suitable for scenarios involving large messages, because a serializable class will load the entire message into memory.
>
> Another point to note is that when creating new BizTalk messages during orchestration development you can specify a .NET class as the message type instead of a schema. This means that you can then read and write data as you would using a normal serializable class and easily pass between orchestrations and .NET components. The downside of course is that you can't make use of features such as promotions and the BizTalk Mapper. Most importantly, the entire message will be loaded into memory and thus doesn't use the streaming model that XLANGMessage typically uses which will cause problems with large messages.
>
> For these reasons this approach isn't commonly used in my experience.

XPath Function

The XPath function is built into the orchestration runtime and can be used within an Expression or Message Assignment shape to retrieve or modify parts of a BizTalk message. In the 2004 release, it was largely undocumented, and its existence still surprises some developers.

The XPath function accepts two parameters: a BizTalk message and the XPath expression. An example of the usage is shown below. Ensure that you pass both parameters to the XPath function because missing one will result in a runtime error rather than a compile error.

```
xpath(OrderMessage, "count(/*[local-name()='Order']/*[local-name()='Items']/
*[local-name()='Item']")
```

XPath is particularly powerful in a number of scenarios and can help to simplify a complex project if used in the right way. The first thing that trips developers up again is the namespace-aware behavior of XPath, meaning that omitting namespaces from an XPath statement causes the XPath statement to fail if the XML nodes you're searching against are qualified with a namespace.

The right way is to fully qualify your namespaces by using the `namespace-uri` function, as follows:

```
/*[local-name()='Order' and namespace-uri()='http://BizTalk_Server_Project1
.Schema1']/*[local-name()='Items' and namespace-uri()='']/*[local-name()='Item'
and namespace-uri()='']
```

However, you can strip the namespaces away by using the `local-name()` function in XPath. Apologies to those schema/XPath purists among you, but as you have probably already noticed, BizTalk sometimes uses this approach when defining XPath expressions.

To aid with the full XPath expression (complete with namespaces), you can cheat slightly by loading the appropriate schema into the BizTalk Schema Editor and selecting the node you wish to use in your XPath expression.

As shown in Figure 5-52, there is a read-only property called Instance XPath that gives you the full XPath expression, complete with the `namespace-uri` function. Copy this to the clipboard, and use it as the base for your XPath expression.

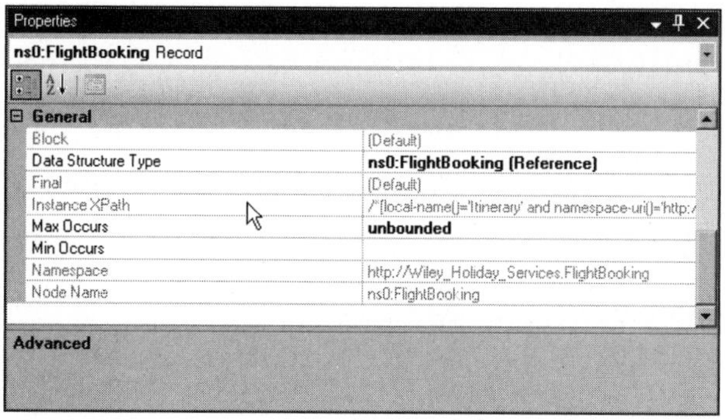

Figure 5-52

The BizTalk documentation has a number of examples of how you can use the XPath function, but we've included a few samples to give you a flavor of what's possible and the types of problems it can solve. Note that the XPath expressions shown below have the `namespace-uri` function omitted for brevity.

Consider the following XML document when reviewing these XPath expressions:

```
<Order>
  <Items>
    <Item Code="ITEM001" Price="23.00" Qty=1>
```

```
            <Item Code="ITEM002" Price="23.00" Qty=1>
            <Item Code="ITEM003" Price="23.00" Qty=1>
        </Items>
    </Order>
```

As part of an orchestration, perhaps you wish to loop around all of the Item elements inside a BizTalk message. To loop around the elements, you need to know how many there are, as there are no enumerator concepts within orchestrations and XML messages.

Using the following XPath expression inside an Expression shape, you can return the number of Item elements and assign them to an orchestration variable for use within a loop condition.

```
count(/*[local-name()='Order']/*[local-name()='Items']/*[local-name()='Item'])
```

When enumerating the Items using the approach detailed above, you may then need to retrieve, say, the Item Code, which is held as an attribute. You can't use distinguished properties because there are multiple Item nodes that aren't supported. Distinguished properties work only if the element appears once in a message.

The following XPath statement can be used to retrieve a particular instance of the Item Code. You need to replace 1 with the particular iteration number using string tokenization.

```
string(/*[local-name()='Order']/*[local-name()='Items']/*[local-name()='Item'][1]/@
Code)
```

Perhaps you need to perform a decision branch within the orchestration, based on the Order Value. Perhaps orders above a certain value need an extra level of authorization. To calculate this order value to check if authorization is required, you will need to add all the Order Item values.

There is no straightforward way to calculate the order value in this way, but the following XPath expression adds all the item values and returns the total, which can be assigned to an orchestration variable and used as part of a Decision shape condition.

```
sum(/*[local-name()='Order']/*[local-name()='Items']/*[local-name()='Item']/@Price)
```

Encoding the XPath expressions into your BizTalk orchestrations obviously presents a manageability issue. If you change your schema during development, you must ensure that you update all orchestrations that use the xpath function. During compilation of your orchestration, you will not receive warnings of any errors; instead, you will experience runtime errors.

An approach to mitigate this is to store the XPath expressions within a .NET helper class or via configuration. This way, you can update the XPath expressions in one place rather than finding all of them across your solution.

Testing XPath Expressions

When developing an XPath expression, I sometimes find it easier to create a Visual Studio unit test to test the XPath expression by using the XPathNavigator class against a sample document. This unit test can then be executed directly within Visual Studio, which is a neater approach than using a temporary console application harness!

This approach gets the XPath expression working correctly before introducing BizTalk orchestration, which can make things harder to debug.

The following is an example of the code required to implement a test:

```
[TestMethod]
public void TestXPath()
{
  using (StreamReader sr = new StreamReader(@"C:\Message.xml"))
  {
      XPathDocument XPathDoc = new XPathDocument(sr);
      XPathNavigator XNav = XPathDoc.CreateNavigator();

      int ItemTotal = (int)nav.Evaluate("count(/*[local-name()='Order']/*[local-
name()='Items']/*[local-name()='Item'])");
  }
}
```

Exceptions

Exception handling is as crucial in BizTalk orchestration as it is in .NET development. Exceptions can occur for a variety of reasons, the most common of which are:

❑   **.NET components** — A base class or custom .NET class invoked by your orchestration can throw exceptions for a variety of reasons, most of which should be documented.

❑   **Throw Exception shape** — Orchestration developers can choose to throw exceptions in the same conceptual way as .NET developers. This can be used to signify a processing error, where you need to either suspend the orchestration or pass it up to an exception handler for resolution.

❑   **BizTalk runtime** — The BizTalk runtime error can throw exceptions for a variety of reasons; perhaps a network failure has caused a loss of connectivity to the BizTalk MessageBox, causing errors during orchestration persistence, XPath problems, and so on.

❑   **Long running-scope** — As you'll see in the next section, a long-running scope can be configured to time out after a certain time, which causes a `Microsoft.XLANG.BaseTypes.TimeOutException` to be thrown.

The general principle of not throwing orchestrations over boundaries still applies, and wherever possible you should catch exceptions and handle them; otherwise, the orchestrations will be suspended in a nonresumable state, meaning that manual intervention is required to resolve the issue, ultimately increasing the total cost of ownership of the solution.

However, if you are absolutely unable to resolve the problem, you should consider logging the exception details to the Windows Event log using custom code held within an Expression shape or, ideally, a .NET class.

You should then suspend the orchestration using the Suspend shape, which will suspend the orchestration within the MessageBox and enable an administrator to resume the orchestration once the problem has been fixed. Because of this, it's crucial that you log all the key information in the Event Viewer. Suspending the orchestration using a Suspend shape will leave it in a suspended-resumable state.

As we cover in Chapter 11, you can use Microsoft Operations Manager (MOM) to monitor such events and flag them for members of your operations staff to resolve.

You should design your orchestration with this in mind and enable the orchestration to retry the operation that failed following a resume, either by using a Loop shape or by invoking a child orchestration using the Call Orchestration shape. A test case should also be created to ensure that this suspend/resume pattern works before finding out in a live environment! An example of this suspend/resume pattern is shown in the "Adding Resilience" section of Chapter 10.

Another alternative that is popular for a system processing critical messages is to pass the message out to a *manual repair* system if any processing steps fail within BizTalk. This enables the message to either be processed manually or resubmitted back into BizTalk; otherwise, the message contents and associated orchestration are hidden away inside the MessageBox, this is covered in Chapter 13. Alternatively, it might be more appropriate to return the message to the sender for some categories of errors.

Orchestration exception handling is broadly similar to the standard C# `try`/`catch` model; a scope shape is used as the `try` element of `try`/`catch`, and by right-clicking a scope you can add an exception handler, which can be used as the `catch` element of `try`/`catch`. Multiple catch sections can be added by choosing Add Exception Handler again.

As with C#, the order of exception handlers is important. In the event of an exception, the exception handlers will be evaluated in the order shown on the Orchestration Designer. You should start with the most specific exception type and finish with least specific (catch-all) handler. You can change the order by dragging the exception handlers in the Scope shape up and down.

Figure 5-53 shows the equivalent of the following .NET exception-handling code:

```
try
{ .. }
catch (InvalidCastException ice)
{
}
catch (ArgumentException ae)
{
}
```

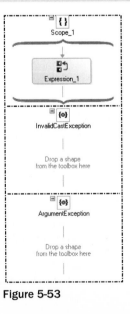

Figure 5-53

Once exception blocks have been added, you must configure each one to handle a specific form of exception. You do this by selecting the exception block and configuring the `Exception Object Type` in the Properties pane.

All the usual .NET exceptions can be selected in this way as long as valid assembly references have been added to the project. The most common BizTalk orchestration exceptions can be found in the `Microsoft.XLANGs.BaseTypes` assembly. The exception selection dialog box is shown in Figure 5-54.

Exception-handling scopes can be nested in the same way as `try`/`catch` blocks, which enable you to perform fairly complex exception handling per your requirements. Exception-handling blocks can be present in long-running scopes but not within an atomic scope, as any errors cause the atomic scope to roll back.

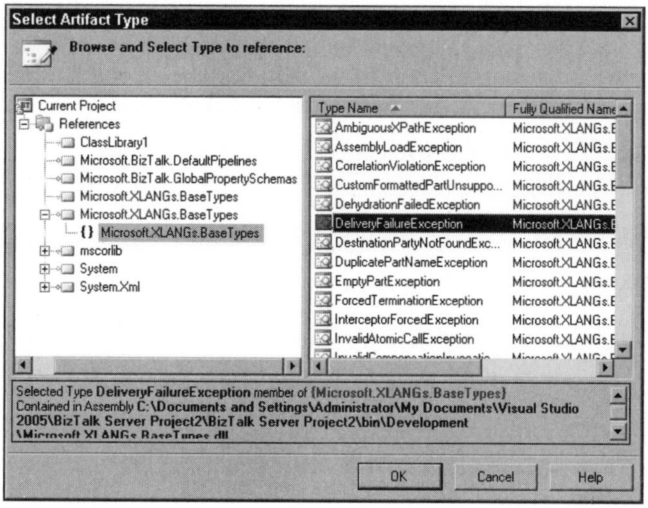

Figure 5-54

Inline Pipeline Execution

BizTalk Server 2006 introduced the concept of being able to invoke a Receive or Send pipeline in line with an orchestration. Such a technique removes the need to involve adapters or the MessageBox infrastructure and thus avoids the overhead associated with them.

Common uses for this technique are when you wish to convert a message from XML to a flat file for transmission, avoiding the standard MessageBox and adapter infrastructure, or more commonly, to take a number of messages and aggregate them into one message.

Another use is for when you receive a message from a method other than an adapter. Perhaps you call a .NET component inline from an orchestration that returns a message in a nonstandard format — you could utilize a Receive pipeline to validate and convert this message to, say, XML.

Such a technique is often considered in low-latency scenarios (see Chapter 10). When you need to extract the most performance out of BizTalk, removing the latency of the MessageBox and adapters is key. You lose the reliability and retry semantics, but this can be mitigated if planned well.

See Chapter 10 to understand how to invoke a receive and send pipeline from a BizTalk orchestration.

Transactions

Now that we've covered coding within BizTalk orchestrations, we'll move on to talk about transactions and how they can be utilized within orchestrations.

Transaction Boundaries

There are three possible discrete transaction boundaries within BizTalk Server. The first boundary surrounds the BizTalk adapter, receive pipeline, and BizTalk MessageBox. The adapter can (transport permitting) enlist in a transaction with the source system, effectively creating a transaction spanning the source system and the in-bound BizTalk architecture. This way, the message will not be removed from the source system until the message is committed into the BizTalk MessageBox and is therefore safe in a durable store.

The second transaction boundary is between the BizTalk MessageBox and orchestrations. This ensures that any messages being processed by an orchestration are handled within the scope of a transaction. If an orchestration fails for whatever reason, the message will be returned to the MessageBox ready for reprocessing or the orchestration itself will resume from a previous checkpoint.

The third transaction boundary is between the BizTalk MessageBox and Send adapter. The adapter can, transport permitting, *flow* the transaction to a destination system, thus creating a transaction spanning from the BizTalk MessageBox to the destination system. This way, the message is not removed from the BizTalk MessageBox until the message has been successfully committed into the destination system.

These transaction boundaries are critical to ensuring that messages are not lost either by BizTalk or by remote systems, and these boundaries provide a high level of transactional integrity for your messages. Figure 5-55 depicts the boundaries.

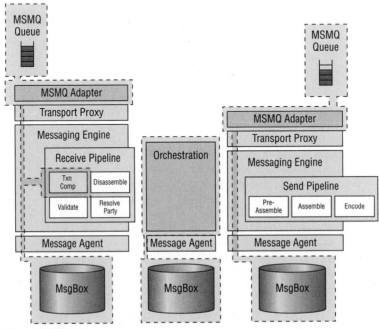

Figure 5-55

The figure depicts the transaction flowing between BizTalk and an MSMQ queue, as both MSMQ and the MSMQ adapter support transactions. However, this is optional depending on your solution. The figure also depicts a custom Receive pipeline component enlisting on the transaction (which is, again, optional).

> I have already covered this in the book but will reiterate it here for completeness. When an orchestration Send shape is executed, it is purely responsible for committing the message to the MessageBox. The Send shape then instantly completes and the orchestration moves onto the next shape.
>
> There is no transaction boundary spanning the orchestration, MessageBox, Pipeline, and Send adapter, as is often assumed; there is a complete and deliberate disconnect.

Compensation

Compensation, as the name implies, is the process by which you can provide a compensating action for an *operation* that has previously occurred, unlike a transactional rollback, which occurs before the operation has been committed.

Compensation is often used for long-running transactions, as there is no other way to roll back things that have happened within the transaction. With atomic scopes, you ensure that everything is happy before committing. Compensation also can be used for atomic scopes where you need to reverse the results of a previously committed transaction.

Compensation is a multistep process; you must provide the code to *undo* the action previously performed. Again, this is different from atomic transactions, as any operations are done within the scope of a transaction and none are committed persistently until the overall transaction has completed.

Compensation blocks can be added to any scope shape configured to be either long running or atomic. These compensation blocks will be executed in reverse order, following an exception being thrown within the orchestration. Compensation blocks can contain any combinations of orchestration shapes.

If you require different ordering of the compensation block invocation, you can control this by using a Compensate shape within a Compensation block or exception handler. Using this, you can perform compensation in any order or miss a compensation block, as required.

In reality, however, compensation should be used with care. It is important that you fully understand the consequences of using it for your scenario.

The reason for this is that there are side effects from transactions that are committed. For example, suppose that a business transaction is constructed from two transactions: #1 – credit payee's account, followed by #2 – debit payer's account.

Let's assume that transaction #2 fails. Therefore, you need to execute the compensating transaction for transaction #1. All's well and good. You simply debit the account the amount that you credited it, and you are back where you started, right?

Well, actually no, because for this scenario when the payee's account exceeds 100,000, he becomes classed as a premier customer. As such, the interest rate applied to his account is automatically adjusted upward. This now means that to correctly compensate you need to execute the business rules to determine whether he is still a premier customer.

This example is relatively trivial, but the point is that many business transactions have side effects. For compensation to work correctly, these side effects need to be accounted for. This usually adds a great deal of complexity, and for many integration scenarios that level of complexity can be overwhelming.

Atomic

An Orchestration Scope shape can be configured with a transaction type of atomic. This signifies that anything executed within the scope will take part in an atomic transaction that conforms to the four usual ACID attributes: atomicity, consistency, isolation, and durability.

- **Atomicity** — All changes effected within the scope of an atomic transaction must complete successfully or all changes must be rolled back. A typical example is that if money is required to be moved between accounts, the atomic transaction must both debit one account and credit another. Creating or deleting money is unacceptable!

- **Consistency** — Once an atomic transaction is committed, it must ensure that any data modified remains consistent; it is not acceptable for an atomic transaction to leave a database in a inconsistent state by invalidating rules or constraints.

- **Isolation** — Any changes made during an atomic transaction must be kept isolated from other read operations until the transaction is completed.

- **Durability** — Once an atomic transaction has successfully committed, the changes must be durable and therefore not held in memory but instead in a durable store such as a SQL Server database. Such changes must be committed to a physical medium, such as a hard drive, to ensure that the changes survive a machine failure. It's not acceptable for data to be subsequently rolled back following a committed atomic transaction.

To provide atomic transaction support, an atomic scope incurs a persistence point at the end of an atomic scope. This is done to ensure that, following the completion of an atomic scope, it cannot be executed again — for example, if the orchestration rolls back following a later failure in the orchestration. Due to the nature of an atomic transaction, the orchestration cannot be dehydrated while within an atomic scope. Therefore, it's wise to ensure that you keep the size of the atomic scope down and, as required consider splitting a large atomic scope into separate discrete atomic scopes and providing compensation handlers.

When would you want to use an atomic scope? There are three main reasons. One is where you need to use a .NET class that is not marked as serializable and you are unable to modify it to make it serializable.

Serialization is critical to orchestration execution, as covered previously in this chapter; however, an atomic scope prevents serialization during execution of an atomic scope, enabling you to use nonserializable components.

Remember that even if you cannot mark a class as serializable, you can instead wrap the class with a thin wrapper that itself is serializable. You must ensure, however, that no data loss will occur if the component is taken out of memory and then reinstantiated. It's worth emphasizing that the use of an atomic scope will produce an extra persistence point in your orchestration, which will introduce performance overhead to your solution. Depending on your solution scenario, this may affect the ability of your solution to scale effectively. It's advisable to consider an alternative to nonserializable classes whenever possible.

The second reason you'd want to use an atomic scope is that you need to call a COM+ component (`ServicedComponent`) that you want to participate in the scope of the orchestration transaction. A .NET class library can be configured to reside in a COM+ component by ensuring that it derives from `System.ServiceModel` and is registered in COM+ with `regsvcs.exe`.

The third reason is to enable orchestration developers to minimize the number of persistence points caused by their solution. As you saw in the "Persistence Points" section of this chapter, an atomic scope itself causes a persistence point, although this can be mitigated if, for example, you wrap two or more Send shapes, each of which incurs a persistence point. In this scenario, you can turn two persistence points into one because the atomic scope optimizes the persistence points down to one by committing both send operations at the same time.

Long Running

Atomic transactions are perfectly suited to short-term operations that require the full ACID behavior and are using technologies that explicitly support transactions. SQL Server, for example, supports distributed transactions natively, whereas the NTFS file system does not, at the time of writing — although support for this is planned.

Even if atomic transactions are supported, they may not be the most appropriate solution to your problem due to the isolation part of ACID. Isolation effectively means that you have to place locks on any data involved in the ACID transaction to prevent modification by other people and, in the strictest sense, even reading of the data (although this can be controlled by lowering the isolation level).

Taking into account a typical BizTalk scenario involving a third party, you would not want a third party to lock any of transactional resources over the Internet or for a long period of time. This is where long-running transactions come into play. They enable you to implement long-running business processes that do not require or cannot support atomicity or isolation. Compensation is instead used to provide a manual form of rollback for your business process — a manual version of atomic transactions' rollback features.

Atomic transactions aren't always suitable, especially when you want to understand if a transaction rolled back for auditing purposes. An atomic transaction effectively erases all the history of a transaction. To this end, you should consider full auditing of such operations and ensure that the auditing operation is not transactional itself. This will ensure that the audit trail is preserved even if the transaction has been rolled back.

Transformations

Message transformation is the process by which you can convert one or more source messages into a new and often entirely different type of message. Transformation is a necessary part of all but the simplest BizTalk solutions.

As covered in Chapter 3, transformation is normally considered an orchestration-only process. As a result, developers rule out a content-based routing solution and utilize orchestrations purely to provide transformation. When using the BizTalk Mapper, you can employ transforms at the port level, thus avoiding the overhead of orchestrations — unless, of course, you need such functionality!

A typical approach when providing a service to multiple partners where you can't prescribe the message format is to accept messages from each partner in their own format but at the adapter level perform a conversion to your *internal* message format. This enables you to design one set of pipeline components and orchestrations, instead of one per each partner message format.

BizTalk Mapper

The BizTalk Mapper provides a graphical design surface for implementing a transformation from one or more XML messages to an output XML message. Under the covers, the BizTalk Mapper design surface creates an XSLT transform, which is then executed by the Mapper at runtime, using the .NET Framework XslTransform class.

The BizTalk Server 2006 release introduced better support for transforming large messages (see the "Virtual Stream — When You Can't Use Forward-Only Streaming" section of Chapter 4).

BizTalk Server 2004, however, utilized the XPathDocument class, which requires the message to be loaded into memory before performing a transform, which caused problems when customers attempted to map large XML messages. The approach used by BizTalk Server 2006 (ScalableXPathDocument) will alleviate this problem but will take longer to transform, as it buffers to disk during transformation.

The BizTalk Mapper provides a library of functoids to aid with message transformation. There are functoids for almost every data transformation operation, and custom functoids can be added as required.

Figure 5-56 shows the BizTalk Mapper designer surface. Note the functoids available on the left-hand side. As you can see, there is an extensive array of functoids present in the Toolbox. On the Mapper design surface, you can see both the source message schema and destination message schema with the grid area in between.

Functoids are then dragged onto the grid area for configuration and joining to message elements and, in some cases, other functoids to provide the desired output.

A BizTalk Map can be executed from a BizTalk orchestration by using a Transform Message shape. As with all message construction operations, this can appear only within a Construct Message shape.

When configuring a Transform Message shape, you are prompted to select the BizTalk map that it should use or you can elect to have it create one for you. The next step is to provide the source and destination messages that will be made available for mapping, as shown in Figure 5-57.

> It's important to note that you can specify multiple source and destination messages as part of this Transform Configuration, which enables you to take two or three messages as an input and aggregate these into one new message adhering to a completely different format.

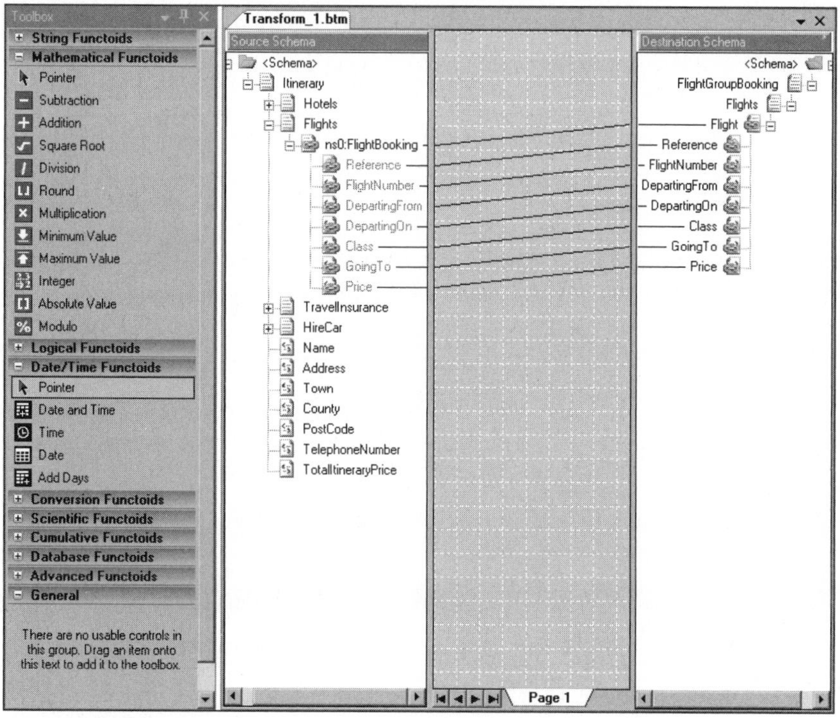

Figure 5-56

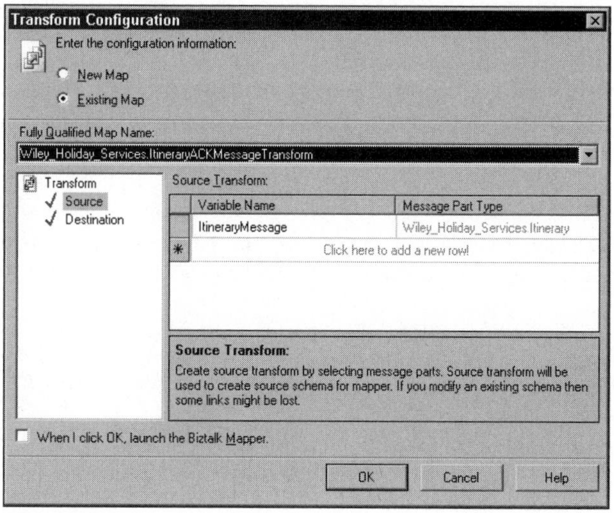

Toolbox

- **String Functoids**
- **Mathematical Functoids**
  - Pointer
  - Subtraction
  - Addition
  - Square Root
  - Division
  - Round
  - Multiplication
  - Minimum Value
  - Maximum Value
  - Integer
  - Absolute Value
  - Modulo
- **Logical Functoids**
- **Date/Time Functoids**
  - Pointer
  - Date and Time
  - Time
  - Date
  - Add Days
- **Conversion Functoids**
- **Scientific Functoids**
- **Cumulative Functoids**
- **Database Functoids**
- **Advanced Functoids**
- **General**

There are no usable controls in this group. Drag an item onto this text to add it to the toolbox.

Transform_1.btm

Source Schema

- `<Schema>`
  - Itinerary
    - Hotels
    - Flights
      - ns0:FlightBooking
        - Reference
        - FlightNumber
        - DepartingFrom
        - DepartingOn
        - Class
        - GoingTo
        - Price
    - TravelInsurance
    - HireCar
    - Name
    - Address
    - Town
    - County
    - PostCode
    - TelephoneNumber
    - TotalItineraryPrice

Destination Schema

- `<Schema>`
  - FlightGroupBooking
    - Flights
      - Flight
        - Reference
        - FlightNumber
        - DepartingFrom
        - DepartingOn
        - Class
        - GoingTo
        - Price

Page 1

Figure 5-56

Transform Configuration

Enter the configuration information:

- ◯ New Map
- ◉ Existing Map

Fully Qualified Map Name:

Wiley_Holiday_Services.ItineraryACK.MessageTransform

Transform
- ✓ Source
- ✓ Destination

Source Transform:

Variable Name	Message Part Type
ItineraryMessage	Wiley_Holiday_Services.Itinerary
Click here to add a new row!	

Source Transform:

Create source transform by selecting message parts. Source transform will be used to create source schema for mapper. If you modify an existing schema then some links might be lost.

☐ When I click OK, launch the Biztalk Mapper.

[OK] [Cancel] [Help]

Figure 5-57

Pages

I have seen many complicated maps created using the BizTalk Mapper, and they become very unwieldy very quickly. Lines criss-cross each other, and you seem to endlessly scroll up and down the large schema trying to work out what message elements and functoids are joined together. The worst one caused the grid view to completely turn black due to the number of lines.

Strangely, most people don't spot the tabs available at the bottom of the grid, myself included, for a long time! These tabs enable you to split the Mapping across multiple pages, thus enabling you to factor parts of your mapping into smaller *chunks*. The resulting map still executes as if it were one entire map; it's purely a viewing trick. The pages can also be named for ease of identification.

Limitations

The BizTalk Mapper is a fantastic tool, but as with everything, it has its limitations. With small-to-medium-sized schemas, you can't really fault it, especially if you make good use of the Pages feature covered above — and this applies to most BizTalk Server projects out there. In my experience, however, large schemas or transformations where the source document bears absolutely no relation to the destination document tend to push the capabilities of the Mapper.

While the BizTalk Mapper is capable of performing the transformations, it can become unwieldy. One particular issue that I've wrestled with is what happens when a source schema utilizes the same type in multiple places. An example is a person. You may have a message schema that includes many instances of this person type: a customer, a supervisor, a friend, a supplier. Now, imagine that you have to transform this concept of a person into a different representation in the destination schema.

You may have to use many functoids and connecting lines to achieve the transformation for one person, which in itself is fine, but imagine having to repeat this person transformation many times throughout your map for each instance of the person type. This sort of repetitive development easily leads to errors and becomes brittle.

Unfortunately, you're not able to factor common parts of your BizTalk map into smaller, reusable parts, which would resolve this issue. It is possible, however to utilize inline XSLT transforms to resolve this particular issue, but this adds further complexity.

Other common problems that customers hit happen when schemas change during development. When you load a map that has had some schema changes, certain connections can be lost if the element has changed, which in a complex map can make it almost impossible to figure out what's been removed.

Default values also suffer from the same problem in that they can be removed following schema changes, and due to the way they are configured, it can be hard to see all the default values that are being used. Instead, you might want to consider using a `Value Mapping` functoid.

Don't get me wrong — for the most part the BizTalk Mapper works extremely well, but in the odd complex case you can end up struggling to make it work for you. I cover a few alternatives below, which may help you with complex scenarios.

Extracting the Generated XSLT

You can extract the XSLT generated by the BizTalk Mapper for possible hand-crafting or for use in another project. To extract the XSLT, right-click your BizTalk Mapper file in the Solution Explorer and choose `Validate Map`.

In the output pane, you will see a number of lines, including one that provides the path to the XSLT file. An example of this is shown below, modified slightly for clarity:

```
Invoking component...
   C:\...\Transform_1.btm: The output XSLT is stored in the following file:
<file:///C:\Documents and Settings\Administrator\Local
Settings\Temp\_MapData\Transform_1.xsl>
   C:\...\ Transform_1.btm: The Extension Object XML is stored in the following
file: <file:///C:\Documents and Settings\Administrator\Local
Settings\Temp\_MapData\Transform_1_extxml.xml>
```

Custom XSLT

For scenarios in which you already have an XSLT or do not want to use the BizTalk Mapper, you can still leverage the Transform Orchestration shape and the built-in messaging support but supply your own XSLT rather than the autogenerated XSLT created by the BizTalk Mapper.

To do this, drag a Transform shape onto your Orchestration Design surface and follow the usual steps to configure the input and output messages. When the BizTalk Mapper design surface is displayed, select the central grid area to view the grid properties. Within the properties of the grid, you can provide the XSLT file via the Custom XSL Path setting.

It's worth noting the new XSLT debugging features of Visual Studio 2005, which you can use to debug BizTalk maps or your own custom XSL transformations. If you want to debug a BizTalk map using this debugger, use the following steps. If you want to debug a custom XSL, follow the steps below starting at number 4.

1. Right-click the BizTalk map, and select Validate Map.

2. In the output window, you'll see a link to the `.xsl`. Click the link to bring it up in Visual Studio.

3. Right-click the XSL document shown in Visual Studio, and select View Source.

4. Set breakpoints in the XSL using either F9 as usual or via the Debug menu.

5. Select Debug XSLT from the XML menu to start the debugger, which will prompt you for a sample input XML document.

You will then be able to step through the XSLT execution, setting breakpoints, evaluating expressions, and viewing the output as you progress.

Figure 5-58 shows an example of the XSLT debugger in action.

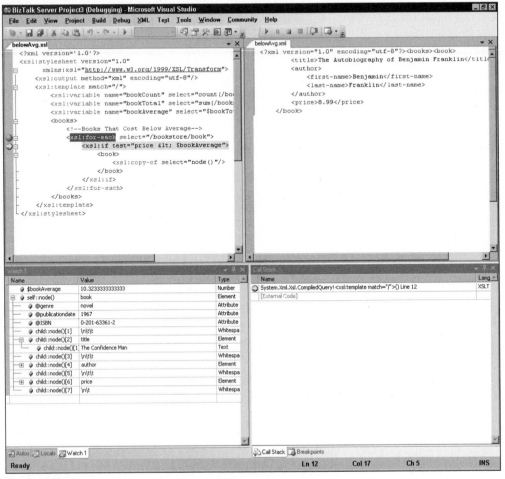

Figure 5-58

You can find more information on how to use the XSLT debugger at `http://msdn2.microsoft.com/en-us/library/ms255605(VS.80).aspx`.

Manual "Mapping"

Many organizations have little or no XSLT skills and don't necessarily wish to develop or maintain applications, due to the perceived complexity required to develop and debug them.

Visual Studio 2005 provided native XSLT debugging features, and a number of partners provide BizTalk Mapper-esque mapping support from within Visual Studio, which may or may not address some of the limitations discussed earlier.

Either way, it's a skill that will be in short supply. Some customers have opted for an approach that any .NET developer can develop, test, and maintain by writing .NET code to perform the conversion.

The first step is to use the XSD.EXE .NET Framework tool to create serializable classes for all the source and destination message types. Then, using the technique covered earlier in the chapter, you can pass the BizTalk messages to your code seamlessly from BizTalk and cast the response from your code to a BizTalk message.

Your custom code can then perform whatever transformation is necessary between the messages by using the .NET Framework base classes. This provides a common and familiar environment to developers and allows for straightforward unit testing.

Debugging

Figuring out what's happening inside your BizTalk solution at runtime can be an overly complex and awkward process. BizTalk Server 2006 improved the visibility of what BizTalk is doing through the BizTalk administration tool (although without the integrated Visual Studio F5 debugging experience, it can be cumbersome at best).

System.Diagnostics

The most popular technique is to utilize the features exposed in the .NET Framework System .Diagnostics namespace. The Debug and Trace functionality provides a quick and easy way for developers to output progress information, message contents, and timing information to aid with development and, in some instances, narrow down a problem when your solution is deployed live.

The System.Diagnostics.Debug.WriteLine method enables developers to output free-form traces for diagnostic purposes. Any trace outputted in this manner will be present only in debug builds and will be removed for release builds, meaning it's an ideal way of providing diagnostics during development.

By default, a trace output in this manner will be handled by the Win32 API OutputDebugString function. If Visual Studio is in Debug mode, this trace will appear in the Output window. Most commonly, DebugView (from www.microsoft.com/technet/sysinternals) is used to provide a viewer for such output. Figure 5-59 shows some sample output displayed by DebugView.

> This is discussed further in Chapter 13 but it's worth noting here that DebugView effectively acts as a debugger and hooks the OUTPUT_DEBUG_STRING_EVENT. As a result, your application (a BizTalk process in this case) will experience a performance impact as the application threads will be suspended while the debug information is output, effectively serializing your application. It's worth noting that if the DebugView tool is not started (and therefore there are no subscribers to the information) the performance impact is negligible and shouldn't, in my experience, be something to worry about, therefore do not be afraid to output information that you feel will be useful.
>
> Be aware that running DebugView during performance testing or on a live server is very likely to significantly impact performance!

The System.Diagnostics.Trace.WriteLine method works in exactly the same way but works in both debug and release builds. Although such tracing will introduce a small amount of performance overhead, you should ensure that you have adequate tracing in all solutions. The performance overhead is negligible compared to the effort required to debug a BizTalk solution with no tracing information.

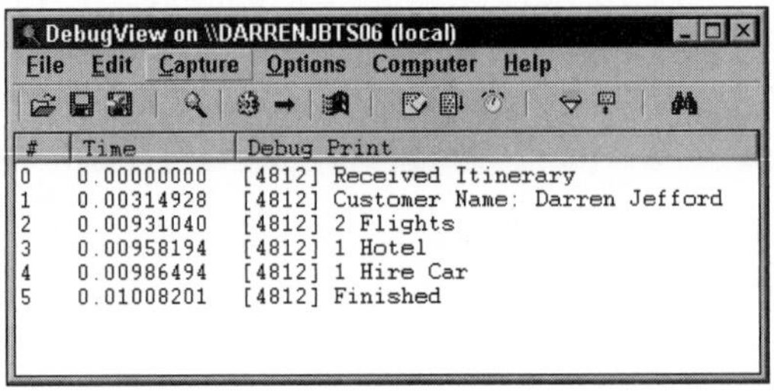

Figure 5-59

Of course, you can implement multiple tracing levels; information, warning, and error levels are a good starting point. This approach enables you to leave error tracing on all the time, and when diagnosing an issue you can turn the volume of tracing up to include information and warnings, as required.

You might be considering the use of the Microsoft Enterprise Library to provide tracing. You can certainly integrate this into your solution, but I've found that it introduces too much complexity and too many problems compared to the now much improved .NET tracing framework, especially with regard to the use of configuration files. Your mileage may vary, but ensure that you prototype how it will work before making a decision for your solution.   See Chapter 13 for more information.

Health and Activity Tracking

Health and Activity Tracking (HAT) was made available in the BizTalk Server 2004 release and was the only real operations tool available. HAT offered the ability to see what orchestrations and messages were currently resident in the MessageBox and to perform administrative operations such as suspending and terminating service instances. It was also possible to see historical information around orchestration execution and messages.

Developers could also use HAT for debugging tasks, including graphically debugging orchestrations.

HAT, however, was widely criticized as being too developer focused and requiring developer-style skills to use it effectively, which is broadly true in hindsight. Although you could do pretty much everything required to administer BizTalk, it was either cumbersome or too slow.

HAT, however, was a thin veneer over WMI (Windows Management Instrumentation) and the BizTalk MessageBox, which made providing a simplified UI or even simple scripts an acceptable workaround for many customers.

As a result, a major focus for the 2006 release was administration tools, and the BizTalk administration tool was introduced and supplanted most of the HAT features by providing a far better UI for viewing orchestrations and messages currently resident in the MessageBox.

HAT still exists in the 2006 release but purely for orchestration development and viewing historical data related to orchestration execution and messages stored in the tracking database.

We cover HAT in more detail in Chapter 11.

BAM

As we cover in Chapter 6, BAM can be used extensively not only to collect and expose data for business users but also to provide data for process tracking and monitoring.

BAM provides a fast and highly scalable mechanism for collecting instrumentation data, which is extremely hard to match via a custom solution.

BPEL4WS

Hopefully, you're broadly familiar with the Web Services Description Language (WSDL) specification; WSDL enables you to describe the public interface of a Web service. The operations and messages are described as part of the WSDL document and allow a potential client to interrogate the service and understand how to communicate successfully with it regardless of platform.

Prior to BizTalk Server 2004, Microsoft developed a propriety orchestration language called XLANG, and other vendors, including IBM, developed their own to address their requirements. As part of the broader standardization efforts, Microsoft and IBM codeveloped the BPEL4WS specification to provide a platform-neutral description of a business process.

The *Business Process Execution Language* (BPEL) was originally positioned as the language in which business processes would be executed, thus removing the proprietary languages used by vendors' products. The theory was that you could take one BPEL document and use it on any platform and vendor combination.

Sadly, the BPEL specification doesn't provide enough semantics for effectively modeling business processes today, which has resulted in most vendors (Microsoft included) either retaining their proprietary language or using BPEL as the basic language but then adding extensive proprietary vendor extensions, meaning that the portability aspect is lost. Many vendors market their products as being BPEL compliant or executing BPEL directly, which is often of limited value due to the lack of semantics available.

Both BizTalk Server 2004 and 2006 support BPEL4WS 1.1 for export and import operations. BizTalk orchestrations can be exported to BPEL4WS, and orchestrations can be created from a provided BPEL document.

Based on this, I like to think of BPEL right now as purely an interchange format in that you can use BizTalk orchestration to design a business process and then export to a BPEL document. You can then take the resulting files and import them into another vendor's tooling.

Right now, you can consider BPEL to be the business process equivalent of WSDL. BPEL4WS enables the public business process contract to be defined; this, in the same way as WSDL, enables a potential business partner or client to understand how to interact with your business process.

Because XLANG offers greater flexibility and capabilities than BPEL, there are restrictions on what you can use in an orchestration to ensure that it can be exported successfully. For example, BPEL has no notion of a Call or Start Orchestration shape and therefore cannot be represented in a BPEL document. The product documentation has a full list of these restrictions.

Summary

This chapter began by introducing the orchestration execution environment and discussing how orchestrations are activated and managed throughout their lifetime by the Orchestration Engine through the use of persistence points and dehydration.

It then discussed how orchestrations are developed, detailing how you can design a business process using orchestration shapes and how complex messaging patterns can be implemented through the use of correlations and convoys. It also described how code can be called from within an orchestration, along with information on transactions and transformations.

This chapter has covered all aspects of BizTalk orchestration, from the fundamentals to the details and, when combined with Chapters 12 and 13, will enable you to design effective orchestrations that make the best use of the BizTalk platform.

Factoring your orchestrations effectively remains the key to a good BizTalk solution. Having one large monolithic orchestration introduces a number of problems, most notably with regard to versioning. Careful refactoring into smaller, discrete orchestrations will make your solution far easier to manage and support moving forward.

The next chapter covers Business Activity Monitoring (BAM), which enables you to instrument your entire BizTalk solution from end to end and provides a view into your BizTalk solution for all stakeholders within your organization (developers, analysts, administrators, etc.)

Business Activity Monitoring

Business Activity Monitoring (BAM) was introduced in the BizTalk Server 2004 release and represents a core component of the BizTalk platform. It was extended further in BizTalk Server 2006. BAM enables end-to-end instrumentation of your BizTalk solution and provides a view into the inner workings of your solution.

BAM is often overlooked due to the official line that identifies it as purely a business tool: to allow the business to "get visibility" of, for example, the number of orders received today. The product documentation fails to highlight how extensive and valuable this component can be to almost all BizTalk solutions. In the context of BizTalk, BAM is to a business process what online analytical processing (OLAP) is to a database.

BAM is as powerful and important as the overall product in many scenarios, and many BizTalk sales have been secured after the customer understands BAM and its capabilities. Indeed, a few companies have purchased BizTalk, at least initially, *just* to use BAM!

This chapter covers the BAM architecture and details some ways in which it can be used to provide a rich view into the system for developers, administrators, and business stakeholders.

Overview

Let's put BAM in context. A typical BizTalk solution ends up being a "black box." You insert messages into it. It whirs, steam blows out the sides, and stuff comes out the other side. Sometimes the stuff comes out hours, days, or even weeks after the initial message; during this period, no one has a really good view of what's going on, except perhaps the developers or IT support staff (who can track orchestration progress using the administration tools). You, on the other hand, can't search for an orchestration handling a specific message (for example, by providing part of the data, such as an identifier).

BAM enables you to easily provide instrumentation of this black box and can be used to give you a view into what your business processes are doing at runtime. The consumers of this instrumentation data don't have to be the notorious business analyst or information worker; instead, they can be anyone involved or interested in the solution. Different types of users can also have different views of the available data, meaning that you can restrict who can see what data. For example, a business will most likely be interested in different data from an engineer supporting the system.

Many organizations have found that embarking on a full-scale process automation project to automate all their business processes can take an incredibly long time and sometimes lead to delivery problems. Some of these problems relate to an organization not understanding exactly what types of business processes are being used, how many activities are processed, or even how long they take to complete. In these instances, BAM can be used to purely instrument these (often) manual processes to provide a view into the business. An educated decision can then be made on which business processes to automate and thus deliver the biggest business impact.

If your BizTalk solution is called by an external system, perhaps an ASP.NET Web application, or uses external resources, such as ASP.NET Web services, you can invoke BAM to provide extra information from components outside of BizTalk, effectively giving you an enterprise-wide view of your business processes.

The data that BAM collects ends up in an opaque SQL Server database you can easily access via your own application, the built-in BAM portal, or tools such as SQL Server Reporting Services or SQL Server business intelligence.

BAM Fundamentals

This section discusses the fundamentals of BAM. We'll cover how you can model the data you want to collect, how it's stored under the covers, and, more importantly, how you can get data into the BAM infrastructure.

Figure 6-1 depicts a simplified view of the BAM architecture that you can refer to as you work through this chapter.

BAM provides a mechanism that can provide a view inside your business process; the business process can be implemented solely in BizTalk or perhaps partitioned between BizTalk, Web services, and so on.

The first step to enabling BAM on your solution is developing an *observation model*, effectively a wish list of information that you want to collect, and it is modeled using an Excel add-in.

The observation model first defines the activities that you want to use. These ultimately become SQL tables and will hold the activity items (data) that you want to collect. The granularity of your activities depends entirely on your solution; we'll demonstrate some examples later in this chapter.

Once you've defined an activity, you must then define the activity items to be held. These activity items are defined as either business milestones or business data items. Milestones are mapped directly to SQL Server `DateTime` columns, and data items map to either SQL Server `varchar`, `int`, or `decimal` columns.

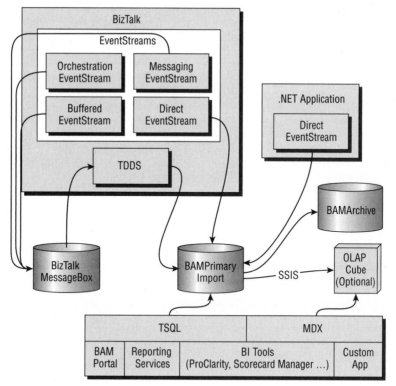

Figure 6-1

Activity views can then be defined, as required, to provide different end users of BAM data with a customized and aggregated view of the BAM data. This is directly analogous to a SQL view. You can at this stage also define measures and dimensions to provide precalculated queries and drill down through any collected data. This will be used to provision an OLAP cube that can be used for later querying. This OLAP step is entirely optional and does not have to be used unless you have specific requirements.

After this observation model has been created, you can use the BAM administration tool to provision all of the database infrastructure required to store this information automatically. The resulting database structure (stored in a SQL database called BAMPrimaryImport) is highly tuned and optimized and performs extremely well under load.

Once the infrastructure is in place, you need to populate it with information. BAM provides EventStreams for this purpose. There are four types of EventStreams (represented as .NET classes): OrchestrationEventStream, BufferedEventStream, MessagingEventStream, and DirectEventStream.

We'll cover the precise differences between the EventStreams later in the chapter, but at a high level OrchestrationEventStream, MessagingEventStream, and BufferedEventStream asynchronously write BAM data into the BAMPrimaryImport database. This is done by temporarily persisting the data destined for the BAM database in the BizTalk MessageBox. The Tracking Data Decode Service (TDDS, or tracking host, as it's sometimes known) is then responsible for moving this information across into the `MessageBox`.

On the other hand, the `DirectEventStream`, as the name implies, writes BAM data directly to the BAMPrimaryImport database without involving the MessageBox hop. The `DirectEventStream` approach will block the caller until the data is written, which is contrast to the other *asynchronous* `EventStreams` that perform faster as they hand off the work to TDDS. This does, however, introduce a lag because activity data will not appear immediately as it would with the `DirectEventStream`.

The `OrchestrationEventStream` and `MessagingEventStream` differ from the `BufferedEventStream` in that they provide transactional consistency with either pipelines or orchestrations. This means that in the case of an orchestration rolling back, for example, any associated BAM entries will also be rolled back. There is also a performance benefit in that in the case of the `OrchestrationEventStream`, it can piggyback the orchestration persistence to write the BAM data, thus incurring less overhead.

These `EventStreams` can be coded against directly to store data as required, but BizTalk solutions can make use of the Tracking Profile Editor to graphically select the information required to be collected, thus creating a tracking profile, which can then be seamlessly deployed to a BizTalk solution without requiring any coding changes.

Once data is in the BAMPrimaryImport database, it can be queried. The database infrastructure created by BAM is openly documented and uses standard SQL tables and views, and can therefore be queried through simple T-SQL statements.

The BAM data can be natively searched and viewed through the built-in BAM portal introduced with BizTalk Server 2006 or with any other SQL-compliant tool, such as SQL Server Reporting Services, Office Business Scorecard Manager, and the like.

As you can see in Figure 6-1, a SQL OLAP cube can be automatically created by the BAM administration tool to provide extra data-mining capabilities. This is populated using a SQL Server Integration Services (SSIS) package, which is created automatically for you.

Last, but not least, there is an SSIS package to support the automatic archiving of aged BAM data in a separate BAMArchive database.

Now that we've set the scene for how BAM works, we'll drill down into the fundamentals in more detail before moving on to demonstrate a working example.

Conceptual Overview

This section provides a conceptual overview of BAM. This introduction will help you understand the functionality and application of BAM as you read through the rest of this chapter.

Activities

You can use the BAM Excel add-in to define BAM activities. These activities will contain the data you wish to collect. It depends on your solution, but quite often you will end up with an activity for each key concept that you wish to collect, so for an order-processing system you may have an activity for an

Order and Line Item. These activities can be linked together in a parent-child relationship to maintain the logical relationships between them, which we'll discuss later.

Activities contain one or more activity items. There are two types of activity items: business milestones (represented as DateTime) and business data (represented as text, integer, or decimal).

After you have defined activities in the Excel spreadsheet, you can use the BAM Management tool (bm.exe) to provision the database infrastructure to support your BAM activities. Each activity is represented as a SQL table, with each activity item represented as a column within the activity.

ActivityIDs

Each instance of an activity is represented by an identifier called an *ActivityID*. This identifier must be unique; otherwise, exceptions will be thrown when you try to create an activity.

Activity Views

BAM activity views are also defined using Microsoft Excel in the same way as BAM activities and are analogous in approach to SQL views. An activity view can enable you to provide a customized view of the activity data for different roles within your organization and to define precalculated queries and dimensions that will be automatically created (via an OLAP cube) when deploying the database infrastructure.

Activity views are optional. If you don't require any of the features they provide, you can access the activity tables directly to retrieve data. Make a decision based on your solution as to whether activity views offer any advantages, but bear in mind that activity views are required to utilize some features of the BAM portal (discussed later in this chapter) and to enable Excel-based PivotCharts.

An activity view can contain activity items across multiple activities, which can prove useful when you're trying to produce a simplified "view" across many activities. Figure 6-2 shows this.

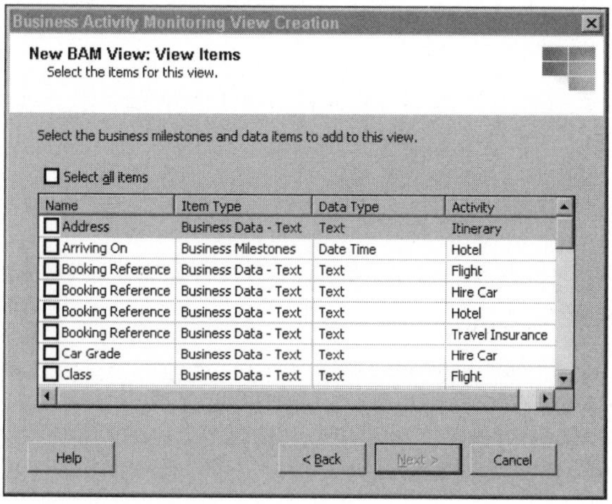

Figure 6-2

You can also rename activity items within an activity view. Renaming proves useful if different areas of your organization have different terms for the same underlying data. Figure 6-3 shows an example.

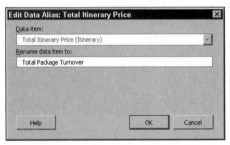

Figure 6-3

You can also request that the duration between two milestones be calculated. This enables you to calculate the execution time of an operation within your business process, which could then be used for service level agreement (SLA) purposes. A Web service call from an orchestration is a good example of where this can be used.

You define start and end business milestones that are populated before and after the Web service call, and the duration will be automatically calculated for you. Figure 6-4 shows an example of this.

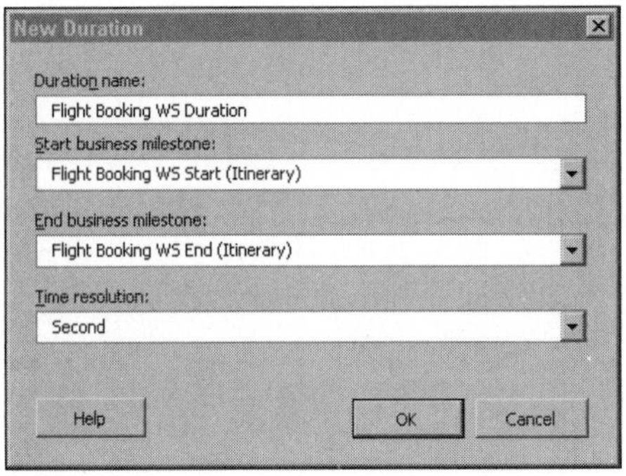

Figure 6-4

Activity views also allow you to define groups, which enable you to group two or more activity items together. Suppose, for example, that your process has two possible outcomes: approved or denied. If you want to calculate the duration of a loan approval process, you don't care whether it's been approved or denied. Instead, you want to calculate the end-to-end time.

Using groups, you can define a finished group and group together the Approved and Denied milestones. The duration is then calculated on whichever activity item is present.

Last, but not least, you can define aggregate dimensions and measures for your view. These are then used to generate the OLAP cube when you provision your database infrastructure using the BAM administration tool.

Measures allow you to define precalculated queries, such as the average age of a loan applicant, the total number of loans received, and the maximum loan amount. These queries are automatically generated when the data is processed into the OLAP cube.

Dimensions allow you to define ways in which your activity items can be organized. The four different types of dimensions are progress, data, time, and numeric range.

> **Bear in mind that activity view items are not visible immediately. Unlike the raw activity data items, the SQL Server Integration Services (SSIS) package (or Data Transformation Services [DTS] package if you are using SQL Server 2000) must be executed to move the information from the BAMPrimaryImport database into the OLAP cube, which is then used when accessing PivotTables and so on.**
>
> **When you define your activity view, you can mark your activity view as Real Time Aggregation (RTA) to enable real-time querying. Some restrictions apply (as covered in the next section).**

Progress Dimension

The progress dimension enables you to view activity data grouped by progress. When you define a progress dimension, you specify one or more milestones present in an activity view.

At its basic level, the progress dimension can show you how many activities have reached the specified milestone. The following table shows a simple example.

Name	Count
Loan Applications Received	5000

From the preceding table, you can see that 5000 loan applications have been received. Using a progress dimension, however, you can drill into the specific status of each of those applications, as shown in the following table.

The following table shows that out of the 5000 loan applications received, 500 are awaiting processing, 3000 have been approved, and 1500 have been denied.

Name	State	Count
Received	Awaiting Processing	500
	Approved	3000
	Denied	1500

Each state shown in the state column is a business milestone that was defined within an activity and selected as part of this progress dimension. The progress dimension thus enables you to quickly and easily identify the status of your business process and identify problems.

Data Dimension

The data dimension enables you to view activity data grouped by data held within the activity itself. When you define a data dimension, you specify one or more data items that will be used when grouping the results.

The following table shows how many total products have been sold, but it doesn't show any more detail as to which products have been sold.

Name	Count
Products Sold	10,000

Defining a data dimension using the product name allows you to group the data, as shown in the following table.

Name	Count
Windows XP	1000
Windows Server 2003	1500
BizTalk Server 2006	7500

Numeric Range Dimension

The numeric range dimension enables you to group data based on *friendly* names assigned to numeric ranges. For example, a loan application between $0 and $5000 might be defined as low-risk loan, but a loan of more than $5000 might be defined as a high-risk loan.

Loan Risk	Count
Low	500
High	500

Time Dimension

The time dimension enables you to view activity data grouped by milestones held within the activity. When you define a time dimension, you specify a business milestone to base the dimension on and a format in which to display the data and time.

The following table shows the number of products sold, grouped using a time dimension that breaks down the sales into year and months. You can control to what granularity the data is grouped.

Year	Month	Count
2007	January	10000
	February	7000
	March	9000

Unlike with the previous dimensions, you can combine the time dimension with the other types of dimensions previously discussed. Defining a time dimension as was done above, but combining it with a data dimension, enables you to group the data as shown in the following table.

Month	Windows XP	Windows Server 2003	BizTalk Server 2006
January	1000	1500	7500
February	2500	3500	1000
March	1500	1000	6500

We've now introduced the concept of activities. You can hold data and activity views, which enable views to be constructed over one or more activities, filtering or renaming items held within these activities to provide a consumer-specific view.

Database Structure

Now that you understand the BAM basics, we'll delve further into the database infrastructure required to support these concepts.

Activities

The database infrastructure used to store your activity data is created automatically by the bm.exe tool during deployment. The infrastructure includes the tables, views, and stored procedures required, resulting in a high-performance storage layer (without any custom database work required).

As discussed earlier in this chapter, each activity that you define is represented as a separate SQL table, as shown in the following table. The RecordID and LastModified columns are reserved internal columns used by BAM. All the columns apart from ActivityID and the reserved columns are marked as nullable, which is necessary because activity items can be written at any point in the activity lifetime (which could be minutes, hours, or weeks).

When you begin an activity, all the activity items are set to NULL and then updated as you call UpdateActivity. The first row shows a fully completed activity; the second row shows an activity still in progress (because the BookingReference column has yet to be updated); the third row shows an activity that has just been created.

RecordID	ActivityID	ArrivalDate	Departure-Date	Booking-Reference	HotelName	LastModified
1	B6820048-255E-4038-A6C3-6DD08 FD6F9A7	16/02/2004 00:00:00	22/02/2004 00:00:00	129AD-3	Wiley Hotels Inc	02/04/2006 15:29:21
2	BC95674C-9EB1-464c-978E-8CC626 B210F5	22/03/2002 00:00:00	29/02/2004 00:00:00	<NULL>	Wiley Hotels Inc	02/04/2006 16:24:11
3	D73D609E-5229-4874-9436-9BC0A1 8FF4B8	<NULL>	<NULL>	<NULL>	<NULL>	18/04/2006 17:02:11

This table structure works fine for low volumes, but as you start to ramp up the volumes (and thus the amount of data within the table), performance will degrade quickly. This performance degradation results because SQL Server caches the data pages in memory, and as the table size increases it's unable to keep the cache completely in memory and physical disk access is required. If you were to mix this writing with live querying, you would find the performance unacceptable.

To resolve this problem, BAM actually creates two SQL tables for each activity: bam_<ActivityName>_Active and bam_<ActivityName>_Completed. Activities that are still active (i.e., EndActivity hasn't been called) are located in the Active table. However, when activities are marked as completed (EndActivity has been called), a trigger fires that moves the row out of the Active table into the Completed table.

This technique keeps the table that's being used for writing as small as possible to improve performance and allows live querying of BAM data that won't interfere with writing.

Activity Views

Any activity views defined in the BAM Excel spreadsheet are also created when you deploy the database infrastructure using bm.exe. If you don't require any of the features and capabilities that activity views provide, you do not have to define them.

An activity view, as covered previously, enables you to group together activity items across different activities in the same way that you can with SQL views. You can then optionally transform the data items and calculate new "measurements" to accompany them.

Activity views are a useful technique when you want to present only a subset of your activity data to the intended audience. After all, business users do not want to see lower-level data, and for security reasons, you might not want to expose developers to some business metrics.

After you define a view via the BAM workbook and deploy the database infrastructure, you will find that a new SSIS package (or DTS package if you are using SQL Server 2000) will be created to support each view.

This SSIS package is responsible for retrieving data held in the activity tables and performing any transformations specified in the view and any cube processing. Figure 6-5 shows an example of an autogenerated SSIS package.

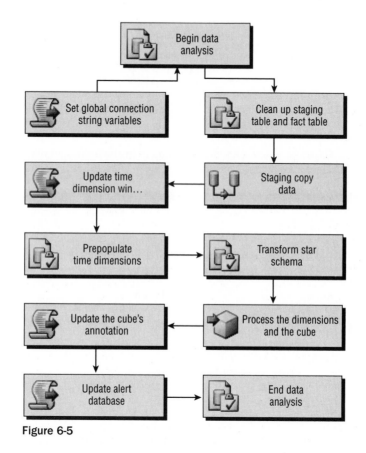

Figure 6-5

This job is unscheduled by default, and you must ensure that it's run at an appropriate interval. Failure to execute the job means that the OLAP cube will not be preloaded with the pending activity data. OLAP cube processing is not an inexpensive operation, so you should only run the job as required (i.e., not every minute). Fifteen minutes is a typical value used, but again it depends on your solution.

When defining an activity view in the BAM workbook, you can specify that a particular activity view be configured for Real Time Aggregation (RTA). As the name implies, RTA enables you to access any view defined transformations in real time without having to run the SSIS package. Figure 6-6 shows the toolbar button to enable RTA.

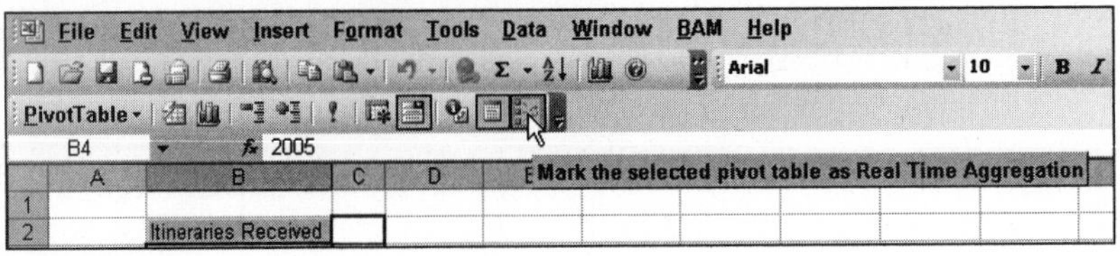

Figure 6-6

You should not enable RTA for all your activity views, because it does have a performance overhead. However, it does prove useful when you have an aggregation that is crucial to monitor or needs real-time visibility (so that you don't have to wait for a daily SSIS package to execute, for example).

RTA is implemented by using SQL triggers created on each activity table. As data arrives in the activity tables, a trigger fires to process the data and create the aggregation view. This view is represented as a SQL view and follows the bam_<ViewName>_<RTAName>_RTAView naming convention.

By default, an RTA view lives for just one day. Any data required for longer than this should really be moved into the OLAP cube for access. You can extend the RTA window by using the bm.exe tool with the set-rtawindow parameter.

Because RTA is implemented via triggers, it directly impacts BAM performance. Any activity writing must wait for the trigger to fire.

A few limitations apply as to what is supported in RTA activity views. Min and Max aggregations are *not* supported; Average, Count, and Sum aggregations are supported.

You can configure security for each activity view with the bm.exe tool, using the add-account parameter.

Partitioning

The BAMPrimaryImport table is primarily designed to store data for current and recently completed activities. For obvious reasons, it is not wise to store many months' or years' worth of information "online" in your BizTalk Server deployment, especially if your data volumes are high.

To address this, BAM has partitioning and archival capabilities out of the box. A Data Maintenance SSIS package (or DTS package if you're using SQL Server 2000) is created when you deploy your database infrastructure and follows the BAM_DM_<ActivityName> naming convention. Note that partitioning and archiving is performed at an activity level.

The DM package handles partitioning and archiving. When the package is executed, a new empty table that mirrors the structure of the existing bam_<ActivityName>_Completed table is created and "swapped" in place of the existing Completed table.

The previous Completed table is then renamed to bam_<ActivityName>_<Guid>, and the relevant views are updated to still retrieve data across the completed table and any other partitions that have been created. This means that your queries, if coded against the views, do not have to update following a partition creation. The same operation happens to the Relationships table for each activity.

Archiving also happens as part of this DM package. Any partitions outside of the configurable online window are purged from the BAMPrimaryImport table and moved to the BAMArchive database, ready for whatever SQL Server archival approach that you use. If the archiving database has not been configured, the data is purged without archiving. Of course, you can still query this historical data once it has been moved into the archive database.

Figure 6-7 shows the SSIS package that is created automatically. Figure 6-8 shows the steps performed and an example of the execution log.

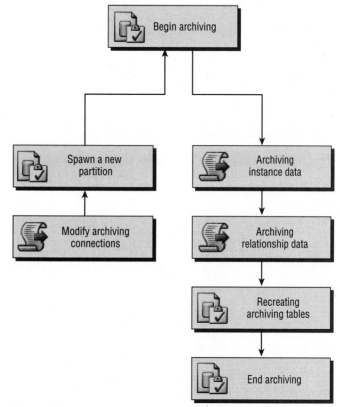

Figure 6-7

You can configure the online window on a per-activity basis by changing the OnlineWindowTimeUnit and OnlineWindowLength settings located in the bam_Metadata_Activities table (which you can find in the BAMPrimaryImport database).

The default for all activities is set to 6 months, meaning that after data has been held in the BAM-PrimaryImport database for 6 months, it is moved to the BAMArchive database. Figure 6-9 shows an example of the bam_Metadata_Activities table.

The DM package is not scheduled by default, but this can easily be scheduled by creating a new SQL Server Agent job that invokes the DM package according to your schedule requirements.

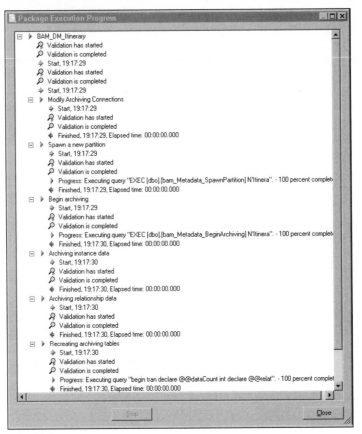

Figure 6-8

	ActivityName	DefinitionXml	OnlineWindowTimeUnit	OnlineWindowTimeLength
▶	Flight	<Activity Name="Flight ...	MONTH	6
	Hire Car	<Activity Name="Hire ...	MONTH	6
	Hotel	<Activity Name="Hotel...	MONTH	6
	Itinerary	<Activity Name="Itiner...	MONTH	6
	Travel Insurance	<Activity Name="Trave...	MONTH	6
*	NULL	NULL	NULL	NULL

Figure 6-9

References

References represent a key area of BAM that you should fully understand. You can use references to great effect to resolve some very complex problems and reduce the amount of code you need to write for your solution.

References are new in BizTalk Server 2006. Relationships between activities existed in the 2004 release, but they have been renamed in BizTalk Server 2006 as *references*. In short, the references capability allows activities to refer to activities, messages, BizTalk artifacts such as orchestrations, or any chunk of data that you provide.

Activity References

The most common form of reference is interlinked activities. Very simple scenarios using BAM might only end up using one activity, but often multiple activities are created, and more often than not they are interrelated.

Or perhaps you need to store multiple "records" that are each represented as a distinct activity. For example, you might receive a travel itinerary into BizTalk as a message. This itinerary message contains details about flight, hotel, hire (rental) car, and travel insurance bookings, and each must be processed individually.

As part of the processing, you need to store the information about each booking along with any booking codes (to be used for tracking of booking progress and to provide business metrics). To support this, you might have an activity for each concept — Itinerary, Flight, Hotel, and Hire Car (each represented as a row in different SQL tables). If you want to identify what constitutes a given itinerary, you must ensure that there is a common identifier in each row that you join together.

Using activity references, you can add a reference from the Itinerary activity to each related activity; under the covers, this is implemented as a join table. Each activity in the BAMPrimaryImport database has an `ActiveRelationships` and `CompletedRelationships` table. This table is effectively a join table that holds two ActivityIDs, the source and target, which allows you to identify interrelated activities. This technique proves particularly useful to enable drill down. For instance, if you were to select an Itinerary activity, you could drill down and see all activities related to it and vice versa. Figure 6-10 illustrates this.

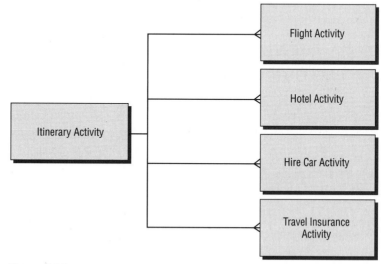

Figure 6-10

The preceding scenario demonstrates a common circumstance in which you need to store multiple instances of an activity; in this case, an itinerary can have multiple flights. Creating multiple Flight activities is straightforward, but you need to link them to an Itinerary; otherwise, they will remain an independent entity.

Adding references between itineraries and flights allows you to easily identify all flights belonging to an itinerary when retrieving activity data. This activity data is used by the BAM portal, which enables you to search for all activities and view anything referenced to it (as is discussed in more depth later in this chapter).

We use this technique heavily in the example scenario later in this chapter, with specific examples that reinforce this concept.

Custom References

Custom references allow you to "refer" data to an activity. A common use of this technique is to store message bodies or another piece of data that doesn't fit contextually within an activity item or is too big.

Using the `AddReference` method on the event streams lets you supply data up to 1MB, which is stored in the `bam_<ActivityName>_ActiveRelationships` or `bam_<ActivityName>_CompletedRelationships` table, depending on the activity status.

The only way to add references in this manner is by using the BAM API directly, which we cover later in this chapter. Message bodies are the most common use of this technique, and custom references provide a way to store the message body for later easy retrieval in case of query. This approach for message body tracking has proven to be faster than the built-in BizTalk Message Body Tracking and also enables a much richer data model by linking activities to the message data that caused those activities.

This technique is typically implemented by creating a custom pipeline component, used in a receiving pipeline that utilizes the `MessagingEventStream`.

Deployment Tool

The BAM Management tool (`bm.exe`), located in the `%PROGRAMFILES%\Microsoft BizTalk Server 2006\Tracking` directory, is used to perform all BAM administration tasks, such as provisioning the BAM databases, deploying activities and views, creating indexes, and so on.

You can find extensive instructions on its use in the BizTalk documentation. This section demonstrates how to deploy and remove the BAM infrastructure using the `bm.exe` tool.

To deploy the BAM infrastructure for the activities and views defined in an Excel workbook, use the following command:

```
bm.exe deploy-all -DefinitionFile:<EXCELWORKBOOK.XLS>
bm.exe deploy-all -DefinitionFile:<BAMDefinition.xml>
```

You can also use the same command but pass the XML representation of the BAM definition, which can be exported from the Excel workbook or perhaps hand-crafted using another tool.

To remove all the tables and views supporting a deployed BAM definition, you must use this command, passing the workbook that was used to deploy the database:

```
bm.exe remove-all -DefinitionFile:<EXCELWORKBOOK.XLS>
bm.exe remove-all -DefinitionFile:<BAMDefinition.xml>
```

You often end up changing the workbook and are then unable to undeploy the database infrastructure, because the definition you're supplying differs from what's deployed. In BizTalk Server 2004, you had to manually remove the tables. With BizTalk Server 2006, however, you can use the `get-defxml` parameter to retrieve the XML definition that was used to originally provision the database, which you can then use to remove the database infrastructure.

Making modifications and additions to your activities is inevitable over time. In the 2004 release of BizTalk, you were required to remove all of your database infrastructure to make changes, which presents an obvious problem for live systems with a lot of data present.

BizTalk 2006, however, introduced the ability to modify your activities by adding new activity items and views on the fly, using the `bm.exe` tool. Use the following command to update an existing BAM database infrastructure:

```
bm.exe update-all -DefinitionFile:<EXCELWORKBOOK.XLS>
bm.exe update-all -DefinitionFile:<BAMDefinition.xml>
```

Alerts

BizTalk Server 2006 included BAM integration with SQL Server Notification Services. The built-in BAM portal enables you to define a query and receive a notification when that query returns data.

For example, you can build a query to identify when a Web service call takes longer than a configured SLA. SQL Server Notification Services can then format a notification and deliver it to you via pluggable delivery channels (e-mail, for instance).

Performance

BAM has been architected with performance in mind and has a number of techniques to maintain performance under heavy concurrent load and large data loads. The BAM event stream APIs are also very fast and when used from BizTalk can "piggyback" orchestration persistence to improve performance further.

For example, the `BufferedEventStream` will provide better performance than the `DirectEventStream`. The caller does not have to wait for the BAM data to be successfully committed to the BAMPrimaryImport database along with the associated processing; instead, the BAM data is written into the BizTalk MessageBox in binary form. The Tracking Host is then responsible for moving this data into the BAMPrimaryImport database, while the calling application can continue processing safe in the knowledge that the BAM data is transactionally secure.

In orchestration scenarios, the `OrchestrationEventStream` will perform even better as it piggybacks any BAM data writes via the orchestration persistence mechanism and thus incurs little or no overhead above and beyond what is already acquired during orchestration processing. Like the `BufferedEventStream`, the BAM data is stored in the BizTalk MessageBox before being moved.

As previously mentioned, utilizing BAM to provide a custom form of message body tracking has been proven in a number of solutions to perform better than the built-in BizTalk message body tracking, and also provides the ability to link these message bodies to the resulting activity information.

Licensing

As discussed previously and demonstrated in the chapter scenario, BAM can prove extremely useful to leverage from non-BizTalk servers — to allow them to contribute data to a BAM activity when the BizTalk server doesn't have visibility or access to key data items that need to be captured, or even enable a solution that doesn't use BizTalk to make use of BAM.

BAM was designed to be host agnostic from the outset and so has a natural way for non-BizTalk servers to write data using the BAM API. BizTalk Server 2004, however, did not allow you to legally use the BAM API on servers not licensed for BizTalk Server.

BizTalk Server 2006 allows the BAM API to be installed on any server without attracting any further licensing fees (a result of the BizTalk Product Group responding to customer feedback). You do, however, have to have licensed BizTalk somewhere within your organization.

You can install the BAM API independently on any non-BizTalk Server using the standard BizTalk installation tool by selecting the BAM Event API component during component selection (under the Additional Software node). You can also select the BAM Client component if you want to install the Excel add-in and the bm.exe administration tool.

This licensing change opens a huge range of possibilities to use BAM across the enterprise, effectively enabling an enterprise-wide instrumentation tool. All systems involved in a solution can contribute data to a central instrumentation database in a very fast and scalable way.

Tracking Profile Editor

The Tracking Profile Editor (TPE) enables you to graphically link orchestration shapes and message data to the relevant items in the observation model that you defined using the Excel spreadsheet.

Linking the items in this way enables you to subscribe to the information. Linking an orchestration shape means that when the shape "fires," the DateTime will be stored as a milestone, and when a Message arrives, any elements subscribed to will be stored as activity data items. This linkage creates a *tracking profile*.

This incredibly powerful technique can be done retrospectively to a live system without requiring any downtime, even if you haven't instrumented your solution previously.

Using the TPE

The TPE tool is located under the Microsoft BizTalk Server 2006 program group. Upon startup, it displays two panes, as shown in Figure 6-11. The first pane is where we will import our BAM activity definition defined previously; the second pane is where we will show orchestrations and messages that will provide the source to our data.

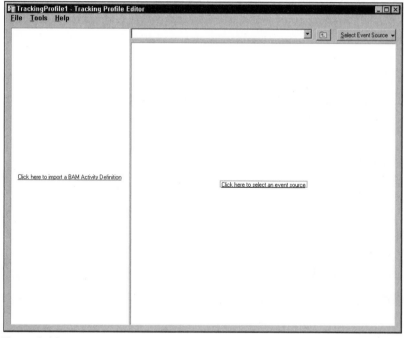

Figure 6-11

Clicking on the hyperlink shown in the BAM Activity Definition pane will allow us to select an activity that has already been deployed using the bm.exe administration tool, which we can then enable for instrumentation, as shown in Figure 6-12.

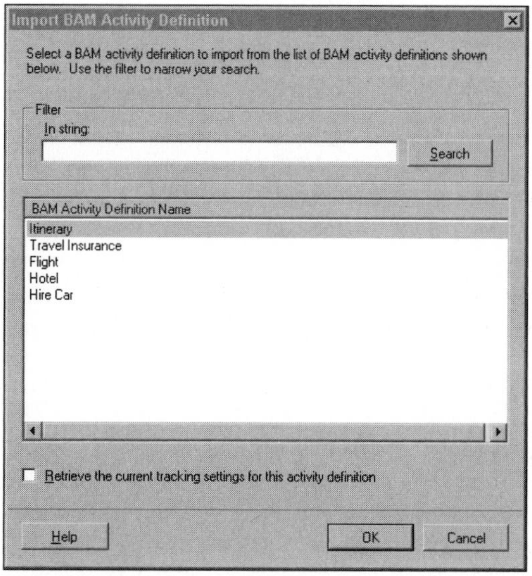

Figure 6-12

Choosing an activity from this dialog box will list all the activity items in the left pane, as shown in Figure 6-13. You can see that business milestones are represented in this tree view by clock symbols, and business data activity items are represented using any document symbol.

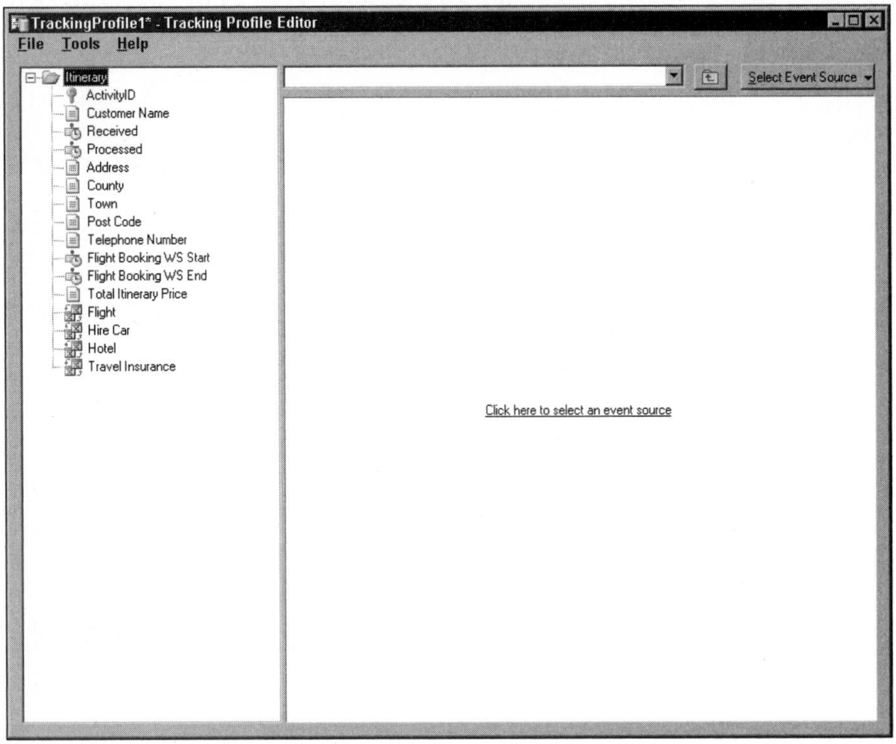

Figure 6-13

Now that we can see the activity items that need to be "hooked up," we need to identify the source of these business data items and the shapes that refer to the business milestones.

BizTalk Server 2006 has four event sources supported by the TPE: `Orchestration Schedule`, `Messaging Payload`, `Context Property`, and `Messaging Property`.

Interceptors

The Event Sources used by TPE when creating a tracking profile are represented as interceptors at runtime. BizTalk ships with an orchestration and messaging interceptor that receive events from the orchestration and messaging engine, respectively.

The tracking profile created by the TPE describes the information that should be collected. At runtime, the interceptor will receive many events from the orchestration and messaging engine but will only action those that have been subscribed to within the tracking profile. For example, each shape within an orchestration will fire an event, but only those subscribed within the tracking profile will be consumed.

This approach of using interceptors enables you to modify your tracking profile on the fly without having to (in this case) modify your orchestrations to manually invoke the interceptor. Of course, this relies on all the events being raised by the appropriate source.

We'll discuss interceptors further later in this chapter and introduce some new interceptors shipped with BizTalk Server 2006 R2 in Chapter 14.

Orchestration Schedule

The Orchestration Schedule refers to a BizTalk orchestration. From this event source, you can view the selected orchestration and hook orchestration shapes up to business milestones, and you can view messages used by the orchestration and hook elements of these messages up to business data activity items.

The key difference between this event source and the other three is that by accessing messages and orchestrations directly, you don't need to configure port mappings (as we discuss in the other event sources). This is because being within the scope of the orchestration TPE knows "where to get the events from."

By dragging orchestration shapes or message items across to the activity definition on the left pane, you are subscribing to the internal events that occur within BizTalk, and in the case of hitting a BizTalk shape, storing the DateTime.

Figure 6-14 shows that we have dragged the Receive Itinerary shape onto the Received milestone on the left side. This subscription means that the DateTime will be recorded in the Itinerary activity when the Receive Itinerary shape is activated.

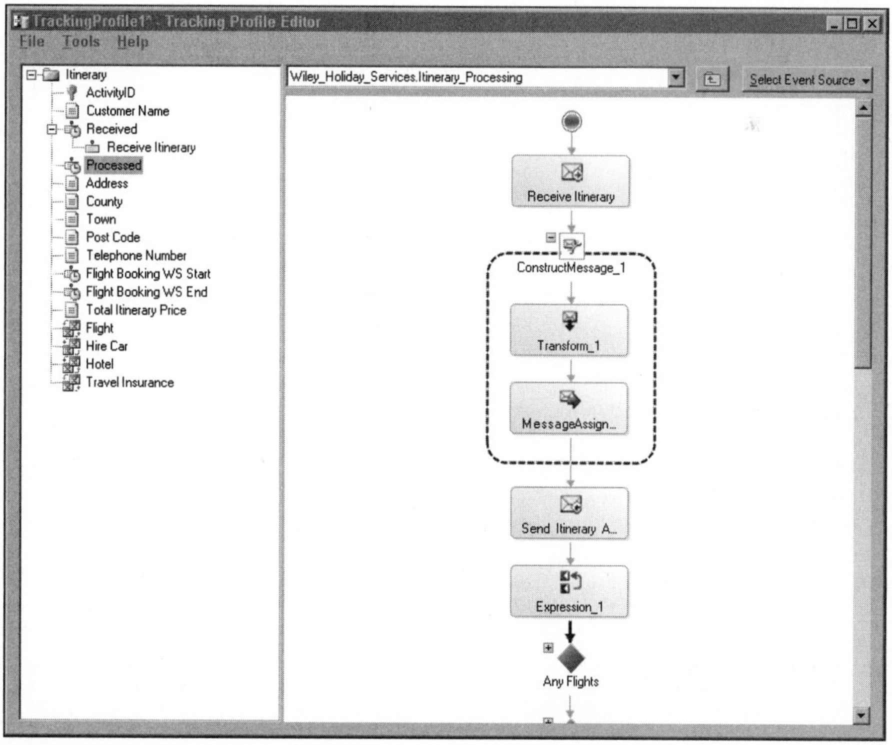

Figure 6-14

241

Any BizTalk messages used by the orchestration can be accessed through this event source, too. Right-clicking on a Send or Receive shape will show three options: Message Payload Schema, Context Property Schema, and Message Property Schema.

The Message Payload Schema option lets you view any part of the XML message referenced by the shape and drag it across onto a business data activity item. Figure 6-15 shows both panes in TPE active, and a few items from the message have been dragged across to the activity definition.

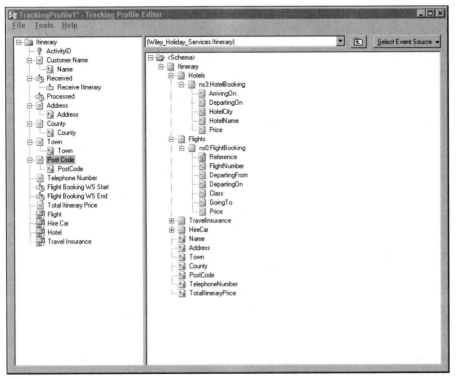

Figure 6-15

The Context Property Schema option that you can select when right-clicking on a Send or Receive shape enables you to view all the context properties that can flow with a BizTalk message. These are "out-of-band" data items that are typically created by adapters and pipelines.

For example, the File adapter will make the originating filename available as a context property on the message, and the SOAP adapter will make available the username that authenticated against Internet Information Services (IIS).

You can drag any of these context items across in the same way as you can with Message Payload Schema items. One thing to be aware of is that not all the context properties will be present in all scenarios. That is, if you don't use the File adapter, you shouldn't expect any of the `FILE.<ContextPropertyName>` properties to be present.

Figure 6-16 shows Context Property Schema items being viewed within TPE.

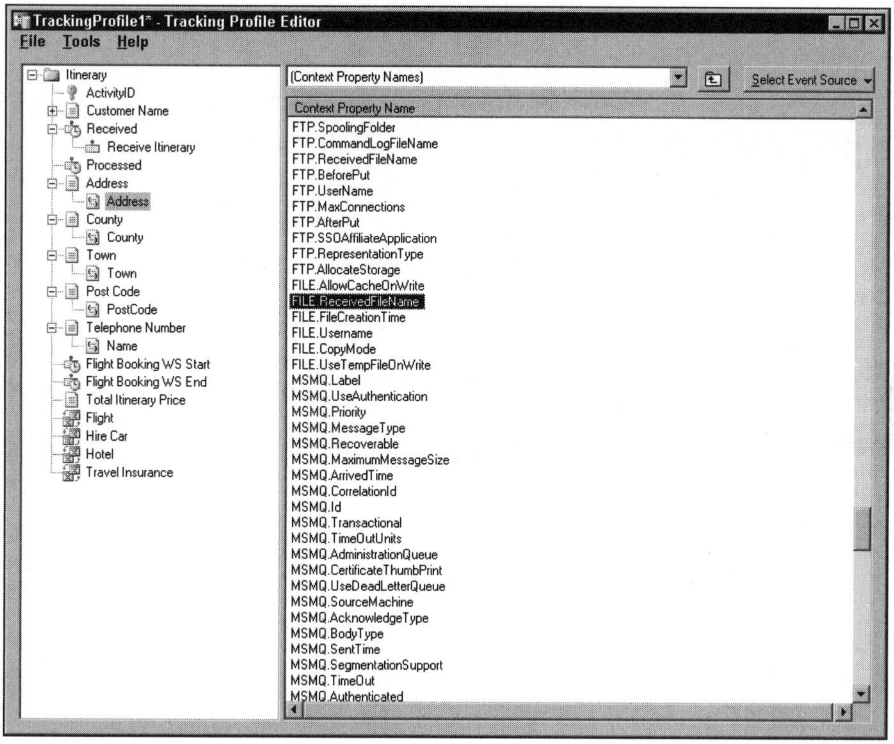

Figure 6-16

The final option when you right-click on a Send or Receive shape is Message Property Schema. This option lets you view all the low-level pipeline-specific settings, such as `InterchangeID`, `PortStartTime`, and the like. This option is less often used from within the context of an Orchestration Schedule event source but exists in case you need to access this information.

Figure 6-17 shows an example.

The Messaging Payload, Context Property, and Messaging Property

These event sources work in exactly the same way as when they are accessed via the Orchestration Schedule event source, the difference being that you have to specify at what send or receive port they should be collected.

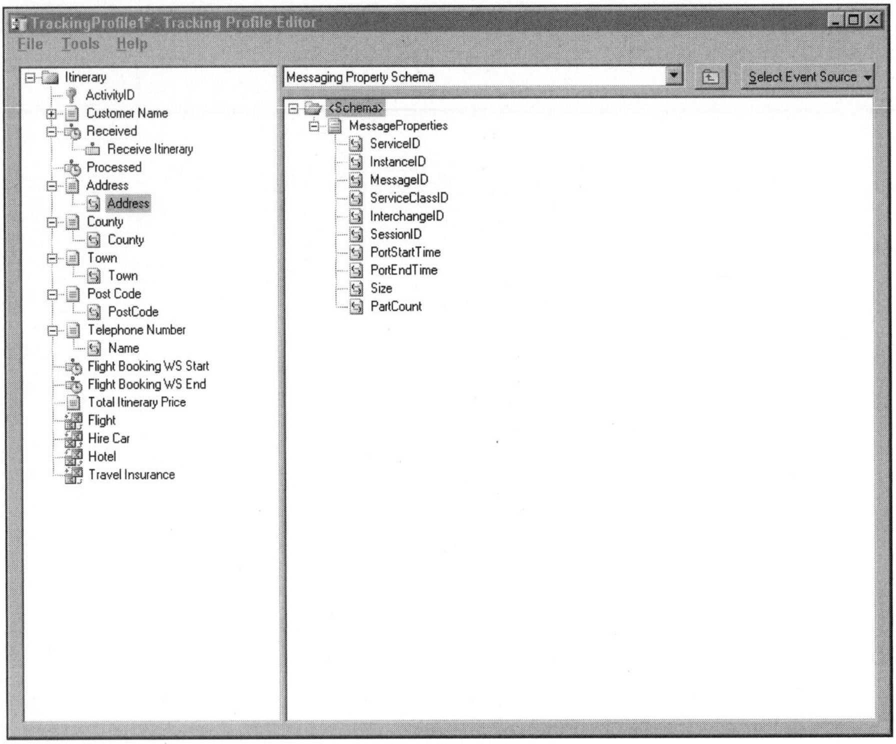

Figure 6-17

> This is a big change from the TPE in BizTalk Server 2004, which could only access messaging information directly used by orchestrations and, frustratingly, could only access elements inside your XML message, not context properties.

Selecting the Messaging Payload event source presents you with a list of all the available schemas, as shown in Figure 6-18.

Selecting a schema will display all the elements within the XML message, which you can then drag across to an activity item on the left side.

The key difference here is that BizTalk doesn't know at what point in processing to collect this information. To indicate where it should collect the messaging information, you must right-click on the activity item you have dragged to the left side and choose the Set Port Mappings option. The shown in Figure 6-19 will appear.

Using this dialog box, you can search and select a port to receive the message you selected in the previous step. BizTalk will automatically retrieve the data you've subscribed to when the message arrives or is sent through the port and store it in the activity.

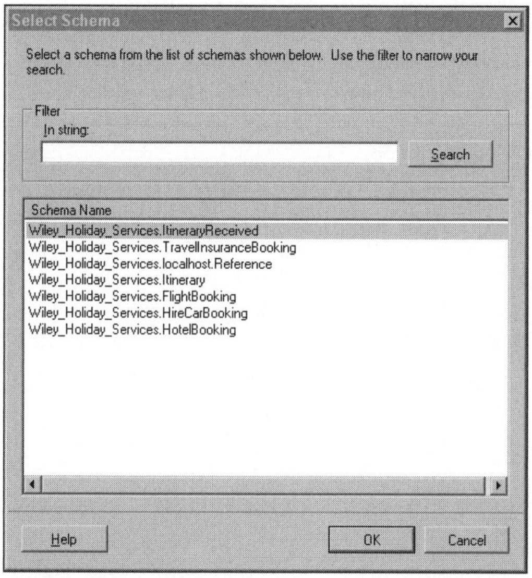

Figure 6-18

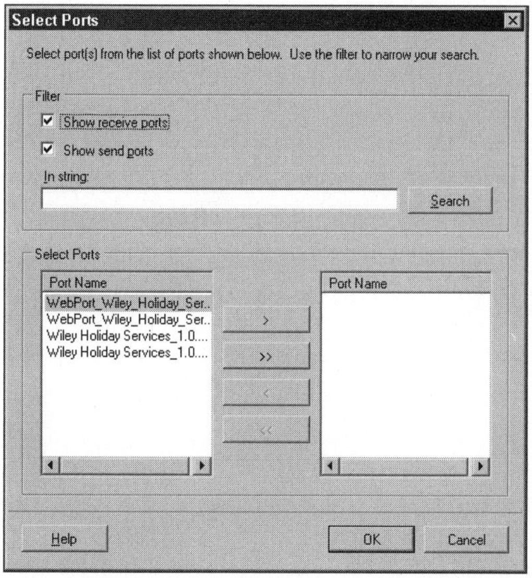

Figure 6-19

You must repeat this process for all activity items from sources other than the Orchestration Schedule event source. Errors are displayed during deployment if you fail to map any activity items.

ActivityIDs

By default, ActivityIDs are created automatically for each activity by obtaining a new globally unique identifier (GUID) at activity-creation time.

For many scenarios, this behavior is fine. If you want to control the ActivityID used for a given activity, however, you can do so by dragging an item of data from a BizTalk message or a context property to the ActivityID node included at the top of your activity definition, which is displayed in the left pane of the TPE.

You must ensure that the item of data you use for an ActivityID is unique; otherwise, BizTalk will throw an exception, and the activity data will not be written.

Continuation

Continuation enables you to contribute to an activity using a different ActivityID than the one that was used to create the activity.

This technique proves useful when another application or system needs to contribute data to an activity but doesn't have access to the unique identifier used to initiate the ActivityID. To enable continuation, you must identify a unique identifier that the other application or system has access to and that you can use as the additional ActivityID.

Remember that if BizTalk itself will be contributing to the activity later in the business process rather than some custom code on another server, you can easily flow an ActivityID using a context property on a message. You shouldn't have to change your BizTalk message to accommodate this extra token, which typically is a bad approach because it ruins the integrity of your business message.

It's important to note that continuation is also required if you use an asynchronous `EventStream`, such as the `OrchestrationEventStream`, even if you are using the same ActivityID throughout.

Due to the asynchronous nature, you can find that activity *writes* may arrive into the BAMPrimaryImport database out of order. Continuation is used to signify which order activity writes should be made available for querying. Out-of-order writes will be hidden temporarily. We'll demonstrate in the "BAM API" section how to correctly enable continuation and crucially how to ensure the use of continuation doesn't lead to orphaned activities.

> It's worth noting that the use of continuations comes with some performance overhead. Wherever possible, it is advisable to utilize a new activity and add references between them to avoid continuations. This applies to scenarios where you need a downstream system to contribute to an activity or are using asynchronous `EventStream`s.
>
> A rule of thumb is that you should not use more than two continuations per activity in general practice.

Figure 6-20 depicts a typical continuation scenario. An Itinerary message that contains a CustomerReference arrives in BizTalk. This CustomerReference is then used as the ActivityID for a new BAM activity. The next step of the process is to book flights using a third-party Flight Booking Web service.

This third-party service has no concept of a CustomerReference because this is a Wiley Travel Services concept and instead requires a BookingID. The Wiley Travel Services solution enables continuation, passing a BookingID as the new continuation identifier.

Once invoked, the Flight Booking Web service uses this BookingID as the BAM ActivityID and writes further information into the activity created by the BizTalk solution.

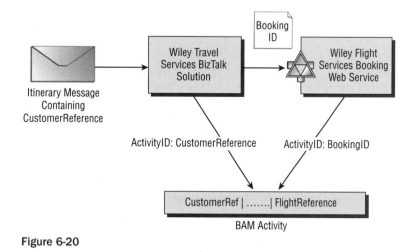

Figure 6-20

Continuation Scenario: Orchestration to Orchestration

To enable continuation using the TPE when two orchestrations are contributing to the same activity, you need to perform the following steps:

1.   Enable continuation and provide the identifier that will be used to identify the activity later on. To do so, right-click the activity name in the left pane of the TPE. Choose New Continuation, and then provide a friendly name for your continuation.

2.   Drag the new ActivityID that you want to use to refer to this activity later from an event source into the new continuation item you created in the preceding step. This step enables your activity to be referred to using this new identifier. Because another orchestration is going to contribute to this activity, you now need to create a ContinuationID item in the activity. This is the method by which two different "sources" can contribute to the same activity instance.

3.   Right-click the activity again and choose New ContinuationID to create a ContinuationID folder and give it the same name as the friendly name you defined previously. From the second orchestration, you can now drag the new identifier to this ContinuationID folder. Continuation is now complete.

Continuation Scenario: Orchestration to Custom Code

In this scenario, an orchestration has created a new activity via the TPE, but some custom code downstream from this orchestration will contribute extra data to the activity.

To enable this, you need to create a continuation folder, which effectively enables continuation for this activity instance. Right-click the activity name in the left pane of the TPE and choose New Continuation. Choose a name for this continuation. The name of the continuation is combined with the value dragged across to create the actual continuation ActivityID.

Then select a piece of data from an event source that will be available inside the custom code and drag this across to the continuation folder you've just created.

Continuation is now enabled. The ActivityID that you will need to use in the custom code is a combination of the continuation folder name and mapped value. So, if your folder were called `Flight` and the mapped value were `REF01`, the resulting continuation ActivityID would be `FlightREF01`.

The following example using `DirectEventStream` demonstrates contributing to an activity after continuation has been enabled within TPE. We will cover the BAM API in more detail in the next section.

```
string ContinuationActivityID = "FlightREF01";
string FlightActivityName = "Flight";
string BookingReferenceActivityItem = "BookingReference";

DirectEventStream des = new DirectEventStream ("Integrated Security=SSPI;Data
Source= MySQLServer;Initial Catalog=BAMPrimaryImport",1);

des.UpdateActivity(FlightActivityName,ContinuationActivityID,
BookingReferenceActivityItem, "BOOKREF42");

des.EndActivity(FlightActivityName,ContinuationActivityID);
```

Continuation Scenario: Custom Code to Orchestration

In scenarios in which custom code creates an activity and the TPE later needs to contribute to the activity instance, continuation must be enabled in the code that creates the ActivityID. This code must preface the ActivityID with some form of prefix.

The following example shows how you might do this. An activity is created and continuation is then enabled and provides a new ActivityID by prefixing the original ActivityID with `CustomCodeToTPE`.

You must always supply a new ActivityID each time you enable continuation; prefixing with a processing step name is a common way of achieving this:

```
string ActivityID = System.Guid.NewGuid().ToString();
string ItineraryActivityName = "Itinerary";

DirectEventStream des = new DirectEventStream ("Integrated Security=SSPI;Data
Source= MySQLServer;Initial Catalog=BAMPrimaryImport",1);

bes.BeginActivity(ItineraryActivityName,ActivityID);
...
bes.EnableContinuation(ItineraryActivityName, ActivityID, "CustomCodeToTPE" +
ActivityID);
bes.EndActivity(ItineraryActivityName,ActivityID);
```

After this is done, you need to create a ContinuationID folder for your tracking profile by right-clicking the activity name in the left pane and choosing New ContinuationID. Type in the prefix added to your ActivityID when enabling continuation.

Finally, drag the final piece that makes up the ActivityID from the appropriate event source to configure continuation inside the TPE.

Relationships

Relationships in TPE enable you to link one activity to another, which we discussed as references earlier in the chapter. An example of a relationship might be between a travel itinerary activity and a flight-booking activity. A flight was booked as part of an overall itinerary and a link must therefore be made between the two.

To enable a relationship between two activities, follow these steps:

1. Right-click the activity name in the left hand of the TPE and choose New Relationship. The name of this relationship folder must be the same as the activity to which you want to link. Therefore, if you want to link a Flight activity to an Itinerary activity, call this folder Itinerary.

2. Drag the ActivityID of the destination activity to this folder. In this case, you drag the ActivityID of the Itinerary activity into this folder. This step allows BAM to identify the exact activity instance to which you are linking.

Looping

Scenarios in which you have repeating constructs in your orchestration require special handling. If you are looping around a repeating element in an XML message, for example, you must create a new activity for each loop iteration, because activity definitions don't have a repeating concept.

In this case, you would have a new tracking definition that has an autogenerated ActivityID or uses a unique property that is available on the message being processed. You would then map the items across the activity definition as usual, the difference being that you will end up with a new activity created for each loop iteration.

Using the relationship feature detailed previously, you would then have to add a relationship back to the parent activity to ensure that you have linkage between parent and children activities.

Deployment

Deployment of a tracking profile defined using the TPE is straightforward. From within the TPE, you can choose Apply Tracking Profile from the Tools menu, at which point the tracking profile is instantly deployed and starts work (without having to restart any BizTalk components).

A deployed activity profile can also be undeployed using the Remove Tracking Profile option from the Tools menu.

To TPE or Not to TPE?

In the BizTalk Server 2004 release, TPE wasn't as feature rich as in BizTalk Server 2006. The 2004 release could not subscribe to data on messages as they came through the pipeline and could not access context properties, which are used often in BizTalk scenarios.

A few limitations apply to what TPE can and cannot do. These limitations are listed in the BizTalk documentation. A notable omission is the ability to use custom references, which allow you to store up to 1MB of information alongside an activity (a useful technique for storing message bodies). However, combining TPE with custom code to perform this is perfectly acceptable.

In addition, the `OrchestrationEventStream` was not exposed initially in the 2004 release. It was also not advisable to mix the use of the TPE and event streams. You had to make a decision one way or the other; more often than not you would end up using the event stream approach.

This is not the case in 2006, which enables the use of the TPE in many more scenarios. It avoids you having to write the BAM API code by hand and allows easy modification of your tracking profile, which to be honest doesn't actually change that often once deployed anyway.

The advantages of using a BAM API approach, which we cover in the next section, is that it is code and therefore debuggable and easy to test through unit tests. You also have more control over the format of the data being stored. Perhaps you want to calculate the total price of an item by adding the item price and tax together, and in scenarios in which you are using BAM from outside BizTalk, you can't, of course, use the TPE (because it relies on the BizTalk infrastructure).

You can use all the concepts that we talk about in the next section (continuation, relationships, and references) through the graphical user interface of the TPE.

Personally, I find it easier to define via code because the UI can be confusing, especially if you're making heavy use of relationships and mixing BAM API code with the TPE. It's better in my view to have everything in one place, where it's easy to test.

The `GeneratedTypedBAMAPI` approach detailed later in this chapter is an easy way to build a simple API around your activities and removes the time-consuming and brittle approach of using the BAM API manually.

This is a personal choice, nothing else. Review both approaches and pick the one most suitable to the problem you're solving. Remember, however, that you can mix them together if that helps.

Another drawback when using TPE in orchestrations is that if an orchestration is changed during the development process, you will need to rerun TPE, wasting a lot of time during development. Even relatively minor changes to orchestrations will make this necessary. You could use TPE right at the end, but although this might reduce the number of times you need to rerun TPE, the chances are that changes will be required to your orchestrations to fix bugs, which means rerunning TPE. Using the API approach detailed in the next section means that you can add your BAM tracking as your solution is developed, leading to a more agile development approach.

BAM API

As discussed earlier, there are four different types of event streams: `DirectEventStream`, `BufferedEventStream`, `OrchestrationEventStream`, and `MessagingEventStream`.

In many scenarios, the TPE will not be used. In such scenarios, you must program against the BAM API directly to provide monitoring data to the runtime; the API is very straightforward.

Creating Activities

To create a new instance of an activity, you need to call the `BeginActivity` method present on all the event streams. In this method, you provide the name of the activity you want to create as a string literal and an ActivityID as a string literal unique within the activity.

```
string ActivityID = System.Guid.NewGuid().ToString();
string FlightActivityName = "Flight";

bes.BeginActivity(FlightActivityName, ActivityID);
```

The `BeginActivity` method creates a new row in the bam_<ActivityName>_Active table, and all data items within the activity are defaulted to NULL.

The ActivityID uniquely identifies this activity and is used in subsequent calls to the BAM API to update data items in this activity.

GUIDs are typically used as ActivityIDs in most scenarios via the `System.Guid.NewGuid().ToString()` approach. If you're using BAM from BizTalk, however, you can make use of the `BTS.InterchangeID` context property, which is held on all BizTalk messages and is guaranteed to be unique for an interchange. The interchange relates to the transfer of the message between the adapter and MessageBox; although if you are splitting messages in the pipeline, this adapter will not be unique. And, if you clone the message inside your solution, you must ensure that you copy this context property to your new message. Of course, you can use a unique identifier of your own choosing, perhaps stored as part of a message that has been received.

Updating Data Items

After an activity has been created using the `BeginActivity` method, you can populate the activity data items at any point in your solution by using the `UpdateActivity` method, as long as the activity hasn't been closed using the `EndActivity` method.

The `UpdateActivity` method updates one or more activity data items in the specified activity that is identified using the passed ActivityID, as follows:

```
string ActivityID = System.Guid.NewGuid().ToString();
string FlightActivityName = "Flight";
string CarrierActivityItem = "Carrier";
string FlightNumberActivityItem = "Flight Number";

DirectEventStream des = new DirectEventStream ("Integrated Security=SSPI;Data
```

```
    Source=MySQLServer;Initial Catalog=BAMPrimaryImport", 1);

    des.BeginActivity(FlightActivityName, ActivityID);

    des.UpdateActivity(FlightActivityName, ActivityID, CarrierActivityItem, "Wiley
    Airlines");

    des.EndActivity(FlightActivityName,ActivityID);
```

If you have multiple activity data items to update, you can provide them all in one `UpdateActivity` statement using the following technique. The BAM API uses the `params` keyword available in the C# language to support this technique. The following code shows the Carrier and Flight Number activity items being written in one call:

```
    string ActivityID = System.Guid.NewGuid().ToString();
    string FlightActivityName = "Flight";
    string CarrierActivityItem = "Carrier";
    string FlightNumberActivityItem = "Flight Number";

    BufferedEventStream bes = new BufferedEventStream("Integrated Security=SSPI;Data
    Source=MYSQLServer;Initial Catalog=BizTalkMsgBoxDb",1);
    bes.BeginActivity(FlightActivityName,ActivityID);

    bes.UpdateActivity(FlightActivityName,ActivityID,CarrierActivityItem, "Wiley
    Airlines",FlightNumberActivityItem,"DJ01");

    bes.EndActivity(FlightActivityName,ActivityID);
```

If you're using the `BufferedEventStream`, the update won't actually happen until you manually flush or reach the flush threshold specified when you constructed the `BufferedEventStream`. In light of this, you should not maintain instances of the `BufferedEventStream` open across, say, orchestration shapes, because you may suffer data loss. The preceding example provides 1 as the flush threshold, meaning you do not have to call flush in this instance.

If you are using the `DirectEventStream`, each call to `UpdateActivity` will result in a database roundtrip, so bear this in mind if you are updating multiple things in short succession and use the multiple-update approach shown above. You can use this approach with any `EventStream` because the API is consistent between them all.

The `DirectEventStream` approach will also raise an exception if it's unable to write the activity data to the BAMPrimaryImport table. Therefore, ensure that you wrap the code in a `try/catch` block to address network connectivity issues or to identify any programming errors (such as providing the wrong type to an activity data item).

Continuation

Continuation has two main roles for BAM. The first role is to enable multiple applications to contribute information to an activity where there may not be a shared identifier across all the systems. The second role is to ensure that all BAM data arrives in the BAMPrimaryImport table in order when you are using an asynchronous event stream such as the `BufferedEventStream`.

When you begin an activity, you pass a unique identifier that is used as the ActivityID. You must then use this activity in all subsequent event stream calls to ensure that you update the same activity instance.

In some systems, you may be unable to pass your initial ActivityID to a downstream system. Therefore, it will be unable to contribute data to your active activity. In these scenarios, you attach another unique identifier to the activity, an identifier that the downstream system does have access to.

For example, a flight-booking service may create a FlightBooking activity using a customer reference that has been passed as an ActivityID but then needs to call an ASP.NET Web service that expects a FlightBooking identifier.

In this scenario, you create a new FlightBooking identifier, and call the EnableContinuation method passing the new identifier. The remote ASP.NET Web service can then call UpdateActivity, passing the new FlightBooking identifier as the ActivityID rather than the original customer reference.

BAM sorts out the *relationship* between the ActivityIDs and writes the data to the correct activity. Refer to Figure 6-20 for a depiction of this scenario. Each time continuation is enabled, you are creating what is known as an *activity segment*.

> **In scenarios in which you are using the same ActivityID but are using an asynchronous event stream, such as the BufferedEventStream and OrchestrationEventStream, you must enable continuation to ensure that data items are written in order. Failure to do this can also lead to orphaned activities and partially completed activities.**

To achieve this, you must create a new ActivityID each time. Typically, we tend to use a simple prefix such as a component or application name.

To enable continuation, you must use the EnableContinuation method. This method takes three parameters: the activity name (as usual), the current ActivityID, and the new ContinuationID that will be used from now on as the ActivityID.

The following code shows how you can enable continuation. After the activity has been created, we call EnableContinuation, passing a new ContinuationID (FBR0402) that can be used by the downstream system and starting a new activity segment.

```
string ActivityID = System.Guid.NewGuid().ToString();
string FlightActivityName = "Flight";
string CarrierActivityItem = "Carrier";

BufferedEventStream bes = new BufferedEventStream("Integrated Security=SSPI;Data
Source=MySQLServer;Initial Catalog=BizTalkMsgBoxDb", 1);

bes.BeginActivity(FlightActivityName,ActivityID);
bes.UpdateActivity(FlightActivityName,ActivityID,CarrierActivityItem, "Wiley
Airlines");
...
bes.EnableContinuation(FlightActivityName,ActivityID,"FBR0402");
bes.EndActivity(FlightActivityName, ActivityID");
```

In the next part of your solution that must update this activity, you must use the ContinuationID — in this case, "FBR0402" — as the ActivityID. The following code shows how you can do this. Note that `BeginActivity` does not have to be called because the activity is already underway.

```
string ContinuationID = "FBR0402";
bes.UpdateActivity("Flight",ContinuationActivityID,"Booking Reference",
"27853-174AZ");
bes.EndActivity("Flight", ContinuationActivityID);
```

You must ensure that you call `EndActivity` in both places. In the first instance of the preceding scenario, you must call `EndActivity`, passing the original ActivityID even though you have already enabled continuation at this point. This then closes this original activity segment; the activity can still be modified but only by using the new ContinuationID.

Then when the second code fragment updates the Activity using the ContinuationID, it must again call `EndActivity` when it has finished writing data to the activity. The ContinuationID must be passed to `EndActivity` in this case, thus closing this activity segment and completing the activity. Of course, you could call `EnableContinuation` before this to enable another activity segment.

Failure to follow these rules will result in orphaned activities in the BAM database. These are represented as activities that remain active and are never moved to the completed table.

Continuation comes with an associated performance cost. Generally, you should not use more than two continuations per activity. If you find yourself using more, you should instead consider using a new activity and use references to link them together.

References

> In BizTalk Server 2004, the `AddRelatedActivity` method on each event stream was used to add relationships between two activities. The new reference functionality in BizTalk Server 2006 supersedes this, but the `AddRelatedActivity` method remains for backward compatibility.
>
> For new code that must relate activities, use the `AddReference` method rather than `AddRelatedActivity`, which as it happens internally now calls `AddReference`.

As mentioned earlier in this chapter, references represent a key area of BAM that you should fully understand. You can use references to great effect to resolve some very complex problems and reduce the amount of code you need to write for your solution.

References are new in BizTalk Server 2006. Relationships between activities existed in the 2004 release but have been included in BizTalk Server 2006 as *references*. In short, the references capability allows activities to refer to activities, messages, BizTalk artifacts such as orchestrations, or any chunk of data that you provide.

Activity References

The most common form of reference is interlinked activities. As detailed in the preceding note, these were exposed via the `AddRelatedActivity` method in the 2004 release of BizTalk, and now via the `AddReference` method.

Very simple scenarios using BAM might only end up using one activity, but most of the time multiple activities are created, and more often than not they are interrelated.

Or perhaps you need to store multiple "records" that are each represented as distinct activities. For example, you might receive a travel itinerary in BizTalk as a message. This itinerary message contains details about flight, hotel, hire car, and travel insurance bookings, and each must be processed individually.

As part of the processing, you need to store the information about each booking along with any booking codes (to be used for tracking of booking progress and to provide business metrics). To support this, you might have an activity for each concept — Itinerary, Flight, Hotel, and Hire Car. In addition, the Itinerary activity must be linked to the Flight, Hotel, and Hire Car activities. Figure 6-21 shows this relationship.

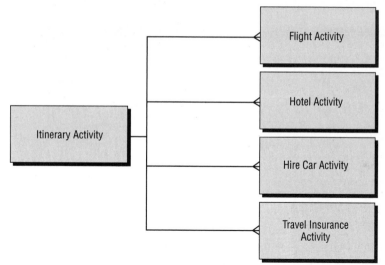

Figure 6-21

The `AddReference` method on each event stream enables you to link two activities together in this manner. Any references are stored in the `bam_<ActivityName>_ActiveRelationships` SQL table initially and then moved to the `bam_<ActivityName>_CompletedRelationships` when the activity has been completed.

Any custom SQL queries should use the associated `bam_<ActivityName>_AllRelationships` SQL view rather than querying the tables directly.

There are two overloads for the `AddReference` method:

```
AddReference(string activityName, string activityID, string referenceType,
        string referenceName, string referenceData)

AddReference(string activityName, string activityID, string referenceType,
        string referenceName, string referenceData, string longreferenceData)
```

The second overload is used for custom references (covered next). An example of using `AddReference` to link the Itinerary and Flight activities is shown below. The `referenceType` parameter is set to `Activity` to indicate an activity reference, and this specific type is used by the BAM portal (covered later) to identify activity references.

```
string FlightActivityID = System.Guid.NewGuid().ToString();
string FlightActivityName = "Flight";
string ItineraryActivityName = "Itinerary";
string ItineraryActivityID = "ITIN0124";

BufferedEventStream bes = new BufferedEventStream("Integrated Security=SSPI;Data
Source=MySQLServer;Initial Catalog=BizTalkMsgBoxDb", 1);

bes.BeginActivity(FlightActivityName, FlightActivityID);
...
bes.AddReference(ItineraryActivityName,ItineraryActivityID,"Activity",
FlightActivityName,FlightActivityID);
bes.EndActivity(FlightActivityName, FlightActivityID");
```

Note that the activities can be linked either way round; that is, you could pass the `FlightActivityName` and `FlightActivityID` parameters first. This just changes which activity relationships table the relationship is added to.

Custom References

Custom references enable you to store data and link it to a given activity. This technique is often used to store large data such as message bodies or JPEGs (perhaps a JPEG of an original paper form that has been scanned and processed).

We covered one overload of the `AddReference` method earlier. The second overload is of specific interest when using custom references. The second overload introduces a `longreferenceData` parameter that can be used to "link" data up to 1MB in size to an activity. The underlying LongReferenceData column is configured with a text SQL data type, meaning that it can store more than 1MB. However, due to the way BAM implements batching under the covers, anything stored over the 1MB can cause batching and therefore performance problems.

The following code fragment shows how to use `AddReference` to, in this case, store a message body.

❑ The first two parameters refer to the Activity and ActivityID that you want to add this custom reference to.

❑ For the third parameter (`referenceType`), you pass `MsgBody`, which is a made-up reference type for the purposes of this code. You can pick any type name, as long as it doesn't clash with the built-in message types.

❑ For the fourth parameter (`referenceName`), you pass the name of the reference for which you pass `MessageBody`.

❑ For the fifth parameter (`referenceData`), you don't actually want to pass anything as you are going to make use of the `longReferenceData` parameter to store the message body. However, you have to pass something, so in this case you take advantage of being able to store the DateTime representing when the message body was stored. You can use this for any purpose (perhaps a digital signature for security reasons).

❑ For the sixth parameter (`longReferenceData`), you store a message body by, in this case, serializing a serializable class into XML:

```
string ItineraryActivityName = "Itinerary";
string ActivityID = System.Guid.NewGuid().ToString();

// Write the Itinerary Body out
System.IO.StringWriter sw = new System.IO.StringWriter();
XmlSerializer xs = new XmlSerializer(typeof(Itinerary));
xs.Serialize(sw, itin);

BufferedEventStream bes = new BufferedEventStream("Integrated Security=SSPI;Data
Source=MySQLServer;Initial Catalog=BizTalkMsgBoxDb", 1);
bes.BeginActivity(ItineraryActivityName, ActivityID);
...
bes.AddReference(ItineraryActivityName, ItineraryActivityID, "MsgBody",
"MessageBody", System.DateTime.Now.ToString(), sw.GetStringBuilder().ToString());

bes.EndActivity(ItineraryActivityName,ActivityID);
```

Generating Typed APIs

For simple scenarios, you will require little in the way of code that drives the BAM API. As you start developing larger solutions with more activities, however, the "instrumentation" code can become unwieldy and brittle.

For example, the BAM definition defined in the Excel spreadsheet will evolve over time, and therefore your "instrumentation" code must be kept in sync with new activities and activity items. In addition, the BAM API is deliberately loosely typed to remain flexible and requires activity names and data items to be supplied as string literals, which can become impossible to manage with large projects because any misspelled activity items will result in a runtime exception. You can easily appreciate the number of string literals required for activity and activity data items in the code samples you've seen so far, let alone a large project.

An approach that I developed while working on a large BizTalk proof of concept was to generate a typed API from the BAM definition spreadsheet and link this to a custom build tool in the BizTalk project — to ensure that the instrumentation façade was always up to date and presented a strongly typed API to the developers, thus reducing the possibility for errors.

I demonstrate the use of this typed API later in this chapter. If you choose to use the BAM API approach for your BAM instrumentation, I strongly recommend you consider using this tool.

You can download the current version of this tool from www.codeplex.com/GenerateTypedBamApi.

Event Streams

The BizTalk Server 2006 release of BAM comes with four event streams: `DirectEventStream`, `BufferedEventStream`, `OrchestrationEventStream`, and `MessagingEventStream`.

`DirectEventStream`, `BufferedEventStream`, `OrchestrationEventStream`, and `MessagingEventStream` were available in BizTalk Server 2004, although the `OrchestrationEventStream` and `MessagingEventStream` were only exposed after the release of BizTalk Server 2004 and are available as a hotfix from Microsoft or in the box with BizTalk Server 2006.

The event streams are used to provide events to the BAM runtime for storage in the BAMPrimaryImport database. Each is useful in a number of different scenarios, as discussed in the following subsections.

The event streams are implemented as .NET class libraries and are located in the `Microsoft.BizTalk.Bam.EventObservation.dll` held in the `%PROGRAMFILES%\Microsoft BizTalk Server 2006\Tracking` directory, apart from the `OrchestrationEventStream`, which is located in the `Microsoft.BizTalk.Bam.XLANGs.dll`.

DirectEventStream

The `DirectEventStream` uses a synchronous database connection to write activity data directly to the BAMPrimaryImport database. Therefore, you have to wait for a database connection to be established to your SQL server and the data to be written before you can continue. The database connection, however, is likely to be cached by the connection pooling feature, which will improve performance slightly. This is directly analogous to you using a `SqlConnection` and `SqlCommand` directly from your own code.

This method proves ideal when you want to write the data and have it appear instantly (low latency) (in contrast to a buffered or asynchronous approach used by the other event streams), but it will have an adverse effect of taking longer to execute and requiring further system resources. This may be acceptable for a low-throughput system, but as you ramp your throughput numbers up, this is likely to prove unacceptable.

The following code shows how you can use the `DirectEventStream` from your custom code. We haven't had to call flush explicitly in this example, because we've set the flush threshold to 1, meaning that it will automatically flush after every call to `UpdateActivity`.

```
using Microsoft.BizTalk.Bam.EventObservation;

string ConnectionString = "Integrated Security=SSPI;Data Source=MySQLServer;Initial
Catalog=BAMPrimaryImport";
string ActivityID = System.Guid.NewGuid().ToString();
string OrderActivityName = "Order";
string NameActivityItem = "Name";

DirectEventStream des = new DirectEventStream( ConnectionString, 1);

des.BeginActivity(OrderActivityName,ActivityID);
des.UpdateActivity(OrderActivityName,ActivityID,NameActivityItem,"Darren Jefford");
des.EndActivity(OrderActivityName, ActivityID);
```

BufferedEventStream

The `BufferedEventStream` provides buffered access to write activity data to the BAM database. Therefore, for the life of the `BufferedEventStream`, you can write multiple activity entries and only require one database roundtrip to persist them all.

The `BufferedEventStream` then stores the activity data in binary form inside the BizTalk Message Box database, which acts as a "store-and-forward" database. The Event Bus Service then processes this data and moves it into the BAMPrimaryImport database.

This method proves ideal when you need to update multiple activities because you reduce the number of database roundtrips, which in turn reduces the processing time of your solution and reduces required system resources. BAM data can then be processed on another machine in the BizTalk group, freeing up the BizTalk servers to get on with processing messages. Typically the `BufferedEventStream` will give better performance than the `DirectEventStream` because the write to the BAM database is decoupled through the BizTalk MessageBox database. You have full control of the buffer size before it's flushed and can force a flush of all pending writes at any time by using the `Flush` method.

The following code shows how you can use the `BufferedEventStream` from your custom code. Note that the `ConnectionString` is now set to point at the `BizTalkMsgBoxDb` rather than the BAMPrimaryImport table used for the `DirectEventSteam`.

```
using Microsoft.BizTalk.Bam.EventObservation;

string ConnectionString = "Integrated Security=SSPI;Data Source=MySQLServer;Initial
Catalog=BizTalkMsgBoxDb";
string ActivityID = System.Guid.NewGuid().ToString();
string OrderActivityName = "Order";
string NameActivityItem = "Name";

BufferedEventStream bes = new BufferedEventStream( ConnectionString, 1);

bes.BeginActivity(OrderActivityName, ActivityID);
bes.UpdateActivity(OrderActivityName,ActivityID,NameActivityItem,"Darren Jefford");
bes.EndActivity(OrderActivityName, ActivityID);
```

Transactional Integrity

In many scenarios in which BAM is used, the data being collected is business critical and must validly represent what's really happened.

Suppose, for instance, that you're processing an order using BizTalk orchestration. At various points in the business process, you record data in BAM, such as the customer's details and items ordered. If at a later point the customer's credit card authorization fails, you might then terminate the business process and roll back any systems you've updated as part of the business process (such as an inventory management application). The same goes for unhandled exception situations within your orchestration.

If you had used the `BufferedEventStream` or `DirectEventStream` to write your BAM activity data, it would have remained present in the BAM database and would have reflected an incorrect view to any business analysis that was performed (such as "How many order have we processed today?").

You could *roll back* the BAM data using compensation (as covered in Chapter 5) in your BizTalk orchestration, but you would have to manually implement this by NULLing activity items out, because there is no supported way to delete activities.

If you are using the preceding event streams, any BAM activity data written is not tied to the execution of the business process, and hence when the orchestration rolls back, the data persists, which is where the OrchestrationEventStream and MessagingEventStream come in.

OrchestrationEventStream

The OrchestrationEventStream writes BAM Activity data into the *state* of the BizTalk orchestration and does not require a database roundtrip each time. When the orchestration completes or reaches a persistence point, the BAM activity data is written into the MessageBox along with the orchestration state.

The Tracking Host built into BizTalk Server then copies the data out of the MessageBox into the BAM PrimaryImport database at regular intervals. It does this typically in batches of 100 items. This offers great performance and scalability because you are effectively piggybacking on the database roundtrips that BizTalk already has to perform and then moving the data to the BAMPrimaryImport database in batches.

Because this data is part of the orchestration state, all data is rolled back along with the orchestration if an error condition is reached. This method gives you complete transactional integrity, unlike the other event stream options, and offers the best performance for an orchestration-based solution.

The OrchestrationEventStream is utilized by the TPE tool. In BizTalk Server 2004, it was an internal component used by TPE and not exposed for general use. The transactional integrity requirement came up during a customer engagement, so it was later exposed in the 2004 release by a hotfix and is in the box with BizTalk Server 2006.

The following code shows how you can use the OrchestrationEventStream from your custom code. Note that because the OrchestrationEventStream is implemented as a static class, there is no need to manually create an event stream each time, and a connection string isn't required, because the OrchestrationEventStream piggybacks the persistence of the orchestration.

```
using Microsoft.BizTalk.Bam.EventObservation;

string ActivityID = System.Guid.NewGuid().ToString();
string OrderActivityName = "Order";
string NameActivityItem = "Name";

OrchestrationEventStream.BeginActivity(OrderActivityName, ActivityID);
OrchestrationEventStream.UpdateActivity(OrderActivityName, ActivityID,
NameActivityItem, "Darren Jefford");
OrchestrationEventStream.EndActivity(OrderActivityName, ActivityID);
```

MessagingEventStream

The MessagingEventStream, like the OrchestrationEventStream, is transactionally consistent. However, instead of being consistent with orchestration execution, it is consistent with pipeline execution. If, for example, the execution of a pipeline fails, any associated BAM data written up to that point using the MessagingEventStream will be rolled back.

Again, like the `OrchestrationEventStream`, it is an asynchronous `EventStream` in that the BAM data is written initially to the BizTalk MessageBox before being transferred to the BAMPrimaryImport database.

To use the `MessagingEventStream`, you will need to write a custom pipeline component (see Chapter 4). Unlike with other `EventStream`s, you do not *construct* an instance of the `MessagingEventStream`; instead, you must instead retrieve an instance from the pipeline context. The following code illustrates an example of using the `MessagingEventStream`:

```
using Microsoft.BizTalk.Bam.EventObservation;

public IBaseMessage Execute(IPipelineContext pc, IBaseMessage inmsg)
{
  EventStream mes = pc.GetEventStream();

  string ActivityID = System.Guid.NewGuid().ToString();
  string OrderActivityName = "Order";
  string NameActivityItem = "Name";

  mes.BeginActivity(OrderActivityName, ActivityID);
  mes.UpdateActivity(OrderActivityName, ActivityID, NameActivityItem, "Darren
Jefford");
  mes.EndActivity(OrderActivityName, ActivityID);
```

You can, of course, use the `Direct` or `Buffered` `EventStream`s as required from within a custom pipeline component, although these will not be transactionally consistent with the pipeline execution.

Custom Interceptor

As we touched on earlier, BAM interceptors enable you to *instrument* parts of your application by raising notable events from within your application to a custom interceptor, which if then subscribed to via configuration can be stored within an activity, using an appropriate BAM `EventStream`.

BizTalk ships with built-in orchestration and messaging interceptors. The Orchestration engine will raise events for many events, such as an Orchestration shape firing, which may then be subscribed to through the creation of a tracking profile.

You can, however, create your own BAM interceptor, which you can use to raise events from within your application and then later subscribe to these as you see fit through configuration. A classic example of BAM interceptors are the new Windows Communication Foundation (WCF) and Windows Workflow Foundation (WF) BAM interceptors shipped with BizTalk Server 2006 R2.

These enable events and data exposed from WCF or WF to be subscribed to through the use of an interceptor configuration file and then be written as part of activities using a BAM `EventStream`, without requiring any changes (apart from configuration) to the WCF service or WF workflow. This is covered further in Chapter 14.

This extremely powerful technique enables applications to raise potentially interesting events with next to no overhead, which can then be subscribed to and collected as required into one central location. Imagine a BizTalk solution that makes use of WCF services and a WF workflow as part of processing and being able to collect information from all areas all through the use of configuration that can be modified on the fly.

Custom interceptors can be implemented through the use of the `BaseInterceptor` class, which is located within the `Microsoft.BizTalk.Bam.EventObservation.dll` held in the `%PROGRAMFILES%\ Microsoft BizTalk Server 2006\Tracking` directory. A sample of an interceptor is included in the BizTalk SDK under `%PROGRAMFILES%\Microsoft BizTalk Server 2006\SDK\Samples\BAM\ BamApiSample`.

It's unlikely that you'll find yourself having to write custom interceptors, because the orchestration and messaging interceptors expose just about everything you'll need, and any data is typically held within BizTalk messages. If, however, you have extensive additional information that you may need to collect moving forward and want to avoid modification to your solution when your tracking requirements change, an interceptor may be a good approach.

We've now covered all of the key fundamentals relating to BAM and will now move on to demonstrate all of these concepts by building a sample application.

Applied BAM

In the remainder of the this chapter, we will build a fictitious solution called *Wiley Travel Services* to demonstrate how BAM can be used throughout a solution to enable a number of real-world scenarios and to demonstrate the features we've discussed.

Wiley Travel Services is a highly simplified sample application in all aspects to ensure the concepts are easy to understand. Wiley Travel Services provides travel agency services such as flight, hotel, and hire car reservations, and travel insurance.

BizTalk is used as part of this solution to physically reserve the services requested as part of an itinerary and will be invoked by a front-end ASP.NET Web application via ASP.NET Web services.

The booking of itinerary services is a time-consuming process because various suppliers operate an asynchronous booking service. To avoid timeout and latency issues, the ASP.NET Web service exposed from the itnerary orchestration will return immediately with an itinerary reference identifier and will carry out the itinerary booking without causing the customer to wait.

Itinerary processing then splits into Flight, Hotel, Hire Car, and Travel Insurance orchestrations. The flight orchestration calls a fictitious external Flight Booking Web service to perform the booking, whereas the remaining orchestrations are stubbed out and just simulate a booking.

Figure 6-22 shows a diagram of the sample architecture.

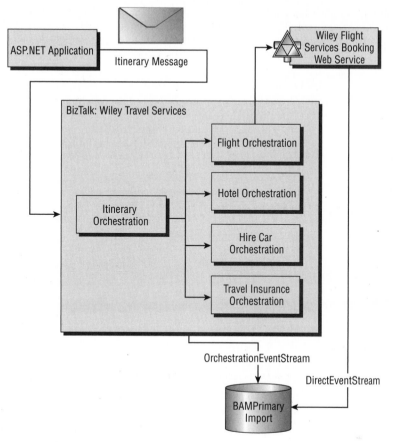

Figure 6-22

Defining Your Activities

The first step in enabling BAM instrumentation of your solution is to define what data you want to collect during the execution of your solution. You do this by defining the activities inside an Excel spreadsheet, using the BAM Excel add-in.

> **BizTalk Server 2004 used a custom** BAM.XLS **file located in the** %PROGRAMFILES%\
> Microsoft BizTalk Server 2004\Tracking **directory. This workbook used Excel macros, which presented some security and trust issues (and hence the move to an Excel add-in).**

As discussed in the "Architecture" section, activities end up as SQL tables in the BAMPrimaryImport database, and each activity item is represented as columns within the SQL table.

As part of the Holiday Services scenario, you want to create five activities to store information on itineraries that have been processed: Itinerary, Flight, Hotel, Hire Car, and Travel Insurance. An itinerary can contain any combination or number of itinerary components, so an itinerary, for example, can contain four flights, two hotel bookings, and no hire car or travel insurance bookings.

The Itinerary activity holds information relating to the customer and general itinerary processing items, and the remaining activities hold the information specific to each itinerary component.

You start by opening Microsoft Excel on a machine with the BizTalk development tools installed. If you don't see a BAM menu, ensure that the add-in is loaded by accessing the Add-Ins option on the Tools menu. Figure 6-23 shows the Add-Ins dialog box.

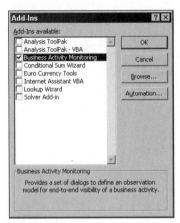

Figure 6-23

From the BAM menu, choose BAM Activity, and then click the New Activity button. We will start with the Itinerary activity, so enter **Itinerary** as the activity name. As part of this activity, we want to store the name, address, county, postal code (ZIP code), and telephone number of the customer, and the total price of the itinerary.

Add each activity item in turn using the New Item button. All the activity items should be created as Business Data — Text except for Total Itinerary Price, which should be set to Decimal.

Next, you need to add the business milestones you want to record. You want to record the date and time when you received the itinerary for processing and when the itinerary finished processing, and also the date and time either side of the Flight Booking Web service call to calculate an average call time.

To do this, you need to create four more business milestone activity items. You should end up with an activity like that shown in Figure 6-24. Note that the last activity item has scrolled off the list but is called Received and is configured as a Business Milestone.

Click OK to Save the activity, and then click New Item to create the Flight activity. As part of this activity, you want to store the flight details following a booking. Create the activity as shown in Figure 6-25, then click OK to save the activity.

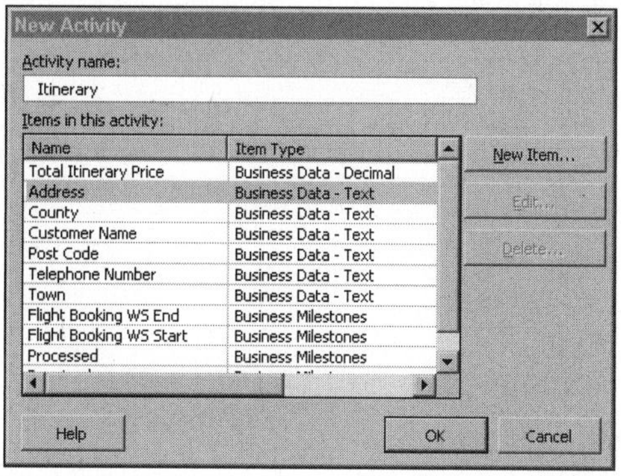

Figure 6-24

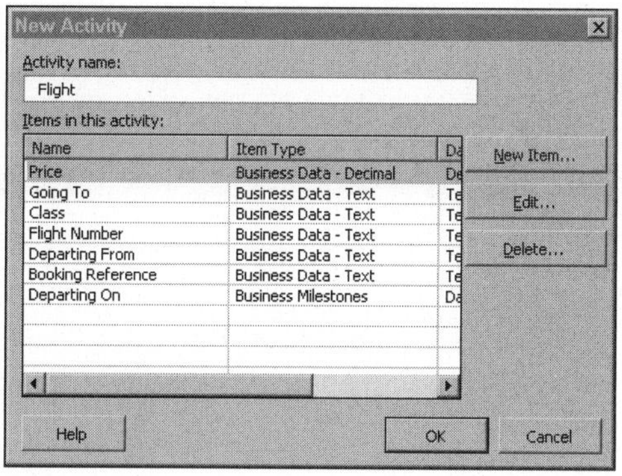

Figure 6-25

The next activity is the Hotel activity. As with the Flight activity, you need to store the hotel details following a booking. Create the activity as shown in Figure 6-26, and then complete the Hire Car and Travel Insurance activities, which are shown in Figures 6-27 and 6-28.

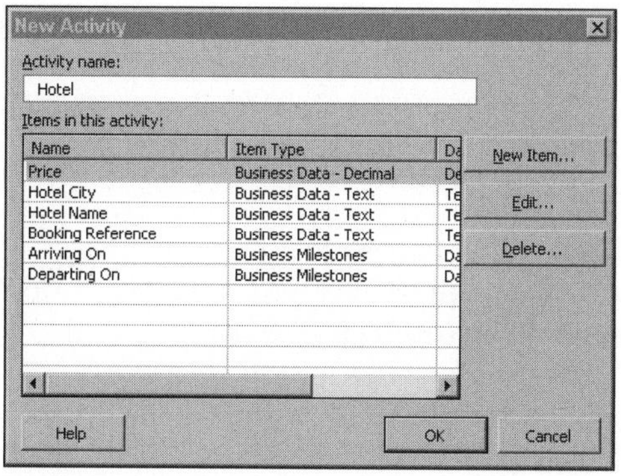

Figure 6-26

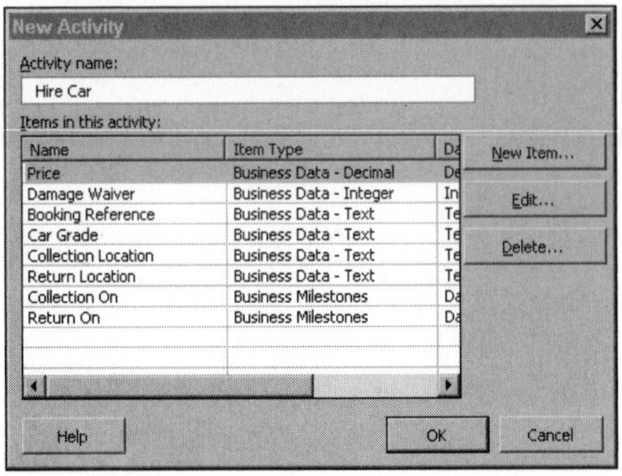

Figure 6-27

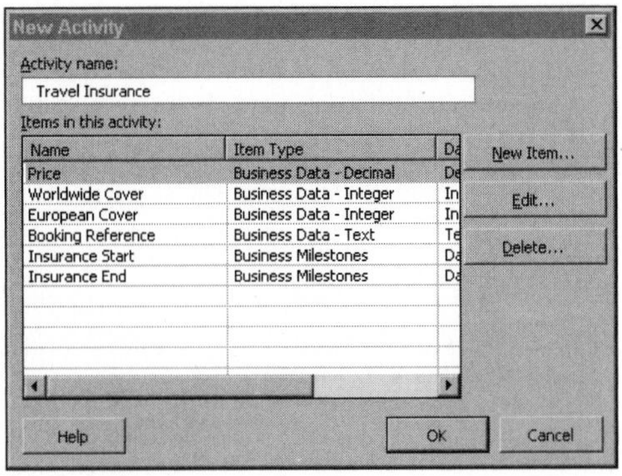

Figure 6-28

All of the activity definitions are now complete. Clicking OK will now bring up the Business Activity Monitoring View Creation Wizard, with which you define the activity views in the following section.

Defining Your Activity Views

Now that you've defined the activities, you can define activity views to pull together the various activity items and permit different roles within the business to view this data. Activity views are an optional step; so, unless you gain some benefit, you can skip this step for your solution. We include them in this solution to demonstrate their effectiveness.

For the purposes of this solution, you will define two views: a Business view and an Operations view. The Operations view will allow the operations staff to view how many itineraries have been received and group this data by time, and also to monitor the average Flight Booking Web service call time to enforce any SLA requirements with the external company.

The Business view allows business staff to view metrics on how many itineraries have been sold and group them over time, and also to view metrics on the various itinerary components to get visibility on how many flights have been sold and to what destinations, for example.

Creating the Operations View

The first step of the wizard is to create a new view. Click Next and enter **Operations View** as the view name. Select the Itinerary Activity, because you don't require any of the data from other activities for this view, as shown in Figure 6-29.

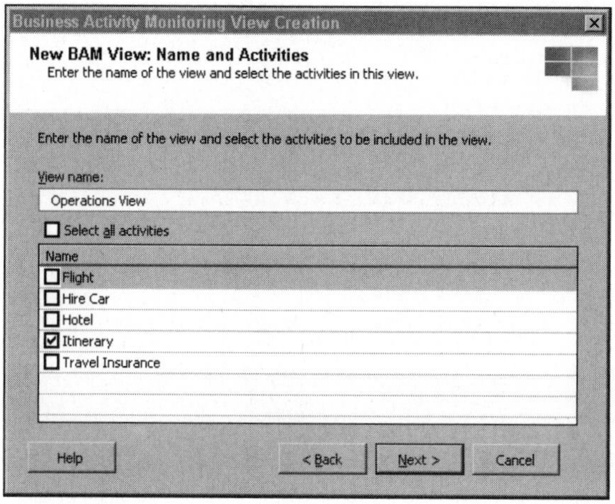

Figure 6-29

Click Next to proceed to the next step. For simplicity, choose Select All Items, and then click Next.

This next step of the wizard enables you to define aliases, durations, and groups with your activity items. Aliases are useful when you need to rename activity items because different business users tend to have different names for the same underlying data. For the purposes of this sample, you just use durations, which will enable BAM to calculate the elapsed time between two milestones automatically.

The first duration definition will be the itinerary processing time. This will be calculated between the Received milestone that was provided when the itinerary arrived at our BizTalk solution and the Processed milestone that was provided when the itinerary finished processing.

Click New Duration and enter **Itinerary Processing Time** as the duration name. Then select the Received and Processed milestone as the Start and End business milestones, respectively. The processing time is very quick for this solution, so select the time resolution of Second. You should end up with a duration defined as shown in Figure 6-30.

The final duration definition will be the Flight Booking Web service call time. This will be calculated between the Flight Booking WS Start and Flight Booking WS End milestones to calculate the elapsed execution time of the Web service.

Create a new duration called **Flight Booking WS Duration** based on the two Flight Booking milestones, and set the time resolution to Second, as shown in Figure 6-31.

As discussed earlier in this chapter, measures are precalculated queries, such as average itinerary processing time, and dimensions are ways in which you can group data, such as grouping the number of itineraries received by time to show how the number has changed over time.

267

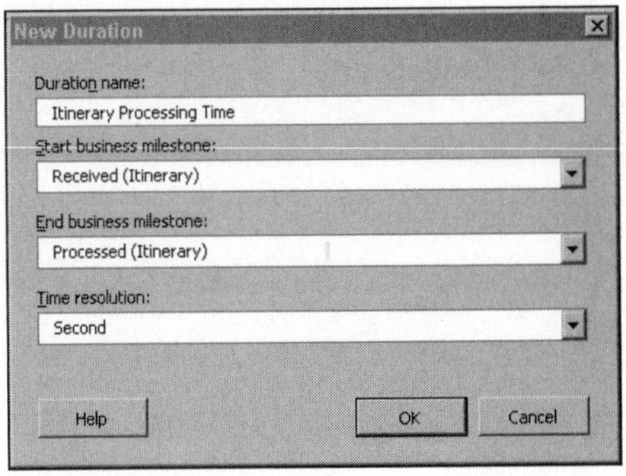

Figure 6-30

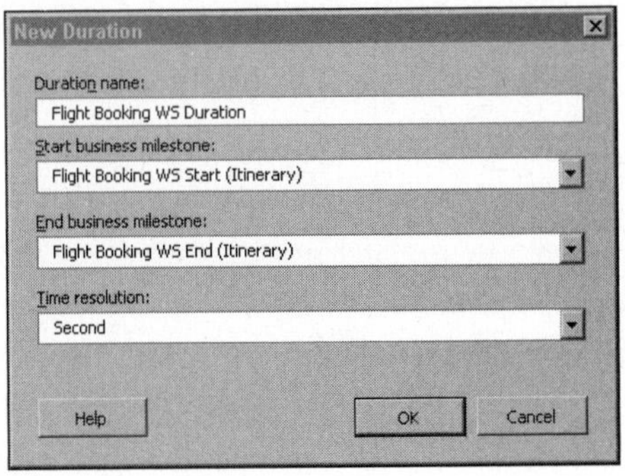

Figure 6-31

The first measure you need is an average of the Flight Booking WS Duration that you defined in the previous step.

Click New Measure, and enter **Av WS Duration** as the measure name. Choose the Flight Booking WS Duration data item, and select Average from the Aggregation Type, as shown in Figure 6-32.

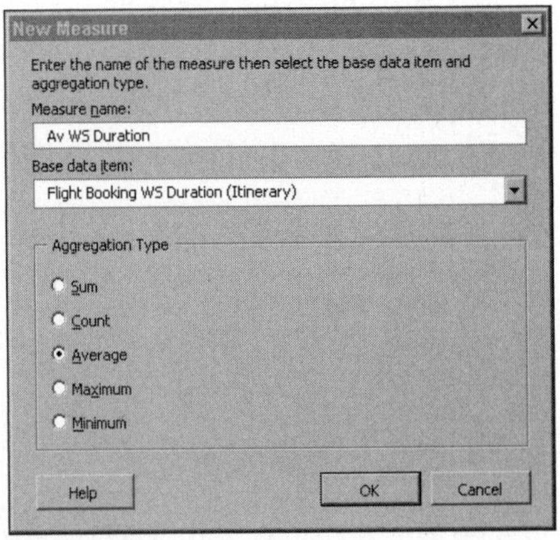

Figure 6-32

The final measure you need is to count the number of itineraries received. To create this, click New Measure, and enter **Itineraries Received** as the measure name. Select Count from the Aggregation Type, and select the Itinerary Activity, as shown in Figure 6-33.

You now need to create a time dimension to allow us to group these measures by time, which will enable you to view these measures over time.

To do this, click New Dimension and enter **Time** as the dimension name. Then select Time Dimension from the Dimension Type drop-down list.

Select Year, Month, Day, Hour, and Minute as the display settings, and you should have a dimension like that shown in Figure 6-34.

Click OK and then Next to view the View Summary page. Then click Next again to complete the view creation.

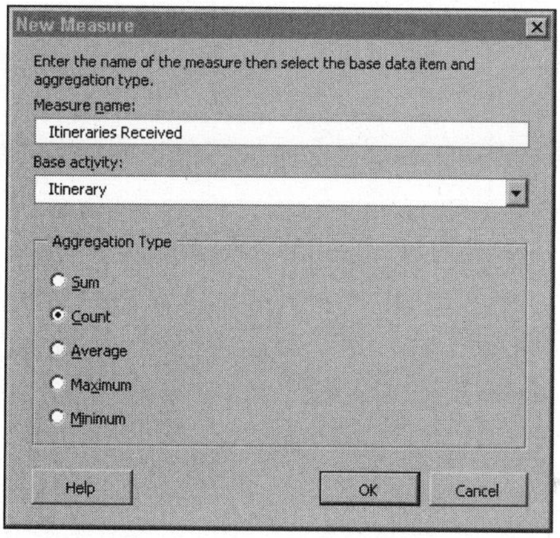

Figure 6-33

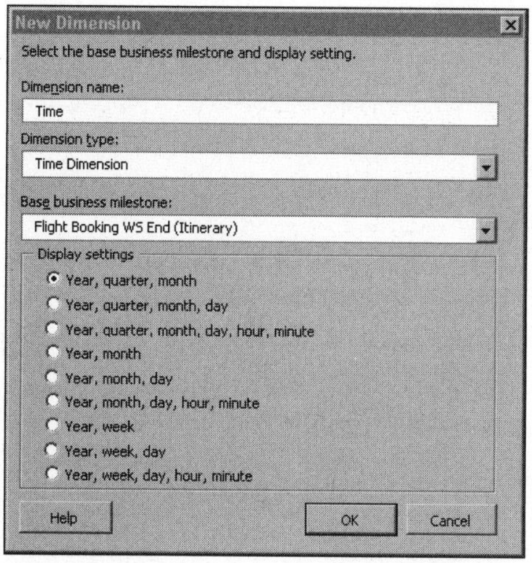

Figure 6-34

Creating the Business View

You've completed the Operations view, so you can now move on to create the Business view. Choose BAM View from the BAM menu, and select Create a new view. Then click Next, and enter **Business View** as the view name.

Choose Select all activities, because you require activity items across all the various activities defined, as shown in Figure 6-35.

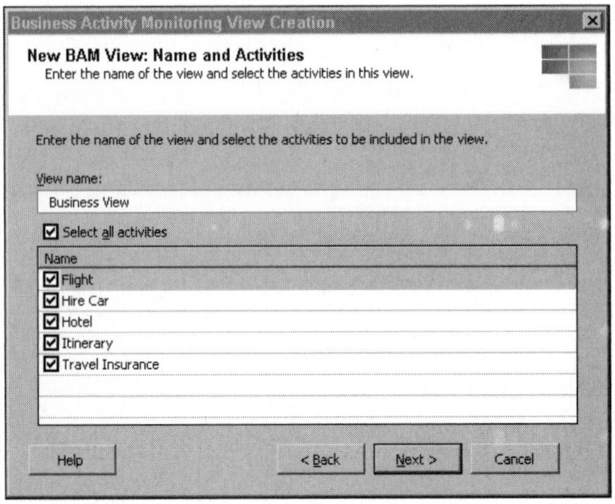

Figure 6-35

The next step of the wizard allows you to pick which activity items you want to include in the view. For the purposes of the sample and clarity, choose Select All Items, and then manually deselect processing-specific activity items such as Booking Reference, Flight Booking WS Start, and Flight Booking WS End, as shown in Figure 6-36, because these are not required for business users. Click Next to proceed.

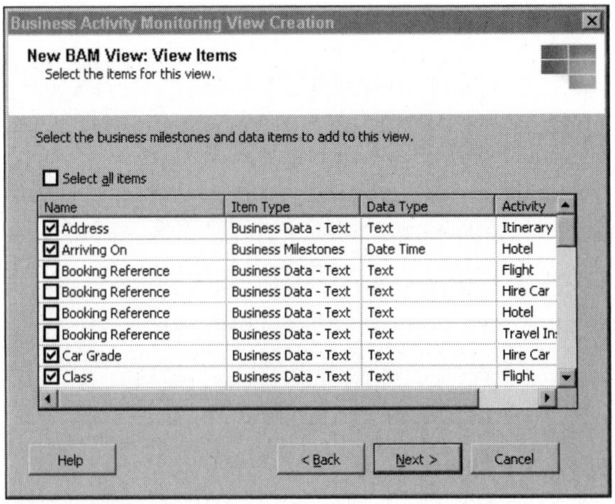

Figure 6-36

This step of the wizard lets you define aliases, durations, and groups with our activity items. As mentioned previously, aliases are useful when you need to rename activity items, because different business users tend to have different names for the same underlying data. For the purposes of this sample, you just use durations, which will enable BAM to calculate the elapsed time between two milestones automatically.

The first duration definition will be the itinerary processing time. This will be calculated between the Received milestone that was provided when the itinerary arrived at the BizTalk solution and the Processed milestone that was provided when the itinerary finished processing.

Click New Duration and enter **Itinerary Processing Time** as the duration name, and select the Received and Processed milestone as the Start and End business milestones, respectively. The processing time is very quick for this solution, so select the time resolution of second. You should end up with a duration defined as shown in Figure 6-37.

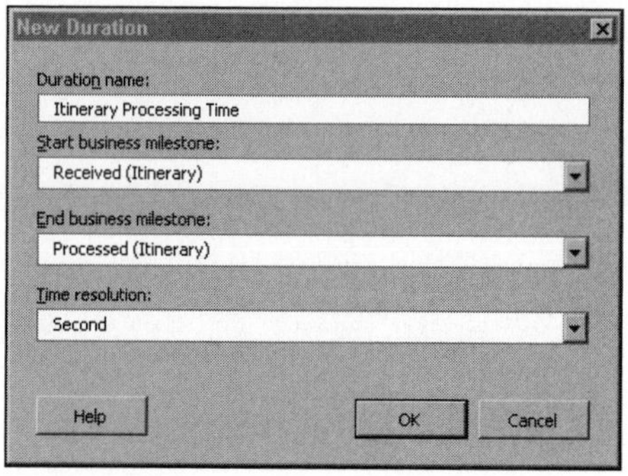

Figure 6-37

The next duration is to calculate the time spent in a hotel. Click New Duration, and enter **Hotel Stay Duration** as the duration name. Select the Arriving On and Departing On milestones, and select Day as the time resolution, as shown in Figure 6-38.

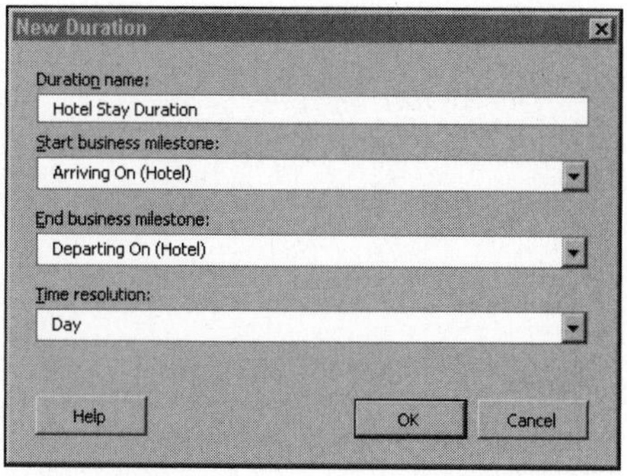

Figure 6-38

Click Next to proceed. You can now define aggregate dimensions and measures.

As discussed earlier in this chapter, measures are precalculated queries, such as average itinerary processing time, and dimensions are ways in which you can group data, such as grouping the number of itineraries received by time to show how the number has changed over time.

The first measure you need is a count of the Itinerary activities received. To create this, click New Measure, and enter **Itineraries Received** as the measure name. Select Count from the Aggregation Type options, and select the Itinerary Activity, as shown in Figure 6-39.

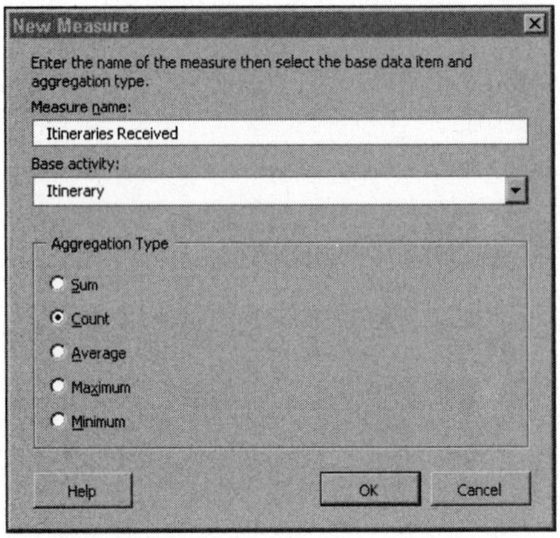

Figure 6-39

Repeat this for each of the Flight, Hotel, and Hire Car activities so that you end up with a Flights Booked, Hotels Booked, and Hire Cars Rented measures, as shown in Figure 6-40.

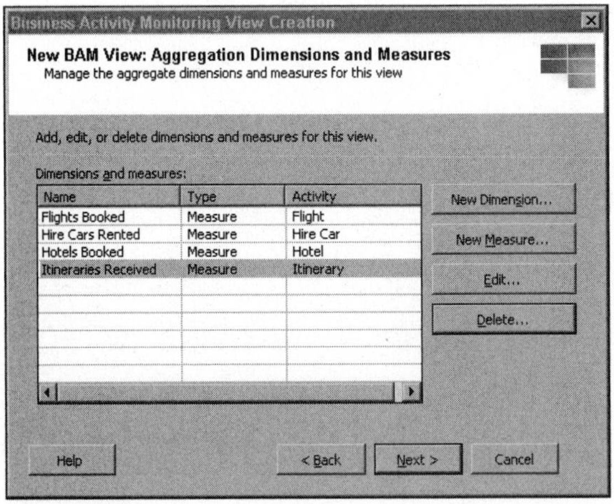

Figure 6-40

The next measure to create is to calculate the sum of all itineraries sold. To do this, you create a new measure called **Sum Itinerary Prices** and select Total Itinerary Price as the Base Data Item and Sum as the Aggregation Type, as shown in Figure 6-41.

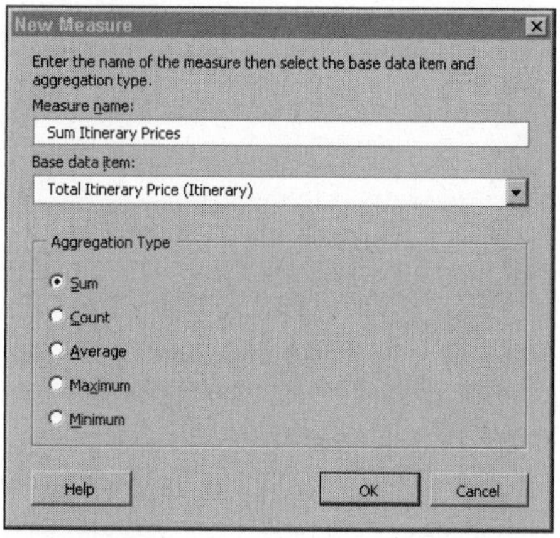

Figure 6-41

The last measure is to calculate the average hotel stay duration, which is based on the duration defined in the previous wizard step. Create a new measure called **Average Hotel Stay** based on the Hotel Stay Duration milestone and select Average as the Aggregation Type, as shown in Figure 6-42.

The final step is to create the dimensions for each activity for which you've created measures. The first dimension is a time dimension on the Itinerary activity, which will allow you to group measures defined on the Itinerary activity by time.

Click New Dimension, and type **Itinerary Received** as the dimension name. Select Time Dimension from the Dimension type drop-down list. You will base this dimension on the Received milestone and select Year, Month, Day, Hour, Minute for the display settings. Figure 6-43 shows this duration definition.

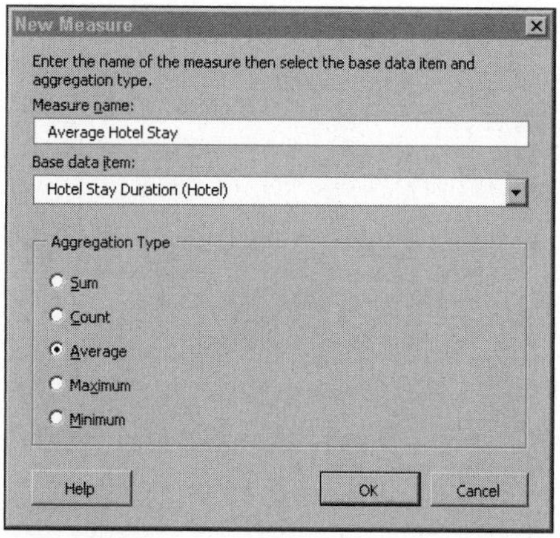

Figure 6-42

273

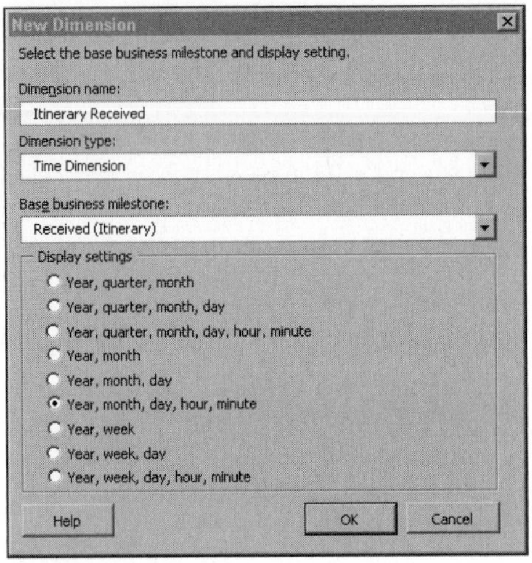

Figure 6-43

The next dimension will be a data dimension, which will allow you to group flights by the destination to identify top destinations, for example.

Click New Dimension and enter **Destination** as the dimension name. Select the Data Dimension from the Dimension Type drop-down list. Select the Going To Activity Item, and click Add to move it across to the Dimension Levels list.

You can add multiple data times to allow a hierarchal grouping. In this instance, however, you only require one activity item, so click OK. Figure 6-44 shows this dimension.

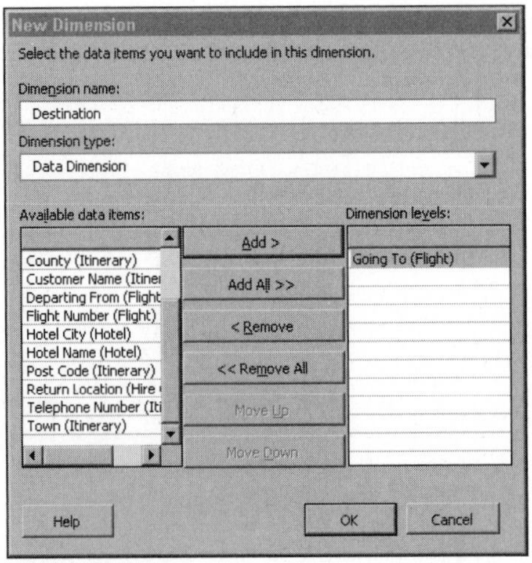

Figure 6-44

The next dimension is the same, but for the Hire Car activity. Create a new data dimension called **Collection Location** based on the Collection Location activity item, as shown in Figure 6-45, and click OK.

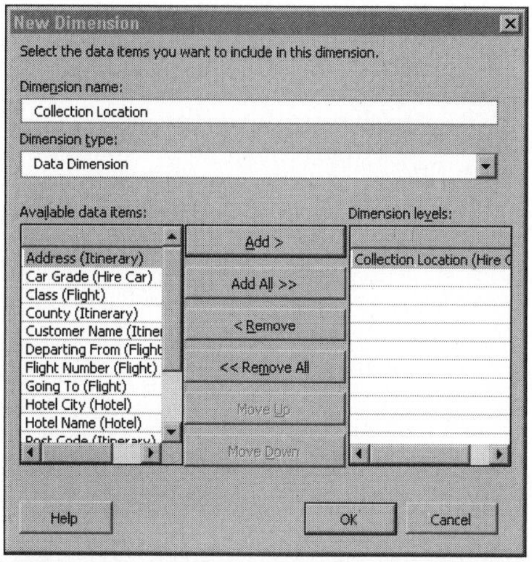

Figure 6-45

The final dimension is the same, but for the Hotel activity. Create a new data dimension called **Hotel City** based on the Hotel City activity item, as shown in Figure 6-46.

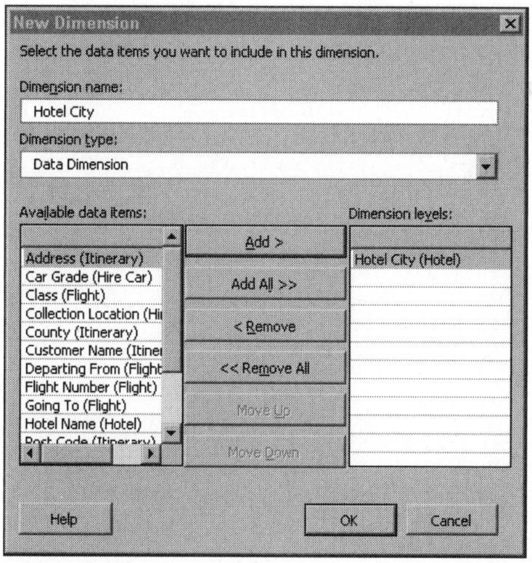

Figure 6-46

You've now finished the activity view definition. Click Next to proceed to the Summary pane, and then click Next again to create the view.

Testing the Views

After you've finished defining your views, you will see that your workbook now has a tab for each view. Within these workbooks, you have one default PivotTable that can be configured using one of your dimensions, this allows you to play with your view to ascertain whether it can model everything you expected.

The spreadsheet helpfully simulates data, which enables you to explore your view in detail. To demonstrate this, select the Operations view and drag Itineraries Received from the PivotTable Field List onto the Drop Data Items Here section. Then drag Time onto the Total column to create a PivotTable, as shown in Figure 6-47.

The final step is to name the PivotTable. Click inside the PivotTable and choose Table Options from the PivotTable toolbar. Then enter **Itineraries Received** as the name.

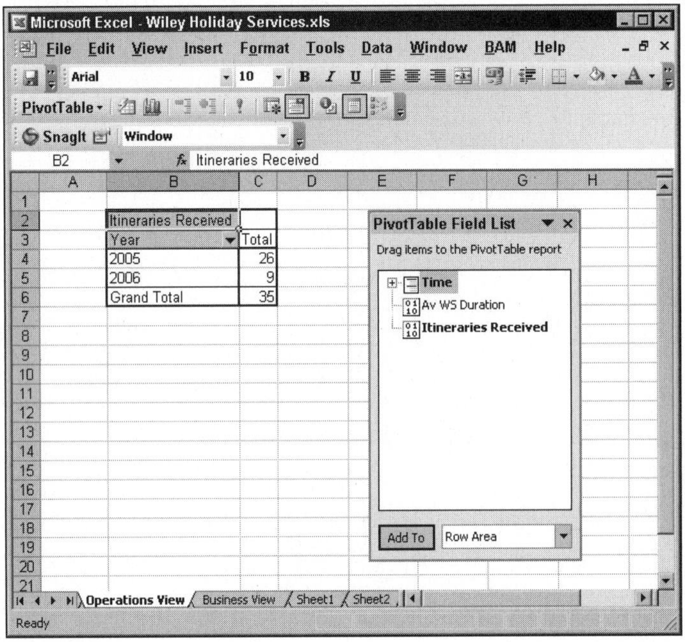

Figure 6-47

Click the Chart Wizard icon from the toolbar to view a chart based on the random data. Doing so can also help you visualize the effectiveness of your views, as shown in Figure 6-48.

Your views are now complete, but you need to configure each of the PivotTables created for you to enable them to be viewed using the BAM portal again. This is an optional step, but I've included it to demonstrate the BAM portal effectively later in this chapter.

You've already configured the Operations view PivotTable, so click the Business View tab to view the Business PivotTables.

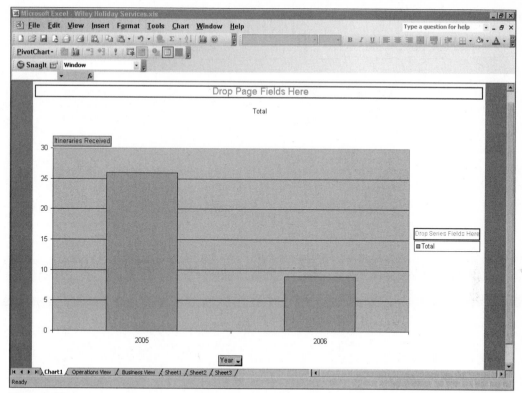

Figure 6-48

Click the first PivotTable, and drag the Flights Booked measure onto the Drop Data Items Here section. Then drag Going To Dimension onto the Total column to create a PivotTable, as shown below. Finally, you have to name the PivotTable. Click inside the PivotTable and choose Table Options from the PivotTable toolbar, and then enter **Flights Booked** as the name.

The PivotTable in Figure 6-49 shows you the number of flights booked grouped by the destination.

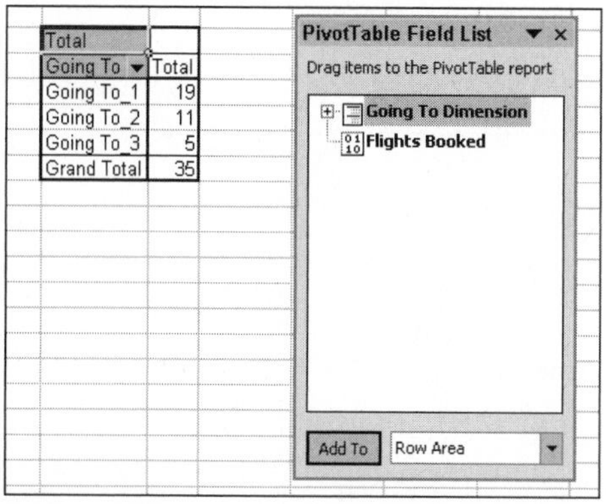

Figure 6-49

Click the second PivotTable and drag the Hire Cars Booked measure onto the Drop Data Items Here section. Then drag the Collection dimension onto the Total column to create a PivotTable, as shown below. Finally, you have to name the PivotTable. Click inside the PivotTable, choose Table Options from the PivotTable toolbar, and then enter **Hire Cars Booked** as the name.

This PivotTable in Figure 6-50 shows you the number of hire cars booked grouped by the collection location.

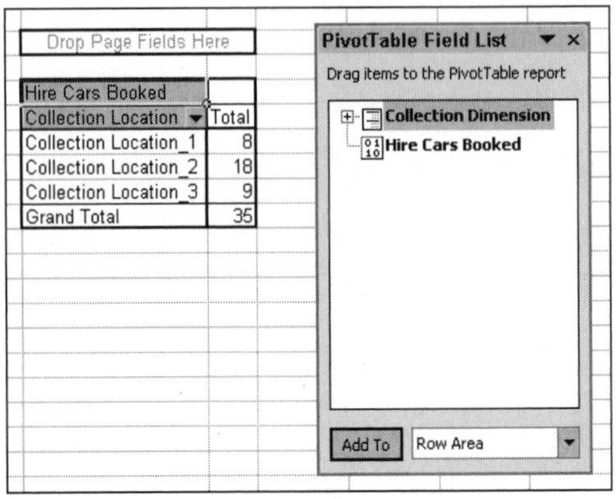

Figure 6-50

Click the third PivotTable and drag the Hotels Booked measure onto the Drop Data Items Here section, and then drag the Hotel dimension onto the Total column to create a PivotTable, as shown below. Finally, you have to name the PivotTable. Click inside the PivotTable and choose Table Options from the PivotTable toolbar, and then enter **Hotels Booked** as the name.

This PivotTable in Figure 6-51 shows you the number of hotels booked grouped by the hotel city.

On the fourth and final PivotTable, drag the Itineraries Received measure onto the Drop Data Items Here section, and then drag the Time dimension onto the Total column to create a PivotTable, as shown below. Finally, you have to name the PivotTable; click inside the PivotTable and choose Table Options from the PivotTable toolbar and type in **Itineraries Received** as the Name.

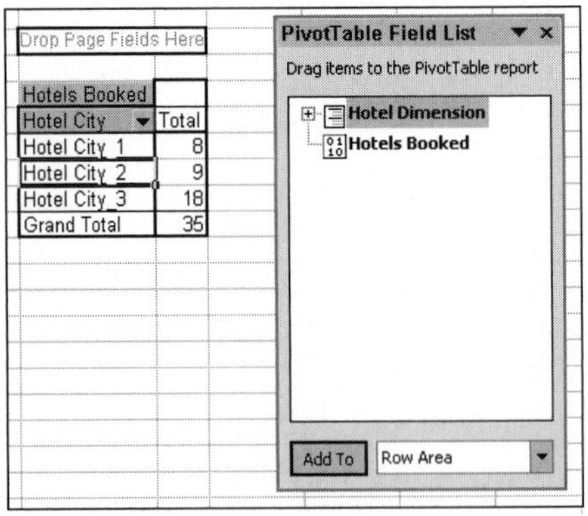

Figure 6-51

This PivotTable in Figure 6-52 shows you the number of itineraries received grouped by time.

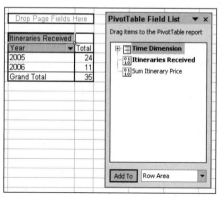

Figure 6-52

Exporting XML

The observation model has now been defined successfully. The final step is to export an XML document that represents this observation model, which we will use in the later steps.

From the BAM menu, select Export XML, and select a directory and filename to where the XML will be exported.

You can now save the Excel spreadsheet and proceed to deploying the database infrastructure to support your observation model.

Deploying the Database Infrastructure

As discussed earlier in this chapter, BAM automatically creates all the tables, views, stored procedures, and packages required for a highly scalable and performant database solution.

The BAM Management tool is called `bm.exe` and is located in the `%PROGRAMFILES%\Microsoft BizTalk Server 2006\Tracking` directory.

Using the `deploy-all` parameter, you can provision the database infrastructure, and using the `remove-all` parameter, you can remove the database infrastructure.

In this case, you want to deploy the database infrastructure, as follows:

```
bm deploy-all -DefinitionFile:"Wiley Travel Services.xls"
```

Figure 6-53 shows the output.

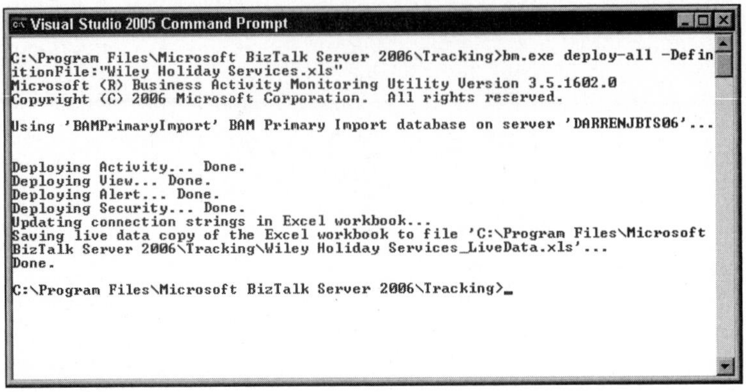

Figure 6-53

Writing Activity Data

So, you've defined an observation model and provisioned the database infrastructure to hold the activity data and produce the views. You now need to write the activity data from your solution.

Two main parts of the sample application need to write data to BAM. Both BizTalk and the Flight Booking Web service contribute data to the observation model, as depicted in Figure 6-54.

The Itinerary orchestration that receives the Itinerary message writes initial data to the Itinerary activity and then calls off to the Flight, Hotel, Hire Car, and Travel Insurance orchestrations, which each writes to its respective activities and links back to the parent Itinerary activity to provide traceability.

The Flight Booking Web service contributes to the Flight activity to provide a booking reference after the flight has been booked, thus demonstrating that BAM can be used on servers without BizTalk Server.

Due to design decisions, we will not use the TPE for this solution. The reasons for this are covered later in the chapter. You will use the GenerateTypedBAMAPI tool discussed previously to generate a typed C# API to write data to your activities, which will then be called from the BizTalk orchestrations. The alternative, of course, is to just use the BAM APIs directly, but that would be cumbersome compared to this approach.

GenerateTypedBAMAPI

GenerateTypedBAMAPI is a simple command-line tool that takes three command-line parameters. The first is to the Excel workbook containing your observation model. The second is the name of the code file that will be created. The third parameter indicates which event stream you want to use. Figure 6-55 shows an example.

Because you are calling directly from a BizTalk orchestration, you need to use the Orchestration-EventStream. Passing Orchestration as the third parameter creates a typed C# API that uses the OrchestrationEventStream under the covers.

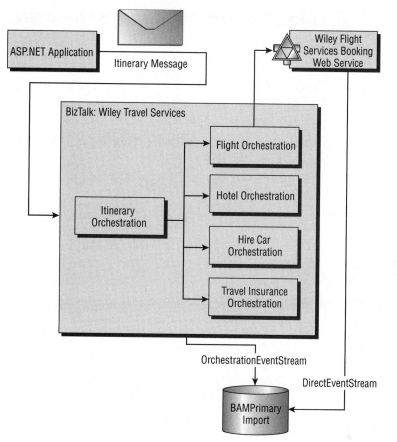

Figure 6-54

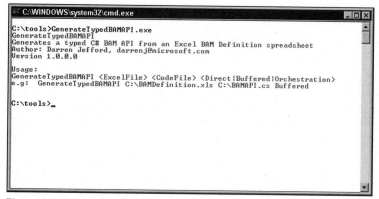

Figure 6-55

So, using the following syntax, you run GenerateTypedBAMAPI against the Excel spreadsheet to create the typed BAM API.

```
GeneratedTypedBAMAPI.exe WileyTravelServices.xls
                TypedBAMAPI.cs Orchestration
```

Figure 6-56 shows the output.

Figure 6-56

The resulting API (in the above example, stored in `TypedBAMAPI.cs`) has a class for each activity containing properties for each activity data item and helper methods to begin and end the activity, as covered in the "GenerateTypedBAMAPI" section. This reduces a huge amount of custom code littered with string literals to activity names and items (very brittle and subject to typos).

Figure 6-57 shows a Visual Studio class diagram to depict the classes created and their contents. As you can see, there is a class for each activity defined and properties on each activity class for each activity item. There are also methods to begin, commit (changes), and end an activity.

Façade

So, now that you've got the typed API, you need to write a simple façade that makes it easy for the BizTalk orchestrations to call into your Instrumentation layer passing messages. This is a common step when using the typed API like this.

As part of this API, you make use of the technique discussed in Chapter 5 whereby you can pass BizTalk messages directly into C# class libraries, which have parameters defined as serializable classes based on the same underlying schema. This makes the whole data transfer process a lot easier.

The `InstrumentationHelpers` class is shown below. As you'd expect, it's very straightforward, with only the `WriteFlights` method doing anything special.

Because the Flight Booking Web service needs to contribute to the activity, you need to keep the activity "active," so you enable continuation to support this, and the Flight Booking Web service is responsible for closing the activity.

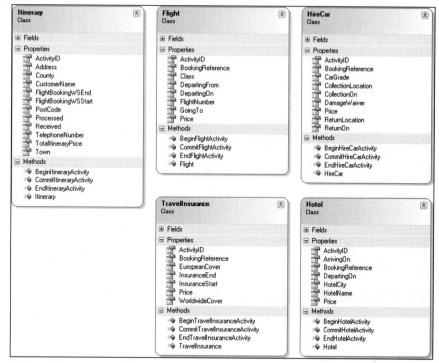

Figure 6-57

As discussed previously, BAM is an ideal choice to store message bodies if you have specific requirements in this area. You will make use of the new BizTalk Server 2006 references functionality to store the
Itinerary message body, which can be used to fault find or provide evidence in case of a dispute.

Each Itinerary component adds a reference back to the Itinerary activity, using the `AddReference`
method. As you'll see later, this enables you to view itineraries and drill into the detail.

```
public static class InstrumentationHelpers
{
  static public void BTSWriteItinerary(string ItineraryActivityID, XLANGMessage
ItineraryMessage)
  {
    Itinerary itin = (Itinerary)ItineraryMessage[0].RetrieveAs(typeof(Itinerary));
    WriteItinerary(ItineraryActivityID, itin);
  }

  static public void WriteItinerary(string ItineraryActivityID, Itinerary itin)
  {
    GeneratedTypedBAMAPI.OrchestrationESAPI.Itinerary Itinerary = new
GeneratedTypedBAMAPI.OrchestrationESAPI.Itinerary(ItineraryActivityID);

    Itinerary.BeginItineraryActivity();

    Itinerary.Address = itin.Address;
```

```
        Itinerary.County = itin.County;
        Itinerary.CustomerName = itin.Name;
        Itinerary.PostCode = itin.PostCode;
        Itinerary.Received = System.DateTime.Now;
        Itinerary.TelephoneNumber = itin.TelephoneNumber;
        Itinerary.Town = itin.Town;
        Itinerary.TotalItineraryPrice = itin.TotalItineraryPrice;

        Itinerary.CommitItineraryActivity();

        // Write the Itinerary Body out
        System.IO.StringWriter sw = new System.IO.StringWriter();
        XmlSerializer xs = new XmlSerializer(typeof(Itinerary));
        xs.Serialize(sw, itin);

        Microsoft.BizTalk.Bam.EventObservation.OrchestrationEventStream.AddReference
("Itinerary", Itinerary.ActivityID, "MsgBody", "MessageBody",
"System.DateTime.Now.ToString(), sw.GetStringBuilder().ToString());

        // Keep the activity open
    }

    static public void BTSFinishItinerary(string ItineraryActivityID)
    {
        GeneratedTypedBAMAPI.OrchestrationESAPI.Itinerary Itinerary =
newGeneratedTypedBAMAPI.OrchestrationESAPI.Itinerary(ItineraryActivityID);
        Itinerary.Processed = System.DateTime.Now;

        Itinerary.CommitItineraryActivity();

        //End the activity now

        Itinerary.EndItineraryActivity();
    }

    static public void BTSWriteFlights(string ItineraryActivityID,
XLANGMessageItineraryMessage)
    {
        Itinerary itin = (Itinerary)ItineraryMessage[0].RetrieveAs(typeof(Itinerary));
        WriteFlights(ItineraryActivityID, itin);
    }

    static public void WriteFlights(string ItineraryActivityID, Itinerary itin)
    {
        foreach (FlightBooking fb in itin.Flights)
        {
            GeneratedTypedBAMAPI.OrchestrationESAPI.Flight Flight = new
GeneratedTypedBAMAPI.OrchestrationESAPI.Flight(fb.Reference);

            Flight.BeginFlightActivity();

            Flight.Class = fb.Class;
            Flight.DepartingFrom = fb.DepartingFrom;
            Flight.DepartingOn = fb.DepartingOn;
```

```
        Flight.FlightNumber = fb.FlightNumber;
        Flight.GoingTo = fb.GoingTo;
        Flight.Price = fb.Price;

        Flight.CommitFlightActivity();

        // Must enable Continuation as we are being async, need
        // to create a new activity ID so we just prefix
        Microsoft.BizTalk.Bam.EventObservation.OrchestrationEventStream.
EnableContinuation("Flight", Flight.ActivityID, "FlightBooking_" +
Flight.ActivityID);

        Flight.EndActivity();
        Microsoft.BizTalk.Bam.EventObservation.OrchestrationEventStream.AddReference
("Itinerary", ItineraryActivityID, "Activity", "Flight", Flight.ActivityID);
    }
}

static public void TimeFlightBookingWSCallStart(string ItineraryActivityID)
{
    GeneratedTypedBAMAPI.OrchestrationESAPI.Itinerary Itinerary = new
GeneratedTypedBAMAPI.OrchestrationESAPI.Itinerary(ItineraryActivityID);
    Itinerary.FlightBookingWSStart = System.DateTime.Now;

    Itinerary.CommitItineraryActivity();
}

static public void TimeFlightBookingWSCallEnd(string ItineraryActivityID)
{
    GeneratedTypedBAMAPI.OrchestrationESAPI.Itinerary Itinerary = new
GeneratedTypedBAMAPI.OrchestrationESAPI.Itinerary(ItineraryActivityID);
    Itinerary.FlightBookingWSEnd = System.DateTime.Now;
    Itinerary.CommitItineraryActivity();
}

static public void BTSWriteHotels(string ItineraryActivityID, XLANGMessage
ItineraryMessage)
{
    Itinerary itin = (Itinerary)ItineraryMessage[0].RetrieveAs(typeof(Itinerary));
    WriteHotels(ItineraryActivityID, itin);
}
static public void WriteHotels(string ItineraryActivityID, Itinerary itin)
{
    foreach (HotelBooking hb in itin.Hotels)
    {
        GeneratedTypedBAMAPI.OrchestrationESAPI.Hotel Hotel = new
GeneratedTypedBAMAPI.OrchestrationESAPI.Hotel(System.Guid.NewGuid().ToString());

        Hotel.BeginHotelActivity();

        Hotel.ArrivingOn = hb.ArrivingOn;
        Hotel.DepartingOn = hb.DepartingOn;
        Hotel.HotelCity = hb.HotelCity;
        Hotel.HotelName = hb.HotelName;
```

```
      Hotel.Price = hb.Price;

      Hotel.BookingReference = "BREF01";

      Hotel.CommitHotelActivity();

      Hotel.EndHotelActivity();

      Microsoft.BizTalk.Bam.EventObservation.OrchestrationEventStream.AddReference
("Itinerary", ItineraryActivityID,"Activity","Hotel", Hotel.ActivityID);
    }
  }

  static public void BTSWriteHireCars(string ItineraryActivityID, XLANGMessage
ItineraryMessage)
  {
    Itinerary itin = (Itinerary)ItineraryMessage[0].RetrieveAs(typeof(Itinerary));
    WriteHireCars(ItineraryActivityID, itin);
  }
  static public void WriteHireCars(string ItineraryActivityID, Itinerary itin)
  {
    foreach (HireCarBooking hb in itin.HireCar)
    {
      GeneratedTypedBAMAPI.OrchestrationESAPI.HireCar HireCar = new
GeneratedTypedBAMAPI.OrchestrationESAPI.HireCar(System.Guid.NewGuid().ToString());

      HireCar.BeginHireCarActivity();

      HireCar.CarGrade = hb.CarGrade;
      HireCar.CollectionLocation = hb.CollectionLocation;
      HireCar.CollectionOn = hb.CollectionOn;

      if (hb.DamageWaiver)
        HireCar.DamageWaiver = 1;
      else
        HireCar.DamageWaiver = 0;

      HireCar.ReturnLocation = hb.ReturnLocation;
      HireCar.ReturnOn = hb.ReturnOn;
      HireCar.Price = hb.Price;

      HireCar.BookingReference = "BREF01";

      HireCar.CommitHireCarActivity();

      HireCar.EndHireCarActivity();

      Microsoft.BizTalk.Bam.EventObservation.OrchestrationEventStream.AddReference
("Itinerary", ItineraryActivityID,"Activity","Hire Car", HireCar.ActivityID);
    }
  }

  static public void BTSWriteTravelInsurance(string ItineraryActivityID,
XLANGMessage ItineraryMessage)
```

```
    {
      Itinerary itin = (Itinerary)ItineraryMessage[0].RetrieveAs(typeof(Itinerary));
      WriteTravelInsurance(ItineraryActivityID, itin);
    }
    static public void WriteTravelInsurance(string ItineraryActivityID, Itinerary
itin)
    {
      foreach (TravelInsuranceBooking tb in itin.TravelInsurance)
      {
        GeneratedTypedBAMAPI.OrchestrationESAPI.TravelInsurance TravelInsurance =
new GeneratedTypedBAMAPI.OrchestrationESAPI.TravelInsurance(System.Guid.NewGuid()
.ToString());

        TravelInsurance.BeginTravelInsuranceActivity();

        TravelInsurance.InsuranceStart = tb.InsuranceStart;
        TravelInsurance.InsuranceEnd = tb.InsuranceEnd;

        if (tb.EuropeanCover)
          TravelInsurance.EuropeanCover = 1;
        else
          TravelInsurance.EuropeanCover = 0;

        if (tb.WorldwideCover)
          TravelInsurance.WorldwideCover = 1;
        else
          TravelInsurance.WorldwideCover = 0;

        TravelInsurance.Price = tb.Price;

        TravelInsurance.BookingReference = "BREF01";

        TravelInsurance.CommitTravelInsuranceActivity();

        TravelInsurance.EndTravelInsuranceActivity();

        Microsoft.BizTalk.Bam.EventObservation.OrchestrationEventStream.AddReference
("Itinerary", ItineraryActivityID,"Activity","Travel Insurance",
TravelInsurance.ActivityID);
      }
    }
}
```

The BizTalk orchestrations call these methods at various points in the processing structure to provide the data. The Flight Booking Web service, however, can't use the OrchestrationEventStream, because BizTalk isn't present; so we opt for using the DirectEventStream directly, as follows.

```
string FlightActivityName = "Flight";

foreach (FlightServices.FlightGroupFlight f in FlightGroupBooking.Flights)
{
  DirectEventStream des = new DirectEventStream("Integrated Security=SSPI;Data
Source=.;Initial Catalog=BAMPrimaryImport",1);
  des.UpdateActivity(FlightActivityName, "FlightBooking_" + f.Reference,
```

```
        "Booking Reference", "BREF01");
    des.EndActivity(FlightActivityName, "FlightBooking_" + f.Reference);
}
```

Using Activity Data

Now that you've defined the observation model, and implemented the Instrumentation layer using the typed BAM API, what can you do with the data that's been collected?

The raw activity data is held in the BAMPrimaryImport database, as covered earlier in this chapter, and can be accessed directly using T-SQL against the appropriate view. There are three main SQL views that you will use to access activity data:

❑   **bam_<ActivityName>_ActiveInstances** — The _ActiveInstances view will return all activities that are currently in the Active state.

❑   **bam_<ActivityName>_CompletedInstances** — The _CompletedInstances view will return all activities that have been marked as completed. Note that any configured continuations must be completed before activities will appear in this view.

❑   **bam_<ActivityName>_AllInstances** — The _AllInstances view will return all activity data, regardless of its state.

It's recommended that you use these SQL views instead of hitting the raw activity tables. The data maintenance (DM) job creates new physical activity tables as part of its processing to implement table partitioning. If you were to query the raw activity tables directly, you would have to update this query each time the DM job executed. This is not the case with the SQL views, because they are dynamically updated as part of the DM job to include the new partitioned tables.

You should also consider querying only the `bam_ActivityName_CompletedInstances` SQL view wherever possible to ensure that your queries do not block or interfere with any live BAM data being written. This shouldn't happen, but it's worth bearing in mind.

Any custom BAM views that you have defined when creating the observation model will also be represented as SQL views. You can view these from within the SQL Management Studio.

If you've made use of references as part of your process, you can find these through the `bam_ActivityName_AllRelationships` view.

Finally (and most importantly), you should expect to add indexes to the automatically generated BAM database tables to support your queries. There is no need to add indexes for general BAM operation, because the entire structure is highly optimized. Custom queries will use the database structure differently and will likely perform poorly if the correct indexes are not applied. The Database Engine Tuning Advisor in SQL Server 2005 can monitor queries and then suggest optimal indexes, which are then applied to activity tables through the `bm.exe` tool. You should not create your own indexes directly using the SQL management tools.

Because the data is held in a straightforward SQL database, it can be integrated into any existing or future systems with ease.

In this section, we cover a variety of ways in which you can leverage this instrumentation data to produce a tracking portal and query the data. The tracking portal concept can be used for multiple purposes: as a support view to provide a way of troubleshooting and diagnosing issues, and as a business user view to track the status and history of business processes.

> As described earlier in this chapter, if you are making use of activity views (as we are in this solution), you must run the BAM_AN_<View Name> SSIS package to load the activity data into the cube. If you fail to do so, the cube won't have the latest data.

SQL Server Reporting Services

We have used SQL Server Reporting Services heavily with a number of projects to provide an extremely easy-to-develop "health portal" that is driven from the data collected by BAM.

> Such an approach has become central to the maintenance and support of many BizTalk solutions, and you should seriously consider a similar approach. Do, however, consider the BAM portal, which we discuss later in the chapter, as it may be enough for your scenario.

SQL Server Reporting Services is a reporting solution included with SQL Server 2005 and available as an add-on for SQL Server 2000.

You can develop reports using Visual Studio, or in SQL Server 2005 using the Report Builder tool. The basis of each report is a SQL query or stored procedure that can then be rendered in a variety of ways. Reports are typically accessed via the Reporting Services portal, the results of which can be exported to PDF, TIF, Excel, and the like.

Itinerary Report

To start off, you need a report that can show all the itineraries that have been processed. From this report, you can then drill down into itineraries for more information. Such a report can be used by operational or front-line support roles to find an itinerary that is being queried and understand what stage of processing it's at. The following steps are for SQL Server Reporting Services 2005.

The first step is to create a new Reporting Services project inside Visual Studio. Choose New Project from the File menu, and select Report Server Project and name it **Wiley Operations Portal**, as shown in Figure 6-58.

A new Visual Studio project will be created that will contain the data source and reports. You start by creating a data source for the report data that will be shared across each report. To do this, right-click Shared Data Sources in the Solution Explorer, and then choose Add New Data Source.

Specify the shared data source name as **BAMPrimaryImport** and enter a connection string that points at your BAMPrimaryImport table, which holds your activity data. If you're running on a local machine, the connection string will be as follows:

```
Data Source=(local);Initial Catalog=BAMPrimaryImport
```

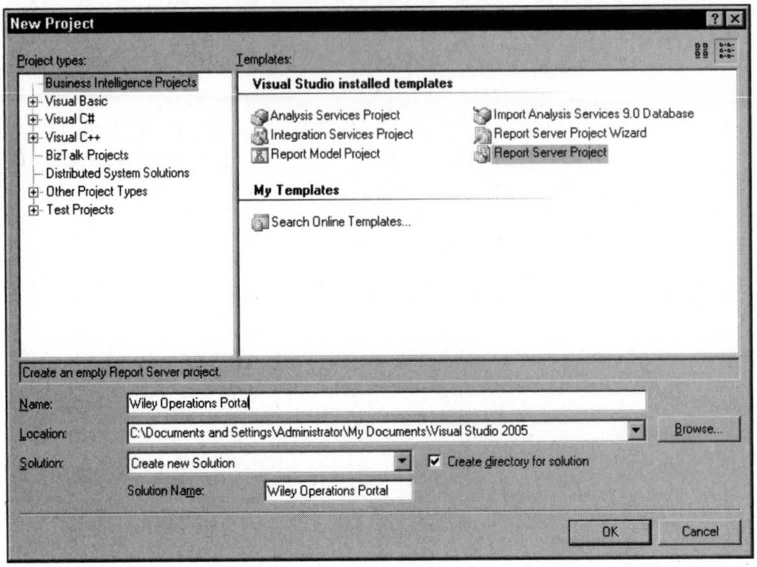

Figure 6-58

Clicking OK creates the data source, and you can now create the itineraries report. Right-click the Reports folder in the Solution Explorer and choose Add New Report.

Select the data source that you created in the previous step, and click Next to display the query builder. In this step, you need to provide the SQL query to return the Itineraries activity data present in the BAMPrimaryImport database.

The following SQL query returns all the completed Itinerary activities by using the bam_Itinerary_CompletedInstances view. Note that the dollar signs ($) present in the columns is BAM's way of dealing with spaces in activity data items:

```
SELECT ActivityID,Customer$Name,Received,Processed,Address,County,Town,Post$Code,
Telephone$Number,Total$Itinerary$Price
FROM bam_Itinerary_CompletedInstances
```

Enter this SQL query into the query builder, and choose Next to choose the report type. For the purposes of this report, choose Tabular, and then click Next to select the Table Design Wizard.

You now define how the data will be presented on the report. Given that there will be a high number of itineraries, you need to group the itineraries somehow.

Grouping by date and then customer is a sensible first choice, so select the Received field and click the Group button to move it across. Then repeat for the Customer Name.

Move the remaining items apart from the ActivityID field into the Details section by selecting them and clicking the Details button. You end up with a table design like that shown in Figure 6-59.

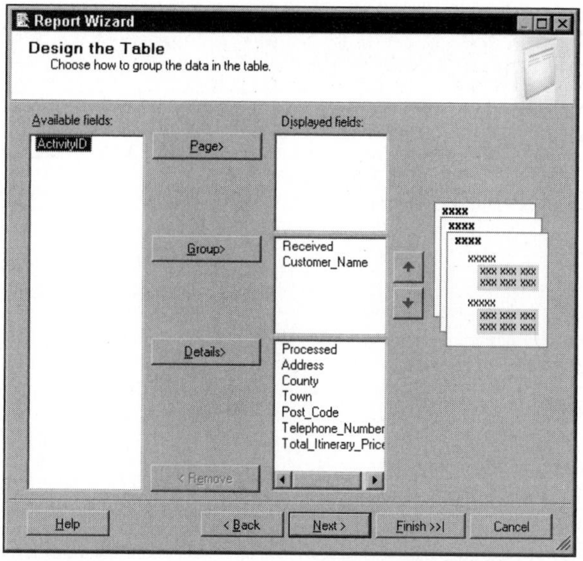

Figure 6-59

Click Next to display the Table Layout Wizard. Select Enable Drilldown, which will allow you to drill farther into each itinerary to show extra information. Then click Next to display the Table Style Wizard.

Choose a wizard style and click Next. Name the report **Itineraries**, and click Finish to create the report.

The report is now shown inside Visual Studio for further customization. Before you execute the report, you need to change the way itineraries will be shown. By default, they will be grouped by the Received field, which is represented as a DateTime. Because each itinerary will have a slightly different DateTime, you need to format this to, say, group by the date rather than down to seconds!

First, click the cell directly below the Received column and change the Format property in the Properties pane to DD/MM/YYYY, as shown in Figure 6-60.

This changes how the date/time is rendered on the report. You now need to change the grouping definition.

Click in the upper left of the table to select the table. Right-click and choose Properties to bring up the Table Properties dialog box. Click the Groups tab, and select the table1_Received group and choose Edit. You need to change the expression to format the date differently; so change the expression to include a reference to the Format method, as shown in Figure 6-61. Then click OK.

You are now ready to run the report. Click the Preview tab to show the report. Figure 6-62 shows an example with the groups expanded.

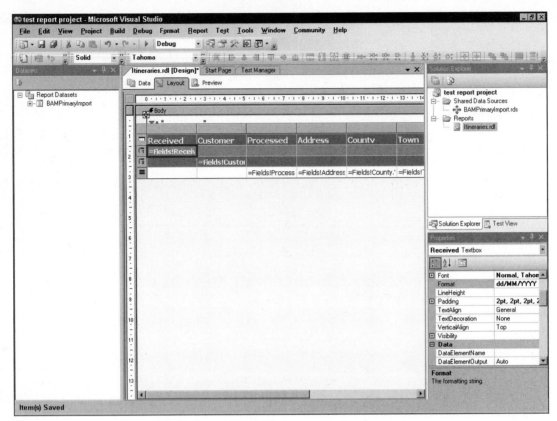

Figure 6-60

Figure 6-61

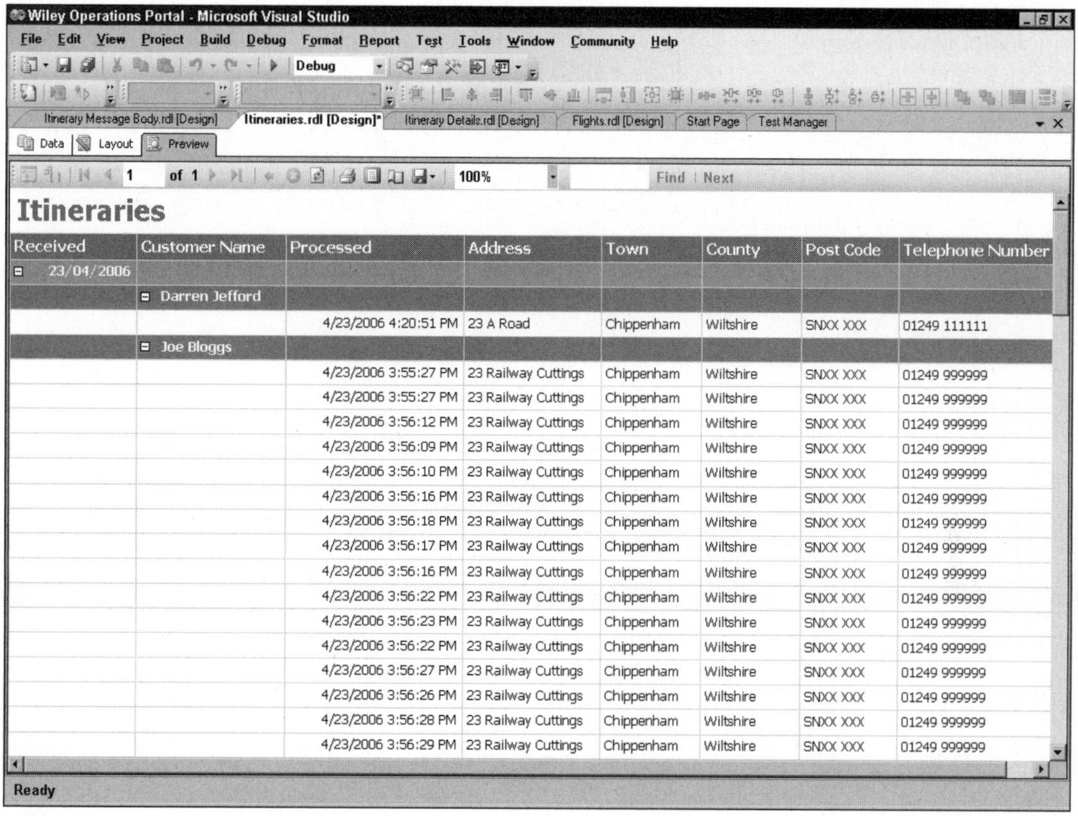

Figure 6-62

Itinerary Details Report

You can now see the itineraries present in the activity tables. However, you also need to be able to view all the itinerary details to view flights, hotels, and so on.

To achieve this, you create an Itinerary Details report that includes all the root itinerary information and a report for each further activity (i.e., one for the Flight activity, Hotel activity, and so on).

You then render these other reports on the main Itinerary Details report to produce a one-stop view of an itinerary. You can then use these individual reports later on to enable retrieval of flight information based on the Flight Reference ID.

You start by building an Itinerary Details report. You don't go through each step here because the steps are similar to the previous steps, but you will see the SQL queries used and the resulting screenshots.

You can use the following SQL query to retrieve all itinerary details. Note that you now have a condition to only return itineraries with the matching ActivityID. Defining a parameter in this way with a report indicates that a parameter must be passed to the report or prompted for during execution:

```
SELECT ActivityID,Customer$Name,Received,Processed,Address,County,Town,Post$Code,
Telephone$Number,Flight$Booking$WS$Start,Flight$Booking$WS$End,Total$Itinerary$Price
FROM bam_Itinerary_CompletedInstances
WHERE ActivityID = @ItineraryActivityID
```

You now need to create the Flight, Hotel, Hire Car, and Travel Insurance reports that will be invoked as part of the Itinerary Details report. Again, the steps are similar to before, so the SQL statements for each one are shown below.

These queries are joining the relevant activity view with the matching AllRelationships view to obtain all activity items referenced by the specified itinerary (identified by the @ItineraryActivityID). Note that these queries are using the _AllInstances view, which will include active and completed activity data. As discussed earlier, you should use this technique sparingly. In this case, however, you may have long-running activities (booking the itinerary components such as hotels may take a while because you need to communicate with a third party), and the report should reflect all current information.

```
SELECT f.*
FROM bam_Flight_AllInstances f, bam_Itinerary_AllRelationships r
WHERE r.ActivityID = @ItineraryActivityID
AND r.ReferenceName = 'Flight'
AND r.ReferenceData = f.ActivityID
AND r.ReferenceType = 'Activity'

SELECT f.*
FROM bam_Hotel_AllInstances f, bam_Itinerary_AllRelationships r
WHERE r.ActivityID = @ItineraryActivityID
AND r.ReferenceName = 'Hotel'
AND r.ReferenceData = f.ActivityID
AND r.ReferenceType = 'Activity'

SELECT h.*
FROM [bam_Hire Car_AllInstances] h, bam_Itinerary_AllRelationships r
WHERE r.ActivityID = @ItineraryActivityID
AND r.ReferenceName = 'Hire Car'
AND r.ReferenceData = h.ActivityID
AND r.ReferenceType = 'Activity'

SELECT t.*
FROM [bam_Travel Insurance_AllInstances] t, bam_Itinerary_AllRelationships r
WHERE r.ActivityID = @ItineraryActivityID
AND r.ReferenceName = 'Travel Insurance'
AND r.ReferenceData = t.ActivityID
AND r.ReferenceType = 'Activity'
```

Now that you have all the reports, you need to render them within the Itinerary Details report. Open the Itinerary Details report, and from the Toolbox drag a subreport item onto the report surface. Repeat this four times.

Click the first subreport and select Flights from the ReportName property to specify which report should be executed. You need to pass the ItineraryActivityID to each report, so scroll up the Properties window to the Parameters collection and select ItineraryActivityID from the drop-down list. (This is derived from the parameter defined in the SQL query.)

In the Parameter Value cell, enter =Parameters!ItineraryActivityID.Value, which specifies that the ItineraryActivityID parameter passed to this report should be passed to the subreport.

Repeat this for the remaining reports, and you should have a report that looks like the one shown in Figure 6-63.

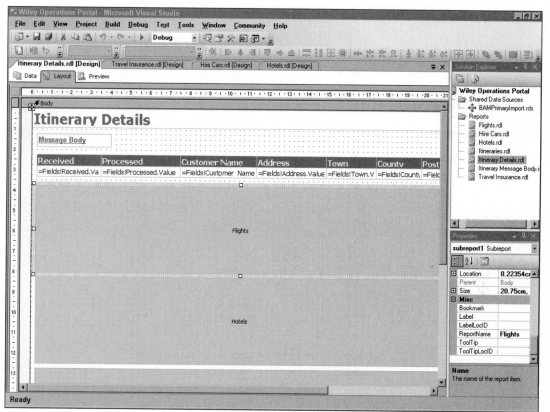

Figure 6-63

You now have an Itinerary Details report, but you need to provide a way to drill down into it from the Itineraries report. There are a few ways of doing this, but the easiest is to provide a link on each itinerary shown in the list.

Bring up the Itineraries report, and select an empty column in the Details row and type in **Details**. In the Properties window, select Action. The Action dialog box appears, as shown in Figure 6-64.

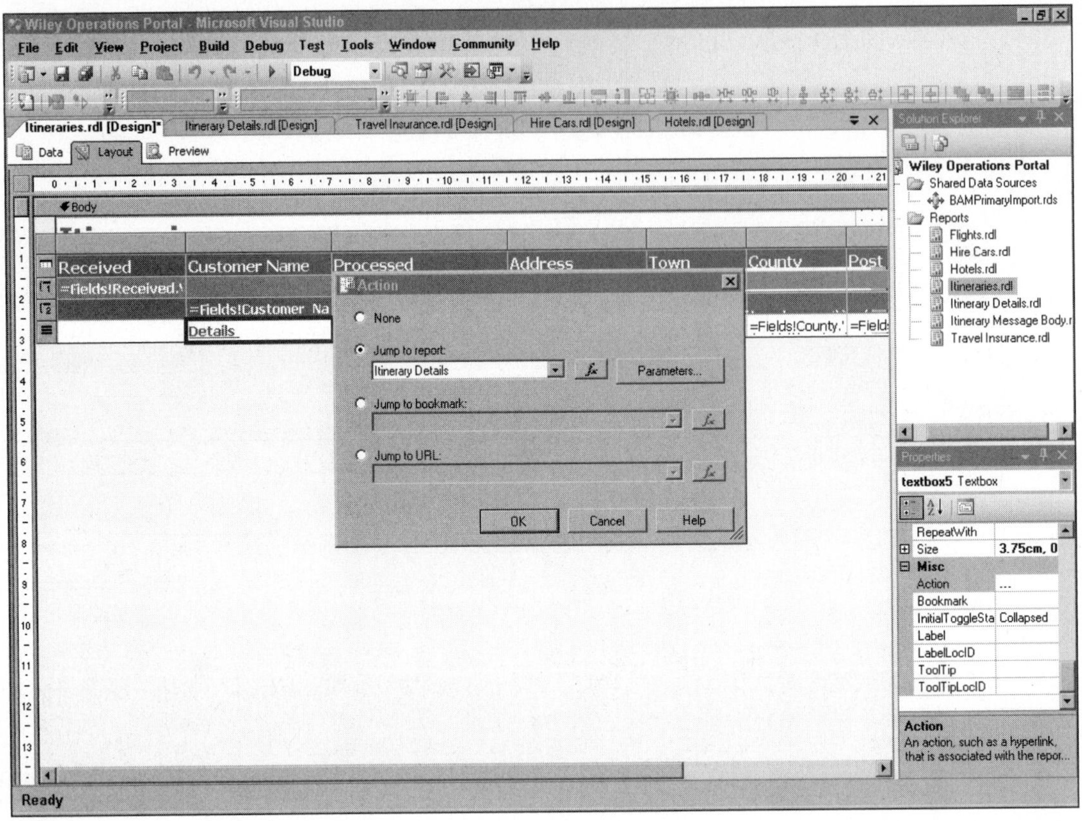

Figure 6-64

Select the Itinerary Details report, and click the Parameters button to specify the ActivityID that will be passed as the ItineraryActivityID, as shown in Figure 6-65. Reporting Services automatically creates a new action for each row pointing at the correct ActivityID.

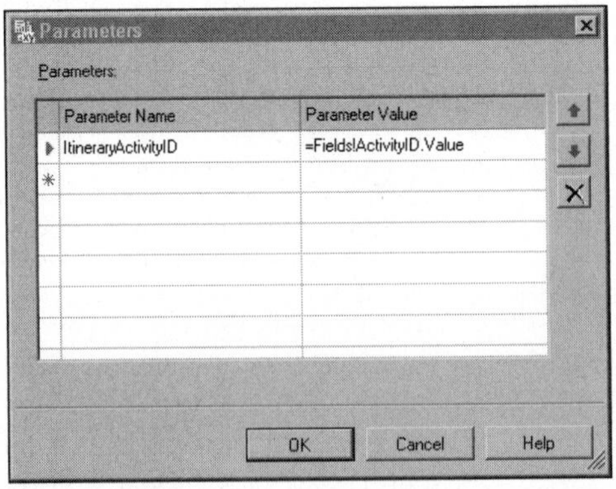

Figure 6-65

The Itinerary Details report is now complete. Click Preview on the Itineraries report to check that everything works, and then click Deploy from the Build menu inside Visual Studio to deploy the Reporting Services site.

Once it is deployed, browse to `http://YOURMACHINE/reports` to view the Report Server website. Figures 6-66, 6-67, and 6-68 show some sample screenshots. As you can see, SQL Server Reporting Services offers an easy and productive mechanism for building a portal against your BAM data.

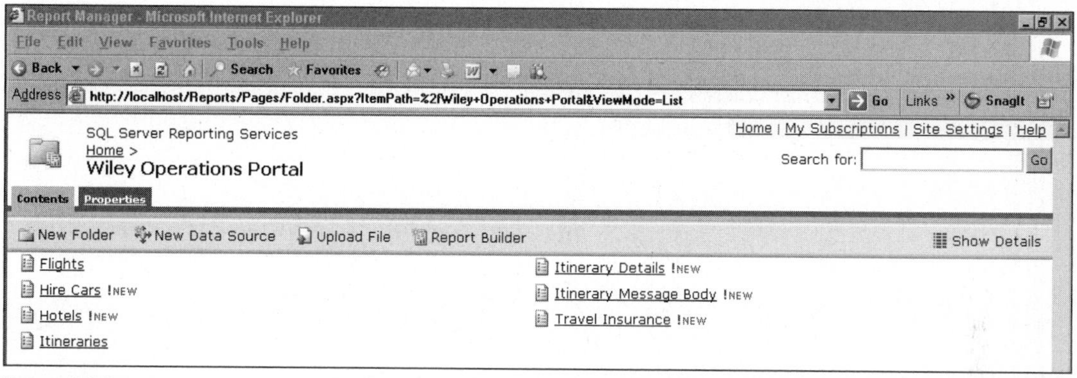

Figure 6-66

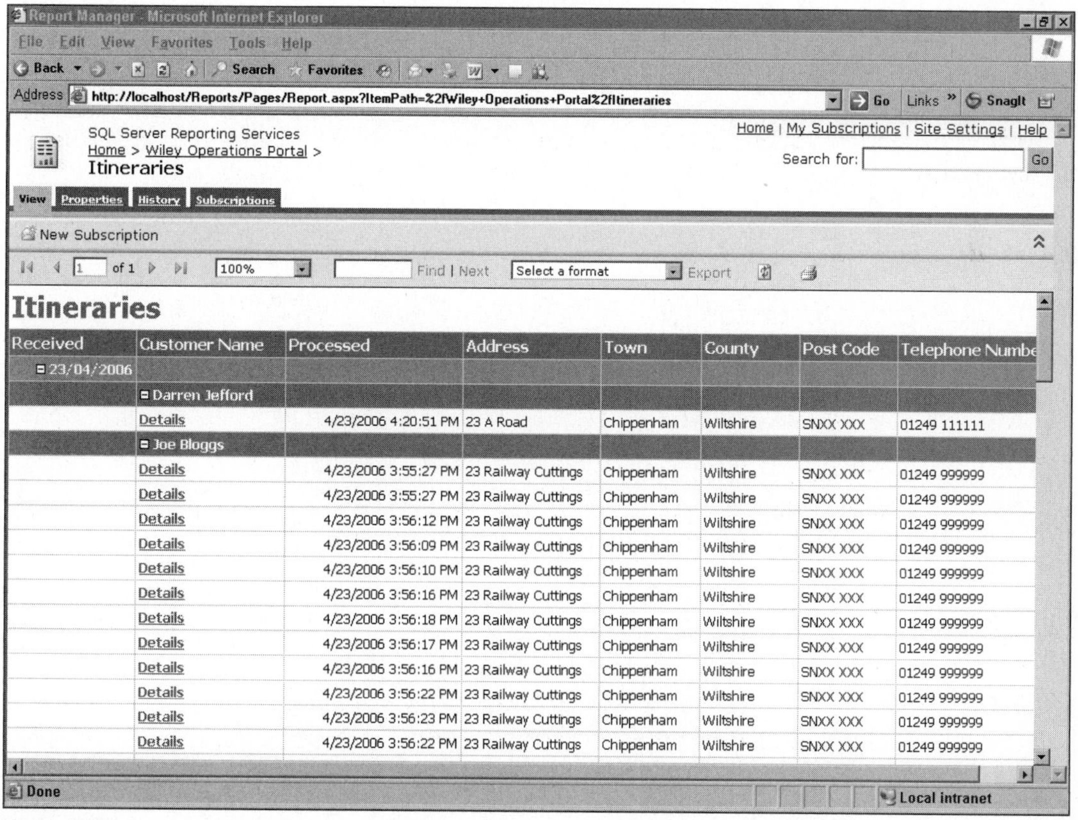

Figure 6-67

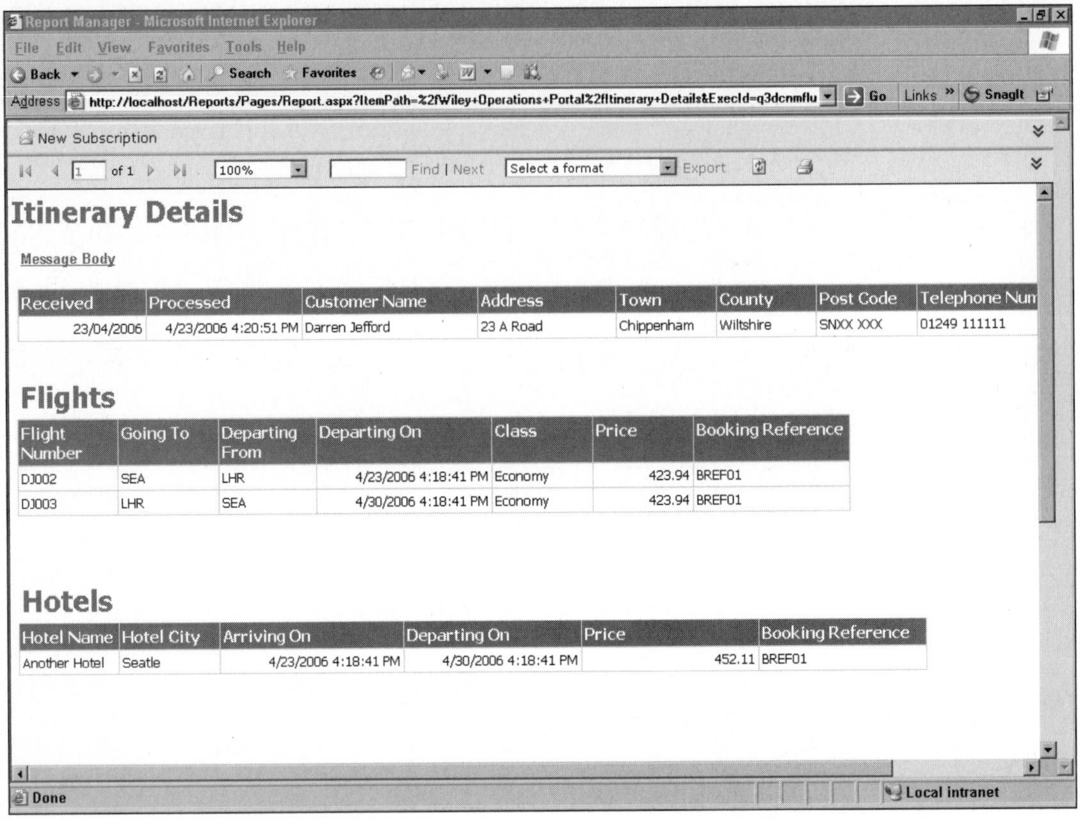

Figure 6-68

Message Body

As part of this solution, you also store the itinerary message body via BAM to be used in case there's any dispute or diagnostics required following processing.

On the Itinerary Details report, you provide a link to an Itinerary Message Body report, which is based on the following SQL query, which retrieves any message bodies linked to the specific itinerary ActivityID:

```
SELECT LongReferenceData
FROM bam_Itinerary_AllRelationships
WHERE ActivityID = @ItineraryActivityID
AND ReferenceType = 'MsgBody'
```

No built-in XML formatting is available with SQL Server Reporting Services, but it can provide a simple view at the very least, as shown in Figure 6-69, and the same SQL query could be performed by a custom application (which might resubmit the data, for example).

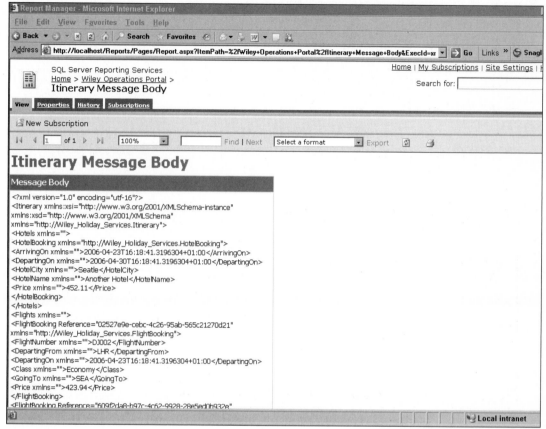

Figure 6-69

BAM Portal

The *BAM portal* was introduced in BizTalk Server 2006 and provides an out-of-the-box portal with which to access BAM data. It is not as feature rich or extensible as the health portal you created earlier in this chapter, but it does offer a portal "for free," which might provide everything you require in your solution.

If you elected to install and configure the BAM portal at installation time, you will find it located at `http://MACHINENAME/bam`. If you were to browse to it when having the Wiley Travel Services BAM definition deployed, you would see the screen shown in Figure 6-70.

Any defined Business views are shown in the pane on the left. As you can see, the Business and Operations views are shown.

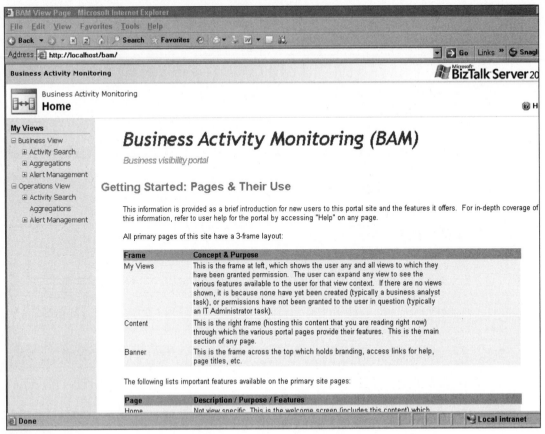

Figure 6-70

Activity Searches

The Activity Search option enables you to search all the activity data present directly from the BAM portal. As shown in Figure 6-71, this enables you to build a query interactively or to select a predefined one.

To demonstrate this, let's build a custom query to find an itinerary. Suppose a customer phones and asks for the status of his booking. Start by choosing the customer name from the Business Data drop-down list in the Query section. Choose Is Exactly as the operator, and enter **Joe Bloggs** as the value. Then select the columns to return in the query. Select Customer Name, Received, Processed, Itinerary Processing Time, and Total Itinerary Price. You should have a query defined, as shown in Figure 6-72.

> Note that only fields present in the activity view will appear. If you've created a restricted view, you will only see fields explicitly added to the view.

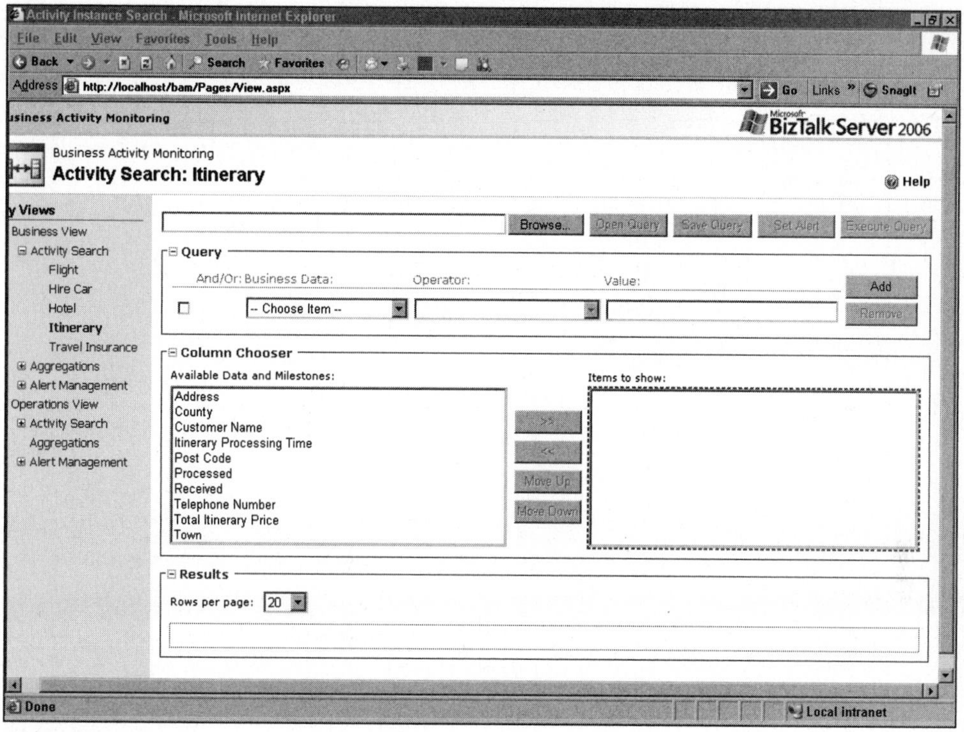

Figure 6-71

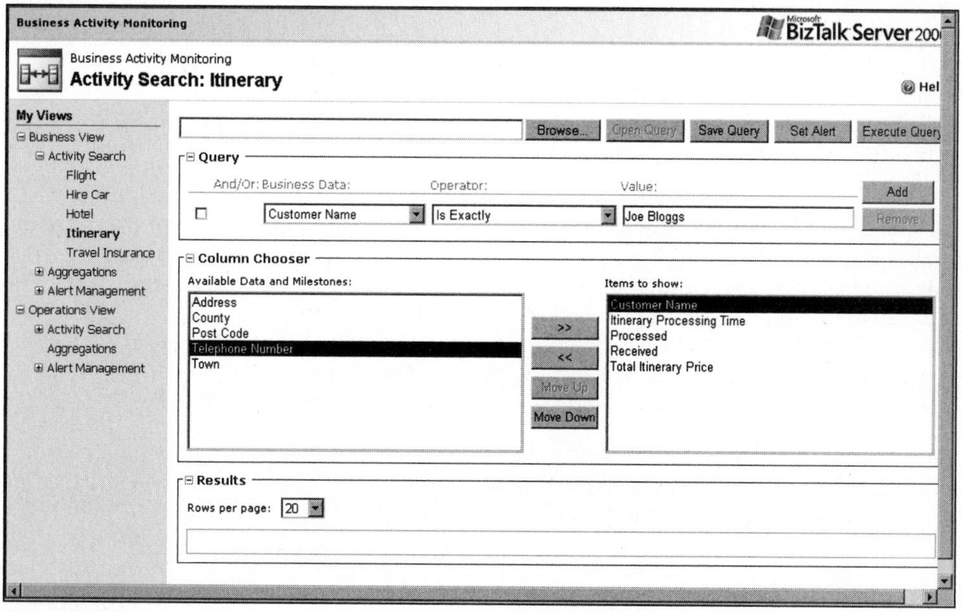

Figure 6-72

Click the Execute Query button to run the query. If any data is present that matches our condition, it displays in the Results pane, as shown in Figure 6-73.

Customer Name ▲	Itinerary Processing Time (Second)	Processed	Received	Total Itinerary Price
Joe Bloggs	84.2700003180653	23/04/2006 16:56:29	23/04/2006 16:55:05	1031.93
Joe Bloggs	89.5366667071357	23/04/2006 17:00:33	23/04/2006 16:59:03	1031.93
Joe Bloggs	82.320000207983	23/04/2006 16:59:34	23/04/2006 16:58:12	1031.93
Joe Bloggs	82.8900000080466	23/04/2006 17:00:57	23/04/2006 16:59:34	1031.93
Joe Bloggs	84.9433332681656	23/04/2006 16:59:12	23/04/2006 16:57:47	1031.93
Joe Bloggs	84.0633333893493	23/04/2006 16:56:28	23/04/2006 16:55:04	1031.93
Joe Bloggs	86.1133329570293	23/04/2006 17:00:42	23/04/2006 16:59:16	1031.93
Joe Bloggs	85.3233333444223	23/04/2006 16:56:17	23/04/2006 16:54:52	1031.93
Joe Bloggs	127.543332916684	23/04/2006 17:00:25	23/04/2006 16:58:17	1031.93
Joe Bloggs	84.0000001480803	23/04/2006 16:56:12	23/04/2006 16:54:48	1031.93
Joe Bloggs	85.9933332307264	23/04/2006 16:56:09	23/04/2006 16:54:43	1031.93
Joe Bloggs	83.8699999731034	23/04/2006 17:00:46	23/04/2006 16:59:22	1031.93
Joe Bloggs	86.4433333044872	23/04/2006 16:56:47	23/04/2006 16:55:21	1031.93
Joe Bloggs	81.9599997717887	23/04/2006 17:00:54	23/04/2006 16:59:32	1031.93
Joe Bloggs	86.4033333957195	23/04/2006 16:56:23	23/04/2006 16:54:57	1031.93
Joe Bloggs	86.1333332257345	23/04/2006 16:59:22	23/04/2006 16:57:56	1031.93
Joe Bloggs	85.7533331494778	23/04/2006 16:59:35	23/04/2006 16:58:09	1031.93
Joe Bloggs	85.2133334381506	23/04/2006 16:56:22	23/04/2006 16:54:57	1031.93
Joe Bloggs	86.6233332082629	23/04/2006 16:56:50	23/04/2006 16:55:23	1031.93
Joe Bloggs	141.546666109934	23/04/2006 17:03:46	23/04/2006 17:01:25	1031.93

1 2 3 4 5 6

Figure 6-73

As you can see, in this particular example a lot of data has been returned and has been automatically paginated. Selecting one of these rows brings up a complete Itinerary Activity view, as shown in Figure 6-74.

In this view, you can see all the activity data captured for the itinerary. You can see when the itinerary was received and when processing was complete. And, because of the way we interrelated activities, you can also see of the child activities that represent the Flight, Hire Car, Hotel, and Travel Insurance activity data.

As you would expect, clicking on one of these related activities brings up the full activity information, too. Figure 6-75 shows an example of the Flight activity. Note that you can drill back up to the related itinerary at this point, too; so searching for a flight booking based on booking reference would allow you to find the related itinerary.

Activity Aggregations

To successfully view any data held in your views, you must run the BAM_AN_<View Name> SSIS package to load the activity data into the cube. If you fail to do this, the cube won't have the latest data, and the BAM portal might not show anything.

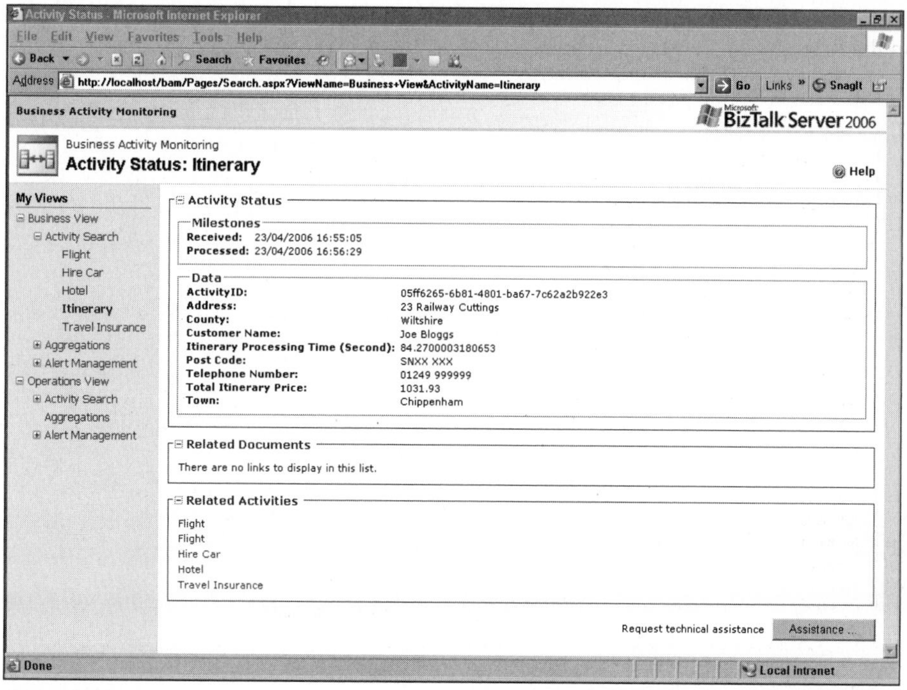

Figure 6-74

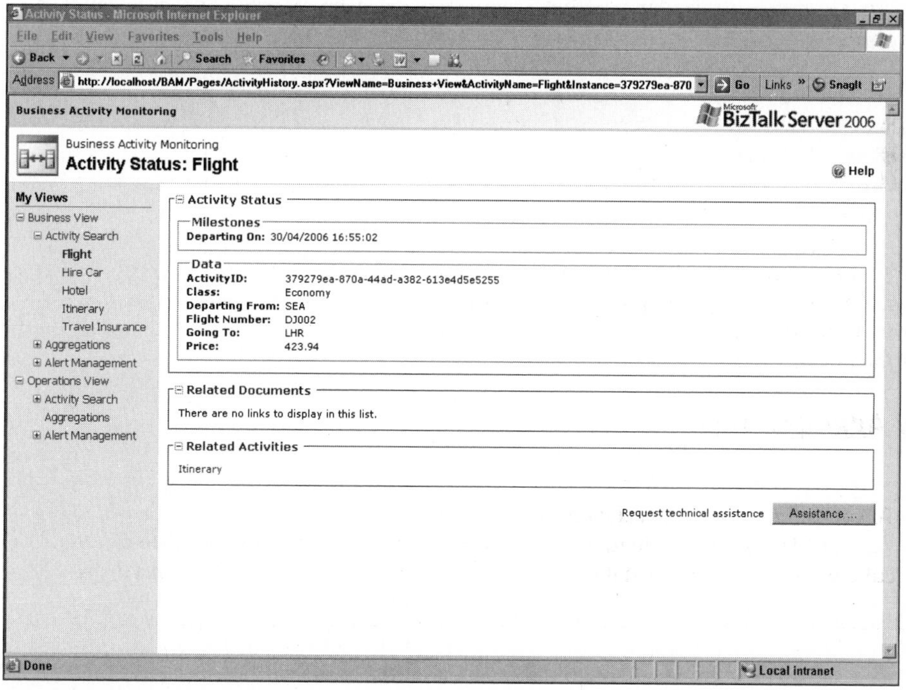

Figure 6-75

Any activity views defined in your observation model are visible via the BAM portal along with any PivotTables that you defined. As part of the sample, you configured a number of PivotTables that are now visible on the BAM portal.

Expanding the Aggregations node shows all the PivotTables that were defined in the BAM spreadsheet.

> If any of your PivotTables are named PivotTable1, PivotTable2, and so on, you must specify a PivotTable name by right-clicking on your PivotTable in Excel and selecting Table Properties.

Clicking one of your PivotTables brings up a PivotTable and Chart view, which leverages the Office Web Components controls. This view enables you to interact with your PivotTable and visualize the data right from within the BAM portal.

Figures 6-76 and 6-77 show examples of the PivotTables viewed directly within the BAM portal.

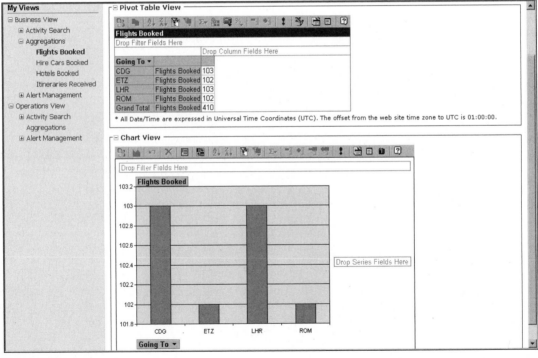

Figure 6-76

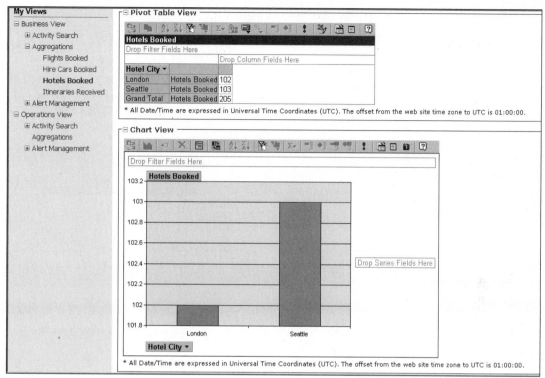

Figure 6-77

Activity Alerts

BizTalk Server 2006 integrates SQL Server Notification Services with BAM and provides an alert and subscriber management system with the BAM portal.

Alerts are driven from predefined activity queries that you define via the Activity Search feature (discussed earlier in this chapter). Figure 6-78 shows a sample query that has been built to show activity details where the Flight Booking Web service duration has gone over the SLA of 5 seconds.

After you have defined the query, you can click the Set Alert button. You can then configure alert information and configure whether to make the alert definition public and let other people subscribe to it. Figure 6-79 shows this configuration screen.

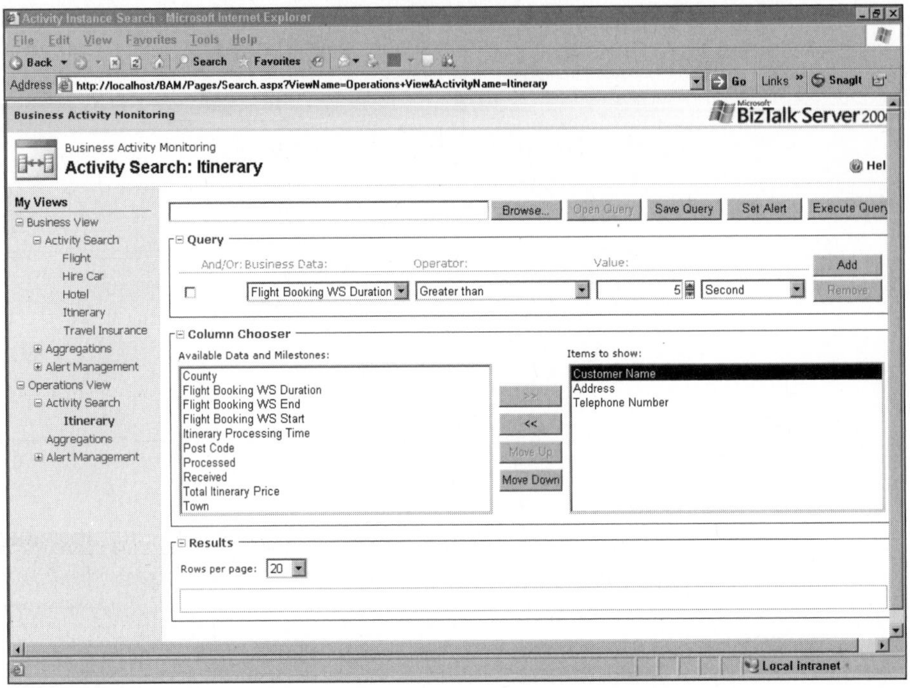

Figure 6-78

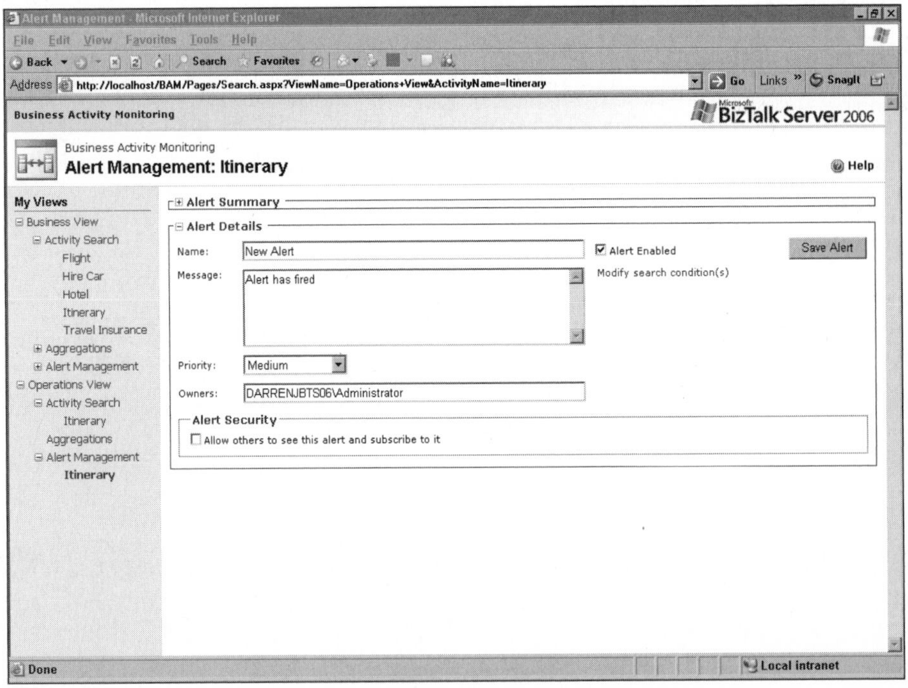

Figure 6-79

After you have defined this alert, users can then subscribe to receive alerts when the condition is met. By default, the e-mail and file transports are provided. Figure 6-80 shows how the users can subscribe to this alert.

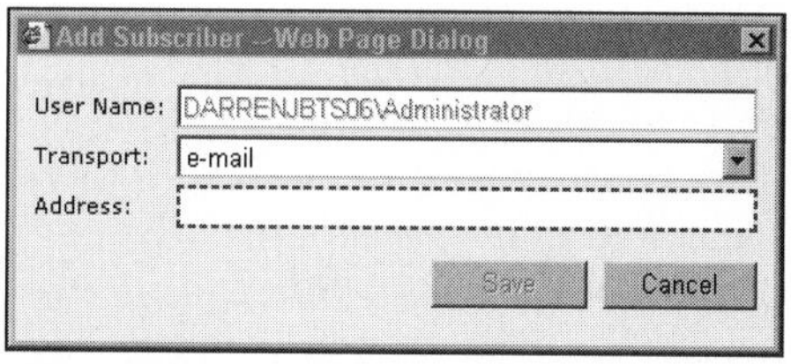

Figure 6-80

Finally, from the Alert Management section of the site, you can see all alerts and active subscriptions (see Figure 6-81).

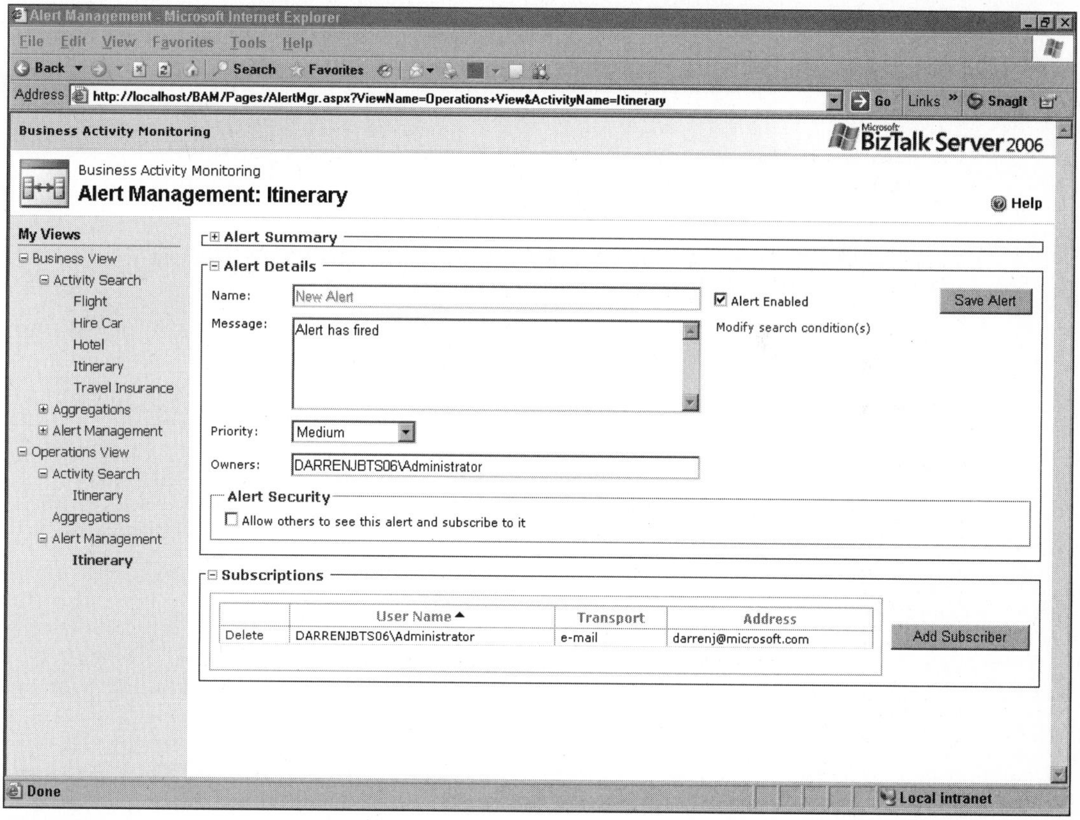

Figure 6-81

MOM Integration

BizTalk Server integrates with Microsoft Operations Manager (MOM) through the installation of the BizTalk Server 2006 MOM Pack. MOM is covered extensively in Chapter 11, but at a high level it provides a central way of monitoring the health of your BizTalk Server solution. For example, you could monitor the duration between two business milestones to determine if a Web service or trading partner is meeting their SLA.

Users of the BAM portal can also raise a request for technical assistance if they spot any problems when reviewing collected BAM data. From within the BAM portal, they can review a BAM activity and then request technical assistance via the Assistance button.

Figure 6-82 shows the technical assistance dialog box. Here the end user can enter some information to assist the system administration in resolving the issue. Once entered, this information, along with any associated metadata (message IDs, orchestration instance IDs, etc.), will be logged to the Event Viewer, which MOM will then consume and raise a support ticket for at the MOM console.

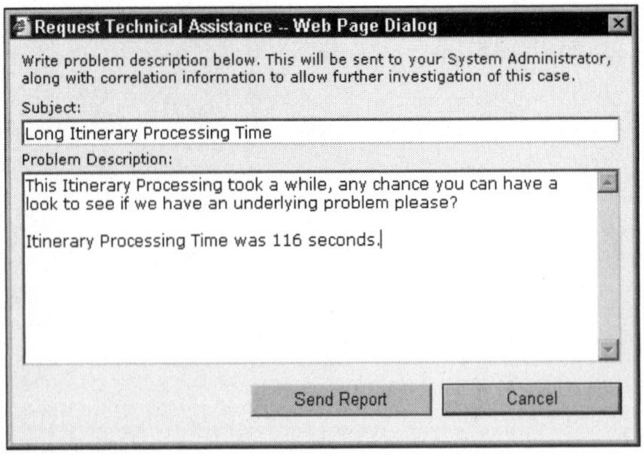

Figure 6-82

The system administrator can then review this support ticket and drill down directly into any associated orchestrations or messages via the Health and Activity tracking tool (HAT), all from the MOM console.

Summary

This chapter introduced the concept of Business Activity Monitoring and highlighted how it can be used to collect real-time information about your business processes implemented both in BizTalk and other Microsoft technologies.

This information can then be used to provide a real-time view into the associated business processes for both operations and business users, or in fact for any stakeholder who has a requirement to access such information.

The built-in BAM portal provides a rich view into data collected via BAM and enables activity data to be searched and viewed in a variety of ways. Because the BAM data is held in SQL tables and views, it's incredibly easy to access the information from a variety of tools, including SQL Server Reporting Services, which can produce a highly detailed tracking portal providing very rich business intelligence.

Performance of any solution is critical, and instrumentation can often impact solution performance. BAM has been designed with this in mind and incurs minimal overhead for your solution through a variety of techniques.

In summary, BAM is an incredibly powerful technology that has a place in almost every BizTalk solution. Once implemented, it can provide highly valuable information with little to no development overhead.

It's also important to note that BAM can be used from within non-BizTalk-based solutions following the BizTalk Server 2006 licensing changes, which can enable a common instrumentation platform across your enterprise.

The next chapter covers the BizTalk Rules Engine, detailing how it works and how it can be used within your solution.

Business Rules Engine

Although most systems today have some form of business rules implemented within them, they are typically implemented in code by developers and therefore require development resources and testing whenever changes are necessary. In contrast, BizTalk Server 2004 introduced the Business Rules Engine (BRE) as a core and stand-alone piece of the BizTalk architecture.

The BRE enables you to abstract these business rules from your solution and allow the owners of such business rules to control them. This abstraction is analogous to BizTalk orchestration, in which we abstract the process flow away from the code and into a business process.

In general, rules engines are highly efficient and can process many hundreds or even thousands of rules in a matter of milliseconds, making them highly desirable for BizTalk-style solutions, which typically process many messages a second.

The mechanics that underpin the BRE are incredibly complex and come across as being pretty inaccessible to almost everyone! So that you don't avoid BRE completely, perhaps to the detriment of a solution, this chapter explains the fundamentals in a clear and concise way. The goal of this chapter is to demystify BRE's complexity and empower you to use the BRE within your solution without resorting to additional (and often inaccessible) reference material.

BRE Basics

This section covers the core BRE concepts that you need to understand before delving into the practical examples throughout the remainder of the chapter.

Rule Expressions

BRE rules are expressed in this following format: IF <CONDITION> THEN <ACTION>. Note that there is no ability to express an ELSE clause. To implement such a clause, you just use an opposite rule.

Rete Analysis Network

A number of algorithms are available to implement rules engines. The BRE, the focus of our attention here, uses the Rete (Latin for "network") algorithm. The Rete alogorithm was designed by Dr. Charles Forgy in 1978, and is available in the public domain. Subsequent to the development of the original Rete algorithm, Rete II and Rete III have been developed. Both offer higher levels of performance but, unlike Rete, are not available in the public domain.

The Rete algorithm, a highly optimized and scalable rules engine algorithm, executes both small and large rulesets quickly (in most cases). It scales particularly well when dealing with a large ruleset (as explained in the following section).

You don't have to understand the intricacies of the Rete engine to appreciate and make full use of the BRE. Therefore, this discussion avoids the complexities and instead provides some examples that explain the fundamentals. If you must know more about Rete, you can find plenty of in-depth discussions on the Internet (but be prepared for some heavy reading).

So, how does the Rete algorithm work? Rules are first translated from their native expression form (IF `<Condition>` THEN `<Action>`) into a *Rete analysis network.* The analysis network in this case relates to an object graph containing four node types: `class`, `select`, `join`, and `terminal`.

Figure 7-1 shows an example analysis network for the following expression, which will help you understand these different node types:

```
IF Loan.Amount < 10,000
AND Customer.Age > 21
THEN Loan.Approved = true
```

A `class` node is a data type that will be used as part of the rule condition. Within the BRE, data types are represented as objects, and therefore data itself is represented as object instances. The example shows a `Customer` data type and an instance of this type, which the BRE will use when evaluating rules. (From this point on, we'll refer to such data as a *fact*, the term used by the BRE.)

A `select` node defines the conditions applied to that class type (or fact) which make up the `<Condition>` part of the rule. Figure 7-1 shows two select nodes, each containing a straightforward and familiar condition.

As the name implies, a `join` node joins up multiple (and therefore successful) flows within a network and passes them on to a terminal node. A terminal node then performs the `action` associated with the rule, thus completing the rule (in Figure 7-1, setting the `Approved` flag on the `Loan` object to `True`).

Let's now walk through the processing steps in Figure 7-1:

1. The facts required for the rule to execute are `Customer` and `Loan`. These must be passed into the BRE. This step is typically referred to as *asserting facts*.

2. Once asserted, the `Customer` and `Loan` facts flow into the network, the `Customer` fact flowing to the `Customer` class node and the `Loan` fact flowing to the `Loan` class node. They then pass on to the select nodes for their respective type.

3. The Customer class will flow to the select node, and the expression Customer.Age > 21 will be evaluated against the Customer fact. If the result of this and the Loan evaluation return True, execution will flow to the join node and then on to the terminal node, where the rule action will be performed. In this case, the Approved flag is set to True on the Loan fact.

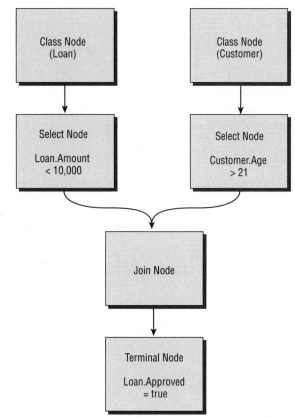

Figure 7-1

Sharing

Now consider what happens to the analysis network if we introduce the following extra rule:

```
IF Customer.Age > 21
THEN Customer.Risk = "Low"
```

You might have noticed that this rule uses the same Customer.Age > 21 condition (*shares* the condition) as the rule in Figure 7-1. Figure 7-2 shows the resulting analysis network. Only the shaded shapes are evaluated as part of the rule's execution.

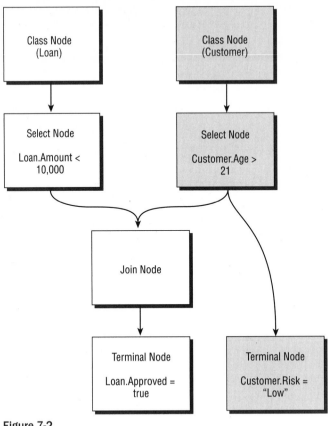

Figure 7-2

Comparing this analysis network with the first example, you can see that the same `select` node is used because the conditions are the same. Because only one condition is used in this rule expression, there is no need for a `join` node. Therefore, the network moves straight to the `terminal` node, which in turn sets the `Loan Risk` to `Low`.

This sharing is particularly important because the Rete algorithm is optimized for such scenarios in which there are shared conditions. Through sharing, an expression is evaluated only one time, rather than for each rule. If both of the following rules were part of a rules policy, for instance, the select node for the `Customer.Age > 21` expression would only be evaluated once:

```
"IF Loan.Amount < 10,000 AND Customer.Age > 21 THEN Loan.Approved = true"
"IF Customer.Age > 21 THEN Loan.Risk = "Low""
```

The Rete algorithm sharing capability thus clearly provides a performance improvement over traditional condition evaluation when you have many rules sharing conditions.

Now consider a slightly more complex sharing example in which an extra fact type, Promotion, is introduced. This example also introduces a new select node to the Loan type. Figure 7-3 shows this example:

```
IF Loan.Amount < 20,000
AND Promotion.EndDate > Loan.ApplicationDate
THEN Loan.APR = 3%
```

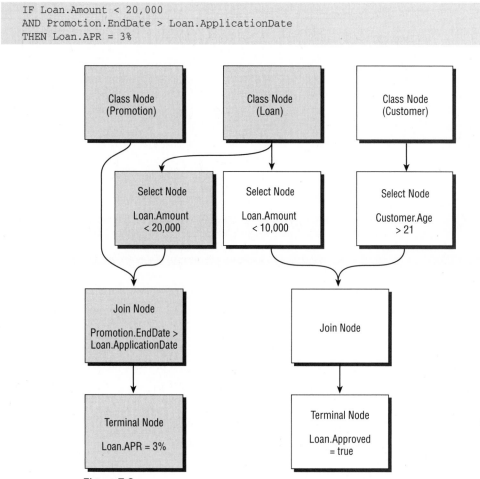

Figure 7-3

Introducing this rule to the analysis network has extended the network further. When we introduce a new condition for the Loan fact (Loan.Amount < 20,000), it is added beneath the class node Loan as a select node.

We have also introduced a new fact type called Promotion that is connected straight to a join node. A select node was not created for the Promotion condition (Promotion.EndDate > Loan.ApplicationDate), because the condition is also dependent on the class node Loan, which will be available only following successful evaluation of the Loan.Amount < 20,000 condition.

A new terminal node has been added to update the APR amount on the Loan object to 3 percent.

As you can see from the previous examples, BRE rules execution is pretty intelligent and shortcuts rules evaluation as appropriate to reduce duplicate condition evaluations. In addition, BRE rules execution avoids parts of the analysis network that are not required to execute rules (particularly important if you have many hundreds of rules).

Evaluating Rules

Now that you understand the analysis network, this section shows you how the rules are actually evaluated. In short, the evaluation process can be broken down into three stages: match, conflict resolution, and action.

The Match Stage

The match process is the process described in the previous section. After the facts have been asserted into the rules engine, you then identify which conditions need to be evaluated to satisfy the rules. As previously mentioned, condition evaluation is shared between rules as required.

The conditions are then evaluated against the rules expression to understand which expressions have resolved to `True`, and the execution flow ultimately ends up at the appropriate `terminal` nodes. When the terminal node is reached, the `actions` associated with the `terminal` node are placed on an `agenda` pending later execution.

The agenda is a queue of rule actions pending execution. Consider the following rules examples to understand what will be placed on the agenda.

The following table lists facts that are asserted into the BRE.

Loan	Amount = "7500" Term = 12 Insurance Required = true
Customer	Name = "Darren Jefford" Age = "28"

The rules policy contains only the following rules

- ❑ **Rule 1** — IF Loan.Amount < 10,000 AND Customer.Age > 21 THEN Loan.Approved = true

- ❑ **Rule 2** — IF Loan.Amount < 10,000 AND Customer.Age < 21 THEN Loan.Approved = false

Following the match process, the agenda will only contain the action for Rule 1 (Loan.Approved = true), which was satisfied because the Customer's age is greater than 21 and the Loan Amount is less than 10,000. Rule 2 was not satisfied because the Age is not less than 21.

For reference, the debug output of the rules execution is shown here. It was captured by hooking up `DebugTrackingInterceptor` (covered later in this chapter). You can clearly see the fact assertion, match, agenda update, and resulting rule firing stages:

```
FACT ACTIVITY 16/09/2006 20:46:02
Rule Engine Instance Identifier: 159a0785-4cd6-4c45-bd17-dda0b7c0aa16
Ruleset Name: Policy1
Operation: Assert
Object Type: LoanFacts.Customer
Object Instance Identifier: 17059405

CONDITION EVALUATION TEST (MATCH) 16/09/2006 20:46:02
Rule Engine Instance Identifier: 159a0785-4cd6-4c45-bd17-dda0b7c0aa16
Ruleset Name: Policy1
Test Expression: LoanFacts.Customer.get_Age > 21
Left Operand Value: 28
Right Operand Value: 21
Test Result: True

CONDITION EVALUATION TEST (MATCH) 16/09/2006 20:46:02
Rule Engine Instance Identifier: 159a0785-4cd6-4c45-bd17-dda0b7c0aa16
Ruleset Name: Policy1
Test Expression: LoanFacts.Customer.get_Age < 21
Left Operand Value: 28
Right Operand Value: 21
Test Result: False

FACT ACTIVITY 16/09/2006 20:46:02
Rule Engine Instance Identifier: 159a0785-4cd6-4c45-bd17-dda0b7c0aa16
Ruleset Name: Policy1
Operation: Assert
Object Type: LoanFacts.Loan
Object Instance Identifier: 29475730

CONDITION EVALUATION TEST (MATCH) 16/09/2006 20:46:02
Rule Engine Instance Identifier: 159a0785-4cd6-4c45-bd17-dda0b7c0aa16
Ruleset Name: Policy1
Test Expression: LoanFacts.Loan.get_Amount < 10000
Left Operand Value: 7500
Right Operand Value: 10000
Test Result: True

AGENDA UPDATE 16/09/2006 20:46:03
Rule Engine Instance Identifier: 159a0785-4cd6-4c45-bd17-dda0b7c0aa16
Ruleset Name: Policy1
Operation: Add
Rule Name: Rule1
Conflict Resolution Criteria: 0

RULE FIRED 16/09/2006 20:46:03
Rule Engine Instance Identifier: 159a0785-4cd6-4c45-bd17-dda0b7c0aa16
Ruleset Name: Policy1
Rule Name: Rule1
Conflict Resolution Criteria: 0
```

The Conflict Resolution Stage

The next step is conflict resolution. This step identifies actions on the agenda that conflict with each other. If both actions were to be performed, which one should "win" over the other action? Obviously, executing each action will cause the last one to "win," which might not be acceptable. To counter this, you can apply a priority to rules that is respected at runtime. In the BRE, higher-priority rules are executed first and so on.

By default, all rules are set to a priority of 0. If a rule's priority isn't set and multiple rules generate the same action, the execution order will be arbitrary because it relies on how the analysis network has been created.

Consider the following example to see how priority works:

Rule 1 (Priority 10)

```
IF Loan.Amount < 20,000
AND Promotion.EndDate > Loan.ApplicationDate
THEN Loan.APR = 3%
```

Rule 2 (Priority 0)

```
If Customer.LoanRisk = "Low"
THEN Loan.APR = 0%
```

The following table lists the facts that are asserted into the rules engine.

Loan	Amount = "10000" Term = 12 Insurance Required = true ApplicationDate = "15/9/2006" LoanRisk = "Low"
Customer	Name = "Darren Jefford" Age = "28"
Promotion	Start Date = "1/9/2006" End Date = "30/9/2006"

Following the match process, the agenda will contain the actions for both Rule 1 and Rule 2 because the conditions were met by both rules. The agenda now contains two conflicting actions, **both** wanting to modify the loan APR.

So, which wins? In the preceding scenario, the APR will be set to 0 percent following execution of the action stage. The actions are executed in priority order, meaning that Rule 1 is executed, which sets the APR to 3 percent. Rule 2 is then executed, setting the APR to 0 percent. Changing the priorities around would, of course, result in the APR being set to 3 percent.

To demonstrate this, consider the following trace, which was captured by executing the preceding rules with no priority set: each rule had equal priority. The trace has been truncated for brevity but shows that both expressions resolve to `True`. Both rules are placed on the agenda and executed with a Conflict Resolution Criteria of 0, which refers to the priority. Both rules are executed in an arbitrary order, which in this case, due to the structure of the analysis network, causes the APR to be set to 3 percent.

```
CONDITION EVALUATION TEST (MATCH) 16/09/2006 23:51:35
Rule Engine Instance Identifier: 79dcf52e-d776-459c-82cb-cc0dcd262646
Ruleset Name: Policy2
Test Expression: LoanFacts.Customer.get_LoanRisk == Low
Left Operand Value: Low
Right Operand Value: Low
Test Result: True

AGENDA UPDATE 16/09/2006 23:51:35
Rule Engine Instance Identifier: 79dcf52e-d776-459c-82cb-cc0dcd262646
Ruleset Name: Policy2
Operation: Add
Rule Name: Low Risk Rule
Conflict Resolution Criteria: 0

CONDITION EVALUATION TEST (MATCH) 16/09/2006 23:51:35
Rule Engine Instance Identifier: 79dcf52e-d776-459c-82cb-cc0dcd262646
Ruleset Name: Policy2
Test Expression: LoanFacts.Loan.get_Amount < 20000
Left Operand Value: 7500
Right Operand Value: 20000
Test Result: True

CONDITION EVALUATION TEST (MATCH) 16/09/2006 23:51:35
Rule Engine Instance Identifier: 79dcf52e-d776-459c-82cb-cc0dcd262646
Ruleset Name: Policy2
Test Expression: LoanFacts.Promotion.get_EndDate > LoanFacts.Loan.get_ApplicationDate
Left Operand Value: 16/10/2006 23:51:33
Right Operand Value: 16/09/2006 23:51:33
Test Result: True

AGENDA UPDATE 16/09/2006 23:51:35
Rule Engine Instance Identifier: 79dcf52e-d776-459c-82cb-cc0dcd262646
Ruleset Name: Policy2
Operation: Add
Rule Name: Loan Promotion Rule
Conflict Resolution Criteria: 0
RULE FIRED 16/09/2006 23:51:35

Rule Engine Instance Identifier: 79dcf52e-d776-459c-82cb-cc0dcd262646
Ruleset Name: Policy2
Rule Name: Low Risk Rule
Conflict Resolution Criteria: 0
RULE FIRED 16/09/2006 23:51:35
Rule Engine Instance Identifier: 79dcf52e-d776-459c-82cb-cc0dcd262646
Ruleset Name: Policy2
Rule Name: Loan Promotion Rule
Conflict Resolution Criteria: 0

Results in the APR set to 3%
```

Now consider a slightly different scenario. Both rules are placed on the agenda as before, but note that the "Loan Promotion" rule has been assigned a Resolution Criteria (Priority) of 10, which means it will be executed first. You can "see" this in the `Rule Fired` statements that are now in reverse to what they were before when they resulted in the APR being set to 3 percent.

```
CONDITION EVALUATION TEST (MATCH) 16/09/2006 23:50:57
Rule Engine Instance Identifier: 6f9915eb-1e19-4f48-b910-df7024fe0018
Ruleset Name: Policy2
Test Expression: LoanFacts.Customer.get_LoanRisk == Low
Left Operand Value: Low
Right Operand Value: Low
Test Result: True

AGENDA UPDATE 16/09/2006 23:50:57
Rule Engine Instance Identifier: 6f9915eb-1e19-4f48-b910-df7024fe0018
Ruleset Name: Policy2
Operation: Add
Rule Name: Low Risk Rule
Conflict Resolution Criteria: 0

CONDITION EVALUATION TEST (MATCH) 16/09/2006 23:50:57
Rule Engine Instance Identifier: 6f9915eb-1e19-4f48-b910-df7024fe0018
Ruleset Name: Policy2
Test Expression: LoanFacts.Loan.get_Amount < 20000
Left Operand Value: 7500
Right Operand Value: 20000
Test Result: True

CONDITION EVALUATION TEST (MATCH) 16/09/2006 23:50:57
Rule Engine Instance Identifier: 6f9915eb-1e19-4f48-b910-df7024fe0018
Ruleset Name: Policy2
Test Expression: LoanFacts.Promotion.get_EndDate > LoanFacts.Loan.get_ApplicationDate
Left Operand Value: 16/10/2006 23:50:55
Right Operand Value: 16/09/2006 23:50:55
Test Result: True

AGENDA UPDATE 16/09/2006 23:50:57
Rule Engine Instance Identifier: 6f9915eb-1e19-4f48-b910-df7024fe0018
Ruleset Name: Policy2
Operation: Add
Rule Name: Loan Promotion Rule
Conflict Resolution Criteria: 10

RULE FIRED 16/09/2006 23:50:57
Rule Engine Instance Identifier: 6f9915eb-1e19-4f48-b910-df7024fe0018
Ruleset Name: Policy2
Rule Name: Loan Promotion Rule
Conflict Resolution Criteria: 10

RULE FIRED 16/09/2006 23:50:57
Rule Engine Instance Identifier: 6f9915eb-1e19-4f48-b910-df7024fe0018
Ruleset Name: Policy2
Rule Name: Low Risk Rule
Conflict Resolution Criteria: 0

Results in the APR set to 0%
```

The Action Stage

When conflict resolution is complete, the agenda contains a list of the actions that need to be executed. Execution of these rules is performed when the `Execute` method is called on the rules engine.

When multiple actions are associated with a rule, they will all be executed in a batch before any actions associated with another rule are executed. All rules executed within a batch will be done so in priority order, highest first.

You can cause rules to be reevaluated following a rule's actions. This process is covered in the following section.

Forward Chaining

Forward chaining is another complex-sounding term, but it actually means something pretty straightforward. Forward chaining describes the ability for one rule's actions to impact facts relied on by another rule and thus require such a rule to be reevaluated to maintain consistency.

Consider this three-rule scenario: Rules 1 and 2 rely on the Loan Risk property to establish which APR the loan should be set to. Rule 3 marks the customer as High Risk if the customer meets the profiling criteria.

```
Rule 1:
IF Customer.LoanRisk = "Low"
THEN Loan.APR = 0%

Rule 2:
IF Customer.LoanRisk = "High"
THEN Loan.APR = 39%

Rule 3:
IF Customer.Age < 21 AND Income < "20,000"
THEN Customer.LoanRisk = "High"
```

A clear dependency exists between these rules. The action of Rule 1 or Rule 2 can be made invalid by Rule 3. The action of Rule 3 modifies the `LoanRisk` fact, which is used as part of the conditions for Rule 1 and Rule 2.

This is where forward chaining comes in. The BRE requires that users create rules with this mind and add an `UPDATE` statement to the rule. This indicates to the BRE that the fact specified with the `UPDATE` statement has changed and that all rules that rely on this fact in a condition should be reevaluated and therefore pass through the match–conflict resolution–action stages again.

A common misconception is that you can resolve this issue by adjusting priority, instead of using the `UPDATE` statement. Adjusting rule priority will not achieve the same result as using the `UPDATE` statement, however, because the match stage has already been executed and the agenda has had the appropriate rules placed upon it.

Adjusting priority only modifies the order in which actions are executed. The `UPDATE` statement forces all rules relying on the fact that has been updated to pass through the match phase again, effectively causing them to be reevaluated.

Therefore, the rules author must understand which rules will impact others and supply the appropriate UPDATE statement to ensure that the results are as intended.

The previous rule statement would need to be modified as follows. Note that the Fact type must be provided to the UPDATE statement, not the individual property. This is dragged from the Facts Explorer onto the UPDATE clause, which is itself created by right-clicking the Actions part of the Rules Editor and choosing UPDATE.

```
Rule 1:
IF Customer.LoanRisk = "Low"
THEN Loan.APR = 0%

Rule 2:
IF Customer.LoanRisk = "High"
THEN Loan.APR = 39%

Rule 3:
IF Customer.Age < 21 AND Income < "20,000"
THEN Customer.LoanRisk = "High"
UPDATE Customer
```

So, with the UPDATE statement in place, you might expect the rule to execute in the way we anticipated. However, if you were to execute the preceding rules as above with the fact base shown in the following table, you would enter a never-ending loop.

Loan	Amount = "10000"
	Term = 12
	Insurance Required = true
	ApplicationDate = "15/9/2006"
	LoanRisk = "Low"
Customer	Name = "Darren Jefford"
	Age = "20"
	Salary = "19000"

So, why do these rules and facts cause a never-ending loop? The addition of the UPDATE Customer statement has effectively caused the Customer fact to be retracted and then reasserted into the BRE. This retraction and reassertion causes all rules relying on the Customer fact to be reevaluated. Remember that we *update* the entire Customer object, so all rules, even if they rely on different properties, must be reevaluated.

In this case, that includes Rule 3, which in this scenario will cause the rule to be placed on the agenda again. When the code is executed, the UPDATE statement is executed again, causing the Customer fact to be reasserted and causing an endless loop.

In scenarios in which you have the fact used in both the conditions and UPDATE part of a rule, you must be aware of such a looping condition and code against it. In this scenario, you can resolve this looping condition. You just add a further condition that causes the rule not to execute if the action statement is already set to the value specified in the THEN clause, as follows:

```
IF Customer.Age < 21 AND Income < "20,000" AND Customer.LoanRisk != "High"
THEN Customer.LoanRisk = "High"
UPDATE Customer
```

Based on the fact base provided before, this modified Rule 3 will execute as normal on the first pass. However, following successful execution of the rule action and the subsequent UPDATE statement, it fails to match when executed again, because Customer.LoanRisk will already equal High.

> *The BRE has a built-in fail-safe to avoid entering an infinite loop. When a loop has been detected (after 65536 loops by default), the BRE throws a* RuleEngineRuntimeExecutionLoopException *and halts execution. The number of loops before declaring an infinite loop can be controlled via the* Maximum Execution Loop Depth *property of the rules policy within the Business Rules Composer. It's advisable to set this to a lower number during development.*

As you can see, the UPDATE statement is a key part of rules development, but it also produces performance overhead. Therefore, design your rules so that they do not require UPDATE statements, if possible; such a design will make your ruleset much easier to understand as well as perform better.

There is no easy visual way to see dependencies between rules or any potential conflicts. Acumen Business has a fantastic tool, Business Rule Manager, that enables you to visualize your rules policy (see Figure 7-4).

The Acumen Business Rule Manager can also be used to work around some of the policy and vocabulary versioning issues discussed later in the chapter. This approach is not supported by Microsoft.

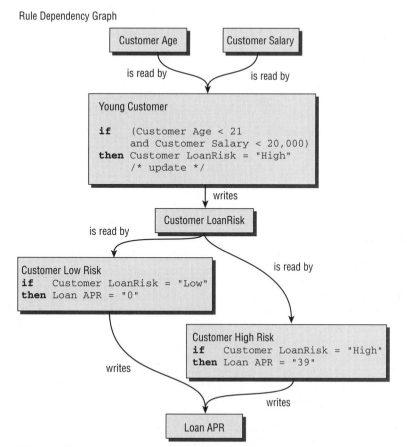

Figure 7-4

Business Rule Composer

The Business Rule Composer is a GUI that enables you to create and modify business rules. It also provides administrative features such as versioning and deployment, and you can install it on its own as part of the BizTalk installation routine.

Figure 7-5 shows the initial view of the Rule Composer when started. The upper-left pane is the Policy Explorer, where you can see all rules policies in the BRE database. Beneath this, you can see the Facts Explorer pane, where data used by rules is defined. On the right side, you can see the rules design surface, where rules are constructed.

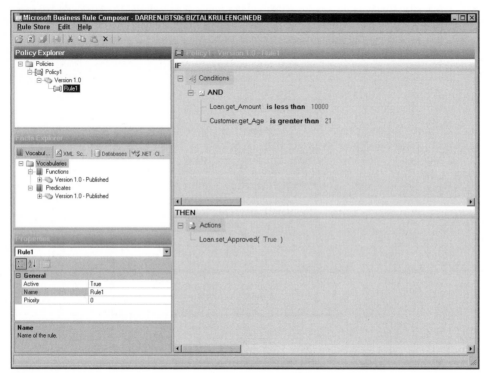

Figure 7-5

Creating Policies

Policies are physical groupings for rules and are the unit of execution. Individual rules cannot be executed. Instead, policies are executed, and all active rules within a group are evaluated during execution. You can deactivate individual rules by setting the `Active` property to `False` through the Rule Composer. You can use the Rule Composer to create policies. To do so, right-click `Policies` in the Policy Explorer pane and choose `Add New Policy`.

Policies are versioned, and a new policy is given a default version of 1.0. Any policy properties or rules can be modified up until the point where a policy has been deployed to the rule store.

There are three states that relate to the lifetime of a policy:

❑ **Editable** — This state is the initial state for a new rules policy. In this state, you can perform any task to the policy (add/remove rules, etc.).

❑ **Published** — After a policy has been published, it becomes read-only and the state cannot be moved back to the editable state. The policy isn't available for use at this stage and is held in a staging area ahead of deployment.

❑ **Deployed** — The Deployed state makes the policy available for execution via the Call Rules shape or the `Policy` class. Once deployed, the policy can be undeployed, making it unavailable for execution.

After a policy has been deployed, you can remove the policy only by undeploying it. Any modification requires a new version of a policy to be created.

Recreating each rule when you introduce a new policy version is tedious, at best. With large numbers of rules, it becomes unacceptable. It's often overlooked, but you can right-click a policy version, as shown in Figure 7-6, and choose Copy.

Figure 7-6

If you then right-click the policy name in the Policy Explorer, you can choose Paste New Version to create a new version of the policy (but complete with all the rules from the previous version). You can then modify or add rules before deploying the policy and making it available.

During rules' development, you may need to publish and/or deploy your rules' policy to run tests. As you'll see later in this chapter, you can use the `PolicyTester` class to enable testing of unpublished or undeployed policies, but there are cases when you may not be able to use this. Invoking rules from an orchestration is a classic example.

In these cases, it can quickly become tedious to create new versions of policies each and every time you need to. There is, however, an unsupported technique often used during development that can enable you to reverse the actions of a publish or deploy activity, thus allowing modification. This should only be used on development workstations and never on live ones.

The SQL statement below demonstrates how a policy called "MyPolicy" with a version of 1.0 can be reset back to its editable state, thus allowing modification. You can then use the Business Rule Composer to publish and deploy the policy as required. Again, please note that this is not supported.

325

```
declare         @RuleSetId int

select @RuleSetId = nRuleSetID
FROM     re_RuleSet
WHERE    strName= "MyPolicy"
AND      nMajor=1 AND nMinor=0

UPDATE   re_ruleset
SET      nStatus = 0
WHERE    nRuleSetID = @RuleSetId

DELETE FROM re_deployment_config WHERE nRuleSetID = @RuleSetId
DELETE FROM re_tracking_id WHERE nRuleSetID = @RuleSetId
```

Creating Rules

Rules are created within the BRE editor. The design surface provides two panes for rules construction: one for the IF part of your rules, and another for the THEN part of your rules.

The IF part of your rule is made up of facts, predicates (>, =, <, etc.), and grouping operators such as AND, OR, and NOT. If you have multiple predicates, you must choose one of the grouping operators.

Figure 7-7 shows an example of a rule to demonstrate how such rules are structured. The rule shown uses an AND condition, two predicates (is less than and is greater than), and an action to call a .NET class method.

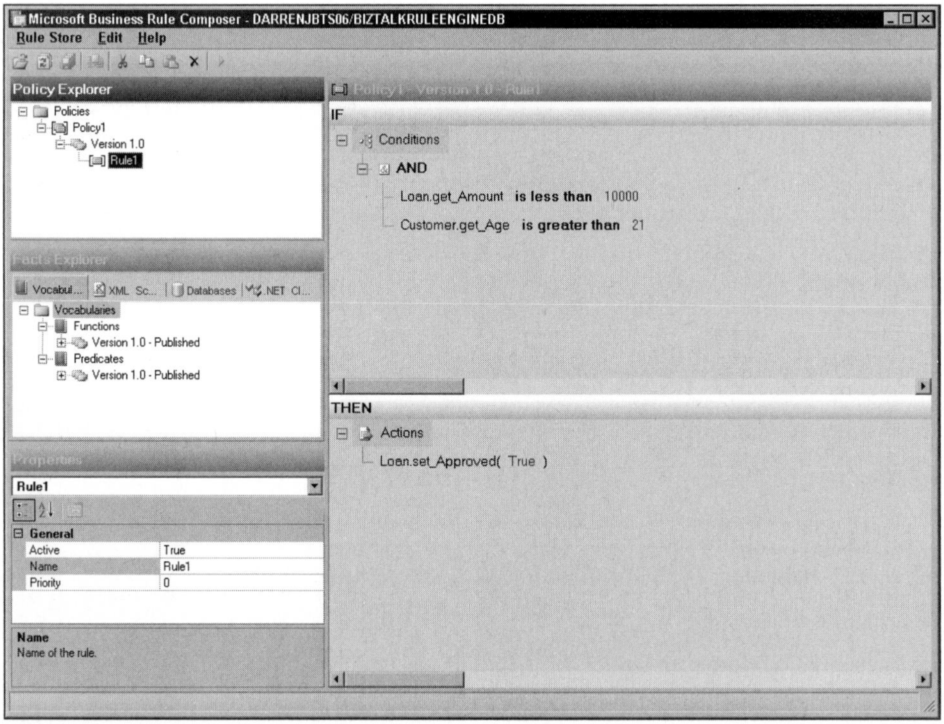

Figure 7-7

Predicates

The following predicates are available to rule developers. These predicates are used when defining the IF part of your rule. The following rule uses both the `GreaterThan` and `Equal` predicates:

```
If Customer.Age > 21 AND LoanRisk = "Low"
```

The predicates available with the BRE are listed here. Most are obvious, but all are included here for reference purposes.

❑ `After` — Can be used only with `System.Date.Time` derived types and enables you to ascertain whether, for example, `LoanApplicationDate` is *after* `PromotionStartDate`

❑ `Before` — Like the `After` predicate, can only be used with `System.Date.Time` derived times and enables you to ascertain whether, for example, `PromotionStartDate` is *before* `LoanApplicationDate`

❑ `Between` — Enables you to ascertain whether a `System.Date.Time` is between two other DateTimes (for example, whether `LoanApplicationDate` is *between* `PromotionStartDate` and `PromotionEndDate`)

❑ `Equal` — Enables you to compare two facts and ascertain whether they match (directly analogous to = in C#).

❑ `Exists` — Enables you to identify whether an XML element or attribute is present in an XML document

❑ `GreaterThan` — Enables you to ascertain whether one fact is greater than another (directly analogous to > in C#)

❑ `GreaterThanEqual` — Enables you to ascertain whether one fact is greater than or equal to another (directly analogous to >= in C#)

❑ `LessThan` — Enables you to ascertain whether one fact is less than to another (directly analogous to < in C#)

❑ `LessThanEqual` — Enables you to ascertain whether one fact is less than or equal to another (directly analogous to <= in C#)

❑ `Match` — Enables you to ascertain whether a regular expression is present in a provided string (for example, `"DB+"` returns true if given a string that starts with the letter D and has one or more B's directly after (e.g., `DB9`)

❑ `NotEqual` — Enables you to ascertain whether one fact is not equal to another (directly analogous to != in C#)

❑ `Range` — Enables you to ascertain whether a fact is between a range of two values. The type representing the lower and upper bounds must be compatible (all integers, decimals, etc.)

BRE Functions

The BRE provides the following five *engine* functions that enable you to control engine behavior as part of your rules execution:

❑ Assert — The Assert function enables you to *assert* a new fact to the BRE for processing. Asserting is the usual step of providing data for the rules to execute upon, but the data is often provided before BRE execution.

In some scenarios, you might want (following a rule being satisfied) to assert additional facts that weren't available prior to the rule policy execution (for example, calling a .NET helper class that returns a new fact passing information that has been retrieved).

❑ Retract — The Retract function enables you to remove a fact from the BRE working memory. When used as part of a rule action, it will remove a specific instance of a fact. Any rules on the agenda that use this fact via predicates or actions will be removed.

❑ RetractByType — Like the Retract function, RetractByType removes all facts matching the passed type from the BRE working memory.

❑ Update — The Update function, which was covered earlier in this chapter, enables you to flag to the BRE that you have changed a fact and that any rules relying on this fact instance should be reevaluated.

These BRE functions are typically used to control the forward-chaining behavior covered earlier in this chapter. If you change a fact relied on by other rules, you must use these engine functions to ensure that these rules are reevaluated. Changes are not detected automatically.

These functions are executed as part of the THEN part of your rule. Therefore, they can be placed only within the THEN part of your rule's definition.

Fact Sources

When creating rules, you can make use of data (or facts) stored in .NET classes, XML schemas, and databases. Obviously, how you access the facts in each of these is different, but this difference is abstracted away from you. You just have to select the data inside these data sources. The BRE handles the retrieval for you.

Rules actions can also update data held in these fact sources. For example, the result of a rule can update a SQL database or change the value of a property inside a .NET class.

Fact sources are controlled within the Business Rules Composer via the Facts Explorer pane. As you can see in Figure 7-8, you can select the required fact type and then drill down to find the data item you want to use.

Figure 7-8

.NET Classes

Any form of .NET class can be used by the BRE as long as it's been registered in the Global Assembly Cache (GAC). In fact, the BRE can use any assembly regardless of whether it's been signed or present in the GAC, but the Rule Composer looks for assemblies only in the GAC.

Within the Business Rule Composer, you can select .NET Classes from the Facts Explorer pane, right-click .NET Assemblies, and then choose Browse to show all the assemblies held in the GAC.

Once this has been done, you will see a list of the all the classes in the pane. From there, you can drill into your class and select the appropriate property or method (as long as it's been marked as public).

Figure 7-9 shows a screen shot of the Facts Explorer pane with a .NET assembly selected.

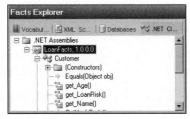

Figure 7-9

Properties and methods of the .NET assembly can then be used as part of the rule's conditions and actions. Just drag the property or method across to the rule's design surface as appropriate.

Figure 7-10 shows a rule using a .NET class within conditions and also setting properties within a .NET class as an action.

After you have defined a rule that makes use of a .NET fact, you then need to make the fact available to the BRE at execution time. This process, as discussed previously, is called assertion.

As discussed later in the chapter, if you use the Call Rules shape, you can easily pass a .NET class instance to the BRE. If you are invoking the BRE directly, however, the following code shows how you assert .NET facts to the BRE:

```
using (Policy LoanPolicy = new Policy("LoanPolicy"))
{
   // Create .NET Classes used as facts
   LoanFacts.Customer Customer = new LoanFacts.Customer(1, "Darren", 20, "Low", 19000);
   LoanFacts.Loan Loan = new LoanFacts.Loan(7500, 12, false, DateTime.Now, "");

   LoanPolicy.Execute(Customer, Loan);
}
```

As you can see, the native class is asserted. No *wrapper* classes are required (as are needed for XML and database fact types).

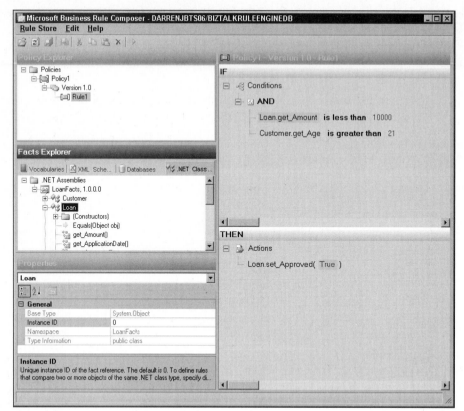

Figure 7-10

XML Schemas

You can also use XML schemas as a source for rules. Although you can view and select elements from an XML schema, you will, of course, have to provide the BRE with an XML document at runtime from which it can retrieve or set elements.

Within the Facts Explorer pane, you can browse to an XML schema file, which will be displayed in the Facts Explorer. You can then drag elements onto the rule's design surface as appropriate. When dragging these elements for use within a rule, you are effectively dragging the XPath statement required to retrieve such rules from an XML document. (Viewing the schema in the pane just makes life easier at the design stage; it's not used at any other time.)

As you'll no doubt see when selecting and dragging elements of your XML document onto your rule's definition, there are two key properties of XML-based facts: the XML selector and XML field. Figure 7-11 shows an example of these.

You can think of the XML selector as the XPath node set that will be asserted into the BRE. In the preceding example, this will be the Itinerary element. If, for example, multiple nodes are returned, each will be asserted into the BRE. The XML field then refers to a child element called TotalItineraryPrice.

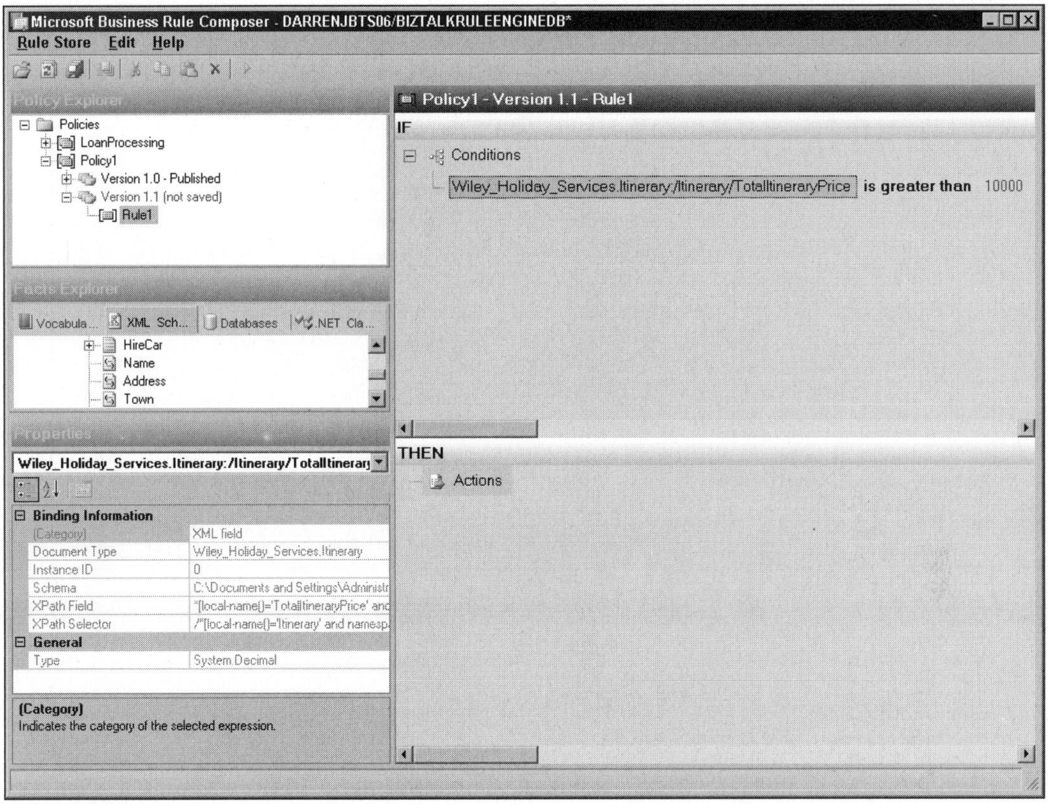

Figure 7-11

It's hard to see the full properties of the XML selector and XPath field in the figure, so they are shown here:

```
XPath Selector: /*[local-name()='Itinerary' and namespace-uri()=
'http://Wiley_Holiday_Services.Itinerary']

XPath Field:/*[local-name()='TotalItineraryPrice' and namespace-uri()="]
```

After you have defined a rule that makes use of an XML-based fact, you must assert the appropriate XML document into the BRE. Native System.Xml.XmlDocument instances cannot be asserted, but must instead be wrapped with a Microsoft.RuleEngine.TypedXmlDocument instance to provide the document type (which isn't otherwise available).

An example of the code required to assert a TypedXmlDocument is shown here. In this example, we use an orchestration message as the source. However, you can start from a straightforward XML document.

```
using (Policy LoanPolicy = new Policy("LoanPolicy"))
{
  // Create a TypedXmlDocument to be used as a fact
  XmlDocument docMyXLANGMessage = MyXLANGMessage;
```

```
    TypedXmlDocument typedXmlDocument = new    TypedXmlDocument
  ("WileyFinancialServices.CreditInformation", docMyXLANGMessage);

    LoanPolicy.Execute(typedXmlDocument);
  }
```

As you see, a Document Type parameter is passed to the constructor of the `TypedXmlDocument`. You can find this parameter by selecting the appropriate schema in the Solution Explorer and viewing the `Fully Qualified Name` in the Properties pane. (This technique is shown later in this chapter in the "Problems" subsection of the "Invoking Rules" section.)

Many people believe that the BRE breaks the BizTalk immutable message behavior in that, via the Call Rules shape, you can pass a message that a rule can then modify as part of its actions. However, the BRE *does not* break the immutability behavior discussed earlier in this book. Instead, it creates a new message and modifies the message reference within the BizTalk orchestration.

> *When a new message is created, it will not contain the context properties present on the previous message. If you have a requirement for these messages, ensure that you create a new message for use by the BRE and then copy the context properties between the old and new messages after the BRE execution has completed.*

Databases

You can access any SQL Server database natively through the Databases section of the Facts Explorer pane. Right-clicking the Servers Node enables you to provide a server name and credentials as appropriate.

> *There is no directly supported way to use data housed in a non–SQL Server database as part of rules execution if you are using the Rules Composer to construct your rules. Of course, you could write a .NET component that provides the capability to retrieve data using a .NET class fact. If you don't use the Rules Composer to construct your rules, you can make use of an `OleDbConnection`.*

After this has been completed, you can then select the database table or column that you require and drag this onto your rule or create a vocabulary definition. Remember that at this stage you are not physically binding to the data source; you are just adding a reference that needs to be resolved at execution time to the real data.

By using tables or columns from the Facts Explorer, you are by default requiring a fact of type `Microsoft.RuleEngine.DataConnection` to be asserted into the BRE. A `DataConnection` is a thin veneer around a normal `System.Data.SqlConnection` and will result in a query being executed to retrieve the data when a rule evaluation is performed. Results from this query are asserted into the BRE as `TypedDataRows`. The BRE takes responsibility for closing the SQL Server connection.

You can, however, specify an alternative binding type when selecting a table or column from the Facts Explorer pane. Within the Properties pane, you can select `Data Table/Data Row` and assert previously populated `DataTable` or `DataRow` instances to the BRE, as shown in Figure 7-12.

> *You might be thinking that perhaps you could populate a non–SQL Server database `DataTable` or `DataRow` to assert as facts to the BRE. Although technically you can do this, it will not work, because during rules creation you must browse a SQL Server database to create the fact or vocabulary definition.*

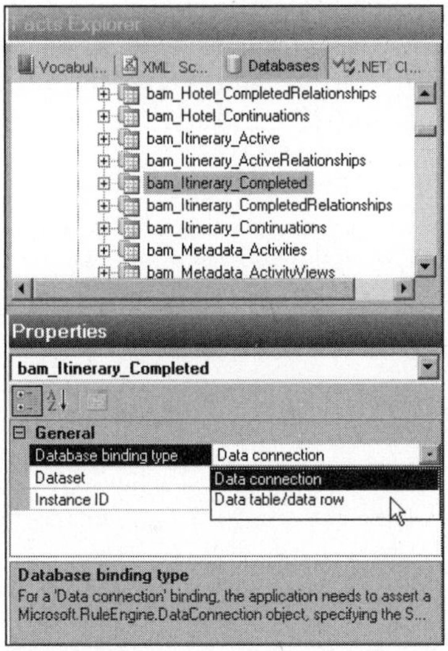

Figure 7-12

In most cases, the default of `DataConnection` should be used, because it offers the best overall performance. (The "BizTalk 2004 Performance Characteristics" paper available at `http://msdn.microsoft.com` covers some test results and details that explain this further.) Another advantage is that the BRE will automatically generate the SQL query to retrieve the required data.

However, in some scenarios the `DataTable/Data Row` option offers significant performance improvements, depending on your rule design.

The following code shows how you can construct a `DataConnection` and assert a `DataConnection` fact into the working memory:

```
using (Policy LoanPolicy = new Policy("LoanPolicy"))
{
  SqlConnection Conn = new SqlConnection( _ConnectionString ))
  DataConnection dc = new DataConnection(""AdventureWorks","Product", Conn);

  LoanPolicy.Execute(dc);
}
```

For scenarios in which each rules policy invocation repeatedly uses the same core data retrieved from a database table that also remains largely static, you can gain a significant performance improvement by caching a `DataTable` within the BRE to avoid the database round trip on each and every rules policy execution.

This is a classic scenario for the use of a Long-Term Fact Retriever to improve execution performance (as covered later in this chapter). Using a database query to retrieve static information required for every policy execution will quickly turn into a bottleneck.

Using a DataConnection as a long-term fact offers little performance gain, because all you are effectively doing is caching a SqlConnection, which is typically backed by connection pooling. The query will still be performed each time rules are evaluated. Caching a DataTable, however, is likely to show a performance benefit, because the data will be cached.

Vocabularies

You will have no doubt observed that the data sources covered previously require fairly in-depth appreciation of the underlying types. This is not particularly a good thing for the typical rules developer, who (more likely than not) is nontechnical.

Vocabularies address this by presenting a business-friendly façade, abstracting away the complexity and enabling data items to be represented with friendly names. A vocabulary is created by selecting Vocabularies in the Facts Explorer, right-clicking Vocabularies, and then choosing Add New Vocabulary.

As with rules policies, vocabularies are versioned. When you create a new vocabulary, a default version 1.0 vocabulary is created for you. In a similar way to policies, vocabularies have states associated with them: Editable and Published. The Rules Composer restricts you to using published vocabularies when creating rules.

Right-clicking a vocabulary version and choosing Add New Definition enables you to then populate this vocabulary, which can contain definitions for the following items:

❑   Constant values, ranges of values, or sets of values

❑   .NET classes or class members

❑   XML document elements or attributes

❑   Database tables or columns

Figure 7-13 shows the first page of the Vocabulary Definition Wizard.

You can also add vocabulary definitions by finding (through the Facts Explorer) the fact you want to add to the vocabulary and dragging it into the vocabulary. You cannot view the Vocabularies pane in the Facts Explorer at the same time; so, while dragging, you need to hover over the Facts Explorer and wait for the Vocabularies pane to appear. You can then drop the fact into a unpublished vocabulary.

Constants, Ranges, and Sets

Vocabularies can contain definitions for constants, which enable you to define a fixed value for use in multiple rules and thus effect a change one time rather than having to do so across multiple rules. You can define constants against the usual types, such as String, Int32, and DateType.

Vocabulary definition is done through the use of a wizard. Figure 7-14 shows Vocabulary Definition Wizard (on the Define a Constant Value page) with a constant called MaximumLoanAmount set to a value of 16000.

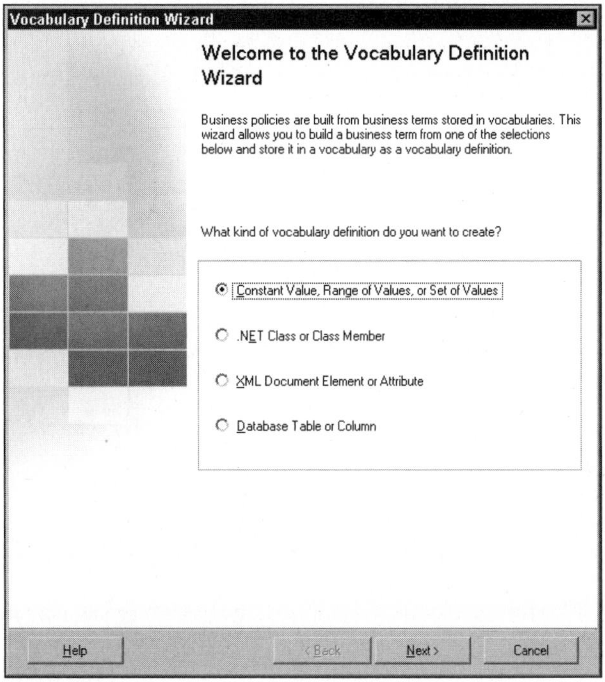

Figure 7-13

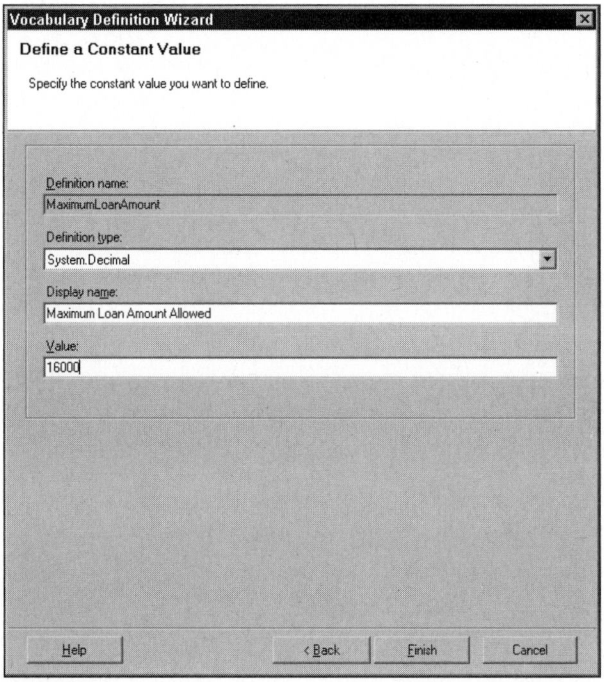

Figure 7-14

Figure 7-15 shows the Vocabulary Definition Wizard (on the Define a Range of Values page) with a definition called `AllowableLoanAmount` that has a lower range of 1000 and an upper range of 16000 configured. The following example shows hard-coded values being used, but it can also utilize constants declared in any published vocabulary.

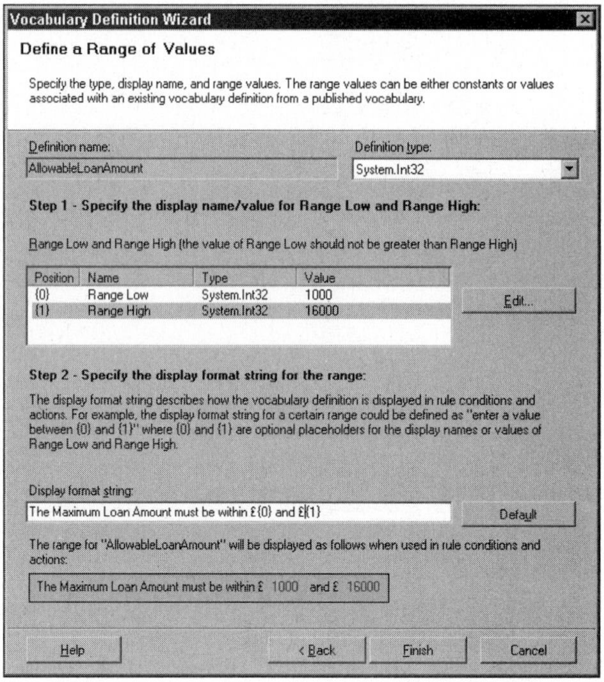

Figure 7-15

Figure 7-16 shows the Vocabulary Definition Wizard (on the Define a Set of Values page with a definition called `LoanTerm` that has a set containing eight values. This example uses hard-coded values, but could, of course, use constants declared within a published vocabulary.

.NET Classes or Members

Vocabularies can contain definitions for .NET classes or members of a specific .NET class. Therefore, rule authors can leverage .NET classes but avoid the technical details involved. For example, a vocabulary definition called `GetCustomerLoanRisk` could be defined that maps to the `Customer` class and specifically the `LoanRisk` property.

As with the previous vocabulary definitions, the creation is done through the use of a wizard. Figure 7-17 shows the creation of a definition called `CustomerLoanRisk` that has been mapped to the LoanFacts assembly and then the `get_LoanRisk` member of the `Customer` class.

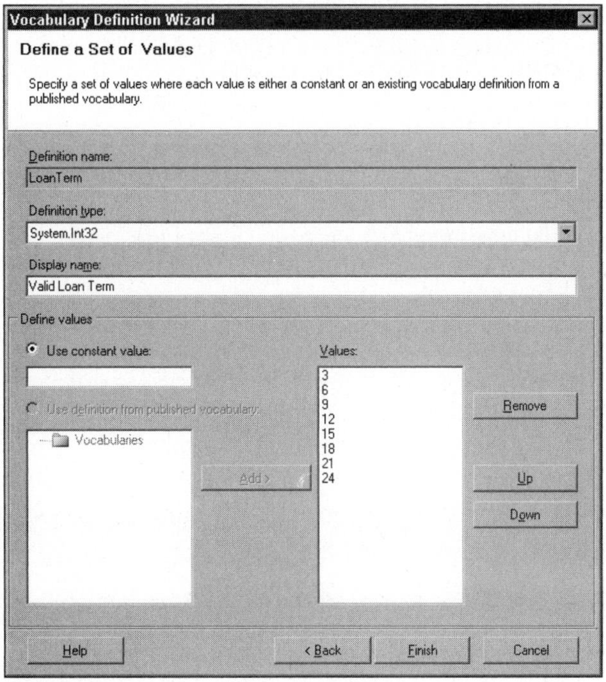

Figure 7-16

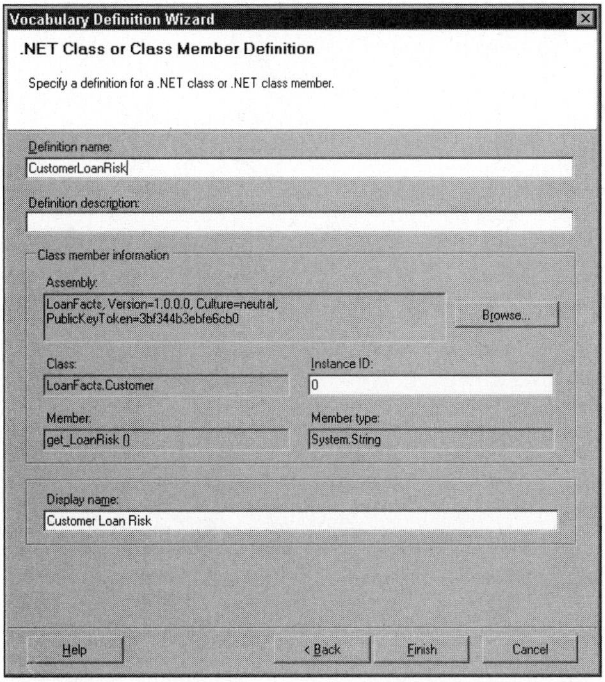

Figure 7-17

As you can see in Figure 7-17, you can provide an instance ID. This instance ID is set to 0 by default. The instance ID enables you to assign a unique instance number, and thus allows you to distinguish between two facts using the same .NET class in a rule definition.

The "Using a Vocabulary" section shows some examples of rules using a .NET class.

Document Elements or Attributes

Vocabularies can also contain definitions for elements or attributes held within an XML document. Rules authors can then use this data from within a rule without having any knowledge or appreciation of the XML document structure or even XPath.

As with all vocabulary definition, creation is done through the use of a wizard. Figure 7-18 shows a vocabulary definition that utilizes the Wiley Travel Services schema used in Chapter 6. When browsing for a schema, you are prompted to select a part of the schema using a tree view. (In this case, the TotalItineraryPrice element has been selected.)

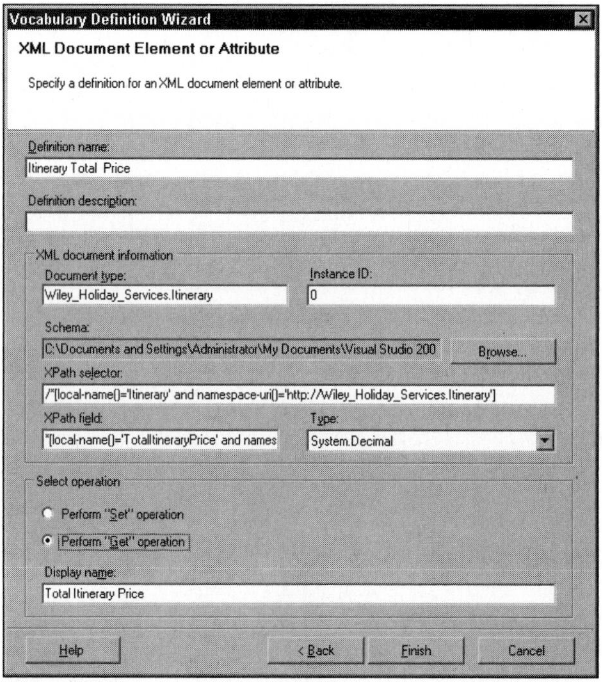

Figure 7-18

As you can see in Figure 7-18, you can configure a vocabulary definition to either perform a Get or Set operation. A Set operation would allow a rule's author to use such a vocabulary definition to set or change part of an XML document for later return to the caller.

Note that the vocabulary definition in this case is purely defining an XPath selector and XPath field, which we covered earlier in the "Data Sources" section.

Database Tables or Columns

Last but not least, vocabularies can contain definitions for data tables or columns. These enable rule authors to use data held in SQL Server database tables without any knowledge of the database server or database semantics.

Figure 7-19 shows a vocabulary definition configured to point at the `bam_Itinerary_Completed` SQL Server database.

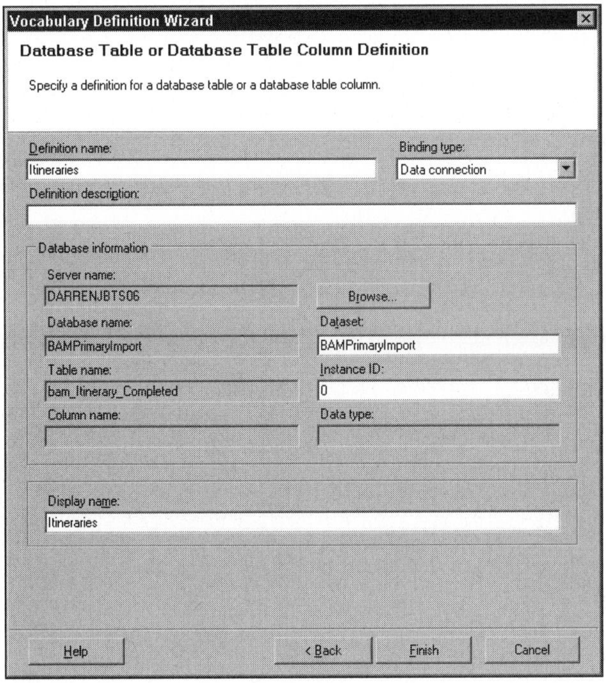

Figure 7-19

Versioning

A vocabulary is treated in a similar way to rules policies: They are versioned and must be published before being used as part of any rules. Any rules making use of a vocabulary bind to the specific vocabulary version and cannot be made either directly or inadvertently to use a new vocabulary version. This is to ensure that the original intent of the rules is not compromised by the underlying definition of a vocabulary changing.

From a usability point of view, this can be frustrating. You have a rules policy containing a stack of rules that uses definitions held within a deployed vocabulary. You then later need to modify a vocabulary definition; perhaps a constant value requires modification following an unexpected business change. You must first create a new vocabulary definition with a new version number and apply your change.

Then you must create a new version of your rules policy. This can be created containing all the rules "as they were." You can then modify each rule, making use of the constant to use the new vocabulary definition and deploy the rules policy.

Of course, any other rules within this policy will still be making use of the original vocabulary version, because the references haven't been changed. All references to vocabularies in rule conditions and actions would need to be updated. This is done by design and required to maintain the integrity of the rules. The preceding example is clearly fabricated, and indeed a constant should not be used for data items that fluctuate and should instead be stored within a fact asserted into the engine, be it a .NET class or database.

> *Acumen Business provides a free downloadable tool called Policy Verificator that, among other things, enables you to update all rules referencing a specific vocabulary version to use a new version without manual modification. You can download this tool from* `http://www.acumenbusiness.com`.

A commonly experienced problem is vocabularies not being made available for use. All vocabularies must be published before being used within a rule. Publishing is straightforward and can be done by right-clicking the desired vocabulary version and choosing Publish, as shown in Figure 7-20.

After a vocabulary has been published, it cannot be "unpublished" for changes. Instead, making any changes requires you to create a new version. You can easily create a new version by right-clicking a vocabulary version, choosing Copy, right-clicking the vocabulary name in the Facts Explorer, and then choosing Paste Vocabulary Version.

When a vocabulary is no longer used by any rules policies, you can delete it. Just right-click the unwanted vocabulary version and choose Delete.

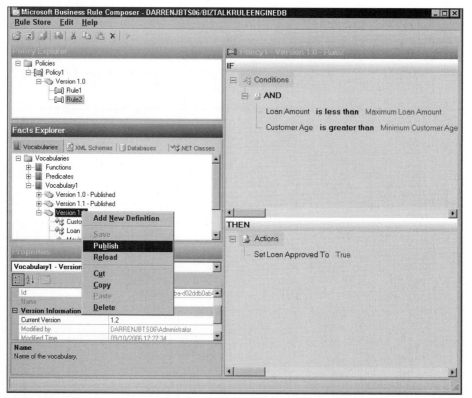

Figure 7-20

During rules development a vocabulary can change many times, and it can quickly become tedious to publish a new version and update any rules that reference the vocabulary each and every time you make a change. There is an unsupported technique often used during development that can enable you to "unpublish" a vocabulary and thus allow modification. This should only be used on development workstations and never on live ones.

The SQL statement shown below demonstrates how a vocabulary called "MyVocabulary" with a version of 1.0 can be set to "unpublished," repeating the statement but using 1 as the nStatus parameter will publish the vocabulary again. You can of course publish it through the Business Rule Composer as usual.

```
UPDATE   re_Voacabulary
SET      nStatus = 0
WHERE    strName = 'MyVocabulary'
AND      nMajor = 1
AND      nMinor = 0
```

Using a Vocabulary

We've covered all the positioning around vocabularies and what a vocabulary can consist of, but let's see what difference a vocabulary can make to a simple rule.

Figure 7-21 shows a rule configured directly against a .NET data source. This simple scenario has a .NET component with a well-defined .NET interface; but of course, this isn't necessarily the case! The rule makes use of a number of methods and uses a few hard-coded values, such as the 21 (which relates to the Minimum Customer Age and is likely to be used in multiple rules, thus leading to an editing nightmare if that changes at some future point).

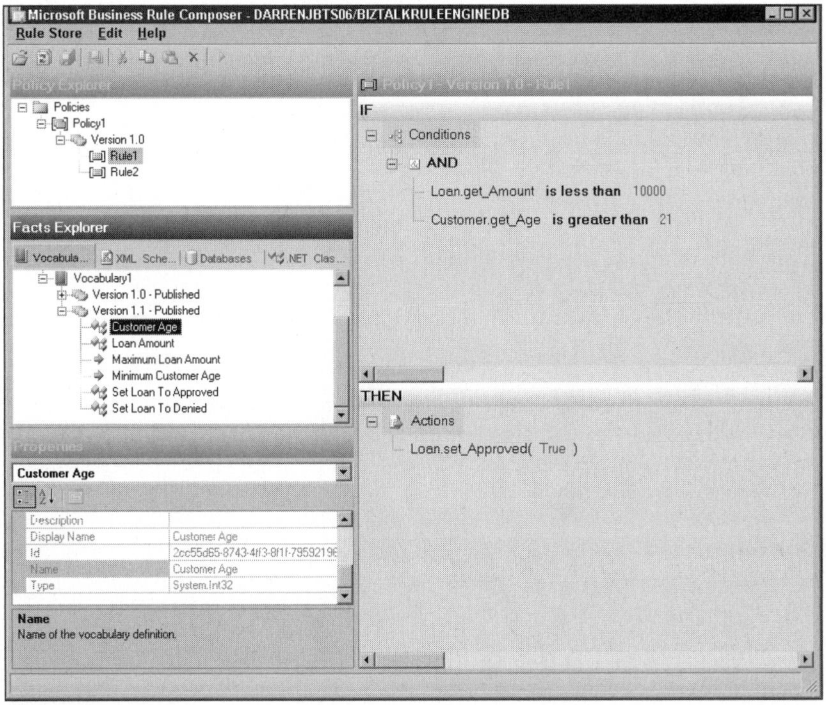

Figure 7-21

Figure 7-22 shows the same rule, but this time using a vocabulary created by a developer for use by a rules author. As you can see, the rule is much easier to read and to construct (using the Vocabulary palette shown on the left side, which is populated with data items expressed in a language familiar to the rules author).

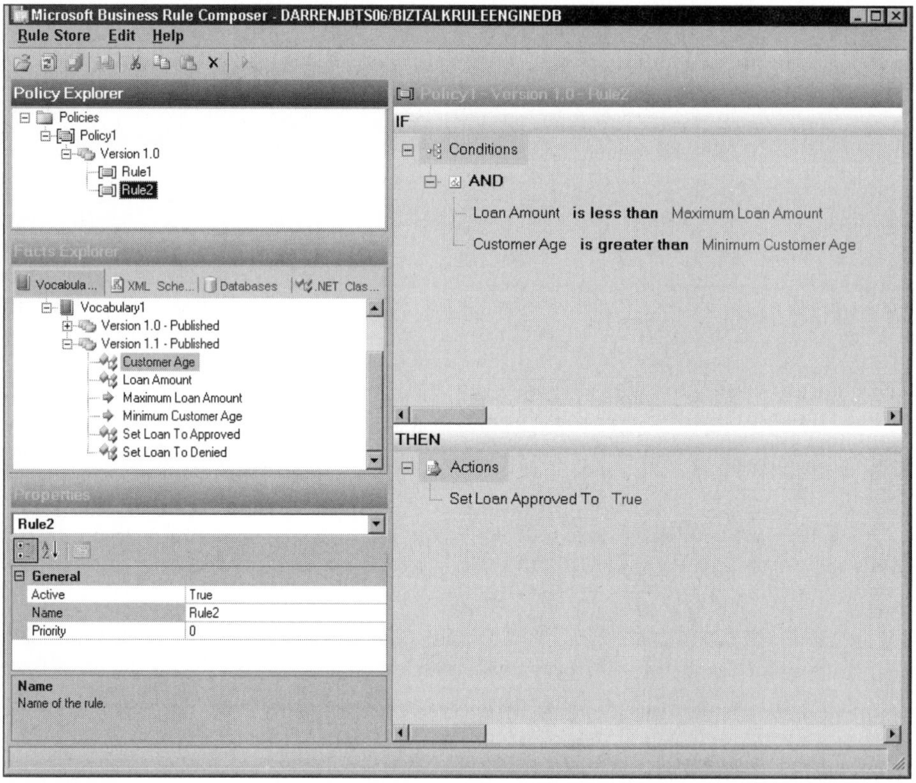

Figure 7-22

The added benefit is that constants have been used to represent the maximum loan amount and minimum customer age, instead of hard-coded values. Therefore, you can keep consistent values for such values that are likely to be shared across rules, and if in the future one of these values needs to be raised, it can be changed in one place.

You can also use .NET class members to help construct rules. Consider the example shown in Figure 7-23, which uses an Add function. Once dragged on, it then renders each parameter on the rules design surface to allow you to provide the parameters. As you can see in the figure, one of the parameters has been supplied, leaving one more to specify.

You can provide a Toolbox of helper functions to add two numbers together or concatenate strings together or pretty much anything you like. The rules developer can then use these easily when constructing rules.

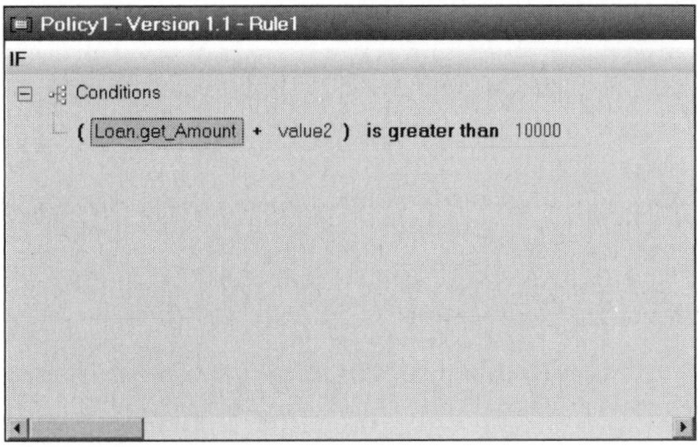

Figure 7-23

By default, you get a Toolbox of functions out of the box, as shown in Figure 7-24, and you can add your own by just writing a standard .NET class and adding the required functions to your vocabulary.

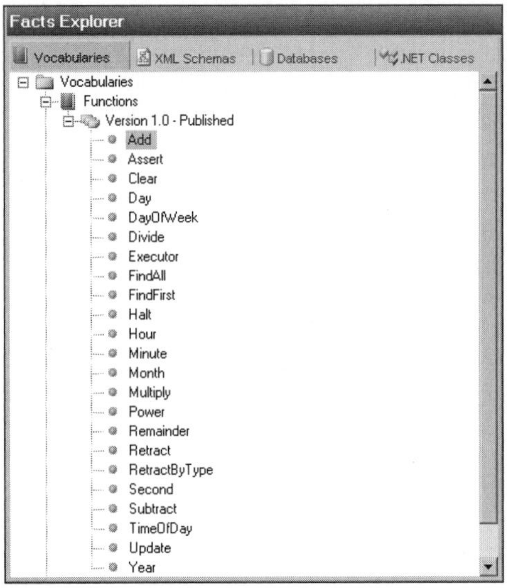

Figure 7-24

Vocabulary API

A question often asked by customers is whether they can construct a vocabulary using code rather than via the Business Rule Composer. The APIs to do this are not documented; therefore, you should consider there to be no supported option to do this.

I see vocabularies as a step performed prior to rules development by developers to provide a *palette* of data and operations that can be leveraged from business rules. The Business Rule Composer provides a helpful interface by which to do this (which should keep you from wanting to create vocabularies manually).

Hosting

The BRE is host agnostic in that it can be hosted in any process, be it BizTalk or a custom application. BizTalk is the natural host and provides deep integration both with the runtime and administration tools.

Although rehostable, the BRE is licensed along with BizTalk Server. Licensing it for use outside of BizTalk might be impractical because of licensing costs. However, using the Rules API, which we cover throughout this chapter, you can invoke rules in any application. Note that the `Policy` class does, however, require the Rules Engine Update Service to be running.

Testing

Testing is an important part of business rules and can be done in two main ways:

❑   BRE authors and developers can test rules in the comfort of the Rules Composer by using the Test Policy feature.

❑   Developers can use test rules by using the `PolicyTester` class.

Both of these methods enable you to test unpublished and undeployed rules, whereas the usual rules execution approach requires that rules be both published and deployed.

Test Policy

To display the Test Policy dialog box, shown in Figure 7-25, right-click a rules policy version in the Policy Explorer and choose Test Policy.

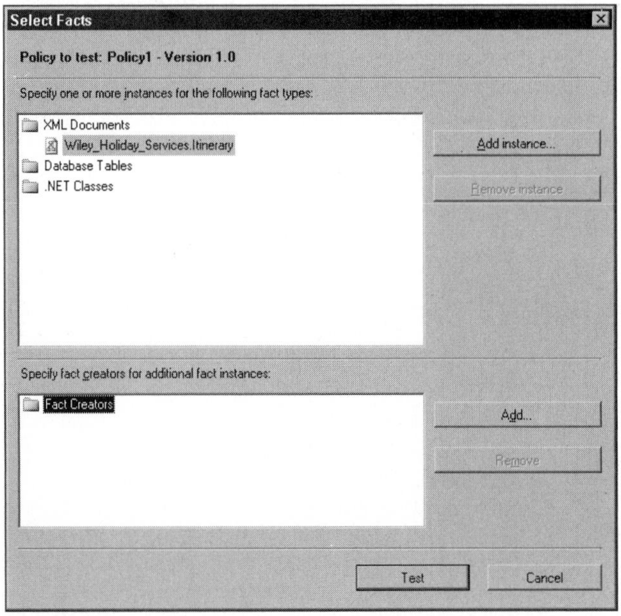

Figure 7-25

344

All the fact types required for the rules policy are displayed, and you can provide instances of these fact types to be used to test the policy. XML- and database-based fact types can be provided automatically by the tool.

To browse to an XML file or select a SQL Server database (or so forth), click Add Instance. If you want to use a .NET-based fact, however, you need to provide a custom fact creator. The custom fact creator will create these types, initialize them, and return them so that they can be asserted into the BRE. Of course, you can use a custom fact creator to assert database and XML facts as required. (You could, perhaps, have a fact creator for each type of test, each asserting different data to produce different results.)

Custom fact creators are straightforward to write and must implement the IFactCreator interface. An example of a custom fact creator is shown here:

```
public class CustomerFactCreator : IFactCreator
{
  object[] IFactCreator.CreateFacts(RuleSetInfo ruleSetInfo)
  {
    object[] facts = new object[2];
    facts[0] = new LoanFacts.Customer(1, "Darren", 28, "Low", 20000);
    facts[1] = new LoanFacts.Loan(5000, 24, false, System.DateTime.Now);
    return facts;
  }

  Type[] IFactCreator.GetFactTypes(RuleSetInfo ruleSetInfo)
  {
     return new Type[] { typeof(LoanFacts.Customer),typeof(LoanFacts.Loan) };
  }
}
```

Whichever approach you use, after a test has been executed, the results are displayed in a fairly complex form (in much the same way as with the Tracking Interceptor covered later in this chapter). The results provide complete details on which facts were asserted, which rules were fired, and so on. However, this type of output is best suited for developers rather than business users.

Figure 7-26 shows an example of the test output.

The PolicyTester Class

As discussed later in this chapter, we usually use the Policy class to execute a rules policy. However, such use requires that a policy be both published and deployed. Therefore, this execution style doesn't prove particularly useful during development when you don't want to be publishing and deploying.

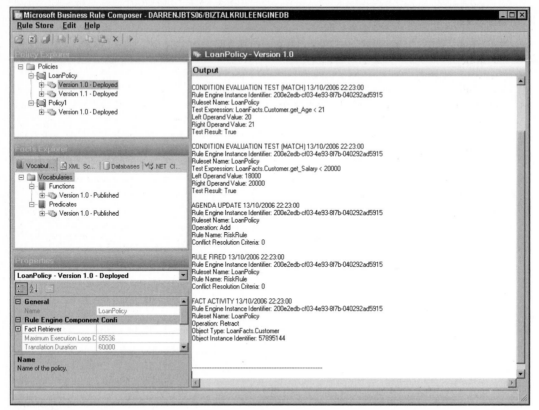

Figure 7-26

The `PolicyTester` class enables you to test policies regardless of whether they are saved, published, or deployed. An example of using the `PolicyTester` class is shown here:

```
// Retrieve the RuleSet
SqlRuleStore RuleStore = new SqlRuleStore("Integrated Security=SSPI;Database=
BizTalkRuleEngineDb;Server=(local)");
        RuleSetInfo RSSetInfo = new RuleSetInfo("Loans", 1, 6);
        RuleSet RSLoans = RuleStore.GetRuleSet(RSSetInfo);

// Configure Short Term Facts
LoanFacts.Customer Customer = new LoanFacts.Customer(1, "Darren", 20, "Low", 19000);
LoanFacts.Loan Loan = new LoanFacts.Loan(7500, 12, false, DateTime.Now, "");
object[] Facts = { Customer, Loan };

using (PolicyTester Tester = new PolicyTester(RSLoans))
{
  DebugTrackingInterceptor Interceptor = new DebugTrackingInterceptor("output.txt");
  Tester.Execute(Facts, Interceptor);
}
```

Invoking Rules

You have two main choices when you are planning to invoke a rules policy from a BizTalk orchestration: the Call Rules shape or a .NET helper class.

The Call Rules shape provides native support for invoking rules policies from BizTalk orchestration and enables you to pass facts required by the rules policy as parameters using a GUI.

BizTalk Server 2004 required that any Call Rules shapes be within an atomic scope (thus incurring an orchestration persistence point each time, which often impaired performance for no direct reason). If you are using BizTalk Server 2004, the advice is to not use the Call Rules shape and instead invoke the BRE directly through an Expression shape or a custom .NET helper class (and thus avoid a persistence point). This restriction was lifted in BizTalk Server 2006, meaning that the Call Rules shape can be used outside of an atomic scope (and thus not incur the persistence point).

In my experience, the Call Rules shape is a bit awkward to use; it will not show the facts required to be *passed* or asserted, but instead requires you to define variables matching the short-term fact types before showing them in the Call Rules Shape user interface, as shown in Figure 7-27.

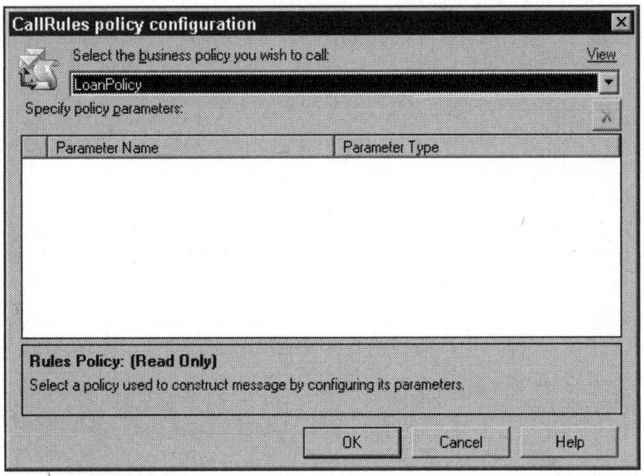

Figure 7-27

The Call Rules shape also doesn't allow you to specify a custom Tracking Interceptor, which, as you will see later in this chapter, can make rules development trickier than it needs to be. However, the Call Rules shape does enable use of the Health and Activity Tracking (HAT) interceptor, which allows past rules execution to be viewed (although I find this cumbersome and prefer the custom Tracking Interceptor approach).

In light of this, I prefer to use a helper .NET class that invokes the rules policy and in turn call this from a BizTalk orchestration. An additional benefit is that this .NET class can then be used outside of BizTalk for, as an example, development and unit testing purposes.

.NET Helper Class

Invoking a rules policy via code is a simple affair and is done using the `Policy` class located in the `Microsoft.RuleEngine` namespace and assembly. The following code shows how a policy can be retrieved, facts asserted, and then executed:

```
using (Policy LoanPolicy = new Policy("LoanPolicy"))
{
  // Create .NET Classes used as facts
  LoanFacts.Customer Customer = new LoanFacts.Customer(1, "Darren", 20, "Low", 19000);
  LoanFacts.Loan Loan = new LoanFacts.Loan(7500, 12, false, DateTime.Now, "");

  // Create a TypedXmlDocument to be used as a fact
  XmlDocument docMyXLANGMessage = MyXLANGMessage;
  TypedXmlDocument typedXmlDocument = new    TypedXmlDocument("WileyFinancialServices.
CreditInformation", docMyXLANGMessage);

  object[] Facts = { Customer, Loan, typedXmlDocument };

  // Execute the Loan Policy passing the facts
  DebugTrackingInterceptor Interceptor = new DebugTrackingInterceptor("output.txt");

  LoanPolicy.Execute(Facts,Interceptor);
}
```

In this example, both .NET classes and an XML message are used as facts. You can, of course, pass any combinations of facts as required by your policy.

You might have noticed the use of the C# `using` statement in the preceding code when constructing a `Policy` class. The `using` statement will call `Dispose` on the object provided to the `using` statement.

The `Policy` class implements `IDispose`, and `Dispose` must, therefore, be called on all policy instances to ensure that each is returned to the policy cache immediately instead of waiting for finalization. I have seen numerous performance problems caused by the policy cache being artificially starved due to unused policies not being returned in a timely manner.

You might be thinking that you can achieve the above from within an Expression shape. You can, but you'll run into problems when you need to assert more than one fact, which in turn requires you to create an array of facts. However, the X# programming language used within Expression shapes has no support for arrays, meaning that you cannot build a fact array used to assert multiple facts. However, in BizTalk Server 2006 you can pass multiple parameters to the `Execute` method of the `Policy` class.

If you are using BizTalk Server 2004, you do not have the parameter option, but you can instead use an `ArrayList` to hold your facts and then use the `ToArray()` method on your `ArrayList` when calling `execute` on the rules engine, as follows:

```
LoanPolicy.Execute(MyFactsArrayList.ToArray());
```

Call Rules Shape

The Call Rules shape is fairly straightforward, but a few tricks are required. First, you drag the Call Rules shape onto your orchestration design surface. Double-click the Call Rules shape to bring up the Configuration dialog box. You then select from all deployed policies and configure the policy parameters (short-terms facts). The Configuration dialog box doesn't show all the possible parameters required by the rules policy. Instead, it requires you to have previous knowledge of the fact types required, in the same way as when you invoke the rules policy via code.

You must define orchestration variables matching the fact types for the parameters to be *shown* in the Configuration dialog box and to be able to pass them. Standard orchestration messages can be passed in place of `TypedXmlDocuments`, but .NET classes must be constructed and initialized, along with `DataConnection`, `TypedDataTable`, and `TypedDataRow` fact types.

.NET class facts are straightforward. You just create the variables of the correct types. However, a few tricks are required for data- and XML-based facts, as covered in the following subsections.

Data Facts

This example shows how to pass a `DataConnection`, but the principles are the same for `TypedDataTable`- and `TypedDataRow`-based facts.

The first step is to define two orchestration variables: one of type `System.Data.SqlClient .SqlConnection` and the other of type `Microsoft.RuleEngine.DataConnection` (which will itself use the `SqlConnection` to perform the SQL query). To do this, you first have to add project assembly references to the `System.Data` and `Microsoft.RuleEngine` assemblies.

Figure 7-28 shows the variables and the properties of the `DataConnection`-based variable.

Both variables must be initialized. The `SqlConnection` needs to be passed a connection string, which is shown hard-coded here but should instead be stored in a configuration file (or preferably the SSO store, which we cover later in this book). The `DataConnection` must be configured to point at the right database and table.

This code is shown here and will be placed in an Expression shape on your orchestration:

```
AdventureWorksConn = new System.Data.SqlClient.SqlConnection("Initial
Catalog=AdventureWorks;Data Source=(local);Trusted_Connection=yes");

DataConnectionAdventureWorks = new Microsoft.RuleEngine.DataConnection
("AdventureWorks","Product", AdventureWorksConn);
```

After this has been done, you can double-click your Call Rules shape and select the policy. A matching policy parameter will display, as shown in Figure 7-29.

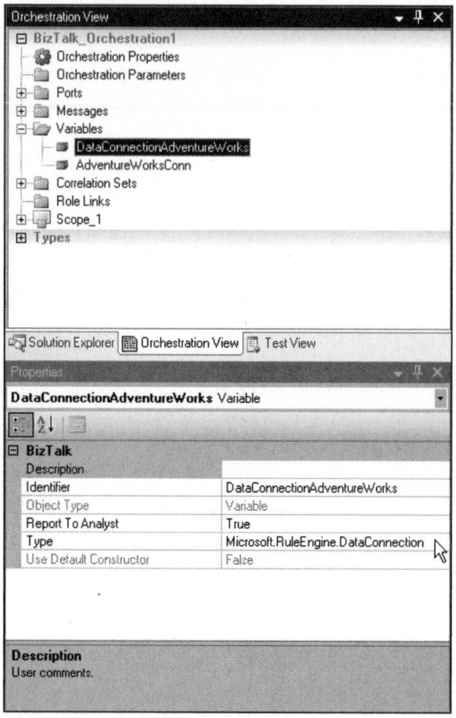

Figure 7-28

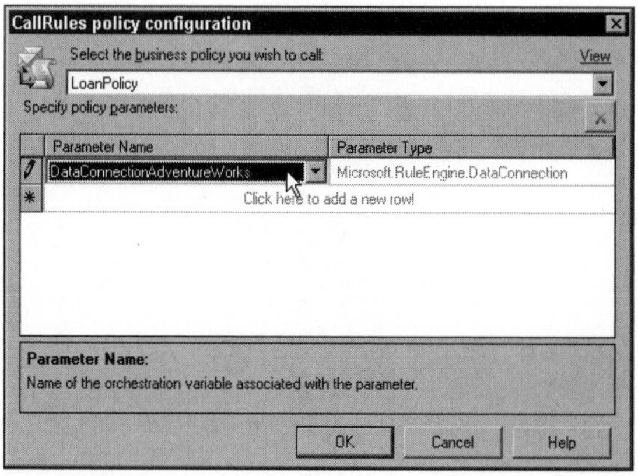

Figure 7-29

XML Facts

This example shows how you can pass an orchestration message to a rules policy expecting a
TypedXmlDocument.

BizTalk Server 2006 seems to do "the right thing." BizTalk Server 2004, however, has an issue that confuses everyone the first time around: You have an orchestration message of the right schema type, but the Call Rules shape refuses to let you pass the message. The problem comes down to the Rule Composer having .NET type for the XML message that differs from the BizTalk orchestration, so the Call Rules Configuration dialog box cannot match the two and, therefore, doesn't display any valid parameters. If you have this problem, ensure that the document type on the XML schema in the Rules Composer is the same as the fully qualified name of your schema.

Figure 7-30 shows the fully qualified name of a schema. To view this, select your schema file in Solution Explorer and review the Properties pane. Here you can see that the fully qualified name is set to `Wiley_Holiday_Services.Itinerary`.

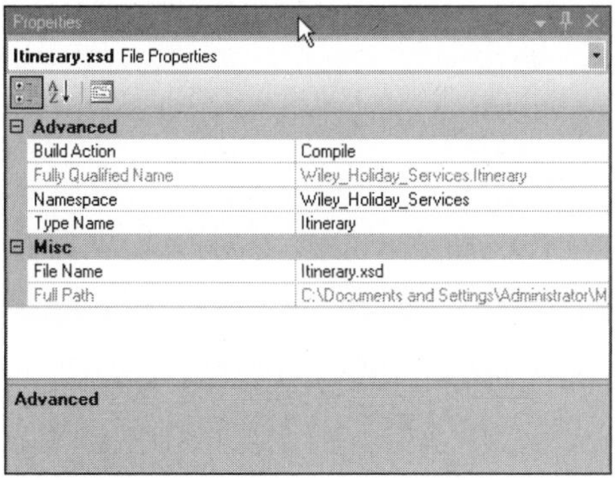

Figure 7-30

Switching to the Rule Composer, select the schema in the XML Schema Facts Explorer pane and ensure that the Document Type property matches (as it does in Figure 7-31).

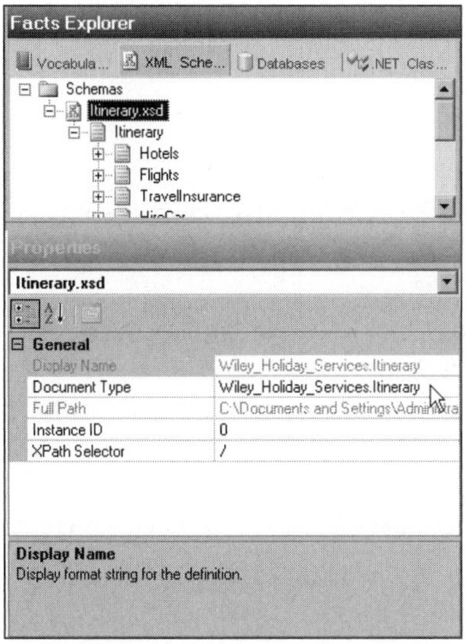

Figure 7-31

Then, when configuring the Call Rules shape, you will see the matching message type appear, as shown in Figure 7-32.

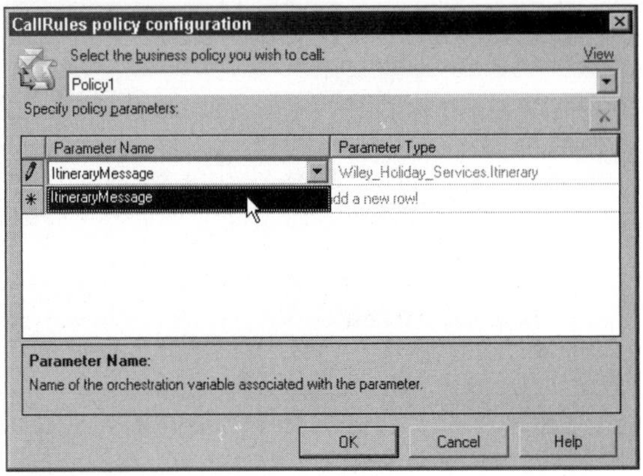

Figure 7-32

Problems

If you run into problems when invoking rules where nothing appears to happen, this usually comes down to the right facts being asserted into the BRE working memory. Utilizing a Tracking Interceptor, as covered later in this chapter, is key to understanding what is being asserted into the BRE, which you can then compare with what is expected.

You can review the expected fact types by reviewing the policy XML by exporting it using the Rules API or by clicking the View hyperlink on the Call Rules Configuration dialog box. Figure 7-32 shows the hyperlink.

The easier option is to use the Rules Composer. Just select the fact type in the Facts Explorer and review the Properties pane to see what type is expected. Figure 7-33 shows a DataTable fact type.

Note that it's set to a DataTable, and therefore expects a fact of type TypedDataTable to be asserted. However, it also expects that the DataSet held within the DataTable should be called BAMPrimaryImport. Therefore, the fact should be constructed as follows to be successfully used by the BRE at execution time:

```
DataSet ds = new DataSet("BAMPrimaryImport");
da.Fill(ds,"bam_Itinerary_Completed");
TypedDataTable tdt = new TypedDataTable(ds.Tables["bam_Itinerary_Completed "]);
engine.Assert(tdt);
```

The same principles apply to other fact types. This debugging technique can save you many frustrating hours!

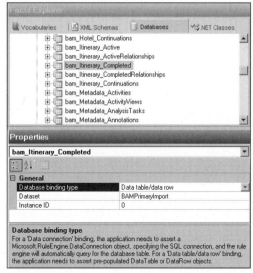

Figure 7-33

Short-Term/Long-Term Facts

Short-term facts are the facts asserted into the BRE prior or during rules execution. After the rules have been executed, the facts are removed from the BRE working memory. Short-term facts are most often used because rules typically rely on instance data passed in at execution time. For scenarios in which the same data is required for many BRE executions, long-term facts should be considered, because the setup cost for these facts will be less because they will be cached across BRE execution.

Retrieving data required for rules execution each and every time a rule is executed is perfectly acceptable for small-scale solutions, but can quickly become a major overhead when it's performed many hundreds of times a second, for example.

Short-term facts, as previously mentioned, are asserted into the engine before execution of the rules and are provided each and every time; they are ideally suited for data that changes frequently or is specific to the request being processed. Long-term facts are suitable for scenarios in which different rules policy executions require the same fact data and that fact data is static or at least changes rarely.

Long-term facts are provided by implementing a custom Fact Retriever, which when configured causes the BRE to call into the Fact Retriever at execution time. The Fact Retriever can assert long-term facts into the BRE that will subsequently be cached by the BRE for future use.

The BRE will still call into your custom Fact Retriever on subsequent rules execution to give you the chance to update stale long-term facts. For example, you might want to use a `DataTable` as a long-term fact but update it every 12 hours.

Long-Term Fact Retriever Example

The example shown here is a Long-Term Fact Retriever implemented for a `DataTable`. In this scenario, each rules policy execution requires the same core data held in a database. To improve performance, this data is retrieved the first time the BRE is executed and then cached for later calls.

In this scenario, you update the `DataTable` long-term fact every 6 hours to reflect perhaps the data changing every 6 hours. Of course, you can customize this to suit your scenario.

To create a Long-Term Fact Retriever, you must first implement the `IFactRetriever` interface, which includes one method called `UpdateFacts`. The `UpdateFacts` method has three parameters, of which `factsHandleIn` is particularly interesting.

The `factsHandleIn` parameter is typed as object and can, therefore, hold anything you want to be passed in to your Fact Retriever. In this example, you store a `System.DataTime` instance that indicates to us when the `DataTable` was last refreshed.

The following example also retracts any previous `DataTable` instances that have been asserted. you do this using the `RetractByType` method instead of the `Retract` method, because you don't maintain a reference to previous `DataTable` instances. You could instead use a simple struct or class containing the `DateTime` and `DataTable` properties and return this as the `factsHandle` that will be passed in on subsequent calls. Then, as you have a reference to the `DataTable` instance, you can retract it directly instead of retracting all instances of a given type.

```
using System.Data;
using System.Data.SqlClient;
using Microsoft.RuleEngine;
public class DBLongTermFactRetriever : IFactRetriever
{
object IFactRetriever.UpdateFacts(  RuleSetInfo ruleSetInfo,
                                    RuleEngine engine,
                                    object factsHandleIn)
{
    object factsHandleOut = null;

    if (factsHandleIn == null)
    {
        // Facts have not been retrieved before
        factsHandleOut = RetrieveFacts(ruleSetInfo, engine, factsHandleIn);
    }
    else
    {
        // If the DataTable was last updated more than 6 hours ago
        // we need to refresh
        System.DateTime LastTimeFactsWereUpdated = (DateTime)factsHandleIn;
        TimeSpan ts = DateTime.Now.Subtract(LastTimeFactsWereUpdated);

        if (ts.Hours > 6)
        {
            // Facts are stale, update them
            factsHandleOut = RetrieveFacts(ruleSetInfo, engine, factsHandleIn);
        }
```

```
            else
            {
                // Facts are not stale, carry on using them.
                factsHandleOut = factsHandleIn;
            }
        }

        return factsHandleOut;
    }

    private object RetrieveFacts(   RuleSetInfo ruleSetInfo,
                                    RuleEngine engine,
                                    object factsHandleIn)
    {
        object factsHandleOut = null;

        using (SqlConnection Conn = new SqlConnection( _ConnectionString ))
        {
            using (SqlDataAdapter da = new SqlDataAdapter("SELECT * FROM Customer",Conn))
            {
                // Ensure that the DataSet name matches the Facts Explorer DataSet Name
                DataSet ds = new DataSet("RulesEngineDemo");
                // Fill the DataSet
                da.Fill(ds,"Customer");

                // If we have asserted a long term fact before we should
                // Retract it to ensure we don't leave stale copies in the
                // engines working memory
                if (factsHandleIn != null)
                {
                    engine.RetractByType(new DataRowType("Customer", "RulesEngineDemo"));
                }

                // Wrap with a TypedDataTable and assert into the rules engine
                TypedDataTable tdt = new TypedDataTable(ds.Tables["Customer"]);
                engine.Assert(tdt);

                factsHandleOut = System.DateTime.Now;
            }
        }

        return factsHandleOut;
    }
```

Many Long-Term Fact Retrievers assert a DataConnection, which, as covered previously in this chapter, offers little performance improvement (because you are effectively just caching a SqlConnection rather than the underlying data).

In the preceding example, you assert a Microsoft.RuleEngine.TypedDataSet class into the BRE; the BRE doesn't natively support DataSets but instead must be wrapped with a TypedDataSet.

To configure the BRE to use a Long-Term Fact Retriever , you must configure the appropriate policy via the Rule Composer to use your Fact Retriever. To do this, select the policy version you want to configure. A Fact Retriever property will appear in the Properties window, as shown in Figure 7-34.

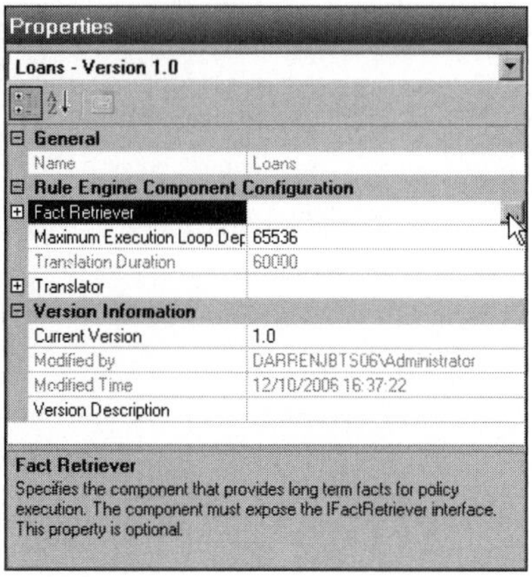

Figure 7-34

Clicking the button, as shown in Figure 7-34, will allow you to select your Custom Fact Retriever assembly; you must ensure that your Fact Retriever assembly has been registered in the Global Assembly Cache (GAC).

When the policy is then deployed, you will find that your Fact Retriever is invoked upon rules execution and will assert the relevant facts into the BRE's working memory. Again, the Debug Interceptor, which we cover in the next section, is invaluable to keep track of what's being asserted and whether the BRE has recognized your fact as something it needs.

The following output shows the `DataTable` being asserted by the Long-Term Fact Retriever, along with a subsequent assertion of a `DataRow` that is asserted as part of the rules evaluation, which in this example utilizes one row from the `DataTable`:

```
FACT ACTIVITY 13/10/2006 15:25:42
Rule Engine Instance Identifier: f3e0a05f-2706-4535-bea2-afaeea1fb8e7
Ruleset Name: Loans
Operation: Assert
Object Type: TypedDataTable:RulesEngineDemo:Customer
Object Instance Identifer: 54861376

FACT ACTIVITY 13/10/2006 15:25:42
Rule Engine Instance Identifier: f3e0a05f-2706-4535-bea2-afaeea1fb8e7
Ruleset Name: Loans
Operation: Assert
Object Type: TypedDataRow:RulesEngineDemo:Customer
Object Instance Identifer: 34723915

CONDITION EVALUATION TEST (MATCH) 13/10/2006 15:25:42
Rule Engine Instance Identifier: f3e0a05f-2706-4535-bea2-afaeea1fb8e7
```

```
Ruleset Name: Loans
Test Expression: TypedDataRow:RulesEngineDemo:Customer.Age < 21
Left Operand Value: 20
Right Operand Value: 21
Test Result: True
```

Tracking Interceptor

When developing and debugging rules, it can sometimes be difficult to understand why the BRE is behaving in the way it is. A Tracking Interceptor enables you to understand exactly what the BRE is doing when executing your rules.

Unfortunately, a custom Tracking Interceptor cannot be configured unless you invoke the BRE directly, which therefore precludes the use of the Call Rules shape. You should consider invoking the BRE directly via .NET code, as covered in the "Invoking Rules" section of this chapter.

The interceptor is incredibly useful for figuring out what the rules engine is doing and why. In my view, you should use it on all BRE projects. It will save you a significant amount of time and hassle.

DebugTrackingInterceptor

A `DebugTrackingInterceptor` ships with the BRE and is located in the standard `Microsoft.RuleEngine` namespace. This Tracking Interceptor can log tracking information to a text file on disk only.

To make use of the interceptor, you must first initialize the interceptor as shown here by passing a file-name for trace output to be written to:

```
DebugTrackingInterceptor interceptor = new
DebugTrackingInterceptor("TrackingOutput.txt");
```

You must then configure the BRE to make use of the interceptor by passing it as a parameter to the `Policy.Execute` method, as follows:

```
DebugTrackingInterceptor Interceptor = new DebugTrackingInterceptor("output.txt");
Policy Policy = new Policy("Policy1");
Policy.Execute(Facts,Interceptor);
```

Once configured in this way, all BRE execution will be written to the file provided in the interceptor constructor. An example of the trace you can expect is shown here:

```
Rule Engine Instance Identifier: 159a0785-4cd6-4c45-bd17-dda0b7c0aa16
Ruleset Name: Policy1
Operation: Assert
Object Type: LoanFacts.Customer
Object Instance Identifier: 17059405

CONDITION EVALUATION TEST (MATCH) 16/09/2006 20:46:02
Rule Engine Instance Identifier: 159a0785-4cd6-4c45-bd17-dda0b7c0aa16
```

```
Ruleset Name: Policy1
Test Expression: LoanFacts.Customer.get_Age > 21
Left Operand Value: 28
Right Operand Value: 21
Test Result: True
```

Custom Interceptors

The built-in `DebugTrackingInterceptor` works well but can prove awkward to use during development and testing because of its dependency on writing trace to file. I find it much easier to display rules output as debug output using, for instance, DebugView from Windows Sysinternals (`www.microsoft.com/technet/sysinternals`).

You can fairly simply display rules output as debug output by creating a custom interceptor. Of course, you can use this approach to write trace to any destination of your choosing, but we'll stick to debug output for now.

Implementation of a custom interceptor requires that you implement the `IRuleSetTrackingInterceptor` interface, which contains a number of methods relating to the different BRE execution stages. These are invoked by the BRE at the appropriate execution time and are listed here.

To help with understanding the examples, the fact in the following trable was asserted into the Rules Engine.

Customer	Name = "Darren Jefford" Age = "28"

`TrackConditionEvaluation` — This method is called when the BRE is evaluating a condition and provides the expression being evaluated and the associated operands as parameters, as follows:

```
CONDITION EVALUATION TEST (MATCH) 16/09/2006 20:46:02
Rule Engine Instance Identifier: 159a0785-4cd6-4c45-bd17-dda0b7c0aa16
Ruleset Name: Policy1
Test Expression: LoanFacts.Customer.get_Age > 21
Left Operand Value: 28
Right Operand Value: 21
Test Result: True
```

❑   `TrackRuleSetEngineAssociation` — This method is called when a `RuleSet` is associated with a `RuleEngine` instance and provides information such as the `Policy Version`, `LastModified DateTime`, and so on. The built-in `DebugTrackingInterceptor` doesn't log this information; if you need it, however, you can do it via your own interceptor.

❑   `TrackRuleFiring` — This method is called when the BRE is executing a rule that has been placed on the agenda following the match/conflict resolution stage. The rule name and conflict resolution details are provided as parameters, as follows:

```
RULE FIRED 16/09/2006 20:46:03
Rule Engine Instance Identifier: 159a0785-4cd6-4c45-bd17-dda0b7c0aa16
```

```
Ruleset Name: Policy1
Rule Name: Rule1
Conflict Resolution Criteria: 0
```

❑   `TrackFactActivity` — This method is called when the BRE performs any fact activity, such as a fact being asserted or retracted. The fact operation and object information are provided as parameters, as follows:

```
FACT ACTIVITY 16/09/2006 20:46:02
Rule Engine Instance Identifier: 159a0785-4cd6-4c45-bd17-dda0b7c0aa16
Ruleset Name: Policy1
Operation: Assert
Object Type: LoanFacts.Customer
Object Instance Identifier: 17059405
```

❑   `TrackAgendaUpdate` — This method is called when the BRE updates the agenda to either add or remove a rule. The agenda operation and rule information are provided as parameters, as follows:

```
AGENDA UPDATE 16/09/2006 20:46:03
Rule Engine Instance Identifier: 159a0785-4cd6-4c45-bd17-dda0b7c0aa16
Ruleset Name: Policy1
Operation: Add
Rule Name: Rule1
Conflict Resolution Criteria: 0
```

Sample Custom Interceptor

I often use the following custom interceptor, which outputs all information via debug output using `System.Diagnostics.Debug.WriteLine()`. The code is provided here for reference, and as you can see, it's pretty straightforward.

The output layout replicates the output provided by the built-in `DebugTrackingInterceptor`. You can, of course, modify this to make it more succinct.

```
namespace RulesEngineDemo
{
    using Microsoft.RuleEngine;
    using System.Diagnostics;

    class RulesDebugInterceptor : IRuleSetTrackingInterceptor
    {
        public void SetTrackingConfig(TrackingConfiguration trackingConfig)
        {
        }

        public void TrackRuleSetEngineAssociation(RuleSetInfo ruleSetInfo,
Guid ruleEngineGuid)
        {
            _RuleSetName = ruleSetInfo.Name;
            _RuleEngineGuid = ruleEngineGuid;

            OutputTraceHeader("RULESET ENGINE ASSOCIATION");
```

```
        }

        public void TrackFactActivity(FactActivityType activityType, string
classType, int classInstanceId)
        {
            OutputTraceHeader("FACT ACTIVITY");
            Debug.WriteLine("Operation: " + activityType);
            Debug.WriteLine("Object Type: " + classType);
            Debug.WriteLine("Object Instance Identifer: " + classInstanceId);
        }

        public void TrackConditionEvaluation(string testExpression, string
leftClassType, int leftClassInstanceId, object leftValue, string rightClassType,
int rightClassInstanceId, object rightValue, bool result)
        {
            OutputTraceHeader("CONDITION EVALUATION TEST (MATCH)");
            Debug.WriteLine("Test Expression: " + testExpression);
            Debug.WriteLine("Left Operand Value: " + leftValue);
            Debug.WriteLine("Right Operand Value: " + rightValue);
            Debug.WriteLine("Test Result: " + result);
        }

        public void TrackRuleFiring(string ruleName, object
conflictResolutionCriteria)
        {
            OutputTraceHeader("RULE FIRED");
            Debug.WriteLine("Rule Name: " + ruleName);
            Debug.WriteLine("Conflict Resolution Criteria: " +
conflictResolutionCriteria.ToString());
        }

        public void TrackAgendaUpdate(bool isAddition, string ruleName, object
conflictResolutionCriteria)
        {
            OutputTraceHeader("AGENDA UPDATE");
            Debug.WriteLine("Operation: " + (isAddition ? "Add" : "Remove"));
            Debug.WriteLine("Rule Name: " + ruleName);
            Debug.WriteLine("Conflict Resolution Criteria: "
 conflictResolutionCriteria.ToString());
        }

        private void OutputTraceHeader(string OperationType)
        {
            Debug.WriteLine(String.Format("\n{0} {1}", OperationType,
System.DateTime.Now));
            Debug.WriteLine("Rule Engine Instance Identifier: " + _RuleEngineGuid);
            Debug.WriteLine("Ruleset Name: " + _RuleSetName);
        }

        private string _RuleSetName;
        private Guid _RuleEngineGuid;
    }
}
```

Rule Store

During development, rules need to be stored in a staging area ahead of being made available for execution. The default store for rules is a SQL Server database, which provides a resilient and easy-to-manage location for rules.

Rules policies or rulesets are represented in an XML document, regardless of status, are stored in the `BizTalkRuleEngineDb` database and then within the `re_ruleset` table as an XML blob. During development of a rules policy, the policy is saved within the database, but it is not available until it's explicitly published and then deployed.

The process of publishing makes that version of a rules policy immutable, in that it can no longer be changed, and a new version must be created to introduce changes. At this stage, rules still cannot be executed until they have been deployed. After a policy has been published, it cannot be unpublished. This restriction provides a form of traceability and auditing of the first stage of the rule's life cycle.

The process of deploying makes the rules policy live and ready for execution. The deploy process can be reversed by undeploying the policy. The publishing step can be seen as a staging ground, enabling you to stage a new rules policy before later making it available for execution.

SQL Server is used as the rule store to provide a highly available and shared store for rules between multiple BizTalk servers. If you are hosting the BRE yourself and not using BizTalk, however, you can also make use of a file-based rule store provided via the `FileRuleStore` class.

Updating and Caching Rules

After a rules policy has been deployed, it is available for use. As previously discussed, the ruleset is represented as an XML blob in the `BizTalkRuleEngineDb`. To execute a rules policy, this XML must be ultimately transformed into a Rete network (which we covered at the beginning of this chapter).

The first stage requires retrieval of the XML from the BRE database. An object model is then created by using the Rules API objects, which we cover in the next section (which demonstrates creation of a rule via code rather than via Rules Composer).

After the object model has been created in-memory, a Rete network is then constructed. It is then used to execute rules. The entire process is called *translation*, and for obvious reasons represents a preprocessing overhead. To counter this overhead, BizTalk takes one of two approaches: the Rules Engine Update Service, which is registered as part of the BizTalk install, or a BRE cache.

The Rules Engine Update Service runs on all BizTalk servers in the BizTalk group and caches the rules policy XML for any BRE invocations on a given server. This optimization means that any rules policies being executed retrieve the XML rules definition locally instead of hitting the SQL Server each time.

To allow for live rules deployment without incurring downtime (such as stopping and starting BizTalk to flush the cache), the service subscribes to policy deploy and undeploy events. When it detects changes, it updates the cache as required.

The Rules Engine Update Service is configured with a default 60 second refresh interval; so if you deploy a new rules policy version, ensure you wait for 60 seconds before assuming that the new policy is in effect. (The refresh interval is configurable via the `PollingInterval` registry entry located under `HKEY_LOCAL_MACHINE\SOFTWARE\Microsoft\BusinessRules\3.0`.)

As mentioned previously, the second approach is a BRE cache. This cache holds instances of the underlying `RulesEngine` class, which are used directly via the `Policy` class or the Call Rules shape in BizTalk orchestration.

`RulesEngine` classes are not designed to be used concurrently, so one instance is required for each caller. Therefore, the cache can hold multiple `RulesEngine` instances for a given rules policy and serve them up as required.

You can construct a `Policy` class or use the Call Rules shape (both perform the same underlying actions) to initially inspect the cache. If a `RulesEngine` instance is available from the cache, it will be returned for use. If one is not available, the cache will construct a new `RulesEngine` instance and return it.

The `RulesEngine` instance is effectively caching the results of translation. This significantly reduces the overhead associated with preparing for rules execution. For solutions that use the BRE, tuning this cache is critical to achieving the best possible performance. We cover how to tune the BRE cache in Chapter 9.

Custom Rules Editor

Many customers that I've worked with have ended up with a requirement to develop a custom UI with which their *businesspeople* can construct rules. We do, of course, have the Business Rule Composer for this purpose, but in some cases customers require a more restricted or cutdown design (to perhaps make it more suitable for a very nontechnical audience). Such a requirement should not be taken lightly, because rules editors not only enable you create new rules but should also perform validation (such as protecting rules designers from creating infinite loops).

The creation of rules via an API is fully supported and is provided within the `Microsoft.RuleEngine` namespace. Via this API, you can produce, for example, an ASP.NET Web application that significantly simplifies the rule design experience.

Rules creation is pretty straightforward and easy to understand using the API. Consider the following code. It implements a rule that uses a .NET class called `Customer` and then deploys the rule to the SQL-based rule store ready for execution. (We cover the custom deployment code in the next section.)

The `PolicyTester` class covered previously in this chapter could be used to directly execute the `RuleSet` when constructed instead of requiring formal deployment, which is used here:

The following rule:

```
IF Customer.Age < 21 AND Customer.Salary < "20,000"
THEN Customer.LoanRisk = "High"
```

is constructed in this code:

```
// Bind to the Customer class we will use in the Rule
ClassBinding CustomerClassBinding = new ClassBinding(typeof(LoanFacts.Customer));

// Create Member bindings for each of the property "getters"
ClassMemberBinding get_Age = new ClassMemberBinding("get_Age", CustomerClassBinding);
ClassMemberBinding get_Salary = new ClassMemberBinding("get_Salary",
CustomerClassBinding);

// Create Constants used in the expressions
Constant MinimumAge = new Constant(21);
Constant MinimumIncome = new Constant(20000);

// Create IF Expressions
LogicalExpression IFCustomerAge = new LessThan(new UserFunction(get_Age), MinimumAge);
LogicalExpression IFCustomerIncome = new LessThan(new UserFunction(get_Salary),
MinimumIncome);

// Create an AND using both IFs created above
LogicalExpressionCollection MultipleExpressions = new LogicalExpressionCollection();
MultipleExpressions.Add(IFCustomerAge);
MultipleExpressions.Add(IFCustomerIncome);
LogicalAnd ANDExpression = new LogicalAnd(MultipleExpressions);

// Create Member bindings for the Method called by the Action
ArgumentCollection argList = new ArgumentCollection();
argList.Add(new Constant("High"));
ClassMemberBinding set_LoanRisk = new ClassMemberBinding("set_LoanRisk",
CustomerClassBinding, argList);

// Create THEN part
ActionCollection THENActions = new ActionCollection();
THENActions.Add(new UserFunction(set_LoanRisk));

// Compose the Rule using the parts
Rule RiskRule = new Rule("RiskRule", 0, ANDExpression, THENActions);

VersionInfo VersionInf = new VersionInfo("Loan Rules", System.DateTime.Now, "Darren
Jefford", 1, 0);

// Create the RuleSet and add the rule
RuleSet LoanRS = new RuleSet("LoanPolicy", VersionInf);
LoanRS.Rules.Add(RiskRule);

// Publish and Deploy the Rule to the SqlRuleStore
IRuleSetDeploymentDriver RSDeployDriver = Configuration.GetDeploymentDriver();
SqlRuleStore SqlStore = (SqlRuleStore)RSDeployDriver.GetRuleStore();

// Add the RuleSet, and publish them (optional);
SqlStore.Add(LoanRS, true);

// Now deploy the RuleSet (optional);
RuleSetInfoCollection RSInfo = SqlStore.GetRuleSets("LoanPolicy",
RuleStore.Filter.LatestPublished);
RSDeployDriver.Deploy(RSInfo);
```

After this code executes, it is then resident in the SQL Rules database and is visible through the Rules Composer, as shown in Figure 7-35.

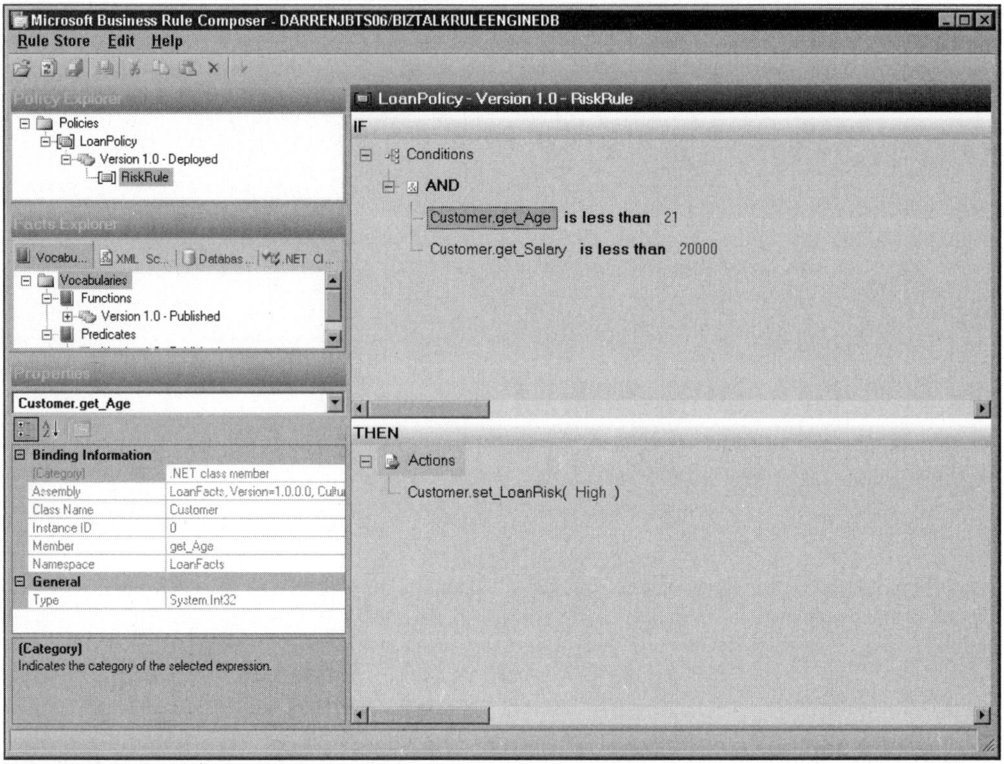

Figure 7-35

The BizTalk 2004 and 2006 SDK have a number of samples underneath the Business Rules subdirectory that demonstrate how to create many rules via the API, including binding to elements of an XML document, a database, and so on.

Deploying Rules

The Rules Engine Deployment Wizard, shown in Figure 7-36, enables you to perform all the deployment tasks required for rules, including deploying a policy that has been published or undeploying a policy that has already been deployed.

You can publish and deploy from within the Business Rules Composer, but in most cases deployment is owned by another department within your organization, which is where the Rules Engine Deployment Wizard comes in.

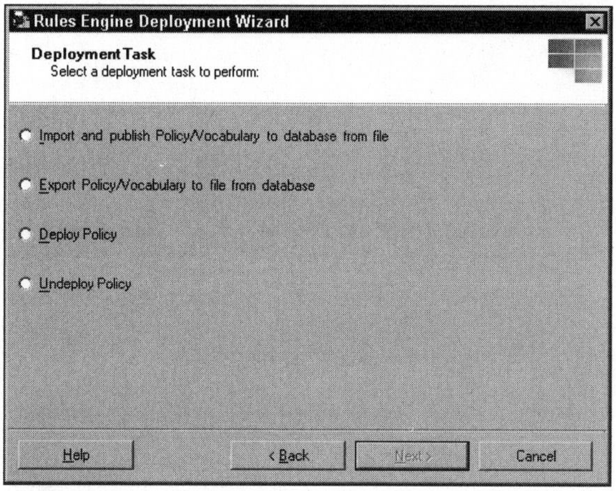

Figure 7-36

The permission to deploy a policy is restricted to BRE administrations; "normal" BRE developers are now allowed to deploy policies. Such permission is granted via the RE_Admin_Users SQL Server role, which by default includes BizTalk administrators.

Programmatically Deploying Rules

The Rules Composer and Deployment Wizard cover almost all deployment cases, apart from a scenario whereby you need to deploy rules from an automated script. A daily build and deployment of your solution is a classic example.

The Deployment Wizard cannot be called from a command line with parameters to automate deployment, which has caused many problems for configuration managers looking to automate the entire build and deployment of a solution.

Although a tool is not available out of the box, you can deploy rules via the Rules Engine API, and specifically the RuleSetDeploymentDriver class. The following example shows the code required to deploy an already published rules policy:

```
RuleSetInfo RSInfo = new RuleSetInfo("Loans",1,8);
IRuleSetDeploymentDriver RSDeployDriver = Configuration.GetDeploymentDriver();
RSDeployDriver.Deploy(RSInfo);
```

This is fine for scenarios in which the rules authors have created their rules and published them ready for deployment. But the more common scenario is a daily build where you have an exported policy file that needs to be added to the rule store, published, and then deployed.

The code required to perform this is shown here. It uses the FileRuleStore to first load the rule's XML into memory, and then walks through all available rulesets (adding, publishing, and deploying in turn).

Note that the `DeploymentDriver` as it's used here will use the configured BRE database, but you can control this to point to any SQL Server rule store, bypassing the server name and database name as constructor parameters.

```
IRuleSetDeploymentDriver RSDeployDriver = Configuration.GetDeploymentDriver();
// Get the default, configured SQL Rule Store
SqlRuleStore SqlStore = (SqlRuleStore)RSDeployDriver.GetRuleStore();

// Load the Exported Rules into a temporary FileRuleStore se we can import
FileRuleStore FileStore = new FileRuleStore("ExportedRules.xml");

RuleSetInfoCollection RSInfoCollection =  FileStore.GetRuleSets(RuleStore.Filter.All);

foreach (RuleSetInfo RSInfo in RSInfoCollection)
{
  // Loop around all RuleSets in FileStore, retrieving them and
  // Adding them to the SQL Store
  RuleSet RS = FileStore.GetRuleSet(RSInfo);

  // Add the RuleSet, and publish them (optional);
  SqlStore.Add(RS,true);

  // Now deploy the RuleSet (optional);
  RSDeployDriver.Deploy(RSInfo);
}
```

Summary

In this chapter, we've covered the principles that underpin the Business Rules Engine to help you understand what happens under the covers and how you should approach the design of your rules.

We've then covered how rules can be constructed using the Rules Composer and the various fact sources that can be used when constructing your rules and how vocabularies can help when creating your rules.

We then finished up by discussing how Long-Term Fact Retrievers can significantly improve the performance of your rules policies if you make use of identical facts regularly. We also covered how the Tracking Interceptor is invaluable when using the Rules Engine.

In the next chapter, we'll cover how your BizTalk solution should be tested and a number of tools that can be used to support your testing.

8

Testing

BizTalk solutions are often deployed at the heart of the business. In many cases, they are the lifeblood of the business. The failure of a BizTalk solution can cause that lifeblood to stop pumping and the business to experience downtime, with a great chance of critical consequences.

Testing can make or break a project, which is ironic because it is all too frequently neglected in software projects. If done well, it can significantly improve the chances of a project's success. If done poorly, then at best your project may not realize its full potential, and at worst it might fail.

As impending project deadlines approach, testing is often one of the first items in the project plan to be squeezed and compromised. Even when project plans are being constructed, testing is often seen as a place to save money. The developers of some projects that rely heavily on BizTalk Server claim it's fine for them to perform only minimal testing because the application is running on top of BizTalk Server, which Microsoft has already thoroughly tested. They think, "What could possibly go wrong?" Well, quite a lot. And when it does, it usually happens quite spectacularly and with maximum visibility to the senior management — and usually just before bonus time!

This chapter examines different testing categories and strategies to de-risk your project and maximize its chances of succeeding. The chapter covers numerous tools and approaches that minimize cost while providing maximum benefit from testing. Although this chapter focuses on testing BizTalk solutions, many of the techniques, tools, and approaches discussed in this chapter can be applied equally well on many server-side software projects that do not use BizTalk Server.

Overview

BizTalk Server is, of course, a server-side product. Server-side code executes under the most extreme conditions. The entire software stack contains many moving parts, from the application right down to the software drivers that communicate with your hardware. High loads are also induced on the hardware stack, whether it is your disk subsystem, network interfaces, or CPUs. These conditions push the entire platform to its limit.

The testing of server-side code differs significantly from the testing of client-side applications. Therefore, you need to approach testing with an entirely different mind-set. It is true that Microsoft has spent many man-years of effort developing and executing tests that cover myriad scenarios and the many features that the product offers. Microsoft performs a comprehensive set of automated test passes over every day's build during the development cycle. In fact, this is the case for all products that Microsoft develops. In itself, that is a huge number of tests. This testing helps Microsoft ensure that on a daily basis no regressions are made to the BizTalk code base. The level of flexibility that BizTalk offers means that it is highly likely that your exact scenario has not been tested by Microsoft in terms of the way that your scenario uses the product. Of course, your custom code and orchestrations will not have been tested by Microsoft. It's also worth considering that the chances are extremely unlikely that your configuration has been tested using the same device drivers and the same hardware as your production environment.

In many ways, BizTalk is an application server. I'm sure you would not consider deploying an ASP.NET application without an adequate level of testing, and a BizTalk solution is no different. So, while you can rely on the BizTalk platform being solid, the only way to gain the same level of confidence in your solution is to thoroughly test it. A lack of sufficient testing leads to many issues, and those issues typically rear their ugly head when you least want them to, usually in a production environment when the system has maximum visibility to the business and your users. This can reflect badly on both the project team that delivered and supports the application and the product itself. As mentioned previously, a BizTalk application is often deployed at the heart of the enterprise running mission-critical systems. As a consequence of this, an outage in some scenarios can result in catastrophic consequences. With that in mind, the level of testing should reflect the consequences of that system failing.

A while back, I reviewed the testing plan for a mission-critical BizTalk project. I was the architect for a large, high-profile enterprise customer. As an architect, I always consider one of my roles is to de-risk the project from a technical perspective to help ensure the project's success. It was going to be delivered by a consultancy that had won the project in a competitive bid against a number of similar consultancies. In these scenarios, budgets are often tight, and areas of the project sometimes need to be "trimmed" to minimize costs and thus maximize the chance of making a profit.

The plan for this particular project was to perform all the end-to-end functional testing manually using a few dozen test scenarios. This included the visual inspection of messages to validate their correct format. In my experience, sadly, this manual approach to testing is often quite common. The messages' format was a type of flat file, and several hundred different schemas were being used. Therefore, the visual inspection was, to put it politely, a little optimistic! A single test pass had been scheduled in the project plan, to be conducted shortly after the code was completed. If the code were to be changed while fixing bugs, for example, we would have no room for performing another test pass due to the length of time required for a manual test pass. Of course, the reality was that subsequent test passes would be necessary, and this would eat into their profit margin.

The test plan assumed that the solution would be built, tested only once, and then go live. (If only life were that easy!) Sadly, this lack of focus on testing is not unusual. For a mission-critical system, however, this was a train crash waiting to happen. I recommended that the solution should be tested using an automated test approach that could be rerun on demand. It would be used to verify the integrity of the code base, and would be used as a regression test pass whenever the code base was changed. Some interesting discussions followed around what the project budget could accommodate. Adopting an automated test approach was viewed as being over elaborate by the consultancy. They felt that it would require a significant development effort, one that they could not accommodate in their budget. To cut the story short, I ended up building an automated test framework that weekend for the project team.

Two months later, we had more than a thousand automated functional tests! This framework provided comprehensive test coverage and a high level of confidence in the solution.

The project ultimately succeeded. In my opinion, the test strategy that we adopted played a key role in ensuring the project's success. That test framework that I built is called BizUnit and has been freely available for some time now to everyone who values testing and wants to maximize the chances of their BizTalk project succeeding. The goal of BizUnit is quite simply to lower the cost of performing automated testing of BizTalk applications. In fairness to the consultancy, they were new to BizTalk at the time. After they understood what BizUnit brought to the table, they fully embraced it and did an amazing job developing a rich set of test cases. In short, they rapidly became one of the best advocates of the approach.

The point of the story is that you really cannot afford *not* to use an automated testing approach for mission-critical BizTalk applications (or, for that matter, any other mission-critical applications). If the project cannot be delivered at or close to budget with the appropriate level of testing, the project should not be initiated (in my opinion). Also, in my experience, the money and time you put into generating automated test assets are investments. Those investments that you made in test assets will repay you each time you rerun the tests.

When considering testing, it is important to think not only about how you perform your testing (manual or automated) but also about the spectrum of test categories applicable and necessary to de-risk your project and ensure that the solution works as desired. The following are some of the main categories of testing that should be considered for a typical BizTalk Server deployment:

- Unit testing
- Functional testing
- Integration testing
- Performance testing and tuning
- Stress testing
- Overload testing
- User acceptance testing
- Disaster recovery testing/dry runs
- Production support testing

If you read through the list and your immediate reaction was along the lines of, "Wow, that's a lot of test categories; we usually only test the first one or two categories," there is a good chance that you are underinvesting in this critical part of your project life cycle. In fact, you might be increasing your project's risk profile.

Throughout the remainder of this chapter, I cover each of those categories in detail, discussing approaches and tools that will enable you to get the most "bang for your buck" out of your testing budget. Of course, different projects have different risk profiles. If you are building a mission-critical system, chances are you should test every category in the preceding list. However, if you are building a tactical solution that is at the other end of the risk spectrum, you can probably skim on some of the test categories. Which categories you test should be a conscious decision. Whatever your project's profile, you need to ensure that you perform the right level of testing to de-risk it.

The Build Process

Before we delve into the various categories of testing, it's important to understand the context of testing within the build process. A solid testing strategy is an integral part of your development process. Microsoft's philosophy, which is deeply entrenched in all its product groups and consulting organizations that develop large mission-critical solutions, is that the build process is the heartbeat of a project. Without a steady heartbeat, you don't know the health of your project. For all you know, it could be dead. The build process is run on a daily schedule, typically starting between midnight and 2 A.M., and consists of the following steps:

1. The source code is synchronized from the source code repository.

2. The source is compiled.

3. The binaries are packaged ready for deployment, be it scripts or MSIs.

4. The solution or product is deployed to a test rig.

5. A series of build verification tests (BVTs) is run. (These are, of course, automated tests.)

6. The results of the build (including results from the compilation, static code analysis, and a comprehensive set of test results) are published to all members of the team.

Typically, the process will have completed by around 6 A.M., in time for the first members of the team to start work on the new day's build (assuming that the daily build is good). If the build is bad, the team must fix it as soon as possible. If you are using an agile methodology, your build process will be initiated for every check-in to the source code repository, the implications of this are that the amount of time taken to execute your BVTs should be shorter.

The daily build process has many advantages. Aside from providing the heartbeat for the project, it forces integration early in your project cycle. Integration is usually a difficult task. Performing these tasks as early and frequently as possible in the project helps to keep the various streams in sync with each other and helps to reduce the risk of the project. Stress and performance testing are typically outside of the daily build process for smaller projects and typically performed on milestone builds.

The daily build process can be used effectively on BizTalk solutions. However, tasks that are typically left to the end need to be done more iteratively. Deployment is an example of this. Although some might consider developing automated deployment scripts up front to be a bit of a burden, it has huge productivity benefits for the developers and tester. Those investments pay productivity dividends each time they are used. Deployment of BizTalk solutions is a typical example of a task that should be automated. During the development process, you have to deploy and undeploy the solution many times. Typically after doing this a few times, it's pretty obvious that automating the deployment is less time-consuming, less error prone, and a lot more fun! In terms of driving the daily build process, Visual Studio Team System and Team Foundation Server is for many the primary choice. An MSBuild script may be used to drive the steps in the build process. An alternative is to use CruiseControl.Net which is also an excellent option for a continuous integration server that works well for these types of projects. You can download CruiseControl.Net from `http://ccnet.thoughtworks.com`.

The BVTs are functional tests that test the quality of the solution and exercise all the main features. They need to be comprehensive enough to indicate the build quality and catch any issues, yet small enough to execute within the allocated build time.

The composition of the BVT test suite depends on what makes sense for a given project. For most projects, it makes sense to separate the various components of the BVT test suite. As shown in Figure 8-1, the BVT suite may be constructed from the following:

❑ **Unit tests** — Because unit tests typically are the first tests to be developed, ideally these would actually be created before the code has been written, using a test-driven development approach. Adding them into the BVTs during the early stages of a project makes a lot of sense. Typically, during this stage there is little test coverage. As the number of functional tests grows and the test coverage increases, the unit tests may be removed from the BVTs.

❑ **Smoke tests** — These are end-to-end functional tests that test the basic functionality of your solution. If these fail, something is seriously wrong. These can usually be run relatively quickly.

❑ **Functional tests** — The functional tests again target end-to-end scenarios, but test *all* the scenarios. For larger projects, it might make sense to further categorize these test cases. Once your solution has been signed off as functionally correct, this test suite will be locked down.

❑ **Regression verification tests** — As solution bugs are found and fixed, test cases should be added to verify that the bug is fixed. These tests are intended to prevent a regression from being introduced back into the solution at a later time. They will typically be edge cases that were not covered in the functional test cases. The regression test suite will grow even after your solution has been deployed in production, if new bugs are discovered and fixed.

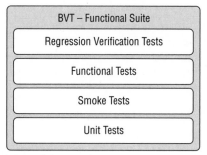

Figure 8-1

For larger projects, the BVTs might be a subset of the full set of functional tests (due to the length of time that they take to run), whereas for smaller projects they will constitute the entire set of functional tests. Of course, to make all this possible, the entire process needs to be automated. Because the focus of this chapter is on testing, this means that your functional tests need to be automated.

Unit Testing

The first of these test categories is unit testing. Unit tests are targeted at the component level. They are tests that typically developers should write, maintain, and run to give them confidence that their components are working correctly before they check in their code changes to the source control system.

As already mentioned, if you are using a test-driven development approach, you will actually develop the unit tests before the code is written, so you will start with your unit tests failing and make the pass by implementing the code. In my view, mock objects provide a powerful tool when writing unit test cases. Mocks allow you to mock up dependencies and thereby enable you to test components in isolation from each other. Mock objects behave and look like the real objects; your component(s) can interact with them as though they were the real thing. You can set expectations on them to define how your component should interact with them. The expectations define which methods should be called, the parameters passed to them, and what the mock will return. At the end of the unit test case, you can ask the mocks to verify that the expectations were met. Failure to meet the expectations will cause a test case to fail. This often means a slightly different way of developing and can be a little alien at first, but it pays huge dividends. In my opinion, RhinoMocks is the best mock library for .NET 2.0 and can be downloaded from `www.codeproject.com/useritems/Rhino_Mocks_22.asp`.

A good unit test should run quickly and clearly indicate whether it has passed or failed. The following are examples where a developer should consider writing a unit test case in the context of a BizTalk solution:

- ❑ Custom helper or utility libraries used by pipeline components, orchestrations, or other components within your solution.

- ❑ Pipeline components. Often, it may be appropriate to test pipeline components independently of BizTalk if the functionality of the component is complex. As mentioned in Visual Studio 2005 Unit Testing and NUnit, the BizTalk SDK contains a tool to help test pipeline components, located at `%PROGRAMFILES%\Microsoft BizTalk Server 2006\SDK\Utilities\PipelineTools\Pipeline.exe`.

Unit testing should be well understood and should be a practice your development team follows already. Some great tools help minimize the overhead of creating, running, and managing unit tests. These tools include Visual Studio 2005 Unit Testing and NUnit. Generally, you would expect developers to run the unit tests (prior to checking their code into the source code repository) for their functional area and any unit tests that they believe relevant to their code check-in.

In case you have not come across either of these tools, the following code illustrates part an NUnit test to validate that a stream compression utility is working as expected. This test is one of many tests for the component. It just tests that a given data stream can be compressed and then uncompressed without any binary differences. This example demonstrates how to use NUnit. The class containing the tests is decorated with the `TestFixture` attribute (if you are using Visual Studio Unit Testing you will decorate your test classes with the TestClass attribute); each method that represents a test is decorated with the `Test` attribute (or the TestMethod attribute for Visual Studio). The `SetUp` attribute identifies the methods that NUnit needs to execute prior to any tests within that class. This is where you place your initialization code. NUnit categorizes test methods as successful if they do not throw an exception outside the scope of the method. The framework contains many helper utilities, such as the `Assert` class used here to check that the return value of a method is the value expected.

```
...
using NUnit.Framework;

namespace BizTalkUnitTests
{
    [TestFixture]
    public class MessageCompressTests
    {
        MessageCompressUtil mcu = new MessageCompressUtil();

        [SetUp]
        public void Init()
        {
```

```
        mcu.Initialize(10);
    }

    [Test]
    public void BasicCompressTest001()
    {
        using (Stream rawData =
            File.Open(@"..\..\CompressTestData001.xml",
            FileMode.Open, FileAccess.Read))
        {
            Stream compressedData, roundTripData;

            compressedData = mcu.Compress(rawData);
            roundTripData = mcu.Uncompress(compressedData);
            Assert.IsTrue(StreamUtils.Compare(
                rawData, roundTripData));
        }
    }
}
}
```

After an assembly containing NUnit tests has been compiled, it can be referenced from the NUnit GUI, which will display the tests from the assembly in the user interface. NUnit is a visual tool that clearly indicates whether a group of tests has been successful. The Console.Out and Console.Error tabs display useful information about the logging and failures for a given set of tests. This information proves helpful in troubleshooting test cases. Figure 8-2 shows a set of unit tests for some BizTalk utility classes.

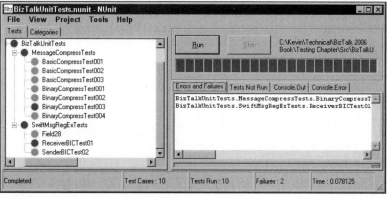

Figure 8-2

You can find more information on NUnit at www.nunit.org.

Functional Testing

Functional tests in the context of BizTalk applications are used to test a specific end-to-end scenario. Generally, you can think of BizTalk as a black box. A functional test may involve feeding an input message with known content to a receive adapter's URL, and then monitoring that the correct number of output message(s) are received on the send side at the correct URLs with the correct content. By passing messages in with known content, you can typically control the path through BizTalk and predict what the expected outputs will be. Of course, many scenarios require known inputs to be orchestrated at the correct time to drive the correct outputs.

Functional testing should cover all the possible paths through your solution — not only those scenarios that you expect in production but also the failure paths that you hope are never exercised in production. The tests should use all in-bound and outbound URLs and all types of messages. All orchestrations should be invoked, and all code branches through those orchestrations should be exercised. The following are some of the considerations when developing functional test cases:

❑ Positive tests

    ❑ Ensure that all combinations of messages and endpoints are passed through the solution to make sure that all message flows are exercised. This may mean using messages with differing content to ensure that all code paths through your orchestrations and custom pipeline components are executed.

    ❑ Ensure that all the different transports are exercised.

    ❑ The message content of all messages that are sent out from the solution should be validated. If XML messages are being sent, they should be validated against their schema. In addition, the values in key fields should be checked using XPath expressions. If flat-file messages are being sent, regular expressions may be the best approach to validate that the content of the message is correct.

    ❑ If your solution uses BAM, your test case should validate that the correct BAM data is being written to the BAMPRimaryImport database.

    ❑ Ensure that all BRE policies and rules are tested.

❑ Negative tests

    ❑ Ensure that invalid messages are passed through the solution to validate that the system handles them correctly. Depending on your strategy, you will need to test that they are rejected before entering BizTalk or that they are suspended by BizTalk.

    ❑ Ensure that all exception blocks in your orchestrations are executed. One of the more common problems is not testing the exception handling in orchestrations.

    ❑ Ensure that the correct error logging takes places upon failure.

Functional testing should be automated. Manual testing is both time-consuming and expensive in terms of resources (and worse, it is prone to human error). Such errors can cause a new test pass to be scheduled in the project plan due to the significant human dependencies. Often, you will be limited as to the time when manual test passes can be made due to the resources required. With automated testing, you invest the development costs associated with building the automated test cases up front and then draw on that investment each time you execute a test pass. Good functional tests should execute relatively quickly and should be repeatable. That is, if the code is written correctly, the functional test should always produce the same result. Poorly written functional tests or poorly written code will result in different test results between test runs, leading to lost cycles spent investigating the causes of failure.

The development time required to write a functional test is also important. Usually, the more expensive it is to create a functional test case, the fewer test cases you are likely to end up with. And of course, that probably means that you will have a lower level of test coverage over your code. One of the most effective approaches to reducing the development cost associated with developing test cases is to invest in a test framework, whether you develop one from scratch or acquire one. A good test framework will enable you to quickly create new test cases. Ultimately, you will end up with more test cases and more of your code being tested. Often, test frameworks use declarative approaches to reduce the amount of code that must be developed.

BizUnit

BizUnit is such a declarative test framework that is designed to enable an engineer to rapidly build test cases. By *declarative*, I mean that the user authors a BizUnit XML test case defining how the tests will be performed. The XML test case is executed by BizUnit. The test result is binary. It either passes or fails. BizUnit is targeted at BizTalk but is in no way tied or restricted to testing BizTalk Server applications.

Because BizUnit is a framework, it needs a driver — an application that hosts and executes the framework, part of which includes telling it which test cases need to be run. You could write some .NET code to drive BizUnit, but a more appropriate host is either Visual Studio 2005 Unit Testing or NUnit. BizUnit has no dependency on either of these, but they both make great BizUnit hosts.

BizUnit defines three stages of a test case: `TestSetup`, `TestExecution`, and `TestCleanup`:

❑   The setup stage is designed to enable the platform to be initialized in the appropriate way for the test to be performed. For example, it could be that to execute the test, some data needs to be inserted into a database table that is later used by the solution during the execute stage.

❑   The execution stage is where the test is actually run. This is where the functionality is actually tested.

❑   The final stage, the cleanup stage, is designed to be used to return the platform the state it was in prior to running the test. It is always executed. The reason the platform should be returned to its starting point is to prevent one test case from interfering with another. For example, consider a scenario in which data is inserted into a database table. The execution of the test will cause this data to be received and processed by BizTalk. If that test fails to execute for whatever reason, the next test that executes might be expecting different data to be present in the database than what is actually there. Thus, if the previous test case did not clean up after itself, the subsequent test case would fail because a different scenario was executed than the one that was supposed to use that data. So one of the guiding principles for BizUnit is that it is the responsibility of every test case to clean up after itself.

Each of these stages contains zero of more *test steps*. A test step is a unit of work. It is a pluggable component designed to perform a specific task. For example, the role of a `FileCreateStep` is to create a file of specific content at a given location and with a given filename. The fact that BizUnit may easily be extended by creating new test steps is key to its flexibility, and key to enabling it to be adapted to a broad range of scenarios. Figure 8-3 shows the format of a BizUnit XML test case, showing the three test stages and their associated test steps.

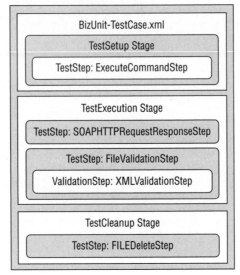

Figure 8-3

To further clarify the format of a BizUnit test case, let's look at an example. The following XML represents the XML for a BizUnit test case named `Test_001_SimpleTest`. The test is simple and is designed to test an uncomplicated BizTalk scenario in which BizTalk receives a file from an input directory and writes a file to an output directory.

```
<TestCase testName="Test_001_SimpleTest">

  <TestSetup>
  </TestSetup>

  <TestExecution>

    <TestStep assemblyPath=""
      typeName="Microsoft.Services.BizTalkApplicationFramework.
        BizUnit.FileCreateStep">
      <SourcePath>..\..\..\TestData\RequestInDoc.xml</SourcePath>
      <CreationPath>
        ..\..\..\InputDir\RequestMsg_{%Guid%}.xml</CreationPath>
    </TestStep>

    <TestStep assemblyPath="" typeName="Microsoft.Services
      .BizTalkApplicationFramework.BizUnit.FileValidateStep">
      <Timeout>3000</Timeout>
      <Directory>..\..\..\OutputDir\</Directory>
      <SearchPattern>ResponseMsg_*.xml</SearchPattern>
      <DeleteFile>true</DeleteFile>

      <ValidationStep assemblyPath="" typeName="Microsoft.Services
        .BizTalkApplicationFramework.BizUnit.XmlValidationStep">
        <XmlSchemaPath>
          ..\..\..\TestData\PurchaseOrder.xsd</XmlSchemaPath>
```

```
        <XmlSchemaNameSpace>
          http://SendMail.PurchaseOrder</XmlSchemaNameSpace>
        <XPathList>
          <XPathValidation query="/*[local-name()='PurchaseOrder' and
            namespace-uri()='http://SendMail.PurchaseOrder']/*[local-
            name()='PONumber' and namespace-uri()='']">PO000105
          </XPathValidation>
        </XPathList>
      </ValidationStep>
    </TestStep>

  </TestExecution>

  <!-- Test cases should always leave the system in the state they found
       it -->
  <TestCleanup>

    <TestStep assemblyPath="" typeName=
      "Microsoft.Services.BizTalkApplicationFramework.BizUnit
        .FileDeleteMultipleStep" failOnError="false">
      <Directory>..\..\..\InputDir\</Directory>
      <SearchPattern>*.xml</SearchPattern>
    </TestStep>

    <TestStep assemblyPath="" typeName=
      "Microsoft.Services.BizTalkApplicationFramework.BizUnit
        .FileDeleteMultipleStep" failOnError="false">
      <Directory>..\..\..\OutputDir\</Directory>
      <SearchPattern>*.xml</SearchPattern>
    </TestStep>

  </TestCleanup>

</TestCase>
```

Here's what the BizUnit test case defines:

1. The `TestSetup` stage contains no test steps. The `TestExecution` stage is the first stage containing test steps and is therefore executed first. The first step is the `FileCreateStep`, which copies the contents of the file `TestData\RequestInDoc.xml`, creating a new file in `InputDir\RequestMsg_{%Guid%}.xml`. The `%Guid%` wildcard will be replaced by a GUID (as covered in more detail later).

2. The second step in the `TestExecution` stage is the `FileValidateStep`. This step waits 3000 milliseconds (3 seconds) for a file in the `OutputDir` with an `.xml` file extension. This is the file that BizTalk creates. This step deletes the file if it is successful. If the `FileValidateStep` finds a file within the specified time, it invokes the `XmlValidationStep`. This is effectively a substep. It validates that the contents of the file found against the `PurchaseOrder.xsd` schema. The validation step also evaluates an XPath expression to check that `PONumber` is equal to `PO000105`. Typically, more than one XPath expression would be executed to check key fields in the document.

3. Finally, two `FileDeleteMultipleStep`'s are executed in the `TestCleanup` stage. This deletes any files that have been left in `InputDir` or `OutputDir` in the event that the test case failed.

A BizUnit test case is executed by creating a new instance of BizUnit and calling the `RunTest` method. If `RunTest` does not throw any exceptions, the test case was successful. The BizUnit constructor takes the name of the test case to be executed. In this case, the XML test case is in the file `Test01_SubmitPO001.xml`. BizUnit may use relative paths to find the test case. The following example illustrates how a BizUnit test case would be executed from Visual Studio 2005 Unit Testing.

```
[TestMethod]
public void Test_01_FILECopyWithXmlValidation()
{
  BizUnit bizUnit =
    new BizUnit(@"..\..\..\TestCases\Test01_SubmitPO001.xml");

  bizUnit.RunTest();
}
```

BizUnit also enables you to perform setup and cleanup at the group level. Typically, you do this for coarse-grained setup and cleanup tasks that need to be executed before or after a collection of tests are run. In some scenarios, this may mean deploying and undeploying your BizTalk solution. When considering test case construction and the granularity of deployment and setup activities, it is important to keep in mind that a functional test should execute in a timely manner. If tests take too long to execute, they won't be broadly adopted and used, and ultimately the benefits from a rigorous automated testing strategy will not be realized.

The following code sample shows how to set up a group-level test case in Visual Studio. Decorating a method with the `ClassInitialize` attribute causes Visual Studio 2005 Unit Test to execute the `Setup` method before the first test case defined in that class is executed. A similar concept exists in NUnit. BizUnit is informed that a test case represents the execution of a test group setup by specifying the `TestGroupPhase.TestGroupSetup` in the BizUnit constructor. By default, if this parameter is not specified, BizUnit will assume that this is a regular test being executed. Setting this will cause the logging to be appropriately written to indicate the test case represents a group setup activity. Similarly, the `ClassCleanup` attribute is used in Visual Studio to mark a method that needs to be executed after the last test has been executed. In this case, it's the BizUnit `TearDown` operation.

```
[ClassInitialize]
static public void SetUp(TestContext context)
{
  BizUnit bizUnit = new BizUnit(@"..\..\..\TestCases\TestSetup.xml",
    BizUnit.TestGroupPhase.TestGroupSetup);

  bizUnit.RunTest();
}

[ClassCleanup]
static public void TearDown()
{
  BizUnit bizUnit = new BizUnit(@"..\..\..\TestCases\TestTearDown.xml",
    BizUnit.TestGroupPhase.TestGroupTearDown);

  bizUnit.RunTest();
}
```

As previously mentioned, a test step is a unit of work that performs a specific task. The failure of a test step results in the failure of the test case. Test steps are driven by configuration that is embedded in the test case XML file; only the test step is required understand this configuration. The configuration for a test case is opaque to BizUnit. The framework does not need to understand the configuration. It is just responsible for passing it to the appropriate test step.

To put this in context, let's look at a slightly more complex example. Suppose that you have an orchestration that is bound to a request-response Web service. The orchestration is responsible for determining the best supplier for a widget. It will select the most appropriate supplier for the purchase of a widget, based on a number of criteria including price, availability, and delivery time. Perhaps this is achieved via the execution of a BRE rule policy. The orchestration sends a request to two back-end systems that represent the two suppliers, one via a file share and the other via a Websphere MQ queue. The orchestration waits for a response from each of the back-end systems (again, one via another file share and the other via another Websphere MQ queue). Then the orchestration determines the best price, builds the response message, and sends it back to the waiting Web service client. The solution uses BAM to track the process flow for the widget requests and their outcome. Figure 8-4 illustrates the scenario from the test perspective.

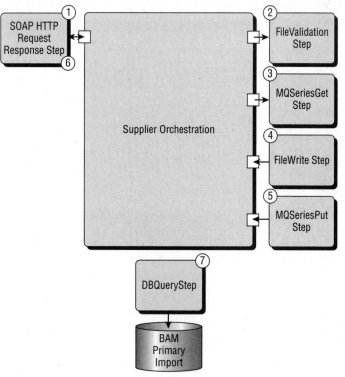

Figure 8-4

It is relatively easy to test this scenario using BizUnit. BizUnit will act as mock services for both the Web service client and the two back-end systems. In addition, BizUnit will be used to query the BAM-PrimaryImport database to check that the correct BAM records have been inserted. The scenario is tested using the following test steps:

1. The SOAPHTTPRequestResponseStep submits a SOAP request to the BizTalk Web service port. The test is executed concurrently by specifying the runConcurrently="true" attribute at the test step level in the configuration file. This attribute tells the BizUnit framework to execute the step on a separate thread. If this attribute is not specified, each individual test step will be run sequentially. Each step will wait for the previous step to complete before it starts. The SOAPHTTPRequestResponseStep step requires a response from BizTalk before it can complete, but the response will only be delivered once the steps after it have completed. Clearly, if all the steps were run sequentially, it could not be completed and would eventually time out. Running the step concurrently enables the subsequent steps to be executed by BizUnit while it waits for its response.

2. The FileValidationStep step is executed while the SOAPHTTPRequestResponseStep step is waiting for the response. The step waits a specified time for a file to be written by BizTalk to the indicated location. Once the file is picked up, the XmlValidationStep step is executed. This validation step is used to validate the data received against a given XSD schema. XPath expressions are evaluated to verify the values of key fields. When performing functional testing, it is important to check not only that messages are delivered to the correct endpoints but also that the content of those messages is correct.

3. The MQSeriesGetStep step waits for a message to be written by BizTalk to a specific queue. The step also executes XmlValidationStep to verify the content of the message.

4. Next, the FileWriteStep step is used to simulate the back-end system sending the response to the file share. BizTalk will receive and process that file when it arrives as though it were sent from the back-end system

5. The MQSeriesPutStep is then used write a message to a specified Websphere MQ queue. Again, BizTalk will receive and process that message when it arrives as though it were sent from the back-end system.

6. The message flow completes when the BizTalk Web service adapter returns the SOAP response to the waiting SOAPHTTPRequestResponseStep. Remember that step was run concurrently; so as long as the timeout has not been exceeded, the response will be processed by the waiting step. The step verifies the response, ensuring that it is as expected.

7. The final step to be executed for the scenario is DBQueryStep. This step is used to query the BAMPrimaryImport database to ensure that the correct tracking data has been written to the database for the flow.

From the preceding example, you can see how easy it is to declaratively define an automated test case for a reasonably complex BizTalk scenario. Creating variations of a given test case is even more trivial and often involves only varying the input data and subsequent verification of output data. Typically, a test matrix should be defined to identify all the possible flows and code paths that need to be tested. One approach to achieve this that I have used on many projects is to use an Excel spreadsheet that defines all the possible combinations of inputs and outputs. BizUnit test cases can then be automatically generated directly from the spreadsheet. The spreadsheet can be filled in by a business analyst who understands the business scenarios but, they would not be required to understand BizTalk, BizUnit, or XML, for that matter.

Creating New BizUnit Test Steps

Because BizUnit is a test framework, it's relatively easy to write new test steps if the step that you need isn't already available. All test steps need to implement the `ITestStep` interface. The interface has a single method, `Execute`, which is called by BizUnit. `Execute` takes an `XmlNode` containing the configuration for that test step and a BizUnit context object. The `Execute` method performs the autonomous action — for example, if it were an `MSMQWriteStep`, it would write a message to an MSMQ queue. The step is considered to pass if an exception is not thrown outside of the `Execute` method.

The following code shows the `ITestStep` interface:

```
public interface ITestStep
{
  void Execute(XmlNode testConfig, Context context);
}
```

Configuring BizUnit

The following XML fragment illustrates the configuration that might be passed to the `FileCreateStep` test step. BizUnit uses the `assemblyPath` and `typeName` attributes to determine which test step to create and execute. In addition to these attributes, BizUnit supports two optional attributes: `runConcurrently` and `failOnError`. The `runConcurrently` attribute defaults to false, whereas the `failOnError` attribute defaults to `true`. Generally, the `failOnError` attribute should be set to `false` in the `TestCleanup` test phase to ensure the best possible attempt of cleaning up the platform following the execution of a test case. The following XML illustrates an XML fragment that would be passed to the `FileCreateStep` test step:

```
<TestStep assemblyPath="" typeName="Microsoft.Services.
    BizTalkApplicationFramework.BizUnit.FileCreateStep">
  <SourcePath>..\..\..\TestData\InDoc1.xml</SourcePath>
  <CreationPath>
    ..\..\..\Rec_03\InDoc1_{%Guid%}.xml
  </CreationPath>
</TestStep>
```

As previously mentioned, the test step is responsible for parsing the XML fragment to get the configuration. As detailed in the following section, the context object has a number of helper methods to aid the process and keep it consistent across test steps. This particular test step has two main properties that it is interested in: `SourcePath` and `CreationPath`. The `FileCreateStep` step will use these to effectively copy the contents of the file specified at `..\..\..\TestData\InDoc1.xml` to the file `..\..\..\Rec_03\InDoc1_{%Guid%}.xml`. Notice that the `CreationPath` has `%Guid%` embedded in it. This is a wildcard for which BizUnit will substitute the correct value. We look at wildcards in more detail shortly.

BizUnit Context Object

As previously mentioned, each test step is passed a context object. The context object is a helper object and serves a number of purposes:

❑ **Configuration helper APIs** — The context contains a number of helper APIs to retrieve configuration values from the XML fragment. The APIs support some useful features that take place under the covers, including the following:

❑ *Substitution of wildcards* — To understand wildcards, it's useful to look at an example. If a `FileCreateStep` needs to write a file with a unique name, the configuration for the target file path may contain a wildcard that is later replaced by a value that will make the filename unique.

The following table lists the wildcards currently supported by BizUnit.

Wildcard	Source String Example	Resulting String
%Guid%	MyFile_%Guid%.xml	MyFile_22D89FA3-3ABA-4f75-B07B-83437C8879B5.xml
%DateTime%	MyFile_%DateTime%.xml	MyFile_210333-14012006.xml
%ServerName%	MyFile_%Guid%_%ServerName%.xml	MyFile_22D89FA3-3ABA-4f75-B07B-83437C8879B5_Thunderbolt.xml

❑   *Fetch from context* — Writing to and reading from the context is explained in more detail below. This feature causes the configuration to be taken from the context object rather than from the test case configuration file. It enables more dynamic behavior in test cases. The code snippet here illustrates the use of this, whereby the `CreationPath` is taken from the context instead of from the XML.

```
<TestStep assemblyPath="" typeName="Microsoft.Services.
    BizTalkApplicationFramework.BizUnit.FileCreateStep">
  <SourcePath>..\..\..\TestData\InDoc1.xml</SourcePath>
  <CreationPath takeFromCtx="DstPath"></CreationPath>
</TestStep>
```

❑   **Flow state between test steps** — For the most part, test steps are autonomous. They are created, executed, and then destroyed (garbage collected). They have no knowledge of which steps are executed before or after them. However, they can be tied declaratively using the configuration. BizUnit provides a mechanism to flow state between test steps within a test case via the context object. There are a number of scenarios in which this is required. For example, suppose that you are using BizUnit to simulate your back-end systems. Suppose further that the back-end system receives a message from BizTalk for which it needs to send an acknowledgment message, but the destination of the acknowledgment message is in the content of the message that it received. Using this feature, the BizUnit step that received the message from BizTalk could extract the destination of the acknowledgment message and save it in the BizUnit context. The next step that is responsible for sending the acknowledgment message would fetch the destination from the BizUnit context.

❑   **Log test step output** — Using the API ensures that the output is logged in a consistent manner to the same target. The logging API supports outputting errors, warnings, and information and provides a similar API to `String.Format`. The following code snippet illustrates the use of the API in the context of a test step:

```
public void Execute(XmlNode testConfig, Context context)
{
    FileStream dstFs = null;
    FileStream srcFs = null;
```

```
    try
    {
      string sourcePath =
        context.ReadConfigAsString( testConfig, "SourcePath" );
      string creationPath = context.ReadConfigAsString(
        testConfig, "CreationPath" );

      context.LogInfo("FileCreateStep about to copy the data from
        File: {0} to the File: {1}", sourcePath, creationPath);
    ...
```

❑ **Test case information** — The context also has APIs to retrieve the test case details. For example, the name of the test case being executed is written to the context object by using the `BizUnitTestCaseName` key, this can be useful for collecting the results associated with a particular test case.

❑ **Executing validation and context-manipulation steps** — The context object has helper methods to execute validation and context-manipulation test steps. This abstracts the execution of these from the test step. The following code snippet illustrates executing the validation test step:

```
public void Execute(XmlNode testConfig, Context context)
{
  MemoryStream data = null;

  try
  {
    ...
    XmlNode validationConfig =
      testConfig.SelectSingleNode("ValidationStep");

    // Load data ...

    // Execute validator...
    context.ExecuteValidator( data, validationConfig );
    ...
```

This section has illustrated how you can use BizUnit to rapidly create automated test cases for BizTalk solutions. BizUnit is simply a test framework that can be used 'as is' or easily extended in order to test your BizTalk scenario, and subsequently drive up the quality of it. BizUnit contains an SDK with a number of examples to help you get started. You can download it from `http://www.codeplex.com/bizunit`.

Code Coverage

If your functional tests are effective, they will exercise all the code paths through your solution, including all the code paths through all your orchestrations and all the code paths through the custom components that you may have written (whether they are utility components, pipeline components, or adapters). You need to be confident that all the code paths have been adequately tested.

Code coverage can also be used to identify dead functions or classes in your code base. In general, code that is not executed or unreachable should be removed from the code base. A common mistake is to just comment out the code rather than remove it. Unfortunately, commented-out code is often untested prior to it being commented out and may therefore have undetected bugs in it. It's safer and better practice to remove the code entirely from the solution in case it is uncommented at a later time.

You can use the Visual Studio Code Coverage tool to perform code coverage of your managed and unmanaged custom code. Running the Code Coverage tool during a functional test pass will enable you to determine the effectiveness of the functional test suite. It will enable you to identify whether additional test cases need to be added and whether there are dead methods that you can remove from the code base. The Visual Studio Code Coverage tool can be driven from the IDE or from the command line. To perform code coverage on assemblies that are hosted by the BizTalk NT service, you need to use the command-line tools. The following steps show how to perform code coverage against a custom pipeline component:

1. Instrument the binaries that you want to perform code coverage on. The tools modify the assemblies, adding instrumentation code that will be used to determine which statements have been executed. This is shown in Figure 8-5. `VsInstr` renames the original assembly to `*.orig` (in this case, `DRPostPipelineComponent.dll.orig`).

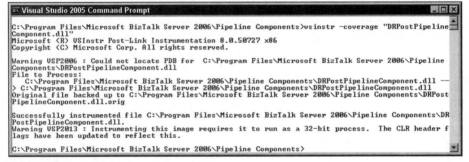

Figure 8-5

2. Start the collection monitor, which is called `VsPerfMon`. `VsPerfMon` needs to be started in code coverage mode. You also need to specify the name of the output file path indicating where the collected coverage data is written, as shown in Figure 8-6.

Figure 8-6

3. Start the BizTalk service and execute the functional tests that you want to determine the code coverage for. `VsPerfMon` will detect when the instrumented assembly is loaded and will indicate that the BizTalk process has been successfully registered, as shown in Figure 8-7. As your functional tests execute, `VsPerfMon` will record which lines of code are executed.

Figure 8-7

4. When the functional tests have completed, stop the BizTalk service. At this point, VsPerfMon will indicate that the process has been unregistered. You can then shut down VsPerfMon, as shown in Figure 8-8.

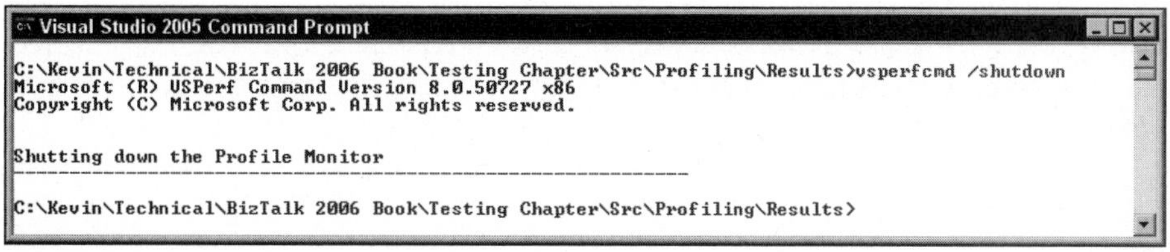

Figure 8-8

5. At this point, you can load the code coverage output file into Visual Studio by double-clicking on it. Figure 8-9 shows the code coverage results window. Each assembly is shown, and the level of code coverage is illustrated. For this scenario, let's look at the assembly DRPostPipelineComponent, which packages the custom pipeline component that we are interested in. By drilling down on this assembly, we can see that the main method Execute has just over 27 percent of its code not being executed. This method is executed for every message that passed through the custom pipeline component, so it's important to understand which portion of the code is not being executed.

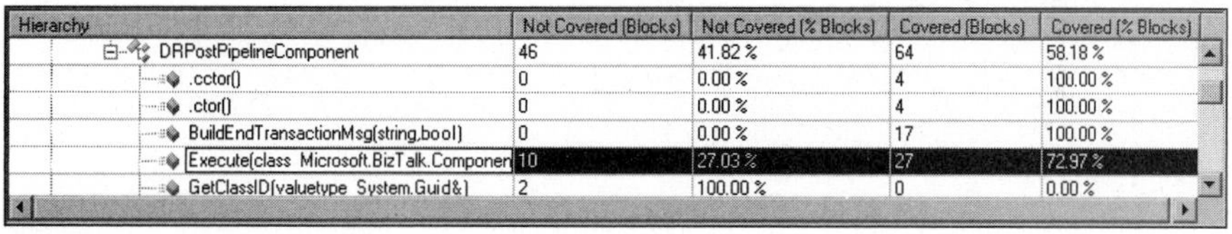

Hierarchy	Not Covered (Blocks)	Not Covered (% Blocks)	Covered (Blocks)	Covered (% Blocks)
DRPostPipelineComponent	46	41.82 %	64	58.18 %
.cctor()	0	0.00 %	4	100.00 %
.ctor()	0	0.00 %	4	100.00 %
BuildEndTransactionMsg(string,bool)	0	0.00 %	17	100.00 %
Execute(class Microsoft.BizTalk.Componen	10	27.03 %	27	72.97 %
GetClassID(valuetype System.Guid&)	2	100.00 %	0	0.00 %

Figure 8-9

At this point, you can look at the code in Visual Studio for the Execute method. Looking at this, you can see that there is a scenario that is not executed for this component. The component handles messages from different ports slightly differently. The code path that processes messages from the NewOrderReceivePort is executed as expected, but the code processing messages from the OrderUpdateReceivePort is not executed. This is a good indication that there is a functional test case missing from the test suite.

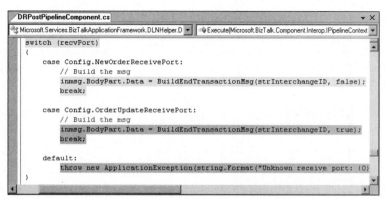

Figure 8-10

Determining the level of code coverage within orchestrations is not so easy. You can sprinkle software trace statements throughout the various branches in the orchestrations and perform some auditing of the trace output collected during the functional test pass. This is somewhat tedious and rather painful. For BizTalk Server 2004, the Orchestration Profiler utility was developed by Jason Birth. (Hopefully, by the time of publication of this book, the 2006 version of the tool will be available, the profiler may be downloaded from `http://www.codeplex.com/BiztalkOrcProfiler`.) The utility is executed during the functional test pass. The utility produces a graphical report indicating the level of code coverage for all the orchestrations. You can use the code coverage output to determine whether additional test cases are required or whether there are branches of orchestrations that may be removed because they are never executed. Figure 8-11 shows the results for an orchestration after running its functional tests. The right branch of the orchestration has clearly not been exercised. Based on this, an additional functional test needs to be authored and added to the functional test cases.

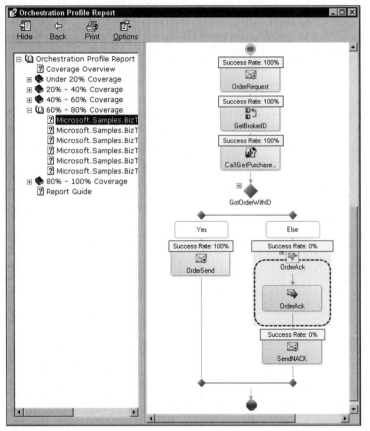

Figure 8-11

Integration Testing

Integration testing is where you wire up your solution to the real systems that it is interfacing with. These do not need to be production versions of those systems. They could be versions of those systems in your integration environment. Integration is often one of the harder tasks from a project perspective and will often flag issues resulting from incorrect assumptions made along the design and development process. Performing integration as early as possible usually makes life easier and helps to reduce project risk. Integration is where you get to validate the assumptions that you might have made about various systems that you interface with. Often, this is a manual process whereby changes to the solution are made to work as desired. (If changes to the solution are made, your functional tests should of course be updated to reflect those changes.)

For most scenarios, it is important to test with real system data rather than data believed to represent the production environment. However, there are scenarios in which getting real data for test purposes is challenging. During a large integration project that I worked on, we had tested the system using our test data. This particular project was a financial system that processed payment messages, so obtaining real messages from the production environment was difficult and presented security issues. Therefore, sanitized data was used that was thought to be similar to the production data. A few weeks before the go-live date, we decided to take a branch feed from the live environment and run it through our integration test rig. We ran about 60,000 messages through the BizTalk solution, fully expecting most to work as expected. To our horror, more than 40 percent of the messages failed with subtle errors. Fortunately for us, those errors boiled down to only half a dozen issues that we subsequently fixed. For that particular project, testing a live feed through the integration environment was a critical decision that helped to ensure the project's success. You really don't want to be finding issues such as those on your first day after go-live! So integration is not only about testing the various system interfaces, it is also about testing the data.

Performance Testing and Tuning

The goal of performance testing and subsequently tuning is to ensure that you get the most "bang for your buck" out of your hardware. Investing in a relatively small amount of performance testing and tuning can pay dividends. Many times, a few tips and tricks can be applied to significantly improve performance and therefore reduce the size of the hardware real estate required to run the solution. For mission-critical deployments that have the equivalent production hardware in the disaster recovery site, these savings can be significant. In addition, this does also translate to operations savings, because you'll need to manage and support fewer servers in production. Performance gains from 30 to 200 percent are not uncommon when tuning BizTalk solutions. Gains such as these translate into significant savings.

Load Profile

When measuring the performance of a given solution, ensure that the load profile is representative of what will be seen in production. For example, suppose you have five endpoints, each bound to a different orchestration. One of those endpoints might handle 80 percent of the messages, and the orchestration bound to that endpoint is expensive in terms of performance. If the solution were to be tested by distributing an even load over all endpoints, the performance of the solution would appear much better than would be seen in a production environment, and any issues related to performance would not be flagged until the solution has gone live. Early detection of any performance issues such as this could lead to the orchestration in question being tuned to increase its performance to an acceptable level. Consider the following when defining the load profile:

❑   A representative number of messages per second should pass through the solution.

❑   The duration of the performance test should be measured such that the "warm-up" period does not skew the results. For example, BizTalk uses an internal caching mechanism for all the artifacts it uses, such as message schemas, pipeline configuration, endpoint configuration, and so on. The first few messages through BizTalk will cause these caches to be loaded. These messages will be processed noticeably more slowly due to the additional amount of work that BizTalk needs to do while processing them. If you are running a scale-out deployment, all the caches on all the servers need to be loaded. Similarly, you might have similar functionality in your own code or back-end systems that are participating in the test. A common approach to this is to induce a burst load before the tests starts in order to load the caches on all servers.

❏ There should be a representative percentage of messages spread across in-bound endpoints. That is, if your application has 10 endpoints and 3 of them handle 70 percent of the load, you need to ensure that your load profile is broadly in line with that distribution.

❏ Similarly, the size and type of those messages distributed across endpoints should be representative of the production environment. The size of the messages being processed will have an effect on performance

❏ The frequency of those messages arriving at in-bound endpoints should be representative of the production environment. For example, are the messages received at a constant rate of, say, 55 messages per second for a 6-hour period, or does the application receive the entire days quota of 1,188,000 messages in a 2-hour period, all of which need to be processed with an average latency of under 10 seconds from end to end? If the latter is the case, your performance requirements are significantly harsher.

❏ If back-end systems cannot be used for performance testing, they should be mocked up, ensuring that they have similar performance characteristics to the production back-end systems.

In addition to ensuring that the correct load profile is used for a given performance test scenario, it is important to ensure that enough runtime metrics are captured during a test run. Generally, these will include performance counters for the operating system, hardware, network, .NET runtime, BizTalk Server, SQL Server, your solution, and any other products being used. Ideally, you need to record this data for each performance run and on each server participating in the test so that it can be analyzed offline. In addition, you should also capture Event Logs and trace files for all the servers to help diagnose any unexpected behaviors.

To ensure that the correct load profile is driven across all your endpoints, you could write some code to help, although there are a number of considerations that would increase the cost of writing a useful performance test framework, including the following:

❏ The framework really needs to be transport agnostic. What you need to do is define the load profile independently of the transport type being used.

❏ You need to write the framework in such a way that the input data is configurable for different endpoints.

❏ You might need to change some of the data in each input file. Perhaps you need to change a transaction reference ID or randomize some portion of the data.

❏ You might need to have some notion of detecting and handling failures, possibly the notion of resending messages when failures occur.

❏ You might need to have your framework ensure that it aggregates the results of all the messages sent across all URLs and stops the test when a given number of messages have been transmitted. Alternatively, you might want the test to run for a given period of time.

❏ You will most likely need to ensure that the message rate adheres to the configured rate.

The list goes on. The point is that writing a tool that can meet the full requirements of performance testing is not the trivial task it might appear to be at first sight. And you don't want to be spending your valuable lab time debugging your load generation framework. Instead, you probably want to be testing and tuning your solution. Fortunately, you don't have to write such a tool, because the BizTalk Server product group made available the load-generation tool that the product group uses to test the BizTalk Server product.

Performance Testing Tools – Load Generation

The Load Generation tool is referred to as LoadGen. It was developed by the BizTalk product group Stress and Performance Testing Team. The team has a fun job: they spend most of their time trying to break BizTalk, sometimes in very imaginative ways! For the most part, their scenarios are based on real-world customer scenarios or variations of them. Another advantage, aside from the tool clearly being fit for purpose, is that because the product group uses it on a daily basis, you can be sure that the tool itself is solid (due to the rigorous testing it has been subjected to). Essentially, LoadGen is an extensible declarative framework that you can use to drive load against BizTalk endpoints to test a wide range of stress- and performance-related scenarios. By *declarative*, I mean that LoadGen is configuration driven. The configuration is in XML format and stored in a file that effectively defines how a test should be executed. We take a closer look at the configuration later.

LoadGen has a modular, extensible design that consists of three layers: presentation, framework, and component. The presentation layer is essentially a command-line driver. Its role is to drive the framework layer. The framework layer parses the configuration and orchestrates the instantiation and execution of the various components in the component layer. The component layer consists of three types of component: load generators, message creators, and throttle controllers. These components are autonomous. You can create your own load generators, message controllers, and throttle controllers and plug them into LoadGen to support any specific needs of your test scenarios. LoadGen is a lightweight tool; its CPU utilization and memory usage are relatively low in most scenarios.

Message creators are optional components that you can use to generate messages. Two modes of creation are supported: synchronous and asynchronous. A synchronous message creator uses a single thread of execution to create messages. It can therefore be used to create messages with incrementing unique transaction reference numbers. However, synchronous generators have no room for scalability, because only a single thread can be used. Therefore, LoadGen cannot guarantee that the message rate will be met. In asynchronous operation, the message creator can use multiple threads of execution, thereby enabling LoadGen to more easily meet the configured message rate. In asynchronous mode, the message creator may randomly modify data for each individual message, but because multiple threads of execution are used, it might not be possible to guarantee unique messages.

The role of a load generator is to transmit messages using a specific transport method and protocol. LoadGen is supplied with load generators to transmit messages using the following transport mechanisms: File, HTTP, SOAP, MSMQ, Websphere MQ, Web services Enhancements, and Windows SharePoint Services.

LoadGen can heuristically throttle the flow of messages that are transmitted based on runtime information. Using runtime information, LoadGen can ensure that a steady rate of messages is transmitted by adjusting the rate up or down. It also enables custom throttling, which may, for example, be based on the number of files in folder, the number of rows in a database table, or the depth of a Websphere MQ queue. This functionality is achieved and customized by using throttle controllers that monitor the message rates to ensure that the configured load generator is generating messages at the configured rate for a given test run (the rate configured in the XML configuration file). The throttle controller notifies the framework when the rate is too high or too low. It does not actually throttle the messages itself. Instead, this role is performed by the LoadGen framework. This simplifies the code that is required to develop a custom throttle controller.

You can use LoadGen to configure a load profile at the URL level. Therefore, a high degree of control is possible when defining the overall load profile for a given system by defining different load profiles for each URL. The end condition for a test is defined by the user. For example, it could be configured to transmit a fixed number of files, or transmit messages for a fixed period of time.

The CommonSection defines default values for load generators, message creators, and throttle controllers. These values can be overridden in any of the Section configurations if required. A sample LoadGen file is shown below. This test sends 100 messages (LotSizePerInterval) every 10 milliseconds (SleepInterval). It uses one thread per load generator (NumThreadsPerSection), which in this scenario is Websphere MQ. LoadGen will stop the test after 10,000 messages have been sent.

Alternatively, a time duration can be used to control the duration of the test. The test case also tells LoadGen to sleep for 1000 milliseconds in the event of a transmission failure (RetryInterval). Like BizTalk, LoadGen is implemented using streaming technology. Therefore, very large messages can be transmitted. The OptimizeLimitFileSize tag defines what should be considered a large message. In this example, a message greater than 204,800 bytes will cause LoadGen to treat those messages differently. Those messages will be processed by streaming them as opposed to loading the entire message into memory, thereby avoiding an out-of-memory condition.

The three Section XML fragments define the three load generators for this scenario, defining the source file for the data to be sent and the Websphere MQ destination queue to which the messages should be sent. As mentioned earlier, each of these sections takes its default configuration from the CommonSection.

```
<LoadGenFramework>
  <CommonSection>
    <LoadGenVersion>2</LoadGenVersion>
    <OptimizeLimitFileSize>204800</OptimizeLimitFileSize>
    <NumThreadsPerSection>1</NumThreadsPerSection>
    <SleepInterval>10</SleepInterval>
    <LotSizePerInterval>100</LotSizePerInterval>
    <RetryInterval>1000</RetryInterval>
    <StopMode Mode="Files">
      <NumFiles>10000</NumFiles>
    </StopMode>
    <Transport Name="MQSeries">
      <Assembly>
        MQSeriesTransport.dll/MQSeriesTransport.MQSeriesTransport
      </Assembly>
    </Transport>
  </CommonSection>

  <Section Name="MQSeriesWoodgroveInbound">
    <SrcFilePath>
      ..\..\..\..\TestCases\TestData\LoanEnquiry.xml
    </SrcFilePath>
```

```xml
      <DstLocation>
        <Parameters>
          <QueueManagerName>QM_Test</QueueManagerName>
          <QueueName>Woodgrove.LoanEnq</QueueName>
          <ChannelDefinition>
            SERVER.CHAN/TCP/BPI4X-C01(1414)</ChannelDefinition>
        </Parameters>
      </DstLocation>
    </Section>

    <Section Name="MQSeriesWoodgroveInbound">
      <SrcFilePath>
        ..\..\..\TestCases\TestData\LoanQuote.xml
      </SrcFilePath>
      <DstLocation>
        <Parameters>
          <QueueManagerName>QM_Test</QueueManagerName>
          <QueueName>Woodgrove.Quotes</QueueName>
          <ChannelDefinition>
            SERVER.CHAN/TCP/BPI4X-C01(1414)
          </ChannelDefinition>
        </Parameters>
      </DstLocation>
    </Section>

    <Section Name="MQSeriesWoodgroveInbound">
      <SrcFilePath>
        ..\..\..\TestCases\TestData\Loan.xml
      </SrcFilePath>
      <DstLocation>
        <Parameters>
          <QueueManagerName>QM_Test</QueueManagerName>
          <QueueName>Woodgrove.Process</QueueName>
          <ChannelDefinition>
            SERVER.CHAN/TCP/BPI4X-C01(1414)
          </ChannelDefinition>
        </Parameters>
      </DstLocation>
    </Section>
  </LoadGenFramework>
```

A LoadGen test case can be executed using the `LoadGenConsole.exe` application. The name of the LoadGen test case is supplied on the command line. Figure 8-12 illustrates starting a LoadGen test and subsequently how the load is throttled to meet the required input message rate.

Identifying Performance Bottlenecks

Performance tuning can be a little like peeling an onion. To optimize performance, you must identify and remove the system bottleneck. After one has been removed, a new bottleneck may be visible. Typically, you will need to identify and remove that, too, and so on until the performance meets the desired level.

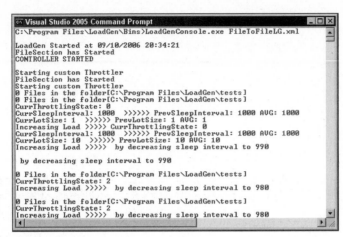

Figure 8-12

The source of performance bottlenecks could be either software or hardware. For instance, the hardware platform might be configured in a less-than-optimal manner, which obviously includes the network. The recommended deployment model for BizTalk is to host the processing and database tiers on separate servers. This recommended setup gives rise to a significant amount of network traffic between the processing tier and the database. Also, a significant amount of network traffic between adapters and the endpoints with which they are communicating will be observed under high-performance scenarios. The best way to identify performance bottlenecks in a BizTalk solution is to isolate the different types of processing to observe their characteristics. Ideally, the isolation of processing needs to be iterative, drilling down until the bottleneck is eventually discovered. Fortunately for us, the BizTalk Server architecture enables a good level of isolation with relatively little effort.

To identify where your performance bottlenecks are, you must first isolate the database work from the processing work. This means ensuring that the database is deployed to a separate server from the BizTalk host instances. If you care about performance, you will have already done this. The BizTalk processing tier is stateless; all the state for messages and orchestrations are persisted in the MessageBox database. Therefore, BizTalk typically drives SQL Server very hard under high performance scenarios. To get the maximum performance out of SQL Server, it needs to "own" the server — that is, it really needs to be the only significant application executing on the server. Deploying two resource-intensive server applications such as BizTalk and SQL causes the two products to fight for system resources.

The next step is to isolate the different types of processing within the processing tier. You do this by creating BizTalk hosts for the different types of processing and pinning the different types of processing to those hosts. Each host instance translates to a separate instance of the BizTalk NT service. By ensuring that the processing for different types of work is performed in a different physical process, you can more easily monitor it to determine its performance characteristics. In addition, you can move it to different physical machines to more easily test different configurations. Typically, this will mean creating three hosts, as follows:

❑ **Receive host** — The receive host should have all in-process receive adapters configured in it. For example, if you are using the File and Websphere MQ receive adapters, the receive handlers for both of these should be configured to use the receive host. This is configured in the BizTalk Server Administration MMC under the adapter node, as shown in Figure 8-13. The effect of this will be to pin the processing on the receive path to the receive host. This includes receiving the messages in the adapter, processing them through the receive pipeline, and executing any configured mapping and then subsequently publishing the message to the MessageBox. All this work will be performed in an instance of the receive host (that is, the same NT service process).

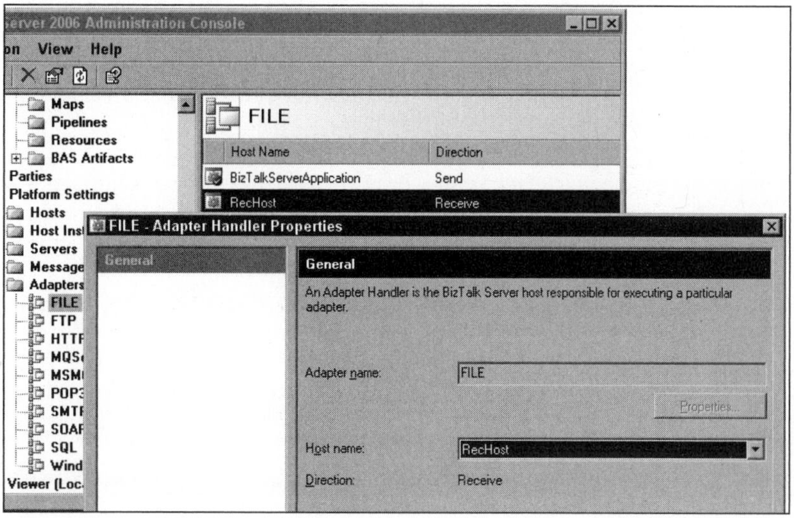

Figure 8-13

❑ **Orchestration host** — The orchestration host should have all orchestrations pinned to it. This will ensure that all orchestrations are executed in the same NT service. You can do this by configuring the bindings for each orchestration to the orchestration host, as shown in Figure 8-14.

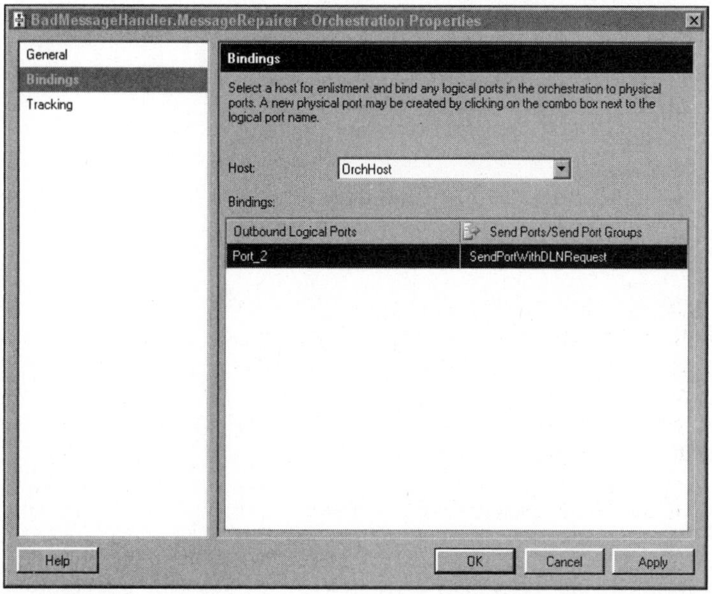

Figure 8-14

- ❑ **Send host** — The send host configuration is similar to the receive host configuration and is achieved in the same manner.

- ❑ **Isolated receive host** — If you are using an isolated adapter such as HTTP or SOAP receive, you need to configure these in an isolated host. The process that they execute in will depend on how you have configured that adapter and its host, because the adapter does not execute in the BizTalk process address space. For example, in the case of HTTP receive running on Windows Server 2003, the process boundary will be defined by the IIS application pool.

After the individual hosts have been created, you need to create host instances on physical servers. It is advantageous to pin a single host instance to a single physical server. For example, if you have four processing nodes, an initial performance pass might be configured with one receive, one send, and two orchestration servers. Ensuring that a single BizTalk process executes on a single machine makes it easier to understand the performance characteristics of that host. With this level of system isolation, it should be possible to determine where the performance bottleneck is (in the database, receive host, orchestration host, or send host).

During a performance run, PerfMon counters for each process corresponding to each host instance and the database server(s) should be collected and analyzed to determine the system performance characteristics. It's always better to record more PerfMon counters than are required, and typically it's easier to record all PerfMon counters from a single machine to get an aggregated view. When deciding which PerfMon counters to record, ensure that you have enough information to help you understand the performance characteristics of the BizTalk receive, orchestration, and send host processes (in addition to he database servers). To do this, you must consider the following categories of PerfMon counters:

- ❑ All process counters for the all BizTalk server host instances and the SQL Server instances
- ❑ All counters for the CPUs on all servers
- ❑ All the memory counters on all servers
- ❑ All the system counters for all servers
- ❑ CLR counters for memory and locks
- ❑ All BizTalk counters that are relevant for a given host (e.g., messaging, adapters, TDDS, message latency, XLang)
- ❑ All SQL Server counters on the database server
- ❑ Disk counters for the database
- ❑ Network interface counters

The following example shows the PerfMon counters for a deployment that has four processing nodes, of which there is one receive host, one send host, and two orchestration hosts, and a single database server:

```
\\btssvr-001\Process(BTSNTSvc)\*
\\btssvr-001\Processor(*)\*
\\btssvr-001\Memory\*
\\btssvr-001\System\*
\\btssvr-001\BizTalk:Messaging(RECVHOST)\*
\\btssvr-001\.NET CLR LocksAndThreads(BTSNTSvc)\*
\\btssvr-001\.NET CLR Memory(BTSNTSvc)\*
```

```
\\btssvr-001\BizTalk:Message Agent(RecHost)\*
\\btssvr-001\BizTalk:Messaging Latency(*)\*
\\btssvr-001\BizTalk:MSMQ Receive Adapter(RecHost)\*
\\btssvr-001\BizTalk:TDDS(*)\*
\\btssvr-001\BizTalk:Message Box:General Counters(*)\*
\\btssvr-001\BizTalk:Message Box:Host Counters(*)\*
\\btssvr-001\Network Interface(*)\*

Repeated for other BizTalk processing servers:
btssvr-002, btssvr-003, and btssvr-004
...

\\dbsvr-01\Process(sqlservr)\*
\\dbsvr-01\Processor(*)\*
\\dbsvr-01\Memory\*
\\dbsvr-01\System\*
\\dbsvr-01\SQLServer:General Statistics\*
\\dbsvr-01\SQLServer:Locks(*)\*
\\dbsvr-01\PhysicalDisk(*)\*
\\dbsvr-01\Network Interface(*)\*
```

The interpretation of `PerfMon` counters is a mixture of common sense and experience; some of the common things to look for include the following, although this is not an exhaustive list of possibilities:

❑ Check that the database server is not maxed out. If the CPU utilization is pegged at 100 percent, the most likely scenario is that your database server is not powerful enough to handle the load that the processing tier is exerting on it, assuming that the deployment and load profile is representative of what you expect to see in production. You could have two database servers, one dedicated to the MessageBox database, which is typically the most resource-intensive database, and the other database server for all of the other BizTalk databases. Alternatively, you might need to scale your MessageBox database server up or out. Usually, it makes more sense to scale it up. Scaling out the MessageBox will mean that you need to move from one database server to three, due to the overhead associated with the scale-out design. On the other hand, SQL Server scales up very well. This is typically not only a more cost-effective approach but also gives better performance for most scenarios. However, before scaling the database server, ensure that your processing tier cannot be optimized to reduce the amount of load that it exerts on the database. For instance, it could be that you have a high number of persistence points in your orchestrations, many of which could be optimized out. Persistence points are discussed in Chapter 5.

❑ Check the CPU utilization on the BizTalk host servers. Is the CPU utilization pegged at or close to 100 percent on any of the servers? Spiking to 100 percent CPU utilization is rarely a problem. However, if the CPU utilization is at 100 percent for a prolonged period on both of the orchestration servers while it's very low on the receive and send servers, it could be that your overall throughput would benefit from deploying an orchestration host on all four servers. However, before you do that, you'll need to further understand what processing is so expensive in the orchestration hosts and tune those first.

❑ If the receive or send host servers are pegged at 100 percent CPU, you need to understand what part of the processing is expensive. Typically, this means understanding whether the CPU is being used mostly in the adapter or pipeline. One way to do this is to eliminate one or the other. Often, if you are using a custom receive pipeline, the best way to do this is to use a pass-through receive pipeline and check whether the performance characteristics remain unchanged. This may mean creating a dummy send port that is bound to your receive port in order to ensure that the receive side messages are published successfully.

❏ If there is low CPU usage on all the BizTalk host servers and the database server CPU utilization is also relatively low, you might have a network problem. Perhaps the disk subsystem on the database server is underperforming or maybe there is significant serialization somewhere. The disk queue lengths and disk idle times on the database disk subsystem generally indicate the performance of the disk subsystem. Monitoring the network interface performance counters will give an indication of the network traffic.

There is no silver bullet to performance tuning, but using a methodical approach and eliminating performance issues as and when you find them helps you to keep moving forward. It requires investigation and experimentation during controlled test passes. It's important not to vary too many things at once. Keep it simple and, where possible, change only a single variable between runs so that the effect of that change can be measured and understood as much as possible. Chapter 9 will drill down further on many of these PerfMon counters and help you to understand what to look for when analyzing them.

Code Profiling

If you can narrow down a performance problem to a specific component, you can try a number of things to identify where the problem lies within that component. Often, it might be necessary to remove that component from the solution to prove or disprove that it is the source of the performance problem. If you own and have access to the source code for that component, you could visually inspect the code, looking for suspicious code.

A good level of software tracing in custom code may be enough to identify where performance problems lie (as long as the software tracing is implemented to include high-resolution timestamps and the ability to determine the code path through a software stack for a given message). This typically means adding a transaction ID that can be used to tie trace statements together from different servers. The BizTalk InterchangeID is often a useful identifier to include in trace statements. For those scenarios where tracing and other approaches cannot be employed, the only approach might be to use code profiling to identify expensive calls. For those scenarios in which the cause of performance problems cannot be found, you can use a profiling tool. Profilers show how often and how expensive method calls are.

Visual Studio 2005 ships with a new code-profiling tool, Visual Studio Profiler. You can configure Visual Studio Profiler to profile managed and unmanaged code, including solely managed or unmanaged applications or mixed applications. The profiler can be used in both sampling and instrumentation modes. Each approach has its own merits. The former is less intrusive but also less accurate. The latter is more accurate but generates a large volume of data and may significantly slow down a solution.

You can use Visual Studio Profiler to rank methods in order of expense (that is, where an excessive amount of time is spent). The "expense" might be resulting from the fact that they are called frequently or just that they are slow. Visual Studio Profiler is a useful tool during performance tuning and troubleshooting to gain greater insight into the runtime behavior of the code, but it should not be the first tool you reach for.

A little known fact is that the Visual Studio Profiler can be installed in stand-alone mode, independently of Visual Studio. You can find the installation executable, VS_Profiler.exe, on the Visual Studio installation media in the \vs\wcu\profiler directory. This is very useful; when you are investigating a performance issue, you probably do not want to install Visual Studio on your BizTalk Server processing machines. This approach gives you a much lighter-weight installation footprint.

> When profiling, it's important to use good symbols — that is, the symbols should match the versions of the binaries that you have installed. Without good symbols you will not get any meaningful results. At a minimum, ensure that you have symbols for your binaries. For some scenarios, it might also be useful to have symbols for the rest of the software stack, including BizTalk Server. Fortunately, Microsoft has published an Internet Symbol Server. Visual Studio can be pointed to this symbol server by setting the environment variable _NT_SYMBOL_PATH to srv*DownloadStore*http://msdl.microsoft.com/download/symbols, where DownloadStore is a cache directory (preferably local); for example, srv*C:\ Symbols*http://msdl.microsoft.com/download/symbols.

You can use Visual Studio Profiler to profile the custom components in the BizTalk solution. The profiling of a service needs to be done from the command line rather than from the Visual Studio IDE. The steps illustrate how you can do so:

1. Enable profiling for managed code. Figure 8-15 shows the command to set up the environment variables required to profile managed code using sampling.

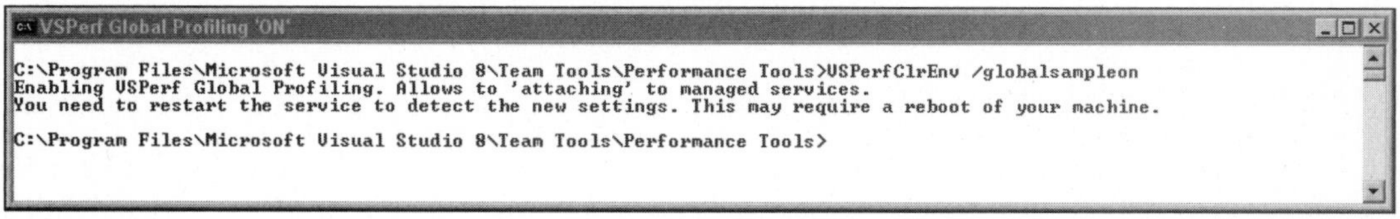

```
C:\Program Files\Microsoft Visual Studio 8\Team Tools\Performance Tools>VSPerfClrEnv /globalsampleon
Enabling VSPerf Global Profiling. Allows to 'attaching' to managed services.
You need to restart the service to detect the new settings. This may require a reboot of your machine.

C:\Program Files\Microsoft Visual Studio 8\Team Tools\Performance Tools>
```

Figure 8-15

2. Restart the machine for the changes to take effect.

3. The BizTalk host instance should be started at this point. Typically, it is advantageous to run a number of messages through BizTalk to prebuild all the internal caches used in BizTalk and possibly your solution as discussed earlier. Failure to do this can skew the profiling results and, for some scenarios, cloak the source of the real issues.

4. Start the profiler. It is configured to use either sampling or instrumentation mode. The /output option creates a .vsp file to store performance data, as shown in Figure 8-16.

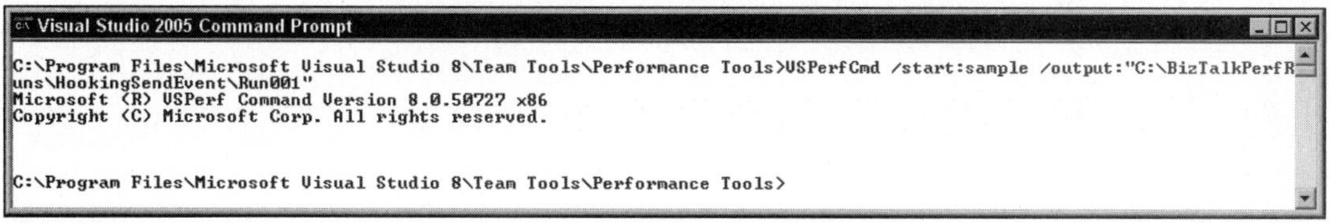

```
C:\Program Files\Microsoft Visual Studio 8\Team Tools\Performance Tools>VSPerfCmd /start:sample /output:"C:\BizTalkPerfR
uns\HookingSendEvent\Run001"
Microsoft (R) VSPerf Command Version 8.0.50727 x86
Copyright (C) Microsoft Corp. All rights reserved.

C:\Program Files\Microsoft Visual Studio 8\Team Tools\Performance Tools>
```

Figure 8-16

5. Attach the profiler to the process. If you cannot determine the process ID of the BizTalk host instance from the task manager, you can use `Process Explorer` from www.microsoft.com/ technet/sysinternals. The example in Figure 8-17 uses the `/counter` option. Prior to Visual Studio SP1, the default settings will not work on Intel Core Duo processors because of some deprecated performance counters on the CPU.

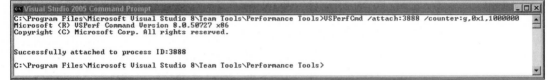

Figure 8-17

6. At this point, a controlled performance run is executed. If you are using sample-based profiling, the run needs to be long enough to get a good sampling.

7. When the performance run is complete, or preferably shortly before it is due to complete, the profiler may be detached and then shut down, as shown in Figure 8-18 and 8-19.

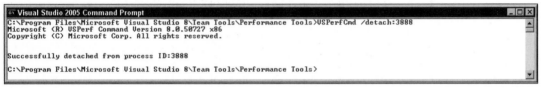

Figure 8-18

Figure 8-19

9. If you have completed your profiling work and you have all the desired results, you can turn profiling off, as shown in Figure 8-20. You must then restart the machine for this to take effect.

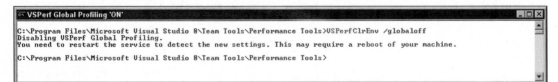

Figure 8-20

At this point, you will have the profiler's performance data stored in a `.vsp` file. You can either generate reports from the `.vsp` using the `VSPerfReport` command-line tool, or you can analyze the results in Visual Studio. To do this, you first need to create a new performance session via the Tools ➪ Performance Tools ➪ New Performance Session menu option, as shown in Figure 8-21.

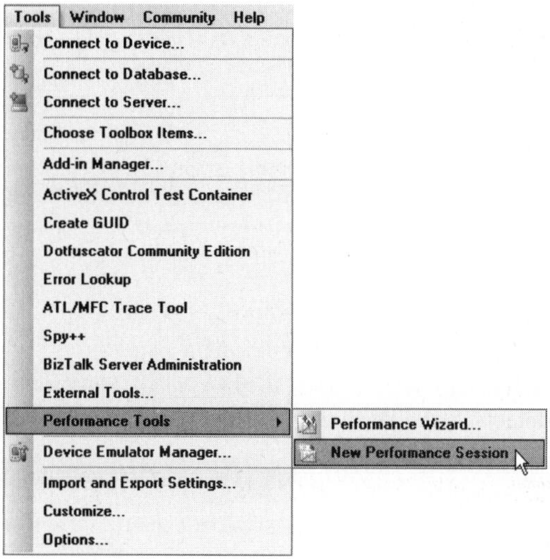

Figure 8-21

After a new session has been created, you can add `.vsp` to the new performance session by using the Performance Explorer (see Figure 8-22).

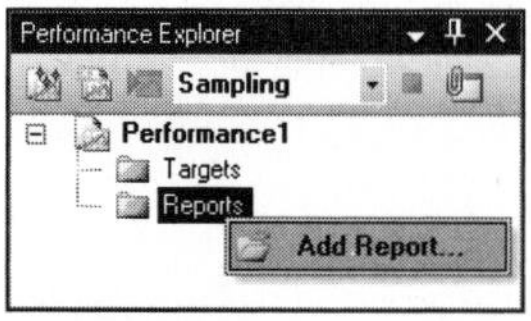

Figure 8-22

Double-clicking the report causes Visual Studio to begin analyzing the data. When complete, the Performance Report Summary will be displayed. To illustrate how the profiler can be used to identify potential performance issues, the following example report is for a custom pipeline component that has a performance issue. The `PoorlyWrittenMethod()` is called from the pipeline component's `IComponent`.`Execute()` implementation. Every message passing through the receive pipeline is processed by this function. The summary in Figure 8-23 shows the top inclusive and exclusive sampled functions. The `PoorlyWrittenMethod()` function is top of the exclusive samples' list. This indicates that this function was found to be executing more often than any other function during the samples that were taken by the profiler. This is a good indication that there is a problem with the function. The summary for the top inclusive sampled functions indicates the functions that were on the stack when the sample was taken.

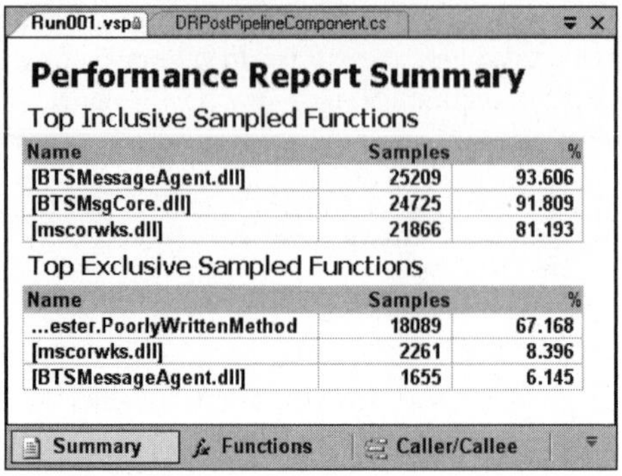

Performance Report Summary

Top Inclusive Sampled Functions

Name	Samples	%
[BTSMessageAgent.dll]	25209	93.606
[BTSMsgCore.dll]	24725	91.809
[mscorwks.dll]	21866	81.193

Top Exclusive Sampled Functions

Name	Samples	%
...ester.PoorlyWrittenMethod	18089	67.168
[mscorwks.dll]	2261	8.396
[BTSMessageAgent.dll]	1655	6.145

Figure 8-23

From the summary view, you can navigate to a number of other views to analyze the data in more detail. Figure 8-24 shows the functions view. Function calls are grouped by modules. Different columns can be added to or removed from the display by right-clicking on the view. The following view below is sorted on inclusive percentage, which is calculated as follows:

```
([Inclusive samples for the function] / [Total inclusive samples taken during
profiling]) * 100
```

The inclusive percentage view is interesting, but notice that near the top is the PoorlyWrittenMethod() in the DeliveryNotificationRequester.dll, which is the assembly for the pipeline component. Looking more closely at this method, you can clearly see that an excessively large portion of the samples are taken while this method is executing. Sorting by Exclusive Percentage shows that, in fact, this function is top at 67.168 percent. At this point, it's clear that there is a serious problem with the function. The next step is to closely examine that function to see why it is so expensive. The Exclusive Percentage is calculated as follows:

```
([Exclusive samples for the function] / [Total exclusive samples taken during
profiling]) * 100
```

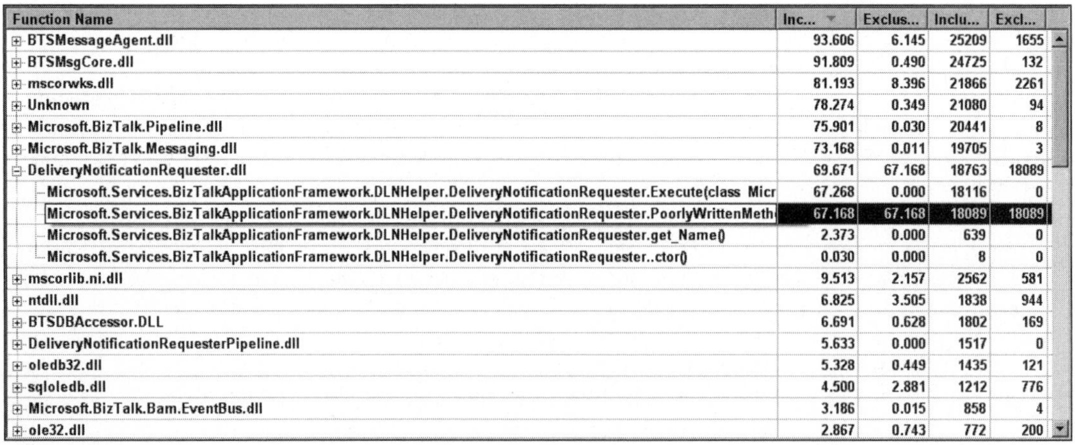

Function Name	Inc... ▼	Exclus...	Inclu...	Excl...
⊞ BTSMessageAgent.dll	93.606	6.145	25209	1655
⊞ BTSMsgCore.dll	91.809	0.490	24725	132
⊞ mscorwks.dll	81.193	8.396	21866	2261
⊞ Unknown	78.274	0.349	21080	94
⊞ Microsoft.BizTalk.Pipeline.dll	75.901	0.030	20441	8
⊞ Microsoft.BizTalk.Messaging.dll	73.168	0.011	19705	3
⊟ DeliveryNotificationRequester.dll	69.671	67.168	18763	18089
— Microsoft.Services.BizTalkApplicationFramework.DLNHelper.DeliveryNotificationRequester.Execute(class Micr	67.268	0.000	18116	0
— Microsoft.Services.BizTalkApplicationFramework.DLNHelper.DeliveryNotificationRequester.PoorlyWrittenMeth	67.168	67.168	18089	18089
— Microsoft.Services.BizTalkApplicationFramework.DLNHelper.DeliveryNotificationRequester.get_Name()	2.373	0.000	639	0
— Microsoft.Services.BizTalkApplicationFramework.DLNHelper.DeliveryNotificationRequester..ctor()	0.030	0.000	8	0
⊞ mscorlib.ni.dll	9.513	2.157	2562	581
⊞ ntdll.dll	6.825	3.505	1838	944
⊞ BTSDBAccessor.DLL	6.691	0.628	1802	169
⊞ DeliveryNotificationRequesterPipeline.dll	5.633	0.000	1517	0
⊞ oledb32.dll	5.328	0.449	1435	121
⊞ sqloledb.dll	4.500	2.881	1212	776
⊞ Microsoft.BizTalk.Bam.EventBus.dll	3.186	0.015	858	4
⊞ ole32.dll	2.867	0.743	772	200

Figure 8-24

For this particular example, the `PoorlyWrittenMethod()` function was fixed, the pipeline component was redeployed, and the solution was again profiled. Figure 8-25 shows that the function is now way down the list and clearly no longer an issue.

Function Name	Inc... ▼	Exclus...	Inclu...	Excl...
⊞ BTSDBAccessor.DLL	19.840	1.856	1785	167
⊞ Microsoft.BizTalk.Messaging.dll	18.995	0.011	1709	1
⊟ DeliveryNotificationRequesterPipeline.dll	17.517	0.000	1576	0
DeliveryNotificationRequesterPipeline.DRXmitterPipeline..ctor()	8.758	0.000	788	0
DeliveryNotificationRequesterPipeline.DLNRequesterSendPipeline..ctor()	8.647	0.000	778	0
DeliveryNotificationRequesterPipeline.DLNRequesterSendPipeline.get_VersionDependentGuid()	0.067	0.000	6	0
DeliveryNotificationRequesterPipeline.DRXmitterPipeline.get_VersionDependentGuid()	0.044	0.000	4	0
⊞ oledb32.dll	15.394	1.145	1385	103
⊞ sqloledb.dll	13.282	8.681	1195	781
⊞ ole32.dll	9.770	2.534	879	228
⊞ DRPostPipelineComponent.dll	9.014	0.000	811	0
⊞ Microsoft.BizTalk.Bam.EventBus.dll	8.959	0.011	806	1
⊞ kernel32.dll	8.214	5.446	739	490
⊟ DeliveryNotificationRequester.dll	7.969	0.000	717	0
Microsoft.Services.BizTalkApplicationFramework.DLNHelper.DeliveryNotificationRequester.get_Name()	7.591	0.000	683	0
Microsoft.Services.BizTalkApplicationFramework.DLNHelper.DeliveryNotificationRequester.Execute(class Micr	0.278	0.000	25	0
Microsoft.Services.BizTalkApplicationFramework.DLNHelper.DeliveryNotificationRequester..ctor()	0.100	0.000	9	0
⊞ Microsoft.BizTalk.Bam.EventObservation.dll	6.691	0.456	602	41
⊞ msadce.dll	5.702	1.534	513	138

Figure 8-25

Automating Performance Testing

Many of the performance lab sessions that I have worked on in the past have required a large matrix of performance results to be collected and analyzed to fully understand the system interactions and dependencies. The configuration, execution, and collection of results can be performed manually, but often doing so proves repetitive and prone to human error. For instance, forgetting to set some configuration can lead to rerunning tests and wasted time. Also, you need to be physically present in the lab to run tests. When performing this type of testing, it's good to consider which reusable assets you can build. In general, building reusable performance test assets will pay dividends. It will enable you to run more scenarios and collect more test data to better understand your performance characteristics and interdependencies. Subsequently, you can use them to jump-start the testing of future projects.

BizUnit lends itself well to these scenarios. You can use it to orchestrate each performance test and collect all the results. The best thing is that you can run the tests overnight so that the results are ready the next morning for analysis. The automation of a series of performance runs generally involves the following test steps:

1. Create a directory to store the test data (performance counters, events logs, software trace logs, and any other test result data useful for subsequent analysis).
2. Clear the event logs on all servers in the rig.
3. Stop the BizTalk hosts on all servers.
4. Clean up the MessageBox database to ensure that there are no residual messages or orchestrations from previous runs.

5. Start the BizTalk hosts.

6. Start the `PerfMon` counters.

7. Send some primer messages to warm up the system caches.

8. Track the test start time in a SQL test results database.

9. Start the performance test. This will, of course, involve starting LoadGen.

10. Wait for the test to complete.

11. Track the test end time in a SQL test results database.

12. Stop the `PerfMon` counters.

13. Save the test data, logs, and so on to the test data directory previously created.

Each individual test will vary its input load to test a different scenario. As mentioned previously, the philosophy of BizUnit is that each test case must clean up after it has executed, regardless of whether it was successful. If a test fails, all the necessary data will be available for analysis to understand why the test failed. When the reasons for its failure are understood, it can be rerun. The failure of that one test should not impact the outcome of any of the other tests.

The BizUnit test case used to drive a performance test is shown here:

```
<TestCase testName="Woodgrove-LoanQuote-001">
  <TestSetup>
    <!-- Ctx prop: name of test run -->
    <TestStep assemblyPath="" typeName="...ContextManipulatorStep">
      <ContextItem contextKey="TestRunName">
        <ItemTest takeFromCtx="BizUnitTestCaseName"></ItemTest>
        <ItemTest>_%DateTime%</ItemTest>
      </ContextItem>
    </TestStep>
    <!-- Ctx prop: name of test dir to store results -->
    <TestStep assemblyPath="" typeName="...ContextManipulatorStep">
      <ContextItem contextKey="TestCaseResultsDir">
        <ItemTest>C:\WoodgrovePerfTests\Results\</ItemTest>
        <ItemTest takeFromCtx="TestRunName"></ItemTest>
      </ContextItem>
    </TestStep>
    <!-- Ctx prop: PerfMon log file -->
    <TestStep assemblyPath="" typeName="...ContextManipulatorStep">
      <ContextItem contextKey="PerfMonFilePath">
        <ItemTest takeFromCtx="TestCaseResultsDir"></ItemTest>
        <ItemTest>\PerfCounters.blg</ItemTest>
      </ContextItem>
    </TestStep>
    <!-- Ctx prop: dest for app event log on BTSSVR-001 -->
    <TestStep assemblyPath="" typeName="...ContextManipulatorStep">
      <ContextItem contextKey="DestPath-BTSSVR-001-AppEventLog">
        <ItemTest takeFromCtx="TestCaseResultsDir"></ItemTest>
        <ItemTest>\BTSSVR-001_ApplicationLog.evt</ItemTest>
      </ContextItem>
    </TestStep>
```

```xml
  <!-- Clear the application event log on BTSSVR-001 -->
  <TestStep assemblyPath="" typeName="...EventLogClearStep">
    <Machine>BTSSVR-001</Machine>
    <EventLog>Application</EventLog>
  </TestStep>

  <!-- Missing Steps: Clear the application logs on all the other
    servers... -->

  <!-- Create the directory to save all the test results -->
  <TestStep assemblyPath="" typeName="...CreateDirectory">
    <DirectoryName takeFromCtx="TestCaseResultsDir" ></DirectoryName>
  </TestStep>
</TestSetup>

<TestExecution>
  <!-- Step 1: Stop BizTalk Hosts -->
  <TestStep assemblyPath="" typeName="...ExecuteCommandStep">
    <ProcessName>C:\WoodgrovePerfTests\Tools\psexec.exe</ProcessName>
    <ProcessParams>\\BTSSVR-001 -i -u "THUNDERBOLT\Administrator" -p
      passW0rd "C:\Windows\System32\Cscript.exe"
C:\WoodgrovePerfTests\Tools\StopBizTalkHostInstances.vbs BTSSVR-001
    </ProcessParams>
    <WorkingDirectory>.</WorkingDirectory>
  </TestStep>

  <!-- Missing Steps: Stop the BizTalk Hosts on all other servers-->

  <!-- Step 2: Clean Up MessageBox -->
  <TestStep assemblyPath="" typeName="...DBExecuteNonQueryStep">
    <DelayBeforeExecution>1</DelayBeforeExecution>
    <ConnectionString>Persist Security Info=False;Integrated
      Security=SSPI;database=BizTalkMsgBoxDb;server=DBSVR-01;Connect
      Timeout=30</ConnectionString>
    <SQLQuery>
      <RawSQLQuery>[dbo].[bts_CleanupMsgbox]</RawSQLQuery>
    </SQLQuery>
  </TestStep>
  <!-- Step 3: Start Perfmon counters -->
  <TestStep assemblyPath="" typeName="...PerfmonCountersStep">
    <PerfmonAction>Start</PerfmonAction>
    <CounterSetName>WoodgrovePerfCounters</CounterSetName>
    <CountersListFilePath>
      ..\..\..\WoodgrovePerfTest\BizUnitTests\PerfCounters\
      PerfMonCounters.txt</CountersListFilePath>
    <SampleInterval>5</SampleInterval>
    <PerfmonLogFilePath takeFromCtx="
      PerfMonFilePath"></PerfmonLogFilePath>
  </TestStep>
  <!-- Step 4: Start BizTalk Hosts -->
  <TestStep assemblyPath="" typeName="...ExecuteCommandStep">
    <ProcessName>C:\WoodgrovePerfTests\Tools\psexec.exe</ProcessName>
    <ProcessParams>\\BTSSVR-001 -i -u "THUNDERBOLT\Administrator" -p
      passW0rd "C:\windows\system32\cscript.exe"
```

```
        C:\WoodgrovePerfTests\Tools\StartBizTalkHostInstances.vbs
      BTSSVR-001</ProcessParams>
    <WorkingDirectory>.</WorkingDirectory>
  </TestStep>


  <!-- Missing Steps: Start the BizTalk Hosts on all other servers-->

  <!-- Step 5: Send Priming messages -->
  <TestStep assemblyPath="" typeName="...LoadGenExecuteStep">
    <LoadGenTestConfig>..\..\..\WoodgrovePerfTest\BizUnitTests\
      LoadGenXmlFiles\LoadQuotes_Primer.xml</LoadGenTestConfig>
  </TestStep>
  <!-- Step 6: Read loadgen file into context variable -->
  <TestStep assemblyPath="" typeName="...FileReadAndLoadToContext">
    <FilePath>
      ..\..\..\WoodgrovePerfTest\BizUnitTests\LoadGenXmlFiles\
      LoadQuotes_Main.xml</FilePath>
    <ContextPropertyName>LoadGenFileContent</ContextPropertyName>
  </TestStep>
  <!-- Step 7: Update test results DB with test start time -->
  <TestStep assemblyPath="" typeName="...DBExecuteNonQueryStep">
    <DelayBeforeExecution>1</DelayBeforeExecution>
    <ConnectionString>Persist Security Info=False;Integrated
      Security=SSPI;database=Woodgrove;server=DBSVR-01;Connect
        Timeout=30</ConnectionString>
    <SQLQuery>
      <RawSQLQuery>INSERT INTO tblPerformanceResults (Test_ID,
        StartTime,LoadGenFile) VALUES ('{0}',GetDate(),'{1}'
        )</RawSQLQuery>
      <SQLQueryParams>
        <SQLQueryParam takeFromCtx="TestRunName"></SQLQueryParam>
        <SQLQueryParam takeFromCtx=
          "LoadGenFileContent"></SQLQueryParam>
      </SQLQueryParams>
    </SQLQuery>
  </TestStep>
  <!-- Step 8: LoadGen: Load actual MQ messages onto queue -->
  <TestStep assemblyPath="" typeName="...LoadGenExecuteStep">
    <LoadGenTestConfig>.
      .\..\..\WoodgrovePerfTest\BizUnitTests\LoadGenXmlFiles\
      LoadQuotes_Main.xml</LoadGenTestConfig>
  </TestStep>
  <!-- Step 9: Delay for 60 secs to allow msgs to start flowing -->
  <TestStep assemblyPath="" typeName="...DelayStep">
    <Delay>60000</Delay>
  </TestStep>
  <!-- Step 10: Wait for Orch Host Queue depth to reach zero -->
  <TestStep assemblyPath="" typeName="...PerfMonCounterMonitorStep">
    <CategoryName>BizTalk:Message Box:Host Counters</CategoryName>
    <CounterName>Host Queue - Length</CounterName>
    <InstanceName>OrchHost:biztalkmsgboxdb:DBSVR-01</InstanceName>
    <Server>DBSVR-01</Server>
    <CounterTargetValue>0</CounterTargetValue>
  </TestStep>
```

```
<!-- Step 11: Update test results DB with test stop time -->
TestStep assemblyPath="" typeName="...DBExecuteNonQueryStep">
  <DelayBeforeExecution>1</DelayBeforeExecution>
  <ConnectionString>Persist Security Info=False;Integrated
    Security=SSPI;database=Woodgrove;server=DBSVR-01;Connect
    Timeout=30</ConnectionString>
  <SQLQuery>
    <RawSQLQuery>UPDATE tblPerformanceResults SET EndTime =
      GetDate() WHERE Test_ID = '{0}'</RawSQLQuery>
    <SQLQueryParams>
      <SQLQueryParam takeFromCtx="TestRunName"></SQLQueryParam>
    </SQLQueryParams>
  </SQLQuery>
</TestStep>
</TestExecution>

<TestCleanup> <!-- Return system to state prior to test -->
  <!-- Stop PerfMon counters -->
  <TestStep assemblyPath="" typeName="...PerfmonCountersStep"
    failOnError="false">
    <PerfmonAction>Stop</PerfmonAction>
    <CounterSetName>WoodgrovePerfCounters</CounterSetName>
  </TestStep>
  <!-- Delete PerfMon counters -->
  <TestStep assemblyPath="" typeName="...ExecuteCommandStep"
    failOnError="false">
    <ProcessName>logman</ProcessName>
    <ProcessParams>delete WoodgrovePerfCounters</ProcessParams>
  </TestStep>
  <!-- Save Event log(s) on locally on each server -->
  <TestStep assemblyPath="" typeName="...EventLogSaveStep"
    failOnError="false">
    <Server>BTSSVR-001</Server>
    <DestinationPath>C:\BTSSVR-001_ApplicationLog.evt
    </DestinationPath>
  </TestStep>
  <!-- Move Event log(s) to Test Case Results folder -->
  <TestStep assemblyPath="" typeName="...FileMoveStep"
    failOnError="false">
    <SourcePath>
      \\BTSSVR-001\C$\BTSSVR-001_ApplicationLog.evt</SourcePath>
    <DestinationPath takeFromCtx=
      "DestPath-BTSSVR-001-AppEventLog"></DestinationPath>
  </TestStep>
</TestCleanup>
</TestCase>
```

You can imagine how much time this approach can save. I have used it in the past to ensure that all the tests are consistently executed. This approach has made it possible to gather a huge amount of data to analyze, which subsequently has lead to the realization of huge performance improvements.

Stress Testing

Some bugs, by their very nature, are extremely difficult to detect, let alone determine their root cause. These types of bugs may include memory leaks, access violations, or race conditions. Often, they are aggravated by the multithreaded execution environment. Bugs of these types can go undiscovered for long periods of time. The code might work as expected until one day the bug shows up and the code stops working. Or a bug might be present for a period of time before anyone notices — perhaps an increase in system load means that the bug can suddenly not be tolerated.

While BizTalk tries to make it as easy as possible to avoid these problems when building your solution, there are plenty of opportunities to introduce issues such as these or even exercise a code path in the software stack where other previously undetected issues may be. To put memory leaks in server-side code into perspective, consider a piece of code that leaks 10 bytes of memory for every message. If your solution were processing 3 million messages a day, that would roughly translate to 30MB of memory leaked in a day. It would not take long before that leak pulled down the process. Race conditions can lead to all sorts of issues, ranging from access violations to incorrect or missing data.

While the CLR helps a great deal to protect you from a number of the issues that would be possible in a native code execution environment, it is no silver bullet for these types of issues. It is still relatively easy to write code that leaks memory, database connections, or other resources. For example, creating and using a COM object though managed code interop is a common issue. Failure to call `Marshal .ReleaseComObject()` on the object will leave it at the mercy of the garbage collector, which will place the object on its finalizer queue. When this happens, the releasing of this memory may take considerably longer, since the object will definitely be promoted to the garbage collector's generation 1 and more than likely be promoted to generation 2. When running under high load and creating a lot of COM objects, it is very likely that the garbage collector will not be able to collect the COM objects in a timely enough manner to release all of the memory associated with them. This will produce all the characteristics and problems of a memory leak. Another common pitfall is not to call `Marshal.ReleaseComObject()` in a loop, which is necessary to ensure that the object is released. This API releases the runtime callable wrapper (RCW) that holds onto the underlying COM object; the API returns the reference count of the RCW. Typically, the RCW reference count will stay at one for more trivial usage scenarios, but depending on your usage of the COM object, the reference counter may go above one. This means that not calling the API in a loop will cause the RCW and subsequently the underlying COM object, not to be released and therefore to be left at the mercy of the garbage collector.

The following code snippet illustrates how to correctly release a reference to a COM object:

```
if ( Marshal.IsComObject(obj) )
{
  while( 0 < Marshal.ReleaseComObject( obj ) )
  {
    ;
  }
}
```

.NET 2.0 introduces a new API to simplify this:

```
if ( Marshal.IsComObject(obj) )
{
```

```
    // This method is new in the .NET Framework version 2.0
    Marshal.FinalReleaseComObject( obj );
}
```

Stress testing should be designed to simulate the operating conditions in a production environment; typically, this should be in line with the most severe conditions that the solution is expected to see. It is important to ensure that your stress tests are executed long enough to uncover any of the issues but short enough to reasonably fit into the project plan. While the BizTalk product group performs stress tests lasting for weeks, unfortunately few BizTalk projects can absorb that level of testing. The duration of a stress run should ideally be long enough to simulate the duration between maintenance windows, since this is typically the longest period of time the system will need to run. That said, some projects may find it difficult to schedule that length of stress run; at a minimum, the solution should be run under a continuous load equal to a minimum of two days' worth of messages. The elapsed time period for the stress run may be compressed by increasing the load. Typically, this level of high-load stress testing will flush out many stress issues, although the longer the test is executed, the more likely issues will be flushed out.

As with performance testing, it is important to monitor and record PerfMon counters so that the results of the stress test may be analyzed offline in the event of issues. The same list of PerfMon counters that were previously discussed should be monitored and recorded. However, the sampling rate will need to be reduced in order to minimize the size of the PerfMon logs. Similarly, the event logs should be saved and checked for errors; while the stress run may have completed successfully, there may have been problems along the way that should be investigated. For example BizTalk will always try to recover from failure scenarios if possible. If connectivity to the database is lost BizTalk will retry to connect to the database. If it cannot reconnect, the BizTalk service will restart itself in order to try to cleanly connect to the database. Ideally, a constant message throughput rate should be observed throughout the test. If the throughput rate steadily degrades, there is almost certainly a problem. Once again, LoadGen is well suited to provide the load profile for BizTalk stress testing; typically, it makes less sense to automate stress tests because of the low number of stress tests that need to be performed.

Mixing It Up

Some systems will inevitably experience periods when they receive high loads of bad messages. Systems prone to such periods are not just those that process messages from external sources; they may also be systems that process messages that originate from other internal applications. It's important to consider these scenarios, too, because memory leaks and other stress-related issues may be associated with the negative scenarios and only be exposed under those conditions. Including a percentage of bad messages throughout the duration of stress runs often proves helpful to flush out problems associated with negative scenarios. Also, varying the load profile and subsequently the rate at which messages are received can prove useful.

Overload Testing

BizTalk uses queues at the database level to persist messages before it processes them. On the receive side, they will sit in the queue until the processing service is ready to pick them up. That could be an orchestration, a send port, or even a receive port, in the case of a two-way receive port. Messages outbound from orchestrations also sit in their respective MessageBox queue prior to being dequeued by their processing service.

The MessageBox queuing decouples the processing of messages. It is designed to enable BizTalk to cope with fluctuations in load both in-bound and outbound from the engine without inducing an adverse effect elsewhere. You can think of it as a mechanism for smoothing out the processing spikes and troughs. For example, the fact that a back-end system is down or busy should not cause the receiving of new messages to be slowed down, within reason of course. For the most part, this works extremely well. When messages are received at a higher rate than the processing of them occurs, they just stack up in the MessageBox queue; that is, the depth of the MessageBox queue increases. At some point, the rate of outbound processing will overtake the rate of in-bound processing, and the queue depth will decrease to a reasonable level.

Sustained periods of high load in-bound can cause the MessageBox queue depth (specifically, I am referring to the depth of the Spool table) to increase when the in-bound processing rate outstrips the outbound processing rate. Usually, this situation does not create a problem. The in-bound rate will eventually drop off, allowing the outbound processing to drain the MessageBox queues. Under most circumstances, the MessageBox queues may build to a depth in the order of millions of messages without serious issue. However, it is important to understand the dynamics of your scenario and how increased queue depths affect the performance and response of your system.

In some scenarios, it might be appropriate to throttle in-bound processing, thereby rejecting new messages after the queue depth has reached a specified depth. Take care, however, to throttle only activation messages, not correlation messages. Suppose, for instance, that an activation message is received that activates a new orchestration. The orchestration sends a message to a back-end system and waits for the response from that back-end system. The response is a correlation message, because it will be correlated to that instance of the orchestration. If all in-bound messages are throttled, however, the correlation message will not be received. In this scenario backlog of orchestrations might be causing the queue depth to increase over an expected threshold. The correlation message is required before the queue depth can drop, since the correlation message will cause the orchestration to complete. With this, we have a catch 22 scenario. Therefore, it is important to consider these limitations carefully when considering whether to throttle in-bound messages.

With BizTalk Server 2006, you can throttle hosts based on the queue depth for that host. (Chapter 9 discusses throttling in more detail.) You configure this in the BizTalk Administration MMC console under Host Properties ➪ Advanced ➪ Throttling Thresholds. You can use the Message Count in Database option to throttle the number of messages that can be received into the MessageBox, as shown in Figure 8-26.

Periods of excessive load can exert pressure not only on BizTalk but also on the various back-end systems with which it integrates. Therefore, it is important to understand the performance characteristics of these systems in the context of the BizTalk solution.

User Acceptance Testing

User acceptance testing should already be well understood. Essentially, the system should be tested by the users who will be using it after it has been deployed to a production environment. For many systems, the BizTalk solution will be invisible to the users; that is, they might be interacting with applications that in turn interact with BizTalk. Regardless of the scenario, the system needs to be tested in the context of the bigger picture. Typically, user acceptance testing should be designed to ensure that the system meets functional requirements. For some scenarios, the nonfunctional requirements might also need to be validated by the users, depending on the scenarios for which the solution has been designed.

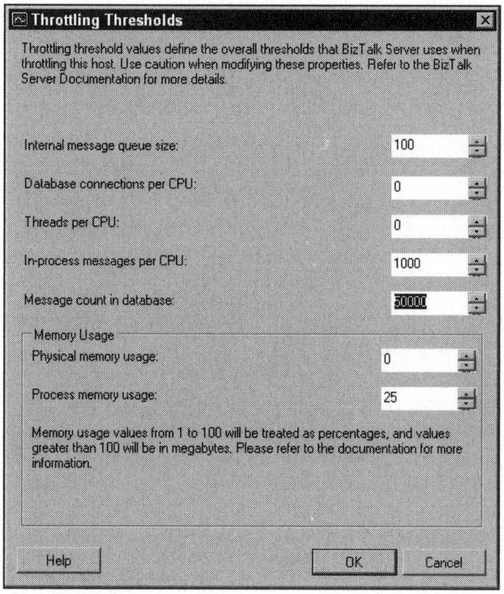

Throttling Thresholds

Throttling threshold values define the overall thresholds that BizTalk Server uses when throttling this host. Use caution when modifying these properties. Refer to the BizTalk Server Documentation for more details.

Internal message queue size: 100

Database connections per CPU: 0

Threads per CPU: 0

In-process messages per CPU: 1000

Message count in database: 50000

Memory Usage
Physical memory usage: 0

Process memory usage: 25

Memory usage values from 1 to 100 will be treated as percentages, and values greater than 100 will be in megabytes. Please refer to the documentation for more information.

Help   OK   Cancel

Figure 8-26

Disaster Recovery Testing

Disaster recovery testing should be designed to test that your solution can cope with a disaster scenario. Disaster scenarios range from minor hardware failures to the loss of your production site. When designing your solution, you must consider the myriad possible failures and have a design or strategy to cope with those.

The disaster recovery test phase is when you get to validate that your solution works as designed under a failure scenario. The following are some of the scenarios that you should consider testing. They might not all be appropriate for your solution; nevertheless, they should trigger some ideas about what you need to test. When thinking about all these types of tests, it is important to remember that failures generally happen under load; therefore, these tests should be carried out when the system is under load, and you should ensure that no data is lost:

❑   **Database cluster failover** — For most BizTalk deployments, the database is deployed in an active-passive cluster. A cluster may failover for a number of reasons, and when it does the chances are you will be processing messages. You may have custom code that is accessing a custom database. You should also ensure that it behaves as designed in a cluster failover scenario.

❑   **Processing node failure** — All BizTalk deployments should have at least two instances of each host instance running on different physical servers. BizTalk is designed to naturally load balance across multiple instances of the same host, and this gives your solution resilience in the event of a failure of one of those servers. This should be tested to ensure that your solution can continue processing. Of course, the throughput will be reduced, but if you have adequately sized your physical architecture, it should be able to keep up with your typical processing rate.

❑ **Network card failure** — Hopefully, your servers will be deployed with dual network cards. The failure of one or both should be tested to ensure that the system behaves as expected.

❑ **Network failure** — The loss of the network should be simulated. When the BizTalk host instances lose connectivity to the database, they will attempt to reconnect by going into retry mode. After the network connectivity has been reestablished, BizTalk should continue processing.

❑ **Full site failure** — The business-critical nature of your system will determine your disaster recovery strategy. This might range from relying on SQL Server database backups to SQL Server log shipping, or for high-end solutions synchronous disk mirroring, whereby every database I/O write to the disk subsystem in your production environment is synchronously mirrored to the disk subsystem at the disaster recovery site. Regardless of your strategy, you need to ensure that it works as designed and that in the event of a critical site failure you can recover to your backup site. This exercise will most likely be time boxed, meaning that your disaster recovery site would need to continue processing within, say, 1 hour of the production site failing. Many financial services' systems have significantly more stringent requirements for this.

❑ **Database restore from backup** — Regardless of your disaster recovery strategy, you should be backing up your databases by using the standard BizTalk scripts. You need to perform a dry run to be sure that you can recover from your database backups (in case doing so might someday be required).

Testing, Documenting, and Fine-Tuning Procedures

Performing a disaster recovery failover generally involves a number of steps, many of which are complex and order dependent. Therefore, a disaster recovery procedure document that details the step-by-step actions to take should be created. The disaster recovery document should be stored in a well-known accessible location (and definitely not just kept in the head of the system expert). A single point of failure should be avoided at all costs. Relying on any single person to be available at the time of a disaster recovery is a recipe for failure. When that person is away from work sick with the flu and his backup person is on vacation, you need someone who can perform the necessary tasks to get your system up and running again with a high degree of confidence.

This disaster recovery procedure should be practiced (prior to going live and then subsequently at regular intervals, preferably at least quarterly). If you are serious about having a disaster recovery capability, it needs to operate like a well-oiled machine, and that means turning the wheels regularly. For some BizTalk deployments, it is possible to run the BizTalk processing tier in an active-active configuration, meaning that BizTalk nodes in the disaster recovery site are always being used. In my view, this is a very good approach and helps to ensure that the disaster recovery site is always in a good state.

Ensuring Zero Data Loss upon Failover

When a system fails, it often fails under high load. Failure often results from the increased stress induced throughout the entire stack (software and hardware). Failover testing while the system is under high load is useful to ensure that you won't lose data during an actual failover scenario and that the system can recover gracefully.

To be honest, testing failover scenarios while the system is not loaded is of limited value. Such testing will give you confidence in your disaster recovery procedures but will do little to increase your confidence in the integrity and resilience of the system. Therefore, the failover testing should be executed while the system is under high load, and all messages should be accounted for to ensure that none are lost.

In some scenarios, messages can be received or sent more than one time in a failure scenario; that is, message duplication can take place. Generally, message duplication is possible when either the receive or send adapters are not transactional. The engine is inherently designed to avoid losing messages, but it may duplicate messages in the event of a nontransactional adapter being used. On the receive side, the messaging engine transactionally persists the in-bound message to the MessageBox before notifying the adapter that it has successfully received the message. This leaves a window of opportunity when the message may be persisted in the MessageBox but still exists at the endpoint.

Consider, for example, the File adapter. The system may fail after a batch of 20 messages submitted by the File adapter has been successfully persisted to the MessageBox but before the engine has notified the File adapter that the batch was submitted or before the adapter has had the opportunity to delete those files from disk. If this happens, the 20 files will still be sitting on the disk waiting to be received when the system comes back up. The problem is that those messages are already sitting in the MessageBox and being processed by BizTalk, and hence all 20 messages will be received twice. Of course, if the Receive adapter were transactional, the messages would be atomically moved from the receive endpoint (which is, in this case, the filesystem to the MessageBox, because both would be enlisted in the same DTC transaction, and for that scenario there is no opportunity to receive messages twice). An idempotent solution such as that described in Chapter 4 could prevent the receiving of duplicate messages when using nontransactional adapters.

On the send side, a similar scenario exists. Again, nontransactional adapters have an opportunity to send messages twice. To take the File adapter as an example again, the BizTalk engine would dequeue a batch of, for instance, 20 messages, process them, and deliver them to the File adapter. The adapter would then transmit 20 files. After the File adapter has successfully transmitted/written 20 files, it notifies the engine that these messages may be deleted from the MessageBox. For a period of time, those messages have been transmitted but not deleted from the MessageBox. The system could potentially fail during that period. If it does fail, those messages will be re-sent when the system comes back up. Again, 20 messages would be transmitted twice.

Microsoft has gone to great lengths to test BizTalk and all the adapters shipped with it to ensure that the product behaves as designed. If you have written a custom adapter, ensure that you have performed enough testing to confirm it behaves as expected. Of course, even if you are using a trusted adapter, it could be misconfigured in many different ways, so this type of testing is still required for most mission-critical deployments.

Production Support Testing

This final test category, production support testing, dovetails with the design and development process. You need to design solutions in a way that allows them to be supported in a "locked-down" production environment. A production environment should be significantly more restricted than the environment where a solution is developed and tested.

This section covers some of the more common issues and problems that you should consider when designing your solution. You should test that your solution can be managed and operated in a production environment as designed. This section does not provide an exhaustive checklist of things to test.

Instead, it examines some of the more common scenarios of which you need to be aware. And this section reminds you to consider the production support scenarios applicable to your specific project and to test that those scenarios work as desired prior to taking your solution live.

Deploying New Solution Artifacts

For many scenarios, you might need to deploy new versions of solution artifacts without halting processing. The two most common artifacts that typically need to be versioned and that frequently cause the most pain are XSD schemas and orchestrations. Although the deployment of a new schema is a relatively trivial task, it is complicated when those schemas are associated with long-running business processes that are in flight and cannot easily be stopped.

Schema versions often have dependent artifacts and components that require an upgrade and redeployment upon version revisions. Changing the version of a schema may require your XSLT maps, orchestrations, and even custom components to be revised. Therefore, you should fully understand the dependency tree for all the artifacts in your solution. You should design the solution in a manner that keeps the artifacts as loosely coupled as possible and packaged in a way that lends itself to deploying new versions of the artifacts with minimal complication. You must design and test the deployment of new versions of orchestrations. For some scenarios, you can drain and then redeploy orchestrations. In other scenarios, however, you cannot drain them, because of the nature of the business processing that they are performing; these scenarios are significantly more complex.

Handling Suspended Messages and Orchestrations

For some scenarios, suspending messages and orchestrations when they encounter problems can cause issues. For example, consider the scenario in which a solution is processing payment messages. The suspension of a message that fails in the receive pipeline means that the payment will not be processed. Instead, it will be persisted in BizTalk's suspend queue. If a suitable strategy has not been designed to handle this situation, you will likely need to save the suspended message to disk, fix it, and resubmit it. This is a manual process; therefore, a large number of suspended messages could mean a significant interruption of business processing and consume a lot of manual labor.

BizTalk Server 2006 enables the routing of suspended messages, meaning that orchestrations or send ports can subscribe to suspended messages. This enables you to design an orchestration to subscribe to failed messages and perform an automated repair of those messages. For some scenarios, it might be appropriate to route the messages back to the sender's "badly formatted error queue" so that the sender can fix them. By doing so, you push the burden back to the source of the bad messages. In other scenarios, it might be more appropriate to save them to disk or perhaps a SharePoint site for manual repair and subsequent resubmission. Regardless of the approach, a strategy for handling badly formatted messages should be designed and then tested.

Similarly, you should design orchestrations in a way that allows graceful suspension. In the event that an orchestration processing a message is suspended, you will need an approach to either get that orchestration running again or to replay the message that it was processing when it was suspended. In terms of gracefully suspended orchestrations, typically this means ensuring that exceptions are not thrown outside of the orchestration. Instead, a `try/catch` block should catch any unhandled exceptions, log the appropriate error information to the Event log, and call `suspend` on the orchestration. Orchestrations should be suspended in such a way that allows the processing to continue when the orchestration is resumed.

Chapter 10 introduces a design pattern for handling failures in orchestrations. The pattern enables orchestrations to be gracefully suspended and then resumed to continue processing at a later time.

Archiving BAM Data

Solutions that depend on BAM need to consider the strategy anticipated to archive historical BAM data. BizTalk provides mechanisms to do this out of the box, but it needs to be enabled. Data-archiving frequency must be considered carefully. Often, this means striking a balance between the amount of BAM data available for historical queries and the amount of disk space required for the `BAMPrimaryImport` database. Of course, performance of your `BAMPrimaryImport` database should also be factored into this. It is not rocket science and is not terribly challenging, but it does need to be planned and tested.

Summary

This chapter has given you insight into how to test an *enterprise-class* BizTalk solution. The content in this chapter is drawn from real-world experience gained while delivering some of the most challenging, mission-critical BizTalk solutions developed to date. Of course, test requirements will vary from project to project and will depend on the risk that a system failure represents for that project. Performing an appropriate level of testing will significantly reduce the risk associated with your project and maximize its chances of success. I have covered the different categories of tests that may be applicable to your project, and talked about approaches to troubleshoot and identify the source of issues. I have also discussed some of the great tools that you can leverage to help your testing.

I have discussed how the test strategy is an integral part of the development process and not an optional addition. If there is one thing you should take away from this chapter, it is to develop automated functional tests. If you do only that, it will dramatically increase the chances of your project succeeding. Automated tests are assets; you invest in building them, and then draw on that investment every time you run them. On the other hand, the adoption of a manual testing approach is a nonscalable approach and will increase the risk associated with your project. Often, this is a cultural change to many organizations, but, if you want to ship rock-solid software, you need to invest in testing, and it needs to be the right type of testing.

Performance and Scalability

Performance testing combined with tuning and troubleshooting is arguably one of the *most crucial* parts of a BizTalk Server solution, and indeed any software solution. Writing code, with BizTalk or any development technology, is relatively straightforward. However, getting it to perform well under load and make the best use of the hardware can prove far harder. If you take away just one thing from this book, remember this: Functional testing, paired with stress and performance testing, is one aspect of any enterprise-class solution that *cannot* be compromised under any circumstances.

The BizTalk platform simplifies performance testing in some aspects, but the actual performance of the system depends on how the solution has been constructed and configured. I've seen many projects assume that performance would be okay and deploy straight to live with little or no testing, resulting in critical problems when the solution was placed under load.

I always try to ensure that developers understand "what things cost" and what a particular feature is doing under the covers, and therefore the likely impact on the overall performance. Having such an appreciation will set up your project for a far greater chance of success. A thorough understanding of orchestration persistence points is a classic example of this.

BizTalk Server is a very powerful product that abstracts complex functionality and techniques by exposing them through a higher-level programming construct and by providing a rich platform. This handles a lot of the heavy lifting for you. Even so, it requires tuning. After all, Microsoft cannot design and build a platform that is "all things to all people."

Chapter 8 introduced some techniques and tools to assist you with testing a BizTalk solution. This chapter expands on those concepts by covering additional performance-testing and -tuning approaches. Testing must be performed often and early in the project life cycle. Parts of your design should be mocked up in the design phase and tested to establish performance levels; assumption is your worst enemy! Many BizTalk applications fail before they ever go live because of a lack of proper nonfunctional preproduction testing.

This chapter covers how you should approach performance and scalability testing of your BizTalk solution and how to monitor the solution performance, again building on what was covered in Chapter 8. This chapter also seeks to demystify the many knobs and levers available for tuning your solution for optimum performance.

This chapter follows a practical layout to aid in your performance testing. It starts with a checklist section that shows you how to confirm whether your environment is configured in a way that avoids negative impacts on performance. The discussion then turns to monitoring, to help you diagnose problems. After that, the chapter focuses on troubleshooting and improving performance.

Laying the Foundations

Before beginning any performance testing, you must ensure that the base environment and software that you're working with is configured correctly. Otherwise, any testing you perform will be highly skewed and will not represent reality. This can lead to many hours or days of wasted effort diagnosing phantom problems — trust me, I've been there!

This section runs through the things that you should ensure are configured correctly in every environment *before* any testing is performed. Everything listed here has affected customers to varying degrees and collectively represents on its own the root of most performance problems (which we as consultants get called out to deal with).

You might also want to review some of the information included in the *Managing A Successful Performance Lab* white paper, published by Microsoft at `http://msdn2.microsoft.com/en-us/library/aa972201.aspx`. This white paper lays out a canonical approach to managing a performance lab and details the process aspects that you should consider.

Hardware

Hardware is critical to the performance of any solution. In this section, we'll discuss areas to be aware of when undertaking performance testing.

Workstation Testing

Some developers attempt to benchmark the performance of their BizTalk solution on their development workstation with both BizTalk Server and SQL Server installed on the same machine. Although this is the natural approach and is sometimes reasonable for non-BizTalk solutions, it's only suitable for functional testing of BizTalk solutions. Using this approach for any form of performance testing is fruitless, largely because of limitations in resources such as the disk, CPU power, and physical memory. Almost immediately, you'll find that BizTalk will be bottlenecked from writing to the disk (i.e., the BizTalk MessageBox).

As discussed later in this section, BizTalk depends heavily on fast disk hardware, which a standard development workstation or server machine does not typically have — unless you're particularly lucky and have a RAID array.

Although you can mitigate this slightly by having separate hard drives with databases and logs separated, it's not a great solution, particularly because SQL Server will attempt to use as much physical memory as possible to improve its performance and also make heavy use of the CPU. If you combine SQL Server with BizTalk Server, which also needs these resources, you'll find they'll contend heavily and this impacts overall performance

In short, perform your functional testing on developer workstations, but then move on to a like-live performance testing rig for performance testing. This rig should be available throughout the development of your project. Any performance numbers you collect from a developer's workstation will be largely useless and not representative of what is possible.

Virtual Machines

For many of the same reasons that apply to workstation testing, it is not advisable to run performance tests on virtualized hardware — the same applies for live servers. Although it's technically possible, my opinion (based on experience with the current generation of hardware and virtualization software) is that virtualization has too much overhead, especially with regard to the SQL Server.

If you do intend to deploy into a virtualized environment, you should perform two sets of performance testing: one on the base hardware and another on the virtualized environment. You can then compare the delta between the two and make an educated decision on the performance degradation that a virtualized environment offers.

Functional and integration-style testing in development environments is well suited to virtualized environments, especially because the environment can be restored to the base build almost instantly (thus saving the time and cost of rebuilding servers). You must have an automated build to enable this, but that is strongly advised anyway.

SQL Server

SQL Server is the heart of any BizTalk solution and its availability and performance are key to the operation of your solution. Your solution's performance will be adversely affected when SQL Server's performance degrades. This could be due to a problem with any of its dependent resources, such as disks, memory pressure, or CPU load.

The size of the machine required to run your scenario is, of course, dependent on your solution and performance requirements. It's important that SQL Server has enough RAM available — typically this will mean at least 4GB. Be aware that you need to set the /3GB and /PAE switches on a SQL Server machine running on 32-bit hardware. Without the /3GB switch, SQL Server is limited to a 2GB process address space.

With the addition of the /PAE switch and the enabling of PAE support in SQL Server (32bit only), the entire memory can be addressed by the operating system. There is a well-known issue with SQL Server 2000 and SP4 in which the server cannot use the entire system memory. For more information, visit http://support.microsoft.com/kb/899761.

In general, Microsoft is moving towards a 64-bit server platform. For SQL Server, this means that you can typically attain better performance by moving to a 64-bit server at little extra cost, which should be the default approach within your organization.

In some scenarios, SQL Server can become a bottleneck for your solution. This is usually experienced as the server being CPU-bound or by seeing heavy lock contention inside the BizTalk MessageBox. A

CPU-bound SQL Server is easy to spot through the % Processor Time performance counter. Lock contention can be identified by monitoring the Lock Timeouts/sec, Average Wait Time (ms), and Lock Waits/sec performance counters, which are discussed later in this chapter.

You might need to scale the MessageBox to meet your performance targets. Before embarking on this, however, you should ensure that you have tuned your solution to minimize the load that it induces on the MessageBox. For example, this means optimizing the persistence points and MessageBox hops for your solution, as discussed in Chapters 5 and 10. Also, you should be sure that SQL Server has enough physical memory available.

Also, if you have multiple BizTalk databases hosted on the same SQL Server machine, it is usually a good idea to try to move all the other BizTalk databases off the MessageBox server before attempting to scale the MessageBox, and to ensure that any database logs are moved onto separate drives.

There are two options around scaling the MessageBox: scale up or scale out. For most scenarios, scaling up will give better price/performance and is arguably easier to manage in a production environment due to the small server estate. Scaling up simply means that you run SQL Server on a machine with more CPUs. SQL will scale up very well. Of course, scaling up could also be achieved by moving to a server with the same number of more performant CPUs.

The second option is to scale out the MessageBox. This is a little more complicated, and in general you should be more cautious about embarking on this approach. Essentially, the MessageBox needs to be scaled from one to three SQL Servers in order to get increased performance. Scaling from one to two MessageBoxes will not give you any significant performance gain. The reason for this is that multiple MessageBoxes will need to be kept synchronized. This requires a distributed transaction across them and the BizTalk processing node. This distributed transaction has associated overhead (setting up, negotiating, committing, etc.), which will be increased if multiple SQL Servers are used for the extra MessageBoxes, due to the network overhead. In addition, you should ensure the message publication is turned off on the master MessageBox to enable it to just evaluate subscriptions and route new messages to the other MessageBox databases for processing.

This routing process uses a round-robin algorithm to ensure that messages are balanced evenly across the two slave MessageBoxes automatically — although it does mean that one of your SQL Servers cannot be used for message publication, which has a performance impact.

Regardless of whether the MessageBoxes are added to the same SQL Server instance or another SQL Server, you should ensure that each MessageBox is stored on its own drive configuration to separate the IO requirements of each MessageBox. Typically, this is performed by exposing another drive letter or LUN from your SAN, as discussed in the "Disks" section of this chapter.

It's worth nothing that any extra SQL Servers used by BizTalk will also need to be clustered for high-availability purposes.

BizTalk Servers

The BizTalk Servers (processing nodes) are where message and orchestration processing takes place. Additional BizTalk Servers can easily be added to a BizTalk group to enable scaling out the processing load, and hardware can obviously be scaled up as appropriate (adding additional processors, for example), although you should always have at least two BizTalk Server nodes that both have instances of all host types for resilience reasons.

BizTalk is primarily a client application to the database server; however, it also has some particular constraints that make selecting an appropriate hardware platform difficult. For instance, a typical server selection will not take into consideration disk performance.

In the interests of conserving physical memory, BizTalk Server can spool large messages (greater than 1MB) to the disk subsystem when necessary through the use of virtual streams, as discussed in Chapter 4. This has the advantage of minimizing the amount of memory used by BizTalk and avoiding out-of-memory conditions, but also has the negative impact of making large message processing dependent on the performance of the disk.

Each BizTalk host process is run under a configured service account. This service account has an associated temporary files folder, which will be used for spooling when a virtual stream is used. Examples of features that may use a virtual stream approach are the BizTalk mapper, SMIME, MSMQT, and so on. It's worth stressing that this spooling approach is not performed for messages under 1MB, and it is used only by certain features of BizTalk Server; streaming is used wherever possible.

In large message-processing scenarios that make use of virtual streams, it is therefore recommended that a high-performance SCSI or SAN disk be attached to the BizTalk Server and the service account's temporary directory be directed to a folder on that drive. This will ensure that the system will not be dependent on the C: drive and Temp folder performance at the same time. See Chapter 4 for more information on this.

It's worth nothing that this is not required in typical BizTalk solutions, only in scenarios making use of virtual streams under the covers. It can be hard to ascertain if virtual streams are actually in use by your solution, so it's advisable to use FileMon (`www.microsoft.com/technet/sysinternals/default.mspx`) to monitor the temporary directory during testing to establish if this is occurring and if you require SAN-attached storage.

The online documentation for BizTalk indicates that the /3GB switch has little or no impact on the system memory footprint. Unfortunately, though technically accurate, the BizTalk server process does not explicitly use the extra memory available by enabling this feature. The underlying .NET 1.1 and 2.0 infrastructure takes advantage of this by increasing the amount of private memory available to the process from 800MB to 1.8GB when this switch is enabled, which can help in some scenarios.

As for selecting the hardware for your BizTalk node, a modern four-way server machine with 2–4GB of RAM performs admirably well in almost all scenarios.

Note that the BizTalk Server licensing is based on physical processor sockets, not cores. Thus, a dual- or quad-core processor can provide significant (but not necessarily double or quadruple) performance improvement over a single-core processor. This should be an important consideration when selecting a server, as the reduced licensing costs combined with the performance improvement can be significant, but bear in mind that you won't necessarily get like-for-like performance when compared to physical processors.

Disks

Some years back during a presentation on performance, my esteemed coauthor Kevin stated, "Put all your money in disks." Although this is obviously a deliberate overgeneralization, it's true in principle.

I can put my hand on my heart and say that a large percentage of BizTalk "performance problems" that I've been called to look at has resulted from disk performance. Either the hardware was not suitable or had not been configured correctly. Code quality and implementation were responsible for the remainder.

Disk performance on each BizTalk server is largely irrelevant. Standard built-in hard drives are perfectly acceptable unless virtual streams are in use (which they rarely are in my experience). However, SQL Server requires a high-performing disk solution.

Storage area network (SAN)–based approaches are often used to provide a high-speed disk solution, and are common in most large independent software vendors (ISVs) and enterprises. A SAN can *project* drive letters, which are, in fact, backed by multiple hard drives configured in the SAN device.

Multiple hard drives used in this way allow the sharing of the read and write load across disks and reduce the likelihood of a having "hot" disks (disks under heavy load). Hot disks effectively parallelize the disk I/O, so this approach increases performance.

SAN storage can be configured in a variety of ways, typically referred to as RAID configurations (redundant array of inexpensive disks). There are many different RAID configurations, each delivering different combinations of redundancy and performance. For an in-depth discussion about RAID and the many configurations, see http://en.wikipedia.org/wiki/RAID.

The default disk configuration tends to be RAID5, which is highly optimized for read operations through the use of striping, which distributes data across multiple disks, thus enabling concurrent reads. However, write operations are expensive, due to the redundancy overheads imposed by RAID5. BizTalk Server solutions impose heavy read and write behavior on the disk array, meaning that RAID5 is not the best option with regard to performance. It's also worth noting that if one disk fails within a RAID5 array, the read performance degrades significantly.

RAID10 (stripe of mirrors) and RAID0+1 (mirror of stripes) offer far higher write performance along with high read performance. These are the recommended disk configurations for SQL Servers used by BizTalk for performance and redundancy reasons. RAID10 is preferred over RAID0+1 because it offers better redundancy.

RAID configuration continues to evolve, and over time further RAID configurations will become available and potentially more desirable than, for instance, RAID10 and RAID0+1. Ensure that the configuration you choose delivers fast reads and writes.

You can identify disk-performance problems by using the `Avg. Disk Queue Length`, `%Disk Idle Time`, `Avg. Disk Sec/Read`, and `Avg. Disk Sec/Write` performance counters. As discussed later in this chapter, the `Avg. Disk Queue Length` counter can be misleading (especially on a SAN), so the other three counters should be used, primarily.

After you have a disk storage system configured, expose at least two drives (or logical unit numbers [LUNs] if you're using a SAN), one for the databases to be stored on and another for the database log files. You might also want to separate logs from different, busy databases to improve performance further. This separates the read and write load on different underlying disks. Of course, when configuring the drives (or LUNs), you must ensure that physical hard drives are not shared, to avoid "hot" disks developing during testing. Such configuration can be complex; you should involve a SAN specialist to get the best performance possible.

It's worth highlighting that, as with all SQL Server databases, the log files require I/O hardware that offers good sequential write performance. Some SAN devices are not great at sequential I/O, although some modern SANs can counter this. You may find that a local (i.e., not SAN) mirror of fast disks offers better performance for database log files and at a lower price.

You should also consider exposing further LUNs for all databases used by BizTalk, including any custom databases.

A good disk storage system may alleviate disk I/O performance issues, but take care to review all BizTalk orchestrations to reduce persistence points as much as possible (although these reduce load on the disk array, reducing the number of them improves overall performance significantly). Chapter 5 covers this in more detail.

Software

Software configuration is a big area, but this section highlights some common oversights around default settings that often thwart performance testing.

Latest Service Packs

Service packs for Microsoft products contain both functional and performance fixes, and you should always install the latest service packs for all Microsoft products before embarking on performance testing. If you install a new service pack at a later point, you should run a functional test pass to ensure your solution works as expected.

More often than not, performance issues identified through performance testing (and subsequently chased down by both customers and Microsoft engineers) have already been "fixed" in the most recent service pack. Therefore, you can save yourself a lot of time by ensuring that you have the latest service packs installed! A service pack includes all hot fixes issued for a product between the release to manufacturing (RTM) of a product and the release of the current service pack. Service packs are cumulative, so they will always include hot fixes included in previous service packs. If you discover a new problem, its severity and impact may warrant the development of a hot fix in conjunction with Premier Support Services (PSS) and the relevant product team. This hot fix will then be rolled up into the next service pack for the product. This is another reason why you should perform performance and stress testing as early in the product cycle as possible. Critical issues take time to fix and could delay your release date.

Note that PSS is a paid-for support service and requires a support contract to be in place with Microsoft. However, if you encounter a bug, the support case will not be chargeable.

Database Location

The BizTalk MessageBox (`BizTalkMsgboxDb`) database and logs should be separated onto different physical volumes/LUNs, with each drive not sharing any underlying physical disks. Using SQL Server 2005 enables you to further split database and logs by supporting UNC-based drives. In some scenarios, based on performance monitoring, it might be useful to exceed the 26-drive-letter limit when distributing the databases components across multiple drives. SQL Server 2005 supports this feature, and it should be a serious decision factor when selecting the version of SQL Server to deploy BizTalk Server on, along with the overall performance gains provided by the 2005 release.

If message tracking is enabled, you might want to also consider moving the tracking database (`BizTalkDtaDb`) onto a separate drive letter, too. If you are using Business Activity Monitoring (BAM) within your solution, the same advice applies for the `BAMPrimaryImport` database

If your databases are already configured to use the local server disks rather than your separate drives, you can easily move them by following these steps. Even if you think the databases are in the right location, double-check! Many performance tests have been thwarted because of the assumption that databases had been moved into the right location!

1. Stop *all* the BizTalk services on all BizTalk servers in your BizTalk group. There will be several of these if you have different hosts configured. They follow the naming convention of BizTalk Server BizTalk Group: <HostName>. You can also do this through the BizTalk Administration Console by stopping active BizTalk host instances.

2. Stop the Enterprise Single Sign-On Service on all BizTalk servers in your BizTalk group. You can instead just stop this service, and any BizTalk Services will be shut down since they are dependent on SSO.

3. Open the SQL Server Management Studio. Right-click the database you want to move. Choose Tasks, and then select Detach, as shown in Figure 9-1. The Detach Database dialog box will be displayed.

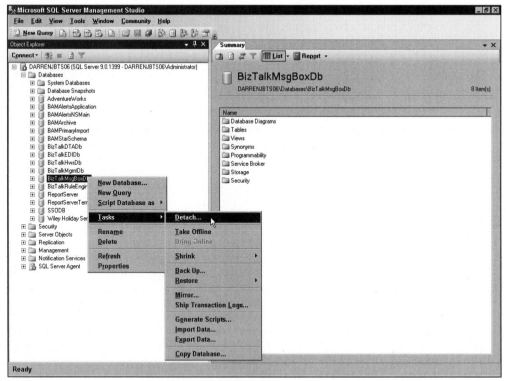

Figure 9-1

4. If all the services have been shut down correctly, no active connections are shown in the dialog box. If any are shown, close the dialog box and ensure that the services are shut down across all BizTalk servers in the BizTalk group. After you confirm, through this dialog box, that there are no active connections, click OK to perform the database detachment.

5. Copy the Database file (`.MDF` extension) and Log file (`.LDF` extension) into the appropriate location from the Data subdirectory (usually located under `%PROGRAMFILES%\Microsoft SQL Server`).

6. Back in SQL Server Management Studio, right-click Databases and choose Attach. The Attach Databases dialog box will appear. Browse to the moved Database and Log files, and choose OK to reattach the database.

The BizTalk MessageBox is a "black box" in that you cannot make changes to the structure, indexes, or stored procedures. Microsoft effectively owns the database structure and offers support in the unlikely event that you run into problems.

All tables and indexes within the MessageBox are configured to use one file group (PRIMARY), which contains one file. Consider the scenario in which an insert is performed in the MessageBox database. The table involved may have binary data (BLOB), internal data (columns and clustered indexes), and finally the nonclustered indexes. As all of these require SQL I/O and can contend with each other, affecting performance.

The use of a modern SAN can mitigate many of these problems through caching and the like. However, if you have access to expert DBAs who understand the MessageBox database structure, the changing of the underlying data storage model of the MessageBox through the use of extra file groups and files is supported. This enables you to move tables and indexes onto different physical volumes/LUNs, thus optimizing usage of your disks and reducing I/O contention and ultimately leading to better overall performance.

This complexity of this procedure should not be underestimated, and you must ensure that you don't adversely impact performance. As SAN technology matures, such an operation may not be required.

You can find additional information on what is and is not allowed to be changed at `http://blogs.msdn.com/Biztalk_Core_Engine`.

Database Autogrowth

When you create a SQL Server database, you can configure the autogrowth function. This function enables SQL Server to automatically grow a database when it runs out of space. Without this capability, the database would run out of space and cause a failure (until an administrator creates additional space). If database growth occurs during testing, it can have a massive impact on the performance of your solution.

Growth can be configured in terms of percent or megabytes. If you configure 10 percent, for example, the database will grow by 10 percent of the total current size each time it gets close to running out of space. When you use megabytes, if you configure, say, 1MB, it will grow by 1MB each time it gets close to running out of space.

By default, the BizTalk MessageBox is set to grow by 1MB. Unfortunately, under load, after 1MB has been added to the database size, it's often immediately exhausted, and the database must grow again, and this pattern repeats continuously. This usually produces a characteristic "saw-tooth" CPU usage profile on the SQL server. Note, however, that this is not as obvious with SQL Server 2005, because it provides new storage faster than previous versions.

The effect of autogrowth on BizTalk Server is that the MessageBox stops responding while growth is performed, which is usually indicated by a complete drop-off in CPU usage on the BizTalk Server for long periods (followed by activity and then another drop-off).

Prior to any testing, the `BizTalkMsgBoxDb` database should be presized to provide more than enough storage, and autogrowth should either be disabled or set to grow a large amount each time.

I personally like to disable autogrowth during testing. That way, if the database does happen to run out of space, I explicitly know. My explicit knowledge is preferable to it just happening under the covers (with performance results skewed without my knowledge and leading to hours of retesting and investigation). However, you might want to test the effect of autogrowth in a specific test so that you can understand the impact when it happens live.

Obviously, it's wise to have autogrowth enabled in live systems to ensure that the system doesn't grind to a halt, unless of course your database administrators have appropriate monitoring and manage the database size manually. You can configure autogrowth and initial size by using SQL Server Management Studio. Right-click the database, choose Properties, and then select the Files page. Figure 9-2 shows the default setting for `BizTalkMsgBoxDb`.

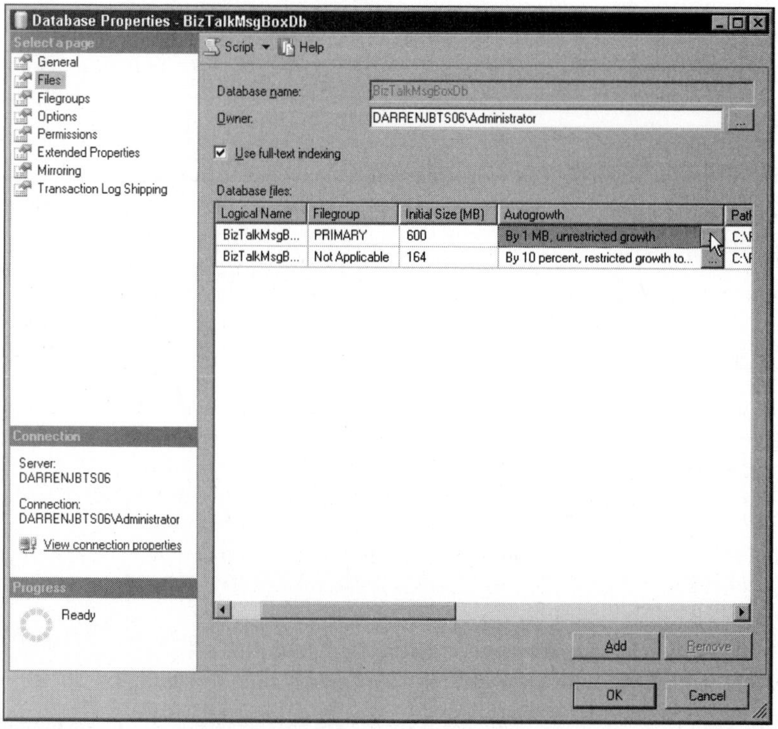

Figure 9-2

SQL Server Agent

Ensure that the SQL Server Agent is started. A default installation of SQL Server leaves the SQL Server Agent disabled. The DTA Purge and Archive, PurgeSubscriptionsJob_BizTalkMsgBoxDb, and TrackedMessages_Copy_BizTalkMsgBoxDb jobs need to run every minute to keep the BizTalk databases in good shape. These jobs are discussed further in Chapter 11, along with how to monitor them using MOM.

Host Configuration

By default, BizTalk Server is installed with two hosts: `BizTalkServerApplication` and `BizTalkServerIsolatedHost`. Most BizTalk artifacts, such as adapters, orchestrations, and send ports, are registered to use the `BizTalkServerApplication` host, with receive elements of adapters such as HTTP and SOAP using the `BizTalkServerIsolatedHost`. Although this default is fine during development, it's not advisable when conducting performance testing.

As mentioned in Chapter 2, a host is represented physically as an operating system process and makes use of threadpools to serve work within this process (apart from isolated hosts, which are of course implemented separate to BizTalk). Consider a scenario in which you have both orchestrations and Receive/Send adapters installed in the same host and actively receiving and processing messages. The host will be busy serving in-bound messages, running orchestrations, and sending new messages out, all of which will be using threads from the finite threadpool.

What typically happens is that the receive or orchestration activity uses up all the available threads in the threadpool, effectively starving the send activity of the ability to process its pending work. Therefore, the recommendation is to start with at least three hosts: one for receive, one for orchestrations, and another for send. This setup keeps busy activities such as receive from starving other parts of the system.

Not configuring hosts in this way generally leads to poorly performing solutions that don't scale well. Adjust them before you begin performance testing. If you do not, you'll end up spending a day or two diagnosing that you're running out of threads! See Chapter 10 for more information.

File Adapter Locations

Wherever possible, use local directories when configuring the File adapter (unless, of course, you have a requirement in your live scenario to use a UNC share, \\MyServer\MyShare). Don't be tempted to use USB flash drives during testing to hold test files; you will suffer from disk-performance problems.

A UNC share requires a network roundtrip to retrieve or transmit files, thus incurring performance overhead. Therefore, a local directory means much faster performance, but be aware that this introduces the potential for data loss, as information will be stored on a local server disk. If the server suffers a hardware failure, you might lose this information unless your server is SAN attached.

If you also have a scenario in which you have multiple servers writing to the same directory on a UNC share, you may experience bottlenecks at the file system level. Having multiple locations across different servers can improve performance.

Virus Scanners

Most servers do not run interactive virus scanners as part of the base build due to the potential performance overhead and often rely on perimeter based security.

You should ensure wherever possible that virus scanners are disabled across your servers to ensure performance isn't affected; the canonical example is the virus scanner slowing the reading or writing of files from a disk drive.

Concurrent Web Service Calls

The HTTP 1.1 Specification states that a "single-user client *should not* maintain more than 2 connections with any server or proxy." This limit ensures that a user cannot overload a remote Web server, and the various Microsoft HTTP stacks all respect this restriction. The SOAP and HTTP adapters all leverage the underlying .NET HTTP stack.

This is fine for *user* scenarios, but when you're calling a Web service from a BizTalk orchestration (via the SOAP adapter) or using the HTTP adapter, you will also be restricted in the same way. Because a server application has no concept of an end user or browser, however, the restriction applies to all requests within your application. The concurrent connection restriction is applied to an AppDomain. Therefore, if the SOAP adapter is *hosted* within a BizTalk host, it will only be able to make two concurrent requests to a given Web server. If you use multiple Web servers as part of your solution, each BizTalk host can make two concurrent calls to each server.

Once two requests are in flight, other requests are queued pending one of the current requests completing. When the requests take a long time, you can find that the queued request times out, causing an exception to be returned to the caller.

As you can imagine, this restriction causes a massive scalability and performance bottleneck for every server left with the default configuration. However, you can easily configure it via the `btsntsvc.exe.config` configuration file located in the `%PROGRAM FILES\Microsoft BizTalk Server 2006` directory.

Open the configuration file, and add the following element under the configuration element. You can set the `MaxConnection` value as high or low as you want. I typically set it to a large number to remove this problem from the equation. This is fine because BizTalk itself throttles the number of send threads it will use. A value of, say, 5000 is more than more than enough. You can, of course, select a lower value, but ensure that it's not too low. ASP.NET 2.0 introduced a self-tuning feature to counter this issue whereby it will set the maxConnection value to a sensible value. This only applies to HTTP or Web Service requests created within ASP.NET 2.0 not BizTalk, so the above still applies to BizTalk solutions.

```
<system.net>
  <connectionManagement>
    <add address="*" maxconnection="5000"/>
  </connectionManagement>
</system.net>
```

It's worth noting that the HTTP adapter exposes a `HTTPOutMaxConnection` registry key to enable configuration of the number of outbound HTTP connections. Setting this overrides any setting you make in the configuration file. See `http://msdn2.microsoft.com/en-us/library/ms961961.aspx` for details on this configuration setting. ASP.NET 2.0 introduced a self-tuning feature to counter this issue whereby it will set the maxConnection value to a sensible value. This only applies to HTTP or Web Service requests created within ASP.NET 2.0 not BizTalk, so the above still applies to BizTalk solutions.

Tracking

Global tracking requires significant overhead (especially if message body tracking is enabled) in BizTalk solutions. Unless you have a specific requirement, it's generally advisable to disable tracking before undertaking testing. You can disable global tracking by changing the `GlobalTrackingOption` column value to 0. You can find the `GlobalTrackingOption` column in the `adm_Group` table within the `BizTalkMgmtDb` database.

Note that if you disable global tracking, you cannot view orchestration execution via Health and Activity Tracking, because it relies, unsurprisingly, on tracking information. Using BAM for such tracking information is compelling and, in my experience, performs extremely well. See Chapter 6 for more information.

Service Class Settings

The Service Class settings reside inside the `adm_ServiceClass` table of the `BizTalkMgmtDb`; it is often the first place some go when problems arise.

I've lost count of the number of times that, during performance testing, someone has fiddled with these settings and then been surprised when they've not had the effect expected (typically because the problem lies elsewhere).

BizTalk comes out of the box with some default performance tuning settings that overall seem to work well for high-throughput scenarios. As covered in Chapter 10, you will have to adjust these to tune the latency out.

You can see these in the `adm_ServiceClass` table of the `BizTalkMgmtDb`. The key columns, along with the default values, are shown here for reference; further values are discussed in Chapter 10.

Name	Low Watermark	High Watermark	Low Sessionmark	High Sessionmark
XLANG/s	10	20	5	10
Messaging InProcess	100	200	2	5
MSMQT	100	200	12	15
Messaging Isolated	100	200	2	5

Service Class settings are split into four different classes: XLANG (orchestrations), Messaging InProcess (adapters/pipelines), MSMQT, and Messaging Isolated (isolated adapters/pipelines).

The Low and High Watermarks specify how many instances of that "service type" can execute at any one time. For XLANG/s, it refers to orchestrations, the `High Watermark` being the maximum number of orchestrations that can be in flight at any one time. When the BizTalk engine hits this watermark, it throttles back to the number specified by the `Low Watermark` and then resumes normal operation.

Low and High Session marks specify the number of concurrent database sessions that can be persisting in-bound messages at any one time for each service class.

Each setting is per processor and per server. Note that BizTalk is not hyperthreading or core aware, so each setting will apply to all processors visible to the operating system, rather than only count processor sockets.

If you have a dual-processor server, for example, the default XLANG Orchestrations settings means that a maximum of 40 orchestrations can be in flight at any time. Quad-processor boxes can have 80, and so on.

Again to highlight the situation with a multiple-core processors, a server fitted with two quad-core processors will appear as eight processors, which, given the default settings, will enable a maximum of 160 orchestrations to be in flight at any time.

Clearing the MessageBox

It can be useful to clear the MessageBox down to its original state between test runs, removing any suspended messages, dehydrated orchestrations, and so on. This should be executed *only* on test boxes and is not supported for use on a live server. You should, in fact, ensure that this stored procedure is not installed on a live server; it can lead to data loss if accidentally executed (which is precisely why the stored procedure is empty by default).

The first step is to create the `bts_CleanupMsgbox` stored procedure by executing the following script: `C:\Program Files\Microsoft BizTalk Server 2006\Schema\msgbox_cleanup_logic.sql`.

Once this is done, you can then run the `bts_CleanupMsgBox` stored procedure, using the SQL administration tools. You should ensure that all BizTalk host instances are stopped and that you have performed an IIS reset using `iisreset.exe` (if you're using the HTTP or SOAP adapters in your solution) before running the stored procedure.

Checklist

We've now covered the key areas that you should ensure are configured correctly. Here's a simple checklist for reference:

- ❑ Have the latest services packs been installed for both BizTalk and SQL Server?
- ❑ Are BizTalk Server and SQL Server installed on separate boxes?
- ❑ Are the databases and logs separated onto separate drive letters and therefore separate physical hard drives?
- ❑ Are the drives used for databases and logs configured on a fast disk array? RAID0 can be used to simulate RAID10/0+1 to reduce cost for your test environments but will offer similar performance.
- ❑ Have the default database for autogrowth settings changed or has autogrowth been disabled?
- ❑ Is the SQL Server Agent running?
- ❑ Have you created separate Receive, Orchestration, and Send hosts and moved the appropriate adapters and orchestrations to the appropriate host?
- ❑ Has the `maxconnection` configuration file setting been changed (if you're using Web services or HTTP as part of your solution)?
- ❑ Have you disabled any virus scanners installed on the servers?
- ❑ Do you have an automated deployment script or installer for your solution to enable easy deployment into the testing environments?

Monitoring

Now that we've covered the configuration of your services, we'll discuss how you can monitor your BizTalk Server solution while subjecting it to load. (The techniques for applying load were covered in Chapter 8.)

Strategy

Performance and scalability testing is pretty straightforward, but without following some basic principles, you can easily find yourself with an unstable system or (and often worse) no understanding of what you've changed and whether you've resolved your issue. There is one golden rule: Change *one* thing at a time and document everything extensively. Here is a bare-bones strategy to follow:

❑ Decide ahead of time what the key measurement of success is going to be. Is the messages/sec (throughput) the most important metric? Is the latency of each message the critical factor?

❑ Use a tool such as Excel to record information about each test that you perform (and include a brief description of the test's purpose). A far better alternative is to write BizUnit tests to automatically store test information in a SQL Server database. This can be customized as you require, see Chapter 8 for more information.

❑ Assign a unique number to each test, and record a brief overview of each test (along with the result and any changes you make). The following table shows an example of such a record. You may, of course, wish to record extra columns.

❑ This information is useful for tracking how tests have progressed. You can also add performance information such as messages/sec to show how performance has changed over time.

❑ Use Counter logs (as discussed in the next section) to collect performance counter information to disk, and store a copy of the Event Viewer in a directory that matches the test number recorded in your test record. As covered in Chapter 8, BizUnit tests can do this automatically for you each time a test is executed.

❑ Don't be tempted to change more than one setting at a time. Doing so means that you cannot say for sure which setting has had the positive (or negative) effect. Running multiple tests can be time-consuming, but modifying too many settings can waste much more time.

❑ Don't be tempted to change settings because you assume that you're going to suffer from issue X or Y. Only change settings that relate to behavior that you can reproduce and explain in your performance test. For example, don't increase the Low Watermark and High Watermark settings for XLANG/s before running any performance tests.

Test Number	Description	Result	Changes Post-Test	BizUnit Test Script
TST01	First performance test: 20x1MB files dropped into directory	Receive port shutdown, no permissions on directory	Granted svcHost permission to c:\drop	Woodgrove-LoanQuote-001
TST02	20x1MB file dropped into directory	Messages loaded, SOAP adapter errored repeatedly, svcSendHost doesn't have permission to call Web service	Granted svcSendHost permission to the Web service	Woodgrove-LoanQuote-001
TST03	20x1MB file dropped into directory	Heavy rate throttling observed on SOAP host		Woodgrove-LoanQuote-001

The outlined strategy is important to implement when performing testing. I cannot emphasize enough the abilities of BizUnit to automate almost all this, which enables test runs to be executed with little to no manual intervention and removes the chance of human error. Chapter 8 covers how you can configure this in more detail.

Microsoft Operations Manager

Chapter 11 discusses the value of Microsoft Operations Manager (MOM), but it's worth mentioning here because you can use the standard BizTalk Management Pack to great effect during performance testing. MOM will automatically highlight some problems immediately (removing the need to manually analyze detailed counters constantly, and may even highlight performance counters and problems you weren't familiar with or problems that you weren't otherwise aware of).

The BizTalk Server MOM Pack monitors a whole range of counters and raises alerts when certain counters exceed certain thresholds. You can also install MOM packs for other products, such as SQL Server, to enable the monitoring of additional servers during testing. You can customize these counters to suit your requirements.

Capturing Performance Counters

It's crucial to ensure that you capture the key performance counters for the operating system — .NET, BizTalk, and SQL Server — for each test that you perform. That way, you have a fighting chance (at least) to understand and, more importantly, explain why a given test has performed the way it has.

When monitoring performance counters, it's important to note that the trend or pattern over time is often more relevant than momentary high values. A sudden short increase in CPU usage isn't necessarily a major problem, but sustained high CPU usage potentially is.

Another important technique is to run a baseline test to understand how the system performs and what the performance counters are showing when under minimal load. This way, you can understand what changes when you apply increasing load.

To effectively monitor a BizTalk Server solution, a multitude of performance counters are required. To make matters worse, there are many servers involved in a typical BizTalk group. Performance Monitor (PerfMon) is the built-in tool for monitoring these performance counters, but it forces you to add counters individually and then again for each server, which, if you have many servers, can take a long time.

Suppose that you have to add 50+ counters to PerfMon. You'll face a time-consuming and error-prone process. You might even miss a performance counter, perhaps on the one server that you need to know about after a test.

It's worth noting that Microsoft Operations Manager (MOM) is very good at monitoring multiple servers in this way. But it is ultimately targeted at operations monitoring, so it isn't flexible enough for performance testing and collection. However, as covered above, it can be useful for monitoring your rig, to highlight problems you might otherwise not have spotted.

To alleviate this pain, I've extended a simple tool developed by a colleague (thanks, James!). This tool uses Excel and enables you to group relevant performance counters by server type. For SQL, for instance, we'll specify some interesting SQL counters. For IIS, on the other hand, we'll capture the relevant IIS counters.

You can find a copy of this Excel workbook populated with the counters covered later in this chapter at www.wrox.com.

It's again worth noting that BizUnit can automate the starting and stopping of performance counter logs and will even copy the resulting log to a configured directory for each test run. This automates a large amount of manual work during testing and removes a lot of errors. At the very least, the Excel workbook is still useful to create the list of performance counters, which BizUnit will then use to create a counter log automatically.

Figure 9-3 shows an example of this performance counter list. Note the server type in the first column, the performance object in the second column, and the performance counter in the third column.

Performance objects such as Processor and BizTalk:Message Agent have multiple instances. Therefore, in the case of Processor, there will be a different numbered instance for each processor installed (especially true with the advent of dual-core processors). In the case of BizTalk:Message Agent, there will be a different named instance for each BizTalk host.

To avoid having to prepopulate the processor numbers of host names, we use * for the performance objects that have multiple instances, which indicates to PerfMon that all instances should be collected.

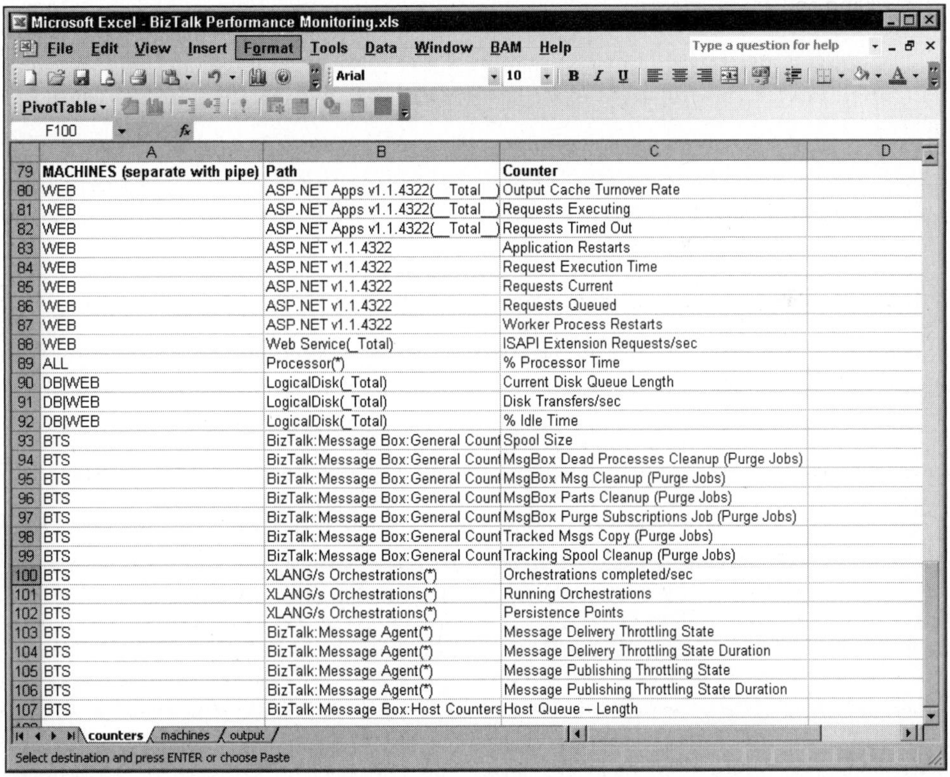

Figure 9-3

The next step is to map physical server names to the server types specified in the previous step. This is done on the `Machines` tab of the Excel workbook and is shown in Figure 9-4. Server types are listed in the first column, with the relevant server name in the second column.

Any counters specified within the `ALL` server type will automatically be added for every physical server listed.

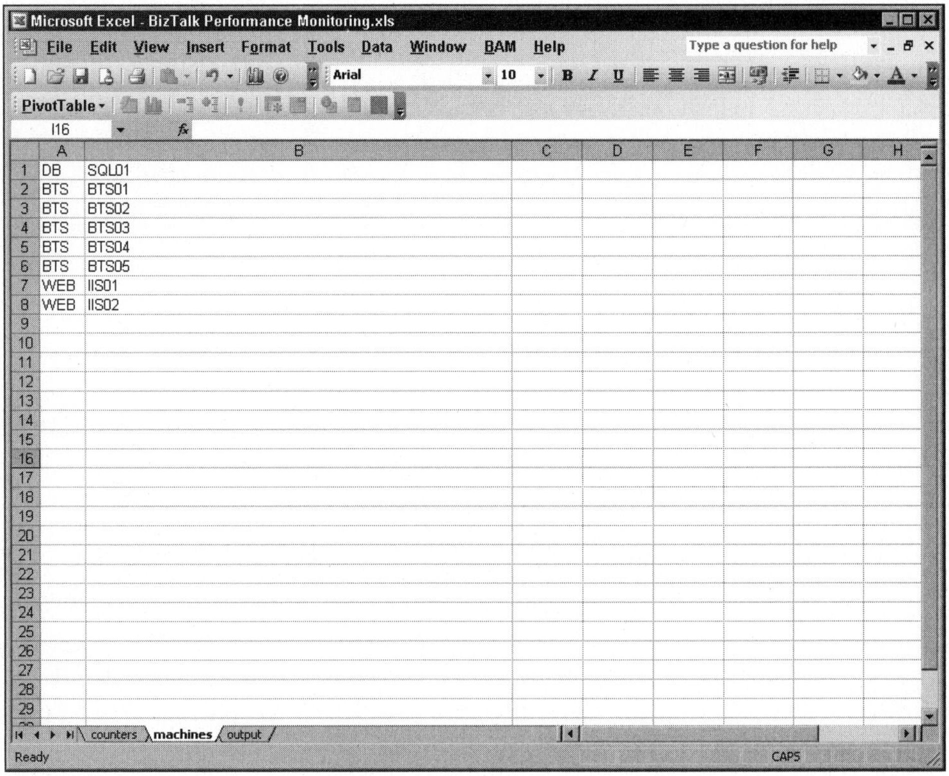

Figure 9-4

The next step uses an Excel macro to generate a text list of all the counters required to be collected. To execute the macro, select the Macro menu, drill into the Macro option, and choose Macros. Run the `CreatePerfCounterElements` macro shown in the resulting dialog box. You might need to adjust your Macro Security to be able to execute this macro.

This macro generates the text list of counters in the `Output` tab of the Excel workbook, as shown in Figure 9-5.

Copy this list of counters to Notepad and save it to a handy location on your machine. Using the built-in Windows command-line tool `LogMan.exe`, you can create a Counter log that will then, by default, collect the specified `PerfMon` counters and store them in a file.

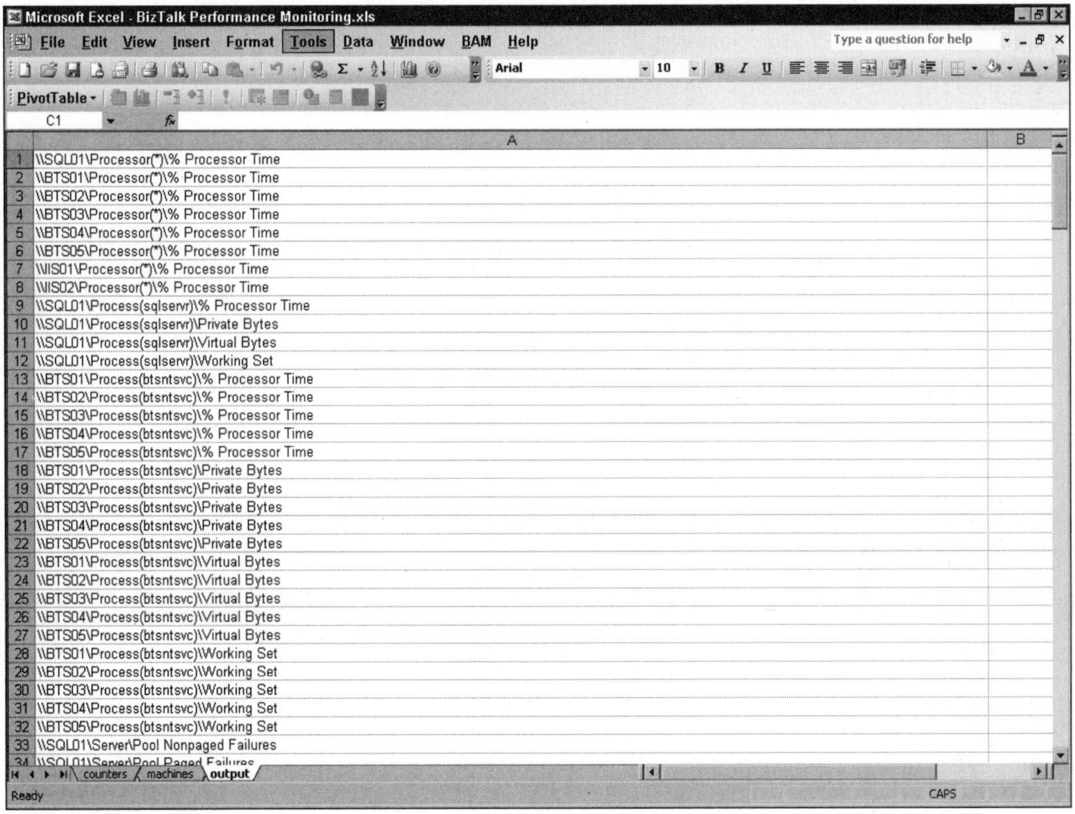

	A	B
1	\\SQL01\Processor(*)\% Processor Time	
2	\\BTS01\Processor(*)\% Processor Time	
3	\\BTS02\Processor(*)\% Processor Time	
4	\\BTS03\Processor(*)\% Processor Time	
5	\\BTS04\Processor(*)\% Processor Time	
6	\\BTS05\Processor(*)\% Processor Time	
7	\\IIS01\Processor(*)\% Processor Time	
8	\\IIS02\Processor(*)\% Processor Time	
9	\\SQL01\Process(sqlservr)\% Processor Time	
10	\\SQL01\Process(sqlservr)\Private Bytes	
11	\\SQL01\Process(sqlservr)\Virtual Bytes	
12	\\SQL01\Process(sqlservr)\Working Set	
13	\\BTS01\Process(btsntsvc)\% Processor Time	
14	\\BTS02\Process(btsntsvc)\% Processor Time	
15	\\BTS03\Process(btsntsvc)\% Processor Time	
16	\\BTS04\Process(btsntsvc)\% Processor Time	
17	\\BTS05\Process(btsntsvc)\% Processor Time	
18	\\BTS01\Process(btsntsvc)\Private Bytes	
19	\\BTS02\Process(btsntsvc)\Private Bytes	
20	\\BTS03\Process(btsntsvc)\Private Bytes	
21	\\BTS04\Process(btsntsvc)\Private Bytes	
22	\\BTS05\Process(btsntsvc)\Private Bytes	
23	\\BTS01\Process(btsntsvc)\Virtual Bytes	
24	\\BTS02\Process(btsntsvc)\Virtual Bytes	
25	\\BTS03\Process(btsntsvc)\Virtual Bytes	
26	\\BTS04\Process(btsntsvc)\Virtual Bytes	
27	\\BTS05\Process(btsntsvc)\Virtual Bytes	
28	\\BTS01\Process(btsntsvc)\Working Set	
29	\\BTS02\Process(btsntsvc)\Working Set	
30	\\BTS03\Process(btsntsvc)\Working Set	
31	\\BTS04\Process(btsntsvc)\Working Set	
32	\\BTS05\Process(btsntsvc)\Working Set	
33	\\SQL01\Server\Pool Nonpaged Failures	
34	\\SQL01\Server\Pool Paged Failures	

Figure 9-5

To create this Counter log, open a command prompt and use the following syntax. This creates a
Counter log called `BizTalkPerformanceTestLog` and adds the counters listed in a file called
`counters.txt`, which was created in the previous step.

```
logman create counter BizTalkPerformanceTestLog -cf counters.txt
```

You can then use `PerfMon` to view the created Counter log, as shown in Figure 9-6.

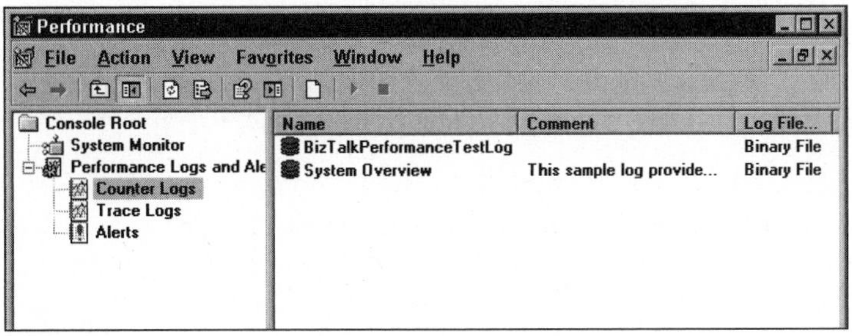

Figure 9-6

433

Double-click the newly created Counter log to review the performance counters added and to configure the interval within which information will be collected. The default of 15 seconds is fine. Figure 9-7 shows an example.

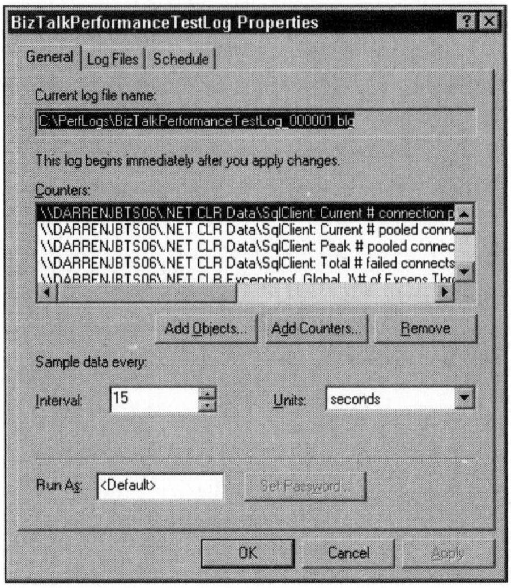

Figure 9-7

> By default, a collection of these performance counters, when started, will show up under the SYSTEM account rather than the account you are logged in to. This is fine if all the counters you want to collect are stored locally. If you are using remote servers, however, the local SYSTEM account will not have permission to collect remote counters. To alleviate this, specify a username and password to run the collection under. You can specify these in the Properties dialog box of your Counter log.

You can start this counter set by right-clicking the Counter log from within the Counter Logs part of PerfMon and selecting Start. Each time you stop a Counter log, a new filename is used, making each Counter log easy to identify.

After a Counter log has been collected, you can view its contents using PerfMon. From the default System Monitor part of PerfMon, click the View Log Data button on the toolbar (depicted as a database shape). Within the dialog box that displays, browse to the Counter Log file and click OK.

You can now add performance counters in the usual way. This time, however, the Add Counters dialog box only shows computers, performance objects, and performance counters that were part of the Counter log. You can even adjust the time range you want to see by clicking the View Log Data button again.

Sadly, this approach doesn't enable you to view the counters in real time while a test is progressing. Therefore, you still need to manually add a basic set of counters if you want to keep track of them as the test progresses. You can, however, do this once and save it for later use.

As we progress through this chapter, we detail the specific performance counters required for BizTalk monitoring. These are used in addition to the *standard* counters you should always use for monitoring across all machines regardless of their role.

Some of the most common are shown in the following tables for reference, but you should expect to add additional counters depending on your scenario.

At the time of writing, there were some problems relating to the remote collection of performance counters exposed by a 32-bit process on a 64-bit machine. Although this shouldn't affect BizTalk processes, you might encounter this problem with IIS, for example. An unsupported technique that might help you is documented at `http://blogs.msdn.com/edglas/archive/2006/09/06/reading-32-bit-counters-on-a-64-bit-machine.aspx`.

Processor	
`% Processor Time (_Total)`	The % Processor Time counter indicates the current amount of processor time being utilized on the system. The `_Total` instance of the counter enables you to aggregate all the processors available within the system.
`%Privileged Time (_Total)`	The `%Privileged Time` counter indicates the current amount of processer time being spent on kernel mode work. A high value may indicate that the server is spending a lot of time performing internal server work rather than processing user mode applications.
Process	
`Private Bytes (BTSNTSvc, sqlservr, w3svc, etc.)`	The `Private Bytes` counter indicates the current number of bytes allocated exclusively to the specified process.
`Virtual Bytes`	The `Virtual Bytes` counter indicates the current number of bytes allocated to the specified process from the virtual address space (`Disk`, etc.)
`Working Set`	The `Working Set` counter indicates the current number of bytes allocated to the specified process across all the various address space types; the memory may not be in active use but is currently allocated to the process.

Continued

Memory

Available Megabytes

The `Available Megabytes` counter indicates the amount of physical memory available to a process or overall system use.

Page Faults/sec

The `Page Faults` counter indicates the number of (soft and hard) page faults that have occurred in the last second. Page faults are normal and occur when a process refers to a page that is not within its own working set.

A soft page fault occurs when the page is loaded elsewhere on the system where it can be referenced directly. A hard page fault occurs when the page is not loaded and the data is fetched from disk, which, of course, takes longer to process.

A high number of page faults can indicate memory pressure that is causing a lot of paging to disk. You can see this by combining this counter with the `Pages/sec` counter and observing if you are experiencing more hard page faults than soft page faults.

Pages/sec

The `Pages/sec` counter indicates the number of hard page faults occurring; as explained in the previous counter, a high number of page faults can indicate memory pressure and overall performance degradation.

System

Context Switches/sec

The `Context Switches/sec` counter indicates the rate at which processors are switching from one thread to another.

A very high value combined with high CPU usage can indicate too many threads running concurrently, causing the processor to spend most of its time switching between threads.

Processor Queue Length

The `Processor Queue Length` counter indicates the number of threads queuing for time on a processor and therefore contending for processing time.

Bear in mind that there is one queue for all processors, so you will need to divide the queue length by the number of processors visible to Windows (including multiple cores).

General guidance is that a queue of 10 or fewer threads is acceptable.

Network Interface

Bytes Received/sec

The `Bytes Received/sec` counter indicates the rate at which bytes are received over a network interface.

Bytes Sent/sec

The `Bytes Sent/sec` counter indicates the rate at which bytes are sent over a network interface.

.NET CLR Memory	
# Bytes in All Heaps	The #Bytes in All Heaps counter indicates the number of bytes allocated across all heaps (Generation 0, 1, 2, and the Large Object Heaps).
#Gen 0 Collections	The #Gen 0 Collections counter indicates the number of Generation 0 collections that have been performed since the start of the application. Objects resident in Generation 0 are the youngest objects in terms of creation and will be moved into Generation 1 if they are still in use when Generation 0 is collected.
#Gen 1 Collections	The #Gen 1 Collections counter indicates the number of Generation 1 collections that have been performed since the start of the application. Objects resident in Generation 1 are *middle-aged* in terms of creation and will be moved into Generation 2 if they are still in use when Generation 1 is collected.
#Gen 2 Collections	The #Gen 2 Collections counter indicates the number of Generation 2 collections that have been performed since the start of the application. Objects resident in Generation 2 are *old* in terms of creation and will remain in the Generation 2 when they are no longer used.
% Time in GC	The % Time in GC counter indicates the amount of time spent in performance garbage collection (GC). This percentage relates to the elapsed time. A high value indicates that many objects are being garbage collected, pointing to potential problems within the code base (many objects being created and thrown away repeatedly).
# of Pinned Objects	The # of Pinned Objects counter indicates the number of objects that are fixed within a generation and can therefore not be moved by the Garbage Collector. Pinned objects are typically used with unmanaged code to enable memory to be directly accessed; hence, they cannot be moved, as this would invalidate memory pointers. A large number of long-lived pinned objects can cause heap fragmentation and out-of-memory errors.
.NET CLR LocksAndThreads	
Contention Rate/sec	The Contention Rate/sec counter indicates the number of attempts to acquire a lock on a managed synchronization object. A high value can indicate contention on a shared piece of data that many concurrent threads need to access and therefore highlights a bottleneck.

Event Viewer

As with all testing, you must ensure that you keep a close eye on the Event Viewer. We all get excited with sudden positive results from particular performance tests, only later to find that it was failing at the first hurdle.

Most software, including BizTalk Server, logs verbosely to the Event Viewer in the case of error — something that your application should also do. Therefore, Event Viewer typically gives you a good idea of what's going on. BizTalk, for example, shuts down receive and send ports after a certain number of errors have occurred and logs this action to the Event Viewer. Much wasted time has been spent trying to figure out why messages weren't being picked up from a file location or sent to a Web service when just a simple glance at the Event Viewer would have highlighted the problem.

As discussed in the "Strategy" section of this chapter, storing the Event Viewer logs following each test is good practice. All you have to do is right-click the Application, Security or System log within Event Viewer, and choose Save Log File As. Then just name the file and save it to the location of your choice. It's advisable to clear the Event log between tests.

It's again worth nothing that, as covered in Chapter 8, BizUnit tests can be configured to automatically clear and store Event logs for each test run.

> *For those of you familiar with BizTalk Server 2004, note that BizTalk throttling conditions are no longer flagged inside the Event Viewer with BizTalk Server 2006. Performance counters now indicate throttling status.*
>
> *Don't (as I did early on with BizTalk Server 2006) assume that throttling is not occurring if there are no Event Viewer messages!*

Managing Servers

When conducting performance tests, you're often using multiple BizTalk servers, each with multiple BizTalk services installed (one for each BizTalk host). Between tests, you often need to restart all the services across all machines (at the least to reset the performance counters and get the environment in a clean state). With BizTalk Server 2004, this was a time-consuming task. BizTalk Server 2006 greatly simplifies this task with the BizTalk administration tool. As always, however, a command-line script is often quicker.

The following code shows a rudimentary *bounce* script that stops and then starts all BizTalk services on all configured BizTalk servers. For your environment, you must add entries to the `strComputerList` array for each BizTalk server.

```
Dim strComputerList(3)
strComputerList(0) = "BTSServer1"
strComputerList(1) = "BTSServer2"
strComputerList(2) = "BTSServer3"
strComputerList(3) = "BTSServer4"

For Each strComputer in strComputerList
   Set objWMIService = GetObject("winmgmts:" _       &
      "{impersonationLevel=impersonate}!\\" & strComputer & "\root\cimv2")

   WScript.Echo "Stopping BizTalk on: " & strComputer

   Set colServiceList = objWMIService.ExecQuery _
      ("Select * from Win32_Service where Name LIKE 'BTSSvc%'")
```

```
   For Each objService in colServiceList
objService.StopService()
Next

   WScript.Echo "Starting BizTalk on: " & strComputer

   For Each objService in colServiceList
objService.StartService()
   Next
   WScript.Echo
Next
```

BizTalk

This section discusses how you should monitor each BizTalk server during performance testing and identifies a number of common stress symptoms.

Performance Counters

I typically recommend the following performance counters to be collected on each BizTalk server. In my experience, these are the most useful. However, you might find other counters helpful in your scenario.

You can add the entire set of performance objects to your PerfMon collector (e.g., BizTalk:Message Box:General Counters), which collects all the individual counters held within. This approach gives you all the information possible but introduces further overhead and storage requirements (and, arguably, confusion when you try to select the right counter during analysis).

Understanding what some performance counters actually represent can prove challenging. It's an often overlooked feature, but within PerfMon you can select a performance counter and click the Explain button for an explanation. Figure 9-8 shows an example.

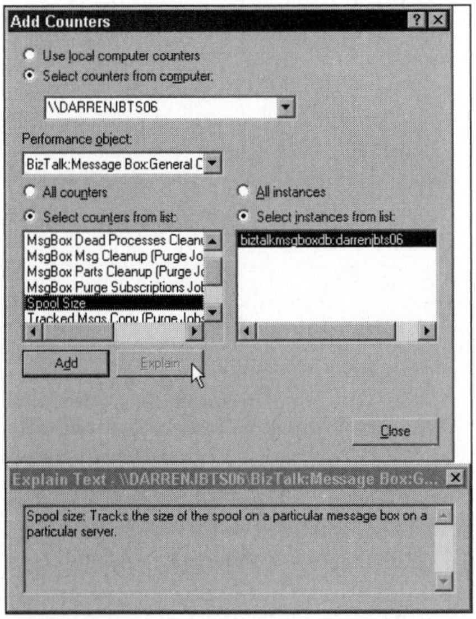

Figure 9-8

For all the counters shown with an asterisk enclosed in parentheses, (*), there will be multiple instances of each counter available. For example, the `BizTalk:Message Box:Host` *counter's performance object will have an instance for each configured BizTalk host. It's important to capture all instances of each performance object.*

BizTalk:Message Box:General Counters(*)	
`Spool Size`	The `Spool Size` counter indicates how many BizTalk messages are currently resident in the Spool table held within the `BizTalkMsgBoxDb`. This counter does not necessarily reflect the number of messages available for consumption by orchestrations and send ports, because it also includes messages currently being processed by an in-bound interchange, any suspended messages, and perhaps messages that haven't yet been removed by the SQL Server Agent jobs. A common example of this that creates confusion is when you are splitting large in-bound messages, which can take 5–10 minutes for large files. During the splitting process, messages are placed in the Spool table but are kept in the scope of a transaction (and therefore not committed until the entire file has been split). If BizTalk "runs out" of work, it will appear to sleep during the period in which the file is being split, despite messages seemingly being available for processing.
`MsgBox Dead Processes Cleanup (Purge Jobs)`	The `MsgBox Dead Process Cleanup (Purge Jobs)` counter reflects the last execution time of this SQL Agent job. This job, under normal operation, should not take more than two seconds to execute. If it takes longer, you should investigate why (SQL Server resource problems, etc.). During processing, an instance of a host reserves a small batch of messages for storage in memory just prior to processing. If the host were to fail, however, the messages would still be *locked* to that host instance. This SQL job ascertains whether a host instance has been terminated and, if so, *unlocks* the messages so that another instance of the same host on another machine can process the messages.
`MsgBox Msg Cleanup (Purge Jobs)`	The `MsgBox Msg Cleanup (Purge Jobs)` counter reflects the last execution time of this SQL Agent job. This job, under normal operation, should not take more than two seconds to execute. If it takes longer, you should investigate why (SQL Server resource problems, etc.). This cleanup job removes all messages that are have been successfully consumed and no longer have any active subscribers.

MsgBox Parts Cleanup (Purge Jobs)	The MsgBox Parts Cleanup (Purge Jobs) counter reflects the last execution time of this SQL Agent job. This job, under normal operation, should not take more than two seconds to execute. If it takes longer, you should investigate why (SQL Server resource problems, etc.). All BizTalk messages consist of one or more parts, which are stored separately within the BizTalk MessageBox. This job detects parts that have no referring messages and removes them.
MsgBox Purge Subscriptions Job (Purge Jobs)	The MsgBox Purge Subscriptions Job (Purge Jobs) counter reflects the last execution time of this SQL Agent Job. This job, under normal operation, should not take more than two seconds to execute. If it takes longer, you should investigate why (SQL Server resource problems, etc.). Subscriptions are created for various reasons during BizTalk operation, and this job removes old subscriptions from the BizTalk MessageBox.
Tracked Msgs Copy (Purge Jobs)	The Tracked Msgs Copy (Purge Jobs) counter reflects the last execution time of this SQL Agent Job. This job, under normal operation, should not take more than two seconds to execute. If it takes longer, you should investigate why (SQL Server resource problems, etc.). When Message Body tracking is enabled, this job copies the message bodies from the BizTalkMsgBoxDb database to the BizTalkDTADb.
Tracking Spool Cleanup (Purge Jobs)	The Tracking Spool Cleanup (Purge Jobs) counter reflects the last execution time of this SQL Agent Job. TThis job, under normal operation, should not take more than two seconds to execute. If it takes longer, you should investigate why (SQL Server resource problems, etc.). The Tracking Spool Cleanup job purges inactive spool tables. Note that this job is disabled by default.
Tracking Data Size	The Tracking Data Size counter reflects the number of entries in the Tracking Data table that need to be processed by the Tracking Data Delivery Service (TDDS). If you have tracking enabled, this data must be copied into the Data Tracking database and will be represented via this counter. If you also utilize an asynchronous BAM event stream, this counter will also reflect these entries prior to TDDS moving them to the BAMPrimaryImport database.

Continued

BizTalk:Message Box:Host Counters(*)	
Host Queue – Length	The `Host Queue - Length` counter reflects the total number of messages currently queued for processing by the specified host.
Host Queue – Suspended Messages – Length	The `Host Queue - Suspended Messages - Length` counter reflects the total number of messages in the host queue that have been suspended.

BizTalk:Messaging Latency(*)	
	These counters and message latency are covered in detail in Chapter 10.
Inbound Latency (sec)	The `Inbound Latency (sec)` counter reflects the average latency in milliseconds from when the Messaging Engine receives a document from the adapter until the time it is published to MessageBox. This includes any pipeline work and is useful to understand how the in-bound part of your solution is performing.
Outbound Latency (sec)	The `Outbound Latency (sec)` counter reflects the average latency in milliseconds from the time when the Messaging Engine receives a document from the MessageBox until the time the document is sent by the adapter. This includes any pipeline work and is useful to understand how the outbound part of your solution is performing.
Outbound Adapter Latency (sec)	The `Outbound Adapter Latency (sec)` counter reflects the average latency in milliseconds from the time when the adapter gets a document from the Messaging Engine until the time it is sent by the adapter. This is different from the previous counter in that it reflects only the time taken by the adapter, not the BizTalk plumbing (pipelines, etc.), and enables you to identify whether the adapter or engine processing is performing badly.
Request-Response Latency (sec)	The `Request-Response Latency (sec)` counter reflects the average latency in milliseconds from the time when the Messaging Engine receives a request document from the adapter until the time a response document is given back to the adapter. This counter proves particularly useful if you are exposing a Web service from BizTalk and want to understand how quickly it is performing within BizTalk itself.

BizTalk:Messaging(*)	
`Active Send Messages`	The `Active Send Messages` counter reflects the number of messages currently in the process of being sent, and includes messages flowing through a pipeline (because this is part of the send process).
`Documents Processed/Sec`	The `Documents Processed/Sec` counter reflects the current rate of messages being processed by BizTalk. Processing includes orchestrations and send ports.
`Documents Received/Sec`	The `Documents Received/Sec` counter reflects the current rate of messages being received by BizTalk.
XLANG/s Orchestrations(*)	
Orchestrations completed/sec	The `Orchestrations completed/sec` counter reflects the current number of orchestrations completing fully (i.e., not dehydrating) every second.
Running Orchestrations	The `Running Orchestrations` counter reflects the total number of orchestrations currently executing.
Persistence Points	The `Persistence Points` counter reflects the total number of persistence points incurred by orchestrations since the BizTalk Host started. Reducing persistence points is key to achieving good performance; see Chapter 14 for further information.
BizTalk:Message Agent(*)	
`Message Delivery Throttling State`	The `Message Delivery Throttling State` counter reflects the current state of message delivery throttling (orchestration and send ports counts as message delivery).
`Message Delivery Throttling State Duration`	The `Message Delivery Throttling State Duration` counter reflects the amount of time the current throttling state has been in force.
`Message Publishing Throttling State`	The Message Publishing Throttling State counter reflects the current state of message publishing throttling. (Receive ports and orchestrations that create messages for transmission count as message publishing.)
`Message Publishing Throttling State Duration`	The `Message Publishing Throttling State Duration` counter reflects the amount of time that the current throttling state has been in force.

Throttling

A thorough understanding of throttling is a cornerstone to effective performance testing and tuning. Although contrived, I like to use a horse-riding analogy to explain throttle. If the horse is going too fast, you pull back on the reins to slow down. You then release the reins when you've reached the desired speed. Throttling effectively pulls the BizTalk reins to settle message receipt and consumption by monitoring many sensors within the system and implementing intelligent resource utilization to achieve a constantly optimum rate.

Throttling is the process by which BizTalk ensures optimum performance and use of system resources (memory, threads, CPU, etc.). Imagine a floodgate scenario in which BizTalk is receiving more messages that it can comfortably process. In such a situation, the *queue* of messages will build continuously because BizTalk cannot process the messages as quickly as it receives them.

If the floodgate scenario exists for a short period of time, such behavior can be accepted. If it is sustained, however, you enter a scenario in which you cannot effectively service the load and run the risk of a potential overload. Perhaps the number of messages reaches a critical level (queue depths), or perhaps the number of concurrent orchestrations being created to service this extreme load puts heavy demands on the CPU, so that it struggles (due to the context switching) to get any other work done.

Throttling exists to protect against such a scenario. The act of throttling in the receive case can restrict the rate at which incoming messages are received until things settle down. This can be achieved for example, by introducing delays or restricting the number of threads. At which point, BizTalk can reset the throttling condition and let things return to normal.

Throttling doesn't just apply to message receipt. It also applies to message consumption and transmission. BizTalk may well be fine to send messages at a rate of 200/sec, for instance, but the destination system may not be able to handle this throughput. In the send case, the engine keeps count of in-flight messages. These are messages that the agent has delivered to an adapter but the adapter has yet to complete transmission. If this in-flight count breaches a configured high watermark, throttling will be introduced and the engine will tell the message agent it does not want any more messages. Once the in-flight count drops below the low watermark the engine tells the message agent to start delivering messages again and throttling will be removed. The same principle applies for Orchestrations.

The other key throttling scenario relates to system resources. If memory is running low within the BizTalk process, for example, the last thing you want to do is process ever-increasing numbers of messages concurrently (despite them being available). In this scenario, you want to back off message processing to attempt to resolve memory usage issues and even aggressively invoke garbage collection (GC).

Throttling is an incredibly powerful technique to ensure the overall health of your BizTalk Server and to maximize the overall throughput possible in your environment. If you question the decisions it makes, it's worth disabling throttling via the Registry (see `http://msdn2.microsoft.com/en-us/library/aa559628.aspx` for more information) and running a performance test to see what happens if it's not in place. Please, however, do *not* do this on a live box!

"Receive" Throttling

Receive throttling is throttling imposed on the receipt of messages into the BizTalk MessageBox and is referred to as *message publishing throttling*. It applies to hosts containing adapters and (often overlooked) also applies to orchestrations that create and publish messages to the MessageBox.

The `Message publishing throttling state` performance counter, in the case of a receive host, indicates the publication of messages to the BizTalk MessageBox is being restricted. That is, BizTalk is restricting the rate at which incoming messages are being committed to the BizTalk MessageBox. This restriction is implemented in a variety of ways, depending on the throttling state, but is typically done by introducing a progressive delay or restricting the number of threads available.

If message publishing throttling is active, the knock-on effect to your system is that you are not receiving messages in the MessageBox as quickly as usual and you face, in the case of MSMQ, a queue that builds up with messages or, in the case of SOAP, the possibility that the request will be blocked for a period of time. The exact behavior depends on the adapter and associated transport method.

Eight possible throttling states apply to message publishing. The throttling state is indicated by the `message publishing throttling state` performance counter. Anything above zero indicates publishing throttling is in force. The message publishing throttling state duration counter indicates how long the current throttling state has been in place for.

❑ **0: No throttling** — This is the default level and indicates that no throttling is currently in force.

❑ **2: Rate** — Rate throttling indicates that messages are being received faster than they are being published, and therefore a backlog is growing. This particular throttling state is common and generally not something to be overly worried about, unless you see rate throttling occurring for extended periods of time.

BizTalk decides to utilize rate throttling by monitoring the rate at which messages are being queued for publishing to the MessageBox and by monitoring the rate at which they are actually physically being published to the MessageBox. If the queued rate exceeds the publishing rate, publishing is not keeping up.

The rate at which publishing requests are occurring, along with the actual publishing operation, is viewable through the `Message publishing incoming rate` and `Message publishing outgoing` rate performance counters.

BizTalk utilizes these performance counters to decide whether rate processing should occur. The calculation it uses to perform this decision is shown below; it is effectively saying: *Use rate throttling if the incoming rate is greater than the rate at which we are physically publishing messages multiplied by an overdrive factor.*

Message publishing incoming rate > (Message publishing outgoing rate * Rate Overdrive factor) (percent)

The `Rate Overdrive factor` used here is configured per host through the BizTalk Administration Console and by default is 125 percent. Figure 9-9 shows the dialog box, which is accessed by right-clicking the appropriate host within the BizTalk Administration Console, choosing Properties, selecting Advanced from the left side of the resulting dialog box, and clicking the Settings button within the Message Publishing Throttling section.

Although the term *rate overdrive* might sound complicated in the case of receive throttling, it is just how much higher you allow the incoming message rate to be than the actual physical publication.

With this default setting of 125 percent, you're effectively saying that you'll allow up to 25 percent over what is currently being physically published (message publishing outgoing rate) to the MessageBox before throttling is introduced. The default value of 125 percent was the optimum setting benchmarked by the BizTalk Product Team.

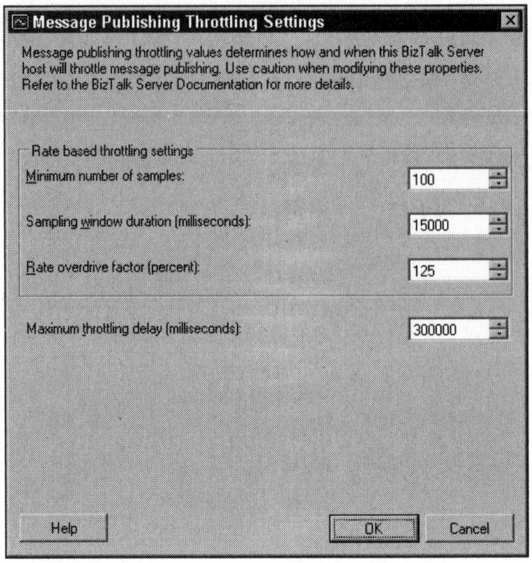

Figure 9-9

As you can see in Figure 9-9, you can control the way in which the BizTalk samples the current state. By default, the sampling window is set to 15000 milliseconds (15 seconds), and the incoming and outgoing rate will be retrieved at least 100 times during this time window to decided whether rate-based throttling needs to be introduced. Setting this to 0 disables rate throttling.

Rate-based throttling is implemented by introducing a progressive delay before the messages are physically published to the message box. You can view the current delay being used via the `Message publishing delay (ms)` performance counter within the `BizTalk:Message Agent` performance object.

❑   **4: Process Memory** — Process memory throttling indicates that the memory being utilized by the BizTalk host's operating system process has exceeded the configured limit. The amount of memory currently utilized by a host process is visible via the process `memory usage (MB)` performance counter located inside the `BizTalk:Message Agent` performance object and includes all types of memory available to the process.

If the memory used by the host process (Working Set) exceeds the process memory usage setting, which is configured via the Throttling Thresholds dialog box, process memory throttling is introduced. The dialog box is shown in Figure 9-10 and is accessed by right-clicking the appropriate host within the BizTalk Administration Console, choosing Properties, selecting Advanced from the left side of the resulting dialog box, and clicking the Settings button within the Throttling Thresholds section.

The default Process memory usage setting is set to 25, as you can see above in Figure 9-10. Values less than 100 are treated as percentages, and values greater than 100 are considered megabytes, thus making the default a percentage: 25 percent.

Thirty-two-bit operating system processes can address a maximum of 2GB memory, regardless of the overall memory installed in the system; therefore, 2GB is used when considering process memory throttling. You can use the /3GB switch in `boot.ini` to address up to 3GB of memory, as required.

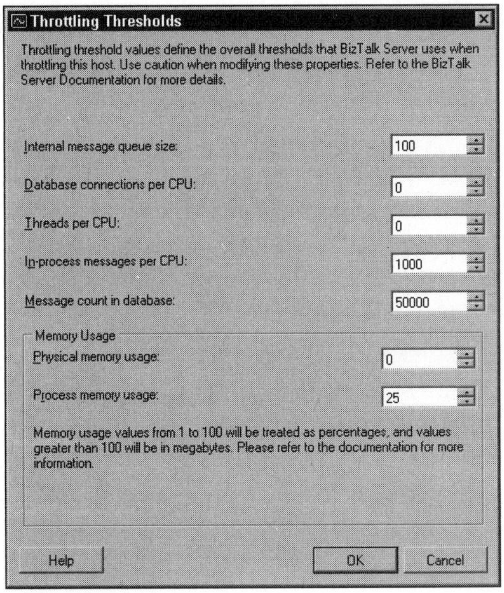

Figure 9-10

So using the defaults, when a BizTalk host operating system process uses more than 512MB of memory (25 percent of 2GB), process memory throttling is introduced, which will restrict the size of the threadpool and/or introduce a progressive delay to message publishing.

❑ **5: System Memory** — System memory throttling indicates that the memory available to the entire computer is potentially running low and you run the risk of an out-of-memory condition. The amount of memory currently being used by the entire computer is viewable via the `Physical memory usage (MB)` performance counter located in the `BizTalk:Message Agent` performance object.

If the physical memory usage exceeds the physical memory usage setting, which is configured via the Throttling Thresholds dialog box (shown in Figure 9-10), system memory throttling is introduced.

The default physical memory usage setting is 0, which means that this particular type of throttling condition is disabled. Setting a value greater than 0 allows this throttling type to be detected and implemented as required.

❑ **6: Database Size** — Database size throttling indicates that messages that have been published to the MessageBox are not being processed and therefore a backlog is building up. The database size is viewable through the `Database Size` performance counter located in the `BizTalk:Message Agent` performance object and takes into account the number of messages in all host queue, spool, and tracking tables.

If the database size increases beyond the `Message count in database` setting, which is configured via the host's Throttling Thresholds dialog box (shown in Figure 9-10), database size throttling is introduced.

The default Message count in database setting is 50000 and means that database size throttling will be introduced if the `Database Size` performance counter reports more than 50000 messages. Note that database size takes into account host queues, and spool and tracking tables, so the sum of these tables may cause throttling to occur.

This throttling condition can also apply if the SQL Server Agent purge jobs are not executed regularly, either due to SQL Server contention or because the SQL Server Agent is not running. The purge jobs are responsible for cleaning up old messages, parts, and the like.

❑   **8: Database Session Count** — Database session count throttling indicates that too many concurrent database connections have been opened by the BizTalk host. The number of database sessions currently open is viewable via the `Database session` performance counter located in the `BizTalk:Message Agent` performance object.

If the number of concurrent database connections exceeds the `Database connections per CPU` setting, which is configured via the host's Throttling Threshold dialog box (shown in Figure 9-10), database session count throttling is introduced.

The default `Database connections per CPU` setting is set to 0, which means that this particular type of throttling is disabled. Specifying a value greater than 0 will enable the detection of database connections and implementation of this type of throttling.

❑   **9: Thread Count** — Thread count throttling indicates that too many threads have been created with the host's operating system process. Too many threads can cause context switching and therefore performance degradation, because too many threads are demanding CPU time. The number of threads currently resident in the process is viewable via the `Thread count` performance counter located in the `BizTalk:Message Agent` performance object.

If the thread count increases beyond the Threads per CPU setting, which is configurable via the host's Throttling Thresholds dialog box (shown in Figure 9-10), thread count throttling is introduced.

The default Threads per CPU setting is set to 0, which means that particular type of throttling is disabled. Specifying a value greater than 0 will allow this type of throttling to be detected and implemented.

❑   **11: User Override** — The User Override throttling type indicates that you have overridden receive throttling via the Registry. Overriding can either be set to 1: Initiate throttling condition or 2: Do not throttle.

"Processing" Throttling

Processing throttling relates to throttling imposed on the processing or consumption of messages from the BizTalk MessageBox and is referred to as *message delivery throttling*. It applies to hosts containing send ports and orchestrations that consume messages from the MessageBox.

The `Message delivery throttling state` performance counter, in the case of an orchestration host, indicates the rate at which messages are being consumed from the MessageBox is being restricted. That is, BizTalk is restricting the rate at which messages are being consumed by BizTalk orchestrations.

If message delivery throttling is under way, the knock-on effect to your system is that you are not processing messages from the MessageBox as quickly as usual, and this could cause a processing backlog.

Eight possible throttling states apply to message publishing. These are indicated by the `message delivery throttling state` performance counter. Anything above zero indicates that publishing throttling is in force. The message delivery throttling state duration counter indicates how long the current throttling state has been in place for.

❑ **0: No Throttling** — This is the default level and indicates that no throttling is currently in force.

❑ **1: Rate** — Rate throttling indicates that messages are being received for processing more quickly than they are being processed, and therefore a backlog is growing. This particular throttling state is common and generally not something to be overly worried about unless you see rate throttling occurring for extended periods of time.

BizTalk decides to utilize rate throttling by monitoring the rate at which messages are being queued for processing and by monitoring the rate at which they are actually physically being processed by orchestrations or send ports. If the queued rate exceeds the processed rate, processing is not keeping up.

The rate at which processing requests are occurring, along with the actual processing operation, is viewable through the `Message delivery incoming rate` and `Message delivery outgoing rate` performance counters.

BizTalk utilizes these counters performance counters to decide whether rate processing should occur. The calculation it uses to perform this decision is shown below. It is effectively saying: *Use rate throttling if the incoming rate is greater than the rate at which we are physically processing messages multiplied by an overdrive factor.*

Message delivery incoming rate > (Message delivery outgoing rate * Rate Overdrive factor (percent))

The rate overdrive factor used here is configured per host through the BizTalk administration tool and defaults to 125 percent. The dialog box is shown in Figure 9-11. You can access this dialog box by right-clicking the appropriate host within the BizTalk administration tool, choosing Properties, selecting Advanced from the left side of the resulting dialog box, and clicking the Settings button within the Message Processing Throttling section.

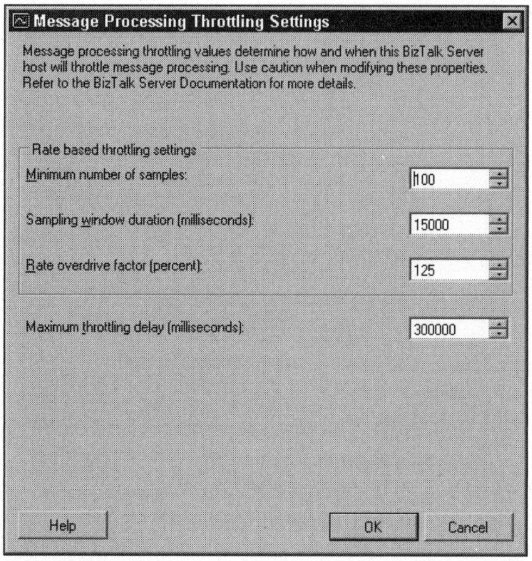

Figure 9-11

Although the term *rate overdrive* might sound complicated, in the case of processing throttling, it is just how much higher you allow the incoming processing rate to be than the actual physical processing rate.

With the default setting of 125 percent, you're effectively saying that you'll handle up to 25 percent over what is currently being physically processed by orchestrations or send ports before throttling is introduced.

The default value of 125 percent was the optimum setting benchmarked by the BizTalk Product Team.

As you can see in Figure 9-11, you can control the way in which the BizTalk samples the current state. By default, the sampling window is set to 15000 milliseconds (15 seconds), and the delivery incoming and delivery outgoing rate will be retrieved at least 100 times during this time window to decided whether rate-based throttling needs to be introduced.

Rate-based throttling is implemented by introducing a progressive delay before the messages are delivered to a send port or orchestration. You can view the current delay being used via the `Message delivery delay (ms)` performance counter within the `BizTalk:Message Agent` performance object.

❑ **3: Unprocessed Message** — Unprocessed message throttling indicates that the number of in-memory messages delivered to the Orchestration or Messaging Engine has reached the maximum configured threshold. This can happen because orchestrations are taking a long time to complete or perhaps adapters responsible for transmitting messages are performing slowly (perhaps due to the destination system).

The number of in-memory messages currently being processed is viewable through the `In-process message count` performance counter.

If the in-process message count increases beyond the `In-Process Messages per CPU` setting, which is configured via the host's Throttling Thresholds dialog box (refer to Figure 9-10), then throttling will be introduced.

The default In-process messages per CPU setting is 1000, which means that unprocessed message throttling will be introduced if the `In-process message count` performance counter reports greater than 1000 messages.

❑ **4: Process Memory, 5: System Memory, 9: Thread Count, 10: User Override** — The last four throttling conditions are implemented identically to receive hosts', so refer to the previous section for information on each of these conditions. You can control the throttling parameters through the same Throttling Thresholds dialog box, which applies to both receive and process throttling.

SQL Server

SQL Server is the heart of any BizTalk group, and the moment it starts to struggle is the moment that the performance of your overall BizTalk group will plateau or even degrade. I've seen many performance-related investigations focus on BizTalk servers, only to find days later that a SQL issue was the root cause.

> *SQL Server tuning is a complex area worthy of an entire book! If you want further information, you should start with the "Troubleshooting Performance Problems in SQL Server 2005" white paper, which you can find at* www.microsoft.com/technet/prodtechnol/sql/2005/tsprfprb.mspx.

Performance Counters

I typically recommend the following performance counters for each SQL server. These represent a small fraction of the available SQL Server counters, but they are of particular note when performing BizTalk Server–focused performance testing.

SQLServer:Locks(*)	
Lock Timeouts/sec	The `Lock Timeouts/sec` counter reflects the number of SQL Server process IDs (SPIDs) that timed out while waiting to acquire locks.
	Lock timeouts are specified by the caller. If you see a large number of lock timeouts, a client has had to wait longer than its specified period to obtain a lock. This can be due to blocking or resource waits.
Average Wait Time (ms)	The `Average Wait Time (ms)` counter reflects the average amount of time spent waiting for locks. A high value typically indicates blocking problems.
	If blocking is suspected, you can use the `sp_blocker_pss80` script for SQL 2000 and SQL 2005 or use the Blocked SPID Process Report in SQL Server 2005. See Chapter 11 for more information.
Lock Waits/sec	The `Lock Waits/sec` counter reflects the number of lock requests that were not granted immediately and therefore required the caller to wait.
	Combining this counter with the previous one enables you to understand how many lock waits are occurring and for how long.
Physical Disk(*)	
Avg Disk Queue Length	The `Avg Disk Queue Length` counter represents the average queue of read and write requests queued for the disk.
	An average value of two per disk is generally regarded as the maximum you should expect to see. Anything higher indicates that BizTalk and SQL Server are blocked waiting for disk I/O, which completely ruins BizTalk and SQL performance results.
	If this occurs, you should consider suspending testing until the disk-performance problems can be resolved; otherwise, the results will not be representative of what is possible.
	I have seen many projects struggle with performance only to find some weeks later that the disk array was not up to scratch or was configured incorrectly.
	If you are using a disk array, divide the Disk Queue Length number by the number of disks (or spindles) used by the disk array. If the resulting number is greater than 2, this indicates disk queuing. It can be hard to use this counter with disk arrays, and experience shows that the following the counters provide easier-to-obtain indications of disk-performance problems.

Continued

451

%Idle Time	The %Idle Time counter represents the percentage of time that the disk has been idle. A very high figure (~100) indicates that the disk is coping perfectly well with the load, but a low number (20) indicates that the disk is struggling and therefore BizTalk performance is suffering significantly. See the preceding counter description (Avg Disk Queue Length) for more details.
Avg. Disk sec/Read	The Avg. Disk sec/Read counter represents the average time that read operations have taken in seconds. As with many of these counters, it depends on the hardware being utilized as to what values indicate problems. You should perform a baseline (low-load) test to understand what the normal range of values should be in your environment. Generally, values of less than 10ms are considered normal; greater than 20ms may indicate problems, and anything over 50ms should be regarded as a severe problem.
Avg. Disk sec/Write	The Avg. Disk sec/Write counter represents the average time that write operations have taken in seconds. As with many of these counters, what values indicate problems depends on the hardware being utilized. You should perform a baseline (low-load) test to gain an understanding of what the normal range of values should be in your environment. Generally, values of less than 10ms are considered normal; values greater than 20ms might indicate problems, and anything over 50ms should be regarded as a severe problem.

Custom SQL Server Databases

It's crucial to fine-tune any custom SQL Server databases that are used as part of your BizTalk solution. Common scenarios in which SQL Server databases are used include access via the SOAP adapter, .NET assemblies, and perhaps Web services that themselves access data held in a SQL Server database.

I've seen no end of problems with databases designed and created by developers with basic SQL Server skills. Database design and index selection are complex tasks and should always involve a database administrator (DBA) wherever possible (to ensure that the overall design is sound and to then help tune the database for the types of queries).

The SQL Server Profiler can help with the tuning stage. The Profiler enables you to record a trace while running a test that will capture queries directed at your database. The Profiler can then suggest indexes and even partitioning to improve performance based on how the database is being used.

You should subject your custom databases to heavy load throughout the development life cycle to ensure that you don't uncover critical problems in the latter stages of your project. Depending on the load, you might want to also consider moving any custom databases from the SQL server used by BizTalk to another, to ensure that they are not competing for resources.

The use of the SQL Server Profiler does not negate the requirement to involve a SQL Server DBA; after all, the Tuning Advisor can only go so far.

I've been involved in scenarios in which I've been able to achieve around 20 percent to 30 percent improvement using my skills and the Tuning Advisor, but then involved a DBA who has achieved around an 80 percent improvement. Deep knowledge of SQL is key!

Dependent Systems

BizTalk can only perform as well as the systems it depends on to complete the steps required for processing a message! *This is an important point to remember.*

If you have a Web service called for each message that takes five seconds to process, for example, this is clearly going to negatively impact the overall performance of your BizTalk solution because the processing of each message will incur this additional overhead.

Because of the scale and power of BizTalk, it can often (at least in default configuration) bring dependent systems to their knees. I've seen many Web servers struggle to meet the requests of just a single BizTalk server. This can be due to BizTalk just generating too much load, but it often highlights a performance or concurrency problem with the service being called. Of course, you can throttle the number and rate of the requests BizTalk Server will send, but this will negatively impact the throughput you can achieve. For that reason, it's key to test and tune any dependent systems heavily and independently of BizTalk prior to embarking on a full integration performance test.

This section focuses on the Internet Information Server (IIS) because it is the most common dependent system used within BizTalk solutions (and because we cannot cover the entire spectrum of dependent systems in one chapter!)

Performance Counters

The following are the most commonly used performance counters for IIS and ASP.NET. Depending on your scenario, you might require more.

Web Service(*)	
Current Connections	The Current Connections counter reflects the total number of concurrent connections to the Web server at the current point in time.
	If you don't see this number go above (2 * *NumberOfBizTalkServers*), you might be experiencing the concurrent connection limit, covered in the "Laying the Foundations" section of this chapter.
	(The *NumberOfBizTalkServers* reflects the number of servers running a host instance that contains the SOAP or HTTP adapter.)

Continued

ASP.NET v2.0.50727(*)	
Request Execution Time	The `Request Execution Time` counter reflects the end-to-end execution time of the last ASP.NET request in milliseconds.
	Execution time of longer than a few hundred milliseconds can indicate slow-performing requests that will have a knock-on effect on how fast BizTalk can process requests and also limit the number of requests per second that IIS can handle.
Requests Queued	The `Requests Queued` counter reflects the number of requests queued pending execution.
	If this counter shows any requests being queued, it indicates that the IIS is struggling to serve the requests, and the request time will be longer than usual.
	Any amount of queuing is typically bad news for overall performance. The requests should be analyzed to understand where the time is being spent. Often, a SQL Server database or component will be found to be the cause.
Requests Wait Time	The `Requests Wait Time` counter reflects the amount of time the last request spent in the request queue.
ASP.NET Apps v2.0.05727	
Requests/Sec	The `Requests/Sec` counter reflects the number of requests per second being received and completed.
Requests Failed	The `Requests Failed` counter reflects the number of requests that result in failure. This number should be 0 in normal circumstances, and any failing requests will likely impact your performance results.

Log Files

IIS log files can be crucial to understanding load patterns, details about individual requests, and which requests are perhaps taking the most the time to complete. Although IIS log files are stored in a clear-text format, they can be hard to analyze effectively. However, they do offer a wealth of information.

Microsoft provides a tool for downloading called Log Parser. Log Parser provides an interactive SQL-like query syntax over IIS log files along with a variety of other log files and sources, including NetMon, Event Viewer, and the Registry.

Log Parser is an amazing tool that can return queries in milliseconds from huge Web server log files and provides a fantastic way to identify which requests are taking a long time within your solution. Thus, it enables you to focus your efforts.

Consider, for instance, the following example. It retrieves the page names of all requests in the log file that have an .ASP extension:

```
LogParser "SELECT cs-uri-stem FROM ex.log WHERE cs-uri-stem LIKE '%.asp'"
```

More usefully, you can also write a query that can retrieve the top *worst-performing* requests. The following example returns these from any number of IIS log files:

```
LogParser "Select Top 20 cs-uri-stem,sc-bytes,sc-status,time-taken FROM ex*.log
ORDER BY time-taken DESC
```

See the Knowledge Base article at http://support.microsoft.com/kb/910447 for further information and for some examples that demonstrate the output of such queries being used to generate graphs (which makes the data easier to analyze).

Common Symptoms

It's not possible to predict or even attempt to document what each performance counter may or may not show during a performance test of your solution. Every solution developed on BizTalk is different, and there are a multitude of reasons why you might see certain behavior during a load test (environment, hardware, message size, etc.).

However, I have included a list of common symptoms that I've seen during performance testing. I've also identified some things to check or consider when you see such behavior. Such "real-world" information is hard to come by, and this should be of great help when you are conducting testing.

Orchestration Completed/Sec Drops Off Suddenly

During performance testing, you might suddenly see that the `Orchestrations completed/sec` performance counter suddenly drops off for a significant period of time in conjunction with the `% Processer Time` counter on the BizTalk servers.

There are a number of potential reasons for such behavior, some of which are covered in the following sections.

Not Enough Work

The most common reason for orchestrations seeming to "drop off" is that there aren't any messages awaiting processing by orchestrations. You can check this by reviewing the `Host Queue-Length` counter for the appropriate BizTalk host.

If the host queue isn't showing any messages, that explains why processing has dropped off. If the host queue is showing messages, however, the drop-off can be due the fact that you are not injecting messages into BizTalk fast enough.

If you are injecting a single message, this scenario doesn't apply. If you are injecting, say, a batch file that requires splitting, however, it could be that you're not feeding the engine fast enough. In-bound debatching can take a long time, especially with large files.

During the debatching process, messages will appear in the host queue performance counter, but they are not actually ready for processing until the entire batch has finished splitting, at which point the messages are "ready" for processing.

This is a common problem. It looks like there are messages to keep BizTalk going, but in fact, you're starving BizTalk of messages that are "ready" for processing. You have to ensure that you are feeding BizTalk hard enough; otherwise, you'll never get sensible performance results.

A technique to establish whether this is the problem is to stop the orchestration or send ports subscribing to your messages via the BizTalk administration tool but *keep* them enlisted to ensure that the subscriptions remain.

Inject a large number of messages, which, because the orchestrations or send ports are stopped, will just queue in the MessageBox. When you have finished injecting messages, start the orchestration or send ports and observe the difference.

If you don't see the drop-offs seen previously, the likely cause was that you were not feeding BizTalk fast enough. Of course, you might reach another bottleneck, but the system should behave much better than before.

This technique of isolating your receive process from your processing process is useful during performance testing because it can help you to identify where your bottleneck lies (in-bound or processing).

SQL Server Problems

Such behavior can also be attributed to the SQL Server performing badly or even performing an operation such as resizing the database. Review the database settings inline with the checklist at the beginning of this chapter. Perhaps also run a SQL trace to ascertain whether the SQL Server is struggling.

Throttling

In extreme cases, throttling can be seen to cause a sudden drop-off. Usually, however, you only observe slight, gradual drop-off because of throttling. To prove whether or not this is a problem, review the `Message Publishing Throttling State` or `Message Delivery Throttling State` performance counter.

High CPU Usage

High CPU usage is not necessarily a problem, because it just highlights the fact that your system is busy processing work. Sustained 100 percent CPU usage, however, indicates that the machine is overloaded. Overloading can indicate that you require another BizTalk server to share the load or that perhaps your solution is using the finite CPU resource in a bad way.

High CPU usage can occur for any number of reasons; a few common reasons are covered in the following sections.

Rules Engine

If you are using the Rules Engine within your solution, and the BizTalk host (normally the Orchestration host) using the BizTalk Rules Engine (BRE) is showing high CPU usage, you may need to review the caching settings for the Rules Engine.

As discussed in Chapter 7, translating the Rules Engine XML into an in-memory model requires an upfront CPU usage cost. To mitigate this overhead, the *translated* rules-engine model is cached when translation is complete, enabling subsequent Rules Engine requests to retrieve the cached in-memory model and thus negating the need for translation each time.

A cached in-memory model can be used one at a time. The default cache size is set to 32, which is easily exhaustible on a standard BizTalk server executing orchestrations that each invoke the Rules Engine.

The cache is kept small by default. Because each in-memory model requires a fair amount of memory, however, you can increase the cache size. But you do need to keep an eye on overall memory usage to ensure that increasing the cache size doesn't cause additional memory-related problems.

It's easy to assume that the cache isn't big enough and increase it. Depending on your workload profile, however, it could be that the cache entries are expiring because they haven't been used for a period of time; the default is set to 3600 seconds (1 hour).

Both settings are controllable via the following Registry key, which you need to apply to each BizTalk server in your BizTalk group:

```
HKEY_LOCAL_MACHINE\SOFTWARE\Microsoft\BusinessRules\3.0
```

The values to modify under this key are `CacheSize` and `CacheTimeout`. In testing, we typically increase the `CacheSize` to 512 as a placeholder value. This doesn't mean 512 policies will be populated in the cache, because entries are only added if the cache is exhausted. However, this way the cache will grow to the required size without being artificially limited.

The configuration settings can also be specified via a configuration file by inserting the configuration elements shown here into the `btsntsvc.exe.config` file in `%PROGRAMFILES%\Microsoft BizTalk Server 2006`:

```
<configSections>
  <section name="Microsoft.RuleEngine" type=
"System.Configuration.SingleTagSectionHandler"/>
</configSections>

<Microsoft.RuleEngine
  CacheEntries="512"
  CacheTimeout="3600" />
```

(See the following section on "High Memory Usage".) Increasing the cache size increases the memory requirements for a BizTalk host process and often triggers process memory throttling. The default of 512MB for a host process must be increased to prevent throttling.

Serialization of Orchestrations

Orchestration serialization is CPU intensive and makes use of the .NET serialization stack. Serialization overhead might be increased further, depending on the number of message and variables you have present within the orchestration.

This isn't usually a major problem, but if your orchestration has many persistence points (as discussed in Chapter 5), you are artificially increasing the usual number of times that orchestration persistence occurs.

Orchestration performance lives and dies by persistence points, and they should be reduced wherever possible. To understand how many persistence points you incur for each logical *transaction*, monitor the `Persistence Points` performance counter in the `XLANG/s Orchestrations` performance object.

Reviewing the number of persistence points in this way enables you to understand how many persistence points are required for just one message. The number of persistence points will differ for each solution and depends on your scenario. (If you're looking for a rule of thumb, I normally consider five to be about average for a complex orchestration.) You should evaluate how many persistence points each orchestration incurs for one message being passed for your solution and try to understand why each one occurs.

Reducing the number of persistence points will reduce the CPU overhead for serialization and improve the overall solution performance.

Bad Code

As with all solutions, poorly implemented custom code can affect the entire end-to-end performance of your solution, and its effects shouldn't be underestimated. As discussed earlier in this chapter, each element of custom code should, wherever possible, be performance tested and tuned in isolation to ensure that it performs in the best possible way. The unit testing and profiling features of Visual Studio 2005 are ideal for this.

Custom code can incur high CPU usage for a multitude of reasons (serialization, XML parsing, etc.). Profiling the code using the Visual Studio Profiler (covered in Chapter 8) should be the first step to understanding where in your code the time is being spent. Then you can tune accordingly.

High Memory Usage

High memory usage or memory leaks are fairly rare in my experience of testing BizTalk Server solutions. One reason for this rarity is that in most cases, pure .NET code is involved, which when combined with garbage collection (GC) means that it is hard to *leak* memory.

Increasing the Rules Engine cache (as discussed earlier in this chapter) can increase memory usage significantly and often causes process memory throttling to be introduced as the BizTalk host process memory usage goes over the default throttling setting of 25 percent (512MB).

Under load, BizTalk suppresses GC because collection is an intensive task. If you monitor private bytes during a test run, for example, you might reasonably think that a "memory leak" is occurring because memory usage is increasing constantly. What you should see is that after a period of time, collection will occur and memory usage will drop.

If the Rules Engine isn't being used and you are still seeing sustained memory usage (usage that isn't released during the test following a collection), you should attempt to isolate the problem by identifying the host involved. If the identified host is hosting receive or send ports, you will need to determine whether the memory usage is due to an adapter or pipeline component. If the host is hosting orchestrations, try to isolate the individual orchestration involved.

You might ultimately need to take a memory dump of the BizTalk host process to understand where the memory is being consumed. A memory dump can be taken using the `adplus` script that ships as part of the Debugging Tools for Windows. You can also download it from `www.microsoft.com/whdc/devtools/debugging/default.mspx`.

You can "tell" `adplus` to capture either a hang or crash dump. In this case, a hang dump should be used because it's nondestructive and allows the process to continue after the dump has been completed.

You can then analyze this dump using `WinDbg` and the SOS Debugger extension. Many guides are available from Microsoft and on the Internet. These guides provide step-by-step instructions on analyzing such a dump file for memory problems. You can find a good example at `http://msdn2.microsoft.com/en-us/library/ms954591.aspx`.

I can also recommend *Debugging Microsoft .NET 2.0 Applications* by John Robbins (Microsoft Press, 2006), which is a fantastic debugging resource.

Web Service Problems (SOAP Adapter)

This section covers two common symptoms of problems: Web service calls performing slowly and the error "Not Enough Free Threads in the ThreadPool Object to Complete Operation."

These symptoms are common when undertaking performance testing of solutions that use the SOAP adapter to call Web services. The error can occur for a number of reasons. The following sections cover some of them.

Thread Starvation

Ensure that you have at least three BizTalk hosts configured: one for receiving, one for orchestrations, and one for sending. Otherwise, if you leave all three types configured in the default `BizTalkServerApplication` host, you will quickly find that they compete against one another for threads.

A common example is a scenario in which orchestrations are processing incoming messages and then generating new messages for transmission via the SOAP adapter to a Web service. You will find that, under load, the orchestrations will use all available threads in the threadpool and not leave any for the SOAP adapter to use to transmit outgoing messages. The SOAP adapter will then raise errors such as "Not Enough Free Threads in the ThreadPool Object to Complete Operation." Of course, the SOAP adapter will then retry according to the retry interval, but such retrying significantly affects overall throughput.

Splitting sending, receiving, and orchestration into separate BizTalk hosts enables each host to have its own threadpool and, therefore, not be affected by another host's activity.

Threadpool Threads Not Created Quickly Enough

This particular problem is covered in depth in Chapter 10, but we highlight the reasoning here for reference.

When BizTalk is ramping up to process a sudden injection of messages, the .NET `ThreadPool` can struggle to create the threads quickly enough to satisfy the demand. This struggle leads to "Not Enough Free Threads in the ThreadPool Object to Complete Operation" errors (or errors with similar wording). This error can also happen after a lull in activity, when threads can be torn down.

The technique to resolve this is to keep a minimum number of threads *warm* and thus always available to incoming requests, which we cover in the next section.

.NET Web Service Stack Uses Two Threads per Request

It's a little-known fact that the .NET Web service stack will use one threadpool worker thread to process the request and then one I/O thread to process the response. In some circumstances, however, multiple worker threads and I/O completion threads can be used. This often leads to confusion when calculating how many worker threads are required. (For example, you select a number and then exhaust it with half the number of requests.)

> *You can find more information about this behavior at* `http://support.microsoft.com/default.aspx?scid=kb;en-us;821268`.

If you do experience such problems, adjust the following Registry settings on all BizTalk servers. By so doing, you should alleviate such issues.

`MinWorkerThreads` indicates the minimum number of threads that should be kept *warm*. Although you won't necessarily see this many threads available via the `Process Thread Count` performance counter, they can be created significantly faster than usual. The rule of thumb for BizTalk servers is that you should set `MinWorkerThreads` to the maximum expected number of concurrent SOAP or HTTP calls, and then add 10 percent for safety. So, if you expect a maximum of 200 concurrent calls, you should set `MinWorkerThreads` to 220 (200 + 10%). Note that this setting is per CPU.

The `MaxWorkerThreads` indicates the maximum number of maximum number of threads that can be available. Setting this value too low can cause the "Not Enough Threads in the ThreadPool" error. Too many threads can cause context switching, but BizTalk itself should have throttled long before that point. Note that this setting is per CPU.

The `MinIOThreads` setting should be changed inline with the `MinWorkerThreads`, because at least one I/O completion port will be used for each request. Doubling of the number is still required because a request may, of course, use multiple I/O threads. Note that this setting is per CPU.

In short, the `Min` and `Max` settings of `WorkerThreads` and `IOThreads` should be kept the same. Modification of these values is done via the Registry, and the keys are shown here. For BizTalk Server 2004, you need to know the GUID for a BizTalk host. However, BizTalk 2006 uses the host name, instead.

The suggested values are:

```
[SYSTEM\CurrentControlSet\Services\BtsSvc{GUID | HostName}]
  [CLR Hosting]
    [MaxIOThreads      = 100] (DWORD)
    [MaxWorkerThreads = 100] (DWORD)
    [MinIOThreads      = 25] (DWORD)
    [MinWorkerThreads = 25] (DWORD)
```

Based on previous results with solutions invoking Web services heavily, I have found the following settings to provide good results. Every solution is different, however, and you should tune your system to the settings that work best for you.

```
[SYSTEM\CurrentControlSet\Services\BtsSvc{GUID | HostName}]
  [CLR Hosting]
    [MaxIOThreads     = 400] (DWORD)
    [MaxWorkerThreads = 400] (DWORD)
    [MinIOThreads     = 220] (DWORD)
    [MinWorkerThreads = 220] (DWORD)
```

Low Throughput (Not Achieving the msg/Sec)

Of all the problems, this must be the most common and typically represents your solution not delivering the required numbers. As you can imagine, this can result from a combination of causes, some of which are covered in the following sections.

Are You Feeding BizTalk with Enough Work?

Ensure that the spool or host queues are not being starved of work. Designing a load injection system that can keep up with power of a large BizTalk solution can be hard, and the use of LoadGen should be considered over a custom load injection tool because it scales well.

Is BizTalk Throttling?

Many of the performance problems related to BizTalk occur because of BizTalk throttling for one reason or another. Monitoring the throttling performance counters is key and will indicate which area of the solution is struggling and causing throttling.

Resolution of the problem will free BizTalk up to operate at its maximum rate. Be aware, however, that resolving one bottleneck invariably leads to another bottleneck being struck!

Are the Dependent Systems Keeping Up?

As discussed earlier in the chapter, BizTalk is only as fast as its weakest link. I often find that SQL Server databases or Web services used by BizTalk initially struggle to keep up with the load imposed on them by BizTalk Server. With profiling and tuning, however, you can often alleviate this during performance testing.

As mentioned earlier, testing of these dependent systems in isolation prior to their being connected up to BizTalk is crucial to the overall design and technology selection.

Add Extra Servers

If your BizTalk Servers are not throttling and the SQL server is not showing signs of stress, you may want to consider adding an extra BizTalk server to distribute the load and add extra processing capability.

If after adding the BizTalk Server you don't experience near to double the throughput, however, you must ensure that any dependent systems, including the SQL server hosting the MessageBox, are not experiencing a bottleneck.

Poorly Performing Disks

As discussed at the beginning of the chapter, you live and die by the performance of your disk arrays. A fast disk array is the key to achieving the required throughput for your solution!

Heavy BAM Usage

If you are using Business Activity Monitoring (BAM) within your solution, you must ensure that you schedule the `BAM_DM_<ActivityName>` SSIS job to be executed at suitable intervals for your scenario.

This Data Maintenance (DM) SSIS package is responsible for partitioning the BAM tables used for insertion of new data. It ensures that the table depths are kept to a minimum, and therefore maintains a high rate of input. (That is, as the data levels increase, the writes don't take longer and longer.)

By default, the Data Maintenance package is not scheduled. However, this can easily be scheduled by creating a new SQL Server Agent Job that invokes the SSIS package according to your schedule requirements.

If you are using an asynchronous event stream (`BufferedEventStream` or `OrchestrationEventStream`), BAM data is initially written to the BizTalk MessageBox and is then copied into the `BAMPrimaryImport` database by the Tracking Data Service (TDDS).

The `Tracking Data Size` performance counter is useful to monitor because this indicates (if global tracking is turned off) how much BAM data is waiting to be moved to `BAMPrimaryImport`. Ideally, this counter should remain low; in high BAM usage scenarios, however, you might see a small backlog build.

In itself, this isn't a problem, because the very nature an asynchronous event stream means that you are not overly worried when the BAM data is made available as long as it gets there. If you do have time-critical issues, consider using the `DirectEventStream`, which is synchronous for data that is time critical. But, of course, this means that the calling system blocks until the data is written to the BAM tables.

Spool Increasing Steadily

If you observe the BizTalk MessageBox Spool increasing steadily, it might indicate a backlog building within your solution. Beware, however, of assuming this if you are processing /debatching a large input file. While this is being done, the spool will increase steadily as the in-bound message is split up. However, these messages cannot be consumed until the entire file has been processed (thus causing the spool to build up, but the spool should then start to drop off).

If this isn't the case, your backlog is building up somewhere. Analyzing each host queue counter will enable you to identify which BizTalk host is running behind (e.g., Receive, Orchestration, or Send). Narrowing down the problem area is critical in such an investigation.

If you find that a host queue is responsible, you first need to understand whether the host is throttling. If it is, the reason for throttling will help to explain what is occurring. (The various throttling states were covered earlier in this chapter.)

If, when you review the BizTalk host queues, you cannot see a host directly responsible for the increasing spool size, ensure that the SQL Server Agent is running (because the various purge jobs need to execute to clear the spool table). This might also indicate that the purge jobs are struggling due to SQL Server contention. (You can use the various purge jobs performance counters to diagnose this further under the `BizTalk:Message Box:General Counters` performance object.)

Summary

This chapter covered the foundations that you should put in place before starting any form of performance testing to ensure that you get the best results possible. Once the foundations are in place, you need to effectively monitor the solution. We've covered the key performance counters to monitor, detailed a few techniques to assist you, and explained in depth how BizTalk throttling works.

We then finished up by discussing a number of common symptoms that are often seen during performance testing. Hopefully, any problems you see during testing are covered in this section.

Performance testing is an absolutely critical part of any BizTalk project. Testing should be performed early and often throughout your development life cycle. Chapter 8 introduced a number of approaches and tools to help with testing, including the BizUnit tool, which automates large parts of your testing process, dramatically increasing productivity and reliability.

The next chapter discusses the topic of low latency and details how latency can be minimized within your solution to meet aggressive low-latency requirements.

10

Low Latency

In some scenarios, the time that BizTalk takes to process individual messages is important, critical even. Perhaps there are users who wait for a user interface that is a thin façade over BizTalk, and the user interface blocks while it is waiting for a response message from BizTalk. Or perhaps BizTalk is deployed as a service and as such is required to meet certain service-level agreements related to message processing. Regardless of why you need to achieve low latency in BizTalk, when designing your system to meet those latency requirements, you need to be aware of the pitfalls and the proactive approaches you can adopt. This chapter discusses what low latency really means for BizTalk, how the BizTalk architecture affects latency, whether you really need low latency, and if you do, how you can tune the product to achieve low latency.

What Is Low Latency?

First, let's discuss what we mean by latency in the context of BizTalk Server. Latency is the time that a message spends within BizTalk, in other words it is the time that BizTalk takes to process a message. For a one-way scenario, this is the time from when the message is received at the Receive adapter to the time when the message is sent out via the Send adapter. For a two-way scenario, the latency is the time from when the message is received to the time when the response message is returned by the Request-Response adapter. Ideally, this should be measured starting at the time the message reaches the Receive adapter and ending at the time the Send adapter completes the transmission of the message — in other words, the amount of time spent in BizTalk.

Out of the box, BizTalk Server is tuned for optimum throughput. In other words, it is tuned to get as many messages through per second as possible. This fact says nothing about how long individual messages take to process. "So what?" you might say. Well, as it turns out, this is at odds with aggressive low-latency processing. In a high-throughput scenario, you may well be able to process 100 messages per second. But the processing time for each message may average 1000 ms (the average time that a message is within BizTalk from the time it is received by the adapter on the receive side to the time it is sent out by the adapter on the send side). Conversely, a low-latency system may only be capable of processing a peak of 40 messages per second, but it may be able to guarantee that every message is processed within 300 ms.

Of course, low latency means different things to different people and different projects. If you are building a financial services messaging platform that is processing stock trades, you might have to guarantee that all messages are processed within 100 ms (your latency requirement). If you can't guarantee this low latency, you risk losing deals. If you are building a travel-booking system that collects all your flight and hotel preferences over a series of screens and then processes your booking on the final screen, however, it might be perfectly acceptable for that last screen to be processed within 30 seconds. The orchestration that performs that processing may involve a large number of complex interactions with back-end systems, the sum of which add up to determine the overall latency for the business transaction. Both scenarios may be considered low-latency requirements, although one of those scenarios is significantly more aggressive than the other. The point is that latency is a relative measurement for your system.

When designing a system that has low-latency requirements, it is important to consider whether it really has low-latency requirements or whether you can design the system in a way that latency is not a key nonfunctional requirement. For example, consider the scenario in which a user submits orders into a Web-based user interface. The orders are sent to BizTalk via a request-response Web service port. The port is bound to an orchestration that processes the message. Perhaps the orchestration in turn needs to communicate to one or more back-end systems before returning a response to the user indicating the outcome of the order. It could be that a tight coupling such as this, between submitting the order and the processing of it, is required. Alternatively, it could also be possible that the order could be persisted in a staging area, with just an order reference ID returned to the user (which they could use at any time to query the status of the order). For that scenario, BizTalk could receive the message from the staging area and process it in batch mode, thereby eliminating the low-latency requirement on BizTalk.

Typically, a user can wait on a user interface for up to 2 seconds. As you approach and exceed that threshold, an application will be perceived to have slow response times, and users are likely to be dissatisfied. Clearly, this means that if your solution involves creating a user interface façade over BizTalk and your user interface blocks while waiting for response messages, your latency requirements should be below 2 seconds. Depending on the scenario, achieving latencies below 2 seconds is achievable for a BizTalk solution that has several MessageBox hops, though some tuning might be necessary to guarantee that messages are processed within those latencies. First, however, you may wish to consider whether you can design your scenario in such a way as to eliminate any low-latency requirements. As we will see shortly, low latency is very achievable using BizTalk, but if it's appropriate, making some minor design changes up front may save you time and effort.

The BizTalk Processing Model

To fully understand how you can fine-tune a BizTalk solution for a low-latency scenario, you need to understand how BizTalk processes messages. Figure 10-1 shows the BizTalk architecture; the flow of a message through BizTalk is illustrated by the arrows on the diagram. I will discuss this flow in more detail shortly. As already discussed earlier in the book, at the center is the MessageBox, a durable publish-subscribe engine built in the database. The MessageBox services all of BizTalk's subservices (referred to as *service classes*). These include the Messaging Engine (in process and out of process), the Orchestration Engine, and the BizTalk Message Queue (MSMQT, T for Transport) adapter.

The flow through BizTalk is as follows:

1.   The MSMQ adapter receives a message from a queue and submits it to the Messaging Engine.

2. The Messaging Engine performs some preprocessing on the message and then executes it through the receive pipeline.

3. The Messaging Engine invokes the Message Agent in order to publish the message to the MessageBox.

4. The message is published to the MessageBox, the subscriptions are evaluated during publication, and a reference to the message is placed in the appropriate application queue in the MessageBox.

5. The Message Agent dequeues the message and passes it to the Orchestration Engine.

6. The Orchestration Engine activates a new instance of the correct type of orchestration.

7. The orchestration processes the message and then posts it to a send port.

8. The Orchestration Engine passes the message to the Message Agent, which, in turn, publishes the message to the MessageBox.

9. The Message Agent dequeues the message and passes it to the Messaging Engine.

10. The Messaging Engine performs some preprocessing of the message and then executes the send pipeline.

11. The Messaging Engine determines which adapter should handle the message — in this case, it is the HTTP adapter. The adapter then sends the message. The Messaging Engine then deletes the message from the MessageBox by invoking API's on the Message Agent.

In addition to the service classes, the MessageBox services the BAM tracking service and the internal caching service. You can control which of these subservices is active in the BizTalk NT Service by the way in which you define your hosts and which servers instances those hosts execute on. However, the subservices don't talk directly to the MessageBox. Instead, they access it via the Message Agent, which works in synergy with the MessageBox to surface the rich publish and subscribe capabilities to the BizTalk service classes. You can think of the Message Agent as the MessageBox API. It is always a singleton per process.

Each service class can be associated with one and only one application queue, although an application queue may service multiple service classes. The Message Agent enables service classes to take advantage of its batching capabilities and provides an API for service classes to deal with both stateless and stateful messages (a stateful message is an orchestration). It will load the balance across multiple instances of the same host running on different servers when dequeuing messages from the MessageBox. The Message Agent also ensures that the right messages are routed to the right process running on the right server. For example, Message Agent ensures that a correlation message received is delivered to the instance of an orchestration that initiated the correlation set for that message, regardless of which server that orchestration is running on.

The Message Agent delivers messages to the various service classes according to the subscriptions configured for those service classes. It achieves this by polling the MessageBox database, checking the application queue to determine whether messages are ready to be dequeued. If the Message Agent finds messages that need to be dequeued, it dequeues them, passes them off to the service class required to process them, and then immediately polls again to fetch the next batch of messages. When the Message Agent no longer finds messages waiting to be dequeued, it pauses before its next poll. This pause/polling interval incrementally increases every time the Message Agent polls and does not find messages that need to be dequeued. This polling interval will eventually reach a maximum polling interval. You can configure this maximum for each service class. We discuss this further later in the chapter.

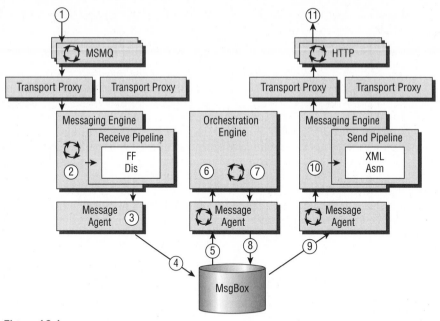

Figure 10-1

The concept behind this polling model is:

- ❏ When the engine is running hot, the cost of polling does not affect performance.

- ❏ When the engine is not running hot, polling on a database doing nothing is relatively cheap and irrelevant, for the most part.

- ❏ When there are messages in the queue, the engine keeps trying to dequeue messages until they have all been processed.

In the scenario shown in Figure 10-1, the message is received by the MSMQ adapter, which submits the message to the Messaging Engine. The Messaging Engine acts as the host for the MSMQ adapter and any other in-process adapters that have been configured. Adapters do not talk directly to the Messaging Engine; instead, they talk to their own instance of a "transport proxy," which is passed to the adapter on startup. In the case of isolated adapters (such as HTTP or SOAP), the adapter itself is the host for the Messaging Engine; the adapter creates its own transport proxy, and under the covers the transport proxy creates the Messaging Engine.

When the Messaging Engine receives the message, it performs some default processing on the message and then executes the message through the correct receive pipeline. After executing the pipeline, if a map has been configured the Messaging Engine executes it. After the message has been processed, it is published via the Message Agent to the MessageBox. Typically, this process takes place for a batch of messages simultaneously rather than for a single message at a time. All APIs from the adapter down to the MessageBox enable this batch-based processing. The engine may subdivide batches as appropriate during the processing for various optimizations. When it does this, all the subbatches are still children of the parent batch and so are all still committed to the MessageBox together. All this processing is accomplished using a relatively flat memory footprint. To be clear, this means that the BizTalk service will try to use a constant amount of memory. In reality, the amount of memory the process uses will fluctuate slightly but should be relatively constant. The entire stack of the engine, from the adapter down to the MessageBox, processes the message in a streaming fashion, thus keeping the memory footprint flat.

In this scenario, the MessageBox evaluates the subscriptions at the time of publication and routes the message to a host queue serviced by the Orchestration Engine. More precisely, the Message Agent hosted by the Orchestration Engine will be polling this queue for new messages. When it discovers the new message has been inserted into the queue that it is servicing, the message will be delivered to the Orchestration Engine. Because the message is an activation message, it will cause the Orchestration Engine to instantiate a new instance of an orchestration of a specified type. The Orchestration Engine will execute the orchestration. The last action in the orchestration is to send a new message to a send port. Again, this is achieved by handing the message off to the Message Agent, which in turn publishes the message to the MessageBox. And again, this process is performed in batches; as detailed in the entire engine stack processes the messages using a forward-only streaming model to ensure that the memory footprint is flat. The Orchestration Engine will use batches where appropriate. For example, both the instance state of the orchestration and the message that it is sending will be persisted to the MessageBox in one atomic operation.

Next, the Message Agent servicing the Messaging Engine hosting the Send adapter will poll the application queue waiting for new messages to arrive. When a new message is inserted into the application queue, it will be delivered to the Messaging Engine. The Messaging Engine maps the message if mapping has been configured, executes the send pipeline, and then delivers the message to the correct adapter (in this case, the HTTP adapter).

The overhead cost of dequeuing and publishing a message is not cheap. BizTalk needs to make a database roundtrip that is an off-machine call. If only a single message were passed to and from the database at any time, the performance would be very poor due to this cost. So, to counter the cost of the roundtrip, BizTalk uses batching, as mentioned earlier. By dequeuing and publishing batches of messages in this way, the roundtrip cost is shared by all messages in the batch, thus reducing the cost.

This architecture means that high message throughput can be achieved using strong transactional semantics. This is good news for many scenarios, because it means that you can process large numbers of messages and they'll be transferred automatically between their source or destination and BizTalk. As mentioned earlier, however, this is at odds with the latency of that processing. Large batches of messages are shuffled around in BizTalk, and although this means that the overall throughput is impressive, the time required for individual messages might be lower than expected because they spend time waiting for their associated batch to be processed. Further, due to the mechanics of the engine, you can see spikes in latencies as different types of processing are performed by the engine.

Measuring Latency

Exactly what constitutes latency will often vary from scenario to scenario. For some scenarios, the latency measure starts when the sending application sends the message and ends when it receives the response. In other words, the time spent on the wire is included in the latency time. For transports that use queuing technology, for example, this could be more significant than, say, a direct TCP/IP transport. Yet, at the other end of the spectrum, the time spent in the adapter is not included. It is acceptable to start measuring at the time when the message reaches the receive pipeline since this period of time may typically be measured in a few milliseconds and is therefore of little interest in the big picture. Of course, this depends on the adapter that you are using.

Out of the box, BizTalk publishes a number of performance counters that you can use to help determine the amount of time messages spend in the BizTalk Engine. None of these counters gives the full latency picture, although the `Request-Response Latency` counter is pretty close. Nevertheless, they are all useful performance counters of which you should be aware.

The following table illustrates the four performance counters published by the Messaging Engine. All these counters are new in BizTalk Server 2006. The counters `Inbound Latency` and `Outbound Latency` measure the time taken in the Messaging Engine between the adapter (receive or send) and the MessageBox. Note, however, that these counters do not take into account the time spent in the MessageBox waiting to be processed. Also note that `Inbound Latency` does not include the time spent in the adapter, but `Outbound Latency` does include the time spent in the adapter.

The `Request-Response Latency` counter measures the time from when the request message is initially submitted into the engine until the time the response message is returned to the waiting Request-Response adapter. This includes the time spent in the MessageBox, but this counter does not include the time spent in the adapter. Typically, this time is short compared to the time spent in the engine; and to be honest, if you really care about the time spent in the entire BizTalk stack, you should arguably measure it outside of BizTalk, anyway. In my experience, for many requirements it is acceptable to ignore the time spent in adapters. You should note that this is not only dependent on the adapter that you are using but also the mode that it is operating in. For example, if the adapter supports batching, the size of the batches that it is using when submitting or sending messages will have an impact on latency. Similarly, if an adapter supports ordered delivery this can also affect latency if the feature is turned on. The counter `Outbound Adapter Latency`, as described below, measures the time taken by the send-side adapter.

Inbound Latency	Average latency in milliseconds from when the Messaging Engine receives a document from the adapter until the time it is published to MessageBox
Outbound Adapter Latency	Average latency in milliseconds from when the adapter gets a document from the Messaging Engine until the time it is sent by the adapter
Outbound Latency	Average latency in milliseconds from when the Messaging Engine receives a document from the MessageBox until the time document is sent by the adapter
Request-Response Latency	Average latency in milliseconds from when the Messaging Engine receives a request document from the adapter until the time a response document is given back to the adapter

So how do you measure end-to-end latency? As mentioned, you could measure this outside of BizTalk. For some scenarios, this will be the desired approach. If you need to measure latency purely to validate your performance, you can use logging technology such as that found in the Enterprise Library or `System.Diagnostics.Trace`. If you need to be able to audit the latency of message processing on a per-message basis, however, you can leverage BAM to provide these capabilities.

Figure 10-2 shows how you can use BAM to measure message latency, note that the MessagingEventStream should typically be used in order to minimize the effect on latency, the DirectEventStream for example could have a significant negative impact on latency. A custom pipeline component is deployed at the beginning of the receive pipeline and at the end of the send pipeline. The receive pipeline component starts a new BAM activity, recording the time that the component processed the message. The activity must use an identifier that can be used to uniquely identify the message as it flows through BizTalk. The most appropriate identifier to use is the BTS.InterchangeID message context property. The interchange ID is a GUID that is created by the engine. It is flowed automatically by the Messaging Engine as the message passes through the pipeline. You should note that the Message ID is typically not appropriate, since the message may be cloned multiple times during its processing, as described in Chapter 4, and each clone will have a unique Message ID. The Orchestration Engine will also flow the BTS.InterchangeID message context property where it can, although you must flow the property yourself in scenarios in which you create new messages. The pipeline component at the end of the send pipeline completes the BAM activity, again specifying the current time; it uses the interchange ID that it retrieves from the message. As with the performance counters, this approach does not include the time spent in the adapters. Unless you have custom adapters, there is no way to obtain the time spent in adapters outside of measuring externally of BizTalk. (For a more in-depth discussion about BAM, see Chapter 6.) Using the approach described in Chapter 6, you could build the ability to query for messages/business transactions within your tracking portal. This can be designed in a way to give rich details around the processing times for messages.

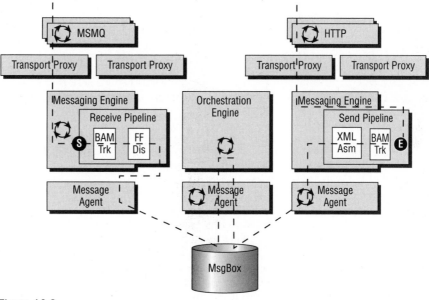

Figure 10-2

Alternatively, you could publish your own PerfMon counters. The reason that the engine can't publish these PerfMon counters for you is because it does not have an inherent knowledge of how your message flows tie together to compose your end-to-end scenario. Using a similar technique to the BAM approach described previously, you could publish PerfMon counters for each message. To do this, you must set a custom message context property for the start time on the message at the start of processing. At the last point in processing, the latency could be calculated by fetching the current time and subtracting the start time that was previously set on the message context. At that point, a `PerfMon` counter could be published. Custom performance counters do give you the ability to publish counters for the end-to-end flow of messages specific to your scenario.

Tuning BizTalk for Low Latency

As previously mentioned, BizTalk is tuned for high throughput out of the box. It usually needs to be explicitly tuned for low latency. For the most part, this tuning is relatively straightforward, although it is important to understand what effects other factors, besides tuning, can have on latency.

The best approach to tuning for low latency is to change the configuration parameters that affect latency one at a time, measuring the difference after each time to evaluate the effect. The first parameters that you must tune are stored in the `BizTalkMgmtDB` database in the `adm_ServiceClass` table. This table has a row for each service class. You should think of a service class as a BizTalk subservice.

There are four types of service classes, as shown in Figure 10-3. The first two should be self-explanatory: XLANG/s is the Orchestration Engine, and Messaging InProcess is the Messaging Engine. You might be surprised to see MSMQT as the third entry. Although MSMQT appears as an adapter, it is actually another service class. The reason for this is its requirements regarding in-order delivery of messages. At this point, you might be thinking that you wouldn't mind writing your own service class. With BizTalk Server 2006, however, you would gain little advantage by doing so. The interfaces that you need to interact with are low level and designed only for internal usage. In addition, they are not tested in the same way that public interfaces are, which means that you would potentially be walking into a world of pain. Previously, the only reason you might have wanted to implement a service class would have been to implement in-order delivery semantics as in the case of MSMQT. In BizTalk Server 2006, the engine exposes this capability for all adapters, so now there really is no reason to do so. The final service class is Messaging Isolated. This entry is again for the Messaging Engine, and it is for all scenarios in which it is hosted by an isolated adapter (for example, the HTTP Receive adapter).

Id	Name	UniqueId	LowWatermark	HighWatermark	BatchSize	MaxReceiveInterval	SingleDequeueSession	SerializeInstanceDelivery	GroupBatchByInsta
1	XLANG/s	226fc6...	10	20	20	500	0	1	0
2	Messaging InProcess	59f295...	100	200	20	500	0	1	0
3	MSMQT	3d7a3f...	100	200	20	500	0	1	1
4	Messaging Isolated	683aed...	100	200	20	500	0	1	0

Figure 10-3

The first parameter that you must tune is `MaxReceiveInterval`. This value is used by each service class when polling the MessageBox. It represents the longest duration between MessageBox polls. As previously mentioned, the engine waits only this long when it has not found any messages in the host queue for a number of polls. Each time that it polls and does not find messages, it incrementally pauses longer before the next poll, eventually reaching the maximum polling interval. As you can see in Figure 10-3, the default value for this is half a second.

To understand how this value affects latency, consider a scenario in which BizTalk is not processing any messages; it's effectively been idle for 20 seconds or so. By this point, the MessageBox is being polled every `MaxReceiveInterval` ms. Let's consider the simplest scenario possible: A message is received by an adapter, published to the MessageBox, routed to a send port, and then sent out via the outbound adapter (that is, a single MessageBox hop). For this scenario, the time that the message spends waiting to be processed will be:

```
Time the message spends waiting (minimum latency) = MaxReceiveInterval - Time since
last poll
```

On average, this will be around 250 ms. If you are really unlucky, it'll be 500 ms. Of course, this does not take into account the time required to actually process the message but just the time that the message spends waiting to be processed. Chances are that your latency will be more than 250 ms. Now let's consider a scenario in which you reduce the value of MaxReceiveInterval to 100 ms. Now your minimum latency is reduced to 50 ms on average; that's a big drop.

If you consider the scenario in which a two-way SOAP receive port is bound to an orchestration, there will be two message box hops: one for the request message, the other for the response message. For this scenario, the average wait time will be 500 ms for the default configuration. Changing the value of MaxReceiveInterval to 100 ms will reduce the average wait time to 100 ms, a difference of some 400 ms. If you are unlucky, the difference in latency could be as high as 800 ms.

As mentioned earlier, you configure these values at the service class level. This will, of course, affect all instances of that service class running on all machines. So, depending on your scenario, you will need to configure MaxReceiveInterval for all service classes involved in your low-latency scenario. For the SOAP scenario described previously, the value of MaxReceiveInterval must be changed for both the XLANG/s and Messaging Isolated rows. At this point, you might be wondering how low you can tune it. The simple answer is this: It depends. Microsoft generally recommends that 100 ms is a sensible minimum value; for most scenarios, this is fine. Latency requirements in the order of 1000 ms are reasonably common and typically quite achievable, although it does depend on the nature of processing. The polling interval is only one function of latency. As with all performance tuning, it's important to modify the MaxReceiveInterval value incrementally and observe the effect, especially if you plan on taking it below 100 ms.

Latencies much lower than 100 ms can be achieved using BizTalk, but this depends on the scenario. A while back, one of our partners who was building a system for a large financial institution asked me to help them meet their nonfunctional requirements. The system they were building processed FIX financial messages. These messages were required to be processed within 100 ms of being received with a latency variation of no greater than one standard deviation. The scenario was a messaging-only scenario. Messages were received by the partner's BizTalk FIX adapter, processed in the receive pipeline, mapped if required for that message, published to the MessageBox, and then sent out again using the partners FIX adapter.

To add to the complexity, the FIX protocol requires messages to be sent out in the same order that they are received — nothing like a bit of serialization in the processing logic to help bump up your latency! Even for a scenario with a single MessageBox hop, this is an aggressive target. With the added in-order requirement, I was sceptical that BizTalk could be tuned to meet the requirement. However, we decided we should try, and so we brought their solution into the Microsoft performance labs.

To cut a long story short, we managed to meet the requirements. We ended up tuning the value of MaxReceiveInterval to 10 ms, which is definitely at the limit of how low it can go. Adjusting the interval much lower will result in excessive load on the MessageBox, which in itself will cause latency to increase. Interestingly, that level of performance was achieved on midrange hardware. We had problems getting the

Storage Area Network (SAN) storage system to perform at the levels that we required, and in the end we used the relatively cheap local disk subsystem in the database server, which was configured as a RAID array. The SAN problems were later discovered to be due to the SAN being misconfigured. The solution scaled well to around 40 messages per second. Up to that point, the latencies of all messages were within the required values, after which the latencies started to climb. For this scenario, scaling beyond 40 messages per second was achieved by adding additional BizTalk groups (or pods, as they are sometimes called), each an independent BizTalk deployment.

This does not mean that you should ignore the Microsoft guidance to keep your value for `MaxReceiveInterval` above 100 ms. However, it does indicate what is possible. In my experience, achieving processing latencies in BizTalk of 100 ms is right at the limit of what is possible with the current BizTalk version.

Next to the `MaxReceiveInterval` in the `adm_ServiceClass` database table is the `BatchSize` column. You might have guessed that `BatchSize` represents the number of messages dequeued by the Message Agent in one batch. The Message Agent will not wait for that number of messages before dequeuing. It dequeues *up to that number* of messages for every dequeue poll that it does. For low-latency scenarios, this value can have an effect. By reducing it, you can significantly improve latency. In addition, a lower batch size sometimes gives more predictable latency numbers. But again, this value should be modified in isolation and monitored to observe its effect. And as previously mentioned, for many scenarios, you might not even have to modify this value.

Host Throttling

The BizTalk documentation on host throttling is extremely good. (Chapter 9 also discusses throttling in detail.) Because the documentation is so good, there is no point repeating it here. Instead, I describe it at a high level and discuss a couple of the new throttling features in BizTalk 2006 that can affect latency.

Host throttling works by continuously monitoring system parameters that affect the engine's performance characteristics. (BizTalk Server 2004 also had the notion of throttling, but it has been significantly improved in the 2006 release.) These system parameters are:

❑   The memory usage, both for the whole system and for the host process

❑   The number of messages being processed (used for outbound throttling only)

❑   Number of threads being used

❑   The size of the database, including the number of messages in each host queue table and the number of messages in the spool and tracking tables

❑   Number of concurrent database connections

❑   Rate of message publishing (in-bound) and processing rate (outbound)

If any of these are exceeded, throttling will be applied. The degree to which BizTalk will be throttled depends on the severity of the throttle condition. Both overthrottling or underthrottling can negatively affect latency, so it's key to ensure that you strike a balance.

BizTalk Server 2006 introduces a new concept in the Message Agent that can help latency. It is called the *pre-dequeue*. Essentially, the Message Agent dequeues messages into an in-memory queue ready to be handed to the processing service class. Previously, the Message Agent dequeued messages from the database and then handed them directly to the service class to process them. This new in-memory queue helps to prevent message starvation during the dequeue process by ensuring that a sufficient number of messages are ready and waiting to be processed.

An example of message starvation is when the send host is ready to process messages but no messages are available for it to process. The default value for this throttling parameter is 100 messages. Increasing it will help with low-latency processing by ensuring that messages are always dequeued and ready to be processed by the engine. A larger memory footprint will be seen when this value is increased because more messages will be held in memory. This might prove more of a problem in scenarios in which large messages are processed. You can modify this value in the Throttling Thresholds dialog box, as shown in Figure 10-4.

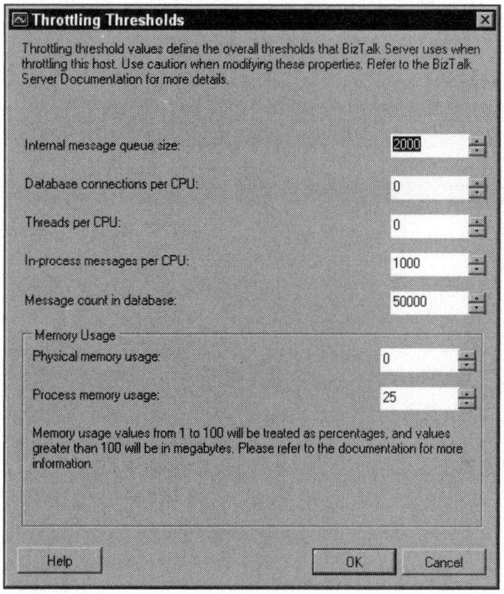

Figure 10-4

In addition, the configurable Sampling window duration (milliseconds) value for both the publishing and processing throttling settings may affect latency. You can effectively disable rate-based throttling by entering a value of zero.

MessageBox Sizing

As CPU utilization of the MessageBox database server rises, it has an impact on latency. As the CPU utilization of the database server approaches 40 percent to 50 percent, you won't see a significant effect on latency. When it breaches that threshold, however, incremental increases in CPU utilization will have an increasing effect on latency. Also, after that point, the latency will fluctuate more and become less predictable. For these reasons, the sizing of your MessageBox database in terms of raw performance is important for low-latency scenarios. If you require low and predictable latencies, size your database server so that your peak load will load the MessageBox database with no more than 50 percent CPU utilization. (Typically, however, it will probably be running at 20 percent to 30 percent CPU utilization.)

Always monitor the MessageBox purge jobs to get an idea of the health of the MessageBox. For low-latency scenarios, this becomes even more important (especially if you are trying to achieve predictable latencies). BizTalk Server 2006 now publishes the durations of the purge jobs using the `PerfMon` counters, as shown following this paragraph. This makes it easy to set a Microsoft Operations Manager 2005 (MOM) trigger on these to notify your operations team when the duration of these jobs increases. Typically, the time taken for these SQL jobs should be less than a second. If their duration starts to climb above that, you will see an impact on latency. This effect is less in BizTalk Server 2006 due to reduced contention on these jobs, but nevertheless they are a good indication of the health of the MessageBox database. Also, you should not try to reduce the frequency at which these jobs run. Reducing the frequency means that jobs have to do more work each time they run and will likely mean that there will be an increase in the amount of time that they take to run (causing spikes in latency while they run).

```
\\btssvr-001\BizTalk:Message Box:General Counters(biztalkmsgboxdb:dbsvr-01)\
MsgBox Dead Processes Cleanup (Purge Jobs)

\\btssvr-001\BizTalk:Message Box:General Counters(biztalkmsgboxdb:dbsvr-01)\
MsgBox Msg Cleanup (Purge Jobs)

\\btssvr-001\BizTalk:Message Box:General Counters(biztalkmsgboxdb:dbsvr-01)\
MsgBox Parts Cleanup (Purge Jobs)

\\btssvr-001\BizTalk:Message Box:General Counters(biztalkmsgboxdb:dbsvr-01)\
MsgBox Purge Subscriptions Job (Purge Jobs)

\\btssvr-001\BizTalk:Message Box:General Counters(biztalkmsgboxdb:dbsvr-01)\
Tracked Msgs Copy (Purge Jobs)

\\btssvr-001\BizTalk:Message Box:General Counters(biztalkmsgboxdb:dbsvr-01)\
Tracking Spool Cleanup (Purge Jobs)
```

The size of all your database log files should be preallocated. Allowing SQL Server to increase the size of log files at runtime will have a big impact on latency and performance as a whole, should SQL Server need to increase the size of the logs files while it is running. For this reason, in a production environment, you should always adjust the size of these as part of the deployment process to avoid SQL Server resizing on the fly.

Disk Subsystem

As with all BizTalk scenarios that require high performance, whether high throughput or low latency, it is important that your database files be stored on a high-performance storage system. Typically, this means using a SAN, although for some scenarios RAID arrays can also provide a good level of performance if configured correctly (striped for performance and mirrored for resilience). The performance of your storage layer will directly impact the performance of your BizTalk solution; BizTalk induces a high load on SQL Server, which in turn induces a lot of I/O on the disk system. So it's worth ensuring that you not only use the best storage that you can, but also that it is correctly configured. Chapter 9 has a more detailed discussion on this subject.

The BizTalk workload imposed on the disk means that the logical unit numbers (LUNs) on your SAN should be configured with as many spindles as possible. When tuning for low latency, you need to understand how your SAN is performing. In generally, you need to know the number of I/O operations performed on the SAN, I/O sizes, disk queue length, and the services times (the length of time that the SAN takes to complete I/O transactions). The tuning of the storage layer is beyond the scope of this book. The key thing to remember is that if you have low-latency requirements (or high-performance requirements), you should ensure that your BizTalk database is deployed to a high-performance storage layer and tuned by a specialist in that area.

Other Things That Affect Latency

Global tracking typically increases latency, largely because of the additional work that needs to be done for every message publication. You can use other approaches in BizTalk to achieve the same or better functionality as global tracking. In general, BAM can provide much richer capabilities for tracking, enabling message context properties to be tracked as well as message bodies. This is discussed in Chapter 6. Although BAM is arguably more appropriate for message body tracking when the size of the messages is under 1MB, for most scenarios BAM provides better performance and has less of an effect on latency. For all BizTalk solutions that I have ever tuned, I turned off global tracking in order to get the optimum performance. For the scenarios that had tracking requirements, I used BAM, which has always given me a greater level of tracking functionality and better performance.

The number of subscriptions that you have configured and the complexity of those subscriptions may affect the throughput for a given scenario. As the number and complexity of subscriptions increases, the cost associated with processing those messages increases. In turn, this might affect the latency for a given throughput volume.

Mixing Low-Latency and High-Throughput Scenarios

I hope by now that you realize low-latency processing and high-throughput processing don't mix well. As you drive your throughput higher, inducing more load on the MessageBox database, you will reach the point when latency starts to suffer. As mentioned earlier, once you exceed 50 percent CPU utilization on your MessageBox database server, latency will start to significantly degrade as the CPU utilization increases incrementally. For scenarios that require the two types of processing (and have strict perform-ance requirements), arguably the only way to go is to use a pod-based deployment, where each pod is dedicated to a specific type of processing (low latency or high throughput). Each pod is a BizTalk group. The important thing is *not* to share the MessageBox database server between pods (see Figure 10-5). If you are using BAM or tracking extensively, each pod should also have its own dedicated BAM and DTA database server. If required, the other BizTalk databases, such as `BizTalkMgmtDb`, `SSODB`, and `BizTalkRuleEngineDb`, could be deployed to a database server shared by both pods (because their per-formance requirements are not very aggressive). Each pod would be tuned and sized for optimum performance, whether low latency or high throughput.

I have worked with a few customers for whom the pod deployment model has been used successfully. Often, this approach is used by a core services team within an organization that is tasked with providing middleware services to the rest of the organization. For this scenario, the core services team typically needs to commit to providing a service-level agreement that requires message processing either at a given throughput rate or within a given latency. Typically for this scenario, they also need to be able to audit each message, demonstrating how long a given message took to process within their middleware service layer.

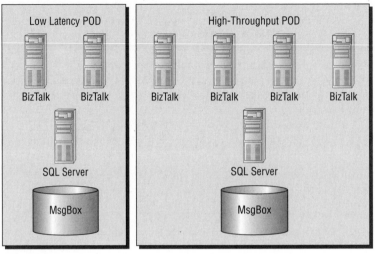

Figure 10-5

You can use a pod for both low-latency and high-throughput messages if you are willing to sacrifice the performance of one or the other. If you can sacrifice your latency under peak load periods, you can most likely get away with a single pod to service both types of requirements. However, this will only work if you don't have very low-latency requirements. Anything less than 1000 ms and the approach may not be appropriate. The deployment will need to be tuned for low latency, but as you process peak loads, the CPU utilization on your MessageBox database server will breach the 50 percent mark. At this point, your latency will start to suffer (as discussed previously), but you will be able to process a higher number of messages and perhaps meet your high-throughput requirements.

On the other hand, if you are willing to sacrifice throughput to keep low latency, you can try a few things. Be aware, however, that this is not easy to get right. That said, the easiest way to do this is to cheat: Just use a service window on your receive ports to protect your low-latency path. The service window may be used to shutdown the receive location during the desired periods. Of course, this "cheat" assumes that you can delay the processing of your high-throughput messages to a time when they do not interfere with your low-latency messages. Effectively, you'd be processing them outside of the core hours when you have low-latency requirements. Of course, this is possible in only a few scenarios.

Assuming that you can't cheat, you could adopt a throttling strategy that throttles the high-throughput messages to enable the low-latency messages to take priority. Throttling can be achieved internally with BizTalk or externally. You can build a throttling mechanism external to BizTalk that monitors your latency processing times. The message processing latencies would be used as a feedback loop to control the throttling of high-throughput receive locations. As the latencies breach a given *high-water mark*, the receive locations servicing high-throughput messages would be stopped. When the latencies fall below a *low-water mark*, the receive locations that service the high-throughput messages would be enabled again. This type of throttling is reasonably easy to implement.

You could use BizTalk to publish custom `PerfMon` counters for the processing latency. A custom NT service that monitors the `PerfMon` counters would read these counters, and disable and enable the configured high-throughput receive locations as the high- and low-latency marks are crossed. The low-water mark must be below the high-water mark to give the system time to recover. The size of the difference is something that needs to be tested and tuned to reach the appropriate behavior. This approach is less likely to work in BizTalk 2004 because of the way the caching service works. Previously, changes to configuration, such as receive locations, were polled periodically (by default, every 60 seconds; this is configured at the group level). BizTalk 2006 uses a new caching service that uses control messages to notify the engine that the cache is invalidated and needs to be reloaded. Consequently, the enabling or disabling of a receive location takes effect much more quickly in BizTalk 2006. Interestingly, this same caching service was present and used in BizTalk 2004, but the service was used only in polling mode due to time constraints around the testing cycle for that feature.

Alternatively, you can use the new BizTalk 2006 host throttling controls (discussed earlier in the chapter) to throttle hosts. For this scenario, you must dedicate a host to either low-latency or high-throughput message processing (because the throttling parameters are applied at the host granularity).

Orchestration Inline Sends

For scenarios in which latency is important, it might be appropriate to send messages directly from an orchestration, thereby avoiding at least one MessageBox hop (two for the scenario in which you are using delivery notifications or two-way sends). In BizTalk Server 2004, inline sends from orchestrations were limited to scenarios in which XML messages were transmitted over the wire, because there was no way to execute a send pipeline from an orchestration. BizTalk Server 2006 enables this scenario. The product group packaged the pipeline manager code, which was previously internal to the messaging engine, into a public assembly, `Microsoft.XLANGs.Pipeline.dll`. You can reference and execute this public assembly from an orchestration. Enabling the execution of pipelines from orchestrations paves the way for inline sends, but it is only part of the story. BizTalk has more than 300 different transport adapters that may be used only via receive and send ports. Therefore, if inline sends are appropriate for your scenario, you will most likely need to write a certain amount of transport code.

Some other scenarios, aside from low-latency ones, can be achieved only by using inline sends. Consider, for example, that you need to atomically transmit two different messages to an MSMQ queue and a SQL Server database. The problem here is that the transaction is scoped between the BizTalk MessageBox and the adapter. (You cannot enlist two different adapters in the same transaction.) The only way to achieve this is to write a custom adapter that sends one message to MSMQ and the other to SQL Server and uses a distributed transaction to ensure that they are atomically written. In addition, you will probably need to define a message with two parts: one for the MSMQ endpoint and the other for the SQL Server endpoint. Unless you do that, there is no way to guarantee that both messages will be delivered to the same instance of the adapter in the same batch. Some projects use compensation to handle this scenario. The transmission of both messages is controlled from an orchestration in which two atomic transactions are used. If the second transaction fails, a compensating transaction is performed to undo the work that was performed in the first transaction. In many situations, this works fine. In others, however, committing the first transaction may cause side effects that are difficult or even impossible to undo. Figure 10-6 illustrates this scenario. The diagram also shows the number of times that messages are published to the MessageBox. You might be wondering where publications 3 and 5 come from. These are internal BizTalk delivery notification messages that the Messaging and Orchestration Engines use to communicate the outcome of the transmission.

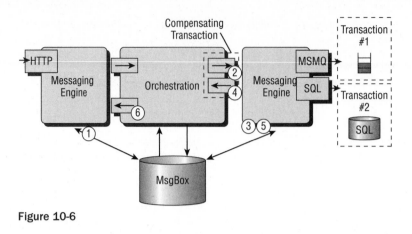

Figure 10-6

You can achieve this same functionality using an orchestration inline send. You can write a custom .NET component that writes the message to both SQL Server and MSMQ while ensuring that both messages are written using the same transaction. In such a case, you don't need the compensation logic, because the same transaction is used to send both messages. Figure 10-7 shows an example of this. Note, also, that the load on the MessageBox is significantly reduced, because only two message publications are now required.

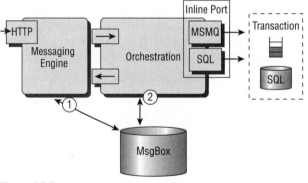

Figure 10-7

What You Lose with Inline Sends

To make an informed decision about using an inline send approach, you need to understand what you lose with that implementation. You lose the support of some 300+ adapters (mentioned previously) available for BizTalk. Obviously, this loss is significant and may be a showstopper if you are not using a transport that you can easily write some .NET code to handle.

In general, adapters are pretty significant server-side components. The BizTalk adapter framework exposes a lot of rich functionality for them to exploit. When coupled with the functionality of the

BizTalk Engine, which acts as their host, they are highly resilient and perform well. The features include the following:

❑ **Batching** — Batching enables an adapter to transmit multiple messages in a single logical batch, thereby amortizing the cost associated with cross-machine calls and transactions.

❑ **Streaming** — Adapters should use streaming to avoid loading the message into memory and running the risk of pulling down the server process due to an out-of-memory condition.

❑ **Retries** — When you are using adapters, the Messaging Engine ensures that transport failures are handled gracefully, logging errors as appropriate and retrying transmissions, messages will be moved to a backup transport should the primary transport be unable to send a message.

❑ **Configuration** — Adapter endpoint configuration is possible. Most scenarios require some transport configuration settings tailored to the endpoint that they are sending to. In addition, you can configure the persistence of secrets (such as user credentials) in a secure manner. All this is handled by the runtime and design-time environments. Storing configuration in a central database means that it only has to be deployed to a single machine, and that database may also easily be backed up.

❑ **Tracking** — When you are sending messages via adapters, the messages that were transmitted over the wire can be tracked and audited (though this approach will not give the best performance; on the upside, however, you do get it for free).

❑ **Mapping** — Documents can be mapped. This may be driven from configuration. Of course, you could move this mapping to your orchestration in the case of an inline send.

❑ **Robust code** — I am sure that your custom code will be of a high quality and robust; even so, BizTalk Server and its adapters have undergone a rigorous testing cycle to ensure that their quality is high. If you do encounter issues with your custom inline send port code, Microsoft and your adapter vendor will be able to provide assistance only for their products. Therefore, develop your code in a way that enables you to troubleshoot in a production environment. Typically, this means ensuring that you appropriately use event logging for error conditions and use software tracing (which you can enable at runtime). This is not necessarily all bad; owning the code can enable you to rapidly fix bugs and deploy patches.

❑ **Initialization of correlation sets** — When sending messages via orchestration ports, the BizTalk engine creates the correlation subscriptions as configured. Bypassing the MessageBox means that this functionality is lost. Later in this chapter, I discuss how you can work around this issue.

❑ **Service windows** — BizTalk send ports support service windows. These enable messages to be transmitted only within the service window.

You need to weigh the functionality of adapters against what you stand to gain by using inline sends. The point is that when it is appropriate to use them, go down that route with your eyes open.

Executing Pipelines from Orchestration

As mentioned earlier, the ability to execute pipelines from orchestrations paves the way to inline sends. So let's consider what is involved and what restrictions apply.

The pipeline manager is exposed to orchestrations in the `XLANGPipelineManager` class, which is packaged in the `Microsoft.XLANGs.Pipeline.dll` assembly. It can be used to execute both receive and send pipelines. Receive pipelines can process a single input message at a time. That input message may be an individual message or a message interchange that may be disassembled into many messages, as discussed in Chapter 4. A send pipeline can take one or more messages and assemble them into a single message as its output. Both send and receive pipelines may be consuming, meaning that they don't produce any messages.

When you are executing pipelines from an orchestration, some restrictions apply. Some of these are common sense, because the pipelines are not hosted by the Messaging Engine and no persistence store backs the execution. When a pipeline is executed from an orchestration, your code needs to handle the input and output from the pipeline, including error conditions. Restrictions include the following:

❑ **Transactional pipeline components are not supported** — If a pipeline component makes a call to fetch the transaction from the pipeline context using `IPipelineContextEx` `.GetTransaction()`, the API will throw a `NotSupportedException` exception. The pipeline components should, therefore, be written in a way to handle this, if possible.

❑ **Recoverable pipelines are not supported** — This scenario needs to be coded around.

❑ **Pipeline components may not use the BAM interceptor** — Pipeline components that fetch the BAM event stream from the pipeline context using the `IPipelineContext.GetEventStream()` API will fail with a `NotSupportedException` exception. They may create an event stream using the BAM APIs, but it will be transitionally decoupled from the pipeline execution. A better approach is to call the BAM event stream from your orchestration to ensure that the BAM event stream is transactionally consistent with the orchestration state.

❑ **BizTalk Server 2004 pipelines will need to be recompiled** — Pipeline assemblies that were compiled against BizTalk Server 2004 must be recompiled against the BizTalk Server 2006 SDK; otherwise, they may not be executed from within an orchestration.

When the Messaging Engine executes a pipeline, it handles the failures. Depending on the scenario, it either suspends the message or, in the case of a Receive adapter, pushes the error back to the adapter for it to determine how to handle the failure. When executed from an orchestration, any error that would result in a message being suspended is indicated by an exception type `Microsoft.XLANGs.Pipeline` `.XLANGPipelineManagerException`.

The orchestration in Figure 10-8 shows the calling of a pipeline. Notice that the pipeline is executed in a message construct shape because the message to send is constructed by executing the pipeline.

A variable of type `Microsoft.XLANGs.Pipeline.SendPipelineInputMessages` is declared for the orchestration called `msgsForPipelineExecution`. This collection of messages will be fed into the send pipeline. For this scenario, it will contain a single message, although for a scenario that assembles an interchange of messages, there will be multiple messages in the collection. The code in the expression shape is shown here. First, the message to process in the pipeline is added to the `msgsForPipelineExecution` collection. Second, the pipeline is executed. Note that the pipeline to be executed is specified using its type. The output from the pipeline will be assigned to `msgOutPO`, this is a BizTalk message that will be sent using a standard send shape as shown in Figure 10-8.

```
msgsForPipelineExecution.Add(msgPO);
msgOutPO = null;

Microsoft.XLANGs.Pipeline.XLANGPipelineManager.ExecuteSendPipeline(
    typeof(InLineSend.InLineSend.FFSendPipeline),
    msgsForPipelineExecution,
    msgOutPO );
```

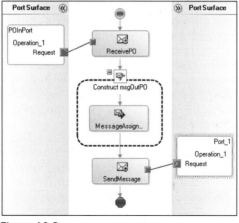

Figure 10-8

Inline Orchestration Send Port

It is arguably more convenient to package up all the code associated with an inline send port in an assembly so that it can be executed as a single API from an orchestration that includes both the pipeline execution code and the transport code. This "packaging" keeps the semantics for executing the inline send port closer to the semantics of sending a message to an orchestration port. This section explains how you can do this. The code is kept relatively simple for explanatory purposes.

Figure 10-9 shows a relatively trivial orchestration that is logically the same as the orchestration in Figure 10-8. However, this orchestration uses an inline send port that is responsible for executing the send pipeline and then transmitting the message.

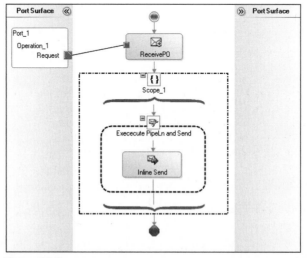

Figure 10-9

The code within the message assignment shape follows this paragraph. It shows how the inline port class can be called from an orchestration. The first point of interest is that the code is executed within an atomic scope. Of course if you are not using a transport that supports transactions, you can avoid using the atomic scope which does have an associated performance cost. This atomic scope is necessary because if we are using a transport that supports transactions, we need to ensure that the message is transmitted in the context of the transaction defined by the orchestration scope. Therefore, we use a transaction whose scope is between the MessageBox and the transport's endpoint, meaning that the message will be atomically moved between the two. BizTalk adapters such as the MSMQ, MQ Series, and the SQL adapter support transactions. For these adapters, it also means that when BizTalk sends messages to an endpoint using one of those adapters, the message is atomically moved between the BizTalk MessageBox and the adapter's endpoint. The difference when using an inline send port is that the transactional semantics are coupled more closely to the orchestration. To get semantics similar to those of an inline port using an adapter requires the use of delivery notifications on your orchestration port. Of course, this does incur two additional MessageBox hops.

```
// First initialize the message that will be returned by the pipeline,
// this will be the message transmitted by the transport
msgOutPO = null;

// Create a new inline send port...
inlineSendPort = new XLANGInlinePort.InlineSendPort();

// Pass the message to the port, specifying the pipeline to execute and
// the URL of the endpoint
inlineSendPort.Send(typeof(InLineSend.InLineSend.FFSendPipeline),
  @"MSMQ://.\Private$\Test01",
  msgPO,
  msgOutPO);
```

So, that was pretty straightforward. Of course, the pipeline to execute is hard-coded, as is the URL of the endpoint. In reality, you'd probably pull the pipeline from a configuration file, the URL of the endpoint would either come from a configuration file or be determined more dynamically. Now let's take a closer look at the code for the inline send port.

The code that follows shows the InlineSendPort class. Note that it is derived from ServicedComponent, because it needs to support transactions for this scenario. The class has a single method used to execute the send port. This method has four parameters: the type of the send pipeline to be executed prior to sending the message, the destination URL where the message should be sent, the message to send to the port (this is the message that will be fed into the pipeline), and the message that will actually be sent. This variable is set by InlineSendPort after the pipeline has been executed. After the Send method has validated the parameters that were passed to it, it executes the send pipeline specified. The FetchTransmitter() method then determines which transport should be used to send the message. This method uses a similar approach used when BizTalk handles a dynamic send, whereby the transport is determined by the alias of the destination URL. The InlineSendPort splits the URL destination using :// as a delimiter. Ideally, you'd want to use the System.Uri class. The portion of the string preceding the delimiter is the alias used to determine which transport class to use to handle the transmission of the message. Ideally, this configuration would not be hard-coded, so that new transports could be added without recompiling the XLANGInlinePort assembly. The appropriate transport is created, and then its Send() method is called, passing the destination URL and the message that was returned by the pipeline execution.

```
using System;
using System.EnterpriseServices;
```

```csharp
using Microsoft.XLANGs.BaseTypes;
using InlineTransmitters;
using XLANGInlinePortFramework;
using System.Runtime.InteropServices;

namespace XLANGInlinePort
{
  [ComVisible(true)]
  [System.EnterpriseServices.Transaction(
    TransactionOption.Supported, Timeout = 3600)]
  [System.EnterpriseServices.JustInTimeActivation(true)]
  public class InlineSendPort : ServicedComponent
  {
    private static readonly string urlSplitter = "://";

    public void Send(Type pipeline, string url,
      XLANGMessage xlangMsg, XLANGMessage outXLANGMsg)
    {
      ArgumentValidation.CheckForNullReference(pipeline, "pipeline");
      ArgumentValidation.CheckForNullReference(url, "url");
      ArgumentValidation.CheckForNullReference(xlangMsg, "inXLANGMsg");

      PipelineUtils.ExecuteSendPipeline(
        pipeline, xlangMsg, outXLANGMsg);

      IInlineTransmitter xMitter = FetchTransmitter(ref url);
      xMitter.Send(url, outXLANGMsg);
    }

    private static IInlineTransmitter FetchTransmitter(
      ref string url)
    {
      int index = url.IndexOf(urlSplitter);
      string alias = url.Substring(0, index).ToLower();

      switch (alias)
      {
        case "http":
          return (IInlineTransmitter)new HTTPTransmitter();

        case "msmq":
          url = url.Substring(index + urlSplitter.Length);
          return (IInlineTransmitter)new MSMQTransmitter();

        case "file":
          url = url.Substring(index + urlSplitter.Length);
          return (IInlineTransmitter)new FILETransmitter();

        default:
          throw new ApplicationException(
            string.Format("Unknown transport alias: {0}",
            alias));
      }
    }
  }
}
```

Before looking at the transport code, let's look at the code to execute the pipeline. That code follows this paragraph. After the `PipelineUtils.ExecuteSendPipeline()` method has checked the input parameters, it takes the type of the pipeline to execute the message to feed into the pipeline and sets the messages produced by executing the pipeline in the `outXLANGMsg` parameter. The method is simple. It creates a new `SendPipelineInputMessages`, adds the input message to the collection, and then passes that collection into the `Microsoft.XLANGs.Pipeline.XLANGPipelineManager` `.ExecuteSendPipeline()` method, which is responsible for executing the pipeline.

```
using System;
using System.Collections.Generic;
using System.Text;
using Microsoft.XLANGs.Pipeline;
using Microsoft.XLANGs.BaseTypes;
using XLANGInlinePortFramework;

namespace XLANGInlinePort
{
  public class PipelineUtils
  {
    public static void ExecuteSendPipeline(Type pipeline,
      XLANGMessage inXLANGMsg, XLANGMessage outXLANGMsg)
    {
      ArgumentValidation.CheckForNullReference(pipeline, "pipeline");
      ArgumentValidation.CheckForNullReference(inXLANGMsg,
        "inXLANGMsg");
      ArgumentValidation.CheckForNullReference(
        outXLANGMsg, "outXLANGMsg");

      SendPipelineInputMessages spim = new SendPipelineInputMessages();
      spim.Add(inXLANGMsg);

      Microsoft.XLANGs.Pipeline.XLANGPipelineManager.
        ExecuteSendPipeline(pipeline, spim, outXLANGMsg);
    }
  }
}
```

For this example, the destination URL is `MSMQ://.\Private$\Test01`. This URL was resolved to the `MSMQTransmitter` by the `InlineSendPort.FetchTransmitter()` method, as described above. The code for the `MSMQTransmitter` follows. This class is decorated with the `TransactionAttribute`, indicating that it supports transactions. This, together with the fact that the send to MSMQ is performed with the `MessageQueueTransactionType.Automatic` option specified, ensures that the message is transmitted using the transaction in the current context (which, if you recall, is actually the transaction as specified in the orchestration's transactional scope). Don't forget that the assembly needs to be registered in COM+ using `regsvcs.exe`.

```
using System;
using System.Messaging;
using System.EnterpriseServices;
using Microsoft.XLANGs.BaseTypes;
using XLANGInlinePortFramework;
using System.IO;
using System.Runtime.InteropServices;
```

```
namespace InlineTransmitters
{
  [ComVisible(true)]
  [System.EnterpriseServices.Transaction(TransactionOption.Supported,
    Timeout = 3600)]
  [System.EnterpriseServices.JustInTimeActivation(true)]
  public class MSMQTransmitter : ServicedComponent, IInlineTransmitter
  {
    public void Send(string url, XLANGMessage xlangMsg)
    {
      ArgumentValidation.CheckForNullReference(url, "url");
      ArgumentValidation.CheckForNullReference(xlangMsg, "xlangMsg");

      XLANGPart part = xlangMsg[0];
      Stream s = (Stream)part.RetrieveAs(typeof(Stream));

      MessageQueue queue = new MessageQueue(url);
      Message msg = new Message();

      msg.BodyStream = s;
      msg.UseDeadLetterQueue = true;

      queue.Send(msg, MessageQueueTransactionType.Automatic);
    }
  }
}
```

From this example, you can see how to achieve an inline send with relatively few lines of code. Also, this approach can be used to build up a library of inline Send adapters that can be dynamically resolved and executed at runtime.

Adding Resilience

As mentioned earlier, bypassing the BizTalk send ports using inline sends causes you to lose a number of services provided by the BizTalk engine, along with a certain amount of resiliency. The Messaging Engine handles transmission failures and carries out the configured retry policy. You can write the inline send port code and the orchestration that calls that code in a way that increases resiliency for an inline send.

Figure 10-10 shows one way to add back some of that resilience. The orchestration shown in the figure uses a Loop shape (which is effectively a C# while statement) to invoke the inline send port. If the inline port fails to send the message successfully, the orchestration will catch the exception. It will write an Event log message detailing why the transmission failed and then suspend the orchestration in a controlled manner so that the orchestration is suspended-resumable. The orchestration is designed so that when it is resumed it will attempt to send the message to the inline send port again. If the send succeeds, it will drop out of the while loop and continue the rest of the processing in the orchestration. Because the orchestration raised an Event log entry detailing why it was suspended, the problem can be fixed and then the orchestration resumed. In addition, if a large number of orchestrations fail — perhaps because the orchestration was sending messages to an MQ Series queue that had exceeded its depth limit — they can be bulk resumed. Retry semantics can either be added to the orchestration or possibly to the inline port code. Be advised, however, that you should avoid *sleeping* in custom code invoked from an orchestration; instead, use a Delay shape in the orchestration. This will enable the Orchestration Engine to use system resources more efficiently. The Orchestration Engine will of course take the Orchestration out of memory by dehydrating it, should it need to.

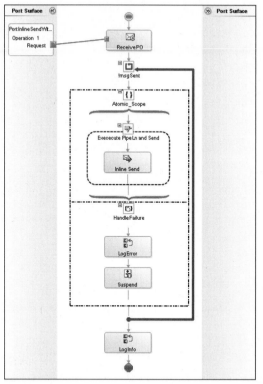

Figure 10-10

Initializing Correlation Sets

Correlation often proves problematic when using inline sends. For example, suppose that you send a message for which you expect a response to the same instance of that orchestration. To achieve this, when BizTalk sends the message via the MessageBox, it initializes a correlation set for that send if configured to do so. This essentially causes a correlation subscription to be atomically created with the message publication to ensure that the response message is delivered to the correct instance of the orchestration. Of course, if you bypass the MessageBox, the correlation subscription will not be created; your orchestration will not get the response that it expects. The Orchestration Compiler is smart enough to catch this, so you will actually get a compile-time error. Unfortunately, no APIs are available to manually create the correlation set. To work around this scenario, you can send a message to a port that consumes the message. Essentially, your orchestration performs a send via an orchestration send port that would be bound to a port with a send pipeline containing a single custom pipeline component that consumes the message. That is, the pipeline component's `Execute` method returns `null`. Because the message passes through the MessageBox, the correlation subscription is created as normal. Subsequent inline sends can be performed as usual. And the correlation subscription ensures that the response messages are delivered as expected. Another approach is to write a no-op adapter that accepts the message and does not send it. Both approaches work.

Figure 10-11 shows a simplified scenario for this approach. In the orchestration shown, a message is received, a message is then sent to a consuming port to initialize the correlation subscription, and then the inline sends are performed in parallel and their responses processed.

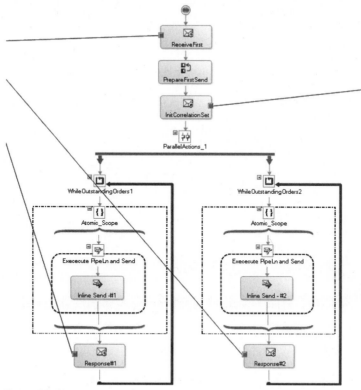

Figure 10-11

It is important to understand that more benefit will be gained as the number of sends in the scenario increases.

Inline Web Service Calls

If your transport is either SOAP or HTTP and you decide to move to an inline send approach, you should be aware of some gotchas. Aggressively calling Web services or a .NET HTTP client inline from an orchestration can result in problems in the threadpool. Especially under high-load scenarios, you can get the following exception thrown when invoking either of these:

```
System.InvalidOperationException: There were not enough free threads in the
ThreadPool object to complete the operation
```

The Microsoft Knowledge Base article at http://support.microsoft.com/kb/815637 gives more information on this error.

To help you understand the problem here, let's first take a look at how the .NET ThreadPool class works and behaves in response to changes in load. The .NET threadpool (ThreadPool) dynamically creates and destroys threads depending on its usage. It has an upper and lower bound for the number of CPU and I/O bound threads in the pool. The number of threads will fluctuate within that range as the workload fluctuates. Any threads that have not been used for 40 seconds will be deleted from the pool. When adding threads to the threadpool, it tries to avoid creating threads more frequently than one every 500 milliseconds.

The .NET threadpool is a singleton per process. At the present time, there is no way to create multiple threadpools in the same process. This means that you share it with not only all of your own code but also with any other .NET components in the same process. Overall, this is a good thing and an efficient way to share system resources. Both the `System.Net.HttpWebRequest` and the `System.Net.HttpWebResponse` classes always use asynchronous methods to complete a request. When the asynchronous request is made, a thread from the threadpool is required to process the response. When a thread cannot be found, an exception of type `System.InvalidOperationException` (as shown above) is thrown from the `System.Net.HttpWebRequest` class instead of enqueuing a new work item on the threadpool.

The problem is that both the Orchestration Engine and the SOAP/HTTP stack share the same .NET process, and hence the same threadpool. For many scenarios, this might not be an issue. For inline Web service/HTTP sends, however, it often is. Both the Orchestration Engine and the SOAP/HTTP stacks make aggressive use of the .NET threadpool; essentially, they compete with each other. Under high-load conditions — particularly when spikes in the load are encountered — there is a good chance that you will run into this issue. There are two approaches that I have used in the past to resolve this. The first is to use the Registry keys that BizTalk exposes to control the minimum and maximum number of threads in the threadpool. In particular, you can prevent threads from being destroyed by adjusting the minimum number of threads in the threadpool. Under burst loads, this helps. Remember, the threadpool will try to create only one thread every 500 milliseconds. Under burst conditions, this can be a major issue if suddenly the threadpool has 100 requests queued up. You can adjust the minimum value such that the pool maintains the full quota of threads and never destroys them.

You can set the Registry keys on a per–BizTalk host basis to control the number of threads in the threadpool There are four Registry keys under the following `CLR Hosting` key for each host instance (as shown in the following table). For example, the Registry key path for the default BizTalk host `BizTalkServerApplication` is:

```
HKLM\SYSTEM\CurrentControlSet\Services\BTSSvc$BizTalkServerApplication\CLR Hosting
```

	Value	Description
MaxWorkerThreads	25	The maximum number of CPU-bound threads in the pool.
MaxIOThreads	25	The maximum number of I/O-bound threads in the pool. The I/O threads are bound to I/O objects, such as a streams or pipes.
MinWorkerThreads	2	The minimum number of CPU-bound threads in the pool. This number cannot be less than the number of CPUs on the machine.
MinIOThreads	2	The minimum number of I/O-bound threads in the pool. This number cannot be less than the number of CPUs on the machine.

Be careful when changing these values. If you increase the maximum values, it is important to incrementally increase them and then observe the behavior change. If you increase the number too much, you might adversely affect performance. The best approach is first to try to increase the minimum value; typically, you should try increasing it to equal the maximum value. When testing the effect of the Registry keys, it is important that you test using maximum loading on the system. In addition, you should burst-load the system after it has been idle for a few minutes so that the threadpool has an opportunity to kill any threads it deems unnecessary. In general, you should focus on the minimum number of worker threads. You can monitor the number of threads in the threadpool during your test scenarios by using the CLR performance counters.

In addition, you might need to adjust the In-process messages per CPU value in the throttling thresholds for the host. This can be adjusted in the Administration Console for BizTalk. You can use this value to limit the number of messages that BizTalk is processing in-memory at any point in time. Typically, you will need to have about 25 percent of the threads in the threadpool available to process the responses from the System.Net.HttpWebRequest or System.Net.HttpWebResponse stacks to avoid the out-of-threads issue. In other words, the minimum number of threads in the threadpool should be 25 percent higher than the number of messages that are being processed at any time.

Adjusting the threadpool configuration should be the first line of attack if you hit the "There were not enough free threads in the ThreadPool object to complete the operation" problem. I have worked on several projects where the Registry keys did not provide the "get out of jail free card" that we needed. Typically, these projects were for high-throughput scenarios that required an inline send approach to meet the aggressive performance requirements. For these scenarios, we used a different approach that is very effective and reliable: process isolation.

The process isolation approach uses the COM+ application hosting model to avoid the issue of too few threads. Figure 10-12 shows the design for inline SOAP/HTTP sends. The code to call the System.Net.HttpWebRequest or System.Net.HttpWebResponse is packaged in a .NET Enterprise Service class. This class executes as a COM+ server, and therefore will be executed in a separate address space from the BizTalk NT service. Of course, process isolation does mean that it will use a different instance of the .NET threadpool. This approach provides a high level of isolation. Because you are in complete control of the work loaded onto the threadpool, its behavior is more predictable.

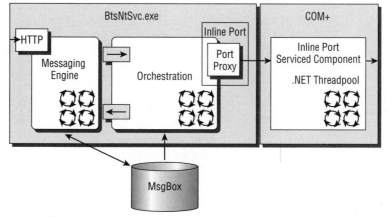

Figure 10-12

The inline port is executed in the same way as the inline port example earlier. Here, the inline port assembly contains the pipeline execution and transport lookup code as before, but this time the transport component is packaged in a separate assembly that is installed as a COM+ server application. The following code shows the inline port code, which is similar to the previous example. The main difference is that the transport interface is changed slightly. The new interface transports the message data as a byte[], because of the problems associated with marshaling an XLANGMessage message over .NET Remoting. Notice also that both the transport component and the XLANGMessage are disposed before the port method returns.

```
...

namespace XLANGInlinePort
{
  ...
  public class InlineSendPort : ServicedComponent
  {
    public void SendViaProxy(Type pipeline, string url, XLANGMessage
      xlangMsg, XLANGMessage outXLANGMsg)
    {
      ArgumentValidation.CheckForNullReference(pipeline, "pipeline");
      ArgumentValidation.CheckForNullReference(url, "url");
      ArgumentValidation.CheckForNullReference(xlangMsg, "inXLANGMsg");
      ArgumentValidation.CheckForNullReference(outXLANGMsg,
        "outXLANGMsg");

      try
      {
        PipelineUtils.ExecuteSendPipeline(pipeline, xlangMsg,
          outXLANGMsg);
        IServicedInlineTransmitter xMitter =
          FetchServicedTransmitter(ref url);

        xMitter.Send(url, StreamHelper.GetMsgBuffer(outXLANGMsg));
      }
      finally
      {
        if (null != xMitter) { ((IDisposable)xMitter).Dispose(); }
        if (null != outXLANGMsg) { outXLANGMsg.Dispose(); }
      }
    }
  }
}
```

The transport component is relatively simple. Most of the error handling has been removed to better show the basic functionality. The transport component is derived from ServicedComponent. It is also decorated to use object pooling.

```
namespace ServicedInlineTransmitters
{
  [ComVisible(true)]
  [System.EnterpriseServices.Transaction(TransactionOption.Supported,
    Timeout = 3600)]
  [System.EnterpriseServices.JustInTimeActivation(true)]
  [ObjectPooling(true, 10, 20)]
```

```
[Guid("FF010F5D-7816-45a7-8313-EE1F3C2B979B")]
public class HTTPServicedTransmitter : ServicedComponent,
  IServicedInlineTransmitter
{
  public void Send(string url, byte[] msg)
  {
    ArgumentValidation.CheckForNullReference(url, "url");
    ArgumentValidation.CheckForNullReference(msg, "msg");

    HttpWebRequest wr = (HttpWebRequest)WebRequest.Create(url);
    wr.Method = "POST";
    wr.Timeout = 10000; //10 seconds
    wr.ContentType = "text/xml; charset=\"utf-8\"";
    wr.ContentLength = msg.Length;

    Stream rs = wr.GetRequestStream();
    rs.Write(msg, 0, msg.Length);

    using(HttpWebResponse webResponse =
      (HttpWebResponse)wr.GetResponse())
    {
      if ((webResponse.StatusCode != HttpStatusCode.OK) &&
        (webResponse.StatusCode != HttpStatusCode.Accepted))
      {
        // Handle Error...and throw
      }
    }
  }
}
```

Modifying the inline send port in this manner gives an effective and flexible approach to handling inline sends. It does add a small overhead associated with the out-of-process call, and the system resources need to be shared with another threadpool (`ThreadPool`) instance. However, in the scenarios that I have worked with in the performance labs, this approach has produced optimum performance combined with solid predictability, which, to be honest, is harder to achieve using the Registry key approach.

Summary

In this chapter, we have discussed exactly what we mean by low latency. Often, this in itself is the source of much confusion. You will now understand the effects that the BizTalk architecture has on latency, since its primary use case out of the box is for high throughput. Understanding the architecture as described in this chapter will help you to exploit it to the fullest and to squeeze the most out of it for your scenario. If BizTalk cannot be tuned to meet your latency requirements, the adoption of an inline send port approach is most likely your best bet to meet your targets. The code samples in this chapter will help you to understand how this can be achieved relatively easily and also help you to design your solution so that you don't lose many of the benefits provided by using send ports.

Finally, this chapter has helped you to understand the various options for how you can measure latencies. Performance counters can be used for a coarse-grained view. Alternatively, BAM can be exploited to provide a message-level view of the latency characteristics of your system.

11

Administration

So the BizTalk application has been developed, and you've successfully completed the functional and nonfunctional testing and have followed all the advice laid out in this book; time to relax, then? Well, actually no. Although the initial development phase is complete, the business is only just about to receive payback for all that investment and hard work.

In order for that to happen, the application needs to meet current and future performance requirements, as well as internal and external service-level agreements. As the initial chapters of this book explained, BizTalk is a resilient technology that can be used to solve common business problems; it provides much of the required plumbing out of the box. It also tends to be used in scenarios involving data that is critical to the successful running of the business, therefore it needs to be maintained appropriately.

Much of my time is spent reviewing customers' designs and deployments of BizTalk — that is, trying to prevent problems. The rest of my time is spent fixing reactive problems for customers. Unfortunately, many problems that occur would have been preventable if the best practices had been followed.

This chapter will cover the best practices that should be followed. This includes the main things to be aware of in any BizTalk deployment; including the common pitfalls and the tasks you should be performing on a regular basis. The chapter explains the underlying reasons why these practices need to be implemented and discusses the consequences of not doing so, to give you a full appreciation of why BizTalk administration is critical to keeping your application up and running. I will then demonstrate the tools you can use to administer and maintain BizTalk, including out-of-the-box tools installed by default and those used in the field by Microsoft Premier Field Engineers. This chapter is a summary of the tools, techniques, and best practices required to administer BizTalk. It covers a wide range rather than a detailed analysis of one or two techniques; therefore, throughout the chapter you will find links to additional information on particular techniques or practices, as appropriate.

What to Manage

BizTalk is made up of mulitple Microsoft components, depending on the installation and configuration options you choose. The components that can be used by BizTalk directly include, but are not limited to, the following:

- ❑ BizTalk Server
- ❑ Enterprise Single Sign-On (ESSO)
- ❑ SQL Server
- ❑ SQL Server Analysis Services
- ❑ Internet Information Services
- ❑ Windows SharePoint Services
- ❑ SQL Notification Services

Figure 11-1 shows how the infrastructure for a typical BizTalk application may look.

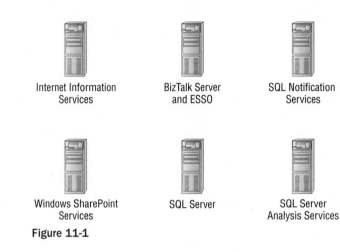

| Internet Information Services | BizTalk Server and ESSO | SQL Notification Services |

| Windows SharePoint Services | SQL Server | SQL Server Analysis Services |

Figure 11-1

As Figure 11-1 illustrates, a number of components are part of a BizTalk application. Each component has to be managed, maintained, and updated correctly. The chapter focuses primarily on the administration of BizTalk, although some of the tools and techniques do involve other components such as SQL Server.

The Administration Toolkit

This section briefly introduces each tool provided with a standard installation of BizTalk Server 2006. The detailed use of them will be covered later in the chapter.

BizTalk Server Administration Console

The BizTalk Server Administration Console was one of the biggest improvements in BizTalk 2006 compared to 2004. It enables users to manage and monitor multiple BizTalk groups from one place. The Console also introduces the concept of applications, allowing BizTalk artifacts (orchestrations, pipelines, and schemas) from the same application to be grouped, configured, and administered together. This means that applications can be started and stopped as a unit; this is a great feature for customers, as in BizTalk 2004 custom scripts would often need to be produced to manage related artifacts. The Console is illustrated in Figure 11-2.

The Console provides the facility to configure applications fully, including creating receive/send ports and binding logical orchestration ports. Right-click the desired application and select Configure to display a wizard prompting you for all the artifacts that need to be configured. This helps ensure that an application is not just partly started (i.e., some receive locations necessary for normal function may be missed out if the artifacts were not grouped this way). Figure 11-3 shows the Configure Application screen in use.

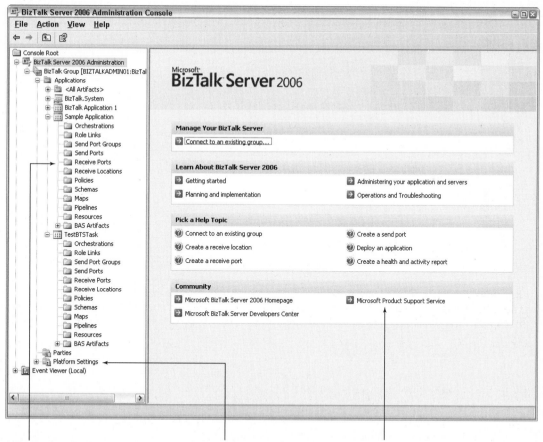

Artifacts are grouped as applications to ease administration.

Host settings can be modified through the Platform Settings node.

Help links are included.

Figure 11-2

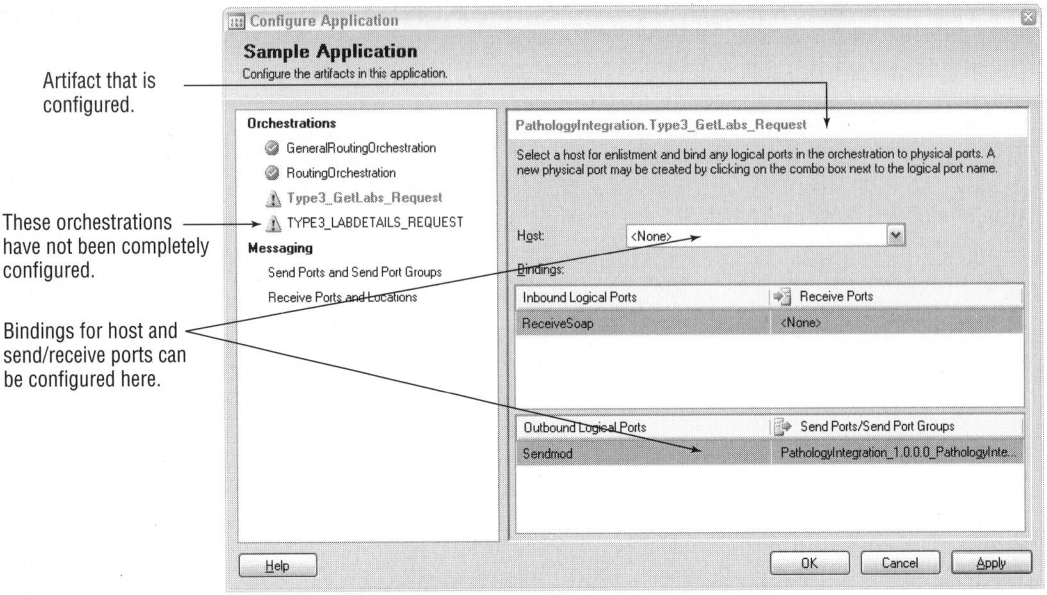

Artifact that is configured.

These orchestrations have not been completely configured.

Bindings for host and send/receive ports can be configured here.

Figure 11-3

Health and Activity Tracking (HAT)

HAT is used primarily to view historical tracking information for messages passing through BizTalk. It allows you to retrospectively view the message flow as a message passes through the pipeline and into the MessageBox, and is then consumed by one or more subscribers. You can use HAT either as an independent tool or in conjunction with the BizTalk Server Administration Console when troubleshooting suspended instances. It provides information about the events during a message flow, the properties, and the message body (if configured).

The Orchestration Debugger allows administrators to view historic information about how the flow of events for an orchestration instance were executed. It also enables developers to set breakpoints before any shape in an orchestration so that specific variable values and message data can be examined while the orchestration is executed. Figure 11-4 shows the results of a HAT query to view tracking information about the last 100 service instances that have been completed. The use of this is covered later in the chapter.

BTSTask and BTSDeploy

BTSTask is a new command-line-based tool that was introduced in BizTalk 2006. It allows application deployment tasks to be performed from the command line. BTSDeploy is included in BizTalk 2006 to support legacy deployment scripts that have a dependency on it; any new scripts should be written using BTSTask. BTSTask is covered in depth later in this chapter.

For more information on both of these tools, see the "Application Deployment Command Line" section of the online documentation, at http://msdn2.microsoft.com/en-us/library/aa560728.aspx.

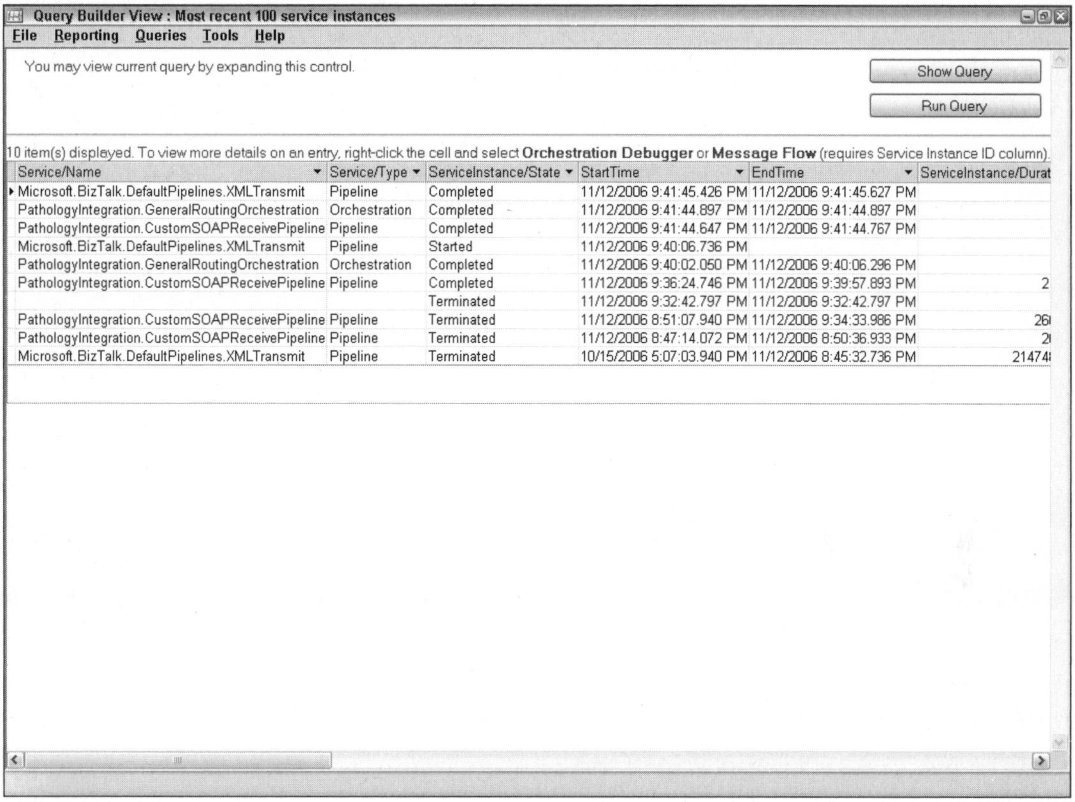

Figure 11-4

WMI

Windows Management Instrumentation (WMI) allows programmatic access to all administrative functions available in BizTalk 2006. This can be used to automate tedious, monotonous tasks and reduce the likelihood of human error. For example, suppose that a BizTalk Server has 50 receive locations, of which 25 use a pipeline. For this pipeline to be updated, all the receive locations using it must first be disabled. This is a boring, monotonous task, which, if done manually, introduces the possibility of human error; that is, an administrator could mistakenly forget to disable one or more receive locations. Automating this process through the use of the WMI classes available would speed the process up and provide a much needed structured approach.

> *Many WMI samples are provided in the* `SDK\Samples\Admin\WMI` *folder in the BizTalk Server 2006 program files directory. These are also documented at the following link to the online documentation:* `http://msdn2.microsoft.com/en-us/library/aa559638.aspx`.

BizTalk Explorer

This is the tool used by developers to manage a single BizTalk Server. It enables them to perform the administrative functions they require without leaving the familiar Visual Studio environment. In BizTalk

2004, the Explorer was used by some administrators in their production environments because it provided much needed functionality that was not available in the Administration Console. In BizTalk 2006, the administration tools have been improved to offer all the functionality of the BizTalk Explorer; therefore, *this tool should only be used in development environments.*

Regular Administration Tasks

This section describes the administrative activities that should be performed on BizTalk environments. This content is primarily aimed at BizTalk 2006, although much of it also applies to 2004. This section assumes some familiarity with the BizTalk Server Administration Console; rather than providing a feature analysis of this and other tools, the following sections show how they should be used in a real-world environment most effectively to perform administrative functions.

Application Deployment

While working with large enterprise customers, I have seen on more than one occasion problems that have been caused by poor application deployment processes. The process of deploying applications should be planned and controlled to minimize the risk of error. The business often dictates that application deployment must occur after hours; therefore, it tends to be done by operations staff that are not familiar with each and every component used by the application.

To reduce the chances of something going wrong, human input should be minimized throughout the deployment process. If something can be automated (for example, enlisting and starting 100 send ports), then it should be! This makes your deployment processes less error prone, more automated, and easier to test. It is important that this automation occurs through all stages of your application development. Following these practices in your development and staging environments helps to ensure that any problems are resolved before they are used in production!

A lot of investment was made in the deployment process for BizTalk 2006. The introduction of the "application" improved the administration tasks of deploying, modifying, updating, and removing related BizTalk artifacts. The application concept makes managing related BizTalk artifacts much more intuitive for developers and administrators by allowing you to deploy and manage artifacts at the application. Developers can use the Application Name property of a BizTalk Visual Studio project to ensure that the project's contents will be contained within that application. Administrators can use the BizTalk Server Administration Console to add and remove artifacts to an application, as well as create new ones. Errors can be grouped in the Console by application; this enables an administrator to quickly track down problems and determine the root cause of issues.

In addition to the Administration Console, BizTalk provides several tools to perform these tasks, such as BizTalk Explorer, BTSTask, and WMI. This section will cover the best practices for application deployment in the different environments you maintain.

Separation of Environments

Unfortunately, I still see customers who do not maintain separate development, staging, and production environments. This is a well-known best practice that is incredibly important; many of the testing techniques covered in Chapter 8 rely on you having these separate environments. Maintaining distinct, tightly controlled environments and adopting strict testing policies greatly increases the chances of problems being detected before it is too late. In my experience, those customers who perform only limited testing in their development environment before their production deployment run an extremely high risk of a serious failure occurring. Anyone who will be deploying a BizTalk application should review Chapter 8 for detailed information on testing and application build best practice.

Wherever possible, the staging environment should be an exact replica of production. This should include the number of servers present, their roles, and any separation by network infrastructure such as firewalls and routers. It is also important that the staging environment is owned and controlled by the operations team, who should use the same processes and procedures that are used to manage the production environment. A recent presentation by a colleague of mine from Microsoft highlighted the problems that they had experienced while working on a project that utilized BizTalk heavily. Many of the problems highlighted were due to there being differences between the environments, which had unforeseen consequences on the application.

If an environment is not an exact replica (or as close as it can be) and your application has not been connected to the systems that it will be communicating with, it becomes very difficult to guarantee that your application and deployment process will work. As discussed in Chapter 9, if an environment is not available that is built on the same (or very similar) infrastructure, it is very difficult to perform tests (such as measuring latency under high load) other than functional application tests. Although the cost of maintaining a staging environment can be significant, the proper use of this as part of your testing process greatly reduces the chance of problems occurring in production. Given that BizTalk is regularly used to build applications that are critical to business operations, can you really afford to take the inherent risk of not following this best practice?

We will now examine the tools that can be used to deploy applications.

Visual Studio and BizTalk Explorer

Visual Studio is the heart of BizTalk development. It provides all the functionality necessary for developers to develop and deploy their applications. To ensure that developers do not need to step outside Visual Studio when developing BizTalk applications, Visual Studio provides BizTalk Explorer. This is the deployment tool that is aimed exclusively at development environments. It provides developers with all the functionality they need to perform the tasks necessary to deploy and configure an application. This includes deploying an assembly to the Management database and the local GAC, creating physical receive locations, as well as send/receive ports, and binding these to the relevant ports in an orchestration.

Developers tend to have one single server that has all the required components installed (such as SQL Server, Visual Studio, BizTalk, etc.). Often when a change is made to an artifact, the developer will want to test it to ensure it works. Therefore, it is essential that the process of deployment and redeployment is as quick and efficient as possible. To speed up the process, the `Redeploy, Install to Global Assembly Cache,` and `Restart Host Instances` properties should all be set to `True`. The properties can be accessed by right-clicking the root of your BizTalk project in Visual Studio and selecting Properties and then Configuration Properties ➪ Deployment.

The `Redeploy` property allows an existing project to be redeployed when the assembly version number is identical. This is ideal when testing small incremental changes in a development environment. The `Install to Global Assembly Cache` property ensures that the assembly will be redeployed to the GAC on the local server. Setting the `Restart Host Instances` property to `true` means that the BizTalk host instances will be restarted on deployment, this ensures that the correct new version of the assembly will be loaded into memory. Setting these properties allows a developer to simply finish the edit that he or she has made to a BizTalk artifact, then right-click the project and select Deploy. The new version of the application will now have been deployed and be ready to test. This efficient process maximizes developer productivity and minimizes the risk of errors occurring (such as forgetting to restart host instances to ensure that the latest version of the assembly is loaded into memory). Therefore, to take advantage of all this, you should ensure that when Visual Studio's BizTalk Explorer is used for deployment the Deployment properties are set as shown in Figure 11-5.

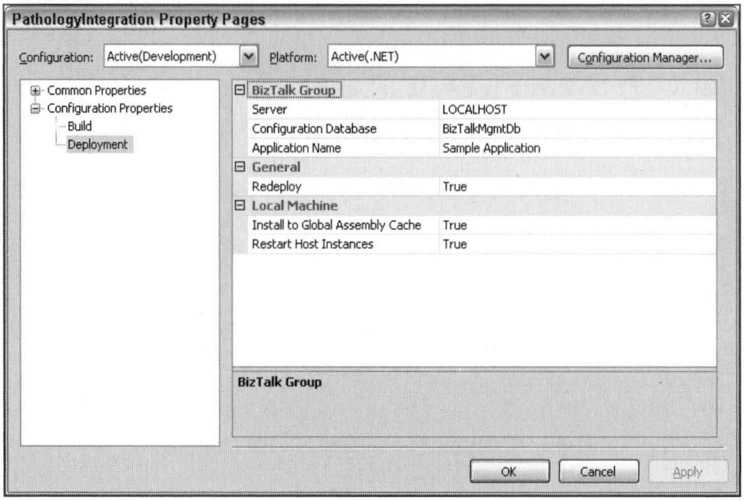

Figure 11-5

You have seen in this section that BizTalk Explorer can be very useful for deploying applications in development environments. It provides all the necessary functionality to enable a developer to quickly and easily deploy to a local development server. However, BizTalk Explorer is not intended for any other use and should certainly never be used within a production environment. There are a number of reasons for this, including:

- ❑   It requires Visual Studio to be present in your production environment.
- ❑   Access to the raw project files is required in order to deploy an application from BizTalk Explorer.
- ❑   The tool allows the user to redeploy assemblies with the same version number, which is not desirable in production.
- ❑   BizTalk Explorer is not application aware (i.e., it will not group artifacts by the application that they belong to).
- ❑   A scripted, automated deployment technique that is less error prone is preferred to the BizTalk Explorer.

In short, you should always use one of the other deployment options in your staging or production environments.

BizTalk Server Administration Console

The BizTalk Server Administration Console provides a graphical interface for all application deployment tasks. The Import and Export Wizards contained within it allow a user to create and import Microsoft

Installer (MSI) files containing BizTalk applications. This can be used to export an application from one environment (for example, development) and import it into another (for example, production). In this section, we will discuss the application concept within BizTalk, the role that MSIs play in deployment, and how the functionality of the Console can be used during deployment to different environments.

The full support of the application concept greatly improves the deployment process when using the Console. An application can contain all the required BizTalk artifacts, such as orchestrations, pipelines, and send/receive ports, but it can also contain other resources. The ability to add additional resources to an application allows an application to contain all the components it depends on. The resources that can be added include, but are not limited to, non-BizTalk assemblies, multiple binding files for different environments, and pre- and postprocessing scripts for custom actions. All these resources can then be serialized into an MSI file that is used for deployment. We will now look at how this is used to ease the pain of deployment.

MSI Usage

MSIs are the standard way of deploying applications on the Microsoft platform. They fully integrate with the Add/Remove Programs screen and most administrators are familiar with them. For this reason, MSI was adopted in BizTalk Server 2006 as the standard method of application deployment across machines and environments. In order for BizTalk to operate correctly, an assembly must be registered in the Management database and the GAC on each BizTalk server. The BizTalk MSI implementation provides a solution for this by allowing the same MSI file to be used in two different ways during deployment:

❑   First, the assembly needs to be registered once in the Management database. This is performed by running the Import MSI File Wizard, which can be done by right-clicking the Applications node in the Console and selecting Import ➪ MSI File. This is commonly referred to as the import process and is covered later in this section.

❑   The second stage is to install all the required assemblies into the GAC on all BizTalk servers. Because the MSI can contain non-BizTalk assemblies and other resources such as scripts, it can be used to automate the deployment of everything that is required by the application. This process is known as the installation process and needs to be performed on each BizTalk server in the group. To perform this, simply double-click the MSI file on the appropriate servers.

Depending on the type of deployment that you are performing, you may or may not have to perform both of the preceding actions. If you are either deploying an application upgrade or setting up a new environment, then you will need to perform both steps. However, if you are simply adding a new server to the BizTalk group, it is likely that only the second step will need to be followed to register the required assemblies on the local machine.

Using Multiple Binding Files

One of the most useful resources that can be added to an application is `System.BizTalk` `.BizTalkBinding`. This allows multiple binding files to be stored within an application, each of which can be associated with one of your environments. This allows one MSI file to be used across all your environments for deployment.

To use multiple binding files, you first need to deploy your application to an environment (typically, the development environment) and create the required ports and bindings for the application using the Console. This registers the configuration in the Management database, which can then be exported to a binding file.

To export a binding file for your application, right-click on the application in the Console and select Export ⇨ Bindings. This will start the Export Bindings Wizard, as shown in Figure 11-6. The Export to File box allows you to configure where the binding file is exported to. The three options available allow you: to export the selected application bindings, to export the whole groups bindings (i.e., bindings for all the applications), or to export the bindings associated with a specific assembly. The wizard also allows you to export any party information present in the group if the Export Global Party Information box is checked. You should select the appropriate option and then click OK to export the bindings to an XML file.

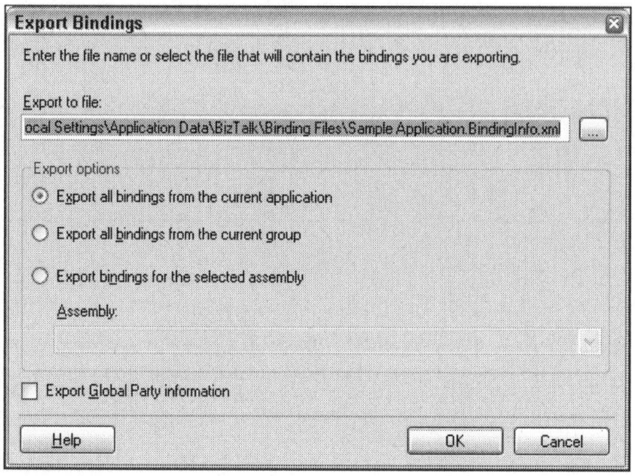

Figure 11-6

A party within BizTalk represents an outside entity that interacts with it. A party is often used in solutions to represent a trading partner or other organization. A party can have a certificate associated with it. When multiple parties are present in a group, BizTalk can determine which party sent a message that has been received by examining its digital signature and resolving this to a known party within BizTalk. This party information can be included in binding files if the Export Global Party Information box is checked. This should be checked only if the group has been configured for party resolution. For more information on this topic, see the "How to Configure BizTalk Server for Party Resolution" section of the online help, at http://msdn2.microsoft.com/en-US/library/aa561268.aspx.

Now that the bindings have been exported to an XML file, this can be customized to suit your environment. To do this, you should now open the binding file that you have just exported in an XML editor. You should see a file similar in structure to that in Figure 11-7. The binding file contains all the bindings that you created previously using the Console (or any other tool, such as BTSTask). Typically, the main differences between environments will be the endpoint configuration. The binding file can be modified to take this into account for each of the environments that you have.

In Figure 11-7, the <address> tag that contains the configuration information for the ReceiveSoap receive location is highlighted. This currently contains the following value: C:\filedrop\RxInitial\ *.xml, which is the File location that it polls to receive messages from. Values such as these can be modified appropriately. For example, in production, it may need to be changed to `\\ReceiveServer\BTSReceiveIN`. Once the file has been modified for the new environment, a version of it should be saved using an appropriate name. You should do this for each of your environments.

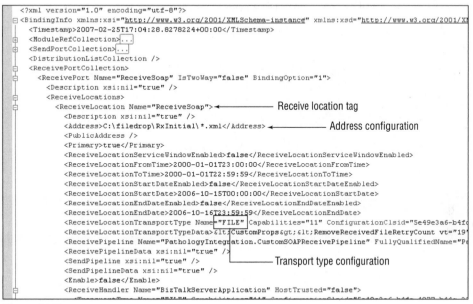

Figure 11-7

For a thorough guide to modifying binding files, see the "Customizing Binding Files" section of the online help, at `http://msdn2.microsoft.com/en-us/library/aa559898.aspx`.

The new binding file(s) can then be added as a resource to your application. To do this, right-click the application in the Console and choose Add ➪ Resources. This will display the Add Resources screen, from which you should click the Add button, and then browse to the new binding file(s) you just created in the Select Files to Add window that appears. Once you have clicked Open in that window, it will return to the Add Resources window. The File Type drop-down list should now be populated with the text `System.BizTalk.BizTalkBinding`. To specify which environment this belongs to, you should enter the name of the environment in the Target Environment box (such as Staging). Your screen should now look similar to Figure 11-8.

If no environment name is entered, the bindings will be applied to all environments. This is almost always not what you want!

Next, select OK to add the binding file as a resource within the application. It is recommended that you perform this process of generating binding files for each of your environments. Once this has been done, when you run the Import MSI File Wizard for an MSI file containing this application, it will prompt you to select the environment that you are importing the application into. This is covered later in the chapter. We will now look at how the Export MSI File Wizard can be used.

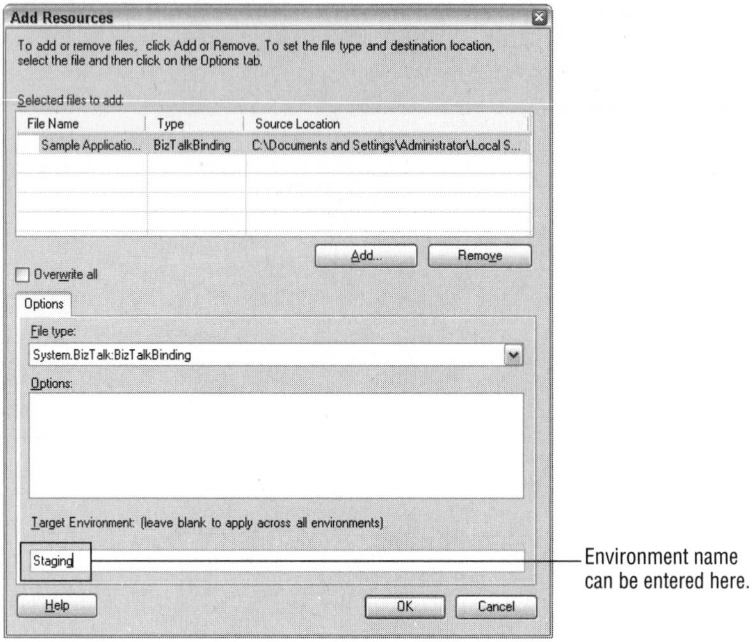

Figure 11-8

If you are using an adapter that requires a username and password to be entered into any send port or receive location that is configured, then note that these passwords are removed during the binding file export process for security reasons. This is so that confidential passwords are not exposed within an organization. Therefore, you will need to reenter the passwords, which can be done either within the binding file or in the BizTalk Server Administration Console, once the bindings have been applied. When binding files are added to an application, passwords are not removed. Therefore, it is recommended that you reenter the password into the binding file to provide as automated a process as possible.

Export MSI File Wizard

Now that you have added the necessary binding file resources to the BizTalk application, you can export it from the original environment. The Export MSI File Wizard is used to do this. Figure 11-9 shows the wizard, which you can start by right-clicking the application in the Administration Console and selecting Export and then MSI file.

As you can see in Figure 11-9, the Export MSI File Wizard allows complete contents of the application to be exported. This includes the bindings associated with the application as well as the artifacts. Figure 11-9 shows that this application contains two binding files. The artifacts that are exported can be configured by selecting or deselecting the various check boxes on the first screen of the wizard. The wizard then prompts you to export any IIS virtual directories that are used. Figure 11-10 shows the wizard being used to export a virtual directory that is used in this application to host the HTTP Receive adapter — BTSHTTPReceive.dll.

Export MSI File Wizard - Sample Application

Select Resources

Select the resources that you want to include in this file.

Welcome to the Export MSI F

Select Resources

Specify IIS Hosts

Dependencies

Destination

Progress

Summary

Select the resources to export:

If you select bindings, all of the bindings for the application will be exported, and not just the bindings for the selected resources.

- ☑ System.BizTalk:BizTalkAssembly
  - ☑ PathologyIntegration, Version=1.0.0.0, Culture=neutral, PublicKeyToken=ce736ː
- ☑ System.BizTalk:BizTalkBinding
  - ☑ Sample Application.BindingInfo.Production.xml
  - ☑ Sample Application.BindingInfo.xml
- ☑ System.BizTalk:WebDirectory
  - ☑ /btshttpreceive
- ☑ Bindings
  - ☑ Global Parties

Help   < Back   Next >   Cancel

Figure 11-9

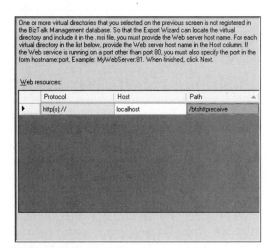

One or more virtual directories that you selected on the previous screen is not registered in the BizTalk Management database. So that the Export Wizard can locate the virtual directory and include it in the .msi file, you must provide the Web server host name. For each virtual directory in the list below, provide the Web server host name in the Host column. If the Web service is running on a port other than port 80, you must also specify the port in the form hostname:port. Example: MyWebServer:81. When finished, click Next.

Web resources:

	Protocol	Host	Path	▲
▶	http(s)://	localhost	/btshttpreceive	

Figure 11-10

Once this step is complete, the wizard will then list any dependencies that the application has. A dependency means that at least one artifact within the application requires another artifact from another application in order to function correctly. This tends to occur when an orchestration requires access to a schema to resolve a message or when one orchestration calls another. If this is the case, it is important to ensure that the dependent application is also present on the BizTalk group and that there is a reference present between the two applications. The wizard then prompts you for a location to create the MSI file. Once this has been done, the wizard completes and the application is exported successfully.

Import MSI File Wizard

So you've now exported your application from the development server, and it includes a number of binding files for each environment. In this section, we will discuss how an application can be deployed into another environment using the BizTalk Server Administration Console and the exported MSI file.

Before you start the import process, it is important to bear the following in mind:

❑ Importing an application does not install the required assemblies on all BizTalk servers. This must be done by double-clicking the MSI on each of the runtime servers.

❑ Importing an application requires that you are a member of the BizTalk Server Administrators group.

❑ Installing the application on a BizTalk server requires that you have write permissions on the local file system.

❑ When an MSI file is imported into an existing application, the application's existing bindings will always be overwritten with those contained within the MSI file. This can be prevented only if the binding files are not selected when running the Export MSI File Wizard.

❑ All hosts that are referenced in the bindings must be present in the new environment. So, if an orchestration is bound to a host named Send, you must have created a host named Send in the environment in which you wish to import the application; otherwise, the import process will fail.

❑ You might need to add a reference to another application during the import operation. If your application depends on another application, then this must be deployed to the group first. The Import MSI File Wizard prompts you to do this. If no reference is made to the application containing the required artifact, the application you have imported will not start correctly.

❑ Consider splitting very large applications into separate MSI files to avoid timeouts. This is because the import process will time out if it exceeds 3600 seconds. You can do this by rerunning the Export MSI File Wizard multiple times and selecting only a subset of components to export each time.

After you've reviewed the preceding list, you should copy the MSI file you created previously to an accessible location. Then, using the BizTalk Server Administration Console, you should connect to the correct group. Within the group, right-click the Applications node and select Import ⇨ MSI file. This will start the Import MSI Wizard. On the welcome screen click the ... button and browse to the location of the MSI file and select Open. Then click Next to open the Application Settings screen, which is shown in Figure 11-11.

The Application Settings screen enables you to choose the name of the application, under Application Name, into which you wish to place the MSI files contents. If you select an application that is not empty (for example, when performing an update) and you want to overwrite existing artifacts, you should ensure that the Overwrite Resources box is checked. The `Available Applications to Add References To` box allows you to create any necessary references to other application within the group. You should do this if an artifact in another application (such as a shared schema or pipeline) is required for this application to run successfully. After selecting the desired options, click next.

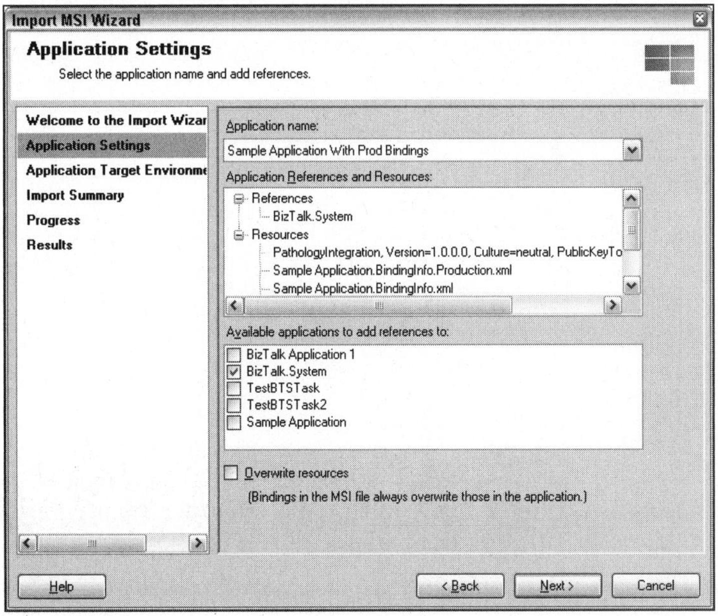

Figure 11-11

This will display the Application Target Environment Settings screen, from which you can select the desired target environment (see Figure 11-12). The environment names used are those that you associated the binding files with when you added them as resources to the application. You should ensure that you select the correct environment so that the correct bindings are applied; otherwise, your application will not work. Then click Next to display the Import Summary screen. You should review this and ensure that it is correct, and then click Import. A Progress screen will then be displayed, followed by the Import Succeeded screen (if the import is successful). If you want to install the application (i.e., register the assemblies in the local GAC), you should check the Run the Application Installation Wizard to install the application on the local computer check box and then click finish. If this option is checked, it will launch the MSI installer. Run this only if the machine that you have run the import on is one of the runtime servers.

Before running the application, you should ensure that the MSI has been installed on each of the BizTalk runtime servers. This will install all the necessary assemblies in the local GAC of the server.

This section has illustrated how the application concept can be used with the BizTalk Server Administration Console to improve the deployment and installation process. Packaging an application and all its required resources in an MSI file streamlines the process and reduces the likelihood of errors occurring. It is important to note that there are many other resources that can be added to an MSI file, which have not been covered here. This includes Business Rule policies and custom pre- and postprocessing scripts to perform additional tasks before or after the import or installation process. The "Deploying and Managing BizTalk Application" section of the online help provides useful information on this and is available at http://msdn2.microsoft.com/en-us/library/aa578693.aspx.

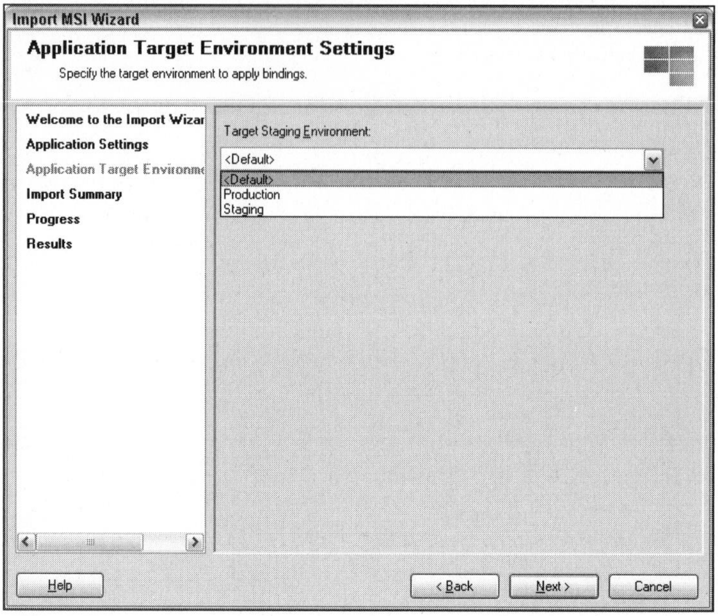

Figure 11-12

BTSTask

As previously mentioned, BTSTask was introduced in BizTalk 2006 to provide a command-line tool that could be used to script the execution of deployment tasks. As the successor to BTSDeploy, BTSTask includes additional functionality, supporting the new deployment features of BizTalk 2006, including the application concept and MSI file functionality.

> *In order to run* BTSTask, *the user account that executes the tool must have the required permissions. Typically, this will be being a member of the BizTalk Server Administrators group and the local administrators group on the machine you would like to deploy the assembly to.*

BTSTask supports the following functionality:

❑ Creating new applications in the Management database

❑ Adding a BizTalk artifact to an application

❑ Exporting/importing an application and artifacts to/from an MSI file

❑ Exporting/importing binding information to/from an XML file

❑ Listing the artifacts that an application contains and their unique identifiers

❑ Listing all the applications in the Management database

❑ Listing the artifacts that are contained within an MSI file

❑ Listing all the artifact types that BizTalk 2006 supports

- ❑ Removing an application from the Management database
- ❑ Removing an artifact from an application
- ❑ Uninstalling an application from the local computer

This functionality allows fairly complicated scripts to be built up very quickly. This section will walk you through how to use BTSTask to create a deployment batch script that creates an application, adds the relevant artifacts to it, and imports a binding file to bind logical and physical send/receive ports. The first stage in the process is typically to create the application; this is the logical bucket that BizTalk 2006 uses to group and manage related artifacts. This is done by opening a command window and using the following -AddApp switch with the BTSTask command:

```
BTSTask -AddApp:<ApplicationName> -Server:<SQL Server> -Database:<Management
Database Name>
```

The following snippet is an actual example taken from a batch script. Note that an error message will be displayed if the application has already been created in the Management database. If you get an error while running the BTSTask command, this script displays an error message and goes to the section in the batch file specified (nextstep). This could be used so that a new application is created only if one doesn't exist; if it does exist, the artifacts can be added to it.

```
BTSTask AddApp -applicationname:TestBTSTask2 -Server:localhost
-Database:BizTalkMgmtDb
If %errorlevel%==1 (
Echo Error Creating Application.  We will and go add artifacts to this application
Goto :nextstep
)
:nextstep
```

This command creates an application named TestBTSTask in the BizTalkMgmtDb database stored on the local SQL Server.

The next stage is to add a resource to the application. In this case, you are going to register a BizTalk assembly in the Management database and register it in the local Global Assembly Cache (GAC). This is done by using the -AddResource switch with the BTSTask command:

```
BTSTask -AddResource -Source:<location of assembly> -ApplicationName:<name of app>
-Type:<Assembly type e.g. System.BizTalk:BizTalkAssembly> /overwrite< this is
optional> -Options:GacOnAdd <optional>
```

Here's an actual example that adds four BizTalk assemblies to the Management database and the local GAC. Note these are all added to the TestBTSTask application created previously:

```
BTSTask AddResource -Source:c:\scripts\assemblies\SampleDeployment.Schema.dll
-ApplicationName:TestBTSTask -Type:System.BizTalk:BizTalkAssembly /overwrite
-Options:GacOnAdd
BTSTask AddResource -Source:c:\scripts\assemblies\SampleDeployment.Maps.dll
-ApplicationName:TestBTSTask -Type:System.BizTalk:BizTalkAssembly /overwrite
-Options:GacOnAdd
BTSTask AddResource -Source:c:\scripts\assemblies\SampleDeployment.Pipelines.dll
-ApplicationName:TestBTSTask -Type:System.BizTalk:BizTalkAssembly /overwrite
-Options:GacOnAdd
```

```
BTSTask AddResource -Source:c:\scripts\assemblies\SampleDeployment.Orch.dll
-ApplicationName:TestBTSTask -Type:System.BizTalk:BizTalkAssembly /overwrite
-Options:GacOnAdd
```

These assemblies are added to the local GAC (this is done with the `GacOnAdd` option) and registers it in the Management database under the application `TestBTSTask`. You also can use the `AddResource` switch to add many other resources, including binding files, .NET assemblies, BAM artifacts (definition of an activity stored in an XML file), certificates, COM components, files, and pre- and postprocessing scripts.

The next stage is to import the binding file for the application. This is done by using the `ImportBindings` switch. The following command imports the binding file into the `TestBTSTask` application:

```
BTSTask ImportBindings -Source:C:\SampleDeployment\Binding\Binding.xml
-ApplicationName:TestBTSTask
```

This section has shown an example of how `BTSTask` can be used to create a batch file that scripts the deployment process of a BizTalk application. You can use `BTSTask` to automate many steps in the deployment process, including importing applications from MSI and exporting them to it, importing/exporting binding files, and many other deployment tasks.

> *This section demonstrated some of the tasks that can be automated. For information on* `BTSTask`, *see* `http://msdn2.microsoft.com/en-us/library/aa560955.aspx`.

Deployment Best Practices

This section provides some additional advice that you should bear in mind when deploying applications.

❑ First, wherever possible you should take advantage of the application concept in BizTalk 2006 and group shared artifacts together where possible; this enables the artifacts to be administered as a single entity within the BizTalk Server Administration Console and makes tasks such as stopping and starting these related artifacts very trivial for an administrator.

❑ Ensure that you add all the required resources to your application before exporting it to MSI. Most importantly, this should include binding files that contain customized information for each of your environments, but it can also include non-BizTalk assemblies that are required and any custom scripts that you need to run.

❑ If certain artifacts are going to be shared across multiple applications — for example, you may have an organizational standard XML schema (or, indeed, so may your trading partners) — they should be placed in a separate application. This keeps the schema from becoming unavailable to other applications that have referenced it because of maintenance being performed on another application.

Note: The following artifacts should also be deployed to separate "shared applications": web sites, policies, and shared certificates.

❑ As stated previously, you should *never* deploy to a production environment using the BizTalk Explorer tool that is built into Visual Studio.

❑ If you are deploying large MSI files (greater than 100MB), you might experience deployment failure. This can be caused by the two COM+ components used during application deployment timing out. To solve this, go to Control Panel ➪ Administrative Tools ➪ Component Services.

When the MMC opens, select Component Services ➪ Computers ➪ My Computer ➪ Com+ Applications. You should then drill down to the `Microsoft.BizTalk.ApplicationDeployment` `.Engine` folder and right-click the `Microsoft.BizTalk.ApplicationDeployment.Group` component. In the properties box that appears, select the Transactions tab and increase the default timeout (which is in seconds). You should also do this for the `Microsoft.BizTalk` `.Deployment.DeployerComponent` component that is located under the `Microsoft` `.BizTalk.Deployment` folder. Figure 11-13 illustrates this.

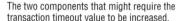
The two components that might require the transaction timeout value to be increased.

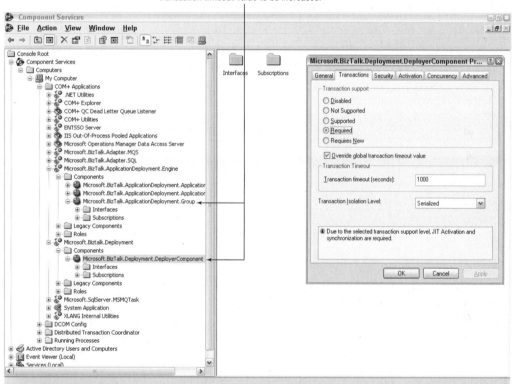

Figure 11-13

Managing Hosts

As discussed previously in this book, hosts are a logical set of BizTalk runtime services to which items can be deployed, including orchestrations, adapter handlers, and receive locations. Once a host has been created, instances of this host can be created on individual servers. This model allows the same host to be hosted on multiple BizTalk Servers in your group, providing reliable processing. As indicated in Chapter 9, "Performance and Scalability," it is recommended that separate hosts be created for the following function-ality: sending, receiving, processing (orchestration), and tracking (see Figure 11-14). It is recommended that you use this instead of the default host configuration in BizTalk, which creates only one in-process host. If this configuration is used, all BizTalk activities (sending, receiving, processing, etc.) will be done within the same process on each of your servers, which can lead to the process running out of threads.

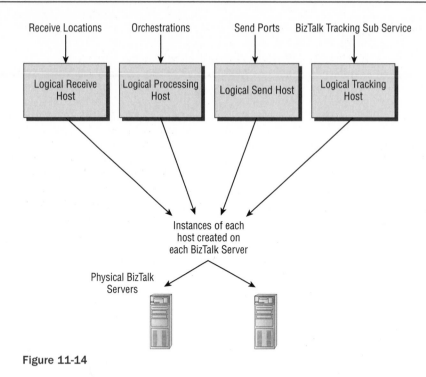

Figure 11-14

Tracking Hosts

It is very important that you have one of your BizTalk hosts configured as a tracking host and that there be at least one host instance for this. Even if tracking is disabled for every send port, receive port, orchestration, and so on, some tracking data is still written to the MesssageBox. If tracking is enabled on a host, this means it runs the Tracking Data Decode Service (TDDS), which is responsible for moving the tracking data from the MessageBox database. TDDS is used to move tracking data to the DTA database, but it is also used to move BAM data if one of the asynchronous event streams has been used, such as `OrchestrationEventStream`, `MessagingEventStream`, or `BufferedEventStream`.

For more information on the BAM event streams and how to use them within your application, see Chapter 6. If none of your hosts are configured as tracking hosts, TDDS will not be running. This can result in a buildup of data in the MessageBox, which can slow down BizTalk's overall performance. As discussed in the previous section, when performing host separation it is recommended that you run tracking within its own dedicated host.

With the default configuration of BizTalk 2006, the initial host created has tracking enabled. You can check to see if tracking is enabled for a host by opening the BizTalk Administration Console, expanding the node for your group, then Platform Settings, and then the Hosts folder. From here, right-click a host and select Properties. The Host Properties window will be opened on the General tab. In the right-hand window under Options is an Allow Host Tracking check box that determines whether the tracking subservice runs within this host. You should check each of your hosts' properties and verify that you have a dedicated tracking host, and that there is at least one running host instance of that tracking host.

Clustering Hosts

Generally, BizTalk can be made highly available by running multiple instances of the same host. This ensures that if one host instance were to fail, the system could continue to process messages on another running host instance. In BizTalk 2006 host clustering support was made available to be used in a limited number of scenarios.

All the out-of-the-box BizTalk adapters, with the exception of the Base EDI adapter, can be clustered. Apart from the scenarios defined in this section, there is no benefit from doing this. Running the same host on multiple BizTalk servers provides high availability, but with the added benefit that all host instances can process messages continuously, not just when failover occurs. Effectively running BizTalk within a clustered host reduces the possible throughput by half, because the host can be active only on one of the clustered nodes at any point in time. Therefore, you should cluster BizTalk hosts only if it is required.

In this section, we will discuss the situations in which you should consider clustering BizTalk hosts.

> *This section discusses when and why you should cluster BizTalk. It does not cover the step-by-step instructions that are required to set up a BizTalk host as a clustered resource. Detailed information on this can be found in the "Using Windows Server Cluster to Provide High Availability for BizTalk Server Hosts" section of the online help, at* http://msdn2.microsoft.com/en-us/library /aa560059.aspx.

FTP Adapter

A host running the FTP Receive adapter should not be configured to run in multiple BizTalk hosts simultaneously. This recommendation is made because the FTP transport does not allow the adapter to lock files while it is in the process of removing them from the FTP server. If multiple instances of the FTP Receive adapter were running, it is possible that multiple copies of the same file could be retrieved and processed by BizTalk. Therefore, to provide high availability for the FTP Receive adapter, you should configure it to run in a clustered BizTalk host instance.

MSMQ Adapter

The Microsoft Message Queuing (MSMQ) adapter does not support remote transactional reads, which means that messages on a remote MSMQ queue cannot be read in a transactional manner. If the message contains critical information (such as payment or workflow data) then this is not acceptable. To enable transactional reads, you must run the MSMQ Receive adapter in a host instance that is local to the MSMQ service. To ensure that this is made highly available, both the MSMQ service and the MSMQ Send and Receive adapters should be configured to run in a cluster group. Clustering the MSMQ Send adapter and the MSMQ service together ensures that the outgoing queue will be highly available.

When making this highly available, you should ensure that you have performed the following actions:

- ❑ Configure the MSMQ service as a clustered resource in a Windows Server cluster group. The cluster should also contain a clustered BizTalk host.

- ❑ Add the MSMQ service as a Resource dependency for the clustered BizTalk host. This is done to ensure that the BizTalk service does not start until after the MSMQ service in the event of a failover.

- ❑ Ensure that the MSMQ Send and Receive adapters are configured in a host instance that is a clustered resource in the same cluster group as the clustered MSMQ service.

POP3 Adapter

Whether this needs to be clustered or not depends on the configuration of the POP3 server that you will be receiving mail from. If the POP3 server allows multiple concurrent connections to the same mailbox, then you need to ensure that the POP3 Receive adapter is running within a single BizTalk host that has been clustered. This recommendation is made to avoid multiple copies of the same e-mail message from being received and processed by BizTalk.

In-Order Delivery

The MSMQ and MQSeries adapters provide the ability to deliver messages into BizTalk in the order in which they were received. To implement this correctly, only a single instance of these Receive adapters should be running at any given time. Therefore, to provide high availability, these should be run within a clustered BizTalk host.

Troubleshooting BizTalk

The ability to troubleshoot and resolve problems as quickly as possible is an essential skill in the modern enterprise. To minimize the number of problems that need to be resolved, rigorous development, coding, testing, deployment, and source code control processes should be followed. However, even if all these aspects are handled correctly and the advice laid out in this book is followed, it is likely that you will at some point have to troubleshoot and resolve an issue. Part of my role at Microsoft involves dealing with critical situations (called *CritSits* internally); these occur when a BizTalk customer somewhere in the world has a problem that results in their system suffering downtime. This section covers the tools used by internal Microsoft engineers to resolve these situations, including the out-of-the-box tools plus others that have been developed by people working in the field to speed up problem resolution.

Checking the Health of Your BizTalk System

As previously stated, most enterprise applications contain many components. This is particularly the case for integration applications that are built on BizTalk. These types of applications are likely to contain and communicate with products from the Microsoft stack and other third parties. Therefore, the health of your application cannot normally be determined merely by the state of BizTalk; it is important that all the components are monitored.

This section will show how the tools provided can be used to monitor the health of BizTalk, and later in the chapter we will cover how Microsoft Operations Manager (MOM) can be used to ease this administrative burden. When reading this section, it is important to bear in mind that in your application you should automate the monitoring of its components where possible. For example, by using MOM you can automatically monitor the health of physical and software components (such as SQL Server, SharePoint, the underlying operating system, server hardware, storage area networks (SAN), and many more). It is beyond the scope of this book to cover all of this; therefore, this chapter focuses solely on monitoring the health of BizTalk.

The Group Hub Page

A new feature implemented in BizTalk 2006, the Group Hub Page provides administrators with an at-a-glance view of the health of the applications running in a group (see Figure 11-15). This can be accessed in the BizTalk Administration Console, through the Group Hub tab of the Group Overview page. The Group Hub Page provides indicators of the health of the overall group and each individual application, allowing problems to be caught at an earlier stage in a more proactive manner. The hub view is separated into four sections, each of which provides different information about the health of the group.

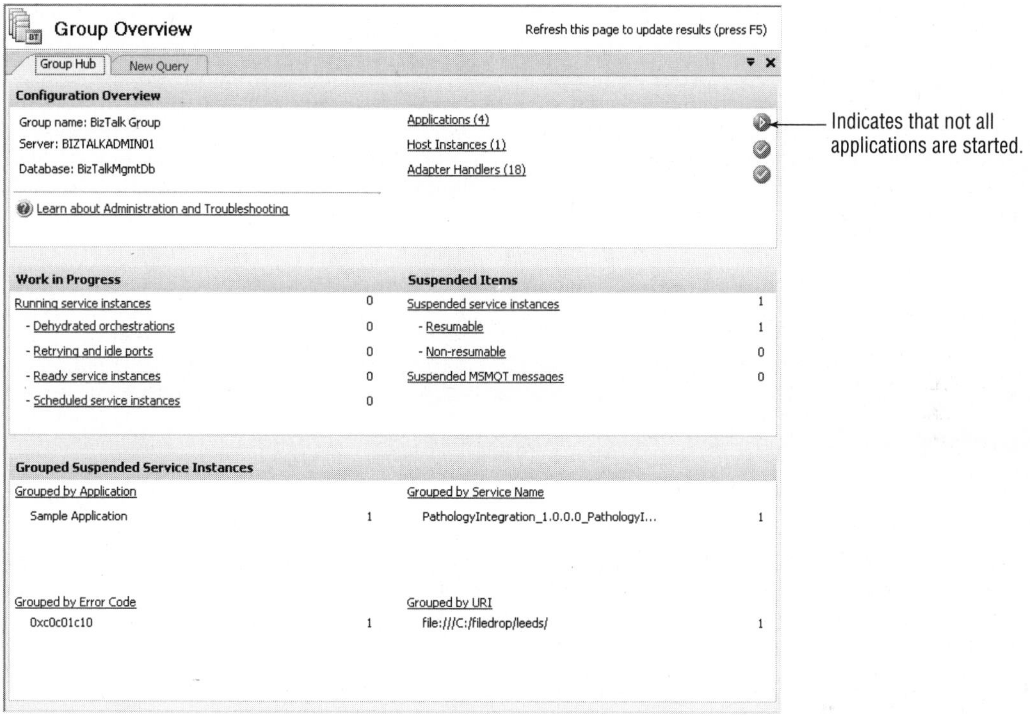

Figure 11-15

- ❏ **Configuration Overview** — The Configuration Overview section provides the group name, the management database location, and the number and status of applications, host instances, and adapter handlers that are present in the group. Figure 11-15 shows the Group Hub Page and an indication that not all applications have been started successfully within this group. Click the icon which is indicated in Figure 11-15 to bring up detailed information about the status of each application.

- ❏ **Work in Progress** — The Work in Progress section displays information on the unsuspended service instances, including those currently running, dehydrated orchestrations, retrying and idle ports, and service instances either in the ready-to-run state or scheduled to run. This enables you to determine at a glance whether the numbers for each of these indicators look okay.

- ❏ **Suspended Items** — The Suspended Items section breaks this figure down into those that are resumable, non-resumable, and BizTalk Message Queuing (MSMQT) messages. You should take immediate action if you see a buildup of suspended service instances. Depending on how the application has been architected, it may be normal to see a small number of suspended service instances; however, a large number tends to indicate a problem, which if left could result in operational issues with your the BizTalk Server.

❑ **Grouped Suspended Service Instances** — The Grouped Suspended Service Instances section displays the suspended service instances information grouped by application name, service name, error code, and URI. This enables you to quickly see common trends (for example, if a trading partner's endpoint was down, this may cause a large backlog of suspended service instances all with the same URI).

To summarize, the Group Hub Page provides a quick insight into the overall health of your BizTalk hub. Troubleshooting suspended instances is much improved in BizTalk 2006, compared to previous versions, due mainly to this. This chapter will go onto cover in greater detail later on how you can use the Group Hub Page alongside the rest of the functionality the Administration Console provides to rapidly resolve problems.

> If you would like to provide a user with low-privilege access, BizTalk provides the BizTalk Server Operators group. This provides members with the permissions required to perform monitoring and troubleshooting actions. However, it does not allow them to make any configuration changes or access sensitive information such as message bodies.

Troubleshooting Suspended Instances

As previously mentioned, the BizTalk Group Hub Page enables you to determine at a glance the health of the group, including the number of suspended instances present. This section will show you how to drill down from the Group Hub Page to determine the root cause of the suspended instances that are present in the MessageBox. The primary tool to do this is the BizTalk Administration Console, as it provides a comprehensive view of what is currently running in the active BizTalk processes.

From the Group Hub Page, it is possible to drill down and find out more information about a problem, including viewing the message body, context information, and the flow of the message as it has traveled through BizTalk. It also allows you to save a message to file for closer inspection, editing, or resubmission. To view suspended service instances that are present in the MessageBox, use either the links on the Suspended Items section or the links under Grouped Suspended Service Instances. In Figure 11-16, the Grouped by Error link from this section has been selected. This opens the query window of the Administration Console, which has been predefined to find suspended service instances and group them by error code.

As you can see in Figure 11-16, the Grouped by Error link has been clicked, which opened a populated query. From this you can see that there is one service instance present with the error code indicated. Right-clicking the row in the Query Results window brings up options that allow you to view the service instances. Bulk operations such as resume and terminate can be performed by right clicking the results displayed in the Query Results window and selecting either Resume Instances or Terminate Instances. This is particularly useful when a trading partner's endpoint has suffered downtime resulting in suspended resumable service instances within BizTalk. Using the bulk operation functionality of the Console, it is now possible to quickly resume all these instances without scripting. The other option that will be displayed is a link to the online help looking up the error code present. This ensures that when troubleshooting failures, administrators are always looking at the current version of the documentation for that error code.

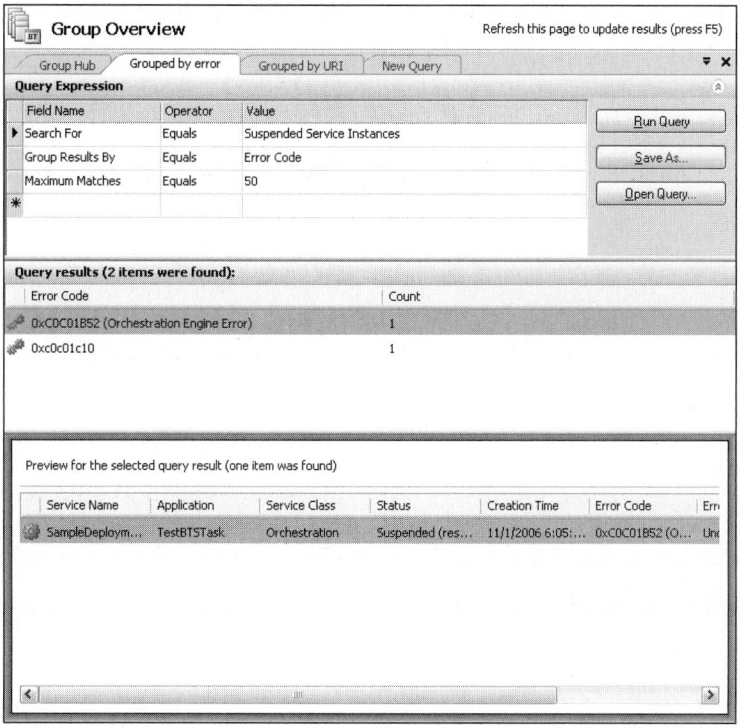

Figure 11-16

Right-clicking on the actual service instance in the Query Results view displays several options. The Service Details option displays the box shown in Figure 11-17. The General tab displays information such as the status of a message, its start time, service class, processing server, and instance ID. The Error Information tab displays the error code and the text related to it; Figure 11-17 shows the text for the error that the File Send adapter has thrown. Finally, the Messages tab allows context information and the message body to be displayed. This Messages tab is particularly useful if the error message displayed indicates that it is due to a message structure problem.

To examine the issue further, it is often necessary to drill down and look at the message flow. To do this, right-click on the instance in the Query Results window (see Figure 11-18) and select Message Flow. This opens HAT, which queries the `BizTalkDTADb` database, the database BizTalk uses to store tracking information. Basically, as (or soon after) a message is processed through the MessageBox, the TDDS copies the context data associated with a message from the tracking data tables to the tracking database.

Context data for a message includes information such as the Message ID, Service Instance ID, any promoted properties that are present in the message, and the Interchange ID. The Interchange ID is the same for all messages that are part of the same interchange — that is, if Message A is processed by Orchestration 1 that produces Message B during a send operation, Messages A and B will both have the same Interchange ID. This enables HAT to show the flow of messages through the workflow.

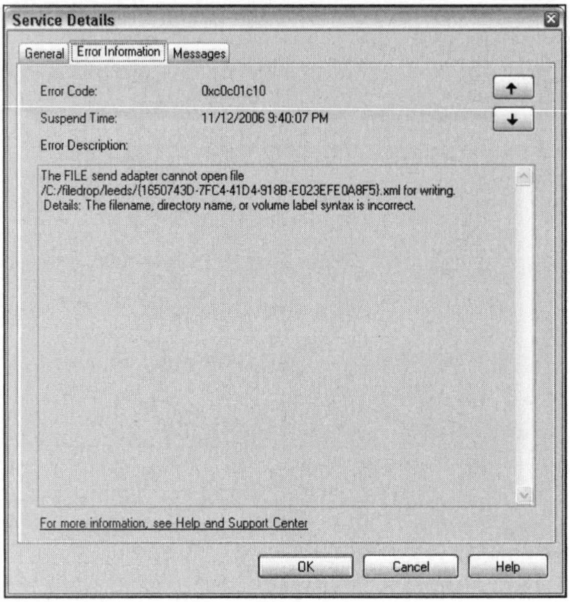

Figure 11-17

To view message flow information and the flow of events in the Orchestration Debugger, you must configure tracking correctly. You can do so by right-clicking on the relevant artifact (receive port, orchestration, or send port) and selecting the Tracking item in the BizTalk Server Administration Console. See the "Configuring Tracking Using BizTalk Administration Console" section of the online documentation, at http://msdn2.microsoft.com/en-us/library/aa559964.aspx.

Figure 11-18 shows the message flow for a suspended service instance — in this case, a send port that has been used by the General Routing orchestration to send a message using the File adapter. The inbound and outbound message can be seen in the message flow. At the top of the screen, the context information (highlighted in the figure) displays properties associated with the instance as well as useful error information. Often, the error information displayed can be used to resolve the issue.

In the case below, the message has failed to transmit due to a problem with the format of the string that the file adapter is trying to write to (that is, no filename has been specified for the message, only a folder). The %MessageID% placeholder should be used to generate a unique identifier for the message. The error information displayed at the top of the screenshot clearly indicates that this is the case. If you require further information about the flow of the message and services (orchestrations and send ports) that were called, you can click on the links for each of them (as indicated for the General Routing orchestration in Figure 11-18).

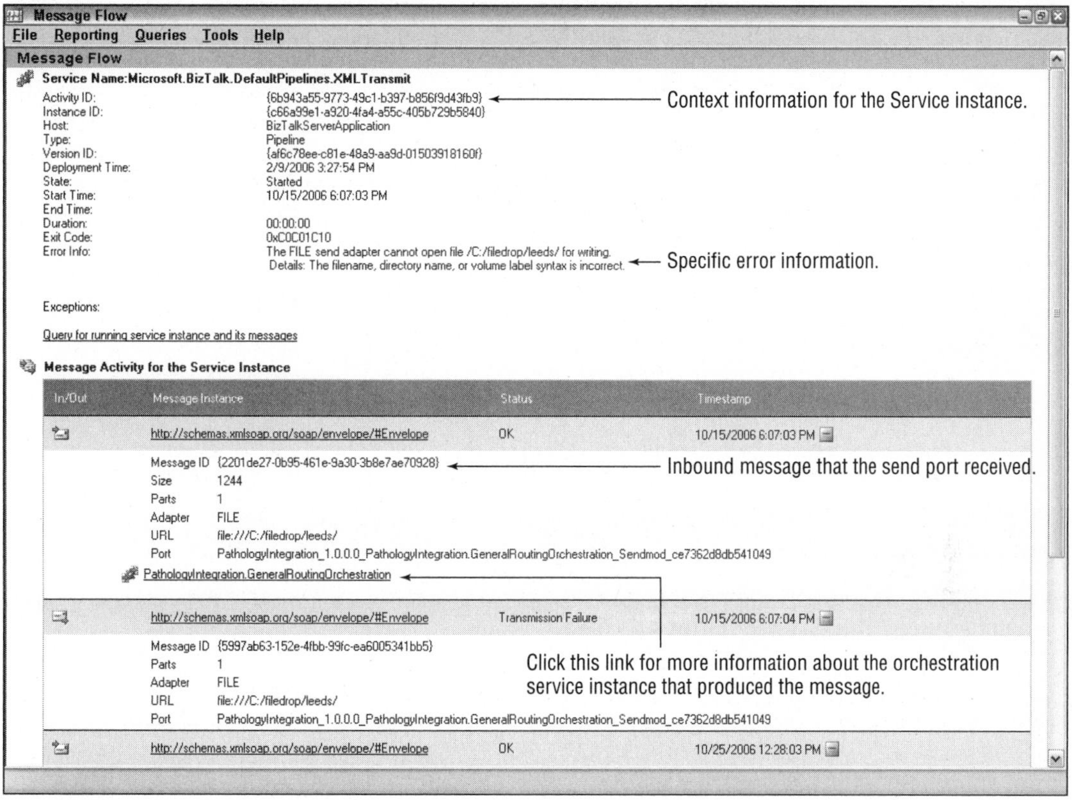

Figure 11-18

If an orchestration service instance is selected, there will be an option to Switch to Orchestration Debugger, which is displayed at the top of the page on the left. Click this to open the Orchestration Debugger, which shows the flow of events as that instance was executed. This enables you to determine the flow through the orchestration for that instance. This is illustrated in Figure 11-19. Timestamps are displayed on the left-hand side when a shape begins and ends execution. These are particularly useful when troubleshooting latency/performance-related issues, as it may be that the bottleneck in a system is not BizTalk but another back-end system that BizTalk communicates with during the execution of the orchestration. You also can insert breakpoints for an orchestration to allow detailed examination of the variables passed to and from the engine during execution. Note that this should *never* be used in production unless absolutely necessary, as setting a breakpoint will result in all instances of the orchestration not processing.

> *For more information on using the Orchestration Debugger, see the "Debugging Orchestrations" section of the online help, at* `http://msdn2.microsoft.com/en-us/library/aa560241.aspx`.

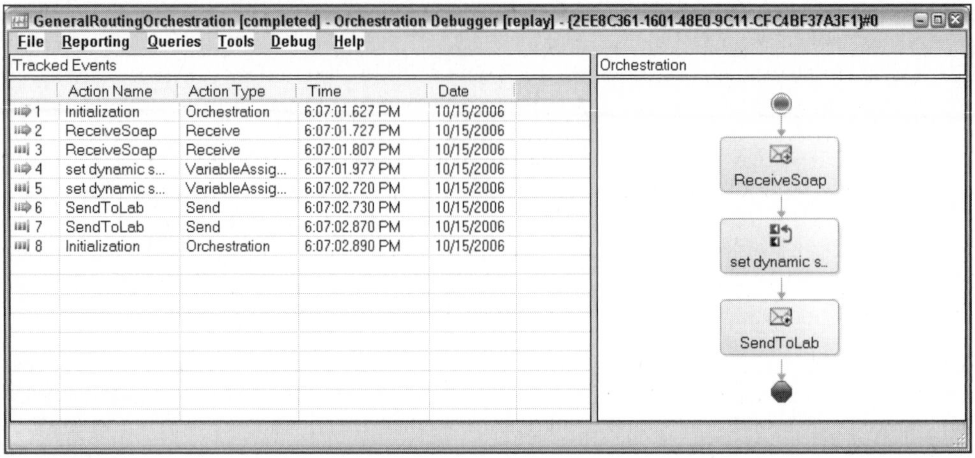

Figure 11-19

Subscriptions

Subscriptions are the technique that BizTalk uses to route messages that match particular parameters to the appropriate processes. BizTalk uses a publish-subscribe routing model to allow a message to be passed to multiple subscribing processes. For more information on the architecture of BizTalk, see Chapter 2. If a message is received by a receive port and has no valid subscriptions, a routing failure report will be thrown. This will be displayed as a suspended service instance on the Group Hub Page.

Routing failure reports are used, instead of discarding the message, because the most common cause for no subscribers being present for a message is due to an orchestration or a send port has not been enlisted correctly. When a send port or orchestration is enlisted, the subscription is configured within the MessageBox. Until this has been done, any message destined for that orchestration/send port will not be delivered for processing. If you see a routing failure report, you should check the Service Details (as shown in Figure 11-17) to view any error information specific to that instance.

The BizTalk Server Administration Console also enables you to view the subscriptions that are currently active in your group. To do this, open the Group Hub Page. At the top of the screen, you will see tabs with any queries you have already run. Click the New Query tab. In the Query Builder will be a drop-down list next to the Search For row that appears at the top. Select Subscriptions and then click Run Query. This will display the first 50 subscriptions found in the MessageBox (the limit automatically added by the Query Builder). If you cannot determine from this list whether the subscription you are searching for is present, you can add another row and specify the service name (i.e., the orchestration name) that you are looking for a subscription for.

Just as when troubleshooting a suspended instance, you can right-click on a result displayed and select Subscription Details. The General tab that is displayed allows you to see information such as whether it is an activation (which initiates a new orchestration) or instance subscription (which is created when responses need to be correlated to an already existing orchestration). The Expression tab enables you to view the expression used to determine which messages should be picked up by this subscription. When looking at the reasons why a message has not been picked up by a particular subscription, this Expression screen and the service details error information tend to be the best resources for finding the root cause.

Essential ESSO Maintenance

Unbeknownst to many customers, BizTalk has a key dependency on Enterprise Single Sign-On (ESSO); this is because there are two uses of ESSO. The first use is to store encrypted user credentials, which can then be transmitted to various systems. Most heterogeneous environments require different credentials to access different systems, often meaning that users have to remember multiple credentials for different systems. This can have negative effects, such as users using simple passwords for systems or even using the same password for all of them and never changing it. This is likely to introduce security vulnerabilities in your system. With ESSO, the credentials are stored securely in the encrypted Single Sign-On (SSODB) database, meaning that users do not have to remember separate credentials for each application they use. This is the most common interpretation of how BizTalk uses ESSO.

However, ESSO is also used to securely store send port and receive location configuration information for BizTalk. Because the information contained in the configuration of these items (URLs, file drop locations, etc.) is often confidential, it needs to be stored safely and securely. This means that the BizTalk service requires access to the ESSO service in order to be able to access this configuration information and, hence, send and receive messages. The SSODB can also be used to store your application configuration data (see Chapters 12 and 13). Therefore, it is essential that you take the steps outlined in this section to ensure ESSO is always available.

The Master Secret Server

ESSO uses the SSODB database to store all encrypted credentials. Information is encrypted and decrypted from this database using a key called the *master secret key*. The first BizTalk Server that is installed in your group will have an ESSO service installed, referred to as the *master secret server* because the master secret key is stored in the registry on this box. On each additional BizTalk Server that is installed in the group, an ESSO service will be present, which has to start up successfully and without errors for BizTalk to start (see Figure 11-20).

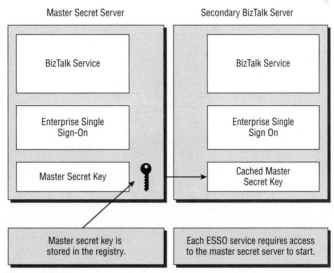

Figure 11-20

For each of these instances of ESSO to start, they require access to the master secret server ESSO instance so that the key can be cached by the service. Access to the master secret server is now not required until the service is restarted. If the master secret server fails, when the other ESSO services restarted, they would no longer be able to access the master secret server and cache a copy of the key. Therefore, they would not be able to access information in the SSODB database and the service would not start correctly. This, in turn, would prevent BizTalk from starting correctly. To resolve this, you would need to recreate the SSODB database, which would require you to reconfigure the full BizTalk group — typically, a lengthy process and one that you want to avoid! Therefore, it is critical that you back up your master secret key and know how to restore it. This section will describe the process.

Backing Up the Master Secret Key

If you have not already done so during setup, it is *essential* that you back up the master secret key. This enables you to promote another server in the group to the master secret server status in the event of its failure and avoids having to reconfigure the full BizTalk group! To do this:

1. Open a command prompt and navigate to `C:\Program Files\Common Files\Enterprise Single Sign-On`.

2. To back up the master secret, run the command `ssoconfig -backupsecret <location of backup file>` (for example, `ssoconfig -backupsecret \\backupserver\master-secret\btsserver.bak`).

3. The utility will prompt you for a password to protect the file and then ask you to reenter this.

   Note that as well as having a copy of the backup file, you should ensure that the password used to protect this is documented somewhere (e.g., in your disaster recovery documentation).

4. The utility will then ask you to add a password hint; make sure that this is something useful that would be understood by another user in your organization.

Alternatively, this can be done from the ESSO Administration Console, which can be accessed from Start ⇨ Programs ⇨ Enterprise Single Sign-On ⇨ SSO Administration. To back up the master secret key, expand the Enterprise Single Sign-On node, right-click System, and then select Backup Secret. When the Backup Secret window appears, enter the relevant information to back up the master secret.

It goes without saying that you need to ensure that the backup file is installed in a secure location that would be easily available in the event of server failure. This should definitely not be the local C:\. *You should ensure that the password used to protect the backup file is also kept secure. If someone has access to the backup file and the password associated with it, they could gain access to the confidential data stored in the SSODB database. Unfortunately, I have seen many customers leave themselves exposed to this.*

Moving the Master Secret Server

It is important that you consider how you are going to keep the master secret server available, if you decide not to cluster the master secret server (see the section below). It can still be made available, but not highly available, by having a well-documented process to promote one of your other ESSO servers to the master secret server and restore the master secret key to it. We will now walk through how this promotion-and-restore process can be done. We are going to assume that ESSO has already been installed and configured on this server and that it is part of the same SSO system.

1. The first step is to change the master secret server name that is stored in the credential database to reference the new master secret server. Log in to the current master secret server (if this is not available, do this on the new master secret server), open Notepad, and paste the following XML into the window:

```
<sso>
  <globalInfo>
      <secretServer>Server Name</secretServer>
  </globalInfo>
</sso>
```

You should replace the `Server Name` text with the name of the new master secret server. Save the file as an `.xml` file in the ESSO installation folder (the default location is `C:\Program Files\Common Files\Enterprise Single Sign-ON`).

2. Open a command prompt and change to the ESSO installation folder (for example, `C:\Program Files\Common Files\Enterprise Single Sign-ON`). Then type the following command, replacing `XMLFILE` with the name of the file you previously saved:

```
ssomanage -updatedb XMLFILE
```

3. The next stage is to log in to the computer you want to promote to master secret server. Restart the ESSO service on this server, and then open the ESSO Administration Console on the computer by going to Start ⇨ Programs ⇨ Enterprise Single Sign-On ⇨ SSO Administration. You need to ensure that you have access to your copy of the master secret key backup and know the password associated with it.

4. To restore the secret, right-click the system node and select Restore Secret. When the Restore Secret window appears, click the Browse button and browse to the location of the master secret backup file you created previously.

5. If required, you can click the Show button to display the password reminder that was set during the backup.

6. Enter the password for the file in the File password box, and then click OK. You should get a dialog box displaying a message indicating the secret has been restored successfully. You have now successfully moved the master secret server.

Clustering Options for the Master Secret Server

Because the master secret server is a single point of failure in your BizTalk group, it should be made highly available. This can be done using Windows clustering. The master secret server must be part of an active-passive cluster configuration. It can either be installed on its own server cluster or as part of one of your existing clusters. Given that the master secret server does not consume many resources, most customers opt to install it on the database cluster that the BizTalk databases use. This avoids the somewhat prohibitive costs of purchasing the additional resources required for an additional cluster but provides a highly available solution. Please note that if you do cluster the master secret server using the

BizTalk database cluster, it is recommended that it is contained in its own cluster group so that if it fails over it does not affect other clustered services such as SQL Server.

> For detailed information on how to cluster the master secret server, see `http://msdn2.microsoft.com/en-us/library/aa561823.aspx`.

Tools to Assist You

Microsoft Product Support Services (PSS) deals with problems of varying severities daily, ranging from minor issues during development to show-stopping issues in production on major systems. In addition to dealing with reactive issues, PSS also offers proactive services, such as architectural reviews and workshops designed to prevent the issues from occurring in the first place. To assist the engineers who perform this work and ensure that they are empowered to diagnose the root cause of an issue and resolve it as quickly as possible, a suite of tools has been developed internally. As the tools become widely used internally, they are often also released as downloads from one of the Microsoft web sites. Unfortunately, many customers are not aware of these tools and end up working much harder than is necessary to resolve an issue or remain dependent on PSS.

The purpose of this section is to empower you to be able to use many of the tools that are used by the PSS and Premier Field Engineers. In summary, this section will enable you to *work smarter, not harder*.

BizTalk Best Practices Analyzer (BPA)

This tool, which primarily examines production and staging environments, is designed to automatically examine a deployment of BizTalk 2006 and generate a list of issues pertaining to a list of best-practice standards. During the many problems that I have been called to resolve for customers, poor configuration has been the cause of a number of these problems. Poor configuration and maintenance can result in needless downtime for the mission-critical applications that often sit on top of this framework. The BPA tool detects common customer mistakes, such as failing to configure the Backup BizTalk Server or DTA Purge and Archive jobs, not backing up the master secret key, and failing to separate the BizTalk database Transaction log and data files. Automatic updates are available with the tool via the Web so that as new issues are discovered they are included in its knowledge base. Therefore, in my opinion, it is absolutely critical that you run this tool against all BizTalk environments as part of your build verification process.

The BPA gathers information from a variety of sources, including Windows Management Instrumentation (WMI), SQL Server, and the registry. The data that is collected from the machine is then analyzed by BPA to evaluate the deployment of BizTalk. No system settings are modified throughout this process.

You can download BPA from the BizTalk Server Best Practices Analyzer link at `www.microsoft.com/technet/prodtechnol/biztalk/downloads/bpa.mspx`.

Once you have downloaded the tool, extract the self-extracting file to a convenient location. From here, you can access the `readme.htm` file, which you should consult before installing or running the tool. In particular, you should note that the tool must be installed on a machine that has BizTalk 2006 running, and the account you either log in as or use to enter the credentials in the tool must be a member of the BizTalk Server Administrators Group as well as an administrator on every machine in the BizTalk Group and member of the SSO Administrators Group.

To start the tool, navigate to the installation directory (default is C:\Program Files\BizTalkBPA) and double-click BizTalkBPA.exe. The program will start and prompt you to download updates from the Internet; updates can also be downloaded manually. The welcome screen will then be displayed, which provides the option to either view existing scans or configure a new one. Figure 11-21 shows the configuration screen for a new scan. This screen allows the scan to be labeled with an identifier (particularly useful if you are scanning a lot of different environments). The location of the management database must then be specified. This is essential because it contains all the configuration information for the group, including the location of all the databases, the number and name of the BizTalk Servers, as well as all artifacts that have been deployed to the group. When you click the Start Scanning button, a progress window will be displayed. The scan should be completed in a couple of minutes but may take longer, depending on the number of servers in the group, load on the BizTalk and SQL Servers, and so on.

Once the scan has completed, an option is displayed to show a summary of the scan. Selecting this displays the summary screen, as shown in Figure 11-22. The report can be displayed in various formats, including a list format that you can skim to gain an idea of the result of the scan, and a tree format that is useful if you would like to drill down from the root to view the results.

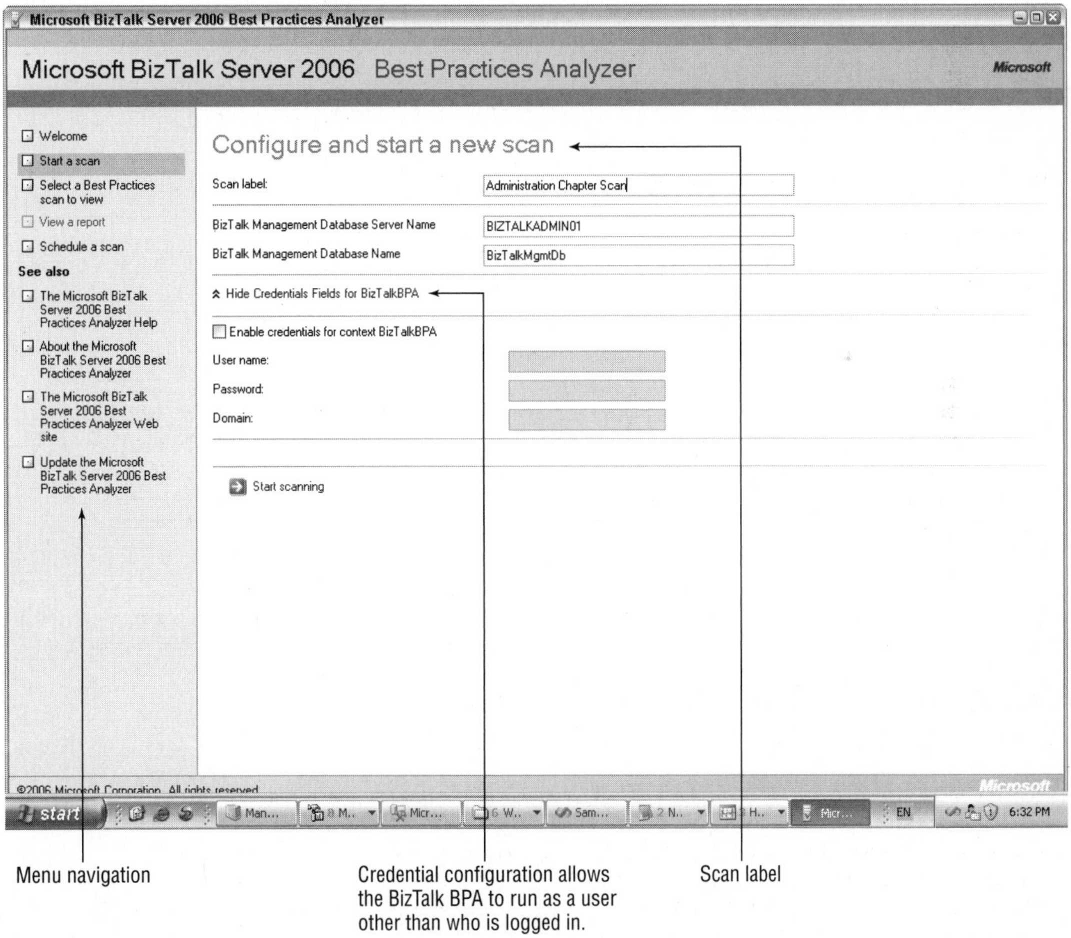

Menu navigation

Credential configuration allows the BizTalk BPA to run as a user other than who is logged in.

Scan label

Figure 11-21

Selecting an individual error provides links to the help file with detailed information on the issue and how to resolve it, as well as the option to remove the item from the report. (Use this only when you are certain that the alert can be ignored.) To view which items have been hidden from the report, select Other Reports and then the Hidden Items tab. It is always useful to check this to make sure that a critical error has not been flagged as hidden by a previous user of the tool. From personal experience, I assure you that the help entries are very useful and also provide links to the relevant section in the BizTalk 2006 online MSDN documentation if you do require any further information or background.

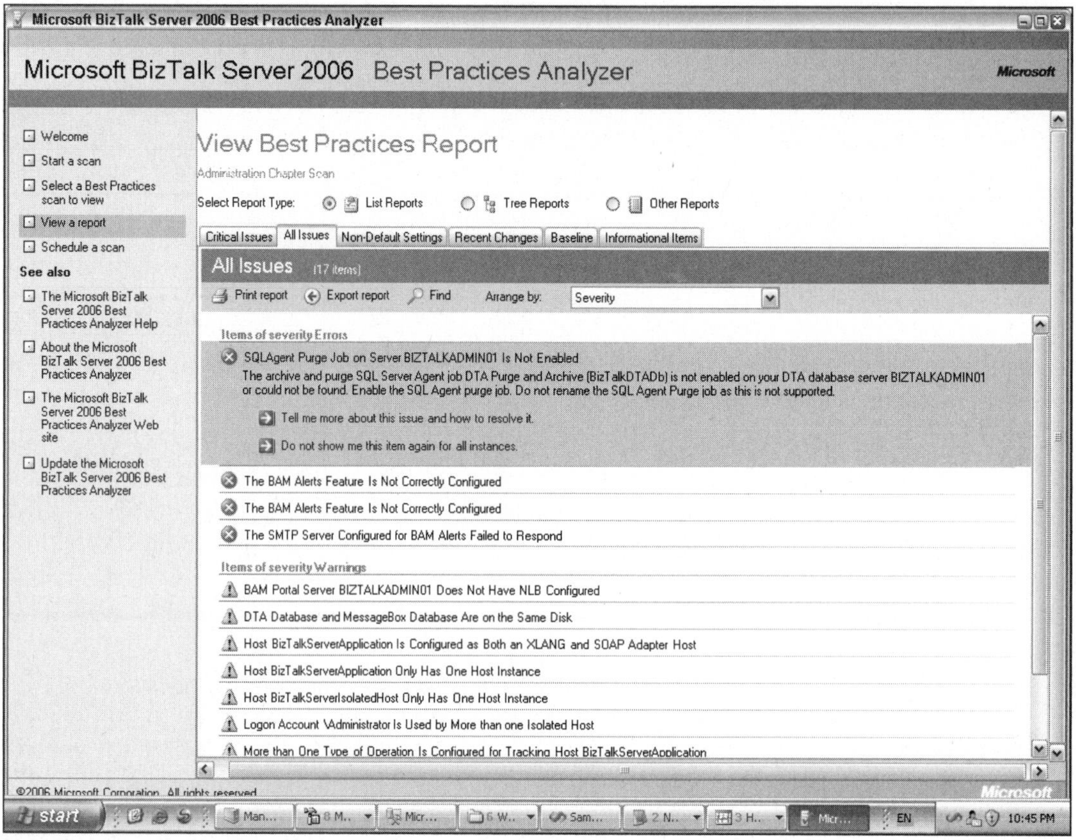

Figure 11-22

Hidden Tools with BizTalk 2006

Unbeknownst to many customers, a number of useful tools are contained in the Support\Tools folder of the BizTalk 2006 CD. There are versions for 32-bit and 64-bit operating systems. These tools were previously available only for internal use by the Product Group and PSS. As a best practice, you should include these tools in your base build for BizTalk. They provide a lot of very useful information. Having these tools preinstalled as part of the base build means that you can collect the information that PSS requires quickly if a problem occurs. This section will cover how and when these tools should be used to help diagnose problems. If you require more detailed information, consult the Readme.doc file, which is contained in the same folder.

> *In addition to installing these tools on your base BizTalk build, you should always create debug symbols for your solution and have them ready in case they are required by PSS (such as when debugging a custom component).*

PSSDiag for BizTalk

PSSDiag (http://support.microsoft.com/kb/830232), an internal tool, was originally available only if you had a PSS call raised with Microsoft and was primarily aimed at troubleshooting SQL Server problems. An external version, which differed slightly, was then released to the Web. Both tools perform similar jobs but differ slightly in the options that they expose. Over the years, this tool has been used on countless PSS cases to collect the following information in an automated way:

❑   Performance counters

❑   SQL Profiler Traces

❑   SQL Blocking Script output

❑   Event logs

❑   The output of other testing tools such as SQLDiag (http://msdn2.microsoft.com/en-us/library/ms162833.aspx)

The data collection can be customized to change the data collected, sample interval, and so on.

In order to automate the collection of data that is necessary to resolve BizTalk issues, PSSDiag has been customized to collect the data that is required by the PSS Engineer to resolve your issue. This tool is included in the Support/Tools folder of the BizTalk 2006 CD.

Running the Tool

To run the tool, you must first download the Platform SDK from http://go.microsoft.com/fwlink/?LinkId=21975. This contains the tracelog.exe file, which is required to collect the BizTalk Trace. Download the installer for your operating system and then start it (Note that you cannot run the PSDK-x86.exe installer unless you have connectivity to the Internet.) When prompted, choose the Custom Installation option. Select a location to install the SDK (default is C:\Program Files\Microsoft Platform SDK), and then, on the Custom Installation screen, clear all available features and make sure that only the tools featured under the Microsoft Windows Core SDK feature are selected. Your screen should look similar to Figure 11-23. From here, click Next and then Next again to start the installation.

You should then copy the contents of the relevant folder from the Support/Tools folder on the BizTalk CD (i.e., x86 folder for Intel 32 bit-based systems) to a location on your computer — for this section, we will assume this is C:\BTS Support Tools. Once the installation of the Platform SDK has been completed, if it asks you to restart the system, select No. You should then locate the BIN folder, which is beneath the Microsoft Platform SDK folder, and copy the Tracelog.exe file from this location to C:\BTS Support Tools.

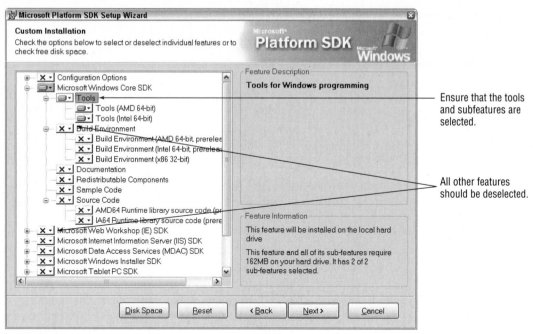

Figure 11-23

To start PSSDiag, go to a command prompt and type **PSSDiag /G**. When prompted for the trace level, enter **–high**. (There are other options, but this is the most useful.) This trace level determines the level of detail that is captured about the engine processing while the trace is run. PSS engineers will typically require a high-level trace in order to troubleshoot a problem. PSSDiag will then be running, as illustrated in Figure 11-24. You should now reproduce the issue you are having. Once the issue has been reproduced successfully, press Ctrl+C to stop PSSDiag. The data will now have been collected in the C:\BTS Support Tools\output folder.

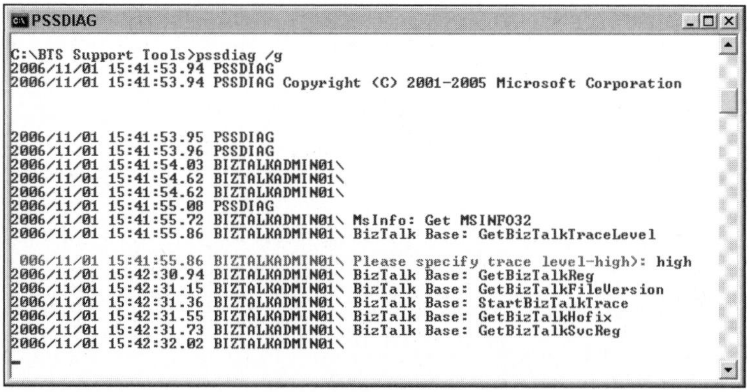

Figure 11-24

Data the Tool Collects

The data that is collected by the tool is stored in the Output folder (in this case, `C:\BTS Support Tools\Output`). The tool collects useful information, including:

❑ **BizTalk Trace** — This binary trace can be formatted internally by PSS to show the engineer what is happening in the BizTalk Engine when the issue is reproduced. Unfortunately, there are no external trace format files available, so the information can be analyzed only by PSS.

❑ **BizTalk HAT information** — A text file is produced in the Output directory that details all the suspended instances present in the MessageBox on the system it was run against.

❑ **Event logs** — The application, security, and system logs are all collected as CSV files. The CSV format is preferable to the EVT format because it preserves all the information from any errors and doesn't require the DLLs that produced the error to be present on the system that the log is analyzed on.

❑ **Performance logs** — The tool collects more than 60 performance counters by default. You can view and edit these by looking at the `PSSDiag.ini` file, located in the `C:\BTS Support Tools` folder.

❑ **BizTalk Registry settings** — All relevant BizTalk Registry keys are exported to a `.reg` file. If the error is occurring only on one system (for example, in production but not staging), you should use the Visual Studio command-prompt tool WinDiff to compare the registry settings between the two environments. You can launch WinDiff by typing **windiff** from a Visual Studio command prompt.

❑ **Attributes (version, size, modified date, etc.) of BizTalk executables** — Attributes provide the file versions of all the main executables used by BizTalk and all its assemblies that are present in the GAC. You also can use WinDiff to compare the file versions if the issue you are experiencing is occurring in only one of your environments. Note that on more than one occasion I have seen customers have an issue occur in one environment only either due to different registry settings or different file versions been present.

❑ **BizTalk hotfix information** — PSS maintains a directory of the changes to version numbers that are made by any hotfix. PSSDiag for BizTalk collects the file versions, attributes, and so on for BizTalk files; therefore, this can be used to determine what hotfixes have been deployed to the system. Note that the tool does not actually list the hotfixes that have been applied to your system; rather, it lists the file version numbers and other information that you can use to determine this. The hotfixes that have been installed for BizTalk can be determined by looking in Add/Remove Programs in Control Panel.

❑ **MSInfo Information** — This collects information regarding your system, such as device drivers that have been installed.

PSSDiag collects the data from your system that either PSS or you can use to find the root cause of the problem. It is certainly much easier to take the BizTalk trace using PSSDiag than doing this manually (see http://support.microsoft.com/kb/835451). In order to speed problem resolution, it is advisable to set up the tool in advance so that it can be run immediately if an issue occurs. This is important because issues can appear intermittently; if the tool has to be set up, you may not have the chance to record the data in time.

Memory Dumps

Sometimes the information that PSSDiag collects may not be enough to determine the root cause of an issue. If you are working with PSS in this situation, it is likely that you will be asked to take a "dump" of the process; this is a copy of what was happening in the process at a point in time. When troubleshooting BizTalk, you typically are interested in mini-dumps (that is, a dump of one particular process), rather than a full dump of the full memory of a machine.

There are two types of mini-dumps that can be taken:

❑ A **hang dump** provides a snapshot of the process at a particular point in time. Usually, this is used when an issue is occurring that causes your process to become unresponsive (for example, it is not making progress or doing useful work, but does not crash). In this scenario, multiple hang dumps will typically be taken. These can then be debugged to determine the cause of the problem, which may be due to an infinite loop. Typically, you will see very high CPU usage for the BizTalk process in Task Manager when this happens. Multiple dumps of a hung process will be taken to see if the threads in the dumps are deadlocked on a common resource.

❑ A **crash dump** is taken when a particular process is crashing under certain conditions. In this situation, a debugger will be attached to a process and, when it crashes, a dump of the memory for that process at that point in time will be written to disk.

Once the dumps have been collected, they can be analyzed by the PSS engineer, who can use them to determine the cause of the problem (whether it is a problem with custom code or a Microsoft component). If the PSS engineer identifies that it is a bug in a Microsoft product, the dump will be analyzed by the Product Group, who will then use it to determine the source of the bug. The PSS engineer can also use this information to see whether the issue experienced by the customer has already been fixed in a previous hotfix. In this situation, PSS will ask the customer to install the hotfix in their environment.

Typically, the tool that is used to collect dumps is ADPlus, which is included in the Debugging tools for Windows (www.microsoft.com/whdc/devtools/debugging/default.mspx). For a knowledge base article detailing how to use ADPlus to troubleshoot hangs and crashes, refer to http://support .microsoft.com/kb/286350. It is suggested that you install the debugging tools proactively on your system as part of your base build and read the information contained at these links to ensure that in the event of a problem you are able to collect the required information for PSS.

BizTalk Assembly Checker and Remote GAC Tool

As you know, the BizTalk artifacts that a developer creates in Visual Studio are compiled into an assembly. When deployed, the versions of assemblies that are present in the Management database must also be present in the local GAC on the BizTalk servers that will be processing these artifacts. If during deployment an updated version of an assembly containing, say, an orchestration is registered in the Management database but is not registered in the GAC on any of the BizTalk Servers that will be processing the artifact, it will lead to suspended service instances if a server attempts to process this orchestration without the assembly being present in the GAC.

To ensure that this doesn't happen, you should ensure that your deployment practices are documented and automated, where possible, and validate that all assemblies have been deployed successfully. The BizTalk Assembly Checker and Remote GAC tool is designed to check the versions of assemblies that are deployed to the Management database. The tool can then verify that they are correctly registered in the GAC on all your BizTalk Servers. If you have multiple servers in your environment, this tool allows you to check that they all have the correct assemblies in the GAC and deploy any that are missing.

Running the Tool

To run the tool, you will need to be logged in with administrative privileges on the machine running the tool. The account must also have DBO permissions on the Management database and administrative privileges on all BizTalk Servers. The machine the tool is running from must have BizTalk Server 2006 installed. Figure 11-25 shows the screen that is displayed when the executable BTSAssemblyChecker.exe is run. Once you have the screen below displayed, you should type in the name of the Management database and server that you would like to connect to and click the Connect button.

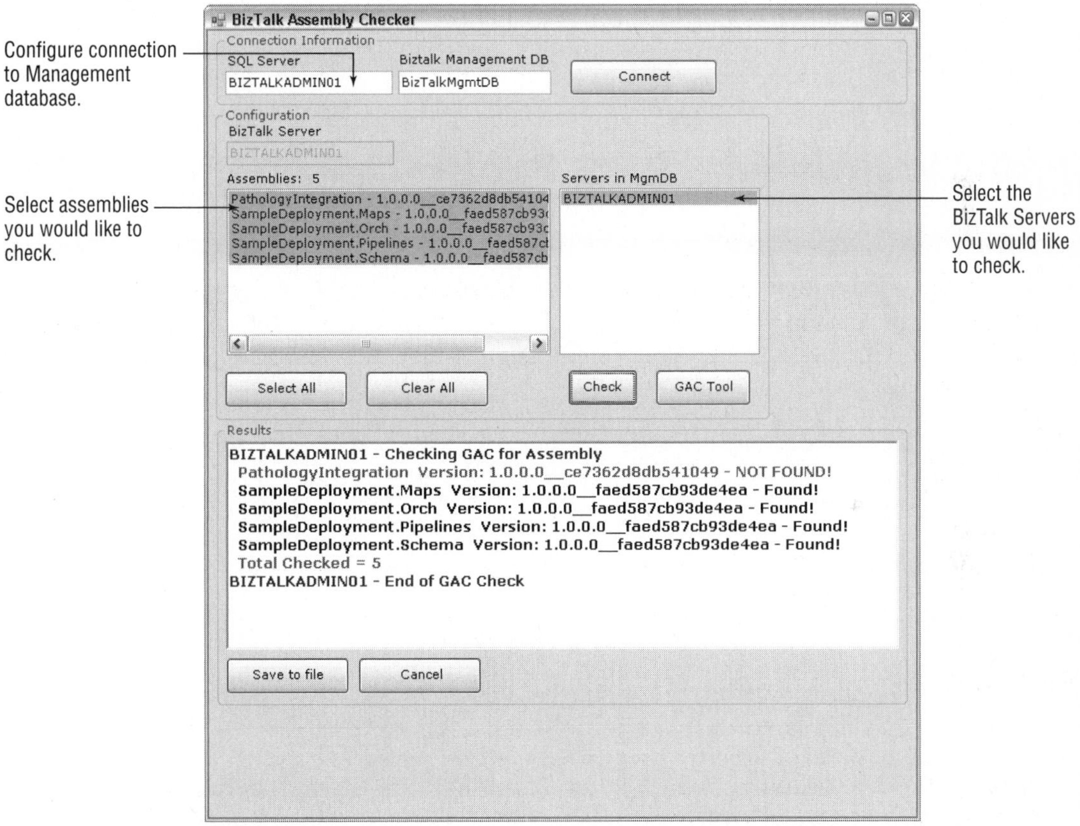

Figure 11-25

This will then display the assemblies that are present in the Management database and the BizTalk servers that are present. You must now configure the product to scan the servers for your chosen assemblies. To do this, hold down the Control key and select the assemblies you would like to check, and then do the same for the servers you would like to check. Then click the Check button. A report will now be displayed in the results window, indicating which assemblies were present and which were missing. This is very useful information that would take a long time to gather manually. As shown in Figure 11-25, one of the assemblies was not present on the server that I scanned. To resolve this, the assembly should be added to the GAC on the local server.

Important Information about the Tool

One of the features of the tool is the ability to register missing assemblies in the GAC automatically on the servers from which they are missing. To use this feature, you must run this tool on a BizTalk server that has the missing assemblies present in the GAC (because the tool copies missing assemblies from the local GAC on the machine it is run on). To use this feature, click the GAC Tool button. This will open a screen that prompts you to select the server and the missing assemblies. You can then check a box to register the assemblies and copy them across to the machine. Unfortunately, this feature does not work in the version of the tool that was included in the BizTalk 2006 CD. If you try to run this, a message box will display the error message GACUtils.CopyFile Error. This bug has now been fixed in the latest version, which you can download from www.gotdotnet.com/workspaces/releases/viewuploads .aspx?id=d59b9df0-5ec5-42e4-8c13-889d6dc4b48f.

Troubleshooting DTC Problems

The Microsoft Distributed Transaction Coordinator (MSDTC) service is the component included with Windows 2000 and above (also available on NT4) that is responsible for providing and coordinating transactions between multiple Windows machines. This is used by COM and .NET to provide transactional capabilities for programs built on either of these systems. To ensure that all operations are transactional in an environment that may potentially contain multiple servers all performing different roles, BizTalk uses MSDTC to ensure that the operations are transactionally consistent. Figure 11-26 shows the high-level architecture for the distributed transaction that is used by BizTalk to dequeue messages in a transactional manner from MQSeries and publish them into the MessageBox.

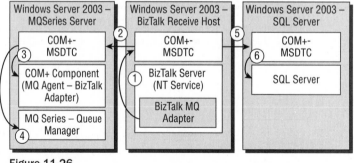

Figure 11-26

Three servers are involved in the transaction: the MQSeries server, the BizTalk Receive host server, and the SQL server that hosts the BizTalk MessageBox. MSDTC is used throughout to ensure that the operation is done atomically (that is, the message is either successfully removed from MQSeries and published into the MessageBox or the transaction is aborted and it remains on the queue). MSDTC is also used whenever BizTalk persists data to the MessageBox (for example, when a persistence point is hit in an orchestration). It is clear from these scenarios that if MSDTC is not working correctly, it is impossible for BizTalk to perform any of these actions in a transactional manner. This section will show how

MSDTC should be configured for normal BizTalk operation as well as the tools that should be used to troubleshoot suspected problems.

Checking Firewall Configuration

BizTalk requires MSDTC to communicate with its databases; MSDTC in turn depends on a remote procedure call (RPC) in order to operate. In the default configuration, the RPC uses a random port above 1024. Organizations often separate their BizTalk and SQL servers using one or more firewalls. This poses a problem for BizTalk because firewall administrators tend to minimize the number of open ports, hence blocking RPC communication and thus stopping BizTalk from communicating with its databases. Many customers have encountered this problem only when they have begun testing in their production environment. The typical reason for this is that their preproduction environment did not have a firewall between the servers. The RPC can be configured to work across a firewall and therefore allow BizTalk to communicate with the SQL Server on the other side. Refer to the knowledge base article "How to configure RPC dynamic port allocation to work with firewalls," at http://support.microsoft.com/kb/154596.

Verifying NetBIOS Resolution

For successful MSDTC operations to occur between machines, both machines must be able to resolve the NetBIOS name to the correct IP address. When troubleshooting any suspected MSDTC issue, you must first check that these names are been resolved correctly. Perform the following steps on each machine:

1. Open a command prompt and type **hostname** to display the NetBIOS name of the machine.

2. Type **ipconfig –all** to list all the IP addresses in use on your system.

3. To verify the resolution of the other machine, type **ping <NetBIOS name of computer>**. If this works successfully, one of the IP addresses associated with the other machine should be returned from the `ping` command.

4. If NetBIOS name resolution is not working, you can either add a record manually to the Hosts or LMHosts file (see http://support.microsoft.com/kb/101927/en-us) or add the entry to the server used for NetBIOS name resolution. This is typically a Windows Internet Name Service (WINS) server. For more information on installing and configuring WINS, see http://technet2.microsoft.com/windowsserver/en/technologies/wins.mspx.

Checking MSDTC Security Options

Windows 2003 SP1 and XP SP2 introduced improved security enhancements for MSDTC access over the network. By default, network DTC access is now disabled on these operating systems, meaning that the machine will not accept or send network DTC traffic. Given that BizTalk requires this, you must modify the default network DTC configuration for proper operation. This is one of the most common MSDTC issues that I have seen when working with customers.

> **Network DTC access is strictly required only if a multibox installation of BizTalk has been done (including separating SQL and BizTalk on separate boxes) or if an adapter that requires MSDTC, such as the MQSeries adapter, is used.**

To configure the correct MSDTC settings:

1. Go to the Administrative Tools folder in Control Panel and double-click Component Services. This will open the Microsoft Management Console (MMC).

2. Expand Component Services and open the Computers folder.

3. Right-click My Computer, select Properties, and then click the MSDTC tab.

4. Configure the MSDTC security settings as shown in the following table. Figure 11-27 shows a typical configuration.

Option	Default Value (XP SP2 or 2003 SP1)	Recommendation
Network DTC Access	Disabled	This should be enabled to allow the MSDTC service to access the network.
Client and Administration		
Allow Remote Clients	Disabled	Leave disabled.
Allow Remote Administration	Disabled	Leave disabled.
Transaction Manager Communication		
Allow Inbound	Disabled	Enable this to allow transactions that originate from a remote computer to run on the local computer.
Allow Outbound	Disabled	Enable this to allow the local machine to initiate a transaction on a remote machine.
Mutual Authentication Required	Enabled	Leave enabled if all machines involved in the communication are running XP SP2, 2003 SP1 or above, as this sets the greatest security mode that is available at present for network communication.
Incoming Caller Authentication Required	Disabled	Enable this if MSDTC is running as a clustered service on any of the machines (for example, when the SQL Server used by BizTalk is clustered). This option requires only the remote connection to be authenticated.
No Authentication Required	Disabled	Enable this if pre–XP SP2 or 2003 SP1 machines are involved in the communication. It can also be used if MSDTC is running on two machines in separate domains that do not have a trust relationship established.
Enable Transaction Internet Protocol (TIP) Transactions	Disabled	Enable this if you are using the BAM Portal.
Enable XA Transactions	Disabled	Enable this if you are communicating with an XA transaction–based system, such as when using the MQSeries adapter.

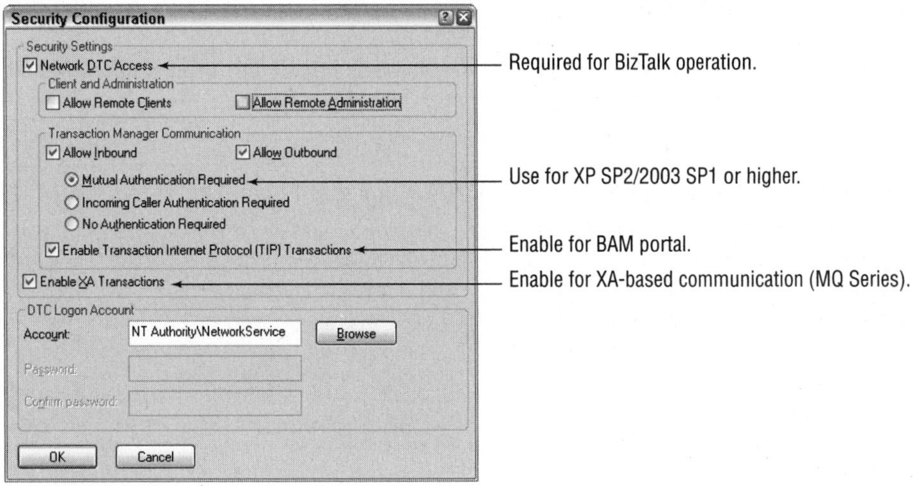

Figure 11-27

Checking Windows XP SP2 Registry Settings

If you are running the BizTalk runtime on Windows XP SP2 in your development environment, read this section carefully. (Note that you should only ever run the BizTalk runtime on Windows XP in development environments.) To enhance security, Windows XP SP2 requires any calls to the RPC interface to be authenticated. If you are running BizTalk or SQL Server on this platform, perform the following procedure to ensure that the EnableAuthEpResolution and RestrictRemoteClients Registry keys exist, and that their values are set as shown in the following table. This ensures that remote machines can access the RPC interface on the machine.

1. Go to Start ⇨ Run, and then enter **regedit.exe**. This will open the Registry Editor.

2. Navigate to HKYEY_LOCAL_MACHINE\SOFTWARE\Policies\Microsoft\Windows NT. (Note that this was one of the keys that was introduced in the fixes included in XP SP2.) There should be an RPC key under this. If it doesn't exist, you must create it.

3. Create the DWORD entries as shown in the following table.

DWORD	Default Value (XP SP2)	Recommendation
EnableAuthEpResolution	0 (disabled)	Set to 1 (enabled) to require clients to authenticate themselves when they make a call to the RPC endpoint mapper to determine which endpoint they need to connect to (for dynamic endpoints).
RestrictRemoteClients	1 (enabled) This setting permits access to interfaces only by using authenticated connections	Set to 0 (disabled) to enable anonymous access to remote interfaces.

4. Close the Registry Editor.

For more information on the RPC changes that were made in the fixes included in XP SP2, see `http://support.microsoft.com/kb/838191`.

Checking DTC Connectivity

The DTCPing and DTCTester tools are very useful for testing DTC connectivity between two servers. They can be used to quickly determine whether DTC is the problem or whether it is another issue. DTCPing allows you to test DTC's underlying dependencies (for example, NETBIOS name resolution and RPC). DTCTester allows you to test that actual DTC transactions can take place against a specified SQL server. It is recommended that when you use the tools, you test connectivity in both directions on both servers to verify that DTC connectivity is functional in both directions.

More information and the downloads for the tools can be found at the following links:

❑ **DTCPing download** — `http://download.microsoft.com/download/d/0/0/d00c8f6b-135d-4441-a97b-9de16a1935c1/dtcping.exe`

❑ **How to use DTCTester (includes download link)** — `http://support.microsoft.com/kb/293799`

❑ **How to troubleshoot MSDTC firewall issues** — `http://support.microsoft.com/default.aspx?scid=kb;EN-US;Q306843`

Preventive Administration Tasks

Many times when looking at the cause of a problem with customers during the aftermath of a serious outage, it is found that simple preventive administration could have either stopped the problem altogether or ensured that it was discovered before causing an outage. This section covers the things that, in my experience, tend to be done only after a serious problem has been experienced. If the customer is lucky, this will be on a staging or development environment; unfortunately for some, this often happens in production. Time and time again, I see customers with problems that have affected their project and sometimes their business that could have been avoided had they taken the time to do some regular preventive administration of their system.

Microsoft Baseline Security Analyzer

The Microsoft Baseline Security Analyzer (MBSA) has identified many issues for me onsite that customers typically miss, such as missing service packs on SQL Server and service accounts that are running with local administrator privileges. This is one of the first tools that I use when performing a Supportability Review of an environment. MBSA checks one or more machine's security updates against those from the Microsoft Update catalog. You can use MBSA to scan all the Microsoft Windows machines in the environment (for example, BizTalk, SQL Server, and any other Windows machine that BizTalk could potentially communicate with, such as SharePoint or IIS). In addition to checking the underlying operating system's security updates, MBSA checks many other components that BizTalk depends on, such as the .NET Framework. It is recommended that you run this tool on a regular basis in all your environments to test your patch management process.

> *For more information on the tool and instruction on how to use it, visit* `http://support` `.microsoft.com/kb/895660` *and* `www.microsoft.com/mbsa`.

UK SDC BizTalk 2006 Documenter

PSS often has to troubleshoot a problem remotely; however, it is often difficult to possess a complete understanding of a customer's environment, and setting up a complete reproduction environment can be quite time-consuming. Sometimes it is not even feasible to do this, due to the dependencies on external systems and other elements. In this situation, the UK SDC BizTalk 2006 Documenter is one of the tools that I request customers to run on their BizTalk environment. This tool generates a compiled help file that contains details of the BizTalk configuration. This output allows you to view all BizTalk artifacts on the system, including schemas, maps, pipelines, and orchestrations, as well as how these are grouped together into applications. PSS often finds this a useful tool for troubleshooting and verifying configuration settings. Customers can also use this for producing accurate, reliable documentation.

> *You can download the UK SDC BizTalk 2006 Documenter from* `http://www.codeplex.com/` `BizTalkDocumenter`.

The tool generates documentation like that shown in Figure 11-28. It allows you to see how the BizTalk artifacts have been separated into applications, how many applications there are, the flow of events in an orchestration, and much more. It is often useful to use this output as a point of reference when looking at error codes, particularly for systems that you do not have access to. For instance, if an error in the Event log indicates a problem with a particular orchestration, you can navigate to the process overview and code elements section of the `.chm` file and understand the flow of messages through the orchestration, as well as any custom code that is called/used within any expression shapes.

The hosts section of the documentation provides information on their configuration, including which service accounts the instances are running as and which orchestrations are running within the host. All this information can be useful when finding the cause of a problem. For instance, if from the output you see that only one in-process host is configured and the system is suffering poor performance, it may be due to thread starvation. (See Chapter 9 for more information on this.)

The installation of this tool is very straightforward. Simply download the Zip file from the aforementioned location. This file contains a single MSI file that should be run on your target system to start the Installation Wizard. The default installation options are perfectly fine for all the situations I have experienced. Once the tool has been installed, you should run it from Start ⇨ Programs ⇨ UK SDC BizTalk 2006 Documenter. This will display the configuration screen shown in Figure 11-29. From here you should specify the server name and database name for the Management database. Optionally, you can output documentation on the rules engine, as well. The Select Documentation Type screen allows you to choose whether to document the configuration for the complete BizTalk group or for only a specific application.

> *The Orchestration Info screen enables you to select and view orchestrations in an ad hoc manner. If the saved orchestration option is chosen from this screen, it outputs a copy of the process flow to a JPEG. This is handy when you need to produce documentation containing screenshots of your orchestrations.*

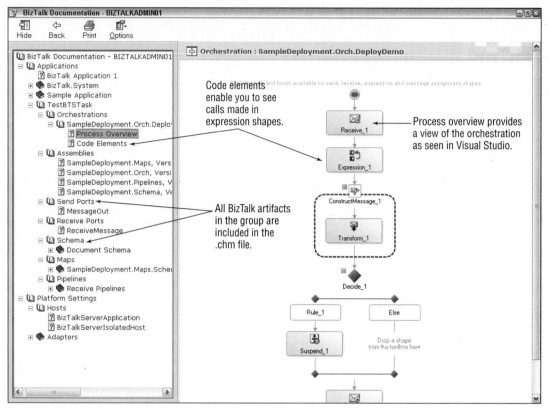

Figure 11-28

MPSReports

MPSReports is a tool that can be used in a similar way to PSSDiag for BizTalk — that is, to gather information from a system that can be used by an experienced engineer to troubleshoot a problem. Unfortunately, no BizTalk-specific version is available right now, although much of the BizTalk-specific troubleshooting information required is already collected by PSSDiag for BizTalk. Additional information about the underlying platform BizTalk is installed on can be required when troubleshooting. This tool collects useful information such as which group policies are applied to a machine, cluster configuration, network configuration, and IIS metabase information.

When troubleshooting issues, I find this tool particularly useful to collect information from the SQL Server(s) that BizTalk is using. The tool collects information without modifying the Registry or any other operating system or application settings. A number of versions are available, each of which collects information tailored to its particular use. The versions available include Directory Services, Networking, Clustering, SQL, Software Update Services, and MDAC. A readme file is included with each version. Typically, the information collected includes all Event logs on the system (normally these are gathered in EVT and TXT format), driver information, hotfix information, .NET Framework version (particularly relevant to BizTalk), network configuration, and system diagnostics information. The tools are very straightforward to run.

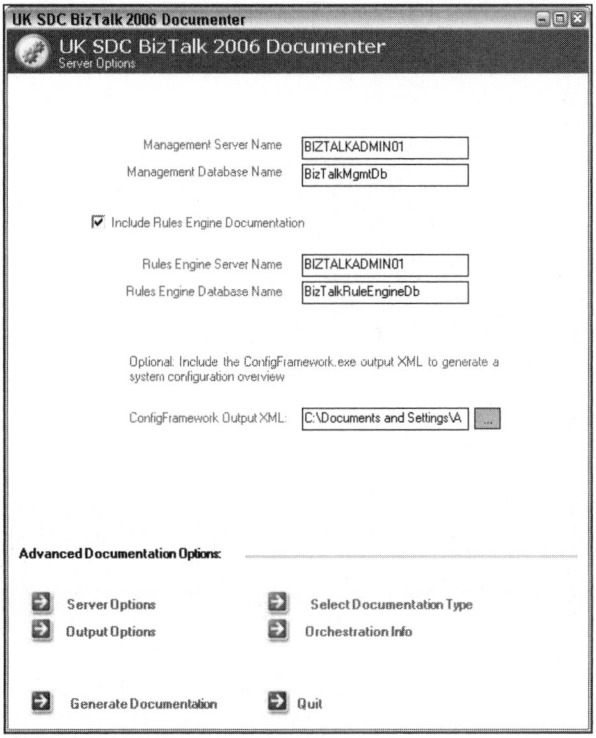

Figure 11-29

You can download the various versions of MPSReports from www.microsoft.com/downloads/
details.aspx?FamilyID=CEBF3C7C-7CA5-408F-88B7-F9C79B7306C0&displaylang=en.

SQL Server — From a BizTalk Perspective

BizTalk servers are essentially stateless. The SQL Server databases store all BizTalk's configuration, tracking, and processing information that they require for normal operation. Of these, the MessageBox is the heart of BizTalk. If it is not performing quickly and efficiently, neither will BizTalk. This section covers the things about SQL Server that all BizTalk developers and administrators should be aware of. This includes a high-level overview of the MessageBox structure, how SQL Server Agent maintains the database, and the BizTalk backup and restoration process. There are entire books written on administering and maintaining SQL Server; therefore, we will cover only the BizTalk-specific piece here. We will begin by describing the structure of the MessageBox.

How Messages Are Stored in the MessageBox

The MessageBox is a huge database that is essentially BizTalk's storage engine during processing. The most important point to make is that *no changes whatsoever* are supported to the MessageBox. You can look at the things we highlight in this section, but you must under no circumstances make any changes, as this may break something that BizTalk relies on. In this section, we are primarily focused on understanding how the physical messages themselves are stored in the MessageBox database.

All physical messages within BizTalk are stored across four tables in the MessageBox database: Spool, MessageParts, Parts, and Fragments. The reason for this is that each message can consist of one or more part, and each part consists of one or more fragments.

The fragmentation of messages within BizTalk can be controlled to some degree. The BizTalk group's large message fragment size setting is used to determine when the Messaging Engine will overflow a message into the MessageBox before it has completed processing. This is done to help avoid out-of-memory (OOM) conditions within the BizTalk process when processing in the context of a receive port. The Message Agent, which runs within the BizTalk service and is the layer of abstraction between the service and the MessageBox (see Chapter 2), also autofragments data. This is done regardless of the fragment size and is done to try to prevent loading too much data into memory during processing when a subscriber receives the message. It means that when the message is delivered to the subscribers, the complete message doesn't need to be loaded into memory by the BizTalk service. The subscriber gets a stream of the message, and the fact that, if they do read past the current loaded buffer, data will loaded on demand is hidden from them.

> To view the Large message fragment size settings, right-click the group node in the BizTalk Server Administration Console and select Properties. The Large message fragment size setting should then be displayed on the Group Properties screen. By default, its value is 102400 bytes.

For every host that is created, a corresponding set of queue tables is made in the MessageBox: the main queue table (which each host polls to collect messages that are pending processing); the scheduled queue table (which is created but never actually used by BizTalk); the state queue table, which holds the list of messages that have been processed but are required later; and the suspended queue table (where suspended messages are stored).

When you configure BizTalk, the default host BizTalkServerApplication is created. If you examine the MessageBox database, you will see the following tables for this host:

- ❑ BizTalkServerApplicationQ (main queue)
- ❑ BizTalkServerApplicationQ_Scheduled (scheduled queue)
- ❑ InstanceStateMessageReferences_BizTalkServerApplication (state queue)
- ❑ BizTalkServerApplicationQ_Suspended (suspended queue)

If you have created any other host in the group, you will see that it has its own corresponding set of queue tables.

These host queues are used only to store references to the actual messages. Each instance of the host runs within its own BTSNTSVC.EXE process and will poll its main queue table as configured, for as long as there is work on the queues to read and there are resources available to process the work. If no work is present on the queue, the polling interval will slow down until it eventually reaches the maximum polling interval. This is configured in the MaxReceiveInterval column of the adm_service class table in the Management database. When a host instance processes a message, it actually retrieves the physical message data from the Spool, MessageParts, Parts, and Fragments tables.

In BizTalk 2006, when a message is routed only to one subscriber, once it has finished processing a reference will immediately be inserted into the MessageZeroSum table, which is used to mark the physical messages for cleanup by a job running within SQL Server Agent. This means that these types of messages will be cleaned up very quickly from the MessageBox database.

For messages going to multiple subscribers, once the message finishes processing, the BizTalk service will not remove the message from the database or insert a reference in the MessageZeroSum table, because it does not know whether there are any more subscribers to the message (for example, if it is referenced in another queue). The reference counts (or number of subscribers) for these messages are maintained by a combination of the following tables: MessageRefCountLog1, MessageRefCountLog2, and MessageRefCountLogTotals. The ActiveRefCountLog table is also used as an auxiliary table. A job running within SQL Server Agent is used to aggregate the reference counts in these tables and determine which messages can be deleted. The Message IDs that can be deleted are then inserted into the MessageZeroSum table, from which another SQL Server Agent job will clean them up.

Figure 11-30 illustrates how the structure described above works. You can see that there is a clear separation of the tables used to store the physical messages and those that hold their references. The reason for the distinction is that each message can have one or more subscribing services that may run in different hosts. Storing only a reference to any message on the host queues enables each message to be processed by multiple hosts but be stored only once. Each instance of a particular host will poll its main queue table (for example, the HostAq table in the figure), which contains the message reference. The message content itself will be accessed through the Spool, MessageParts, Parts, and Fragments tables.

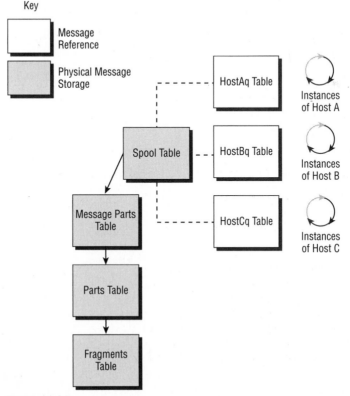

Figure 11-30

SQL Server Agent Jobs

A set of SQL Server Agent jobs is installed and enabled when BizTalk is installed. The purpose of these is to automate the necessary administrative tasks for the MessageBox and other BizTalk databases. It is important that these jobs run successfully; failure can result in the performance of your BizTalk system degrading and eventually lead to the system being in an unmanageable state. This section provides an overview of the job functionality and then looks at some tasks in more detail.

Job Overview

Before going any further, we need to introduce the specific jobs that BizTalk uses. The following table lists the jobs that are installed with the product. The jobs perform maintenance activities on the Management, DTA, MessageBox, and Rules Engine databases.

The `Backup BizTalk Server` and `DTA Purge and Archive` jobs are disabled by default because they require additional configuration. (These jobs are covered in more detail in the section "Archiving and Purging Options," later in this chapter.) The `MessageBox_Message_Cleanup_BizTalkMsgBoxDb` job is also disabled by default because it is called during the execution of the `MessageBox_Message_ManageRefCountLog_BizTalkMsgBoxDb` job and should not be scheduled directly. You should ensure that all other SQL Agent jobs in this table are enabled.

It is recommended that you monitor these jobs for failures. You might want to consider monitoring the duration time for the jobs. If the time that they are taking to run increases significantly, it can be the sign of a problem. This typically happens when the SQL Server is under heavy load and might be a sign that the system has exceeded its maximum sustainable throughput. It is worthwhile noting that the Backup BizTalk Server, DTA Purge and Archive, and Tracked Messages Copy jobs are likely to take the longest to complete. This is due to the amount of processing that they perform. Finally, you should ensure that the startup type for the SQL Server Agent service is set to automatic and that this is also being monitored. Microsoft Operations Manger (MOM) can be used to monitor this for you.

Job	Description
Backup BizTalk Server (BizTalkMgmtDb)	Backs up all BizTalk databases.
CleanupBTFExpiredEntriesJob_ BizTalkMgmtDb	Performs cleanup of expired BizTalk Framework (BTF) entries in the Management database.
DTA Purge and Archive (BizTalkDTADb)	Automates the purging and archiving of the BizTalk tracking database.
MessageBox_DeadProcesses_Cleanup_ BizTalkMsgBoxDb	Checks for stopped BizTalk services (hosts) and releases all work that was held by those services so that another host can process it.
MessageBox_Message_Cleanup_ BizTalkMsgBoxDb	Removes any messages with no subscribers left from the MessageBox. Note that this job is never scheduled; it is called by `MessageBox_Message_ManageRefCountLog_BizTalkMsgBoxDb`.

Job	Description
`MessageBox_Message_ManageRefCountLog_BizTalkMsgBoxDb`	A parent job that calls the `MessageBox_Message_Cleanup_BizTalkMsgBoxDb` job to clean up any messages with no more subscribers.
`MessageBox_Parts_Cleanup_BizTalkMsgBoxDb`	Cleans up any message parts that are no longer referenced by any of the messages within BizTalk.
`MessageBox_UpdateStats_BizTalkMsgBoxDb`	Updates the statistics on the MessageBox.
`Operations_OperateOnInstances_OnMaster_BizTalkMsgBoxDb`	Manages the maintenance in multi-MessageBox scenarios; it performs operational actions to the master MessageBox after they have been performed on the other MessageBox databases.
`PurgeSubscriptionsJob_BizTalkMsgBoxDb`	Cleans up any subscriptions that are no longer required in the MessageBox.
`Rules_Database_Cleanup_BizTalkRuleEngineDb`	Removes old audit data and policy deployment history data from the Rules Engine database.
`TrackedMessages_Copy_BizTalkMsgBoxDb`	Copies tracked message bodies from the MessageBox database to the BizTalk DTA tracking database.

Removing Physical Messages from the MessageBox

We've already described how the physical messages are stored separately to any references to them. This section will show you how these physical messages are removed from the MessageBox. The removal process is done by SQL Server Agent in order to avoid potential lock contention issues and to maximize I/O usage.

The `MessageBox_Message_Cleanup_BizTalkMsgBoxDb` job is used to delete the physical messages from the MessageBox database when there are no longer any outstanding references to them. This job is disabled by default because it is called by the `MessageBox_Message_ManageRefCountLog_BizTalkMsgBoxDb` job, which runs continuously and will never complete. Because the `MessageBox_Message_ManageRefCountLog_BizTalkMsgBoxDb` job loops continuously and never actually completes, the job history will never show that it has been completed successfully.

The job was designed to run constantly because SQL Server Agent has a minimum interval of one minute. At very high transaction rates, it is possible that so much load could be generated in one minute that the job would not be able to catch up with the backlog. Running the job in an infinite loop allows the deletes to occur constantly. This enables BizTalk to provide consistent performance when under high load.

Some customers I have worked with have assumed that this was a problem and disabled the job. You should never do this, because the cleanup job (`MessageBox_Message_Cleanup_BizTalkMsgBoxDb`) will then never be called. It is *very* important that this is not done because it will result in physical messages with no subscribers remaining in the MessageBox database, which will slow down and eventually stop BizTalk.

This example should illustrate to you how important these jobs are to the proper functioning of BizTalk. SQL Server Agent performs essential database maintenance, without which BizTalk performance will degrade and it will eventually stop. For more information on the jobs, see `http://msdn2.microsoft`
`.com/en-US/library/aa561960.aspx`. We will now look at how a backup is handled by the `Backup BizTalk Server` job.

Backing Up the BizTalk Databases — The Supported Method

I have lost count of the number of conversations I have had with customers regarding the supported backup methods of the BizTalk databases and whether third-party backup utilities can be used. First, let me make it clear that the supported method of backing up the BizTalk databases is to use the provided Backup BizTalk Server SQL Agent job. The only exception to this is some of the Business Activity Services (BAS) and Business Activity Monitoring (BAM) databases, which have different backup and restore characteristics. The reasons for this dependency on the SQL Agent job is that the BizTalk service writes to multiple databases using distributed transactions, including the MessageBox, DTA, Management, and BAM Primary Import databases. In order for the backup and corresponding restore process to work, all these databases must be restored to a consistent transactional state.

> **This section focuses on backing up the main BizTalk databases that are used by the majority of customers. If you are using BAM (specifically, the SQL Analysis Services functionality), BAS, or the BASE EDI adapter, there are additional configuration steps that need to be taken for them to be backed up and restored successfully. These are not documented here. If you are using these, please see the following section of the online help:** `http://msdn2.microsoft.com/en-us/library/`
> `aa560972.aspx.`

The Backup BizTalk Server job ensures that all databases are backed up in a manner that allows them to be restored to this state. The job is installed onto the SQL Server that has the Management database, and consists of two steps. The first step in the job performs a full backup of the BizTalk databases and stores these files in one location. The second part of the job performs a "named" distributed transaction across all databases that are included in the backup job. This blocks all new transactions on the BizTalk databases and lets existing ones complete before this transaction commits itself.

The mark in the log that is inserted by this named transaction represents a transactionally consistent point in all BizTalk databases. Because a distributed transaction is used which uses MSDTC, this will be a consistent transactional point in all the logs even if the databases are located on separate SQL servers. This means that if you restore all the databases to this point, you can guarantee that the BizTalk group will function correctly. It is because of this requirement for Transaction log marking that the `Backup BizTalk Server` job is the required method of backup and that no third-party SQL Server backup utilities are supported.

This section will outline the configuration that is needed for the job. First, you need to ensure that the account you use to log in to back up the databases is a member of the sysadmin role on the SQL Server that contains the Management database. If the BizTalk databases are spread across multiple servers, the user account can be added to the BTS_BACKUP_USERS role; this means that sysadmin permissions are only required on the Management Database server that controls the process. The account that you use should be a domain account, and it should be a member of the BTS_BACKUP_USERS role on all SQL Servers. To configure the job, perform the following steps:

Note that the following instructions are for using SQL Server 2005's Management Studio. In SQL Server 2000, the job can be configured using the Enterprise Manager in a similar manner. For detailed instructions, see http://msdn2.microsoft.com/en-us/library/aa546765.aspx.

1. Open SQL Server Management Studio and connect to the server that contains the Management database.

2. Expand the server and select SQL Server Agent ⇨ Jobs. Double-click the Backup BizTalk Server Job to open the Job Properties – Backup BizTalk Server (BizTalkMgmtDb) screen.

3. Select the Steps page from the Job Properties – Backup BizTalk Server (BizTalkMgmtDb) screen and double-click step 1, BackupFull. This will open the Job Step Properties – BackupFull screen.

   The command section in this window contains the following:

   ```
   exec [dbo].[sp_BackupAllFull_Schedule] 'd' /* Frequency */, 'BTS' /* Name */,
   '<destination path>' /* location of backup files */
   ```

   Replace <destination path> with the full path (including quotes) of the location where you would like to store your backup files (for example, \\backupserver\biztalk\dbfiles\). You should not store these files on the same server that the databases reside on. Ensure that the location specified is a UNC path, to avoid data loss in the event of server failure. The frequency of the job, which is by default set to d for daily, can be configured with the following values: w (weekly), m (monthly), y (yearly), and h (hourly). In most scenarios, the default daily backup is sufficient. Once this has been configured, click OK.

4. Double-click step 2, MarkAndBackupLog. This will open the Job Step Properties – MarkAndBackupLog screen.

   The command section in this window contains the following:

   ```
   exec [dbo].[sp_MarkAll] 'BTS' /*  Log mark name */,'<destination path>'  /*
   location of backup files */.
   ```

   Replace <destination path> with the full path to the location you would like to store your backup log files (for example, \\backupserver\biztalk\logfiles). This should be on a separate server to protect against loss of data, and you should ensure that this location is a UNC path so that the server that will be used by BizTalk log shipping to restore these files in the event of failure can access them. Once this has been done, click OK.

5. Double-click step 3, Clear Backup History. Check that the command section of the resulting properties window contains the following:

   ```
   exec [dbo].[sp_DeleteBackupHistory] @DaysToKeep=14
   ```

Configuring the DaysToKeep parameter, which has a default value of 14, adjusts how many days the mark name is stored in the MarkLog table in the BizTalk databases. This table contains all the marks that have been used as the named transaction. This step was implemented to ensure that this table does not grow excessively large in any of the databases. The default value for DaysToKeep is fine for normal operation. Adjust this only if you have a specific reason that requires you keep this information for a longer period.

6. Click the Schedules tab in the Job Properties – Backup BizTalk Server (BizTalkMgmtDb) window, and then double-click the MarkAndBackupLogSched row in the Schedule list section. On the Job Schedule Properties – MarkAndBackupLogSched screen that opens (see Figure 11-31), you can see that the job is configured to run every 15 minutes by default. Note that this means in the event of a failure, up to 15 minutes' worth of data would be lost and unrecoverable. With the default full backup frequency set to daily, these settings mean that a full backup will occur daily at midnight and a log backup will be made every 15 minutes. If this level of data loss is unacceptable, you can reduce the interval between backups by modifying the schedule in the Job Schedule Properties – MarkAndBackupLogSched screen opened earlier in this step.

For more information on backing up and restoring the BizTalk databases, see http://msdn2 .microsoft.com/en-us/library/aa560972.aspx.

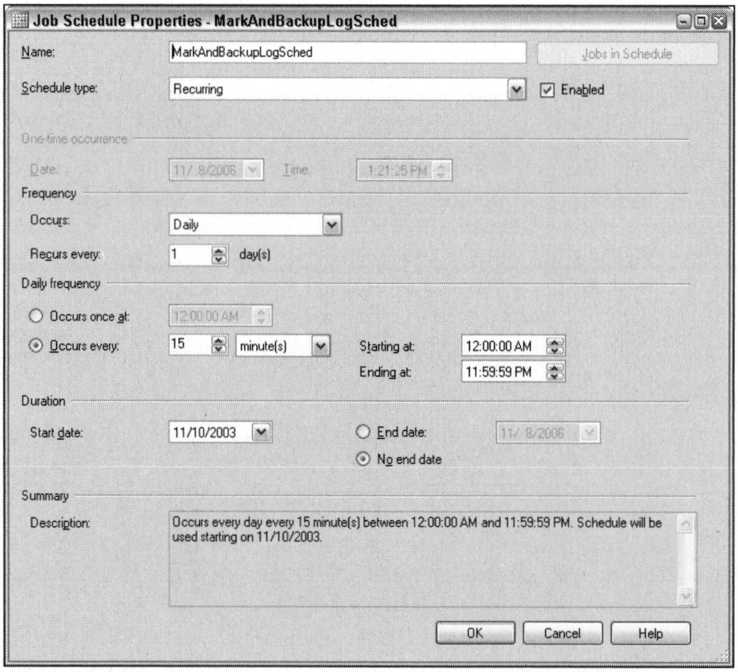

Figure 11-31

There may be situations when you want to do a complete backup of the databases and not wait for the scheduled hourly, daily, weekly, monthly, or yearly backup. This is particularly the case when you are going to install a BizTalk hotfix or service pack. You often want to minimize the time necessary to recover in the event of failure.

If a full backup is forced, it will mean that the next time the Backup BizTalk server job is run the full backup step will run before the log mark and backup step. If the databases then need to be restored to this point, only one backup and one log file need to be restored for each BizTalk database, thereby reducing the recovery time significantly.

You can do this by opening the adm_ForceFullBackup table located in the Management database. You should then set the ForceFull column value to `true`, forcing a full backup of all databases when the next backup job is run. After a full backup has been completed, this value will be reset to `false`.

Adding Custom Databases to the Backup Job

In many situations, it is important to keep custom databases in sync with BizTalk. A good example of this is when you have an atomic scope in an orchestration that writes data to a third-party database. At that point, you are participating in a distributed transaction with the MessageBox and you need to ensure that it is in sync. Therefore, it is important that when the BizTalk databases are restored, the database that the application depends on is also restored to the same point. For this reason, a set of T-SQL scripts is included in the Installation directory of BizTalk.

To add a custom database to the Backup BizTalk Server job, perform the following steps:

1. Navigate to the Schema directory in the BizTalk Installation folder (`C:\Program Files\ Microsoft BizTalk Server 2006\Schema`).

2. Using SQL Server Management Studio, run the `Backup_Setup_All_Procs.sql` and `Backup_Setup_All_Tables.sql` scripts in the custom database. These will create all the necessary tables, stored procedures, and database roles for the database to be included in the backup job.

3. If the SQL Server holding the custom database is on a separate server to the Management database, you need to add it as a linked server on the Management server.

4. The account running the job (by default, the SQL Agent Service Account) must be a domain account that has a SQL login either directly or through a group membership on each SQL server. If this is not created, you must create it.

5. Add a new user in the custom database, and point this to the login configured in the preceding step. You should then make this user a member of the BTS_BACKUP_USERS role, which was created when the T-SQL scripts were executed in step 2

6. Add a row in the adm_OtherBackupDatabases table (in the Management database for the custom database), as illustrated in Figure 11-32.

7. To verify that this has worked, you should run the Backup BizTalk Server. Do this by right-clicking on the job in the Server Name ⇨ SQL Server Agent ⇨ Jobs folder in SQL Server Management Studio. Select the Start Job at Step option. In the Start Job on *<Server Name>* screen (where *<Server Name>* is the name of your SQL server), click Start to run the job.

8. The Start Jobs – *<Server Name>* screen will now appear as the job is executing. Verify that this displays that the job has completed successfully, and then click Close.

9. Open the location that you configured earlier to store your Transaction log backups. There should now be a Transaction log backup in this folder for your custom database. It will be named as follows:

```
<Server Name>_<Your Custom Database Name>_Log_<Mark Name>_<Date-time
representation>.bak
```

For example:

```
BIZTALKADMIN01_SSODB_Log_BTS_2007_02_17_18_59_30_567.bak
```

10. To verify that the full backup of the database is working, either wait until your next scheduled full backup or change the ForceFull column value to `true` in the adm_ForceFullBackup table in the Management database. Then execute the job (repeat steps 7–8). Once this has completed successfully, check the location you configured previously to store your full backup files. There should now be a full backup file in this folder for your custom database. It will be named as follows:

```
<Server Name>_<Your Custom Database Name>_Full_<Mark Name>_<Date-time
representation>.bak
```

For example:

```
BIZTALKADMIN01_BizTalkMsgBoxDb_Full_BTS_2007_02_17_18_59_13_643.bak
```

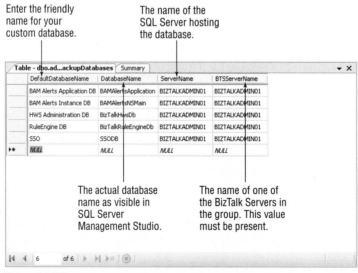

Figure 11-32

Log Shipping

Recovery from failure is one of the most asked about topics when I speak to system administrators. They want to understand what options are available to them with BizTalk and how they should implement it. In BizTalk Server 2006, log shipping is the recommended method of recovery. This is because a set of SQL Server Agent jobs is provided that automate a lot of things that would need to be done manually.

This includes applying the last set of full database backups followed sequentially by the Transaction log backups for each of the databases that are included with the Backup BizTalk Server job. The final Transaction log for each of the databases would then need to be restored to the mark in the log, to ensure that they were in a consistent transactional state. Without guaranteeing all this, it is likely that the BizTalk group will not function correctly. Therefore, it is strongly recommended that you use the built-in log shipping jobs that BizTalk provides.

The primary focus of this section is on ensuring that you have a thorough understanding of what log shipping is and the common pitfalls that you should be aware of. We will refer to the log shipping configuration steps when necessary. These are extremely well documented in the "Backing Up and Restoring BizTalk Server Databases" section of the online MSDN documentation at http://msdn2.microsoft.com/en-us/library/aa561125.aspx.

Before delving into the BizTalk specifics, we will discuss the general architecture and purpose of log shipping. Log shipping is a process that allows SQL Server to move Transaction logs from one SQL server to another standby SQL server. These logs are then automatically applied in sequential order to the standby SQL server, which will now only be slightly out of sync with the active server. This means that in the event that your production site fails, an application can be redirected to your standby SQL Server, thus minimizing the downtime for users of the system.

Log shipping protects against both hardware and software failures. This provides organizations with a relatively inexpensive, high-availability solution, which is not limited by proximity. Because log shipping restores the logs sequentially when they are received at the standby SQL server, it can be placed in a remote location to protect against catastrophic failure such as site loss. The standby SQL server does not need to be an exact replica of the source SQL Server, which helps minimize costs further.

The main downside to the log shipping story is that the standby SQL server will always be out of sync with the source SQL server. This can be reduced to several minutes if a high-speed network is used between the sites. But losing even a few minutes of data can be unacceptable for some systems, such as trading systems for financial organizations. Therefore, log shipping should be used only to protect you in the event of a disaster (such as when you lose the disk with the data file on it).

To make SQL Server highly available, it is recommended that clustering be used to protect against other failures, such as when the SQL service stops responding on a server node. This use of clustering with a shared disk array means that a failover can occur within the production site with no data loss whatsoever. Data will be lost only if the production site was completely lost and log shipping was used to resume service on the standby SQL server.

Log Shipping in BizTalk

As discussed previously in this chapter, BizTalk depends on a number of SQL Server databases. The BizTalk runtime uses DTC transactions across these databases; therefore, the backup and restore model needs to provide a consistent point in time to restore to. Without this, it would not be possible to guarantee that the restore process would leave the BizTalk group in a functioning state.

The Backup BizTalk Server job uses log marks that are consistent across all the databases. This provides you with the synchronized point in the log that you require for restoration. BizTalk provides SQL Server Agent jobs, which are installed when log shipping is configured, that perform this restoration to the last Transaction log mark. It is for this reason that it is recommended you use the BizTalk log shipping feature.

Configuring Log Shipping

To set up BizTalk log shipping, it is essential that you ensure that the Backup BizTalk Server job is configured correctly, as described in the preceding section. In particular, ensure that the path you specified to store the database and log backup files is a UNC path (for example, `\\BizTalkBackupServer\Data`). This means that the backup files will be readily available in the event of server failure. You also need to ensure that the same version of SQL Server is used on both the source and the destination systems. Log shipping from one version of SQL Server to another is not supported.

After you have verified this, the destination system can now be set up for log shipping. Step-by-step instructions are provided in the "How to Configure the Destination System for Log Shipping" section of the online help (`http://msdn2.microsoft.com/en-us/library/aa560961.aspx`). It is strongly recommended that you review this before progressing any further.

First, you need to ensure that you are logged in as a member of the BizTalk Server Administrators group. You should also ensure that you have performed a full backup of the standby SQL Server and all its databases (including the Master and MSDB databases). Then you must connect to SQL Server Management Studio and specify the name of the standby SQL Server that you want to configure. You are then required to run two scripts, which are located in the Schema subfolder for BizTalk (by default, `C:\Program Files\Microsoft BizTalk Server 2006\Schema`).

The first script that has to be run is `LogShipping_Destination_Schema.sql`. This creates the required tables in the Master database on the server. These are used to store the list of databases being recovered, copies of the backup history (taken from the Management database), and the configuration of the SQL Server Agent jobs on the source SQL Server.

The next script that should be run is `LogShipping_Destination_Logic.sql`, which implements the artifacts required (including stored procedures and database roles).

You are now required to execute the `bts_ConfigureBizTalkLogShipping` stored procedure, which was created in the Master database by executing the SQL scripts. To enable you to execute the next stored procedure, you have to enable Ad Hoc Distributed Queries using SQL Server Surface Area Configuration.

Open Start ➪ All Programs ➪ Microsoft SQL Server 2005 ➪ Configuration Tools ➪ SQL Server Surface Area Configuration, and then click Surface Area Configuration for Features. On the Surface Area Configuration for Features screen, expand MSSQLServer ➪ Database Engine ➪ Ad Hoc Remote Queries. Check the box labeled Enable OPENROWSET and OPENDATASOURCE support, click OK, and then close the SQL Server Surface Area Configuration tool.

Using SQL Server Management Studio, ensure that you are connected to your standby SQL Server and open a new query window using the New Query button on the toolbar. Then execute the stored procedure using the following syntax:

```
exec bts_ConfigureBizTalkLogShipping @nvcDescription = '<Name of Log Shipping
Solution>',
@nvcMgmtDatabaseName = '<Name of your Management database>',
@nvcMgmtServerName = '<Name of your Source Management SQL server>',
@SourceServerName = null, -- null indicates that this destination server restores
all databases
@fLinkServers = 1 -- 1 automatically links the server to the management database
```

You will need to replace the parameter `@nvcMgmtDatabaseName` with the name of the Management database. Then replace `@nvcMgmtServerName` with the name of the source SQL server. The `@SourceServerName` parameter needs to be altered only if you have multiple source SQL servers and you are restoring these to more than one standby SQL server — for example, if you had separated your MessageBox database on its own SQL Server and you had another server for the other BizTalk databases.

If you were going to use BizTalk log shipping to restore all these databases onto one standby SQL server, you could leave this parameter as null. If you wanted to maintain two standby SQL Servers, you would need to execute this stored procedure on each standby SQL Server and specify which was its source server (for example, `@SourceServerName='FirstSQLServer'`). For more detailed instructions, see the previously given link to the documentation.

Under SQL Server Agent ➪ Jobs in SQL Server Management Studio, you will see that three new jobs have been created:

- ❑ **BTS Log Shipping Get Backup History** — This job moves backup history records to the standby SQL server and runs every minute.

- ❑ **BTS Server Log Shipping Restore Databases** — This job is responsible for restoring the backup files from the source SQL server to the standby SQL server. This runs every minute and will continue while there are backup files to restore.

- ❑ **BTS Log Shipping Restore to Mark** — This job restores all the databases to the last available log mark and recreates all the SQL Server Agent jobs on the standby SQL server.

The final step of the configuration process is to edit the `SampleUpdateInfo.xml` file that is used as part of the recovery process. This must be done on one of your BizTalk servers. Make sure that you make a note of which one it has been done on; it is needed for the recovery process. It is included in the `Schema\Restore` subfolder of the `BizTalk Program Files` directory.

You should open this file and replace all instances of `"SourceServer"` and `"DestinationServer"` with the names of your source and standby SQL servers, respectively. Ensure that you keep the quotation marks around these names. If you have the BAM, Human Workflow Services, Rules Engine, or EDI databases installed, you will have to uncomment these, as appropriate. Be especially careful with the BAM and Rules Engine databases. These are components that are commonly used but are commented out by default in this file. If you're using multiple message boxes, an additional `MessageBoxDB` line will need to be added in. Be careful to ensure that `IsMaster="0"` is set for all the non-master databases.

Restoring the Databases Using Log Shipping

We will now describe how the databases are restored to the standby SQL Server. If a failure occurs and your production SQL Server is unavailable due to a catastrophic failure (such as site loss), the first step that you need to do is to disable the three log shipping jobs on the standby SQL Server. To do this, right-click the following jobs in SQL Server Management Studio and select Disable:

- ❏ BTS Log Shipping Get Backup History
- ❏ BTS Server Log Shipping Restore Databases
- ❏ BTS Log Shipping Restore to Mark

Some of the BizTalk databases contain a reference to the physical SQL server that they are stored on. The next stage is to update these databases so that they no long reference the product SQL server (which is now unavailable). To do this, on the BizTalk server where you previously edited the `SampleUpdateInfo.xml` file, open a command prompt and navigate to the `Schema\Restore` subdirectory of the `BizTalk Program` Files directory. Enter the following command (this only needs to be run on the server):

```
cscript UpdateDatabase.vbs SampleUpdateInfo.xml
```

Each BizTalk Server maintains a Registry key that tells it the location of its Management database. The server polls the management database this references to update its admin cache periodically (this is set to 60 seconds by default). In order for the restore process to work, this Registry key must be updated.

A script is provided with the product to automate this. You are required to first copy the `Sample-UpdateInfo.xml` file to the `Schema\Restore` subdirectory of the `BizTalk Program Files` directory on all the BizTalk servers in your group. After you've done this, navigate to this directory on each of the BizTalk servers and run the following command:

```
cscript UpdateRegistry.vbs SampleUpdateInfo.xml
```

The final step is to restart all the BizTalk services, including the ESSO service and the Rules Engine Update service (if it is used). The Windows Management Instrumentation service must also be restarted. This must be done on all BizTalk servers and can be done using the Services MMS (access it by going to Start ⇨ Run and typing **Services.msc**). To access the group in the BizTalk Server Administration Console, you will also need to register the new group. (This is necessary because the Management database is now on a SQL server with a different name.)

The last thing that you need to configure is the Backup BizTalk Server job. Ensure that this is enabled and writing the backup files to a shared storage area (refer to earlier instructions, if necessary). Once this has been done, your group should be up and running. If you want to fall back to the source SQL Server at some point in the future, you should repeat this process, substituting the appropriate values for source and standby SQL Server, where necessary.

> *The full online documentation for restoring the BizTalk databases is available at* `http://msdn2` `.microsoft.com/en-us/library/aa546753.aspx`.

DTA Purging and Archiving

With the default out-of-the-box configuration for tracking, as messages are processed through BizTalk, each host instance will serialize tracking data and store it in one of the tracking data tables. The tracking

data tables are in the MessageBox and are named in the following format:
TrackingData_<Number>_<Number> (for example, TrackingData_0_3).

> This tracking data table format is new for BizTalk Server 2006. In BizTalk Server
> 2004, there was only one table, the TrackingData table. This has now been parti-
> tioned and replaced with a view called the TrackingData view, which is a union of
> the partitioned tables.

This tracking data is then asynchronously copied across to the DTA database by the BizTalk host that is
configured as the tracking host. The tracking host runs the Tracking Data Decode Service (TDDS), the
subservice responsible for moving tracking data from the MessageBox to the DTA database. Figure 11-33
illustrates the process.

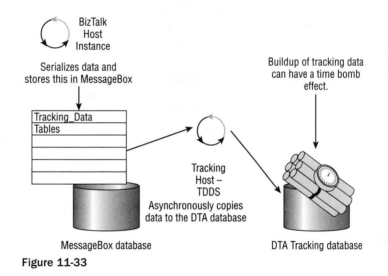

Figure 11-33

Over time, as more data passes through BizTalk, the DTA database will continue to grow in size. As
the size increases, it will take progressively longer for TDDS to insert data into this database. This may
result in TDDS generating errors and a backlog of tracking data building up in the MessageBox. Both
outcomes are likely to result in decreased SQL Server performance, which will directly affect the performance of your BizTalk group.

I often refer to DTA database maintenance as the ticking bomb within the product. If it is addressed and
managed appropriately, it is not an issue and the situation can be diffused; however, if left unchecked,
it can result in server performance degrading quite spectacularly! By default, there is no purging and
archiving enabled on your DTA database, because it is up to you, the customer, to determine how much
tracking data you need to keep in the DTA. In some cases, there will be legal requirements for keeping x
number of years' worth of data. Therefore, you *must* configure this for each and every installation of
BizTalk.

Archiving and Purging Options

BizTalk Server 2006 is the first version of the product to ship with a fully supported SQL Server Agent job for DTA database maintenance. Previous versions of the product provided sample scripts for archiving and purging tracking data. Both of these processes are now provided through the DTA Purge and Archive job. (This is now included in Service Pack 2 for BizTalk Server 2004.)

This job is disabled by default but must be enabled to ensure that you keep a healthy system. The purging and archiving job measures the age of an item based on the time since it was first inserted into the DTA database. A live window of data is defined in the job configuration. If the data is older than this live window, it will be removed by the purging and archiving job when it is executed. This section will discuss the two types of purging (soft and hard) that are used.

Soft purging deals only with completed instances. You can configure the process by editing the Archive and Purge (step 1) of the DTA Purge and Archive job. To do this, perform the following steps:

1. Open SQL Server Management Studio and connect to the server that contains the DTA database.

2. Expand the server and select SQL Server Agent ⇨ Jobs. Double-click the DTA Purge and Archive (BizTalkDTADb) job to open the Job Properties – DTA Purge and Archive (BizTalkDTADb) window.

3. Select Steps from the Job Properties – DTA Purge and Archive (BizTalkDTADb) window and then double-click step 1, Archive and Purge, to open the Job Step Properties – Archive and Purge window.

The command section in this window should contain the following:

```
exec dtasp_BackupAndPurgeTrackingDatabase
0, --@nLiveHours tinyint, --Any completed instance older than the live hours
+live days
1, --@nLiveDays tinyint = 0, --will be deleted along with all associated data
30, --@nHardDeleteDays tinyint = 0, --all data older than this will be deleted.
null, --@nvcFolder nvarchar(1024) = null, --folder for backup files
null, --@nvcValidatingServer sysname = null,
0 --@fForceBackup int = 0 --
```

In the configuration, the sum of the Livedays and LiveHours parameters is the live window for which tracking data will be kept in the tracking database. Any data associated with a completed instance that is older than this window is deleted when the DTA Purge and Archive job is executed. By default, the job is configured with a live window of one day, which means any data older than this will be purged and archived. Before running the job, you must first set the @nvcFolder parameter with the location you would like the DTA archive files to be stored — for example:

```
'\\BackupServer\DTAArchive', --@nvcFolder nvarchar(1024) = null, --folder for
backup files
```

In order for the job to purge data, the archive of this data must be completed. If the archive is successful, any data associated with completed instances that is older than one day will be purged from the DTA database. To ensure that data is purged only if it has been included in an archive backup, the timestamp of the last backup is included in the Tracking database, and the backups are overlapped to a certain degree to ensure no tracking data is purged without having been archived.

The second type of purging available is *hard purge*. This deals with incomplete instances that are in the Tracking database. This is useful in many situations, including when you have looping orchestrations that run indefinitely over a long period of time. Left unaddressed, this could result in the DTA database growing and these instances never being purged. Hard purging allows all data older than the specified value of the parameter @nHardDeleteDays to be purged, with the exception of that data that indicates the existence of an instance. The value of this parameter should always be greater than your soft purge window.

> **You must ensure that on the General page in the Job Properties DTA Purge and Archive (BizTalkDTADb) screen, the Enabled box is checked. Without enabling it, the job will not run as scheduled. The job is scheduled by default to run every minute.**

Configuring Credentials for the Job

By default, the DTA Purge and Archive job will run as the SQL Server Agent service account. For added security, and to prevent the possibility of elevation of privileges, you can configure the job to run in the context of an account that is a member of the BTS_BACKUP_USERS role. This is created in the DTA database when BizTalk is installed. To do this, you first need to create the SQL login by performing the following steps:

1. If you do not already have an account you can use, you need to create one. This should almost always be a domain account; the only case where local computer accounts are supported is if all BizTalk components are installed on a single server. Create the account using either the Active Directory Users & Computers (domain accounts) or Computer Management (local accounts) consoles.

2. Open SQL Server Management Studio and connect to the server containing the DTA database using an account that is a member of the sysadmin role.

3. Expand the server and select Security ➪ Logins. If the login does not exist, right-click on the Logins folder and select New Login, which will display the Login – New configuration window.

4. Enter the name of the account you want to use in the Login Name box (for example, BIZTALK-ADMIN01\DTAPurge), ensure that Windows Authentication is selected, and then click OK to close the window.

5. In SQL Server Management Studio, expand the server and select Databases ➪ BizTalkDTADb ➪ Security ➪ Users. If the login that you are using is not already present (or is not a member of any groups that are referenced), you will need to right-click the Users folder and select New User. This will open the Database User – New window.

6. In the Database User – New window, enter a representative username, such as DTAPurge, in the User Name: box.

7. Enter the login name in the Login Name: box (for example, BIZTALKADMIN01\DTAPurge).

8. Ensure that the box next to BTS_BACKUP_USERS under Database role membership is checked, as shown in Figure 11-34. This adds the user to the appropriate database role.

9. Click OK to exit the Database User – New window.

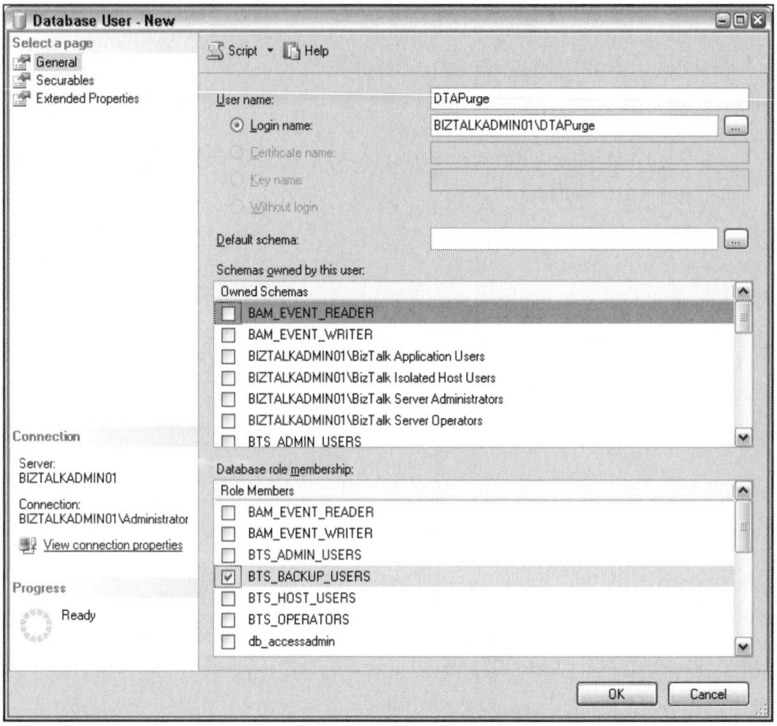

Figure 11-34

To configure the job to run in the context of the account you just configured, you will need to ensure that a credential has been added for the account. This basically allows SQL Server 2005 to store a copy of the password so that it can run processes in its context. To do this, perform the following steps:

1. Navigate to the Security ➪ Credentials folder for your server in SQL Server Management Studio.

2. Right-click Credentials and select New Credential. In the New Credential screen, enter an appropriate name in the Credential Name box. In the Identity box, enter the login name (for example, BIZTALKADMIN01\DTAPURGE). In the Password box, enter the password associated with the account, and then confirm this in the Confirm password box. The DTA Purge and Archive job executes T-SQL, which always runs in the context of the owner of the job (this is the SQL Server Agent service account by default). To configure the DTA Purge and Archive job to run in the new context, navigate to the SQL Server Agent ➪ Jobs folder for your server in SQL Server Management Studio. Then double-click the DTA Purge and Archive Job (BizTalkDTADb to open the Job Properties – DTA Purge and Archive (BizTalkDTADb) window.

3. On the General page in this window, enter the login name for the account you just configured (for example, BIZTALKADMIN01\DTAPurge) in the Owner box, as illustrated in Figure 11-35. This determines the context under which the job will run. Click OK to close the window.

4. To verify that the job is working correctly, right-click the DTA Purge and Archive (BizTalkDTADb) job and select the Start Job at Step option. This will open the Start Jobs – *<Server Name>* window

(for example, Start Jobs – BizTalkAdmin01). After a few minutes (it might take longer if your DTA database is very large), the window should display a message indicating that the job has completed successfully. Click Close to close the window. You have now configured the DTA Purge and Archive job to run in the context of an account with only the required permissions.

Configuring DTA Purging Only

If you do not want to archive any data, it is possible to configure the job to purge data only. This can be configured by changing the stored procedure that is called by the DTA Purge and Archive job. To do this, navigate to the Jobs folder under SQL Server Agent in SQL Management Studio (2005) or Enterprise Manager (2000) and double-click the DTA Purge and Archive job.

In the window that appears, click Steps (located in the left-hand pane). Then double-click step 1 Archive and Purge in the Job step list to display the Job Step Properties – Archive and Purge window. From here, you will need to edit the command section for this step so that the dtasp_PurgeTrackingDatabase stored procedure is called rather than dtasp_BackupAndPurgeTrackingDatabase.

This stored procedure also requires only four parameters to be passed to it. The @nHours and @nDays parameters determine the live window after which completed instances will be purged from the DTA. The @nHardDays parameter determines the window for incomplete instances. Finally, the @dtLastBackup parameter should be set to the current UTC time by setting it to GetUTCDate(). If this is set to null, data will not be purged from the DTA. Figure 11-36 shows what your command section should look like.

You can see from the figure that the @nvcFolder, @nvcValidatingServer, and @fForceBackup parameters are no longer required and should either be removed or commented out using the -- syntax. (They are commented out in Figure 11-36.)

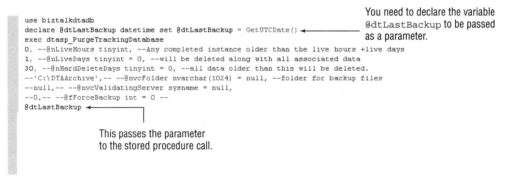

Figure 11-36

For more information on DTA purging and archiving, see the "Archiving and Purging the BizTalk Tracking Database" section of the online help, at http://msdn2.microsoft.com/en-us/library/aa560754.aspx.

Checking the Performance of Your BizTalk Database Server

Many times while working with a customer, I have wanted to determine the performance of the underlying SQL Server hosting the BizTalk databases. This is particularly the case when the SQL Server is not dedicated solely for BizTalk. Recently, I was troubleshooting a performance problem for a company that was using BizTalk to do the back-end processing for any orders made through their web site, and it was performing incredibly slowly!

The customers' perception was that this was due to BizTalk and therefore they had raised a Severity A case with Microsoft, which meant I was dispatched to resolve it. After a detailed examination, I discovered that one of the other databases on the same SQL Server had a table with 12 million rows of data (approximately 12GB). The column that was been queried in a select query by a Web application did not have any index on it; therefore, SQL Server 2000 had to perform a full table scan each time a query was run on the server. This was leading to average disk queue lengths of greater than 1000, which, of course, caused BizTalk to grind to a halt!

This section will show you some of the tools and techniques that you can use to check the performance of SQL Server.

SQL Server 2005 Management Studio Reports

The SQL Server 2005 Management Studio has a little-known but fantastic feature. When you install SQL Server 2005, behind the scenes a trace of the system is enabled by default that collects information on the performance of the SQL Server.

The information that is collected can be easily analyzed using the out-of-the-box reports provided. To get access to this type of information in SQL Server 2000, you would have to run a SQL Profiler trace, which can be done manually or using PSSDiag. SQL Profiler traces contain a lot of detailed information that is very useful but often difficult to analyze due to the volume of data that is collected. Therefore, Read80Trace, a utility to report on this information (see http://support.microsoft.com/kb/887057), is often used to format the data collected into an .htm file.

Only then would it be possible to analyze the data easily to determine which queries were most "expensive" in terms of duration, CPU time, and so on. This is a lengthy process and relies on the Profiler trace running when the performance issue occurs — not particularly suited to troubleshooting performance problems that occur unpredictably and intermittently.

In SQL Server 2005, this information is readily available for you, and ad hoc reports can be generated through the Management Studio. To view these reports, open the Management Studio and connect to the desired SQL server.

In my experience, you will normally be interested in the server(s) that has the MessageBox, DTA, and BAM databases on, as these are the databases that BizTalk uses the most. Once you have connected, select the root node for your SQL Server.

This will display the Summary screen for the SQL server. In the right-hand summary window, select the Report menu, which will display the list of available reports. Your screen should now look similar to Figure 11-37. To view a report, simply select it from the drop-down list that is displayed.

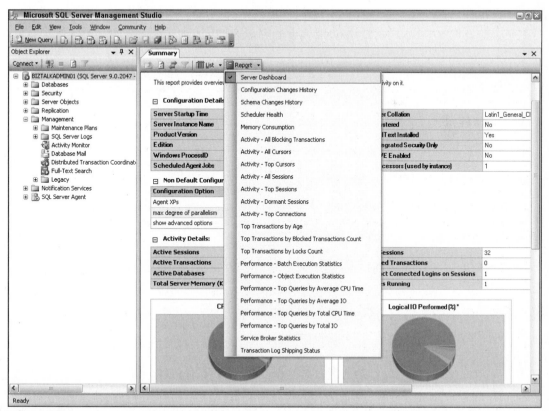

Figure 11-37

Of particular interest are the Performance reports, especially the Performance – Top Queries by Average CPU Time and Performance – Top Queries by Average IO reports. These reports render the data collected by the default background SQL Profiler trace in SQL Reporting Services.

They are very user-friendly and allow the user to drill down to the required level of detail. Figure 11-38 shows how the Performance – Top Queries by Average CPU Time report displays the actual T-SQL that was executed by the worst performing queries. (This is visible in the Query Text column in the report.) These reports give you the ability to analyze a lot of data quickly and easily. Because the default trace is enabled on a standard installation, they can also be used in a postmortem situation.

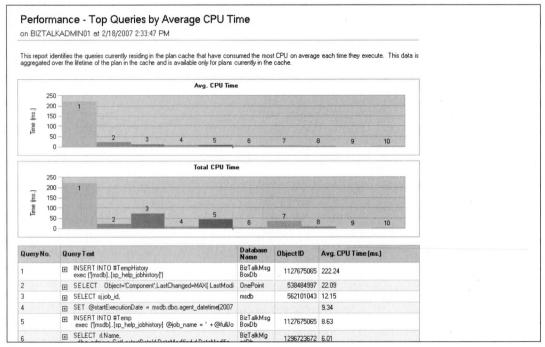

Figure 11-38

For a full tutorial on the functionality of SQL Server Management Studio and information on the default trace that is enabled, see the following links:

❑ **SQL Management Tutorials** — http://msdn2.microsoft.com/en-us/library/ms167593.aspx

❑ **Default Trace Information** — http://msdn2.microsoft.com/en-us/library/ms175513.aspx

Database Separation

It is recommended that you separate database and log files on separate drives. In addition, the MessageBox should have its own dedicated drives for the MessageBox database file and Transaction log, if additional performance is required. For detailed information on this, see Chapter 9.

BizTalk Monitoring

As has been stated repeatedly throughout this book, applications built using BizTalk are typically part of the lifeblood of an organization. For example, if you work for a bank that is using BizTalk to process all payments received from and sent to other financial institutions, it is essential that this system stay up. If it does not, the consequences can be severe both personally to the administrator of the system who may be "asked" to leave and to the organization as a whole, which could face regulatory fines, bad publicity, and the like.

Remember that the availability of your BizTalk application depends on a number of components, including ESSO, SQL Server, the underlying OS, and usually many more. Therefore, it is essential that you reduce the difficulty associated with monitoring a system and do your utmost to avoid the avoidable wherever possible.

The goal of monitoring is to minimize the direct and indirect costs (losses through downtime, etc.) associated with operations and to simplify the identification and root-cause resolution of issues. Monitoring should also provide administrators with enough information to deal with problems proactively (before they affect the level of service that the business receives). This section will discuss the monitoring product that Microsoft provides and how to configure it to monitor BizTalk and its dependant components.

Microsoft Operations Manager

Many products are available that allow you to monitor systems; the most important thing is that you do some monitoring. Many times I have reviewed a customer's BizTalk infrastructure design and have seen no mention of monitoring whatsoever. When questioned about this, many just assume that a problem won't happen and they don't need to. This is at best a very naïve approach. In my opinion, monitoring should be an essential part of *any* enterprise application that you are going to deploy.

Microsoft Operations Manger (MOM) is the product that Microsoft produces and recommends organizations use to monitor all their server-based products. MOM 2005, which at the time of writing is the latest released version of the product (until System Center Operations Manager 2007 ships), allows you to monitor the state of an application based on the state of each of the underlying components it depends on. Each component is measured against a set of criteria defined by the group that produced it. This troubleshooting and diagnostic information is stored in a Management Pack.

Each Microsoft Server product (including BizTalk, ESSO, Windows, and SQL Server) ships with a Management Pack. This allows you to set up MOM to monitor all the components in your BizTalk group quickly, accurately, and reliably through the common MOM interface and tools. Customers are usually very impressed when I show them the value of monitoring BizTalk with MOM. With minimal configuration, MOM enables you to monitor effectively and helps increase availability of service. This section is not meant be an in-depth guide to MOM (there are complete books on this); instead, it is designed to demonstrate some of the functions that can be performed.

If you require additional in-depth technical information on MOM, see the following links:

❑   **MOM 2005 Technical Resources** — www.microsoft.com/mom/techinfo/default.mspx

❑   **MOM 2005 for Beginners (includes online virtual labs)** — www.microsoft.com/Mom/techinfo/training/getstarted.mspx

MOM Architecture

Before delving too deeply into the BizTalk specifics, we'll do a quick overview of the main components involved in MOM, as illustrated in Figure 11-39.

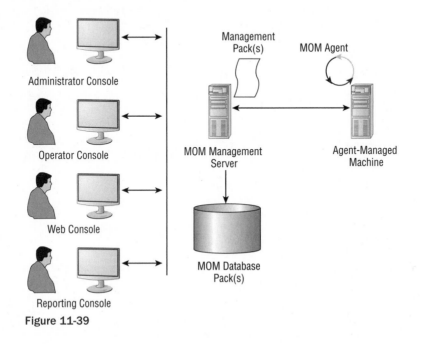

Figure 11-39

A MOM Management group consists of at least one Management server and the MOM database in any MOM environment. The MOM database is the store where all operational data is kept. Typically, machines are managed by installing a MOM Agent on the machine, which is responsible for sending and receiving data to one or more Management servers. Note that it is possible to have machines that are not managed by agents. A number of Management Packs are installed on the Management server, each of which is tailored to a particular component (SQL, Windows, etc.). This is done through rules that determine what data is collected from managed machines in the Management group.

The Administrator Console enables a user to configure the managed machines in the group, deploy agents to machines, and add and remove management packs to and from the group.

The Operator Console provides a detailed insight into the data in the MOM database, including the health of the computers that are managed, and the ability to view alerts at different levels (overall alerts and alerts for a specific product). The Operator Console also provides you with the ability to assign alerts to individual operators and maintain a company knowledgebase for alerts, which can be used to help other users resolve an issue should it recur in the future.

The Web Console, essentially a lightweight, Web-based version of the Operator Console, is designed to provide the functionality to a wider audience who do not require the in-depth view that the Operator Console provides.

Finally, the Reporting Console, a browser-based reporting tool built using SQL Reporting services, provides various reports that can be used to present the appropriate data from the MOM database to various types of users in your organization.

Deployment Considerations

Installing MOM using the standard configuration is quite straightforward. However, *be warned* that it is most certainly not a trivial task to deploy it so that it will provide you with all the information required, in a timely manner, and so that it is highly available. It is essential that you engage the right resources to ensure that your deployment is done efficiently and effectively. Full books and numerous white papers have been written on this topic; therefore, this chapter will not cover it and will instead focus on the functionality that is provided through the BizTalk and ESSO Management Packs.

> For the definitive guide to planning and deploying MOM, see the "Mom 2005 Planning and Deployment Resources" section at www.microsoft.com/mom/techinfo/planning/default.mspx.

BizTalk Management Packs

There are two separate Management Packs for BizTalk and ESSO:

❑   The **BizTalk Management Pack** is designed to allow MOM to capture events and `PerfMon` counters specific to the product and to raise alerts when operator intervention is required.

❑   The **ESSO Management Pack** can be used to monitor ESSO events and `PerfMon` counters.

For a complete monitoring solution, both packs should be deployed in all scenarios because BizTalk has a dependency on the ESSO service for normal operation. This section will walk you through the deployment process for each of these packs. We will assume that you have already followed the MOM 2005 Planning and Deployment documentation to set up your infrastructure.

> The BAM Wizard was included with the MOM 2005 Resource Kit and enables a MOM Management Pack to be created that raises alerts when the BAM Key Performance Indicators (KPIs) deviate from their normal values. Unfortunately, the BAM Wizard is no longer supported in BizTalk Server 2006. If you are running BizTalk Server 2004 and want to find out more information about this, please visit www.microsoft.com/mom/downloads/2005/reskit/default.mspx.

When you first start MOM 2005 after the initial installation, you should use the Administrator Console (available from the Microsoft Operations Manager 2005 folder in the Programs menu), as shown in Figure 11-40.

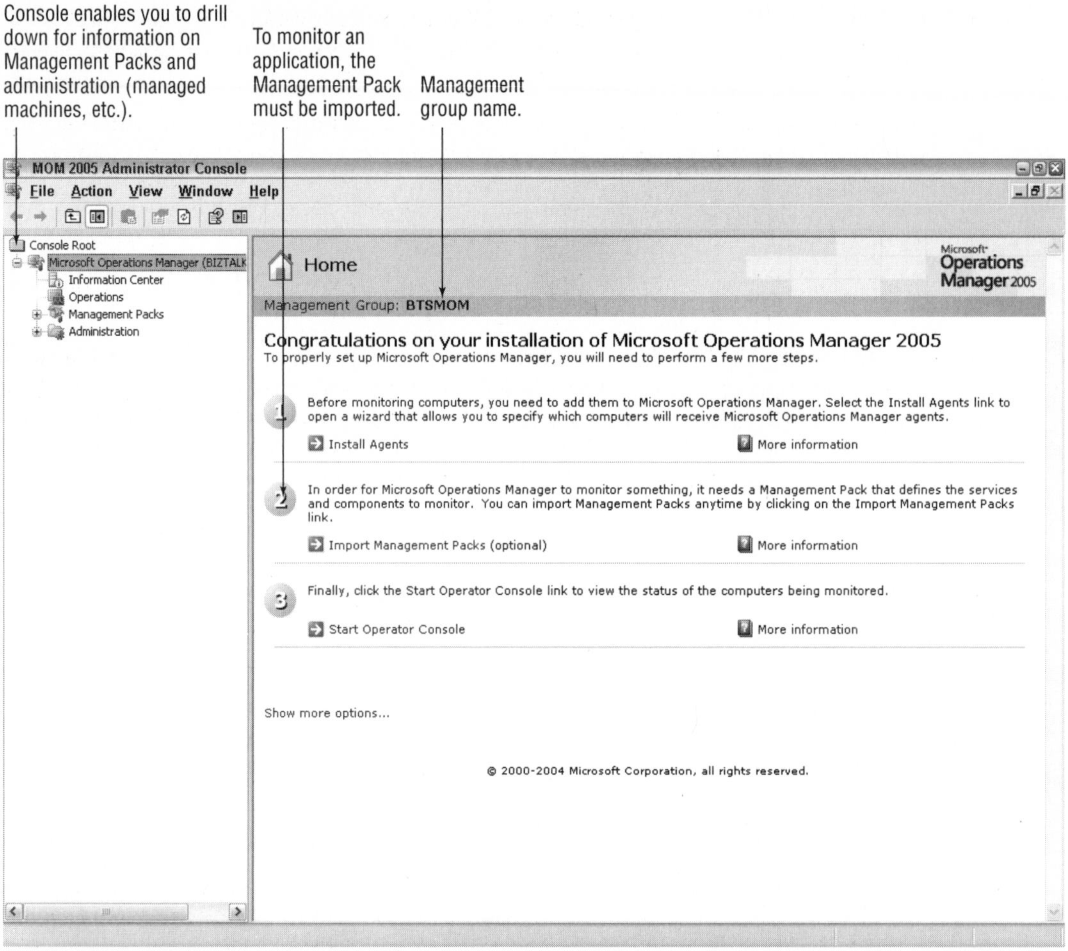

Console enables you to drill down for information on Management Packs and administration (managed machines, etc.).

To monitor an application, the Management Pack must be imported.

Management group name.

Figure 11-40

We will now deploy the necessary MOM Agent. To do so, perform the following steps:

1. Open the Administrator Console by selecting Start ➪ All Programs ➪ Microsoft Operations Manager 2005 ➪ Administrator Console. When the console opens, click the Install/Uninstall Agents Wizard button (located in the right-hand pane). This will start the Install/Uninstall Agents Wizard, which is responsible for installing and removing the MOM Agent from computers. The MOM Agent is the piece of software that sits on each server monitored by MOM and allows all the information to be gathered on the central MOM Management Server.

2. Follow the Install/Uninstall Agents Wizard and ensure that the agent has been deployed to all the servers within your BizTalk infrastructure. Note that MOM should always be installed on a separate infrastructure to your BizTalk environment and, unless your SQL server is clustered, it is desirable for it to have its own SQL environment. If it does share a cluster with the BizTalk SQL server, it should reside on its own instance of SQL on the cluster. Now that the necessary MOM Agents have been deployed, you can install the necessary Management Packs.

3. Download the self-extracting BizTalk and ESSO Management Pack executable from `www.microsoft.com/downloads/details.aspx?FamilyID=9E07C538-9ED4-41EA-9914-35DF6EFFB078&displaylang=en`.

After you've extracted it, you will notice four files: two documents and two `.akm` files, which are the two management packs. Before importing the BizTalk Management Packs, you need to deploy the pack for the underlying operating system. These are included in the Management-Packs folder of the installation media or can be downloaded from the Management Pack Catalog at `www.microsoft.com/technet/prodtechnol/mom/mom2005/catalog.aspx`.

4. Click the Import/Export Management Packs button on the MOM Administrator Console Home page to start the Import/Export Management Packs Wizard.

5. Click Next on the initial welcome screen. On the following screen, ensure that Import Management Packs and/or reports is selected, and then click Next. You will then be asked to specify a location to search for Management Packs (`.akm` files). You should browse or enter the location of the ManagementPacks folder on your installation media. (If you do not have this, you will need to download them from the Management Pack Catalog.) The next screen asks you to specify which management packs you would like to import. It is suggested that you import the following:

- ❑ `MicrosoftBaselineSecurityAnalyzer.akm`
- ❑ `MicrosoftOperationsManager2005.akm` (Management Pack for MOM itself)
- ❑ `MicrosoftActiveDirectory.akm`
- ❑ `MicrosoftBaseOperatingSystem.akm`
- ❑ `MicrosoftWindowsDNS.akm`
- ❑ `MicrosoftWindowsIIS.akm`
- ❑ `MicrosoftWindowsServerClusters.akm` (if you use this)

These are typically the main components involved in a BizTalk application, and they should be monitored as well to provide complete coverage. Note that if you wish to use MOM to monitor SQL Server 2005, you have to download the SQL 2005 Management Pack from the Management Pack Catalog. Hold down the Control key while selecting the Management Packs, to select more than one at a time. The screen should look similar to Figure 11-41.

6. Once you have selected the Management Packs, complete the wizard by clicking Next on the remaining screens.

7. Repeat steps 4–6, only this time install the BizTalk and ESSO Management Packs that are in the directory where you extracted them earlier.

After completing these steps, if you expand the Management Packs node of the Administrator Console and then the Rule Groups node, you should see a selection of rules grouped into different categories, including Microsoft BizTalk Server 2006 and Microsoft Enterprise Single Sign-On.

If you expand the Microsoft BizTalk Server 2006 rule group, you will see that it is broken up into three subgroups — BAM, BAS, and BizTalk Server Core — each of which is in turn separated into Event Rules, Alert Rules, and Performance Rules.

The Performance Rules are quite self-explanatory and are used to gather performance data to monitor the component. Alert Rules allow the MOM administrator to post process Performance Rules or Event Rules. For example, an Alert Rule could be created to send an e-mail to all system administrators if one of the Performance Rules or Event Rules generated an alert with a Service Unavailable severity.

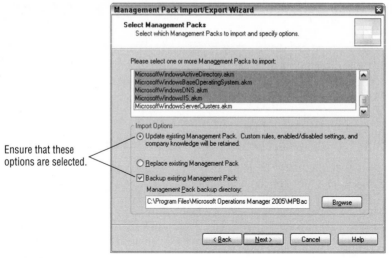

Ensure that these options are selected.

Figure 11-41

The Event Rules are essentially for two purposes: availability monitoring and health monitoring. Availability monitoring rules are designed to provide the administrator with information regarding the current operative state of the BizTalk Server (for example, to verify that it is up and able to process messages). All types of rules are configured by default to suppress repeated identical alerts, so as not to overwhelm the administrator with data.

Although the BizTalk and ESSO Management Packs provide a great deal of functionality out of the box, they do require additional configuration once they have been imported. Some rules are not enabled by default, as they require additional configuration. To look at this, open the Administrator Console and expand Management Packs ⇨ Rule Groups ⇨ Microsoft BizTalk Server 2006 (enabled) ⇨ BAM (enabled) ⇨ Performance Rules (5). If you look at the enabled column in the right-hand pane, you will see that the Total TDDS Failed Batches Exceeded Limit and the Total TDDS Events Failed Exceeded Limit rules are disabled by default (see Figure 11-42).

Both of these performance rules will generate an alert when a threshold, which has to be configured by you, is met. To illustrate how to configure the threshold, I will walk through how we configure the threshold for the Total TDDS Failed Batches Exceeded Limit rule.

First, double-click the Total TDDS Failed Batches Exceeded Limit rule. In the Threshold Rule Properties window (see Figure 11-43) that appears, click the Threshold tab.

On this tab you can alter the value of the threshold and determine whether the alert will fire if any sampled value is over the threshold, or if an average is required over a specified number of values. Once the threshold has been set appropriately, you can enable the rule by selecting the General tab, checking the This Rule Is Enabled box, and clicking OK.

This example illustrates that you should constantly be reviewing your MOM configuration to ensure that your monitoring strategy is effective. Review all the rules in all your rule groups periodically to ensure that they are enabled/disabled, as appropriate.

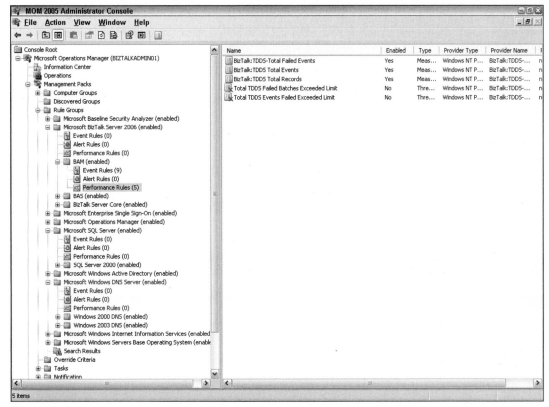

Figure 11-42

Figure 11-43

Now that the MOM agent has been deployed to each of the servers in your BizTalk infrastructure, the relevant rule groups will automatically be applied to the servers. This is done through the Computer Attributes node, which is below the Management Packs node; in here are the identifiers that are used by the agent to determine whether a server has a particular product installed. For example, if you double-click BizTalkServer2006Attribute, you will see that the `SOFTWARE\Microsoft\BizTalk Server\3.0\ProductVersion` Registry key is used to determine whether BizTalk is installed on the machine.

Creating Rules to Monitor BizTalk SQL Agent Jobs

It is possible to modify a rule in the Management Pack and to create new rules based on existing ones. The BizTalk Management Pack includes two Event Rules (disabled by default):

❏ Critical Error: A BizTalk SQL Server Agent job failed -Backup BizTalk Server

❏ Critical Error: A BizTalk SQL Server Agent job failed -Tracked Message Copy

These rules are configured to monitor the Backup BizTalk Server and Tracked Message Copy SQL Server Agent jobs. This section will walk you through creating a copy of one of these rules to monitor the DTA Purge and Archive job.

1. In the MOM Administrator Console, browse to Management Packs ➪ Microsoft BizTalk Server 2006 (enabled) ➪ BizTalk Server Core (enabled) ➪ Event Rules. Right-click the rule named Critical Error: A BizTalk SQL Server Agent Job Failed – Backup BizTalk Server, and select Copy.

2. Right-click on Event Rules under BizTalk Server Core and select Paste. This will create a rule with the name Copy of Critical Error: A BizTalk SQL Server Agent Job Failed – Backup BizTalk Server.

3. Rename this to something that represents that it will monitor the DTA Purge and Archive job (for example, Critical Error: A BizTalk SQL Server Agent Job Failed – DTA Purge and Archive).

4. Click on the Criteria tab; you will see the criteria that are used to match only a SQL Server Agent Event ID for the Backup BizTalk Server Job Failing. Click the Advanced button to edit the regular expression used.

5. Select Parameter 1 and click the Remove button. This will automatically populate the Define More Criteria box.

6. Change the wildcard in the Value box from *Backup BizTalk Server* to *DTA Purge and Archive* (see Figure 11-44).

7. Click Add to List, and then the Close button. Then check the This Rule Is Enabled box on the General tab, and choose OK to close the Event Rules Properties window.

Congratulations! You have created a rule that can be used to monitor for the failure of the DTA Purge and Archive Job. If required, you can now enable the rules that were precreated for you to monitor the Backup BizTalk Server and Tracked Message Copy jobs.

If you would like to create a rule to monitor any of the other SQL Agent jobs, follow the preceding steps and insert the appropriate wildcard for parameter 1. (Be careful what parameter you use.)

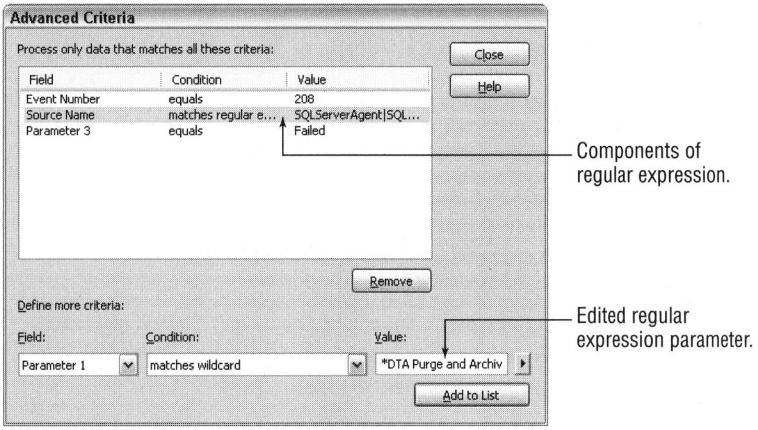

Figure 11-44

It is *very important* to note that for these rules to work, you need to ensure that the SQL Server used by BizTalk is included in the BizTalk Server 2006 computer group. To do this, in the Administrator Console expand the Management Packs node, select Computer Groups, then right-click BizTalk Server 2006 and select Properties. On the window that is displayed, click the Included Computers tab and verify that all your BizTalk and SQL Server machines are present in the group. If they are not, click the Add button and then browse the network to add in all BizTalk and SQL Server machines.

Hopefully, this example has shown you how useful the Management Pack can be and how it can be customized. For more information on customizing the Management Pack, see the online help section "Customizing the BizTalk Server 2006 Management Pack" at `http://msdn2.microsoft.com/en-US/library/aa560501.aspx`. We will now walk through the Operator Console, which allows you to view alerts as they are raised.

MOM Operator Console

The Administrator Console that was used previously allows you to deploy, configure, and manage MOM Agents and Management Packs, as well as providing the ability to customize Management Packs. The Operator Console provides a rich view of the data that MOM collects. To open it, select Operator Console from the Microsoft Operations Manager 2005 folder in the Programs menu. The Operator Console will default to the Alert Views tab.

Various alert views are available. All alerts for all rule groups are displayed by default. To view only the open BizTalk Core alerts, expand the Alert Views root, select Microsoft BizTalk Server, and then click BizTalk Server 2006 Core Open Alerts. If no alerts are displayed, try sending a message that you know will be suspended. You should get an alert similar to Figure 11-45. On the right-hand side, you will notice the Tasks pane. If this is not displayed, click the Tasks button on the menu bar to display it. The Task pane contains tasks that can be used to assist you in finding the root cause of a problem. There are typically tasks for every management pack, and BizTalk is no exception to this.

View filtered to
display only core
BizTalk open alerts.

System health traffic
light indicator.

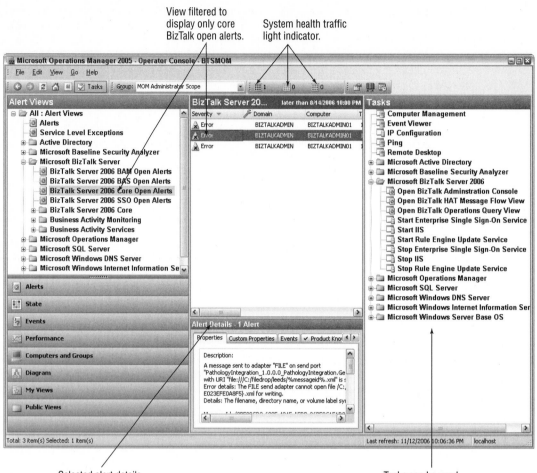

Selected alert details.

Tasks can be used
to help diagnose the
root cause of problems.

Figure 11-45

To use a task, select an alert in the middle pane. From here, you can perform such BizTalk tasks as view
the instance in HAT (this requires HAT to be installed on the machine the Console is running on) and
view the BizTalk Administration Console Operations view. Certain tasks may not be able to run for a particular warning. For example, in the case when a message was suspended but has since been resumed, the
error would show up in the Alerts view; however, if you attempted to run the Open BizTalk Operations
Query View task, it would not work because the instance is no longer present in the MessageBox.

When using the Operations Console, it is important to bear in mind that other components can cause
problems with BizTalk — for example, if a network card has failed or if the underlying operating system
has a problem. Therefore, you should always work from the ground up, which means not underestimat-
ing the power of basic tasks — for example, using the Ping task to test connectivity to the BizTalk server
that generated the error.

The Operator Console has many other uses. The traffic light indicator for System State categorizes errors; any critical errors are flagged as red. Figure 11-45 shows that there is one critical error, which actually turned out to be due to the BAM Alerts Service not starting correctly. This provides a good example of how you can use MOM to gain an at-a-glance view of how healthy your system is. The left-hand window also contains several other useful views, including the Performance view, which you can use to graphically display the performance monitor data collected by the BizTalk Management Pack.

> *We have really just scratched the surface in terms of what MOM can achieve. You should read the online MOM documentation in the links that were provided earlier. Every BizTalk administrator should also review the "Monitoring BizTalk Server Using MOM" section of the online help, at* http://msdn2.microsoft.com/en-US/library/aa577973.aspx.

Summary

Administering BizTalk is not a trivial task. This chapter began by illustrating that a BizTalk application typically involves lots of components, including IIS, SQL Server, SharePoint, and others, all of which need to be managed and maintained effectively. We then highlighted the tools that BizTalk comes with, such as the BizTalk Administration Console and BTSTask, which are incredibly powerful in the right hands.

It is very important that all application deployments are planned and controlled. The BizTalk Administration Console allows you to import and export MSI files containing the BizTalk application and other resources, such as additional .NET assemblies that may be required. The preparation before any deployment should not just be limited to making sure that the application code is right. It is important to ensure that all the necessary processes and procedures have been agreed upon and documented, and that proper training has been provided to the necessary personnel. Training BizTalk operations staff is often the most neglected area. This is dangerous because it can lead to mistakes being made that result in downtime. Wherever possible, you should automate administrative tasks. BizTalk provides BTSTask to automate deployment tasks.

To take advantage of BizTalk's scalability, it is important to separate the send, receive, processing, and tracking functions into their own dedicated hosts. This means that all the functions run in separate threads, thus eliminating the possibility of thread starvation.

We also noted that, no matter how many best practices are followed, the ability to troubleshoot is essential. You should ensure that your operations staff is familiar with how to drill down using the BizTalk Administration Console. The Group Hub Page provides gives a great at-a-glance view of the BizTalk group, which allows the user to quickly find the root cause of an issue. Setting up other tools as part of your base BizTalk server build, such as PSSDiag, the BizTalk BPA, and MBSA, enables you to get the information that you require quickly should a problem occur.

It is also important to note that many issues can be avoided by performing simple proactive maintenance. For example, you should always ensure that the master secret key has been backed up and that its restore process is documented and has been tested. Running the BizTalk BPA tool will identify many of the common configuration errors that customers make. Make use of the tools that other products provide, such as the built-in reporting functionality in SQL Server Management Studio. This is especially important if it is shared with other applications, as these may have an impact on it.

I cannot stress enough how important it is that you have an automated monitoring solution in place. Many instances of BizTalk downtime could have been avoided if there had been some monitoring in place. BizTalk provides a fully customizable Management Pack for MOM, which allows you to monitor the servers and automate problem resolution. Management Packs are also available for every Microsoft Server product, which means that MOM can be used to monitor all the components that BizTalk relies on.

The next chapter covers the End-to-End scenarios that ship with BizTalk. These are incredibly useful because they show how Microsoft experts have designed and implemented BizTalk solutions to solve complex customer problems.

12

End-to-End Scenarios

End-to-end scenarios (E2E) are somewhat of a trade secret, despite the fact that there is a huge amount of supporting documentation and all the source ships as part of the BizTalk SDK. They are sometimes referred to as *super samples*, but, in my opinion, this does them something of a disservice.

The E2E team was the first customer of BizTalk Server (2004 and 2006 releases) and was required to sign off on BizTalk Server 2006 being fit for release. The team worked with a number of high-profile and innovative customers to ensure that BizTalk could meet their highly challenging requirements, and helped the customers design and implement their scenarios in the best possible way.

The E2E team then distilled the important techniques and approaches used within these scenarios to architect and design three E2E scenarios (based on real-world customer scenarios).

The implementation of these three scenarios was performed by a dedicated team and leveraged best practices throughout. To address each scenario's requirements, a number of frequently requested BizTalk features were developed as part of the scenario, which we'll cover later in this chapter.

Each scenario was then put through highly challenging, production-quality performance testing. The results were then used to improve BizTalk's overall performance before launch.

Key people from the Microsoft field community were also rotated through the E2E team at regular intervals to provide further real-world experience and guidance and also to work on these scenarios. One deliverable of such a rotation was the development of the LoadGen performance-testing tool covered in Chapter 8, which was used by the E2E team for their testing.

Typical Microsoft SDK samples are good at providing simple demonstrations of specific technologies, but they often don't demonstrate best practices. This does not apply to the scenarios, which represent our current best practices for BizTalk solutions.

In short, these scenarios are invaluable to every BizTalk customer. They provide real-world guidance on how to solve complex problems and, even better, provide the full source code, enabling you to lift useful parts or approaches for use in your solution.

> *Because the scenarios are part of the BizTalk SDK, they are not supported in the same formal way as the BizTalk Server product. So you shouldn't expect Product Support Services–style support. However, Microsoft will provide developer-style assistance in case you run into problems, along with the usual community-based resources, such as newsgroups. It's worth remembering, however, that the scenario code was fully tested to production-quality levels, which should minimize potential problems.*

The Scenarios

The highly comprehensive documentation that ships with the E2E scenarios provides detailed information on each scenario along with explanation on all the patterns and approaches used throughout.

It doesn't make sense to re-create all the documentation within this chapter; instead, we will focus on introducing each scenario in turn and highlighting key features that might be useful to your scenario. In fact, a number of the patterns and techniques we've covered throughout this book are actually implemented as part of these scenarios.

The Business Process Management Scenario

The Business Process Management (BPM) scenario covers a cable TV ordering system for a customer called Southridge Video. At a high level, the solution enables call center users to activate, modify, or cancel a cable subscription and to update in-flight cable activation requests.

The business requirements imposed by Southridge Video follow. Because the scenario is based on a real-world scenario, most of them will apply to scenarios that you might develop.

❑   **Long-running processes** — A given cable order request may be completed very quickly or may last for up to a year. This poses a number of challenges for the overall solution, most notably the ability to change the business process during this time.

❑   **Process changes** — The business process, and therefore the implementation, will evolve over time and should require minimal changes to the overall solution and have little or no impact on any running processes.

❑   **Modify in-flight processes** — While an order is in flight through the solution, there is a requirement that any specific order can be modified or canceled as required. An in-flight order will be represented as an orchestration instance that needs to be interrupted.

❑   **End-to-end tracking** — The progress of an order throughout the solution should be fully visible to Southridge Video.

❑   **No suspended messages** — Suspended messages present administrative overhead and also a stalled cable order. Therefore, suspended messages should be eradicated and any failures should be passed to the Operations team to enable manual repair.

Figure 12-1 shows the overall scenario architecture.

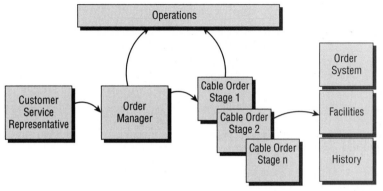

Figure 12-1

Highlights

The overall BPM scenario is very complex and can seem overwhelming to some people. In light of this, I've highlighted a number of aspects of the solution below that are of specific interest, particularly innovative, and of use to many solutions developed using BizTalk Server.

The reasoning behind each design choice in the scenario along with complete technical information is covered in the BizTalk documentation, and you can, of course, use parts of the solution in your own scenario as required. As with all SDK samples, you should understand the implementation fully; Microsoft provides no support for such samples as discussed earlier.

Process Manager Pattern

The Southridge Video ordering process can execute over a long period of time (weeks, months, or even a year). Although the business process could be implemented with one or two orchestrations, this would seriously hamper the ability to modify the business process implementation over time, because any orchestration changes could not be picked up by in-flight orchestrations, as they were already instantiated.

To address this, the business process can be split up into multiple discrete parts, instead of one large monolithic orchestration. Thus, these individual orchestrations would complete individually during the business process. This, of course, then enables orchestrations involved in the latter stages of processing to be modified and then picked up as required during execution of the process.

Although this enables modification of the business process implementation, it doesn't address the scenario in which the business process changes significantly, perhaps through the addition of an extra processing step. A monolithic or fixed business process would require changes to incorporate a further step.

To address both requirements, the BPM scenario implements the Process Manager pattern, which is designed for scenarios in which you don't necessarily know what processing steps are required at design time. You can find more information on this pattern at www.enterpriseintegrationpatterns.com/ ProcessManager.html.

The number of stages is a configuration setting that the BPM scenario has chosen to store within the SSO store. The `OrderManager` orchestration retrieves this number when it is activated and iterates through the number of stages, starting at 1 and ending at the total number of stages configured.

The `OrderManager` orchestration cannot bind directly to each processing stage orchestration, as this would require the `OrderManager` orchestration to change each time new stages were introduced. To counter this, a technique using inverse direct bound ports is used. This is covered in more depth in Chapter 5.

In short, a logical port (`StagePort`), which is configured as an inverse direct bound port, is created on the `OrderManager` orchestration. This is used to communicate with all stage-processing orchestrations. This port is configured to use the `Direct` port binding, and the `Port on partner orchestration` setting is pointed at itself (the `StagePort`). This implies no direct bindings between orchestrations.

A stage-processing orchestration (e.g., `CableOrder1.odx`) has a logical port, which uses the same port type as that used by the `OrderManager` `StagePort`. This port is also configured to use the Direct port binding, and the `Port on partner orchestration` setting is pointed at the `StagePort` port defined on the `OrderManager` orchestration.

This configuration is effectively saying that messages sent through the `StagePort` port on the `OrderManager` orchestration will be delivered to anyone who is listening to messages from this send port. The Process Stage orchestration is itself saying that it will receive messages sent from the `OrderManager` orchestration through the `StagePort` port — a form of backward subscription, if you will. The `OrderManager` orchestration is effectively broadcasting via the `StagePort` port to anyone subscribing to the port.

The BizTalk message representing an order (`OrderMessageMsg`) is configured as a multipart message. The first part contains the order content, and the second part contains the routing information.

When the orchestration needs to pass the Order to the next stage of processing, it updates the routing information with the next stage number. Stage-processing orchestrations then subscribe to Messages of this type with the relevant stage number. This is an important step. If the stage-processing orchestrations were not filtered on the relevant stage number, they would receive all messages of this type because they would all be subscribing to the same message type. The filter enables routing to the right stage-processing orchestration.

Figure 12-2 shows an example of a stage-processing orchestration subscription.

The general rule of when to split orchestrations into separate stages for a pattern like this is after your orchestration has hit a long-running persistence point, such as a Receive or Delay shape. This technique then reduces the amount of time an orchestration is in flight and enables new processing stages to be added or modified easily. If the entire process were implemented as one monolithic orchestration, you would not be able to add new processing stages to in-flight orchestrations, which is a critical requirement for this scenario, as an order can be active for many months.

Interrupting In-Flight Orchestrations

The BPM scenario supports the ability for an order that is currently being processed to be altered in flight. Once the `OrderManager` has started a stage-processing orchestration, it waits on a listen shape that is configured to list for an Order Update, Stage Completed, or Stage Terminated message.

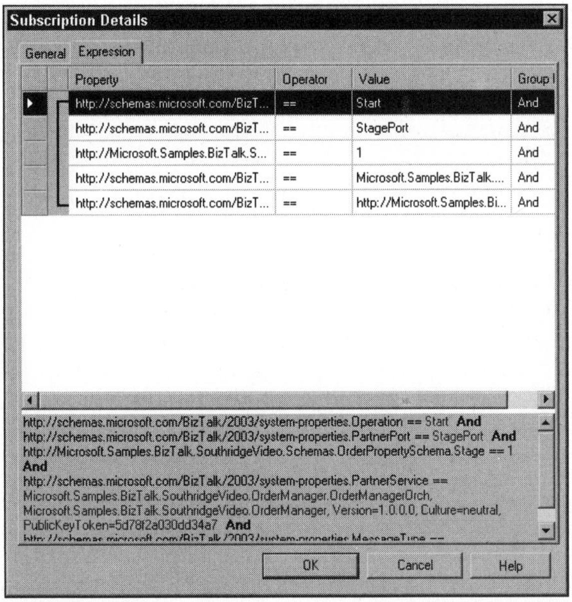

Figure 12-2

If an Order Update message arrives, the order processing needs to be interrupted to take into consideration the order change. An Order Update can be a cancellation or a simple update of the details.

Either way, the `InterruptOrch` orchestration is invoked. It can be found in the `Interrupted.odx` file of the `OrderManager` project. This orchestration simply constructs an interrupt message and sends it via an inverse direct bound port, which, like that detailed in the previous section, enables any interested orchestration to receive the interrupt message.

In this scenario, each Processing Stage orchestration has a port defined using the same port type, thus enabling it to receive interrupt messages. Each Processing Stage orchestration is then required to call the `CheckInterruptOrch` orchestration, which can be found in the `CheckInterrupt.odx` file of the `OrderManager` project.

The Processing Stage orchestrations call the `CheckInterrupt` orchestration at regular convenient intervals to see if an interrupt has been requested. The `CheckInterrupt` orchestration is shown in Figure 12-3.

As you can see, the CheckInterrupt orchestration uses a Listen shape with two branches. The first branch attempts to receive an interrupt message, whereas the second branch uses a Delay shape to wait for a delay period of 0.

The Listen shape will execute the first branch first. Therefore, if an interrupt message has been sent, it will be retrieved and the second branch will never execute, whereas if an interrupt message has not been sent, the Delay Branch will fire and ultimately return to the calling orchestration.

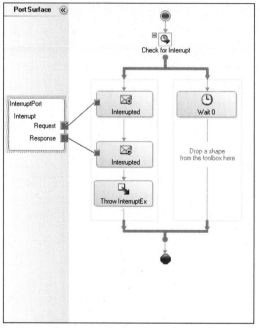

Figure 12-3

> Remember that branches in scenarios like this are executed in order from left to right until the *listen* condition is satisfied.

If an interrupt message is returned, an exception is returned to the calling orchestration, which itself will terminate the orchestration and the OrderManager orchestration that starts processing of the order again from the beginning.

Any interrupt processing is logged comprehensively using BAM providing end-to-end instrumentation of what has happened during order processing.

Single Sign-On Store Used for Configuration Data

The BPM scenario elects to store configuration data inside the SSO store. As we cover in Chapter 13, this approach enables configuration data to be stored in a central store rather than individual configuration files located across all BizTalk Servers, which can lead to inconsistent configuration problems.

Once configuration data is stored in the SSO store, it can then easily be accessed by multiple BizTalk Servers. It is then cached manually to reduce the latency of configuration requests. This approach is utilized by the BizTalk adapters and pipeline components to store configuration data, including sensitive usernames and passwords. These are stored in encrypted form by SSO.

The code implemented for this can be found in the SSOConfigHelper.cs file, located inside the Utilities subproject. SSOConfigHelper is implemented as a helper class to enable orchestrations to easily retrieve configuration data. It also implements an internal cache to reduce the latency of configuration setting retrieval.

An example of the configuration data being read can be found in the `OrderManager` orchestration inside the `Initialize Stages` expression. The scripts to create the SSO Application and to populate the data can be found in the `CreateSouthridgeVideoApplication.cmd` script file, which is located in the `SDK\Scenarios\BPM\Scripts` directory.

End-to-End Order Tracking

The BPM scenario implements end-to-end order tracking by using Business Activity Monitoring (BAM). The scenario records data directly using the BAM API and the `OrchestrationEventStream`. See Chapter 6 for an in-depth discussion of these concepts and why the Tracking Profile Editor might not be suitable for your scenario.

A façade over the `OrchestrationEventStream` was developed to provide a process specific façade to the orchestration developers, which can then call methods like `RequestReceivedFromVendor` or `RepliedToRequester`, passing the required data. The various façade classes can be found in the `ServiceLevelTracking` subproject.

The BAM definition is defined using Excel and can be found in the `SDK\Scenarios\BPM\BAM` subdirectory.

Ops Adapter

The BPM scenario ensures that all exceptions are caught within orchestrations, and in the case of messages that are suspended by BizTalk (i.e., a malformed in-bound message), a send port (`BizTalkErrors-SP`) is created that subscribes to all messages where the context property `ErrorReport.ErrorType` exists.

Catching these *errors* is the first step; the next and most important step is providing these to somebody to implement a form of *manual repair*.

As part of its implementation, the BPM scenario has provided an Ops adapter, which is a fully featured BizTalk adapter built on the Adapter Framework. The Ops adapter receives a message and then invokes a preconfigured .NET assembly that is responsible for routing or storing the message for repair. The .NET assembly can be configured through the usual adapter configuration in the BizTalk Administration Tool (see Figure 12-4).

The .NET assembly used by the Ops adapter must implement the `IOpsAIC` interface. This can be found in the `IOpsAIC.cs` file within the `IOPsAIC` project of the `OpsAdapter` solution in the `SDK\Scenarios\BPM\OpsAdapter` folder. The .NET assembly must also be located in the Global Assembly Cache, because reflection is used by the Ops adapter.

The supplied .NET assembly invoked by the Ops adapter is the `OperationsClient`, which uses Remoting to communicate with the `OperationsServer`, which uses an `OperationsHandler` that dumps messages via the `Trace` class. Although this implementation of an `OperationsClient` isn't particularly useful, it demonstrates how you can plug in your own operations client with ease.

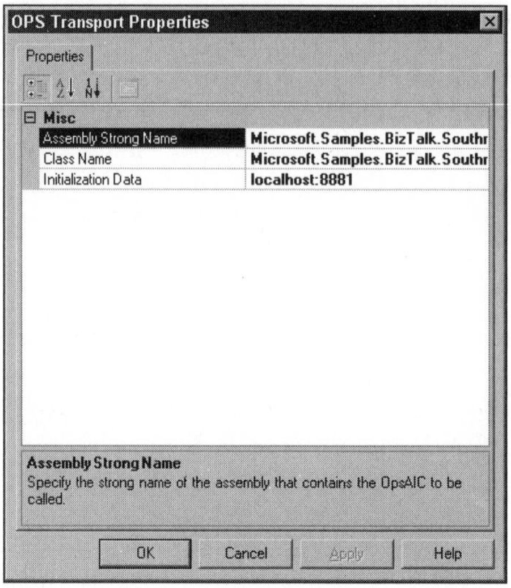

Figure 12-4

It's also worth noting the Ops adapter has been developed with all the adapter best practices in mind and has been fully tested as part of the scenario testing. Therefore, it could be used as the basis for your own adapter.

Tracing

The BPM scenario, along with the other scenarios, makes good use of the `System.Diagnostics.Trace` class to provide basic developer-level tracing of the overall solution.

Default configuration means that any trace information will be output to the debug console. A tool like DebugView from Windows Sysinternals (`www.microsoft.com/technet/sysinternals`) can be used to view along with the output pane of Visual Studio.

Installation

Again, the BizTalk documentation for the BPM scenario is extremely comprehensive, and the configuration of some scenarios can be fiddly, so refer to the "Deploying the Business Process Management Solution" section of the BizTalk Server documentation.

If you want to review the source code for the scenario, you can find the scenario installed at `%PROGRAM-FILES%\Microsoft BizTalk Server 2006\SDK\Scenarios\BPM`.

The Service-Oriented Scenario

The Serviced-Oriented (SO) scenario covers a solution developed for Woodgrove Bank, which is required to offer a credit balance retrieval service for its customers.

To retrieve a balance, the scenario implementation must communicate with a SAP system hosted on a mainframe via the SAP adapter to retrieve the credit limit. The scenario must then communicate with a mainframe system via Host Integration Server to retrieve the total amount of pending transactions. Finally, it must communicate with a payment-tracking system via MQSeries to retrieve recent payments made on the account.

Figure 12-5 shows the overall scenario architecture.

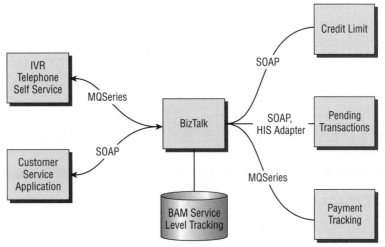

Figure 12-5

Once the responses have received, they need to be aggregated, and a response must be returned to the caller. The caller can request a balance in two ways, either via a self-service telephone system (Interactive Voice Recognition [IVR]) communicating with the service via MQSeries or via a call center with a member of staff using a Windows Forms application that communicates with the solution via a Web service.

Because the customer is waiting *synchronously* for the result, performance is paramount. It's unacceptable for the customer to have to wait for a significant amount of time. Woodgrove Bank has imposed the following performance requirements on the BizTalk part of the solution. (The latency incurred by accessing the supporting systems is not included in these requirements.)

❑ Must support a sustained throughput of 40 incoming requests per second.

❑ Must support a peak throughput of 100 incoming requests per second.

❑ Ninety percent of requests must be processed from end to end within 1000 milliseconds.

❑ Ninety-five percent of requests must be processed end-to-end within 2000 milliseconds.

❑ One hundred percent of requests must be processed from end to end within 5000 milliseconds.

Highlights

The SO scenario and the BPM scenario represent scenarios that BizTalk is frequently used to solve. I've highlighted a number of key techniques, some of which are likely to be of use in your solution.

As with the BPM scenario, the reasoning behind each design choice in the scenario, along with complete technical information, is covered in the BizTalk documentation. You can, of course, use parts of the solution in your own scenarios as required. (See the chapter introduction for a discussion of the support you can expect for the scenario code.)

Also refer to Chapter 10 for an explanation of the requirements and trade-offs, and also information on how you can reduce latency further by adjusting the out-of-the-box configuration settings.

The Scatter Gather Pattern

Within the scenario implementation, three supporting systems must be communicated with in order to receive all the information required to service the user's request. In light of the stringent latency requirements, these requests should be processed in parallel to enable the three requests to be undertaken at the same time, instead of waiting for each request to finish before starting the next.

There are a number of implementation approaches for this requirement, which is based on the Scatter Gather pattern. You can find more information on this at `www.enterpriseintegrationpatterns.com/BroadcastAggregate.html`.

A loosely coupled implementation could have been implemented, allowing for easy addition of new systems. However, because we know which systems we need to call and there is no requirement to add new systems, we directly invoke the systems and therefore avoid the performance overhead associated with a loosely coupled system. It's important to remember the specific business requirements when designing a low-latency implementation.

The `CustomerService` orchestration utilizes the Parallel shape with multiple branches to send messages to multiple systems concurrently. (Refer to Chapter 5 for a full explanation of how the Parallel shape works.) Remember that the Parallel shape works concurrently not in terms of threading but in terms of the business process, so only one branch will be executed at any one point in time.

Figure 12-6 shows a fragment of the `CustomerService` orchestration. You can see that a Receive shape is used within each branch to retrieve the response following an initial send — both of which are highlighted in Figure 12-6. All branches must complete before the orchestration can complete.

The Aggregator Pattern

After the three responses have been retrieved from the supporting systems, the responses need to be aggregated to form a single response to the client.

A common pattern used to implement this is the Aggregator pattern, which is detailed at `www.enterpriseintegrationpatterns.com/Aggregator.html`.

The ability to perform aggregation using the BizTalk Mapper is often overlooked but in fact provides a very convenient and practical solution for such a pattern. When configuring a Transform shape, you can supply multiple input messages, which can then be used as part of the map design to form a single output message, using connectors and functoids, as required.

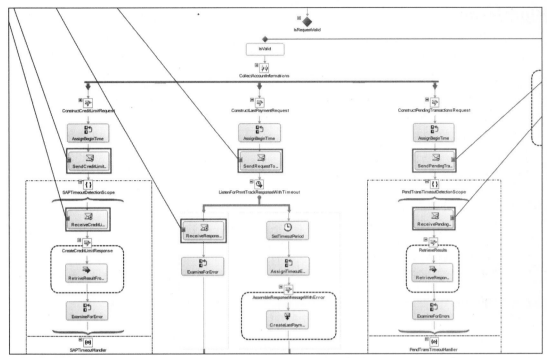

Figure 12-6

Figure 12-7 shows an example of configuring a Transform shape with multiple input messages.

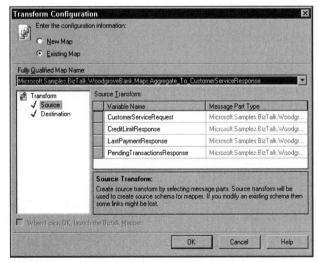

Figure 12-7

Inline Pipeline Invocation

As detailed earlier in this chapter, the performance of the SO scenario is paramount because customers are synchronously waiting for a response. Anything that can be done to reduce the request latency will have a direct effect on the end-user experience.

The SO scenario demonstrates the technique, introduced in Chapter 10, of invoking send pipelines inline directly from the BizTalk orchestration. This avoids the latency incurred by first publishing messages to the BizTalk MessageBox and then having the appropriate send port retrieve the message, and the reverse process for the response messages.

Three implementations of the orchestrations required for the SO scenario are included, each located within its own subproject of the overall solution: `Orchestrations.Adapter`, `Orchestrations.Inline`, and `Orchestrations.Stub`.

The `Adapter` version of the orchestrations uses the send and receive shapes, as usual, and therefore should demonstrate the greatest amount of latency. The `Inline` version invokes the supporting systems directly, avoiding adapters, and therefore reduces the overall latency. The `Stub` version calls *stub* Web service versions of the supporting system, which is ideal for a developer configuration, where the developers may not have access to a SAP system.

When testing the solution using the client, you can elect to use any of these methods and observe the performance benefit of each solution.

The `Orchestrations.Inline` version of the orchestrations uses three helper classes to invoke the supporting systems. Calls to the Pending Transactions system (`Microsoft.Samples.BizTalk .WoodgroveBank.PendingTransactionsCall`) and the Credit Limit (`Microsoft.Samples .BizTalk.WoodgroveBank.SAPCall`) system are both done inline without using adapters and use a Web service. Note the custom exception- and timeout-handling implementations, which are required because adapters are not being used.

The call to the payment-tracking system is performed inline, using the MQSeries Client API. However, in this case, receive and send pipelines must be used to process the messages. The send pipeline (`PaymentTrackerSendPipeline.btp`) is called to generate a request message, which is then sent to the MQSeries queue, using the `PaymentTrackerCall` class. The response is then passed through a receive pipeline (`PaymentTrackerReceivePipeline.btp`).

Service-Level Tracking

The SO scenario provides full service-level tracking of requests through the end-to-end solution by utilizing BAM. BAM is used via the `OrchestrationEventStream` API in the same way as in the BPM scenario; refer to the previous section for further information.

Full timing information for each part of the system is stored, providing fine-grained information on where time is being spent, and any error details are also stored. The built-in BAM portal can be used to query the data, along with any other SQL-aware data tool.

The BAM definition is defined using Excel and can be found in the `SDK\Scenarios\SO\BTSSoln\BAM` subdirectory.

Stubs

The SO scenario provides three stubs for the supporting systems; these are implemented as three Web services that mimic these systems. These were implemented for use by, say, a developer who may not have access to these systems during development. They also enable the system to work "in a box," which can be a useful technique if you must perform performance testing off site without access to these systems. The performance results, however, may not be indicative, as the stubs won't be able to replicate the real-life behavior of these systems when under sustained, concurrent load.

SSO for LOB Credential Storage

Like the BPM scenario, SSO is used for storage of configuration details. In addition to this approach, the SSO scenario stores credentials that are required to be supplied when communicating with the supporting systems.

Unlike "clear text" configuration data, credentials for these line-of-business systems must be secured appropriately, which SSO does, and the adapters usually hide this from you.

The "Using SSO Efficiently in the Service Oriented Solution" section of the BizTalk documentation covers this in depth (see `http://msdn2.microsoft.com/en-us/library/aa561067.aspx`).

Latency Control

The SSO scenario provides a sample Windows Forms–based application that can be used to drive the scenario. As you can see in Figure 12-8, the client enables you to select the transport type (SOAP or MQSeries) and, in the case of the SOAP transport, which implementation type (Adapter, Inline, or Stub).

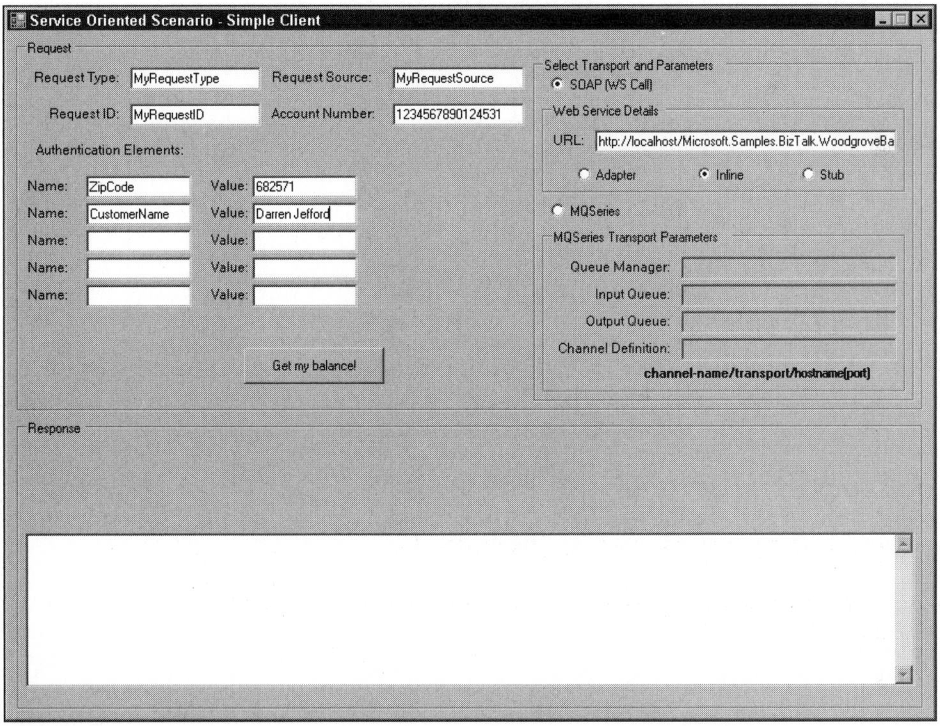

Figure 12-8

You can use this application to understand the performance benefits associated with each approach.

Installation

As with the previous scenarios, the BizTalk documentation for this SO scenario is extremely comprehensive. Refer to the "Deploying the Service Oriented Solution" section of the BizTalk Server documentation.

To review the source code, you can find the scenario installed at `%PROGRAMFILES%\Microsoft BizTalk Server 2006\SDK\Scenarios\SO`.

The Business-to-Business Scenario

The Business-to-Business scenario (B2B) covers a solution developed by a fictional company called LitWare, which provides a distribution network that enables customers and brokers to place orders with vendors.

The primary focus of the scenario is to enable orders received from customers to be routed to the appropriate vendors for processing. Each order, depending on its contents, will require different vendors to be used, and they will change over time. In light of this, the scenario is loosely coupled to enable easy modification of vendors and suppliers, and provides a centralized way of modifying this information.

The scenario makes use of the Trading Partner Management System to enable business users to control customers and vendors involved in the trading partner *network* without having to modify the technical solution. Generic orchestrations then identify how to communicate with these partners by retrieving profile information from the Trading Partner database.

> *The design and implementation of the scenario was done with the BizTalk Server 2006 release and does not take into consideration the new EDI features provided with BizTalk Server 2006 R2. If you choose to adopt some of the approaches within the scenario for your solution, you may want to review the EDI documentation for R2 to understand if other alternatives are available.*

Highlights

In line with the previous scenarios, there is complete documentation for the B2B scenario within the BizTalk documentation. A number of solution highlights are covered below to pull out techniques that are often of use in general BizTalk solutions, not just B2B.

The Message Broker Pattern

A number of distinct business processes are used within the B2B scenario, including processing new orders, updating orders, and updating trading partners.

Each order may contain one or more orders, all of which could be destined for a different destination *partner* to fulfil the order, and these trading partners will change over time.

In light of this, a flexible and dynamic routing pattern must be implemented that allows for constant changes and flexibility in these trading partners. The B2B scenario implements a pattern based on the

Message Broker pattern. You can find out more at `www.enterpriseintegrationpatterns.com/MessageBroker.html`.

In this scenario, all partner information is held within the Trading Partner Management system that the BizTalk orchestrations use to route order messages and retrieve e-mail addresses to send order acknowledgments to vendors. This centralized storage of routing information, coupled with generic (i.e., not partner-specific) orchestrations, is a great example of the Message Broker pattern.

The Splitter Pattern

An order message submitted to the B2B scenario can contain one or more discrete orders, each of which may need to be processed by a different vendor. To enable this, the `ConfirmOrderWithVendors` orchestration implements a version of the Splitter pattern. You can find more on this pattern at `www.enterpriseintegrationpatterns.com/Sequencer.html`.

The orchestration retrieves each order within the message in turn and submits it to the appropriate vendor. The Splitter pattern is implemented using an XPath expression to count the number of orders held within a message and then uses another XPath expression to retrieve each order within the scope of an orchestration Loop shape.

Dynamic Send Ports

During order processing, an order acknowledgement e-mail must be sent to the vendor. Because the order-processing orchestration (`ConfirmOrderWithVendors`) is used for all vendor types, it must retrieve the vendor's e-mail address from the Trading Partner Management system and then send the e-mail.

A dynamic port is used to implement this requirement. This enables the orchestration to dynamically configure a send port with the vendor's e-mail address. This technique means that a send port doesn't have to be created for each possible vendor; instead, a dynamic port is used with a BizTalk orchestration, which is then configured with the required adapter and address information at runtime.

Trading Partner Management

The B2B scenario makes use of the Trading Partner Management functionality included within BizTalk to identify the partners that should be used to fulfil a given order. Given the flux of new trading partners being added, modified, or removed, business users are given the ability to control trading partners.

The `GetUserProfile` orchestration within the scenario accesses trading partner information using a custom `TPMAccess` Web service, which is a simplified wrapper around the standard Trading Partner Management Web service.

Trading partners are managed through the Business Activity Services site via a set of customized InfoPath forms provided as part of the B2B scenario.

Creating Empty Messages

Often within a BizTalk solution you have a requirement to create a new message. Although you can do so through the use of a Transform shape, if you have no use for a BizTalk map, this is a cumbersome approach.

Chapter 5 introduced this approach: A helper class, through the use of a serializable class created via the `xsd.exe` tool, exposes a method whose return value can be cast directly to a BizTalk message. This approach enables a new message to be easily integrated within a BizTalk orchestration.

The B2B scenario implements a similar approach. However, instead of using serializable classes, it stores the underlying XML representing an empty message inside a resource file that is retrieved by an orchestration by using the `ResourceHelper` class, which you can find with `helper.cs` in the `Utilities` project.

The serialization approach, while perhaps slightly neater and easier to use, introduces extra performance overhead because you make use of the .NET serialization stack. This probably won't be that noticeable but under load may become overhead you cannot tolerate.

This approach may be a better solution in that case, but remember that you will always have to update the XML held within the resource whenever the schema changes, whereas the serialization approach is derived directly from the XML schema used by BizTalk.

You should test and make the choice based on your solution and requirements; the result of both approaches is the same.

Installation

Again, the BizTalk documentation for the B2B scenario is extremely comprehensive, and the configuration of some scenarios can be fiddly. Refer to the "Deploying a Business-to-Business Solution" section of the BizTalk Server documentation for more information.

To review the source code for the scenario, you can find the scenario installed at `%PROGRAMFILES%\ Microsoft BizTalk Server 2006\SDK\Scenarios\B2B`.

Summary

This chapter introduced the E2E scenarios and positioned the investment that the BizTalk product team made in order to ensure that the BizTalk 2006 release would enable customers to effectively develop and deploy complex, mission-critical solutions.

The next chapter continues the theme of best practices, covering scenarios from the processing large messages debatching of messages to the loose coupling of your orchestration.

13

BizTalk Best Practices

This chapter covers some best practices that we have developed and implemented as part of various cutting-edge BizTalk projects. There is often more than one way of solving a problem using the tools available, and sometimes you only find the *right* way after learning the hard way the first time around.

Each of the areas that we cover in this chapter has been key to developing these solutions. They have either greatly simplified a solution, significantly improved performance, or resolved a complicated design goal previously deemed impossible or unworkable.

Processing Large Messages

In my experience, solutions that must process large messages from end to end tend to be fairly rare. Generally, large input files can be debatched by a receive pipeline into smaller discrete messages. This debatching removes the need to worry about a large message and enables processing to be parallelized.

However, development of a BizTalk solution that must deal with large messages through pipelines and orchestrations can often prove problematic.

The golden rule when dealing with large messages might seem obvious, but it is often broken: You *must* limit or (the ideal approach) remove any operations that require the entire message to be loaded into memory.

BizTalk itself operates a streaming approach whereby the message is read through the use of a stream, meaning that the entire message doesn't have to be present in memory at any point in time. (This is discussed in detail in Chapter 4.) This streaming approach is used by the built-in pipeline components such as the Flat File Disassembler, XML Disassembler, and in fact the whole BizTalk engine, meaning that BizTalk will do the *right thing* with regard to processing large messages, but you need to ensure that any custom pipeline components, orchestrations, or helper classes follow this approach.

An exception to this rule occurs when XML messages containing a CDATA element that holds a large payload (greater than 1MB) are received. CDATA elements cannot be streamed; they must be requested in their entirety.

The BizTalk Mapper uses XSLT under the covers, which in normal cases requires that the entire message be loaded into memory to perform a transformation. This was true for the BizTalk Mapper in the 2004 release of BizTalk. Under any load whatsoever, this requirement causes "out-of-memory" problems pretty quickly (and therefore ruled out the mapping of large messages in BizTalk Server 2004).

In contrast, BizTalk Server 2006 has implemented a virtual stream mechanism. If the message size is over 1MB, it is spilled over into a temporary file, thus keeping the memory usage flat during mapping. Of course, this swapping incurs performance overhead, but this is much better than running out of memory! Small messages will continue be mapped in memory. This approached is covered in Chapter 4.

In my experience, custom pipeline components or helper classes invoked from orchestration are often the cause of problems when dealing with large messages because they load the entire message into memory. An operation such as using the XmlDocument will load the entire message into memory and ruin the flat-memory model of pipeline execution, because it does not make use of a streaming approach.

As covered in Chapter 4, you should wherever possible avoid this by using a forward-only streaming approach, which minimizes the amount of data held in memory. If this isn't possible, you can use the VirtualStream implementation shipped as part of the BizTalk SDK.

The VirtualStream implementation wraps any .NET stream, and when memory use exceeds a configured limit (normally 1MB), it is swapped out to disk (similar to BizTalk maps in BizTalk Server 2006). Of course, this swapping also impacts performance due to the disk I/O overhead.

Executing rules against a large XML message is something to avoid. The BizTalk Rules Engine (BRE) requires that XML messages be asserted into the BRE memory using a TypedXmlDocument based on an XmlDocument (which therefore requires the entire message to be loaded into memory).

When monitoring a BizTalk solution's memory use that does make use of, for instance, an XmlDocument to load a large message, you will observe that the amount of memory used for, say, a 100MB message can be around 10x the actual message size. This disparity results because the XmlDocument needs to build an in-memory representation of the XML document, which requires significant memory over and above that needed for the raw data.

If you must process a large message end to end through BizTalk, it's generally advisable to implement some form of debatching or splitting mechanism in-bound to carve up the message into messages of a manageable size. The results of processing these messages can be aggregated as required to perform a single response by using a sequential convoy pattern.

As with every design decision made with a BizTalk solution, ensure that you prototype and test any design to understand fully the impacts and requirements it imposes. If you fail to do so (with, for instance, how you process large messages), you might have to fundamentally alter the architecture of your solution late in its development life cycle and thus delay the project.

Looping/Storing Messages

Often, and especially when dealing with sequential convoy scenarios, you need somewhere to store multiple messages. Take a look at the orchestration fragment shown in Figure 13-1.

Figure 13-1

As you can see, each loop iteration invokes the Receive shape to receive another message and store it in the same BizTalk message variable, thus losing a reference to the message stored in the last iteration.

XLANG doesn't support arrays, so you cannot leverage an array of BizTalk messages to store each message. (You could use a .NET ArrayList, but iteration is hard without using nonserializable types.) However, you can take advantage of a couple of workarounds, depending on your requirements.

You must bear in mind, however, the memory and orchestration state overhead of such a solution. Obviously, storing many messages in this way will use increasing amounts of memory, so you should ensure that you fully test this aspect of your solution. In addition, each extra message stored through either method will incur extra orchestration state, which will be persisted during dehydration, thus increasing SQL I/O and CPU overhead. While this isn't necessarily a problem, you should bear it in mind and potentially make use of the virtual stream approach, as appropriate.

❑ **Use a multipart message** — As the name implies, a multipart message can contain any number of parts, which can be dynamically created. The "Creating a Multipart BizTalk Message" section of Chapter 5 shows an example.

❑ **Use a custom .NET class that exposes a method that accepts a parameter of type XLANG-Message** — This custom .NET class can then convert the message into whichever format is required — perhaps a serializable class (as long as the message isn't large) — and store it inside a collection (thus enabling subsequent retrieval or processing by the .NET component).

Storing Configuration Data

Storage of application configuration data is a problem in any BizTalk project. You might have string literals used by orchestrations or .NET assemblies that should be made configurable to enable change after compilation, endpoint URLs for dynamic sends, caching of data, and so on. Because orchestrations and

.NET assemblies are represented as DLLs, they cannot have standard .NET-style configuration files. Instead, any configuration entries must be placed in the loading application's configuration file (`YourLoadingApplication.exe.config`). You can then access these entries via the usual `AppSettings` approach.

For BizTalk-based solutions, the loading application is always the BizTalk service: `btsntsvc.exe`. You can find this service in `%PROGRAMFILES%\Microsoft BizTalk Server 2006`. Of course, any parts of your solution hosted by other applications such as IIS will introduce another configuration file (e.g., `web.config`).

If you add custom entries such as the ones shown here to the existing `btsntsvc.exe.config file`, you can retrieve them using the following code:

```
<configuration>
  <appSettings>
    <add key ="AServerName" value="MYSERVER1"/>
  </appSettings>
</configuration>

string ServerName = ConfigurationManager.AppSettings["AServerName"];
```

Although this works fine, it does require a sensitive configuration file to be updated. If you make a typo in `btsntsvc.exe.config`, it will cause the BizTalk Service to fail when starting. Therefore, modification is something your administrator is likely to discourage.

It also requires the configuration data to be spread across each of your BizTalk servers and therefore be not stored in one central location. This can lead to servers using stale configuration data and therefore experiencing intermittent errors. The BizTalk service also has to be restarted to pick up new configuration data, which can prove awkward with a live system.

Security is another issue. Perhaps you don't want a particular configuration value to be generally visible to server administrators. Because it's in clear text, however, you don't have much choice, unless you implement custom encryption. An approach that I've used heavily with customers is to use the Single Sign-On (SSO) store. SSO is already in place for every BizTalk Server installation. Adapters already use SSO to store adapter configuration data and secure information such as usernames and passwords and other configuration information. It's important to note that SSO doesn't only have to be used to store *secrets*.

SSO data is cached on each server within the SSO service process and thus avoids the penalty of having to look up configuration data across the network each time it's needed. In addition, it has a built-in cache-refresh feature.

As you may notice when reviewing the End-to End (E2E) scenarios, the supplied usage of the SSO for configuration data implements a custom form of caching locally within the BizTalk process. This is to reduce cross-process calls between the BizTalk and SSO operating-system processes. This isn't major performance overhead in most instances; however, the E2E team had very stringent latency requirements for the SO scenario and therefore optimized everything they could to ensure that they met their performance numbers. You can adopt this approach, as required.

In short, SSO does everything you require. Configuration data is stored securely in one place, enabling you to store sensitive information without having to implement custom security approaches, and it can be quickly accessed via a local cache.

So how do you go about storing and retrieving configuration data in the SSO store? Documentation is fairly light, and there are limited built-in administrative tools to assist you. That said, the benefits outweigh this slight pain.

Fortunately, the End-to-End scenarios team has provided a tool to get and set configuration data as part of the scenario shipped with BizTalk Server 2006. We cover this more in Chapter 12, but for this sample we'll use the `BTSScnSSOApplicationConfig.exe` tool supplied as part of the scenarios. You can find this tool in the `%PROGRAMFILES%\SDK\Scenarios\Common\SSOApplicationConfig` directory after you've compiled it.

First, you must define the schema of your configuration data. You do so by creating an XML document, an example of which is shown below.

You must supply some identification information about the application using the SSO data and specify the administrator or administrative group allowed to administer this SSO application. You then supply the user who can access this SSO application.

You must then supply a `field` element for each piece of configuration data that you want to store. In this case, we specify a `Database Connection` and a `Number` to control the number of times that an orchestration will attempt a manual retry. The `Masked` property prevents an administrator from retrieving these properties.

```
<sso>
  <application name="Wiley.HolidayServices">
    <description>Wiley Holiday Services SSO Config Demo</description>
    <contact>darren@domain.com</contact>
    <appAdminAccount>BizTalk Server Administrators</appAdminAccount>
    <appUserAccount>BizTalk Application Users</appUserAccount>
    <field ordinal="0" label="Reserved" masked="no"/>
    <field ordinal="1" label="DBConn" masked="yes" />
    <field ordinal="2" label="MaxNumberOfManualRetries" masked="no" />
    <flags configStoreApp="yes" allowLocalAccounts="yes" enableApp="yes" />
  </application>
</sso>
```

After this file has been created, you need to create the SSO application. You create it with the following command line:

```
%COMMONPROGRAMFILES%\Enterprise Single Sign-On\ssomanage.exe –createapps
<YourApplicationSSOConfig>.xml
```

It's worth noting that a new Enterprise Single Sign-On MMC snap-in has now been released that enables you to create applications, add fields, and so on. You might want to review this approach, although the preceding approach should probably be used to enable the creation to be scripted for deployment onto multiple servers.

Now that you have the configuration placeholders, you need to populate them using `BTSScnSSO-ApplicationConfig`, the tool supplied by the End-to-End scenarios team. The source code required to set configuration data is straightforward and is supplied, enabling you to build a friendlier Windows Forms application, for example.

The following command sets the properties `DBConn` and `MaxNumberOfManualRetries`. Note that this particular tool requires that the value of each property not contain spaces.

```
BTSScnSSOApplicationConfig.exe -set Wiley.HolidayServices ConfigPro
perties DBConn Server=MyDBServer;Database=AdventureWorks;Trusted_Connection=yes
MaxNumberOfManualRetries 6
```

You can then use the following command to retrieve the value to ensure that it has been written. Note that the `DBConn` property will not be returned because it has been marked (in the first step) as requiring masking.

```
BTSScnSSOApplicationConfig.exe -get Wiley.HolidayServices ConfigProperties
MaxNumberOfManualRetries
```

Now that you've got data in the SSO store, how can you use it from within your BizTalk solution? With the same API used by `BTSScnSSOApplicationConfig`, you can retrieve these configuration values with ease.

First, you add an assembly reference to `Microsoft.BizTalk.Interop.SSOClient.dll`, which you can find in `%COMMONPROGRAMFILES%\Enterprise Single Sign-On`. Then, using the `SSOStore` class, you can retrieve the configuration properties, as shown here:

```
ISSOConfigStore SSOStore = new ISSOConfigStore();
APropertyBag PropBag = new APropertyBag();

SSOStore.GetConfigInfo("Litware.B2BHub", "ConfigProperties",
  SSOFlag.SSO_FLAG_RUNTIME, PropBag);

object propValue;
PropBag.Read("DBConn", out propValue, 0);

string DBConnectionString = (string)propValue;
```

As you can see from the preceding code, it's pretty simple. However, it does use of a custom property bag called `APropertyBag`. Therefore, you must create your own Property Bag class that derives from `IPropertyBag`. You custom property bag will hold the various configuration properties (which, of course, can be any serializable type).

An example property bag implementation is shown here. Note the use of `HybridDictionary`, which is included for performance reasons. A dictionary performs better than a hash table when it contains few entries. As the number of entries increases, however, a hash table performs better. The `HybridDictionary` will select the most appropriate collection type.

```
internal class APropertyBag : IPropertyBag
{
  private HybridDictionary _ConfigurationDictionary;

  public APropertyBag()
  {
    _ConfigurationDictionary = new HybridDictionary();
  }
```

```
public void Read(string propName, out object ptrVar, int errorLog)
{
  try
  {
    ptrVar = _ConfigurationDictionary[propName];
  }
  catch (System.ArgumentOutOfRangeException)
  {
    ptrVar = "";
  }
}

public void Write(string propName, ref object ptrVar)
{
  _ConfigurationDictionary[propName] = ptrVar;
}
}
```

In short, the SSO store provides a scalable, secure, and easy-to-administer store for your configuration data. You do have to jump through more hoops initially, but the subsequent benefits outweigh the initial development investment.

Most scenarios provide a strongly typed façade class around the API shown here to present a simplified access mechanism for orchestration and .NET developers.

Subscribing to Failure Messages

As discussed later in this chapter, suspended messages can cause administrative problems. BizTalk suspends messages following an error condition. Error conditions vary from simple message-integrity problems (not adhering to the schema, for example) to more serious orchestration failures (such as an uncaught exception thrown by the BizTalk engine or a custom component).

Some error conditions can be caught and handled by the developer (for example, the use of a Scope shape within an orchestration with an exception handler configured or the use of a `try`/`catch` block within a pipeline component). Other error conditions cannot, by default, be caught by a developer (for example, a malformed message received by the `XmlReceive` pipeline). In these cases, the exception is propagated to the BizTalk runtime, which either returns an error to the client (in the case of a Receive pipeline connected to a request/response adapter) or (as in all other cases) places the message in the MessageBox but marks it as suspended.

You can view suspended messages through the BizTalk administration tool. In some cases, a suspended message may be resumed. Resumption causes BizTalk to reattempt processing. Such resumption is common when an orchestration was not enlisted when the message arrived, for instance. The orchestration not being enlisted means no subscription for the message would have been present (and therefore the message was then suspended).

In other more serious cases, such as malformed messages, you cannot resume the message. Instead, you must view the message through the BizTalk administration tool and either save the message contents to disk for manual repair or return it to the sender. Doing so imposes administrative overhead and requires that your front-line administration team be taught additional skills. To address this common problem, BizTalk 2006 enables you to subscribe to messages that would have otherwise been suspended. You have similar potential to do so with BizTalk 2004 by subscribing to NACK messages using an orchestration, although the NACK only has a reference to the actual message. This means that you'll need to retrieve the contents manually by using WMI.

The ability to subscribe to failed messages is called *failed message routing* and can be used on messages being processed by receive or send ports. It works off a set of newly introduced context properties under the `ErrorReport` namespace that will be placed on messages that would otherwise have been disabled. To enable failed message routing, you must check the Generate Error report for Failed Messages option when creating your receive or sent port. Failed message routing in covered in more detail in Chapter 4.

An orchestration or send port can then subscribe to these properties, as required. The most common subscriber is an orchestration, which (as you know) can be implemented to perform just about any task you might require. A common technique used by customers is to build a "manual repair" application that first- or second-line support can use to fix the message. Such an application can easily be developed using Business Activity Monitoring (BAM).

A BAM activity can be created to represent items under repair, and a BAM custom reference can be used to store the message body, even if it's large. An ASP.NET Web application can be used to query the `BAMPrimaryImport` SQL database to retrieve the message and present it to the user. If the message can be repaired, it can then be submitted directly back into BizTalk (via a Web service, for example).

A manual repair facility such as this can be integrated into the tracking portal concept, which is covered in Chapter 6. However you choose to integrate it, you can present a simple user interface to end users with little development investment because the database is autogenerated using BAM, and your application does little more than a SQL query. It's worth noting that the A4Swift accelerator implements a repair facility by routing messages to SharePoint, where they can be fixed and then submitted back into BizTalk. Unfortunately, this implementation is specific to the accelerator and cannot be used by other solutions.

Messages suspended following an orchestration error can still be suspended, but these can be mitigated through careful orchestration design that catches all exceptions and hands off failure messages to a manual repair application.

No Suspended Messages/Orchestrations

Suspension of messages and orchestrations by BizTalk is rarely a desirable outcome within any BizTalk solution. A suspended message or orchestration could represent a significant amount of money to you or a customer (perhaps even risking an important order) and can present a performance problem if you have many congesting the MessageBox.

Depending on the type of suspension, it might not be resumable, meaning you have a *dead* orchestration or message that contains important information that still needs to be processed. At this stage, your only option is to save any referenced messages to disk and resubmit or manually process them, incurring often unacceptable administration overhead.

An alternate approach discussed previously is to manually repair the application. If you enable failed message routing on all receive or send ports and ensure that all exceptions are caught inside your orchestrations and subsequently pass the messages to manual repair, you can then almost entirely remove the potential for suspended messages and enable easy identification of failed messages through your custom repair application.

This repair application can then enable quick and easy resolution of any problems without having to train administration staff to understand BizTalk concepts such as orchestrations and messages, and the steps to resolve them. Instead, this enables other roles within your organization to perform the repair operation.

Loosely Coupling

This section covers more of a pattern than a best practice per se, but it is still incredibly valuable to understand before designing orchestrations.

Long-running business processes are fully supported using BizTalk orchestration. A given business process may last for days, weeks, or months, depending on your requirements. However, these long-running processes may introduce problems when you want to upgrade your solution.

It's not practical (and often not even possible) to wait for all long-running processes to finish before performing an upgrade.

Most medium-to-large business process implementations are factored into multiple orchestrations rather than one large, monolithic orchestration. Multiple orchestrations such as these are used for manageability reasons, such as allowing multiple developers to work on implementing a business process and keeping the physical size of the orchestration small.

In addition, with multiple orchestrations, you upgrade one small piece of your business process rather than the entire business process. As discussed in Chapter 5, an orchestration is compiled down into a .NET assembly that must be strongly named (and therefore you can deploy one or more versions of the same assembly side by side by using the Global Assembly Cache [GAC]).

All seems great! But not quite. The natural way to invoke these child orchestrations is by using the Call Orchestration or Start Orchestration shape, which directly binds to a specific assembly name and version, and will therefore always use the orchestration version it was compiled against and will require a recompilation and deployment to upgrade.

A solution to this is to loosely couple orchestrations. With this mechanism, you post a BizTalk message back into the MessageBox via a direct port, thus enabling the next orchestration to subscribe to the message and continue with the business process. This method places no direct binding between orchestrations and purely relies on the MessageBox to route the message to the next orchestration. This method resolves our original versioning issue, and also enables a number of other interesting scenarios.

Having a loosely coupled model such as this enables insertion of new business process steps with no effect on the running system. You can deploy a new orchestration that subscribes to a message, enlist, start, and away you go.

So how do you go about implementing a loosely coupled system? Generally speaking, you will probably want to use the same underlying BizTalk message throughout and not want to constantly map to a new message type to avoid the performance overhead and indeed the associated maps.

If an orchestration is invoked following arrival of a message and then subsequently posts the same message back to the MessageBox via a direct port, it will be launched again, thus entering a infinite loop. To combat this and enable the next orchestration to consume the message, you must expose some form of status flag on your message.

This status flag can either be a number or string literal, and each orchestration is responsible for updating the flag before posting to the MessageBox. Each downstream orchestration then configures a filter on the Receive shape to subscribe to the same message type but a specific status value.

Figure 13-2 shows the Filter Expression dialog box used to apply a filter to a Receive shape. In this case, you can see that we have selected a ProcessingState property and specified that this orchestration is interested in a ProcessingStage of 2.

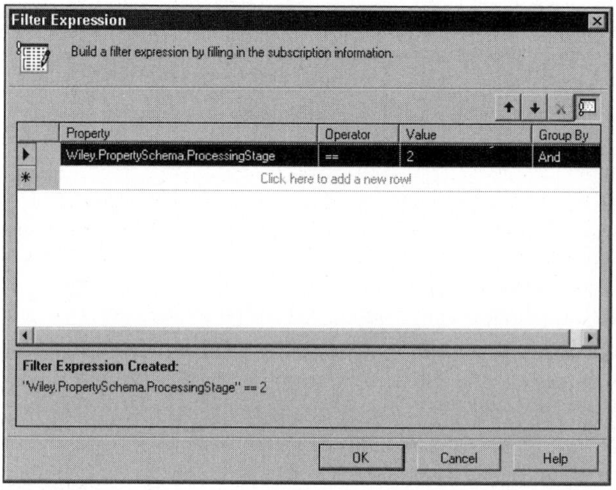

Figure 13-2

Implementing loosely coupled orchestrations in this way does incur extra overhead, because you are transferring orchestration control via the BizTalk MessageBox. Therefore, you should not consider this pattern for low-latency scenarios that require the message to be processed from end to end in the fastest possible time.

A BizTalk message context property is typically used to hold the status flag, which abstracts any processing instructions away from the underlying message data. This context property must be promoted (using a property promotion) to enable orchestration subscriptions to make use of it via Receive shape filters. An alternative approach is to use a multipart message with two parts, one for the message body and another to hold "routing" information such as this status flag. This approach is used within the BPM scenario covered in Chapter 12.

We covered how to create a custom context property in the "Advanced Property Promotion" section of Chapter 5. You will need to create a custom pipeline component for this solution to *promote* your custom context property to allow for routing. This pipeline component should also set the default value for the status flag to ensure that the first orchestration in the sequence executes when the message is published. This is a simple technique, but highly powerful, so let's consider a fictional scenario to formalize your understanding.

Wiley Holiday Services implements a Travel Booking service and exposes a number of Web services and schemas that third parties can use to book travel itineraries. Most third parties invoke these Web services from within their systems, and this enables Wiley Holiday Services to develop one solution to suit all third parties.

However, some third parties cannot use these schemas or even call Web services (perhaps because of their choice of technology/platform). Although this might seem surprising, it happens more often than you'd think! In these scenarios, Wiley Holiday Services needs to get these special third parties on board and provide a custom implementation to handle their flat-file–based messages.

For cost reasons, this onboarding process should require minimal development and administration and should not require the overall solution to be modified (and thus impact availability). The onboarding is achieved is follows:

1. A new receive location can be created using the File adapter. A custom receive pipeline is developed to use the Flat File Disassembler, along with a flat-file schema to convert the incoming flat file to an XML file.

2. A new third-party–specific orchestration is then developed that, among other processing steps (hence the requirement for an orchestration), maps the custom XML schema format to the internal and generic travel itinerary schema. This new message is then posted to the MessageBox, which is then consumed by the Itinerary Processing orchestration used for all travel itinerary processing.

This minimal development can be done quickly and can be deployed with no impact on the live system, thus enabling rapid onboarding of new trading partners.

To optimize this approach, you could configure the receive location with multiple maps; doing so enables you to transform incoming trading-partner–specific messages to your generic format before the message is published to the MessageBox. By so doing, you can use exactly the same infrastructure that is used by messages arriving in the native schema format and avoid the requirement for a extra orchestration unless of course in the scenario above you need to perform extra processing.

One drawback to a decoupled scenario is that you cannot perform classic exception handling around the entire process because it's split up across different orchestrations that are not invoked directly. However, you can make use of a neat technique that enables you to reinsert a message following manual repair.

If an orchestration in your processing sequence encounters an error during processing, it can place the message in manual repair, as discussed previously in this chapter, along with the processing stage value. Once repaired, the message can then be reinserted along with the processing stage value, thus causing the original orchestration that encountered the error to collect the message and resume processing. With this approach, you avoid having to restart the entire process.

In summary, loosely coupling enables a long-running business process to be executed in smaller, short-lived orchestrations. This, in turn, enables straightforward versioning, modification, and onboarding of new trading partners with next to no development overhead or effect on a live system.

Process Manager Pattern

The Process Manager pattern (www.enterpriseintegrationpatterns.com/ProcessManager.html) is another approach to solving the problem of large, long-running business processes. Instead of implementing a loosely coupled approach using the MessageBox (as discussed previously), you can use a parent orchestration to control which orchestration should be called next.

When finished, each child orchestration then returns control to the parent orchestration, which makes a decision on the next orchestration to be called. This decision can be implemented via configuration or the Rules Engine, thus enabling on-the-fly modification of your business process.

Because you require this return path to the calling orchestration, you cannot use the approach detailed before. Therefore, you must instead invoke orchestrations directly, but not in such a way that binds the parent orchestration to a specific orchestration/assembly version (which, of course, would prevent us being able to upgrade one piece of the solution).

Using a technique called *inverse direct partner binding*, you can enable this scenario, which is put to great use in the Business Process Management (BPM) scenario in Chapter 12.

Instrumenting Your Solution

Although BizTalk itself enables you to observe which BizTalk artifacts are executing and to review the execution path of an orchestration, it doesn't provide the type of developer-level tracing usually expected to aid with debugging of a solution.

BAM provides highly scalable and high-performing instrumentation for your solution. BAM enables you to record milestones, data, timings, and even messages related to the execution of your business processes. Indeed, it enables you to record any aspect of your entire solution, including .NET components and Web services. See Chapter 6 for more information about how you can use BAM and for an example of a tracking portal, which can provide a friendlier view inside your BizTalk solution.

BAM is ill-suited for developer-level instrumentation, which typically logs information such as method parameters, method timings, and thread identifiers to help developers understand how the solution is executing at a code level. However, BAM can be used for the timing element to enable quick identification of components or methods with long execution times.

In these cases, consider using the much improved .NET 2.0 System.Diagnostics namespace to provide tracing to a variety of listeners, including the debug console, files, and the event log. You can also develop custom listeners with ease. Another option is the Enterprise Library provided by the Patterns and Practices team at Microsoft. The Enterprise Library provides a number of application blocks, including a Logging and Instrumentation block that ships with a number of sinks (among others, Database, Message Queue, Text File, and Event Log). As with custom listeners, you can develop custom sinks.

Review both options and choose the best option for your scenario. Remember, however, the somewhat greater complexity of the Enterprise Library (especially with regard to configuration) and the overhead of the logging and application block as compared to `System.Diagnostics` functionality (significantly reworked for the .NET 2.0 Framework release).

Whichever instrumentation technique you select, you *must* ensure that the entire instrumentation call is as fast as possible to reduce the impact on the running system when enabled. For example, a SQL Server database used as the sink for log entries will incur SQL Server and network overhead that is significantly greater than, for instance, writing to a local log file. A popular method is to utilize an MSMQ queue to post log entries, which are then pulled off by a separate process and written to a SQL Server database. This can also be used to ensure that audit entries cannot be lost, as both MSMQ and SQL server can be used within the scope of a transaction.

Multiple levels of instrumentation can prove useful and enable you, for instance, to leave basic instrumentation always turned on and to then ratchet up the detail level of instrumentation when you encounter problems. As always, however, ensure that you run performance tests with instrumentation turned off and on to understand the impact of enabling high levels of instrumentation and ensure that it doesn't bring the system to its knees!

Event Tracing for Windows (ETW) is a kernel-mode instrumentation layer and is by far the fastest method of instrumentation. As such, almost all Microsoft products, including BizTalk, use it. At the time of this writing, however, no sink was available for either Enterprise Library or the `System.Diagnostics` namespace, despite the now deprecated Enterprise Instrumentation Framework (EIF) shipping with a version. The Orcas release of Visual Studio, however, is currently scheduled to supply an ETW listener which can be plugged into the `System.Diagnostics` architecture which will likely become the de facto standard in time.

For developer-level tracing the tracing classes held within the `System.Diagnostics` namespace is often used along with the Windows `Sysinternals DebugView` tool (`http://www.microsoft.com/technet/sysinternals/default.mspx`). In default configuration all trace will be output using the Win32 OutputDebugString function which DebugView can monitor.

This approach works extremely well, but you should be aware of the associated performance overhead. `DebugView` effectively acts as a debugger and hooks the `OUTPUT_DEBUG_STRING_EVENT` event. As a result, your application (a BizTalk process in this case) will experience a performance impact as the application threads will be suspended while the debug information is output, effectively serializing your application. It's worth noting that if the `DebugView` tool is not started (and therefore there are no subscribers to the information) the performance impact is negligible and shouldn't in my experience be something to worry about, therefore, do not be afraid to output information that you feel will be useful.

Either way you should insure that your tracing code is implemented such that it can be disabled to reduce the performance overhead, typically you will need the ability to enable it at run-time. When carrying out performance testing you will most likely want to disable tracing, although gaining an understanding of the overhead is also valuable.

In my view the performance hit associated with software tracing is outweighed by the ability to diagnose run-time issues in a nonintrusive manner. As discussed in Chapter 4, most Microsoft products, including BizTalk Server, rely heavily on software tracing which the product group leverage to diagnose customer issues offline. Just be aware that running DebugView during performance testing or on a live server is very likely to significantly impact performance!

First In, First Out

While writing this book, I received a number of requests for a worked example that shows how first in, first out (FIFO) behavior can be implemented using BizTalk. I had planned to include an example as part of this chapter, but a white paper on BizTalk and FIFO has been published that covers FIFO in great detail and it didn't make sense to repeat it here.

You can find this white paper at www.microsoft.com/downloads/details.aspx?familyid= F4FF7AFC-81A2-4B89-AE0D-3746B39D9198&displaylang=en&displaylang=en.

Summary

This chapter covered a number of best practices that you should consider when architecting or developing a BizTalk solution. We covered how you should approach solutions that process large messages, and then moved on to cover how configuration data can be stored in a central secure location by using SSO. Finally, we detailed how your orchestrations can be designed to enable them to be easily versioned and maintained.

The next chapter introduces Windows Workflow Foundation and describes how it fits next to BizTalk Server.

14

Windows Workflow Foundation and BizTalk

The arrival of Windows Workflow Foundation (WF) has caused a significant amount of confusion throughout the architect and developer community. After all, on the surface, WF can be construed as *replacing* elements of BizTalk Server. This leads to an inevitable question: Why should you pay for BizTalk when you have WF available for free?

This truth is, however, that WF and BizTalk complement one another and can work extremely well together to meet and exceed your solution requirements.

This chapter covers the basic principles of WF and then discusses how the BizTalk Server vision fits with WF. It then details which technology you might elect to use for a given scenario, and provides an overview of how Office 2007 and Windows SharePoint Services 3 (which both leverage WF) can work together with BizTalk to enable compelling and exceed, up until now, seamlessly integrated solutions.

This chapter is not meant to provide anything more than an overview of WF to help position it alongside BizTalk. A number of great books are available that cover WF in depth. The best at the time of writing is *Essential Windows Workflow Foundation* by Dharma Shukla and Bob Schmidt.

Introducing Windows Workflow Foundation

This section introduces WF and its key concepts. WF is worthy of a book in its own right, so consider this a primer to help you to understand what WF offers. By the end of this chapter, you should clearly understand how WF synergizes with BizTalk Server.

Workflows

A workflow represents the implementation of a particular *process* in the same way as a BizTalk orchestration. In fact, the team behind BizTalk Orchestration (XLANG) formed a large part of the WF development team! It's worth noting that all software, not just BizTalk, has elements of workflow, but these are typically represented as code. A common workflow foundation such as the one provided by WF enables workflow to be expressed and used across any application on the Microsoft platform in a clear and consistent way.

BizTalk orchestrations allow the implementation of *sequential processes*. Sequential processes are well suited for system-based workflow in which the steps are known ahead of time and executed in an identical manner each time.

Figure 14-1 shows an example sequential process designed using WF.

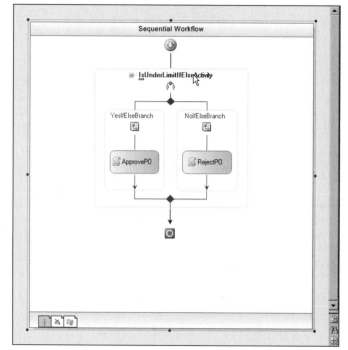

Figure 14-1

WF workflows can be implemented out of the box as either sequential workflows or state machine workflows. You can also customize your own workflow type as required through the extensibility points provided. This is a significant departure from the fixed sequential process used by BizTalk orchestrations.

As previously mentioned, sequential workflows work well with fixed sets of steps. In contrast, state machine workflows work well when the workflow includes human interaction, because such interaction often follows a less fixed way of moving through the workflow.

606

Figure 14-2 shows a classic state machine workflow that was designed within the WF Workflow Designer. This workflow is included as part of the Windows SDK samples and details the states an order may need to go through.

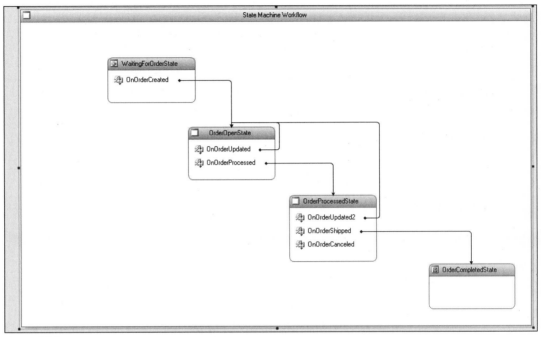

Figure 14-2

The default state of the workflow in Figure 14-2 is `WaitingForOrderState`. When the `OnOrderCreated` event is raised, the workflow moves to the `OpenOrderState`. When in the `OpenOrderState`, the order can be updated or canceled. If the `OnOrderProcessed` event is raised, the workflow moves to the `OrderProcessedState`.

In the `OrderProcessedState`, the order can be updated, a process that moves it back to `Open-OrderState`. When, eventually, the `OnOrderShipped` event is raised, the workflow moves to the `OrderCompletedState`. In contrast, modeling such a workflow using a sequential process approach would be very hard to develop and maintain.

Activities

WF activities represent a task or a unit of work within a workflow. BizTalk orchestration shapes are directly analogous to an activity. Unlike BizTalk orchestrations, custom activities (or shapes) can be developed for use within your workflows.

Activities can also be designed to encompass other activities to provide a composite activity. This technique proves useful for wrapping up complex activity combinations into an abstracted activity such as

"Update Backend System," which itself might represent a complex interaction to which the end user does not need to have in-depth exposure.

Figure 14-3 shows an example of the activities available with WF.

Figure 14-3

Custom activities are straightforward to create and must inherit from the `Activity` base class. Composite activities must derive from the `CompositeActivity` base class. To provide extra functionality, you can also create custom activities by deriving from an existing activity and adding the desired additional functionality.

It's expected that WF activities will be available from a number of third-party sources over time. Such sources will potentially provide a rich *market* of activities for use within your WF workflows. You'll also learn how you can use these WF activities with the SharePoint Workflow Designer later in this chapter.

Hosting

The WF runtime is not represented as a Windows service or any form of physical *application* that must be launched to execute workflows. Instead, it's provided as a library that must be loaded by a *hosting* process.

A hosting process can be any form of Windows *application* (conventional application, web application, or Windows service) as long as it can load the .NET Framework (version 2.0). This hosting process is responsible for instantiating the WF runtime. The host then communicates with the runtime as required to manage workflow instances.

Consistent with WF providing a workflow *framework*, WF is designed to be hosted within any form of application so as to provide workflow capability. WF ships with one host (`WorkflowWebHostingModule`), which is an HTTP module that supports routing of page or Web service requests to the appropriate workflow instance.

Any other hosting application must instantiate the WF runtime manually, which fortunately is a simple task. The code required to do this within a Windows Forms application is shown here for reference:

```
using (WorkflowRuntime workflowRuntime = new WorkflowRuntime())
{
  workflowRuntime.StartRuntime();

  workflowRuntime.WorkflowCompleted += OnWorkflowCompleted;
  workflowRuntime.WorkflowTerminated += OnWorkflowTerminated;

  Type type = typeof(MySimpeWorkflow);
  workflowRuntime.CreateWorkflow(type).Start();

  // Running Workflow, wait until termination or completion

  waitHandle.WaitOne();

  workflowRuntime.StopRuntime();
}

static void OnWorkflowCompleted(object sender, WorkflowCompletedEventArgs instance)
{
  // Workflow Completed, return
  waitHandle.Set();
}

static void OnWorkflowTerminated(object sender, WorkflowTerminatedEventArgs e)
{
  // Workflow Terminated, log and return
  System.Diagnostics.Trace.WriteLine(e.Exception.Message);
  waitHandle.Set();
}
```

Runtime Services

The WF runtime requires three different types of *runtime services* to execute workflows:

❑ Persistence

❑ Tracking

❑ Workflow Scheduling

The following subsections cover each of these.

Persistence Service

For exactly the same reasons that BizTalk orchestrations use persistence points and dehydration, WF workflows use persistence points. The WF runtime uses pluggable persistence services to provide this persistence, rather than mandating one fixed way of persisting the state of a workflow.

Consider a Windows Forms application hosting WF. This scenario might not require any form of durable persistence store, because the workflows might only be resident in memory momentarily and do not execute across different instances of the application over time.

Contrast the preceding scenario with an ASP.NET-hosted workflow, perhaps via an ASP.NET Web application. In this case, a specific workflow instance quite possibly will be required to execute across different page requests. Keeping the workflow instance in memory presents potential scalability problems (especially when you have many hundreds of workflow instances in memory at any given time), and therefore it needs to be removed from memory while inactive.

Typically, ASP.NET Web applications load balance requests across multiple servers. If the workflow instance is held in memory on Server A and a subsequent request is load-balanced to Server B, the workflow instance will not be available. In addition, the workflow instance will be lost if, for instance, the server crashes. In such a situation, you risk the data loss and any *progress* within the workflow.

For these scenarios, persistence provides the mechanism for a workflow instance to be serialized out of memory into some form of storage. The storage is typically (but not exclusively) durable — an example would be SQL Server, which can then be made available to multiple servers and provides a resilient storage system.

During a workflow execution, you might also require the workflow to sleep for a given time period (minutes, days, or even weeks). Therefore, it's not sustainable to keep the workflow instance in memory during the period. After all, the application hosting the application might need to restart. And, of course, having many instances hanging around in memory poses scalability problems.

If a workflow instance is serialized out to a durable store such as a SQL database, you need to monitor any *sleeps* in progress and ensure (from the persistence store) workflow reactivation upon completion of the sleep time.

WF provides one persistence service out of the box: `SqlWorkflowPersistanceService`. As the name implies, this service enables workflow instances to be persisted to a SQL Server database (also provided via a SQL Script) and to provide timer services to enable workflows to be reactivated. This persistence service handles the usual locking semantics that you would expect for use in multithreaded environment.

The `SqlWorkflowPersistenceService` serializes the state of the workflow into a binary representation and uses the `System.IO.Compression.GZipStream` class to compress this before storage in the SQL Server database.

This approach is almost identical to the approach taken by BizTalk in that it uses a binary representation and GZIP compression. Unlike with BizTalk, however, you can write your own persistence service that serializes workflow state into whatever format or medium that you require. And, unlike with BizTalk, you can implement your own persistence service that you can plug in to the WF runtime. This persistence service can then represent the workflow state in a format of your choosing and store wherever is appropriate.

You can create a custom persistence service by deriving it from the supplied `WorkflowPersistence-Service` abstract class.

Tracking Service

A WF tracking service enables you to track the execution of a workflow instance. Such tracking can help you understand, for example, how long a workflow took to execute start to finish, which *route* through a workflow was taken, or when activities executed as part of a workflow were called and completed (again providing timing information).

Workflow tracking is directly analogous to Business Activity Monitoring (BAM) in that it enables you to directly pull out *data* used within a workflow or metadata around activities and store it somewhere. By so doing, you enable users, support staff, and even customers to understand the progress of a workflow without having to understand the implementation details of a workflow.

WF provides one tracking service out of the box: `SqlTrackingService`. As the name implies, this tracking service enables you to persist tracking data to a SQL Server database (also provided via a SQL Script).

Another tracking service (`ConsoleTrackingServiceSample`) is provided as an unsupported sample. It outputs tracking information to the Console, which unless you are hosting within a Console application is of limited use. Of course, you can modify the sample to use the `System.Diagnostics.Trace` class, for example. Doing so would enable you to route trace to the Debug Console for viewing via the Windows Sysinternals DebugView tool or to a file.

You can add multiple tracking services to a workflow runtime, even on the fly. Therefore, you can enable, for example, a standard database tracking service to be used and then a debug tracking service to be plugged in as required.

Implementation and configuration of a tracking service is one step. The next is to actually specify what information will be *tracked*. You do this through the creation of a tracking profile. Again, this is a term that you are likely already familiar with. It is used to describe what data BAM will collect and store (hence the Tracking Profile Editor [TPE] tool that enables a tracking profile to be created using a graphical drag-and-drop tool).

WF provides all the framework to enable a BAM-style solution. However, it doesn't provide concrete enterprise-scale implementations. There is no tool with which you can create a tracking profile. Instead, you must do this programmatically or by creating an XML file adhering to the appropriate schema.

Of course, there is nothing stopping you (or a partner) from creating a WF version of the BizTalk Tracking Profile Editor to simplify the creation of a tracking profile. In fact, a workflow `TrackingProfileDesigner` sample that enables you to graphically design a tracking profile is included as part of the Windows SDK (but is unsupported).

You must also consider the way in which you will expose this tracking data to potential *consumers*, because there is no out-of-the-box ability to do this (unlike with the BizTalk BAM portal).

The Windows SDK also ships with a `WorkflowMonitor` sample that enables real-time (or after-the-fact) monitoring of workflow execution. Figure 14-4 shows an example that demonstrates a workflow that has executed through to completion. On the left side, note the list of activities that were executed.

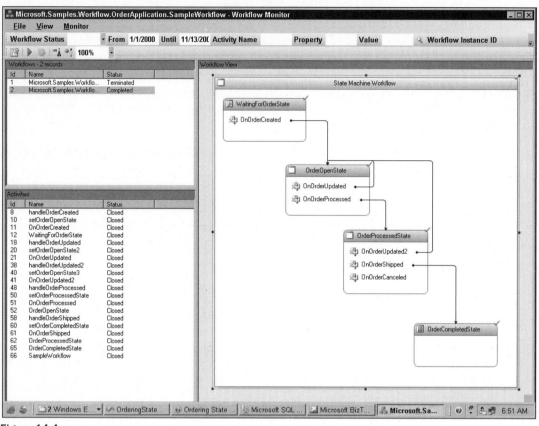

Figure 14-4

Workflow Scheduling Service

The WF runtime requires threads to start or schedule workflow instances. Being host agnostic, WF provides a scheduling service that enables custom services to be plugged in to provide the ability to schedule new workflow instances that are appropriate to the host being used.

WF ships with two scheduling services: `DefaultWorkflowSchedulerService` and `ManualWorkflow-SchedulerService`. The `DefaultWorkflowSchedulerService` is likely to be the only scheduler service you'll use (unless you are hosting within ASP.NET) and dispenses threads from the CLR `ThreadPool`.

The `ManualWorkflowSchedulerService` is designed for use within ASP.NET hosting scenarios. The `DefaultWorkflowSchedulerService` would work within ASP.NET. However, it would result in each Page or Service request causing an additional thread to be used while leaving the invocation thread servicing the Page or Service request idle. On a busy system, this can lead to scalability problems.

To counter this, the `ManualWorkflowSchedulerService` uses the thread already allocated to the Page or Service request (instead of using the CLR `ThreadPool`). Thus, `ManualWorkflowSchedulerService` effectively *donates* the thread for the duration of the WF execution.

As with all WF runtime services, you can create custom scheduling services by deriving from the `WorkflowSchedulerService` abstract class.

Workflow Designer

Unlike the BizTalk Orchestration Designer, which along with orchestration *shapes* is not customizable in any way, the WF Designer is completely customizable and even rehostable within an application of your choice.

Therefore, you can rehost the design surface within your own application to enable users to construct their own workflows within a simplified environment. After all, not everyone finds Visual Studio user-friendly!

The Workflow Designer is not necessarily only to be used when designing workflows; it could be used to create a WF monitoring tool that can show workflow progress graphically.

Rules Engine

Like BizTalk, WF provides a Rules Engine for use within workflows. And just like the BizTalk Rules Engine (BRE), the WF Rules Engine enables you to abstract business rules from the physical code implementation (allowing them to change independently of the workflow itself).

The WF Rules Engine implements a Forward Execution processing algorithm rather than the Rete processing algorithm used by the BRE. As discussed in Chapter 7, the Rete algorithm performs well when rules' conditions are shared, because this process of sharing reduces processing overhead.

Generally, however, it's been found that most rules policies don't share that many conditions; hence, another approach to executing rules can result in better performance and flexibility.

Unlike the BRE, the WF Rules Engine is extremely approachable for developers and doesn't require in-depth knowledge to get started, which, as it happens, was a major design goal. Be aware, however, that the tooling of it has been aimed solely at developers rather than business users.

Unlike the IF `<CONDITION>` THEN `<ACTION>` rule expressions used by BRE, WF rules follow the IF `<CONDITION>` THEN `<ACTION>` ELSE `<ACTION>` expression format. In many cases, this latter format makes life a lot easier because, as you might recall from Chapter 7, the BRE requires an *opposite* rule to be created to provide an *else* part.

Rules depend on data to make their decision. Unlike the BRE, which enables the use of different data sources such as .NET or data held within a database, the WF Rules Engine can work only with instances of .NET classes. This means that you need to wrap any form of data source required with a .NET class.

Rules can be used directly as conditions on selected activities (`IFElseBranch`, `While`, `Replicator`, and `ConditionActivityGroup`) or by directly invoking a policy (as you would do using BizTalk).

Rules construction is performed directly through the Rule Condition Editor, as shown in Figure 14-5. The Rule Condition Editor provides full code completion to the developer.

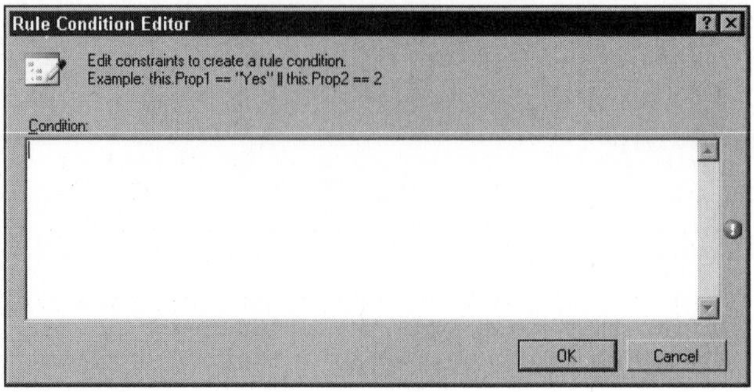

Figure 14-5

Alternatively, you can create a full ruleset (a collection of rules) and invoke it via the Policy activity. In this case, the Rule Set Editor is used. It provides a rich user interface with which to construct rules, as shown in Figure 14-6. Note that, at the time of this writing, you cannot expose this control from within your own application.

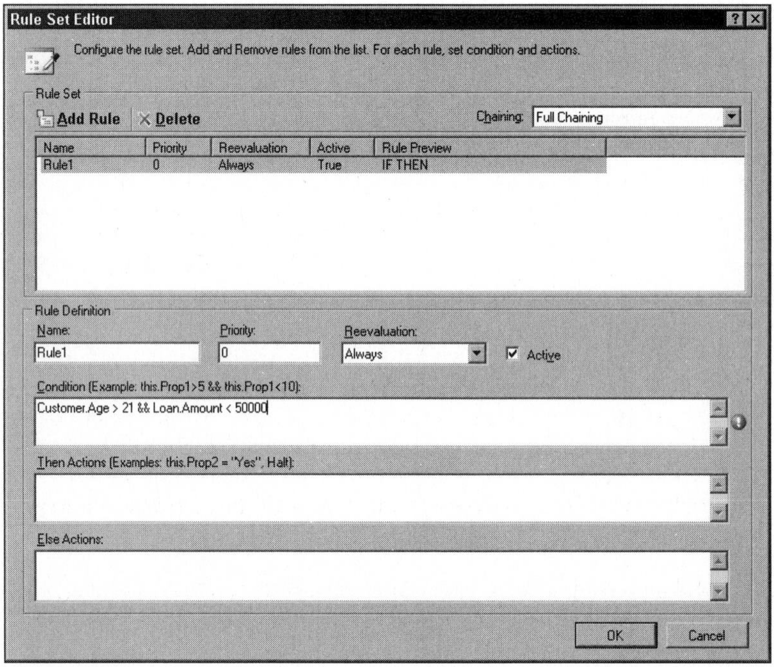

Figure 14-6

The WF Rules Engine, like the rest of WF, is fully extensible and even enables you to invoke the Rules Engine via code directly and outside of the context of Windows WF. Therefore, you can add Rules Engine capabilities to a solution that don't make any other use of WF and more importantly without attracting any licensing costs.

BizTalk provides a Rules Engine database to store rulesets centrally across multiple servers and to provide versioning and staging ahead of deployment. This isn't supported out of the box with WF, but it's entirely possible through the extensibility model provided.

By default, rules are stored in an XML file (which forms part of the resulting .NET assembly). However, you can modify this to store the rules' XML in a database such as BizTalk Server, for instance, which will enable the rules to be changed without deploying a new version of the .NET assembly.

The rules-editing experience provided by WF is aimed at developers rather than business users (who happen to be the main target audience for the Business Rules Composer provided by BizTalk), although the success of this can be questioned, as it can often be construed as too complex for a typical business user.

However, you could implement your own tool to provide a simpler WF rules-editing feature and even add vocabulary support (which is also not available within the WF engine).

BizTalk Server and Windows Workflow

Now that you know a little more about WF, you might be wondering (as many do) what the value of BizTalk is, given the release of WF? We'll now position the two technologies and cover some scenarios where they should be used.

Positioning

As you've probably already realized from this chapter, WF is incredibly powerful and extensible. However, it's just a *foundation* for providing workflow in your application. By itself, it is not suitable as an enterprise business process management/workflow tool. Consider the requirement to communicate with a variety of systems during workflow execution. BizTalk provides a wide range of adapters and pipeline components to make this integration process easy.

Of course, you can use it as the basis for such a tool. In fact, the next major release of BizTalk Server (post–BizTalk Server 2006 R2) supposedly will use WF in place of the proprietary BizTalk Orchestration Engine (XLANG). BizTalk itself will then have to provide enterprise-class and scalable runtime services to achieve the sort of performance demanded by customers. A custom WF scheduling service is likely to be required to allow BizTalk to precisely control which threads are available and to implement throttling, for example.

Custom persistence services will need to be developed to provide all the rich features currently available in BizTalk Server. One of the challenges we have with BizTalk Server today concerns low latency, in that the MessageBox roundtrip can be expensive.

Imagine if, as a BizTalk developer, you could *plug in* a form of in-memory persistence store for low-latency scenarios. Of course, your plug-in wouldn't offer the resilience of SQL, but depending on the message payload, this might be acceptable for your solution. The WF architecture makes such a proposition reality.

So back to how to position WF and BizTalk. In short, WF is absolutely the right choice for workflow *within* your application. For workflow bridging *between* applications, however, BizTalk is the right choice.

WF is a great choice in many situations. For example, you can use it with an ASP.NET Web application, to control page navigation. Until now any navigation relies on hard-coded page transfers, thus making modification difficult.

You could use it within an ASP.NET or a WCF service, for example, to control retrieval of back-end data (perhaps using the Rules Engine), and indeed any processing that involves human interaction.

However, BizTalk remains the best choice for scenarios requiring connectivity to a variety of technologies and vendors. BizTalk provides the connectivity capability via the use of adapters, content-based routing, durable transactional message storage, message transformation, side-by-side deployment versioning of orchestrations and rules, multihost scalability architecture, BRE, BAM, administration tools, and integration with MOM.

As discussed in Chapter 2, you've always been able to write a BizTalk-esque style of solution. You could argue that, with the advent of Windows Communication Foundation (WCF) and WF, we've made such a proposition slightly easier, but as ever the devil is in the details, and the difficulty of developing an enterprise-class, mission-critical server product should not be underestimated. I suggest that you review the "Why BizTalk" section of Chapter 2 which contrasts a custom-built solution with a BizTalk solution to highlight the things that you should be aware of when making a decision.

A rule of thumb, as mentioned earlier, is to think of WF for use *within* your application and BizTalk Server for use *between* your applications. There will always be gray areas, but it's important to remember that Windows Workflow Foundation is a foundation for enabling a common approach to workflow across many applications, both Microsoft and your own.

BizTalk Version "Next" (vNext)

The next major release of BizTalk Server is currently expected to use WF alongside the proprietary XLANG Orchestration Engine. In addition, a number of workflow runtime services will likely be provided by BizTalk to offer the features that you would expect from a premium server.

The proprietary Adapter and Pipeline model is also likely to be replaced by WCF. You can see the first signs of this effort with the new .NET Adapter Framework that will be built on top of WCF and supplied with BizTalk Server 2006 R2.

Effectively, therefore, adapters in the medium-to-long term will be able to be used by anything on the Microsoft platform, thus extending the value proposition of adapters across the Microsoft stack and not just BizTalk. WCF should also simplify the development of adapters, which today is quite complex.

All these plans are still yet to be confirmed, but this is the general approach being considered by the BizTalk Product Team. Such architecture upheaval might make you wonder about backward compatibility. Backward compatibility is a top issue for the BizTalk team and features heavily during planning for the next release.

BAM Interceptor for Windows Workflow

BizTalk Server 2006 R2 is currently expected to include a BAM Interceptor for WF (and WCF). This interceptor will allow events raised by a workflow to be collected and stored as part of a BAM activity.

This interceptor enables, for example, BizTalk Server to be used to process part of a business process but then perhaps hand it off to a user for a manual authorization step. This manual authorization step might be a custom application that itself leverages WF.

Any progress or data used as part of this workflow can then be stored via the interceptor in the BAM database alongside any data collected by the BizTalk Server, and indeed any other part of your end-to-end solution, by using the BAM API.

This is an incredibly powerful proposition because it allows tracking across your entire solution (or even enterprise) and drives BAM instrumentation even further across the Microsoft platform.

In contrast to the BAM API, which requires custom code to be written to collect extra information, interceptors just require configuration to *select* the information you wish to collect and they will then store the information in the BAM database.

Remember, as discussed in Chapter 6, you can use BAM anywhere in your enterprise without buying any additional licenses as long as a BizTalk server is involved in the end-to-process in some way. You just need to have purchased BizTalk at least once in your organization. This was correct at the time of writing, however, you should check the license agreement for the R2 release as this may introduce changes.

The BAM Interceptor writes tracking data transactionally with a workflow transaction to ensure that the tracking data is consistent with the actual workflow execution. That is, if a workflow has to be rolled back for whatever reason, the tracking data is also be rolled back. This is directly analogous to the `OrchestrationEventStream` in BizTalk.

You can enable BAM Interception without any modification to your workflow. You just add it as a new tracking service (`Microsoft.BizTalk.Bam.Interceptors.Workflow.BamTrackingService`), which can be added via configuration or manually via the WF runtime.

A connection string pointing at the appropriate `BAMPrimaryImport` database must also be supplied along with the polling interval for retrieving configuration data (thus allowing on-the-fly modification of the tracking profile). Example code showing how to add the BAM interceptor to the WF runtime is shown here:

```
Using Microsoft.BizTalk.Bam.Interceptors.Workflow;
BamTrackingService BAMTS = new BamTrackingService("Data Source=(local);Initial
Catalog=BAMPrimaryImport;Integrated Security=SSPI;", 5);
runtime.AddService(BAMTS);
```

The next step is to configure the interceptor using an Interceptor Configuration file that is responsible for identifying which events we're interested in and storing them in the BAM database. At the time of this writing, there was no editor to create this tracking profile nor was there one planned for the R2 release. A custom XML file has to be created by hand that adheres to the Tracking Interceptor schema. An alternative, custom solution that you may wish to consider is to create a graphical designer using the Microsoft DSL Tools toolkit, which enables a Visual Studio–hosted graphical designer to be created with relative ease.

The Tracking Interceptor Configuration file is pretty complex at first glance, but it makes sense after you use it longer. At the time of this writing, basic documentation was available that detailed the schema and some sample fragments. We'll now walk through a sample and show all the key parts of the Interceptor Configuration file.

The first element of the configuration file defines an `EventSource`. The `Name` attribute should be a unique name of your choosing and is used later on in the file. The `Technology` attribute should be set to WF for use with Windows Workflow, and the `Manifest` should be the full qualified workflow type. An example is shown here:

```
<ic:EventSource Name="MySampleBAMTrackingWorkflow" Technology="WF"
Manifest="MySampleBAMTrackingWorkflow.Workflow1, MySampleBAMTrackingWorkflow,
Version=1.0.0.0, Culture=neutral, PublicKeyToken=null">
</ic:EventSource>
```

The next element of the configuration file details the name of the BAM activity that we are going to use to store data, as follows:

```
<ic:BamActivity Name="MyActivity">
```

You now need to record the timestamp when a workflow was created in our BAM activity. To do this, you create an `OnEvent` element with a `Name` attribute set to a unique name, and the `Source` attribute set to the `EventSource` name that we defined earlier in the file via the `Source` attribute of the `EventSource` element.

The `IsBegin` and `IsEnd` attributes relate to whether this event creates a new activity or ends an existing activity. Because this is the first event you are tracking, you set `IsBegin` to `true` and `IsEnd` to `false`, as follows:

```
<ic:OnEvent Name="MyEvent1" Source="MySampleBAMTrackingWorkflow" IsBegin="true"
IsEnd="false">
```

You now need to provide a filter to enable the interceptor to filter out events that you are not interested in. Because you want to store the Workflow Creation time, you are interested in the workflow `Created` event. (A full list of exposed events is included in the interceptor documentation.)

The example shown here uses the WF Interceptor operation called `GetWorkflowEvent` to filter on workflow creation events and passes the `Created` event as a parameter:

```
<ic:Filter>
   <ic:Expression>
    <wf:Operation Name="GetWorkflowEvent"/>
    <ic:Operation Name="Constant">
       <ic:Argument>Created</ic:Argument>
    </ic:Operation>
    <ic:Operation Name="Equals"/>
   </ic:Expression>
</ic:Filter>
```

Because tracking data is collected asynchronously, you need to have a unique identifier for use as the `ActivityID` and to route subsequent tracking entries to the right activity instance. To do this, you retrieve the workflow `InstanceID` by using the `GetContextProperty` operation passing a context property name of `InstanceID`.

An example is shown here:

```
<!-- Get Unique ID -->
<ic:CorrelationID>
  <ic:Expression>
    <wf:Operation Name="GetContextProperty">
      <wf:Argument>InstanceId</wf:Argument>
    </wf:Operation>
  </ic:Expression>
</ic:CorrelationID>
```

After you've successfully identified a tracking point (Workflow Created), the final step is to populate the BAM activity with the data you're interested in. You do this via the Update element, which expects a DataItemName attribute that relates directly to a BAM activity item name and a Type attribute that should match the BAM activity item type.

In addition, the following example also retrieves the EventTime property from the tracking event (this represents the timestamp of the workflow creation) and stores it in the WorkflowStarted BAM activity item.

```
<!-- Retrieve the EventTime of when this Workflow was started -->
  <ic:Update DataItemName="WorkflowStarted" Type="DATETIME">
    <ic:Expression>
      <wf:Operation Name="GetContextProperty">
        <wf:Argument>EventTime</wf:Argument>
      </wf:Operation>
    </ic:Expression>
  </ic:Update>
</ic:OnEvent>
```

We've now covered all the steps required to complete a single tracking entry. A full Tracking Configuration file is shown below. This file tracks Workflow Creation and Completion milestones, Completion of a Code Activity milestone, and the retrieval of a custom Workflow property. This Tracking Configuration file uses a number of techniques and should assist with writing your own custom interceptor.

```
<?xml version="1.0" encoding="utf-8"?>
<ic:InterceptorConfiguration xmlns:ic="http://schemas.microsoft.com/BizTalkServer/
2004/10/BAM/InterceptorConfiguration" xmlns:wf="http://schemas.microsoft.com/
BizTalkServer/2004/10/BAM/WorkflowInterceptorConfiguration" >

  <ic:EventSource Name="MySampleBAMTrackingWorkflow" Technology="WF"
Manifest="MySampleBAMTrackingWorkflow.Workflow1, MySampleBAMTrackingWorkflow,
Version=1.0.0.0, Culture=neutral, PublicKeyToken=null">
  </ic:EventSource>

<ic:BamActivity Name="MyActivity">

  <!--Track Workflow Started Event-->

  <ic:OnEvent Name="MyEvent1" Source="MySampleBAMTrackingWorkflow"
      IsBegin="true" IsEnd="false">
  <ic:Filter>
    <ic:Expression>
```

```
        <wf:Operation Name="GetWorkflowEvent"/>
        <ic:Operation Name="Constant">
          <ic:Argument>Created</ic:Argument>
        </ic:Operation>
        <ic:Operation Name="Equals"/>
      </ic:Expression>
    </ic:Filter>

    <!-- Get Unique ID -->
    <ic:CorrelationID>
      <ic:Expression>
        <wf:Operation Name="GetContextProperty">
          <wf:Argument>InstanceId</wf:Argument>
        </wf:Operation>
      </ic:Expression>
    </ic:CorrelationID>

    <!-- Retrieve the EventTime of when this Workflow was started -->
    <ic:Update DataItemName="WorkflowStarted" Type="DATETIME">
      <ic:Expression>
        <wf:Operation Name="GetContextProperty">
          <wf:Argument>EventTime</wf:Argument>
        </wf:Operation>
        </ic:Expression>
      </ic:Update>
    </ic:OnEvent>

      <!--Track Code Activity Completed Event-->

    <ic:OnEvent Name="MyEvent2" Source="MySampleBAMTrackingWorkflow"
      IsBegin="false" IsEnd="false">
      <ic:Filter>
        <ic:Expression>
          <wf:Operation Name="GetActivityName"/>
          <ic:Operation Name="Constant">
            <ic:Argument>codeActivity1</ic:Argument>
          </ic:Operation>
          <ic:Operation Name="Equals"/>
          <wf:Operation Name="GetActivityEvent"/>
          <ic:Operation Name="Constant">
            <ic:Argument>Closed</ic:Argument>
          </ic:Operation>
          <ic:Operation Name="Equals"/>
          <ic:Operation Name="And"/>
        </ic:Expression>
      </ic:Filter>

      <!-- Get Unique ID -->
      <ic:CorrelationID>
        <ic:Expression>
          <wf:Operation Name="GetContextProperty">
            <wf:Argument>InstanceId</wf:Argument>
          </wf:Operation>
        </ic:Expression>
      </ic:CorrelationID>
```

```xml
      <!-- Retrieve the EventTime of when this Activity finished -->
    <ic:Update DataItemName="CodeActivityCompleted" Type="DATETIME">
      <ic:Expression>
        <wf:Operation Name="GetContextProperty">
          <wf:Argument>EventTime</wf:Argument>
        </wf:Operation>
      </ic:Expression>
    </ic:Update>
  </ic:OnEvent>

  <!--Track Workflow Completed Event-->

  <ic:OnEvent Name="MyEvent3" Source="MySampleBAMTrackingWorkflow"
     IsBegin="false" IsEnd="true">
    <ic:Filter>
      <ic:Expression>
        <wf:Operation Name="GetWorkflowEvent"/>
        <ic:Operation Name="Constant">
          <ic:Argument>Completed</ic:Argument>
        </ic:Operation>
        <ic:Operation Name="Equals"/>
      </ic:Expression>
    </ic:Filter>


    <!-- Get Unique ID -->
    <ic:CorrelationID>
      <ic:Expression>
        <wf:Operation Name="GetContextProperty">
          <wf:Argument>InstanceId</wf:Argument>
        </wf:Operation>
      </ic:Expression>
    </ic:CorrelationID>

    <!-- Retrieve the EventTime of when this Workflow was ended-->
    <ic:Update DataItemName="WorkflowEnded" Type="DATETIME">
      <ic:Expression>
        <wf:Operation Name="GetContextProperty">
          <wf:Argument>EventTime</wf:Argument>
        </wf:Operation>
      </ic:Expression>
    </ic:Update>

    <ic:Update DataItemName="Some Data" Type="NVARCHAR">
      <ic:Expression>
        <wf:Operation Name="GetWorkflowProperty">
          <wf:Argument>MyCustomProperty</wf:Argument>
        </wf:Operation>
      </ic:Expression>
    </ic:Update>
  </ic:OnEvent>

</ic:BamActivity>
</ic:InterceptorConfiguration>
```

Assuming that the BAM Definition has already been deployed (see Chapter 6 for more details), we can now go ahead and deploy the Interceptor Configuration file. This is done using the BM.exe tool with a deploy-interceptor parameter. Validation against the deployed BAM activities will occur during deployment.

```
bm deploy-interceptor -Filename:BAMTrackingInterceptorConfig.xml
```

Once it is deployed, you can then start your workflow. You should see all the data specified in the Interceptor Configuration file being tracked in the appropriate Activity table. Figure 14-7 shows an example.

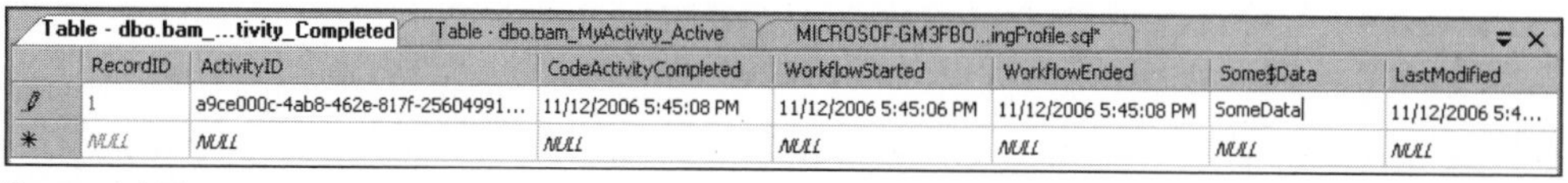

Figure 14-7

To further prove how deep the integration of WF and BizTalk is, consider Figure 14-8. This figure depicts the BAM portal successfully showing the BAM data stored by the Windows Workflow BAM Interceptor.

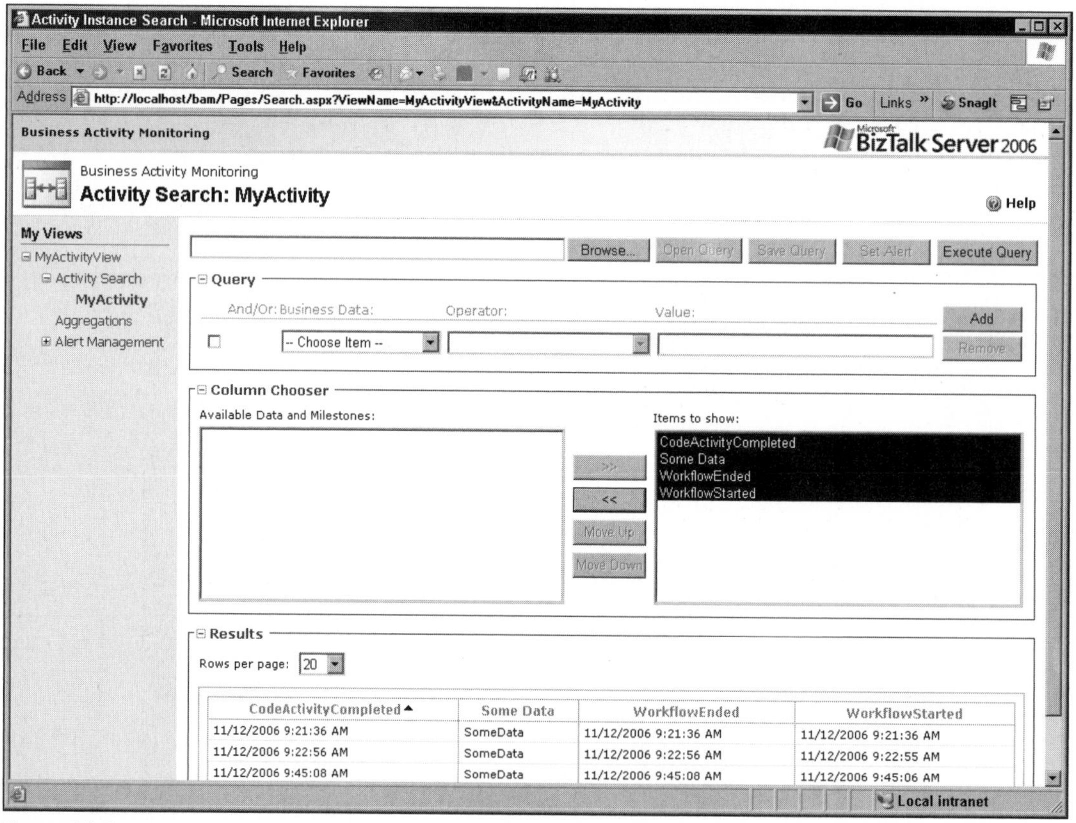

Figure 14-8

BizTalk, WF, and SharePoint

WF is currently being embedded within a number of Microsoft products. The first to market is Windows SharePoint Services 3, which acts as a host to WF.

You can create workflows, such as document approval, by using WF and then deploy them to a SharePoint server. These workflows can then be started following the arrival of a document into a document library. Alternatively, a user can manually start a workflow with a given document via the SharePoint portal site.

In the case of a document approval, you need to route the approval task to the approver. You can create a task on the SharePoint portal for the approver, which they can then use to perform the approval process. You can also synchronize these SharePoint tasks with Outlook to increase visibility.

Again, because SharePoint is hosting WF, it has provided a custom tracking service that enables you to view pending workflows via the portal and ascertain what progress has been made. It's worth noting, however, that you cannot, at the time of this writing, plug the WF BAM Interceptor into the WF runtime hosted by Sharepoint because the tracking configuration is not exposed. Discussions are underway to address this.

> *For more in-depth information about the workflow features of WSS3 and Office 2007, you might want to review the excellent article "Understanding Workflow in Windows SharePoint Services and the 2007 Microsoft Office System," by David Chappell. You can find it at* www.microsoft.com/downloads/ details.aspx?familyid=dbbd82c7-9bde-4974-8443-67b8f30126a8&displaylang=en.

One thing that I want to draw your attention to is the new SharePoint Designer. It ships as part of Office 2007. This tool, among other things, enables an end user (who is, most definitely, not a developer) to construct new workflows that can then be deployed for use by SharePoint.

The SharePoint Designer, as you can see in Figures 14-9 and 14-10, presents a completely different workflow design experience and enables you to construct workflows in a completely new way.

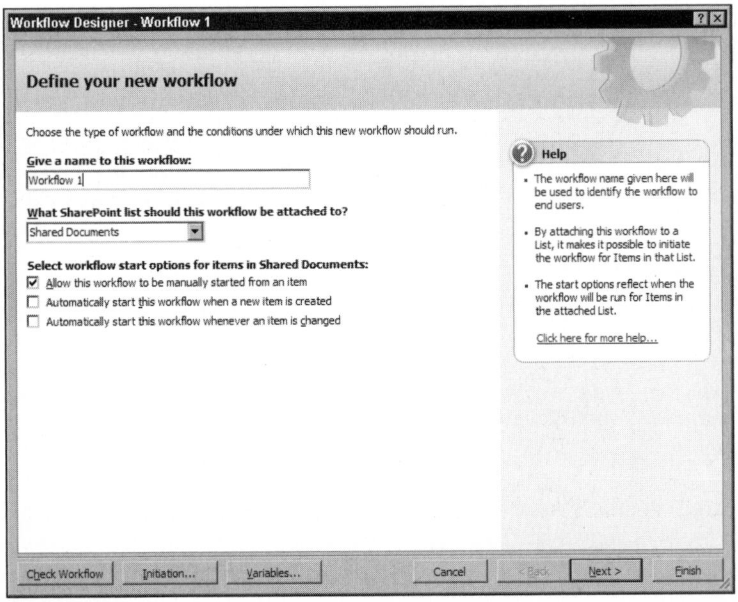

Figure 14-9

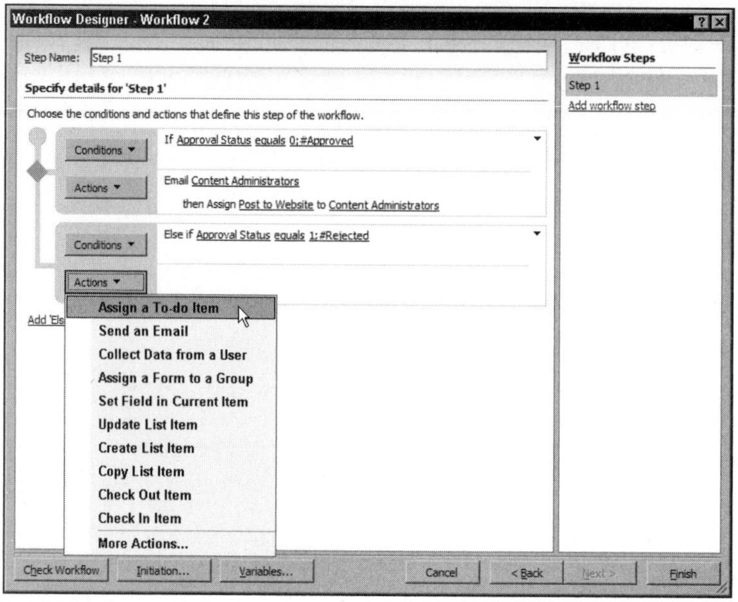

Figure 14-10

As you can see in Figure 14-10, you can construct a workflow similarly to the way you construct mail rules within Microsoft Outlook. The workflow shown in the figure can make use of a number of actions. These actions are workflow activities, and the workflow being built is a sequential workflow.

This enables you to write your own activities and make them available through this workflow design tool to allow end users to construct ever more complicated workflows. As discussed earlier in this chapter, you can build composite activities that contain a complex set of activity interactions to perform a process.

In short, the SharePoint Designer is an incredibly powerful workflow design tool that can truly enable end users to construct workflows to simplify collaboration and business processes.

A classic use case for such document workflow is BizTalk, which during order processing, can post an XML message to a SharePoint portal for an approval process. InfoPath (which is also WF-enabled) can then render the XML message and a form and use Windows SharePoint Services to execute a workflow.

Summary

In this closing chapter, we have introduced Windows Workflow and the underpinning concepts and architecture. Some concepts are very similar to BizTalk Server, a result of many BizTalk team members helping to design and develop WF.

A key message through this section of the book is how WF provides a workflow foundation for use within your own application rather than a complete enterprise server rivaling BizTalk Server.

We then positioned WF and BizTalk Server by highlighting the key differences that you should consider and explaining that WF can be thought of as enabling workflow *within* your application rather than between applications through the use of its rich runtime services such as adapters.

Hopefully, this chapter will prove useful when the inevitable question comes up within your organization: "Why should you pay for BizTalk when you have WF available for free?"

Index

A

A4Swift accelerator, 104
access violations, 406
ACID, 210, 211
  attributes, 210
  transactions, 147
ACK messages. *See* Acknowledgment messages
Acknowledge context property, 66, 67, 68
Acknowledgment (ACK) messages, 196, 197
AckRequired property, 92
  reading/writing/promoting, 93
action stage, 321
activating receive, 141, 142
  Receive shape and, 142
Active Send Messages counter, 443
ActiveInstances view, 288
ActiveRelationships table, 235
activities, BAM, 224–225. *See also* specific activities
  creation, 251
    Wiley Travel Services and, 263–266
  database infrastructure for, 229–230
activities, WF, 607–608
activity aggregations, 302–305
  PivotTables and, 302–305
activity alerts, 237
  Wiley Travel Services and, 305–307
activity references, 235–236, 255–256
activity searches, 300–302

activity segment, 253
activity views, BAM, 223, 225–229. *See also specific activity views*
  BAM portal and, 225
  bm.exe tool and security for, 232
  database infrastructure for, 230–232
  defined
    View Creation Wizard and, 266–275
    Wiley Travel Services and, 266–275
  SQL views *v.*, 225, 230
  tested
    PivotTables and, 276–279
    Wiley Travel Services and, 276–279
ActivityIDs, 225, 246
  TPE and, 246
Acumen Business, 340
  Rule Manager, 323
adapter(s), 21, 37–87, 89. *See also specific adapters*
  architecture, 38
  BizTalk processing model and, 467, 468, 469
  communication semantics, 39
  configuration settings, 47
    SSO database and, 47
  correlation sets and, 481
  custom, 37, 55
    WCF, 85–86
    writing, 55–56
  endpoint configuration, 481
  features of, 481
  functionality of, 481

adapter(s) (*continued*)
hosts and, 46–47
in-box, 37, 56–87
  LOB integration and, 56
inline sends *v.*, 480, 481
mapping and, 481
one-way, 39
overview, 37–38
passwords and, 506
pipelines *v.*, 89–90
service windows and, 481
streaming and, 481
tracking and, 481
two-way, 39
Adapter Framework, .NET 3.0, 55, 56, 87
Add Generated Items wizard, 2, 71
AddDocument method, 126
AddReference method, 236, 254, 255
overloads, 256–257
AddRelatedActivity method, 254, 255
administration, 495–574
application deployment, 500–513
best practices, 495–574
BizTalk application components, 496
BizTalk monitoring, 516–522, 563–573
  MOM and, 563–573
BizTalk troubleshooting, 516–522
DTA purging and archiving, 554–560
ESSO maintenance, 523–526
host management, 513–516
log shipping, 551–554
MSDTC problems, 534–538
SQL Server, 541–562
  BizTalk perspective on, 541–562
  performance determination, 417, 418,
    560–562
SQL Server Agent jobs, 544–546
tasks, 500
  preventative, 538–541, 573
  regular, 500–538
tools, 496–500, 526–534
  hidden, 528–534

**Administration Console. *See* BizTalk Server
  2006 Administration Console**
AdminQueue context property, 66, 67
ADPlus, 532
adplus script, 459
**AffiliateApplicationName context property,
  73, 81**
After predicate, 327
AfterPut context property, 85
Agent, MOM, 564, 566–567
Aggregator pattern, 584–585
information link for, 584
Alert Rules, 567, 568
alerts, BAM portal, 237
Wiley Travel Services and, 305–307
all execution mode, 98
all recognized execution mode, 98
AllInstances view, 288
AllowCacheOnWrite context property, 57, 58
**APIs. *See* application programming
  interfaces**
AppDomain, 11
application deployment, 500–513
best practices, 512–513
BizTalk Explorer and, 501–502
BizTalk Server Administration Console and,
  502–510
environment separation and, 500–501
Visual Studio and, 501–502
**"Application Deployment Command Line,"
  498**
Application Name property, 500
**application programming interfaces
  (APIs), 7**
BAM, 251
BizTalk processing model and, 467, 468,
  469
pipeline, 106
test steps and, 382–383
typed, 257
vocabulary, 343
application queue, 467

Application Settings screen, 508, 509
Application Target Environment Settings
    screen, 509, 510
AppSpecific context property, 66, 67, 68
APropertyBag, 596
ArbitraryXPathPropertyHandler sample, 116
archiving, 224, 232, 233, 413. *See also* DTA
    purging and archiving
ArrivedTime context property, 66, 67, 68
artifacts, BizTalk, 497
ASP.NET
  Application, 263
  performance counters, 453–454
  Web services, 222, 262
Assemble method, 126
Assemble stage, 23, 106
  message assembling, 106
  message formatting, 106
  orchestration and, 106
assemblers, BTF, 111, 112, 126
assemblies, 96. *See also* .NET assemblies
AssemblyName context property, 73
Assert function, 328
asserting facts, 312
atomic scope, 210–211
  COM+ components and, 200, 211
  persistence points and, 147, 211
  reasons for, 210–211
  transactable adapter and, 197
atomicity, 210
Attachments context property, 81
attributes
  ACID, 210
  PSSDiag and, 531
  XML document, 338
Authenticated context property, 66, 67, 68
AuthenticationScheme context property,
    73, 81
AuthLevel context property, 66, 67
autogrowth, database, 423–424
Av WS Duration, 268

Available Megabytes counter, 436
Average Hotel Stay, 273
Average Wait Time (ms) counter, 451
Avg Disk Queue Length counter, 420, 451
Avg Disk sec/Read counter, 420, 452
Avg Disk sec/Write counter, 420, 452

B

B2B scenario. *See* Business-to-Business
    scenario
Backup BizTalk Server job, 544, 546–550
Backup Transport configuration dialog
    box, 49
backups
  BAM, 546
  complete, 549
  database, 546–550
    custom databases added to, 549–550
    more information on, 548
    restore from, 410
  SQL Server Analysis Services, 546
bad code, 458
BAM. *See* Business Activity Monitoring
BAM interceptor for WF, 616–622
BAM_AN_View NameSSIS package,
    289, 302
BAMArchive database, 224, 233
bam_Metadata_Activities table, 233, 234
BAMPrimaryImport database, 223, 227,
    232, 263, 288, 289
  performance, 413
BAS. *See* Business Activity Services
Base EDI adapter, 515, 546
BaseAdapter sample, 55
BaseInterceptor class, 262
batching, 54, 481
  BizTalk processing model and, 468, 469
  File adapter and, 54
  SOAP adapter and, 54
BatchSize, 474

Before predicate, 327
BeforePut context property, 85
BeginActivity method, 251
best practices. *See also* **administration**
  administration, 495–574
  application deployment, 512–513
  BizTalk development, 591–604
    FIFO behavior, 604
    large message processing, 591–592
    looping/storing messages, 593
    loosely coupling, 599–602
    Process Manager pattern, 602
    solution instrumentation, 602–604
    storing configuration data, 593–597
    subscribing to failure messages, 597–598
    suspended messages/orchestrations,
        598–599
  BPA and, 526–528
  E2E and, 575
Between predicate, 327
binding files, 503
  customizing, 505
  modifying, 505
  multiple, 503–506
  passwords and, 506
Birth, Jason, 386
bit shovelers, 37, 89
  SOAP adapter and, 89
BizTalk 2006 CD, hidden tools in, 528–534
BizTalk application, 496
  administration. *See* administration.
  components, 496, 573
    BizTalk Server, 496
    ESSO, 496
    IIS, 496
    SQL Notification Services, 496
    SQL Server, 496
    SQL Server Analysis Services, 496
    Windows SharePoint Services, 496
  infrastructure, 496

  monitoring of, 516–522, 563–573
    MOM and, 563–573
BizTalk artifacts, 497
**BizTalk Assembly Checker and Remote GAC
    tool, 532–534**
  important information on, 534
  running, 533–534
BizTalk best practices, 591–604. *See also*
    best practices
**BizTalk Best Practices Analyzer (BPA),
    526–528, 573**
  download, 526
  link, 526
BizTalk counters, 394
BizTalk Explorer, 499–500
  production environments and, 502, 512
  Visual Studio and, 501–502
BizTalk Framework (BTF), 95, 109–112
  assemblers, 111, 112, 126
  disassemblers, 110, 111, 126
  reliable messages
    receiving, 110–111
    sending, 111–112
BizTalk hotfix information, PSSDiag and, 531
BizTalk log shipping, 551–554
BizTalk Management Pack, 565–570, 574
  Event Rules, 570–571
BizTalk Mapper, 76–77, 212–214, 592
  designer surface, 212, 213
  limitations, 214
BizTalk Message Queue, 466
BizTalk MessageBox. *See* **MessageBox**
BizTalk Messaging counters, 443
BizTalk Messaging Latency counters, 442
**BizTalk perspective, on SQL Server,
    541–562**
BizTalk processing model, 466–469
  adapters in, 467, 468, 469
  APIs in, 467, 468, 469
  batching in, 468, 469

maps in, 468, 469

Message Agent in, 467, 468, 469

message flow in, 466–469

Messaging Engine in, 466, 467, 468, 469

MSMQ adapter in, 466, 468

Orchestration Engine in, 467, 468, 469

orchestration in, 467, 468, 469

receive pipeline in, 467, 468, 469

send pipeline in, 467, 468, 469

send port in, 467

subscriptions and, 467, 468, 469

BizTalk registry settings, PSSDiag and, 531

BizTalk runtime error, 205

exceptions and, 205

BizTalk Server

administration, 495–574

application deployment and, 501–502

architecture, 15–36, 466–469

overview, 20

BizTalk application components and, 496

fictional scenario, 15–20

phase 1, 15–17

phase 2, 17–18

phase 3, 18–20

low latency and tuning, 472–474

MOM integration with, 308

monitoring, 516–522, 563–573

Operators group, 518

Pipeline Component Project, 117

power of, 415

R2 release, 55, 56

SDK, 55

SharePoint, WF and, 623–624

technologies for, 1–12

testing, 367–413. *See also* testing.

WF v., 605, 615–625. *See also* Windows Workflow Foundation.

BizTalk Server 2006 Administration Console, 24, 497–498, 573

application deployment, 502–510

MSI usage, 503–510

import and export wizards, 502–503

passwords and, 506

subscription query feature of, 24

BizTalk Server Administrators Group, 526

BizTalk Servers (processing nodes), 418–419

BizTalk throttling, 461, 478

BizTalk Trace, PSSDiag and, 531

BizTalk troubleshooting, 516–522

BizTalk Version "Next" (vNext), 616

BizTalk vNext. *See* BizTalk Version "Next"

BizTalkServerApplication host, 35, 425

BizTalkServerIsolatedHost, 35, 425

BizUnit, 375–383, 463

configuration, 381

context object, 381–383

download, 383

performance testing and, 401

SDK, 383

test cases, 375

automated, 383

examples, 376–380

execution, 378

failure, 379, 402

group-level, 378

information, 383

LoadGen, 391

performance test and, 402–405

stages, 375

XML, 375, 376

test steps, 375, 379

API and, 382–383

automated performance testing, 401–402

context-manipulation, 383

creation, 381

BizUnit (*continued*)
failure, 379, 402
flow state between, 382
validation, 383
wildcards, 381–382
black box, 221, 222, 373, 423
bm.exe tool, 225, 229, 230
activity view security with, 232
deploy-all command, 236
remove-all command, 237
RTA window extension, 232
update-all command, 237
BodyType context property, 68
Booking ID, 247
bottlenecks, performance, 391–396
host creation and, 392–394
source of, 392
bounce **script, 438–439**
BPA. *See* BizTalk Best Practices Analyzer
BPEL. *See* Business Process Execution
Language
BPEL4WS specification, 219
BPM scenario. *See* Business Process
Management scenario
branches, 579, 580
BRE. *See* Business Rules Engine
BTF. *See* BizTalk Framework
BTS Log Shipping Get Backup History job,
553, 554
BTS Log Shipping Restore to Mark job,
553, 554
BTS Server Log Shipping Restore Databases
job, 553, 554
bts_CleanupMsgbox stored procedure, 428
BTSDeploy, 498, 510
BTSDoStuffFacade method, 201, 202
BTS.InterchangeID context property, 251
BTS.IsReliable message context property,
112
BTS.ReceivePortName context property,
62, 63

BTSScnSSOApplicationConfig.exe tool,
595, 596
BTSTask, 498, 510–512, 573
examples, 511–512
deployment batch script, 511–512
functionality, 510–511
BufferedEventStream, 223, 237, 251,
252, 259
MessagingEventStream *v.,* 224
OrchestrationEventStream *v.,* 224
bugs, 406
stress testing and, 406–407
build process, 370–371. *See also* testing
daily schedule, 370
build verification tests (BVTs), 370, 371
components, 371
Business Activity Monitoring (BAM), 33–34,
219, 220, 221–309, 602
activities, 224–225
creation, 251, 263–266
database infrastructure for, 229–230
activity views, 225–229
database infrastructure for, 230–232
Wiley Travel Services and, 266–279
administration tool, 223, 226
applied, 262–308
architecture, 223
archiving, 224, 232, 233, 413
backup/restore and, 546
BPM scenario and, 581
conceptual overview, 224–229
continuation in, 246–249, 252–254
data items updated in, 251–252
deployment tool, 236–237
dimensions and, 227–229
end-to-end order tracking and, 581
event streams, 258–261
Excel add-in, 222, 224, 238, 263
fundamentals, 222–224
heavy usage, 462

interceptors, 617, 240–241
  custom, 261–262
  for WF, 616–622
latency measurement with, 471
licensing, 238, 309
Management tool, 225
message body storage with, 53
OLAP v., 221
overview, 221–222
partitioning, 232–234
performance, 237–238
portal, 33, 224, 299
  activity views and, 225
  alerts and, 237, 305–307
  health portal v., 299
  location, 299
  Wiley Travel Services and, 299–308, 309
references, 234–236, 254–257
TPE and, 33, 238–250
tracking service, 467
transactional integrity, 259–260
View Creation Wizard, 266
  activity views defined with, 266–275
Wiley Travel Services and, 262–308
Business Activity Services (BAS), 546
business data items, 222, 225, 240
business logic, 34
business milestones, 222, 225, 240
**Business Process Execution Language
  (BPEL), 219**
**Business Process Management (BPM)
  scenario, 576–582**
  architecture, 577
  BAM and, 581
  documentation, 576, 582
  end-to-end order tracking in, 581
  highlights, 577–582
  in-flight orchestrations, 578
    interruption of, 578–580
  installation, 582

Ops adapter and, 581–582
Process Management pattern, 577–578
source code, 582
Southridge Video business requirements,
  576–577
SSO store in, 580–581
tracing and, 582
**Business Rule Composer, 34, 177,
  324–326, 362, 366**
Business Rule Manager, Acumen, 323
Business Rule policies, 509
business rules, 311
  caching, 361–362
  creation, 324, 326
    custom, 362–364
  deployment, 364–366
    automated script and, 365–366
  design surface, 324
  evaluation, 316–321
    action stage, 321
    conflict resolution stage, 318–320
    match stage, 316–318
  expression, 311
  invoking, 347–353
    Call Rules shape and, 347, 349–352
    .NET helper class and, 347, 348
    problems in, 352, 353
  storage, 361
  updating, 361–362
**Business Rules Engine (BRE), 34, 177–178,
  311–366**
  databases, 332–334
  DebugTrackingInterceptor, 317, 357–358
  forward chaining, 321–323
  functions, 327–328
  host agnostic status, 344
  hosting, 344
  Long-Term Fact Retrievers, 354, 366
    example, 354–357
  long-term facts, 353

Business Rules Engine (BRE) (*continued*)
.NET classes and, 329–330
orchestration drop off and, 456–457
predicates, 327
Rete analysis network and, 312–316
rules, 311
creation, 324, 326, 362–364
deployment, 364–366
evaluation, 316–321
expression, 311
invoking, 347–353
storage, 361
updating/caching, 361–362
short-term facts, 353
testing, 344–346
PolicyTester class, 344, 345–346
Test Policy, 344–345
Tracking Interceptor, 357, 366
custom, 358–360
vocabularies, 334–343
XML schemas and, 330–332
Business View
creation, 270–275
testing, 276–279
**Business-to-Business (B2B) scenario,
588–590**
documentation, 588, 590
dynamic send ports in, 589
empty message creation in, 589–590
highlights, 588–590
installation, 590
LitWare and, 588
Message Broker pattern, 588–589
source code, 590
Splitter pattern, 589
Trading Partner Management System and,
588, 589
BVTs. *See* build verification tests
Bytes Received/ sec counter, 436
Bytes Sent/ sec counter, 436
#Bytes in All Heaps counter, 437

C

C#, 134, 136
orchestration and, 138–140
source files, 139, 140
CacheSize, 457
CacheTimeout, 457
Call Orchestration shape, 177, 599
invoking orchestration with, 142
Call Rules Configuration dialog box, 352
Call Rules shape, 177
data facts and, 349–350
HAT tool and, 347
invoking rules and, 347, 349–352
XML facts and, 350–352
Called Orchestration property, 176
CanRecognizeData, 128
CategoryTypes.CATID_Any, 118
**CategoryTypes.CATID_PipelineComponent,
118**
CBR. *See* content-based routing
CC context property, 81, 82
CDATA elements, 592
Certificate context property, 81
Chappell, David, 623
checklist, performance test, 416–428
summary, 428
chunking, 66, 67
Class context property, 66, 67
class node, 312, 313
cleanup stage, 375
CleanupBTFExpiredEntriesJob, 544
ClientCertificate context property, 73
**ClientConnectionTimeout context
property, 73**
CLR. *See* common language runtime
clustering
hosts, 515–516
detailed information on, 515
FTP adapter and, 515
in-order delivery and, 516

MSMQ adapter and, 515
POP3 adapter and, 516
Master Secret Server, 525–526
detailed information on, 526
code, bad, 458
code coverage, 383–386
functional testing and, 383–386
orchestrations and, 386
pipeline component, 384–385
Code Coverage tool, Visual Studio, 384
code profiling, 396–401
symbols and, 397
coding, orchestration and, 197–207
Collection Location, 275
columns, vocabularies and, 339
COM+ components, 200, 211
atomic scope and, 200, 211
COM objects, 406
stress testing and, 406, 407
common language runtime (CLR), 11
counters, 394, 437
stress testing and, 406
CommonSection, 390
communication semantics, 39
compensation, 209–210
CompletedInstances view, 288
CompletedRelationships table, 235
completion ports, 114
component layer, LoadGen, 389
compression stream implementation, 121–124
compression/decompression pipeline component, 117
CompressionStream class, 120, 121, 122
implementation for, 122–124
concurrent Web Service calls, 426
ConfigAdapterWSPort context property, 68
ConfigCustomTemplatesDocLib context property, 68
ConfigCustomTemplatesNamespaceCol context property, 68

ConfigNamespaceAliases context property, 68
ConfigOfficeIntegration context property, 68
ConfigOverwrite context property, 68
ConfigPropertiesXml context property, 68
ConfigTemplatesDocLib context property, 68
ConfigTemplatesNamespaceCol context property, 68
ConfigTimeout context property, 68
configuration data
SSO store and, 594–597
storage of, 593–597
configuration helper APIs, 381–382
Configuration Overview section, 517
"Configuring Tracking Using BizTalk Administration Console," 520
conflict resolution stage, 318–320
connectionString context property, 72
consistency, 210
constants, 334
vocabularies and, 334–336
Construct Message shape, 166, 178, 184
consuming pipeline, 95
content-based routing (CBR), 31, 181
File adapter and, 59–64
Contention Rate/ sec counter, 437
ContentType context property, 81
context data, message, 519
context object, BizUnit, 381–383
context properties, 53. *See also specific context properties*
dynamic send ports, 44, 53
EDI adapter, 82–83
File adapter, 57–58
FTP adapter, 85
HTTP adapter, 80–81
MQSeries adapter, 84
MSMQ adapter, 67–68
MSMQT adapter, 66
POP3 adapter, 82
sample file, 52

context properties (*continued*)
SMTP adapter, 81
SOAP adapter, 73
SQL adapter, 72
WSS adapter, 68–69
Context Property, 240, 243–245
Schema, 242, 243
TPE and, 243–245
Context Property notation, 183, 184
Context Switches/ sec counter, 436
continuation, 246–249, 252–254
event streams and, 246, 253
scenario
custom code to orchestration, 248–249
orchestration to custom code, 247–248
orchestration to orchestration, 247
TPE and, 246–249
continuous integration server, 370
convoy(s), 55, 192. *See also specific convoys*
orchestrations and, 55, 192–196
race condition and, 192–193
singleton pattern and, 193–194
types, 194–196
ConvoySetInstances table, 187
CopyMode context property, 57, 58
correlation, 186–192
File adapter and, 187
mechanics of, 187
message, 186–192
MQSeries adapter and, 187
MSMQ adapter and, 187
sequential convoy and, 188
walk-through, 188–192
Correlation Properties dialog box, 190
Correlation Set properties window, 189
correlation sets
adapters and, 481
initializing, 488–489
low latency and, 488–489
CorrelationId context property, 66, 67, 68

count function, 5–6
Counter log, 432, 433, 434
counters. *See specific counters*
Covast (www.covast.com), 82
Covast EDI adapter, 82. *See also* EDI adapter
CPU counters, 394
CPU usage, orchestration drop off from, 456
crash dumps, 532
credentials, 557
DTA Purge and Archive job and configuration of, 557–559
ESSO and, 523
critical errors, 570, 573
CritSits, 516
cross-field validation, 104
CrossFieldCheck pipeline component, 99, 100
CruiseControl.Net, 370
Current Connections counter, 453
custom references, 236, 256–257
custom rules editor, 362–364
CustomerReference, 246, 247

D

daily schedule, build process, 370
data agnostic, 89
data dimension, 228, 274
data facts, Call Rules shape and, 349–350
data items. *See* business data items
data maintenance (DM) job, 288
Data Table/Data Row, 332, 333
data tables, vocabularies and, 339
Data Transformation Services (DTS) package, 227, 231
Data Maintenance, 232, 233
database(s), 332–334, 541. *See also* MessageBox
autogrowth, 423
testing and, 423–424

backup, 546–550
 custom databases added to, 549–550
 more information on, 548
 BRE and, 332–334
 custom, 452–453
  back up, 549–550
  tuning, 452–453
 location, 421–423
  testing and, 421–423
 restoring, 554
  log shipping and, 554
 separation, 562
database administrators (DBAs), 452
database cluster failover, 409
Database Engine Tuning Advisor, 288
database infrastructure
 activities, 229–230
 activity views, 230–232
 Wiley Travel Services, 279–280
database restore, from backup, 410
database session count throttling, 448
Database session performance counter, 448
Database Size performance counter, 447
database size throttling, 447–448
DataConnection, 332, 333, 334
Date context property, 82
DateTime wildcard, 382
DB2 adapter, Microsoft BizTalk, 56
DBAs. See database administrators
debugging
 HAT and, 218
 orchestrations, 217–218, 498
 XSLT, 215–216
Debugging Microsoft .NET 2.0 Applications
  (Robbins), 459
"Debugging Orchestrations," 521
Debugging Tools for Windows, 459, 532
 link, 532
DebugTrackingInterceptor, 317, 357–358
DebugView, 217, 218, 358, 582, 603, 604

Decide shape, 171–172
 Expression shape and, 197
Decision shape, 135
Decode stage, 22, 100–101
decompression stream implementation,
  124–125
DecompressionStream class, 120, 124
 implementation for, 125
Decompressor pipeline component, 99, 100
default namespace, 3
Define a Range of Values page, 336
Deflate algorithm, 121, 122
DeflateStream class, 121
dehydration, 8
 calculations, 150
 orchestration, 32, 149–150
Delay shape, 32, 171
 orchestration with, 487
 persistence points and, 148
delivery notifications, 170, 196–197
DeliveryReceipt context property, 81
Demilitarized Zone (DMZ), 73
dependencies, 507
dependent systems, 453–454
 low throughput and, 461
deployed state, 325
"Deploying a Business-to-Business Solution,"
  590
"Deploying and Managing BizTalk
  Application," 509
"Deploying the Business Process
  Management Solution," 582
"Deploying the Service Oriented Solution,"
  588
deployment. See also application
  deployment
 failure, 512
  large MSI files and, 512–513
deployment batch script, 511–512
deployment tool, 236–237
 TPE and, 249

Designer
OBDA, 160–164
Orchestration, 31, 165
Schema, 179
SharePoint, 623–624
Visio, 160–164
WF, 613
Destination, 274
development environments, 500, 501
dimensions, 34, 226, 227–229. *See also*
   specific dimensions
types, 227
direct ports, 155–156
binding, 155, 156
filter expressions and, 156
partner ports and, 157–160
self-correlating ports and, 156–157
DirectEventStream, 223, 224, 237, 251,
   252, 258, 263
Disassemble method, 126
Disassemble stage, 22, 101–103
large interchanges in, 102–103
probing capabilities, 102
processing in, 101–102
recoverable interchanges in, 103
disassemblers, BTF, 110, 111, 126
disassembly, 96
disaster recover testing, 409–411
documenting/ fine-tuning procedures, 410
scenarios for, 409–410
test categories and, 369
zero data loss and, 410–411
disaster recovery failover, 410–411
disk(s), 419–421
performance, 420, 462
   low throughput and, 462
subsystem, 476–477
   low latency and, 476–477
disk counters, 394
% Disk Idle Time counter, 420, 452
DispositionNotificationTo context property, 82

distinguished promotions, 80, 172,
   179–180
property promotions *v.,* 181
DM job. *See* **data maintenance job**
DMZ. *See* **Demilitarized Zone**
document object model. *See* **DOM**
Document Type Definition (DTD), 2
documentRootElementName context
   property, 72
Documents Processed/Sec counter, 443
Documents Received/Sec counter, 443
documentTargetNamespace context
   property, 72
DOM (document object model), 115
traversing, 200
DoStuff method, 202
double-hop, 64, 65
drop off, of orchestrations, 455–458
reasons for, 455–458
   BRE, 456–457
   high CPU usage, 456
   not enough work, 455–456
   serialization of orchestrations, 457–458
   SQL Server problems, 456
   throttling, 456
DTA Purge and Archive job, 425, 544
configuration
   credentials, 557–559
   DTA purging only in, 556–560
DTA purging and archiving, 554–560
options, 556–557
DTA purging, configuration for, 559–560
DTC service. *See* **Microsoft Distributed**
   Transaction Coordinator service
DTCPing tool, 538
DTCTester tool, 538
DTD. *See* **Document Type Definition**
DTS package. *See* **Data Transformation**
   Services package
durability, 210
DWORD entries, 538

E

E2E scenarios. *See* **End-to-end scenarios**
EDI adapter, 82–83
  context properties, 82–83
  Covast, 82
EDIFACT (Electronic Data Interchange), 82, 101
EDIINT AS2, 82
editable state
  policies, 325
  vocabularies, 334
EIF. *See* **Enterprise Instrumentation Framework**
Electronic Data Interchange. *See* **EDIFACT**
elements, XML document, 338
EmailBodyFile context property, 81
EmailBodyFileCharset context property, 81
EmailBodyText context property, 81
EmailBodyTextCharset context property, 81
Enable routing for failed messages, 105
  receive port and, 105
EnableChunkedEncoding context property, 81
EnableContinuation method, 253, 254
Encode stage, 23, 107
End Point Manager (EPM), 20, 38
EndActivity method, 251
end-to-end order tracking, 576, 581
  BAM and, 581
End-to-end (E2E) scenarios, 575–590. *See also* **Business Process Management scenario; Business-to-Business scenario; Service-Oriented scenario**
  B2B scenario, 588–590
  best practices, 575
  BPM scenario, 576–582
  documentation, 576
  SO scenario, 582–588
  support for, 576
engine functions, 327–328
enlistments, 45
  send port, 45

Enterprise Instrumentation Framework (EIF), 603
Enterprise Library, Microsoft, 218, 602, 603
Enterprise Single Sign-On (ESSO), 496
  Administration Console, 524
  BizTalk application components and, 496
  credentials and, 523
  maintenance, 523–526
  uses of, 523
environments, 500
  development, 500, 501
  production, 500, 501
    BizTalk Explorer and, 502, 512
  separation of, 500–501
  staging, 500, 501
EPM. *See* **End Point Manager**
Equal predicate, 327
EqualsPredicates table, 27
ErrorReport message context properties, 105
ErrorType property, 105
***Essential Windows Workflow Foundation* (Shukla and Schmidt), 605**
ESSO. *See* **Enterprise Single Sign-On**
ESSO Management Pack, 565–570
ETW. *See* **Event Tracing for Windows**
event logs, PSSDiag and, 529, 531
Event Rules, BizTalk Management Pack, 567, 568, 570–571
Event Sources, 240
event streams, 223, 251, 258–261, 514
  continuation and, 246, 253
Event Tracing for Windows (ETW), 603
Event Viewer, 438
  throttling conditions and, 438
EventingReadStream, 127
Excel, Microsoft, 263
  BAM Excel add-in, 222, 224, 238, 263
  performance counters list in, 430, 431
exception(s), 205–207
  BizTalk runtime error and, 205
  handling, 206

exception(s) *(continued)*
long-running scope and, 205
.NET assemblies and, 205
reasons for, 205
Throw Exception shape and, 205
Execute method, 120, 321
execution modes, pipeline stage, 98
execution stage, 375
Exists predicate, 327
expectations, 372
Explorer. *See* BizTalk Explorer
Export Bindings Wizard, 504
Export Global Party Information box, 504
Export MSI File Wizard, 198, 506–507
Export XML, 279
Expression Editor shape, 180
Expression shape, 197–198
Decide shape and, 197
Message Assignment shape and, 197
expressions, 3. *See also specific expressions*
Extensible Markup Language. *See* XML
Extensible Style Language Transformation.
    ***See* XSLT**
Extension context property, 66, 67

F

façade, 282
helper method, 201
vocabularies and, 334
Wiley Travel Services and, 282–288
fact sources, 328
facts, 312. *See also specific facts*
Facts Explorer pane, 324, 328, 332
failed message routing, 598
failover, 409
database cluster, 409
disaster recovery, 410–411
testing, 410–411
zero data loss upon, 410–411

failure(s)
deployment, 512–513
large MSI files and, 512–513
full site, 410
log shipping and, 551–554
master secret server, 524, 525
network, 410
network card, 410
orchestration, 412–413
pipeline, 104–105
processing node, 409
recovery from, 551
test case, 379, 402
test step, 379, 402
zero data loss upon, 410–411
failure messages, 597
subscribing to, 597–598
FailureCategory property, 105
FailureCode property, 105
***Fetch from context* feature, 382**
FIFO behavior. *See* first-in, first-out behavior
File adapter, 39, 57
batching and, 54
CBR with, 59–64
receive port in, 59–61
security in, 63–64
send port in, 61–63
context properties, 57–58
correlation and, 187
in-order delivery and, 54–55
locations, 425
File adapter-specific configuration dialog
    box, 59, 60
File Transfer Protocol. *See* FTP
FileCreationTime context property, 57, 58
FileMon, 419
Filename context property, 68, 69
FileReceive, 43
FileRuleStore class, 361
FileSystemWatcher class, 16, 18
Filter Expression property, 170

filter expressions, 143, 144, 156
  direct ports and, 156
filters, 42–43, 156. *See also specific filters*
  Receive shape with, 43
firewall configuration, MSDTC and, 535
first recognized execution mode, 98
first-in, first-out (FIFO) behavior, 604
  white paper for, 604
Flat File Disassembler pipeline
    component, 23
flat memory footprint, 468, 469
Flight activity, 235, 236, 255, 264–265
Flight Booking Web service, 263, 280,
    281, 282
  BookingID and, 247
Flight Booking WS Duration, 267, 268
Flight orchestration, 263, 280
Flight report, 294
Flights Booked, 277
flow control shapes, 170–177
flow state, between test steps, 382
adm_ForceFullBackup table, 549
Forgy, Charles, 312
forward chaining, 321–323
Forward Execution processing
    algorithm, 613
  Rete algorithm v., 613
forward partner direct binding, 157–158
  configuration, 158–159
forward-only streams, 94, 469
  virtual streams v., 129, 592
Fragments table, 542, 543
framework layer, LoadGen, 389
From context property, 81, 82
FTP (File Transfer Protocol), 84
FTP adapter, 46, 47, 84–85
  clustering hosts and, 515
  context properties, 85
FTP specification, 85
full site failure, 410

functional testing, 371, 373–386, 415
  automated, 374, 413
  BizUnit, 375–383
  BVTs in, 370, 371
  code coverage and, 383–386
  importance of, 415
  manual, 374, 413
  negative tests in, 374
  positive tests in, 374
  test categories and, 369
functions, XPath, 5–6, 202–205. *See also
    specific functions*
  parameters of, 202

G

GAC. *See* Global Assembly Cache
garbage collector (GC), 114, 437
GC. *See* garbage collector
General Routing orchestration, 520, 521
GenerateTypedBAMAPI, 250, 280,
    281, 282
#Gen 0 Collections counter, 437
#Gen 1 Collections counter, 437
#Gen 2 Collections counter, 437
GetNext method, 102, 126
Global Assembly Cache (GAC), 150. *See
    also* BizTalk Assembly Checker and
    Remote GAC tool
  .NET assemblies and, 198, 199, 329
  versioning and, 150–151
global tracking. *See* tracking, global
globally unique identifiers. *See* GUIDs
GlobalTrackingOption column, 426, 427
GreaterThan predicate, 327
GreaterThanEqual predicate, 327
Group Hub Page, 516–518, 573
  sections of, 517–518
  suspended instances and, 518–522
Grouped by Error link, 518, 519

"Grouped Suspended Service Instances," **518**
Guid wildcard, **382**
GUIDs (globally unique identifiers), **186,
246, 251**
GZip algorithm, **121, 122**
GZipStream class, **121, 124**

H

hang dumps, **532**
hard purging, **556**
hardware configurations, performance
testing and, **416–421**
HashAlg context property, **66, 67**
HAT tool. *See* Health and Activity Tracking
tool
Headers context property, **82**
Health and Activity Tracking (HAT) tool, **21,
218, 498, 499**
Call Rules shape and, 347
debugging with, 218
PSSDiag and, 531
health portal, **289.** *See also* **Business
Activity Monitoring, portal**
BAM portal *v.,* 299
hidden tools, BizTalk 2006 CD, **528–534**
high memory usage, **458–459**
High Sessionmarks, **427**
High Watermarks, **427**
high-throughput scenarios, low latency and,
477–479
Hire Car activity, **235, 255, 265, 266**
Hire Car Orchestration, **263, 280**
Hire Car report, **294**
Hire Cars Booked, **278**
HIS 2006. *See* Host Integration Server 2006
Hoogendoorn, Martijn, **117**
host(s), **34–36, 38, 425.** *See also specific
hosts*
adapters and, 46–47

agnostic, 238
  BRE as, 344
clustering, 515–516
  detailed information on, 515
  FTP adapter and, 515
  in-order delivery and, 516
  MSMQ adapter and, 515
  POP3 adapter and, 516
configuration, 425
creation, performance bottlenecks and,
  392–394
default, 35, 513
management, 513–516
queues, 542
separation of, 513, 514
WF and, 608–609
Host Application adapter, Microsoft
  BizTalk, **56**
Host Files adapter, Microsoft BizTalk, **57**
Host Integration Server (HIS) 2006, **56**
Host Queue - Length counter, **442**
Host Queue - Suspended Messages - Length
  counter, **442**
Host Service Account, **70**
Host System 2006, **56**
  adapters, 56–57
host throttling, **474–475, 479**
  low latency and, 474–475
HostAq table, **543**
HostBq table, **543**
HostCq table, **543**
hosting process, **608**
Hosts file, **535**
Hotel activity, **235, 255, 265**
Hotel City, **275**
Hotel orchestration, **263, 280**
Hotel report, **294**
Hotel Stay Duration, **271**
Hotels Booked, **278**
HTTP 1.1 specification, **72, 426**
HTTP 200 response code, **72, 73**

HTTP adapter, 80–81
 context properties, 80–81
HTTP protocol, in-order delivery and, 55
HTTPOutMaxConnection registry key, 426
HybridDictionary, 596

I

IAssemblerComponent, 126
IBaseComponent, 118
IBaseMessage, 90–91. *See also* **message(s)**
 class diagram for, 91
IBaseMessageContext, 92
 .Promote, 116
 .Write, 116
IBaseMessagePart, 91
 .Data, 120
 .GetOriginalDataStream, 120
IBasePropertyBag, 92
IBTMessage, 90
IComponent, 120
 Execute method, 120
IComponentUI, 119–120
 Icon property, 119, 120
 Validate method, 119
Icon property, 119, 120
Id context property, 68
id function, 6
idempotency, 110, 111
IDisassemblerComponent, 126
IF -CONDITION- Then -ACTION-, 311
IIS. *See* **Internet Information Server**
ILDasm, 92, 93, 140
Import MSI File Wizard, 505, 508–510
 guidelines before using, 508
Import Summary screen, 509
InArchivedMsgUrl context property, 68
Inbound Latency (sec) counter, 442, 470
Inbound Maps section, 42
InboundHttpHeaders context property, 81

InboundResponseQueue context property, 66, 67
InboundTransportLocation context property, 68, 105
InCreated context property, 68, 69
InCreatedBy context property, 68, 69
InEditUrl context property, 68, 69
InFileSize context property, 68, 69
in-flight orchestrations, 578
 interruption of, 578–580
in-flight processes, 576
InfoPath, Microsoft, 12
InIconUrl context property, 69
InItemId context property, 68, 69
InLastModifedBy context property, 68, 69
InLastModified context property, 68
inline orchestration send port, low latency and, 483–487
inline pipeline execution, 207
 SO scenario and, 586
inline sends. *See* **orchestration(s), inline sends**
inline Web Service calls, low latency and, 489–493
InLineSendPort class, 484
 code for, 484–485
InListName context property, 68, 69
InListUrl context property, 68, 69
InOfficeIntegration context property, 68, 69
in-order delivery, 54–55
 clustering hosts and, 516
 File adapter and, 54–55
 HTTP protocol and, 55
 MSMQ and, 55
 MSMQT and, 65, 66
in-process hosts, 35
In-process message count, 450
InPropertiesXml context property, 68, 69
Install to Global Assembly Cache property, 501
Instrumentation layer, 282, 288

InstrumentationHelpers class, 282
integration testing, 386–387
  test categories and, 369
IntelliSense functionality, 197
interceptors, BAM, 240–241, 617
  custom, 261–262
  TPE and, 240–241
interchange(s), 101
  large, 102–103
  recoverable, 103
InterchangeID, 396
interfaces, pipeline, 118–120
internal caching service, 467
internal port type, 154, 155
Internet Information Server (IIS), 35
  BizTalk application components and, 496
  log files, 454, 455
  performance counters, 453–454
Internet Symbol Server, 397
InTitle context property, 68, 69
inverse partner direct binding, 157, 158,
    578, 579, 602
  configuration, 159–160
I/O completion port, 114
IPersistPropertyBag, 118–119
  Load method, 119
  Save method, 119
IPipelineContext, 116
IPipelineContextEx, 116
  .GetTransaction, 97
IProbeMessage interface, 98, 126, 128
IPropertyBag, 596
IRuleSetTrackingInterceptor interface, 358
IsAuthenticated context property, 66, 67
IsFirstInTransaction context property, 66, 67
IsIconUrl context property, 68
IsLastInTransaction context property, 66, 67
isolated hosts, 35
isolated receive host, 394
isolation, 210, 211
IsSecurityEnabled context property, 66, 67

IsXactMsg context property, 66, 67
Item Code, 204
Itineraries Received, 269, 272, 273, 276, 278
Itinerary activity, 235, 255, 264, 280
itinerary details report, 293–298
Itinerary message, 263, 280
  CustomerReference and, 246, 247
Itinerary orchestration, 263, 280
Itinerary Processing Time, 267, 271
itinerary report, 289–293
ITransaction, 116
iWay, 37
IXPathNavigable interface, 130
IXPathNavigable.CreateNavigator
    method, 130

J

JD Edwards EnterpriseOne, 56
JD Edwards OneWorld XE, 56
jobs, SQL Server Agent, 544–546. See also
    specific jobs
  overview/list of, 544–545
join node, 312, 313

L

Label context property, 66, 67
LabelValue context property, 68
Large message fragment size, 96, 102
  settings, 542
Large message threshold, 96, 102
last function, 6
latency, 465. See also low latency
  control, 587–588
  measurement of, 469–472
    BAM and, 471
LessThan predicate, 327
licensing, BAM, 238
line-of-business (LOB) adapter pack, 56, 87

line-of-business (LOB) credential storage, 587
line-of-business (LOB) integration, 56
  in-box adapters and, 56, 87
listen condition, 580
Listen shape, 142, 174–176, 579
  left-to-right behavior of, 176
LitWare. *See* Business-to-Business
  scenario
LMHosts file, 535
Load Generation tool, 389–391
Load method, 119
load profile, 387–389
LoadGen, 389–391, 407, 575
  layers, 389
LoadGenConsole.exe application, 391
LOB integration. *See* line-of-business
  integration
local-name function, 5, 6, 203
Lock Timeout / sec counter, 418, 451
Lock Waits / sec counter, 418, 451
log files, 454–455
  IIS, 454, 455
Log Parser, 454–455
log shipping, 551
  BizTalk, 551–554
    configuration, 552–553
    database restore with, 554
  failure recovery and, 551–554
log test step output, 382–383
logical ports, 153–160
  binding, 155–160
  creation, 153–154
  Port Configuration Wizard and, 153–160
  type, 154–155
logical processing host, 514
logical receive host, 514
logical send host, 514
logical tracking host, 514
logical unit numbers (LUNs), 420,
  421, 477
long-running business processes, 576
  loosely coupling and, 599–602

long-running scope, 205, 211
  exceptions and, 205
  persistence points and, 148
long-running transactions, 211
Long-Term Fact Retrievers, 354, 366
  example, 354–357
long-term facts, 353
Loop shape, 171
  orchestration with, 487, 488
looping constructs, 136, 137
  TPE and, 249
looping/storing messages, 593
loosely coupling, 599–602
  long-running business processes and,
    599–602
  orchestrations and, 599–602
loosely typed errors, 200
low latency, 465–493. *See also* latency
  BizTalk processing model and, 466–469
  definition of, 465–466
  disk subsystem and, 476–477
  global tracking and, 477
  high-throughput scenarios and, 477–479
  host throttling and, 474–475
  initializing correlation sets and, 488–489
  inline orchestration send port and,
    483–487
  inline Web Service calls and, 489–493
  MessageBox sizing and, 475–476
  orchestration inline sends and, 479–480
    limitations in, 480–481
  pipeline execution from orchestrations and,
    481–483
  subscriptions and, 477
  tuning BizTalk for, 472–474
Low Sessionmarks, 427
low throughput, 461–462
  BizTalk throttling and, 461
  dependent systems and, 461
  disk performance and, 462
Low Watermarks, 427
LUNs. *See* logical unit numbers

M

main queue, 542
Management Packs
  Biz Talk, 565–570, 574
    Event Rules, 570–571
  ESSO, 565–570
Management Studio, SQL Server 2005. *See*
    SQL Server 2005 Management Studio
Managing A Successful Performance Lab
    white paper, 416
manual mapping, 216–217
map(s), 41–42. *See also* BizTalk Mapper
  adapters and, 481
  BizTalk processing model and, 468, 469
  on receive port, 42
MarkableForwardOnlyEventingReadStream,
    126, 128–129
  Probe and, 128–129
Marshal.ReleaseComObject ( ), 406
master secret key, 523, 573
  backing up, 524, 573
  restoring, 524–525
master secret server, 523–526
  clustering options, 525–526
    detailed information on, 526
  failure, 524, 525
  moving, 524–525
Match predicate, 327
match stage, 316–318
maxconnection configuration setting, 428
MaxIOThreads, 490
MaxReceiveInterval, 472, 473, 474
MaxRedirects context property, 81
MaxThreshold, 150
MaxWorkerThreads, 460, 490
MBSA. *See* Microsoft Baseline Security
    Analyzer
measures, 34, 226, 227
memory counters, 394, 436

memory dumps, 459
  mini, 532
  PSSDiag tool and, 532
memory leaks, 406, 458–459
memory streams, 94
memory usage, high, 458–459
message(s), 21, 90. *See also specific*
    messages
  BizTalk processing model and flow of,
    466–469
  bodies
    BAM and, 53
    SQL Server Reporting Services and,
        298–299
    storage, 53
    tracking, 50–53
  class diagram for, 91
  context data, 518
  context properties, 92–93, 166, 178–179
    key for, 92
    namespace for, 92
    reading/writing/promoting, 92–93
    tracking, 50
  correlation, 186–192
  creation, 166
  empty, 589
    creation of, 589–590
  failure, 597
    subscribing to, 597–598
  large, 591
    processing, 591–592
  looping, 593
  malformed, 597
  MessageBox and removal of, 545
  MessageBox and storage of, 541–543
  multipart, 166, 593
    creation, 166–169
  orchestrations and, 165–169, 178–197
  parts, 91–92
  probing, 102

processing, 466–469
size, 96
starvation, 475
storing, 593
suspended, 412, 576, 597, 598–599
suspended instance and, 520, 521
transformation, 211–212
Message Agent, 25
APIs, 138
BizTalk processing model and, 467,
468, 469
counters, 443
pipeline architecture and, 94
role of, 467
Message Assignment shape, 178, 184, 186
Expression shape and, 197
Message Broker pattern, 588–589
B2B scenario and, 588–589
Message Count, 408
message creators, 389
**Message delivery delay (ms) performance
counter, 450**
Message delivery incoming rate, 449
Message delivery outgoing rate, 449
message delivery throttling, 448–450
**Message Delivery Throttling State counter,
443, 448, 456**
throttling states, 449–450
**Message Delivery Throttling State Duration
counter, 443, 449**
**Message Processing Throttling Settings
dialog box, 449, 450**
message publishing throttling, 444–447
**Message Publishing Throttling Settings
dialog box, 445, 446**
**Message Publishing Throttling State
counter, 443, 456**
throttling states, 445–448
**Message Publishing Throttling State
Duration counter, 443, 445**

Message Transform shape, 178
MessageBox, 25–31, 223, 224, 466, 541
clearing, 428
counters, 440–442
host, 442
message removal from, 545–546
message storage in, 541–543
pipeline architecture and, 94
publish-subscribe design of, 26
queuing, 407, 408
scaling, 418
sizing, 475–476
low latency and, 475–476
**MessageBox_DeadProcesses_Cleanup
job, 544**
MessageBox_Message_Cleanup job, 544
**MessageBox_Message_ManageRefCountLog
job, 545**
MessageBox_Parts_Cleanup job, 545
MessageBox_UpdateStats job, 545
MessageContextPropertyBase, 184, 186
MessageDataPropertyBase, 184
%MessageID% placeholder, 520
MessageParts table, 542, 543
**MessagePartsAttachments context
property, 81**
MessageRefCountLog tables, 543
MessageType context property, 68
MessageZeroSum table, 543
Messaging Engine
BizTalk processing model and, 466, 467,
468, 469
message processing, 95
large, 96, 102–103
performance counters, 470
pipeline architecture and, 94
**Messaging InProcess service class
settings, 427**
**Messaging Isolated service class
settings, 427**

Messaging Payload, 240, 243–245
Schema, 242
TPE and, 243–245
Messaging Property, 240, 243–245
Schema, 242, 243, 244
TPE and, 243–245
MessagingEventStream, 223, 236, 251, 260–261, 471
BufferedEventStream *v.*, 224
MethodName context property, 73
Microsoft Baseline Security Analyzer (MBSA), 538–539, 573
Microsoft Distributed Transaction Coordinator (MSDTC) service, 534
configuration, 536–537
troubleshooting, 534–538
connectivity, 538
firewall configuration, 535
NetBIOS resolution, 535
security options, 535–537
Windows XP SP2 registry settings, 537–538
Microsoft Installer (MSI) files, 503–510
deployment failure and large, 512–513
Export MSI File Wizard and, 506–507
Import MSI File Wizard and, 508–510
multiple binding files in, 503–506
resources added to, 509
Microsoft ISA Server, 73
Microsoft Message Queuing adapter. *See* MSMQ adapter
Microsoft Office 2007, 605, 623
Microsoft Operations Manager (MOM), 205, 430
Agent, 564, 566–567
architecture, 564–565
BAM and, 308
BizTalk monitoring with, 563–573
BizTalk Server integration with, 308
deployment considerations, 565

hardware/software component monitoring with, 516
Management Packs and, 565–570
BizTalk, 565–570, 574
ESSO, 565–570
Operator Console, 564, 571–573
performance testing and, 430
technical information on, 563
Microsoft service packs, 421
milestones. *See* business milestones
MIME (Multipurpose Internet Mail Extensions), 91
decoding, 82, 101, 104
encoding, 91, 107
MinIOThreads, 460, 490
MinThreshold, 150
MinWorkerThreads, 460, 490
mock objects, 371–372
MOM 2005 for Beginners link, 563
MOM 2005 Technical Resources link, 563
monitoring, 428–455. *See also* Business Activity Monitoring; performance testing
automated, 500, 574
BizTalk, 516–522, 563–573
MOM and, 563–573
goal of, 563
managing servers and, 438–439
performance counters, 430–437
performance testing and, 428–455
persistence points, 149
"Monitoring BizTalk Server Using MOM," 573
MPSReports tool, 540–541
download, 541
versions of, 540
MQ Extended Client, 83
MQSeries adapter, 57, 83–84, 516
context properties, 84
correlation and, 187
MSBuild script, 370

MSDTC service. *See* **Microsoft Distributed Transaction Coordinator service**
MsgBox Dead Process Cleanup (Purge Jobs) counter, 440
MsgBox Msg Cleanup (Purge Jobs) counter, 440
MsgBox Parts Cleanup (Purge Jobs) counter, 441
MsgBox Purge Subscriptions Job (Purge Jobs) counter, 441
MsgID context property, 66, 67
msg/Sec, 461
  problems, 461–462
MSI files. *See* **Microsoft Installer files**
MSIL, 138
MSMQ (Microsoft Message Queuing) adapter, 55, 66–68, 516
  BizTalk processing model and, 466, 468
  clustering hosts and, 515
  context properties, 67–68
  correlation and, 187
  in-order delivery and, 55, 67
  MSMQT *v.,* 64–65, 67
MSMQC. *See* **MSMQ adapter**
MSMQT adapter, 64–66
  context properties, 66
  in-order delivery and, 65, 66
  installation, 66
  MSMQ *v.,* 64–65, 67
MSMQT service class settings, 427
multiple binding files, 503–506
Multipurpose Internet Mail Extensions. *See* **MIME**

N

NACK messages. *See* **Negative Acknowledgment messages**
name function, 6

namespace(s)
  aliases, 4
  default, 3
  message property, 92
  System.Diagnostics, 602
  XML, 2–3, 13
namespace-uri function, 6, 203
Negative Acknowledgment (NACK) messages, 196, 197, 598
  example, 197
NetBIOS resolution, MSDTC and, 535
.NET 3.0 Adapter Framework, 55, 56, 87
.NET assemblies, 198
  calling, 198–202
    best practice advice for, 200–202
  exceptions and, 205
  GAC and, 198, 199, 329
.NET classes, 329
  BRE and, 329–330
  vocabularies and, 334, 336–338
.NET CLR LocksAndThreads counters, 437
.NET CLR memory counters, 437
.NET helper class, 347
  invoking rules and, 347, 348
.NET tracing framework, 218
.NET Web service stack, 460
  multiple threads and, 460–461
network card failure, 410
Network DTC access, 535, 536
network failure, 410
network interface counters, 394, 436
node set, 4
node types, 312. *See also specific nodes*
non-uniform sequential convoy, 195
"Not Enough Threads in the ThreadPool" error, 460, 489, 491
NotEqual predicate, 327
notifications, BAM portal, 237
NumberOfBizTalkServers, **453**
numeric range dimension, 228
NUnit, 372–373, 375, 378

O

OBDA. *See* **Orchestration Designer for Business Analysts**
observation model, 222
  Wiley Travel Services, 263–279
ODBC Adapter for Oracle Database, 56
ODX file, 134, 138
Office 2007. *See* **Microsoft Office 2007**
Office Business Scorecard Manager, 224
OLAP. *See* **online analytical processing**
One-Way messaging, 153
online analytical processing (OLAP)
  BAM *v.*, 221
  cube, 34, 223, 224, 225, 226, 227
    processing, 231
OOM conditions. *See* **out-of-memory conditions**
Operations View
  creation, 267–269
  testing, 276–279
Operations_OperateOnInstances_OnMaster job, 545
Operator Console, MOM, 564, 571–573
Operators group, BizTalk Server, 518
Ops adapter, 581–582
  BPM scenario and, 581–582
Oracle adapter, 56, 87
orchestration(s), 31–32, 133–220. *See also* *specific orchestrations*
  activation, 141–143
    activating receive, 142
    invoked, 142–143
  Assemble stage and, 106
  BizTalk processing model and, 467, 468, 469
  C# and, 138–140
  calling .NET components from, 198–202
    best practice advice, 200–202

code coverage within, 386
coding and, 197–207
compiled, 134
convoys and, 55, 192–196
counters, 443
dead, 598
debugging, 217–218, 498
dehydration, 32, 149–150
Delay shape and, 487
development, 160–220
drop off of, 455–458
execution environment, 133–160
failure, 412–413
fundamentals, 133–160
General Routing, 520, 521
host, 393
implementation, 134–141
in-flight, 578
  interruption of, 578–580
inline sends, 479–480
  adapter functionality *v.*, 480–481
  limitations of, 480–481
  low latency and, 479–481
logical ports, 153–160
Loop shape and, 487, 488
loosely coupling and, 599–602
messages and, 165–169, 178–197
performance, 455–458
persistence points, 144–149, 457, 458
pipeline execution from, 481–483
  low latency and, 481–483
  restrictions for, 482
Reflector tool and, 141
serialization, 457–458
SOAP adapter and, 73–75
subscriptions, 23–25, 142, 143–144
suspended, 412–413, 598–599
transactions within, 208–209
versioning, 150–152, 220

X# and, 137–138
XML representation, 134–137
zoom support, 165
Orchestration Compiler, 488
Orchestration Debugger, 498, 520, 521, 522
information on, 521
Orchestration Designer, 31, 165
Orchestration Designer for Business Analysts (OBDA), 160–164
download, 160
fictional business process, 160–161
orchestration in, 161–162
Orchestration Engine, 466
BizTalk processing model and, 467, 468, 469
Orchestration Info screen, 539
Orchestration Profiler utility, 386
download, 386
Orchestration Schedule, 240, 241
TPE and, 241–243
Orchestration Scope shape, 210
Orchestration Variable pane, 199
OrchestrationEventStream, 223, 237, 251, 260, 263
BufferedEventStream v., 224
Orchestrations completed/ sec performance counter, 443, 455
problems with, 455–458
Order Value, 204
OriginatorPID context property, 104
Outbound Adapter Latency (sec) counter, 442, 470
Outbound Latency (sec) counter, 442, 470
Outbound Maps section, 42
out-of-memory (OOM) conditions, 542
OUTPUT_DEBUG_STRING_EVENT, 217
outputRootElementName context property, 72
overload testing, 407–408, 409
test categories and, 369
Overwrite Resources box, 508

P

PAE switches, 417
Page Faults counter, 436
Pages/sec counter, 436
parallel convoys, 174, 195–196
example, 196
Parallel shape, 142, 172–174
persistence points and, 146
params keyword, 252
parties, 504
partitioning, 232–234
partner ports, 157–160
direct ports and, 157–160
Parts table, 542, 543
Party Resolution pipeline component, 104
pass-through pipelines, 98, 108
PassThruReceive pipeline, 22, 108
PassThruTransmit pipeline, 22, 108
Password context property, 57, 58, 73, 81, 85
passwords, 506
adapters and, 506
binding files and, 506
BizTalk Server Administration Console and, 506
People Soft, 56
PerfMon counters, 394, 430
categories, 394
example, 394–395
interpretation of, 395–396
stress testing and, 407
Performance - Top Queries by Average CPU Time report, 562
Performance - Top Queries by Average IO report, 562
Performance Characteristics white paper, 103
performance counters, 430
ASP.NET, 453–454
BizTalk, 439–443
capturing, 430–437

performance counters (*continued*)
  Database session, 448
  Database Size, 447
  Excel list of, 430, 431
  IIS, 453–454
  Message delivery delay (ms), 450
  Messaging Engine, 470
  monitoring, 430–437
  Orchestrations completed/ sec, 443, 455
    problems with, 455–458
  persistence points, 149, 458
  Physical memory usage (MB), 447
  Process Thread Count, 460
  PSSDiag and, 529
  SQL Server, 451–452
  standard, 435–437
  Thread count, 448
performance lab, management of, 416
performance logs, PSSDiag and, 531
Performance Monitor, 430
Performance reports, 562
Performance rules, 567, 568
performance testing, 387–405, 415–463
  automated, 401–405
    test steps in, 401–402
  BizUnit and, 401
  bottlenecks in, 391–396
  checklist, 416–428
    summary, 428
  code profiling, 396–401
  databases and, 421–424
    autogrowth, 423–424
    location, 421–423
  foundations/configurations before,
      416–428, 428
    hardware, 416–421
    software, 421–428
  importance of, 415, 463
  Load Generation tool, 389–391
  load profile, 387–389

  MOM and, 430
  monitoring and, 428–455
  strategy, 429–430
  symptoms during, 455–463
  test case for, 402–405
  test categories and, 369
  tools, 389–391
  tracking and, 426–427
  tuning and, 391–396, 415
  virus scanners and, 425–426
performance tuning. *See* tuning
persistence points, 144–149
  atomic scope and, 147, 211
  Delay shape and, 148
  end of orchestration and, 148
  long-running scope and, 148
  monitoring of, 149
  orchestration and, 144–149, 457, 458
  Parallel shape and, 146
  performance counter, 149, 458
  Receive shape and, 148
  reduction of, 443
  Send shape and, 145–146
  Start Orchestration shape and, 148
  Suspend shape and, 148
Persistence Points counter, 443
persistence service, WF, 609, 610–611
Physical memory usage (MB) performance
    counter, 447
pinned objects, 437
# of Pinned Objects counter, 437
pipeline(s), 22–23, 89–131. *See also*
    specific pipelines
  adapters *v.*, 89–90
  API, 106
  architecture, 93–107
  component development, 113–131
    assemblers/disassemblers, 126
    compression stream implementation,
      121–124

decompression stream implementation, 124–125
guidelines, 114–116
interfaces/attributes, 118–120
Pipeline Component Wizard, 117
stream implementation, 114–115, 126–130
testing, 130–131
components, 23
code coverage, 384–385
compression/decompression, 117
testing, 372
threads in, 114
configuration, 107–108
instance-based, 107–108
type-based, 107
default, 108–109
failures, 104–105
interfaces/attributes, 118–120
orchestrations and execution of, 481–483
low latency and, 481–483
pass-through, 98, 108
stages, 22–23, 98–100
execution modes, 98
receive, 22, 100–104
send, 23, 106–107
templates, 98
location of, 99
testing, 130–131, 372
transactions and, 97–98, 116
Pipeline Component Project, BizTalk Server, 117
Pipeline Component Wizard, 117
Pipeline Designer, 119
Pipeline Manager, 90
PipelineCompressionComponent, 118
Pipeline.exe utility, 130–131
location, 130
PivotCharts, 225

PivotTables, 227, 276
activity aggregations and, 302–305
activity views tested and, 276–279
pod deployment model, 477–478
pods, 477, 478
policies, 34, 324
creation, 324–326
deployed state, 325
editable state, 325
published state, 325
versioning, 325
Policy class, 325, 344, 345, 348, 362
Policy Explorer, 324
policy files, 98
example, 98–99
Policy Verificator, 340
PolicyTester class, 344, 345–346
polling model, 467, 468
pollingInterval context property, 72
pollingUnitOfMeasure context property, 72
pollWhileDataFound context property, 72
POP3 adapter, 82
clustering hosts and, 516
context properties, 82
port(s), 39. *See also specific ports*
binding, 155–160
creation, 153–154
types, 154–155
Port Binding dialog box, 74, 75
Port Configuration Wizard, 74, 75, 154
logical ports and, 153–160
port binding, 155–160
port creation, 153–154
port type selection, 154–155
Port Type dialog box, 74, 75
portals. *See* **Business Activity Monitoring, portal; health portal**
position function, 6
Pre-Assemble stage, 23, 106
pre-dequeue, 474–475

Predicate SQL tables, 26
predicates, 327. *See also specific predicates*
presentation layer, LoadGen, 389
Priority context property, 66, 67, 68
Private Bytes counter, 435
private port type, 154
% Privileged Time counter, 435
Probe method, 102, 128
    MarkableForwardOnlyEventingReadStream
        and, 128–129
probing components, 128
process changes, 576
process counters, 394, 435
process isolation approach, 491–492
Process Manager pattern, 159
    best practices, 602
    BPM scenario and, 577–578
process memory throttling, 446–447, 450
Process Thread Count performance
    counter, 460
processing flag, 170
processing model. *See* BizTalk processing
    model
processing node failure, 409
processing nodes (BizTalk Servers),
    418–419
processing throttling, 448–450
processor counters, 435
% Processor Time counter, 418, 435
Processor Queue Length counter, 436
Product Support Services (PSS), 115, 421
production environments, 500, 501
    BizTalk Explorer and, 502, 512
production support testing, 411–413
    archiving BAM data in, 413
    deploying new solution artifacts and, 412
    suspended messages and orchestrations in,
        412–413
    test categories and, 369

Profiler, SQL Server, 452, 453
profiling. *See* code profiling
progress dimension, 227
promotions, 179. *See also specific
    promotions*
Property Bag class, 596
property promotions, 41, 181–183
    advanced, 183–186
    distinguished promotions *v.*, 181
    walk-through, 181–183
ProxyAddress context property, 73
ProxyName context property, 81
ProxyPassword context property, 73, 81
ProxyPort context property, 73, 81
ProxyUserName context property, 73, 81
PSS. *See* Product Support Services
PSSDiag tool, 529–532, 573
    attributes of BizTalk executables
        and, 531
    BizTalk hotfix information and, 531
    BizTalk registry settings and, 531
    BizTalk Trace and, 531
    data collection by, 529, 531
    event logs and, 529, 531
    HAT information and, 531
    memory dumps and, 532
    performance counters and, 529
    performance logs and, 531
    running, 529–530
    SQL Blocking Script output and, 529
    SQL profiler traces and, 529
    SQLDiag and, 529
    system information and, 531
public port type, 154, 155
published state
    policies, 325
    vocabularies, 334
publish-subscribe design, 26, 192, 522
    MessageBox, 26

purge jobs, 476
Purge Jobs counters, 440, 441
PurgeSubscriptionJob, 545
PurgeSubscriptionJob_BizTalkMsgBoxDb
    job, 425
purging. *See* DTA purging and archiving

Q

Query Results window, 519, 521
queues. *See specific queues*
Quick Promotion, 183

R

race conditions, 192–193
    stress testing and, 406
RAID configurations, 420
RAID0, 428
RAID0+1, 420
RAID5, 420
RAID10, 420
RAID10/0+1, 428
Range predicate, 327
ranges, 334
    vocabularies and, 336
rate overdrive, 445, 449, 450
rate throttling, 445, 449–450
Read method, 124
ReadReceipt context property, 81
Real Time Aggregation (RTA), 227, 231, 232
    toolbar button to enable, 232
receive host, 392–393
    isolated, 394
    logical, 514
Receive Itinerary shape, 241
Receive Location Properties dialog box,
    59, 60

receive pipelines, 22, 90
    BizTalk processing model and, 467,
        468, 469
    stages, 22, 100–104
receive port(s), 39–40
    Enable routing for failed messages at, 105
    File adapter and, 59–61
    maps on, 42
    read/write permissions for, 63
    shut down of, 64
Receive Port Properties dialog box, 50, 59
    Tracking section of, 50–51
Receive shape, 32, 169–170
    activating receive and, 142
    filters on, 43
    persistence points and, 148
receive throttling, 444–447
ReceivedFileName context property, 57,
    58, 85
ReceivePortName property, 105
Recipient List pattern, 159
recoverable interchanges, 103
Redeploy property, 501
references, 234–236, 254–257
    activity, 235–236, 255–256
    custom, 236, 256–257
Reflector tool, 140
    orchestration and, 141
Registry Editor, 537, 538
regression verification tests, 371
relationships, TPE, 249
reliable messaging, 109
    BTF, 110–112
        receiving, 110–111
        sending, 111–112
    transport-agnostic, 109
    WS-, 109
remote procedure call (RPC), 535
    configuration information, 535

ReplyBy context property, 81
ReplyTo context property, 82
Report Server website, 297
RepresentationType context property, 85
Request Execution Time counter, 454
request-response, 39
Request-Response Latency (sec) counter,
    442, 470
Request/Response messaging, 153
Requests Failed counter, 454
Requests Queued counter, 454
Requests Wait Time counter, 454
Requests/Sec counter, 454
RequestTimeout context property, 81
Resolve Party stage, 22, 104
ResponseQueue context property, 66, 67, 68
Restart Host Instances property, 501
restoration
    BizTalk database, 554
    from database backup, 410
    master secret key, 524–525
    SQL Server Analysis Services, 546
Rete algorithm, 34, 312
    Forward Execution processing algorithm
        v., 613
    II, III, 312
    sharing capability, 314
Rete analysis network, 312–316
    processing steps, 312–313
    sharing, 313–316
Retract function, 328
RetractByType function, 328
retries, 481
RetrieveAs XLANGPart method, 201
retry semantics, 47–49
RhinoMocks, 372
RNFT command, 85
RNTO command, 85
Robbins, John, 459
Roeder, Lutz, 140

roundtripping, 162
RPC. See remote procedure call
RTA. See Real Time Aggregation
Rule Condition Editor, 613
Rule Set Editor, 614
rule store, 361
rules, business. See business rules
Rules Engine API, 365
Rules Engine cache, 458
Rules Engine Deployment Wizard, 364, 365
Rules Engine Update Service, 344, 361, 362
rules engines, 311. See also Business Rules
    Engine; Workflow Rules Engine
Rules_Database_Cleanup job, 545
RuleSetDeploymentDriver class, 365
Running Orchestrations counter, 443
RunTest method, 378
runtime services, WF, 609–613
    persistence, 609, 610–611
    tracking, 609, 611–612
    workflow scheduling, 609, 612–613

S

SAN storage. See storage area network
    storage
SAP adapter, 56, 87
Save method, 119
SAX parsers. See Simple API for XML
    parsers
scalability testing, 415–463. See also
    performance testing
    strategy, 429–430
scalable streams, 129. See also virtual
    streams
ScalableXPathDocument class, 130
ScalableXPathNavigator class, 130
scale out, 418
scale up, 418

Scatter Gather pattern, 156, 584
  information link for, 584
scenarios. *See* **End-to-end scenarios**
scheduled queue, 542
Schema Designer, 179
schemas, XML, 1–2, 12. *See also specific*
    schemas
  BRE and, 330–332
  person description in, 2
  serializable classes generated from, 8–11
Schmidt, Bob, 605
SDK (software development kit), 55
Secure Multipurpose Internet Mail
    Extensions. *See* **SMIME**
Secure Password Authentication (SPA), 82
security identifier (SID), 104
segments, 139
select node, 312, 313
self-correlating ports, 156–157
  configuration, 156–157
  direct ports and, 156–157
send host, 394
  logical, 514
send pipelines, 22, 90
  BizTalk processing model and, 467, 468, 469
  stages, 23, 106–107
send port(s), 40–41
  BizTalk processing model and, 467
  dynamic, 44
    B2B scenario and, 589
    context properties for, 44, 53
  enlistment, 45
  File adapter and, 61–63
  retry settings for, 48–49
  service window on, 49, 50
  WSS adapter and, 69–70
send port filters, 43
Send Port Group Properties dialog box, 41
send port groups, 40
Send Port Properties dialog box, 61
  Filters section, 62, 63

send port subscription, 25
Send shape, 170
  persistence points and, 145–146
  transaction boundary and, 209
SenderID context property, 66, 67
send-wait-retry pattern, 175
SentTime context property, 66, 67, 68
sequential convoys, 194
  correlation and, 188
sequential processes, 606
serializable classes, 7–12, 13, 201
  BizTalk development and, 12
  performance and, 11–12
  schema and generation of, 8–11
serialization, 106
  orchestration, 457–458
server agnostic, 145
ServerName wildcard, 382
servers, managing, 438–439
service classes, 466, 467, 472
  Messaging InProcess, 427, 472
  Messaging Isolated, 427, 472
  MSMQT, 427, 472
  settings, 427–428
  XLANG, 427, 472
service instances, 139
service level agreement (SLA), 226
service packs, Microsoft, 421
service window(s), 49
  adapters and, 481
  on send port, 49, 50
Service-Oriented (SO) scenario, 582–588
  Aggregator pattern, 584–585
  documentation, 584, 588
  highlights, 584–588
  inline pipeline invocation, 586
  installation, 588
  latency control and, 587–588
  Scatter Gather pattern, 584
  service-level tracking, 586
  source code, 588

Service-Oriented (SO) scenario (*continued*)
SSO and, 587
stubs and, 587
Woodgrove Bank performance
requirements, 583
services, 139
sets, 334
vocabularies and, 334–336
setup stage, 375
sgen.exe., 11
shapes, 31. *See also specific shapes*
**SharePoint. *See* Windows SharePoint
Services**
SharePoint Designer, 623–624
**sharing, Rete analysis network and,
313–316**
short-term facts, 353
Shukla, Dharma, 605
SID. *See* security identifier
Siebel eBusiness Applications adapter, 56, 87
Signature context property, 66, 67
**SignatureCertificate context property,
104, 126**
Simple API for XML (SAX) parsers, 114
Simple Object Access Protocol. *See* SOAP
**Single Sign-On database (SSOD),
32–33, 523**
adapter configuration settings in, 47
Single Sign-On (SSO) store, 580–581
BPM scenario and, 580–581
configuration data and, 594–597
SO scenario and, 587
singleton pattern, 193–194
SLA. *See* service level agreement
**SMIME (Secure Multipurpose Internet Mail
Extensions)**
decoding, 101, 104
virtual stream and, 129
encoding, 107
smoke tests, 371

SMTP adapter, 81
context properties, 81
SMTPAuthenticate context property, 81
SMTPHost context property, 81
SO scenario. *See* Service-Oriented scenario
SOAP (Simple Object Access Protocol), 7
SOAP adapter, 39, 72–73
batching and, 54
bit shoveler and, 89
BizTalk messages and, 76
context properties, 73
manual message construction and, 77–79
message parts and, 91
orchestration and, 73–75
port creation in, 74–75
walk-through, 73–80
Web service problems, 459–461
SOAP envelope, 7
soft purging, 556
**software configuration, performance testing
and, 421–428**
software development kit. *See* SDK
software tracing, 115–116, 602, 603
solicit-response, 39
Solicit/Response messaging, 153
SourceMachineGuid context property, 66, 67
SourcePartyID context property, 104
**Southridge Video. *See* Business Process
Management scenario**
SPA. *See* Secure Password Authentication
Splitter pattern, 589
B2B scenario and, 589
information link for, 589
spool, 462
steady increase of, 462–463
Spool Size counter, 440
Spool table, 542, 543
SQL adapter, 71–72
context properties, 72
SQL Blocking Script output, PSSDiag and, 529
SQL databases. *See* database(s)

SQL Notification Services, 496
  BizTalk application components and, 496
SQL Server, 417–418
  BizTalk application components and, 496
  BizTalk perspective on, 541–562
  business intelligence, 222
  counters, 394
  performance counters, 451–452
  performance/availability, 417, 418, 560–562
  problems, 456
    orchestration drop off from, 456
  Profiler, 452, 453
  profiler traces, 28
    details, 28–29
    PSSDiag and, 529
  Reporting Services, 222, 224, 289, 309
    Wiley Travel Services and, 289–299
  tuning, 450
SQL Server 2005 Management Studio, 288, 561
  reports, 560–562, 573
  tutorial, 562
SQL Server Agent, 425
  jobs, 544–546. *See also specific jobs.*
    more information on, 546
SQL Server Analysis Services, 496
  backup/restore for, 546
  BizTalk application components and, 496
SQL Server Integration Services (SSIS), 103
  interchange splits by, 103
  package, 224, 227, 231
    autogenerated, 231
    Data Maintenance, 232, 233
SQL tables, 222, 229, 230
SQL views, 223, 288
  activity views *v.*, 225, 230
sqlCommand context property, 72
SQLDiag, 529
  PSSDiag and, 529
SQS Debugger extension, 459

SSIS. *See* **SQL Server Integration Services**
SSO store. *See* **Single Sign-On store**
SSOAffiliateApplication context property, 85
SSOD. *See* **Single Sign-On database**
stage-processing orchestration subscription, 578, 579
staging environments, 500, 501
Start Orchestration shape, 176–177, 599
  invoking orchestration with, 142, 143
  persistence points and, 148
starvation
  message, 475
  thread, 459, 539, 573
state queue, 542
storage area network (SAN) storage, 420, 474, 477
stores, 7, 8
Stream.CanSeek property, 104
Stream.Read, 121
streams, 7, 591. *See also specific streams*
  adapters and, 481
  compressing, 121–124
  decompressing, 124–125
  pipeline components and, 114–115, 121–130
  wrapper, 127
Stream.Write, 121
stress testing, 406–407, 415
  bugs and, 406–407
  CLR and, 406
  COM objects and, 406, 407
  importance of, 415
  PerMon counters and, 407
  race conditions and, 406
  test categories and, 369
stubs, 587
subbatches, 102
Subject context property, 81, 82
SubmissionHandle context property, 81

subscription(s), 23–25, 142, 143–144. *See also specific subscriptions*
  BizTalk processing model and, 467, 468, 469
  low latency and, 477
  troubleshooting, 522
***Substitution of wildcards* feature, 381–382**
Sum Itinerary Prices, 273
***super samples,* 575**
Suspend shape, 205
  persistence points and, 148
suspended instances, 518
  message flow for, 520, 521
  troubleshooting, 518–522
Suspended Items section, 517–518
suspended queue, 542
SWIFT messages, 104
symbol server, 397
symbols, 397
  code profiling and, 397
  debug, 529
**symptoms, during performance testing,
    455–463**
system counters, 394, 436
system memory throttling, 447, 450
System.BizTalk.BizTalkBinding, 503
System.Diagnostics, 217–218, 602, 603
System.Diagnostics.Debug.WriteLine ( ), 359
System.Diagnostics.Trace class, 582
**System.Diagnostics.Trace.Writeline
    method, 217**
System.XML types, 147

T

TDDS. *See* **Tracking Data Decode Service**
Team Foundation Server, 370
Team System, 370
terminal node, 312, 313

test cases, 375. *See also* **BizUnit**
  automated, 383
  examples, 376–380
  execution, 378
  failure, 379, 402
  group-level, 378
  information, 383
  LoadGen, 391
  performance test and, 402–405
  stages, 375
  XML, 375, 376
Test Policy, 344–345
test steps, 375, 379
  API and, 382–383
  automated performance testing, 401–402
  context-manipulation, 383
  creation, 381
  failure, 379, 402
  flow state between, 382
  validation, 383
TestBTSTask application, 51
TestCleanup, 375
TestExecution, 375
testing, 367–413. *See also specific
    testings*
  automated, 369
    functional, 374, 413
    performance, 401–405
  BRE, 344–346
  build process and, 370–371
  categories, 369
  disaster recover, 369, 409–411
  failover, 410–411
  functional, 369, 371, 373–386, 413, 415
    BVT, 370, 371
  integration, 369, 386–387
  manual, 369
  Operations View, 276–279
  overload, 369, 407–408, 409

overview, 367–369

performance, 369, 387–405, 415–463

pipelines, 130–131, 372

production support, 369, 411–413

scalability, 415–463

stress, 369, 406–407, 415

unit, 369, 371–373

user acceptance, 369, 408

workstation, 416–417

XPath expressions, 204–205

tests. *See specific tests*

TestSetup, 375

Thomas, Stephen W., 187

thread(s), 114

.NET Web service stack and multiple, 460–461

in pipeline components, 114

starvation, 459, 539, 573

Thread count performance counter, 448

thread count throttling, 448, 450

ThreadPool class, .NET, 16, 114, 459, 489, 490

problems, 459–460, 489–490

throttle controllers, 389, 390

throttling, 444–450, 478

BizTalk, 461, 478

disabling, 444

Event Viewer and, 438

host, 474–475, 479

message delivery, 448–450

message publishing, 444–447

orchestration drop-off from, 456

processing, 448–450

receive, 444–448

throttling states, message publishing, 445–448

Throttling Thresholds dialog box, 446, 447, 450

throughput, low, 461–462

Throw Exception shape, 205

exceptions and, 205

TIBO Enterprise Message Service, 56

TIBO Rendezvous adapter, 56, 87

time dimension, 228–229, 269, 273, 274

% Time in GC counter, 437

TimeSpan, 171

TimeToReachQueue context property, 66, 67

To context property, 82

tools. *See also specific tools*

administration, 496–500, 526–534

hidden, 528–534

BizTalk 2006 CD, 528–534

performance testing, 389–391

TPE. *See* Tracking Profile Editor

tracing, 115–116, 602, 603

BPM scenario and, 582

tracing framework, .NET, 218

TrackAgendaUpdate method, 359

TrackConditionEvaluation method, 358

Tracked Messages Copy job, 544, 545

Tracked Msgs Copy (Purged Jobs) counter, 441

TrackedMessages_Copy_BizTalkMsgBoxDb job, 425

TrackFactActivity method, 359

tracking, 50–53

adapters and, 481

end-to-end order, 576, 581

global, 426–427

low latency and, 477

message bodies, 50–53

message properties, 50

performance testing and, 426–427

service-level, 586

Tracking Data Decode Service (TDDS), 223–224, 441, 514

Tracking Data Size counter, 441, 462

tracking data tables, 554–555

tracking hosts, 35, 224, 237, 514

logical, 514

Tracking Interceptor, 357, 366

custom, 358–359

sample, 359–360

Tracking Interceptor Configuration file, 617–622

tracking portal concept, 288–289

tracking profile, 238

Tracking Profile Editor (TPE), 33, 224, 238–250

ActivityIDs and, 246

Context property and, 243–245

continuation and, 246–249

deployment and, 249

interceptors and, 240–241

limitations, 250

looping and, 249

Messaging Payload and, 243–245

Messaging property and, 243–245

Orchestration Schedule and, 241–243

relationships, 249

using, 238–240

tracking service, WF, 609, 611–612

Tracking Spool Cleanup (Purge Jobs) counter, 441

TrackRuleFiring method, 358

TrackRuleSetEngineAssociation method, 358

Trading Partner Management System, 588

B2B scenario and, 588, 589

transactable adapter, 197

atomic scope and, 197

transaction(s), 97

ACID, 147

boundaries, 208–209

Send shape and, 209

distributed, 97

DTC, 102

orchestrations and, 208–209

pipelines and, 97–98, 116

transactional integrity, BAM, 259–260

transactional reads, 515

TransactionId context property, 66, 67

Transform Message shape, 212

configuration, 212, 213

Transform shape, 585

transformations, 211–212

translation, 361

TransmittedFileLocation context property, 68

transport agnostic, 89

reliable messaging, 109

transport proxy, 468

Travel Insurance activity, 235, 255, 265, 266

Travel Insurance orchestration, 263, 280

Travel Insurance report, 294

troubleshooting, 415, 573. *See also* **testing**

BizTalk, 516–522

MSDTC problems, 534–538

subscriptions, 522

suspended instances, 518–522

"Troubleshooting Performance Problems in SQL Server 2005" **white paper, 450**

try/catch model, 206, 207

T-SQL statements, 224

tuning, 391–396, 415. *See also* **performance testing**

custom databases, 452–453

disaster recover testing and, 410

SQL Server, 450

Tuning Advisor, 453

U

UK SDC BizTalk 2006 Documenter tool, 539–540

download, 539

UNC share, 425

"Understanding Workflow for Windows SharePoint Services and the 2007 Microsoft Office System" (Chappell), 623
uniform sequential convoys, 194
unique identifier, 186
unit testing, 371–373
  test categories and, 369
Unit Testing, Visual Studio 2005, 372, 375, 378
UnknownHeaders context property, 73
unprocessed message throttling, 450
Update function, 328
UPDATE statement, 321, 322, 323
UpdateActivity method, 251
Url context property, 68, 69
USB flash drives, 425
UseHandlerProxySettings context property, 81
UseHandlerSetting context property, 73
UseProxy context property, 73, 81
user acceptance testing, 408
  test categories and, 369
User Override throttling type, 448, 450
UserDefined context property, 73
UserHttpHeaders context property, 81
UserName context property, 73, 81, 85
UseSoap12 context property, 73
UseSSO context property, 73, 81
UseTempFileOnWrite context property, 57, 58
"Using SSO Efficiently in the Service Oriented Solution," 587
using statement, .NET, 114

V

Validate method, 119
Validate stage, 22, 103–104
variables, 198

Variables node, 198
Version context property, 66, 67
versioning, 45
  GAC and, 150–151
  orchestrations, 150–152, 220
  policies, 325
  vocabularies, 334, 339–341
Virtual Bytes counter, 435
virtual machines, 417
virtual streams, 129–130, 419, 592
  forward-only streams v., 129, 592
  location of, 130
  SMIME decoding and, 129
VirtualStream implementation, 592
virus scanners, 425–426
  performance testing and, 425–426
Visio 2003, Microsoft, 160
  orchestration imported into, 162–163
Visio Designer, 160–164
  walk-through, 160–164
Visual Studio
  2005 Unit Testing, 372, 375, 378
  application deployment and, 501–502
  BizTalk Explorer and, 501–502
  class diagram, 282, 283
  Code Coverage tool, 384
  Orcas release of, 603
  Profiler, 396–397
    custom component profiling with, 397–401
vocabularies, 34, 334–343
  API, 343
  constants and, 334–336
  data tables/columns and, 339
  editable state, 334
  façade and, 334
  .NET classes and, 334, 336–338
  published state, 334
  ranges and, 334–336
  sets and, 334–336

vocabularies (*continued*)
using, 341–343
versioning, 334, 339–341
XML document elements/attributes
and, 338
Vocabulary Definition Wizard, 334, 335
VsPerfMon, 384, 385
VS_Profiler.exe, 396

W

W3C standard. *See* World Wide Web
Consortium standard
wait points, 32
WCF adapter. *See* Windows Communication
Foundation adapter
Web Service calls
concurrent, 426
inline, 489–493
low latency and, 489–493
Web Service problems, SOAP adapter,
459–461
Web Services Description Language (WSDL)
specification, 219
Web Services Enhancements (WSE)
adapter, 86
WebSphere MQ adapter, Microsoft BizTalk,
57, 83
WebSphere MQ Server for Windows, 57
WF. *See* Windows Workflow Foundation
wildcards, BizUnit, 381–382
DateTime, 382
Guid, 382
ServerName, 382
Wiley Operations Portal, 289
Wiley Travel Services/BAM instrumentation,
262–308
activity data
using, 288–289
writing, 280–288

architecture diagram, 263
BAM portal, 299–308, 309
activity aggregations, 302–305
activity alerts, 305–307
activity searches, 300–302
database infrastructure deployment,
279–280
façade, 282–288
MOM integration, 308
observation model
activities created, 263–266
activity views defined, 266–275
activity views tested, 276–279
Export XML, 279
SQL Server Reporting Services, 289–299
itinerary details report, 293–298
itinerary report, 289–293
message body, 298–299
WinDbg, 459
WinDiff, 531
Windows Communication Foundation (WCF)
adapter, 55, 85
custom adapters and, 85–86
WCF-BasicHttp adapter, 86
WCF-Custom adapter, 86
WCF-CustomIsolated adapter, 86
WCF-NetMsmq adapter, 86
WCF-NetNamedPipe adapter, 86
WCF-NetTcp adapter, 86
WCF-WSHttp adapter, 85–86
Windows Internet Name Service (WINS)
server, 535
installation/configuration
information, 535
Windows Management Instrumentation
(WMI), 218, 499
samples, 499
Windows SharePoint Services (WSS),
496, 605
adapter, 68–71
context properties, 68–69

send port and, 69–70
walk-through, 69–71
BizTalk application components and, 496
Transport Properties dialog box, 69, 70
WF, BizTalk and, 605, 623–624
Windows Sysinternals, 358, 582, 603
Windows Workflow Foundation (WF), 605–625
activities, 607–608
BAM interceptor for, 616–622
BizTalkServer v., 605, 615–625
Designer, 613
as foundation, 615, 624
hosting process, 608–609
introduction to, 605–615
key concepts, 605–615
Rules Engine, 613–615
runtime services, 609–613
  persistence, 609, 610–611
  tracking, 609, 611–612
  workflow scheduling, 609, 612–613
SharePoint, BizTalk and, 623–624
workflows, 606–607
Windows XP SP2 registry settings, MSDTC and, 537–538
WindowsUser context property, 104
WINS server. *See* **Windows Internet Name Service server**
wire stream, 94
wish list, 33
WMI. *See* **Windows Management Instrumentation**
Woodgrove Bank. *See* **Service-Oriented scenario**
Work in Progress section, 517
Workflow Rules Engine, 613–615
workflow scheduling, WF, 609, 612–613
workflows, 606–607
default state, 607
state machine, 607

WorkflowWebHostingModule, 609
Working Set counter, 435
workstation testing, 416–417
World Wide Web Consortium (W3C) standard, 1
wrapper classes, 329
wrapper streams, 127
Write method, 124
WS:* specifications, 85
WSDL specification. *See* **Web Services Description Language specification**
WSE adapter. *See* **Web Services Enhancements adapter**
WS-Reliable Messaging, 109
WSS. *See* **Windows SharePoint Services**

X

X#, 134, 136, 137, 138
compiler, 138
orchestration and, 137–138
X12, 82
XLANG, 219
compiler, 145
counters, 443
runtime engine, 138
service class settings, 427
XLANGMessage, 90, 593
XLANGs.BaseTypes assembly, 207
XML (Extensible Markup Language), 1
Disassembler, 115
Disassembler component, 182
documents, 1–2
  attributes, 338
  elements, 338
  vocabularies and, 338
facts, 350
  Call Rules shape and, 350–352

XML (Extensible Markup Language)
  (*continued*)
  field, 330, 331
  orchestration and, 134–137
  schemas, 1–2, 12. *See also* schemas, XML.
  selector, 330, 331
  Validator, 104
XmlDocument, 115
XMLReader class, 114, 115
XmlReceive pipeline, 22, 109
XmlSerializer, 11
XmlTransmit pipeline, 22, 109
XPath, 3–6, 13
  functions, 5–6, 202–205
    parameters of, 202
XPath expressions, 202, 203, 204
  testing, 204–205

XPathDocument, 5
XPathNavigator class, 5, 130
XSD.EXE, 9
XSD.EXE.NET Framework tool, 217
XsharpP.exe, 138
XSLT (Extensible Style Language
  Transformation)
  custom, 215–216
  debugging features, 215–216
  extraction, 215
  language, 5
XslTransform class, 16, 212

Z

zoom support, 165